MACROECONOMICS

MACROECONOMICS

A EUROPEAN PERSPECTIVE
2nd edition

Olivier Blanchard, Alessia Amighini
and Francesco Giavazzi

PEARSON

Harlow, England • London • New York • Boston • San Francisco • Toronto • Sydney
Auckland • Singapore • Hong Kong • Tokyo • Seoul • Taipei • New Delhi
Cape Town • São Paulo • Mexico City • Madrid • Amsterdam • Munich • Paris • Milan

PEARSON EDUCATION LIMITED
Edinburgh Gate
Harlow CM20 2JE
United Kingdom
Tel: +44 (0)1279 623623
Web: www.pearson.com/uk

First published 2010 (print)
Second edition published 2013 (print and electronic)

The Financial Times. With a worldwide network of highly respected journalists, *The Financial Times* provides global business news, insightful opinion and expert analysis of business, finance and politics. With over 500 journalists reporting from 50 countries worldwide, our in-depth coverage of international news is objectively reported and analysed from an independent, global perspective. To find out more, visit www.ft.com/pearsonoffer.

ISBN: 978-0-273-77168-5 (print)
 978-0-273-77180-7 (PDF)
 978-0-273-78081-6 (eText)

British Library Cataloguing-in-Publication Data
A catalogue record for the print edition is available from the British Library

Library of Congress Cataloging-in-Publication Data
Blanchard, Olivier (Olivier J.)
 Macroeconomics : a European perspective / Olivier Blanchard, Alessia Amighini and Francesco Giavazzi. – 2nd edition.
 pages cm.
 Includes index.
 ISBN 978-0-273-77168-5 (pbk.)
 1. Macroeconomics–Europe. I. Amighini, Alessia. II. Title.
 HB172.5.B574 2013
 339.094–dc23

10 9 8 7 6 5 4 3
17 16 15

Print edition typeset in 9.5/12.5pt Charter by 35
Print edition printed and bound by L.E.G.O. S.p.A., Italy

NOTE THAT ANY PAGE CROSS REFERENCES REFER TO THE PRINT EDITION

BRIEF CONTENTS

CONTENTS

Supporting resources

Visit **www.MyEconLab.com** to find valuable online resources.

MyEconLab for students
- A personalised study plan with self-assessment questions to check your understanding
- Multiple-choice questions to test your learning
- Extensive annotated hotlinks to relevant websites
- An online glossary to explain key terms with flashcards to test your knowledge
- Pearson e-text with search tool to help locate specific items of content

MyEconLab for instructors
- Customisable testbank of question material that can be set as tests and homework assignments
- E-mail results and profile tools to send results of quizzes to instructors
- Downloadable PowerPoint slides
- Complete instructor's manual and solutions guide to end of chapter questions.
- Economics Experiments that provide you with engaging activities that allow your students to apply their knowledge to real-life situations
- Online help and support to assist with website usage and troubleshooting

For more information please contact your local Pearson Education sales representative or visit **www.pearsoned.co.uk/blanchard**

LIST OF FIGURES

LIST OF TABLES

LIST OF FOCUS BOXES

ABOUT THE AUTHORS

Olivier Blanchard is the Class of 1941 Professor of Economics at MIT. He did his undergraduate work in France and received a PhD in economics from MIT in 1977. He taught at Harvard from 1977 to 1982, and has taught at MIT since 1983. He has frequently received the award for best teacher in the department for economics.

He has done research on many macroeconomic issues, from the effects of fiscal policy, to the role of expectations, price rigidities, speculative bubbles, unemployment in Western Europe, transition in Eastern Europe, labour market institutions and unemployment, and, most recently, the financial and macroeconomic crisis. He has done work for many governments and many international organisations, including the World Bank, the IMF, the OECD, the European Commission and the EBRD. He has published more than 160 articles and edited or written more than 15 books, including *Lectures on Macroeconomics* with Stanley Fischer.

He is a research associate of the National Bureau of Economic Research, a fellow of the Econometric Society, a member of the American Academy of Arts and Sciences, and a past vice president of the American Economic Association. He is a past member of the French Council of Economic Advisers, and a past editor of the *Quarterly Journal of Economics* and of the *American Economic Journal: Macroeconomics*. He is currently on leave from MIT, working as the chief economist of the IMF.

Olivier Blanchard lives in Washington with his wife, Noelle, and has three daughters, Marie, Serena and Giulia.

Francesco Giavazzi is Professor of Economics at Bocconi University in Milan and has been, for many years, a visiting professor at MIT where he has often taught the basic macroeconomics course for undergraduates. After studying electrical engineering in Milan, he received a PhD in economics from MIT in 1978. He then taught at the University of Essex.

His research has focused on fiscal policy, exchange rates and the creation of the European Monetary Union. His books include *Limiting Exchange Rate Flexibility: the European Monetary System* with Alberto Giovannini and *The Future of Europe: Reform or Decline* with Alberto Alesina.

He has frequently advised governments and central banks: he was the Houblon-Norman Fellow at the Bank of England, evaluated IMF research, assessed Sweden's central bank for the Swedish Parliament with Fredrik Mishkin, and is currently an adviser to the French Treasury. He was also the macroeconomics editor of the *European Economic Review*.

Francesco Giavazzi divides his life between Milan and Cambridge (Massachusetts), although his best days are spent skiing in the Dolomites and rowing along the canals of Venice.

Alessia Amighini is Assistant Professor of Economics at Università del Piemonte Orientale in Novara (Italy) and Adjoint Professor of International Economics at the Catholic University in Milan. After graduating from Bocconi University in 1996, she received a PhD in Development Economics from the University of Florence, and then

worked as an Associate Economist at the Macroeconomics and Development Policies Branch of UNCTAD (Geneva) from 2003 to 2006.

She lives in Milan with her husband and two children.

PUBLISHER'S ACKNOWLEDGEMENTS

We are grateful to the following for permission to reproduce copyright material:

CARTOONS

Cartoons on page 22, page 42 from Universal Press Syndicate, reproduced with permission; Cartoon on page 39 from www.cartoonstock.com, reproduced with permission, CartoonStock.com; Cartoon on page 336 from Chappatte, in L'Hebdo, www.globecartoon.com, copyright globecartoon.com; Cartoon on page 349 from www.cartoonstock.com, CartoonStock.com; Cartoon on page 373 from Tribune Media Services (c) 1994. All rights reserved. Distributed by Tribune Media Services; Cartoon 22.1 from *Haitzinger Karikaturen 2004*, Munchen: Bruckmann (Haitzinger, Horst 2004) p. 9, Horst Haitzinger

FIGURES

Figure 1.1 from IMF, World Economic Outlook Database, Spring 2009, p. 1, reproduced with permission; Figure 3.5 from Google Trends. "Great Depression", World Search (c) 2012 Google; Figure 5.13 from G. Peersman and F. Smets, The monetary transmission mechanism in the Euro area: More evidence from Var analysis, European Central Bank, Working Paper No. 91, December 2001, http://www.ecb.int/pub/pdf/scpwps/ecbwp091.pdf; Figure 5.14 from Panel B, Chart I, pag. 92 ECB Monthly Bullettin May 2010, http://www.ecb.int/pub/pdf/mobu/mb201005en.pdf, Available free from ECB website. Reproduced with permission; Figure 6.1 from UK office for National Statistics, Source: Office for National Statistics licensed under the Open Government Licence v.1.0.; Figure 6.5 from Bank of England, Table: interest and exchange rate data, http://www.bankofengland.co.uk/boeapps/iadb/index.asp?; Figure 7.3 from The role of financial markets' openness in the transmission of shocks in Europe, *National Institute of Economic and Social Research, Discussion Paper No. 271*, p. 18 (Al-Eyd, Ali, Barrell, Ray and Holland, Dawn 2006); Figure 7.6 from Is there life outside the ERM? An evaluation of the effects of sterling's devaluation on the UK Economy, *International Journal of Finance & Economics*, vol. 2(3), July, pp. 199–216 (Hughes Hallett, Andrew J. & Wren-Lewis, S. 1997) (c) John Wiley & Sons, Ltd. Reproduced with permission; Figure 8.1 from Eurostat, http://epp.eurostat.ec.europa.eu, © European Union, 1995–2013, © European Communities, 1995-2010; Figure 9.10 from *Macroeconomic Policy in a World Economy*, W.W. Norton (Taylor, John 1993) Fig. 5-1A, p. 138, reproduced with permission from the author; Figure 9.19 from International Energy Agency (2008) Worldwide trends in energy use and efficiency: Key insights from IEA indicator analysis, http://www.iea.org/papers/2008/indicators_2008.pdf (c) OECD/IEA, 2008; Figure 13.2 from Economic growth and subjective well being: Reassessing the Easterlin paradox, *Brookings Papers on Economic Activity*, Spring fig. 4 (Stevenson, Betsey and Wolfers, Justin 2008), reproduced with permission; Figure 13.2 from Betsey Stevenson and Justin Wolfers, "Economic Growth and Subjective Well Being: Reassessing the Easterlin Paradox Brookings papers on Economic Activity, Spring 2008", fig. 4, http://www.nber.org/papers/w14282; Figure 13.3 from Penn World Tables http://pwt.econ.upenn.edu/php_site/pwt_index.php; Figure 15.5 from Hybrid Corn: An exploration in the economics of technological change, *Econometrica*, October, pp. 25–34 (Griliches, Zvi 1957), reproduced with permission; Figure 16.2 from Eurostat, http://epp.eurostat.ec.europa.eu, © European Union, © European Communities, 1995–2010; Figures 16.3, 16.5, 18.5, 20.13 from Bank of England; Figure 18.6 from Barry Eichengreen, Kevin O'Rourke, "A Tale of Two Depressions", voxeu.org, September 2009, http://voxeu.org/index.php?q=node/3421#apr609; Figure 19.3 from ECB Interest rate and Money Growth Rules, *Rotterdam, Erasmus University, mimeo* (Smant, D. J. C.); Figure 19.4 from ECB, Monthly bulletin, August 2009., http://www.ecb.int/pub/pdf/mobu/mb200908en.pdf, European Central Bank, data available free of charge from http://www.ecb.europa.eu/home; Figures 20.7, 20.9 from IMF, World Economic Outlook, April 2009, p. 4, reproduced with permission; Figure 20.8 from IMF, World Economic Outlook, April 2009, p. 7, reproduced with permission; Figure 20.10 from IMF, World Economic Outlook, April 2009, p. 30, reproduced with permission; Figure 20.12 from Philip R Lane (2011) The Irish Crisis, CEPR Discussion Papers No. 8287 www.cepr.org/pubs/dps/DP8287.asp, reproduced with permission; Figure 20.15 from International Monetary Fund, World Economic Outlook Database, September 2011, reproduced with permission; Figure 20.17 from IMF, World Economic Outlook, Chapter 4, October

2009, http://www.imf.org/external/pubs/ft/weo/2009/02/index.htm#ch4fig, reproduced with permission; Figure 21.7 from Estimating fiscal limits: The case of Greece, Working Paper, Bank of Canada (Bi, Huixin and Traum, Nora), November 2012, reproduced with permission; Figure 22.1 from Political and monetary institutions and public financial policies in the industrial countries, *Economic Policy*, October pp. 341–392 (Grilli, Vittorio, Masciandaro, Donato and Tabellini, Guido 1991), Copyright (c) 2013 John Wiley & Sons. Reproduced with permission of John Wiley & Sons Ltd.; Figures 23.2, 23.3, 23.4, 23.5 from Francesco Giavazzi and Frederic S. Mishkin, "An evaluation of Swedish Monetary policy between 1995 and 2005", Finance Committee, Swedish Parliament, http://people.su.se/~leosven/papers/Giavazzi-Mishkin%20200607_RFR1_eng.pdf, reproduced with permission

TABLES

Table 1.1 from European Commission, http://ec.europa.eu/economy_finance/publications/european_economy/2011/pdf/2011-05-13-stat-annex_en.pdf (c) European Communities 2012, © European Communities, 1995–2010; Table 1.4 from IMF, World Economic Outlook Database, http://www.imf.org/external/pubs/ft/weo/2011/01/weodata/index.aspx, reproduced with permission; Table 4.1 from IMF, http://www.imf.org/external/np/sta/cofer/eng/index.htm, reproduced with permission; Table 6.1 from Eurostat, http://epp.eurostat.ec.europa.eu, © European Union, 1995–2013, © European Communities, 1995–2010; Table 6.2 from UK Office for National Statistics, Source: Office for National Statistics licensed under the Open Government Licence v.1.0.; Table 6.3 from UK Office of National Statistics, http://www.statistics.gov.uk/pdfdir/bop0909.pdf, Source: Office for National Statistics licensed under the Open Government Licence v.1.0.; Table 6.4 after Central Statistics Office Ireland; Table 11.3 from Ten Years of Mrs T, *NBER Macroeconomics Annual*, Vol. 4, pp. 13–72 (Bean, Charles and Symons, James 1989); Table 13.1 from Penn World Tables, http://pwt.econ.upenn.edu/php_site/pwt_index.php, Alan Heston, Robert Summers and Bettina Aten, Penn World Table Version 7.0, Center for International Comparisons of Production, Income and Prices at the University of Pennsylvania, May 2011, reproduced with permission; Table 14.1 from Economic reconstruction in France, 1945–58 in Dornbusch, R., Nolling, W. and Layard, R. (eds) *Postwar Economic Reconstruction and Lessons for the East Today* (Saint-Paul, G. 1993) (c) 1993 Massachusetts Institute of Technology, by permission on the MIT Press; Table 17.1 from 'Choice, chance and wealth dispersion at retirement' in Ogura, S., Tachibanaki, T. and Wise, D. A. (eds) *Aging Issues in United States and Japan*, University of Chicago Press (Venti, S. and Wise, D. 2001) Table A.1 (c) 2001 by The National Bureau of Economic Research. All rights reserved; Table 19.1 from WTO statistics, country profiles, trade to GDP ratio, http://stat.wto.org/CountryProfile/WSDBCountryPFHome.aspx?Language=E, reproduced with permission; Table 19.2 from GEOGRAPHIC MOBILITY IN THE EUROPEAN UNION: OPTIMIZING ITS ECONOMIC AND SOCIAL BENEFITS, IZA Research Report No. 19, 2008, p. 133, reproduced with permission; Table 19.4 from Eurostat, http://epp.eurostat.ec.europa.eu/portal/page/portal/statistics/search_database, © European Union, 1995–2013, © European Communities, 1995–2010; Tables 22.1, 22.2 from Comparing empirical models of the Euro economy, *Economic Modelling*, Vol. 21, pp. 735–758 (Wallis, Kenneth F. 2004), Elsevier (c) 2004, with permission from Elsevier

TEXT

Box on page 4 after History of the European Union, http://europa.eu/abc/history/index_en.htm (c) European Communities 2012; Box on page 223 from The role of monetary policy, *American Economic Review*, vol. 58(1), pp. 1–17 (Friedman, Milton 1968); Box on page 259 adapted from Ten Years of Mrs T, *Discussion Paper 316*, Vol. 4, pp.13–72 (Bean, Charles and Symons, James 1989), CEPR; Box on page 311 from Economic reconstruction in France, 1945–58 in Dornbusch, R., Nolling, W. and Layard, R. (eds) *Postwar Economic Reconstruction and Lessons for the East Today* (Saint-Paul, G. 1993) (c) 1993 Massachusetts Institute of Technology, by permission of the MIT Press; Box on page 335 adapted from Hybrid Corn: An exploration in the economics of technological change, *Econometrica*, October, pp. 25–34 (Griliches, Zvi 1957), reproduced with permission

In some instances we have been unable to trace the owners of copyright material, and we would appreciate any information that would enable us to do so.

GUIDED TOUR

Chapter **Introductions** include a news story or example to illustrate a macroeconomic concept or theme that is built upon within the chapter.

Chapter 4

FINANCIAL MARKETS

During the recent financial crisis that hit the USA and most of the world starting in 2007, central banks around the world had a particularly hard time. They were asked to design measures to help economies out of the recession and to enable the financial sector to recover and strengthen in the future. Over these years, central banks were often in the headlines explaining what their strategies and priorities were.

However in tranquil times too, barely a day goes by without the media speculating as to whether the central bank – either the ECB (short for European Central Bank) in the euro area, the Bank of England in the UK, the Riksbank in Sweden or the Fed (short for the Federal Reserve Bank) in the USA – is going to introduce some monetary policy measure, e.g. to change the interest rate, and how that change is likely to affect the economy. The chairmen of these central banks are very influential policy makers in their countries. Among them the chairman of the Fed – Ben Bernanke and his predecessor, Alan Greenspan, chairman of the Fed during 1987–2006 – is widely perceived as the most powerful policy maker in the USA, if not in the world. The President of the ECB – currently Mario Draghi – is probably the single most influential policy maker in the euro area.

The model of economic activity we developed earlier (see Chapter 3) did not include an interest rate, so there was no role for the central bank and its president.

This was an oversimplification, and it is time to relax it. In this chapter, we shall introduce the simplest model needed to think about the determination of the interest rate and the role of the central bank, a model in which people face a simple portfolio choice: whether to hold money or to hold bonds. In that model, we can think of the interest rate as determined by the demand for money and the supply of money. Then, in the next chapter, we shall look at how the interest rate in turn affects demand and output. This simple model does not, however, do justice to the complexity of the financial system. When we focus on the crisis later (see Chapter 20), we shall look at the financial sector in more detail, but it is better to keep things simple until then.

The chapter has four sections:

● Section 4.1 looks at the demand for money.

● Section 4.2 assumes that the central bank directly controls the supply of money and shows how the interest rate is determined by the condition that the demand for money be equal to its supply.

● Section 4.3 introduces banks as suppliers of money, revisits interest rates and how they are determined and describes the role of the central bank in this process.

● Section 4.4, an optional section, presents two alternative ways of looking at the equilibrium. One focuses on the interbank market, the other focuses on the money multiplier.

Focus boxes expand on macroeconomic events or examples.

FOCUS
Deficit reduction: good or bad for investment?

You may have heard this argument in some form before: 'Private saving goes either towards financing the budget deficit or financing investment. It does not take a genius to conclude that reducing the budget deficit leaves more saving available for investment, so investment increases.'

This argument sounds simple and convincing. How do we reconcile it with what we just saw, namely that a deficit reduction may decrease rather than increase investment?

To make progress, first go back to equation (3.10) (in Chapter 3). There we learned that we can also think of the goods–market equilibrium condition as:

$$\text{Investment} = \text{Private saving} + \text{Public saving}$$
$$I = S + (\hat{T} - \hat{G})$$

In equilibrium, investment is indeed equal to private saving plus public saving. If public saving is positive, the government is said to be running a budget surplus; if public saving is negative, the government is said to be running a budget deficit. So it is true that, given private saving, if the government reduces its deficit – either by increasing taxes or reducing government spending so that $\hat{T} - \hat{G}$ goes up – investment must go up: given S, $\hat{T} - \hat{G}$ going up implies that I goes up.

The crucial part of this statement, however, is 'given private saving'. The point is that a fiscal contraction affects private saving as well: the contraction leads to lower output and therefore to lower income. As consumption goes down by less than income, private saving also goes down. And it may go down by more than the reduction in the budget deficit, leading to a decrease rather than an increase in investment. In terms of the equation above: if S decreases by more than $\hat{T} - \hat{G}$ increases, then I will decrease, not increase.

To sum up, a fiscal contraction may decrease investment. Or, looking at the reverse policy, a fiscal expansion – a decrease in taxes or an increase in spending – may actually increase investment.

Monetary policy, activity and the interest rate

Increase in M ⇔ monetary expansion. Decrease in M ⇔ Monetary contraction ⇔ Monetary tightening. ➤ An increase in the money supply is called a **monetary expansion**. A decrease in the money supply is called a **monetary contraction** or **monetary tightening**.

Let's take the case of a monetary expansion. Suppose that the central bank increases nominal money, M, through an open market operation. Given our assumption that the price level is fixed in the short run, this increase in nominal money leads to a one-for-one increase in real money, M/P. Let us denote the initial real money supply by M/P, the new higher one by M'/P, and trace in Figure 5.9 the effects of the money supply increase on output and the interest rate.

For a given price level P : M increases by 10% ⇒ M/P increases by 10%. ➤

● Again, step 1 is to see whether and how the IS and the LM curves shift.

Let's look at the IS curve first. The money supply does not *directly* affect either the supply of or the demand for goods. In other words, M does not appear in the IS relation. *Money does not appear in the IS relation ⇔ Money does not shift the IS curve.* ➤ Thus, a change in M does not shift the IS curve.

Money enters the LM relation, however, so the LM curve shifts when the money supply changes. As we saw in section 5.2, an increase in the money supply shifts the LM curve down, from LM to LM': at a given level of income, an increase in money leads *Money appears in the LM relation ⇔ Money shifts the LM curve.* ➤ to a decrease in the interest rate.

● Step 2 is to see how these shifts affect the equilibrium. The monetary expansion shifts the LM curve. It does not shift the IS curve. The economy moves along the IS curve, and *The increase in M shifts the LM curve down. It does not shift the IS curve. The economy moves along the IS curve.* ➤ the equilibrium moves from point A to point A'. Output increases from Y to Y', and the interest rate decreases from i to i'.

● Step 3 is to say it in words: the increase in money leads to a lower interest rate. The lower interest rate leads to an increase in investment and, in turn, to an increase in demand and output.

Margin notes create a classroom-like dialogue, remind the student of key terms and issues, and add context to the main text.

At the end of each chapter, a short **Summary** will help consolidate learning, bringing together the key concepts of the chapter to assist with review and revision.

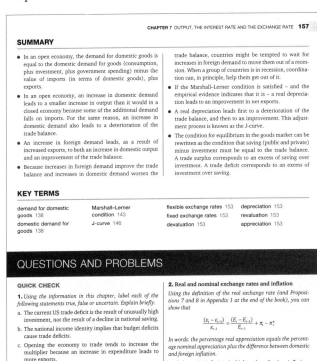

End of chapter questions remind students what they have just read and test that students have understood the chapter.

Key terms are highlighted in the text when they first appear. These terms are also included in the **Glossary** at the end of the book and on the website.

GUIDED TOUR TO MyEconLab®

MyEconLab is an online assessment and revision tool that puts you in control of your learning through a suite of study and practice tools tied to the online eText.

How do I use MyEconLab?

The **Course Home page** is where you can view announcements from your instructor and see an overview of your personal progress.

View the **Calendar** to see the dates for online homework, quizzes and tests that your instructor has set for you.

Your lecturer may have chosen **MyEconLab** to provide online homework, quizzes and texts. Check here to access the homework that has been set for you.

Practice tests for each chapter of the textbook enable you to check your understanding and identify the areas in which you need to do further work. Lecturers can customise and assign the practice tests or students can complete the tests on their own.

Keep track of your results in your own gradebook.

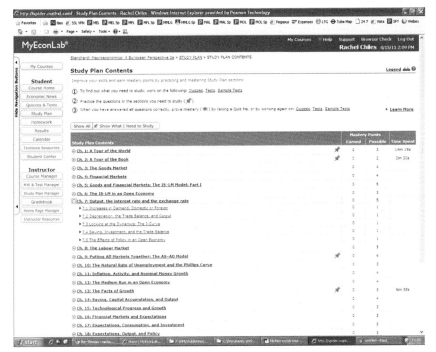

Work through the questions in your personalised **Study Plan** at your own pace. Because the Study Plan is tailored to each student, you will be able to study more efficiently by only reviewing areas where you still need practice. The Study Plan also saves your results, helping you see at a glance exactly which topics you need to review.

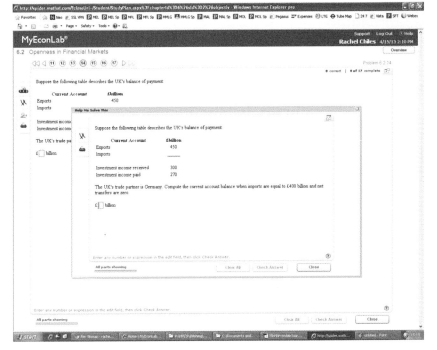

Additional instruction is provided in the form of detailed, step-by-step solutions to worked exercises. The figures in many of the exercises in **MyEconLab** are generated algorithmically, containing different values each time they are used. This means that you can practise individual concepts as often as you like.

There is also a link to the **eText** from every question in the Study Plan, so you can easily review and master the content.

View supporting multimedia resources such as links to the eText and **Glossary Flashcards**.

Lecturer training and support

Our dedicated team of Technology Specialists offer personalised training and support for **MyEconLab**, ensuring that you can maximise the benefits of **MyEconLab**. To make contact with your Technology Specialist, please email **feedback-cw@pearson.com**.

For a visual walkthrough of how to make the most of **MyEconLab**, visit **www.MyEconLab.com**.

To find details of your local sales representatives, go to **www.pearsoned.co.uk/replocator**.

PREFACE

The European edition of *Macroeconomics* is based on the well-tested US edition and on the experience of previous European editions in national languages – French, German, Spanish and Italian – some of which have been used in universities around Europe for many years (the Italian edition since 1998).

We had three goals in preparing this new edition:

- To provide an integrated view of macroeconomics.

  The book is built on one underlying model, a model that draws the implications of equilibrium conditions in three sets of markets: the goods market, the financial markets and the labour market. Depending on the issue at hand, the parts of the model relevant to the issue are developed in more detail while the other parts are simplified or lurk in the background. But the underlying model is always the same. This way, you will see macroeconomics as a coherent whole, not a collection of models. And you will be able to make sense not only of past macroeconomic events, but also of those that unfold in the future.

- To make close contact with current macroeconomic events.

  What makes macroeconomics exciting is the light it sheds on what is happening around the world, from the economic impact of the introduction of the euro in Western Europe, to the large US current account deficits, to the economic rise of China and other large emerging economies, and last but not least to the origins of the world crisis that started in 2007. These events – and many more – are described, not in footnotes but in the text or in detailed boxes. Each box shows how you can use what you have learned to get an understanding of these events. Our belief is that these boxes not only convey the 'life' of macroeconomics, but also reinforce the lessons from the models, making them more concrete and easier to grasp.

- To focus on European events, both from the viewpoint of the euro area and from viewpoint of the countries outside the euro: Sweden, Denmark and the UK in particular.

  Throught this edition we make a particular effort to use data, figures and examples mainly taken from the European experience. Two chapters are specifically dedicated to Europe. They describe the long process that led some countries to adopt the euro and others to decide not to adopt it. We have also added many new 'boxes' focusing on Europe – for example, on inflation targeting in Sweden, on the major macroeconometric models used in the euro area, on Poland's macroeconomic performance during the crisis, on the costs and benefits of a monetary union, on how to measure expected inflation in the euro area, and on the criticisms to the Growth and Stability Pact.

The second European edition further adapts the study of macroeconomics to the European context:

- As European economies are among the most open to the rest of the world, this edition includes the study of the open economy fully in the Core. How the open economy works in the short- and in the medium-run is studied by extending immediately the closed-economy model respectively in The Short-run and The Medium-run sections of the book.

- Europe being at the centre of a severe crisis that has recently cast doubts on the viability and on the future of the European project, this edition includes an up-to-date presentation of European events in a part fully dedicated to Europe, which includes a chapter describing how it was that the euro ended up in such a mess, a chapter on the recent economic crisis from a European perspective, and a chapter on high public debt as the major legacy of the recent crisis.

AUTHOR ACKNOWLEDGMENTS

This book builds on previous US, European and foreign editions, and the list of people who helped and made comments on them has grown too long to be given here. This particular edition would not have been possible without the dedication and the effort of Caterina Rho. We are particularly grateful to Kate Brewin for her patience and support, to Lucy Chantler whose work on the final manuscript was invaluable, and to all the team at Pearson who contributed to this project. We are also grateful to the academic staff who reviewed the material: Bertrand Candelon, Maastricht University School of Business and Economics; George Chouliarakis, University of Manchester; Martin Floden, Stockholm School of Economics; Michael Funke, Hamburg University; Pekka Ilmakunnas, School of Economics, Aalto University; Paul Scanlon, Trinity College Dublin; Jennifer Smith, University of Warwick; and Gianluigi Vernasca, University of Essex.

INTRODUCTION

The first two chapters of this book introduce you to the issues and the approach of macroeconomics.

Chapter 1 A tour of the world

Chapter 1 takes you on a macroeconomic tour of the world, from the recession that started in 2008, to the troubles of the euro area and the problem of unemployment in Europe, to the extraordinary growth in China and three other emerging economies: Brazil, India and Russia.

Chapter 2 A tour of the book

Chapter 2 takes you on a tour of the book. It defines the three central variables of macroeconomics: output, unemployment and inflation. It introduces the three concepts around which the book is organised: the short run, the medium run and the long run.

A TOUR OF THE WORLD

What is macroeconomics? The best way to answer is not to give you a formal definition, but rather to take you on an economic tour of the world, to describe both the main economic evolutions and the issues that keep macroeconomists and macroeconomic policy makers awake at night.

The truth is, at the time of writing (spring 2012), they are not sleeping well, and have not slept well in a long time. In 2008, the world economy entered a major macroeconomic crisis, the deepest one since the Great Depression. World output growth, which typically runs at 4 to 5% a year, was actually negative in 2009. Since then, growth has turned positive, and the world economy is slowly recovering. But the crisis has left a number of scars, and many worries remain.

However, the current difficulties, albeit very serious, could overshadow the fact that for over two decades the world economy has grown more rapidly than ever before, not only in advanced economies, but also (and actually at a higher pace) in emerging and developing countries, as shown in Figure 1.1. Notice two features of Figure 1.1: first, the impressive growth of emerging and developing economies since the 1990s, which largely contributed to the good performance of world output for almost two decades; second, the dramatic decrease of output growth (which actually turned negative in advanced economies) since 2008.

There is no way we can take you on a full tour of the world, so we shall give you a sense of these evolutions, and of some of the issues confronting different countries today: Europe, the USA, and a number of emerging countries – economies that have grown at an extraordinary pace and are now large enough to make a difference for the rest of the world – the largest of which are the so-called BRIC countries (Brazil, the Russian Federation, India and China).

- Section 1.1 looks at the European Union.

- Section 1.2 looks at the USA.

- Section 1.3 looks at the four largest emerging economies.

- Section 1.4 draws some conclusions and introduces some of the questions which will be answered in this book.

Read this chapter as you would read an article in a newspaper. Do not worry about the exact meaning of the words, or about understanding all the arguments in detail: the words will be defined, and the arguments will be developed in later chapters. Regard it as background, intended to introduce you to the issues of macroeconomics. If you enjoy reading this chapter, you will probably enjoy reading this book. Indeed, once you have read the book, come back to this chapter; see where you stand on the issues, and judge how much progress you have made in your study of macroeconomics.

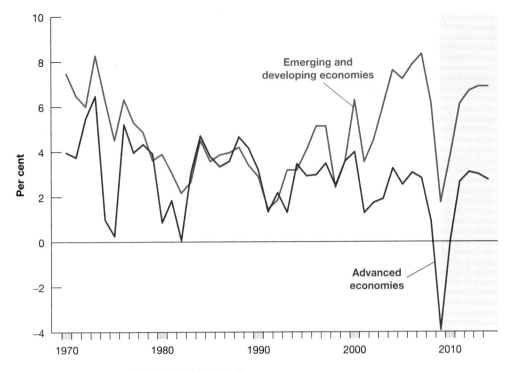

Figure 1.1

Real GDP growth in advanced, emerging and developing economies since 1970

From 2008–2010 GDP growth declined all over the world. In advanced economies it turned negative.

Source: IMF, *World Economic Outlook*, Spring 2009, p. 1. (Data from 2010 onwards are forecasts.)

1.1 EUROPE AND THE EURO

In 1957, six European countries decided to form a common market – an economic zone where people and goods could move freely. Since then, 21 more countries have joined, bringing the total to 27. This group is now known as the European Union, or **EU-27** for short (if you want to know more about the history of European enlargements, read the Focus on 'The history of EU enlargements in a nutshell'). The group of 27 countries forms a formidable economic power: their combined output (around €12,700 billion in 2011) now exceeds the output of the USA (around €10,600 billion in 2011), and many of them have a standard of living – a level of output per person – not far from that of the USA.

When macroeconomists study an economy, they first look at three variables:

- *Output* – the level of production of the economy as a whole – and its rate of growth.
- The *unemployment rate* – the proportion of workers in the economy who are not employed and are looking for a job.
- The *inflation rate* – the rate at which the average price of the goods in the economy is increasing over time.

Table 1.1 reports these data for the EU-27. The first column gives the share of output on the total output of the EU-27. Within the EU-27, the countries that have adopted a single

Table 1.1 Growth, unemployment and inflation in the EU since 1991

	Share of EU-27	Output growth rate[a]		Unemployment rate[b]		Inflation rate[c]	
	2011	1991–2000	2001–2011	1991–2000	2001–2011	1991–2000	2001–2011
EU-27	100	4.9	3.4	9.2	9.1	2.7	1.9
Euro area	75	2.2	1.2	9.6	9.4	2.5	1.0
Germany	20	2.1	1.1	7.8	7.9	1.7	1.7
France	16	2.0	1.2	10.5	9.2	1.4	1.8
Italy	13	1.6	0.4	10.4	8.1	3.8	2.0
UK	12	2.5	1.6	7.9	6.8	2.9	2.3
Spain	9	2.8	2.0	15.7	16	4.1	2.1
Poland	3	3.8	3.9	–	14.3	25.6	2.6
Czech Republic	1	0.3	3.2	–	12.1	12.1	1.9

[a] Output growth rate: annual rate of growth of output (real GDP).
[b] Unemployment rate: average over the year.
[c] Inflation rate: annual rate of change of the price level (GDP deflator).

Source: Statistical Annex of the European Economy, Spring 2012.

FOCUS
The history of EU enlargements in a nutshell

The EU begins life in the 1950s. At that time it was called the European Economic Community. The six founding members – Belgium, Germany, France, Italy, Luxembourg and the Netherlands created a new way of coming together to manage their joint interests, based essentially on economic integration. In 1957, the Treaty of Rome created the European Economic Community (EEC), a common market initially limited to agricultural products among the six member countries.

The first enlargement takes place when Denmark, Ireland and the UK join the EU on 1 January 1973, raising the number of member states to nine. Towards the end of that decade, the European Parliament increases its influence in EU affairs and in 1979 all citizens can, for the first time, elect its members directly.

In 1981 Greece becomes the 10th member of the EU and Spain and Portugal follow in 1986. In 1987 the Single European Act is signed, a treaty establishing the principle of the free flow of trade across EU borders, and creates the Single Market. Unification of Germany in 1990 brings in the Länder from Eastern Germany.

In the 1990s, with the collapse of communism across central and Eastern Europe, the process of economic integration accelerates. In 1993 the Single Market is completed with the 'four freedoms' of movement of goods, services, people and money. The 1990s is also the decade of two treaties, the 'Maastricht' Treaty which establishes the monetary union and the European Central Bank in 1993 and the Treaty of Amsterdam in 1999. In 1995, the EU gains three more new members: Austria, Finland and Sweden. A small village in Luxembourg gives its name to the 'Schengen' agreements that gradually allow people to travel within the EU without having their passports checked at the borders.

The 2000s is a decade of further expansion. A new currency is created, the euro, which becomes the common currency for many Europeans. The political divisions between east and west Europe are finally declared healed in 2004, when the Czech Republic, Estonia, Cyprus, Latvia, Lithuania, Hungary, Malta, Poland, Slovenia and Slovakia join the EU, followed in 2007 by Bulgaria and Romania. Croatia will join on 1 July 2013. Five candidates, Iceland, the Former Yugoslav Republic of Macedonia, Montenegro, Serbia and Turkey, have since applied for membership.

Source: This box is adapted from Eurostat, *Europe in Figures 1–1 Eurostat Yearbook 2011.*

currency, the euro, account for slightly more than three-quarters (75%) of this total. The four largest EU economies together (Germany, the UK, France and Italy) account for 61% of the EU-27's gross domestic product (GDP) in 2011. The next columns give the average value of the rate of growth of output, the unemployment rate and the inflation rate for the period 1991–2000, and for the period 2001–2011.

The main conclusion to draw from the table is that the economic performance of European countries after the turn of the millennium has not been as good as it was in the 1990s:

- Average annual output growth from 2001 to 2011 was 1.5 percentage points lower than in the previous decade in the EU-27 (only 1 percentage point lower in the euro area). This reflected a signicant slowdown in all of the largest European economies since 2008, and a recession in 2009, when GDP contracted by more than 4%.
- Low output growth was accompanied by persistently high unemployment. Although the average unemployment rate from 2001 to 2011 has slightly decreased with respect to the 1990s, in the euro area it is still 9.4%, reflecting the high unemployment rate in the largest economies in continental Europe, especially Spain, where unemployment was higher than 20% in 2011.
- The only good news is about inflation. Average annual inflation was 1.9% in the EU and 1% in the euro area.
- In the economies of central Europe (Poland and the Czech Republic in Table 1.1) inflation jumped when these economies made the transition to market economies and previously regulated prices were liberalised, but it stabilised in the following decade, surprisingly rapidly.

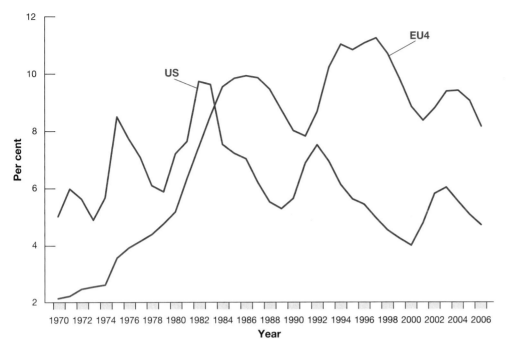

Figure 1.2

The unemployment rate in continental Europe and the USA since 1970

Until the beginning of the 1980s, the unemployment rate in the four major European countries was lower than the US rate, but then it rapidly increased.

At the time of writing, all attention is on the crisis of the euro and of government debt of euro area countries (we will tell you more about this in Chapter 20). Although short-run problems dominate the debate, European macroeconomists are still also concerned about three main issues that have been at the heart of the economic debate for a long time.

The first is, not surprisingly, high unemployment. High unemployment has not always been the norm in Europe. Figure 1.2 plots the evolution of the unemployment rate in the four largest continental European countries (Germany, France, Italy and Spain) taken as a whole, and in the USA, since 1970. Note how low the unemployment rate was in these European countries in the early 1970s. At that time, Americans used to refer to Europe as the land of the *unemployment miracle*; US macroeconomists travelled to Europe hoping to discover the secrets of that miracle. By the late 1970s, however, the miracle had vanished. Since then, unemployment in the four largest continental European countries has been much higher than in the USA. Despite a decrease since the late 1990s, it stood at 7.5% in 2008 and increased to 12% in 2010. Although the recent increase is due to the recession that hit the world economy since 2008, the unemployment rate in Europe is constantly nearly 2 percentage points higher than the unemployment rate in the USA. We will study the causes of the high unemployment rate in Europe later (see Chapter 10).

The second is the growth of income per person (or per capita). Table 1.2 shows income per person in some European countries and in those that have adopted the euro, relative to the USA. Income per person in the USA is set equal to 100 in each year so that, for example, the number 71.5 for the euro area in 1970 means that in that year per capita income in the euro area was 28.5% (100 − 71.5) lower than that in the USA. Europe emerged from the Second World War largely destroyed, but in the fifties and sixties the gap with the USA shrank rapidly: in 1980, euro area countries had reached almost 77% of US income per

Table 1.2 Income per capita in Europe compared to the USA (USA = 100)

	1970	1980	1990	2000	2005	2011
Euro area (EA-12)	71.5	76.9	75.7	71.2	70.0	74.3
Italy	67.8	75.7	76.5	73.0	66.3	69.4
France	71.6	78.2	75.1	72.1	69.9	72.7
Germany	89.3	94.4	92.6	74.0	73.8	81.8

Source: OECD *Economic Outlook* database.

Note in Table 1.2 the effect of German reunification: the data until 1990 refer to West Germany only. The data from 2000 onwards refer to all of Germany including the East which is on average poorer than the West.

capita. However, since then the gap has started to grow. Why? To answer this question, we need to understand the factors that contribute to economic growth over time. We will tackle this when discussing the sources of growth later (see Chapter 14).

The third issue is associated with the introduction, in 1999, of a common currency, the euro. After fourteen years, many questions remain. What has the euro done for Europe? What macroeconomic changes has it brought about? How should macroeconomic policy be conducted in this new environment? Should those European countries that originally decided to opt out of the common currency area now change their minds?

Supporters of the euro point first to its enormous symbolic importance. In light of the many wars that Europeans fought against each other over many centuries, what better proof that the page has definitely been turned than the adoption of a common currency? They also point to the economic advantages of having a common currency: no more changes in the relative price of currencies for European firms to worry about, no more need to change currencies when travelling between euro countries. Together with the removal of other obstacles to trade among European countries, the euro will contribute, they argue, to the creation of a large, if not the largest, single economic zone in the world. There is little question that the move to the euro is indeed one of the main economic events of the start of the twenty-first century.

Others worry that the symbolism of the euro has brought serious economic costs. They point out that a common currency means a common monetary policy, and that means the same interest rate across the euro countries. What if, they argue, one country plunges into recession while another is in the middle of an economic boom as is today the case, for instance in Spain and Germany? The first country needs lower interest rates to increase spending and output; the second country needs higher interest rates to slow down its economy. If interest rates have to be the same in both countries, what will happen? Isn't there the risk that one country will remain in recession for a long time or that the other will not be able to slow down its booming economy?

One important benefit has come to those countries that entered the euro with high public debt, such as Italy (where the ratio of debt to gross domestic product is above 120%), and has come in the form of a sharp reduction of interest rates. Before the euro, nominal interest rates in Italy were above 10% and every year the government had to use an amount of tax revenue as high as 12% of GDP (120×0.10) to pay the interest bill on the public debt. By 2005, after adopting the euro, nominal interest rates had fallen below 3% and the interest bill on the public debt (whose stock in 2005 was not much smaller than at the time Italy joined the euro) had fallen below 4% of GDP: a saving of 8 percentage points of GDP. Why have interest rates dropped so much? Mainly because interest rates reflect a country's credibility at maintaining low inflation: the European Central Bank enjoys a better reputation than the Bank of Italy and this is reflected in much lower interest rates. Since the cost of public debt is the interest that the state pays to holders of public bonds, the lower the interest rate, the lower the cost of debt.

At the time of writing the euro is in big trouble. Many euro area countries accumulated large public debts during the crisis and some of them find it increasingly difficult to finance interest payments on their debt. Investors have been losing confidence on the ability of some countries to repay their debt and are willing to continue buying euro area government bonds only at increasingly higher interest rates. The euro area is in the middle of a public debt crisis and the survival of the euro can no longer be taken for granted. We will discuss the first thirteen years of the euro and how it was that it found itself in such big trouble later (see Chapters 19 and 20).

1.2 THE ECONOMIC OUTLOOK IN THE USA

At the time of writing, the USA is still in the middle of the severe recession triggered by the biggest financial crisis since the Great Depression back in 1929. The economic outlook in the USA is gloomy, as GDP contracted by almost 3% in 2009, after a sharp slowdown the

Table 1.3 Growth, unemployment and inflation in the USA since 1991

Output growth rate[a]		Unemployment rate[b]		Inflation rate[c]	
1991–2000	2001–2011	1991–2000	2001–2011	1991–2000	2001–2011
3.3	1.6	4.8	6.2	2.8	2.3

[a] Output growth rate: annual rate of growth of output (GDP).
[b] Unemployment rate: average over the year.
[c] Inflation rate: annual rate of change of the price level (GDP deflator).

previous year. However, as we saw at the beginning of this chapter, this should not overlook the fact that US economic performance has been remarkable over the past two decades. To put the current numbers in perspective, Table 1.3 gives the same basic numbers for the US economy as Table 1.1 gives for the EU. The columns show the average value of the rate of growth of output, the unemployment rate and the inflation rate for the period 1991–2000, and for the period 2001–2011.

From an economic point of view, there is no question that the 1990s were amongst the best years in recent memory. Look at the column giving the numbers for the period 1991–2000:

- The average rate of growth was 3.3% per year, substantially higher than the average growth rate in the previous two decades.
- The average unemployment rate was 4.8%, again substantially lower than the average unemployment rate in the previous two decades.
- The average inflation rate was 2.8%, slightly higher than in Europe, but lower than the average inflation rate over the previous two decades.

In the recent past, however, the US economy has slowed down. Output did not grow in 2008 and decreased in 2009; it rebounded in 2010, but then growth decreased again. As a result, average growth for 2001–2011 substantially declined compared to the 1990s. What are the reasons for the recent slowdown? Between 2007 and 2008, families in the USA were hit by four economic shocks which occurred over a short period of time: an increase in oil prices, though now partially reversed; a fall in the price of their homes; a fall of the stock market; and a restriction of credit.

Let us start with the oil price increase. Figure 1.3 gives an idea of the size of the oil shock which occurred in the summer of 2008, comparing it with the oil price increases that have occurred since the end of the Second World War. (The chart shows the price of oil at constant US dollars, that is, taking into account the fact that, in the meantime, all prices went up.) Earlier this decade, a barrel of oil cost $20; in the summer of 2008, it reached $145 before returning to around $50: an increase of two and a half times compared to that in 2000–2001. Oil in the spring of 2012 was back to $106 per barrel. The easiest way to understand the effects of oil prices on importing countries is the following. If oil imports become more expensive, this means that in order to import the same amount of oil, importing countries will have to transfer a greater share of their income to the oil producing countries. This will contribute to impoverishing importers and to reducing their consumption.

The second shock that hit the US economy was a fall in house prices. Figure 1.4 shows house prices in the USA at constant prices, that is, adjusted for inflation, from 1890 until 2009. The graph relates house prices (adjusted for inflation) to three variables: population growth, construction costs and interest rates. The point is that none of these three factors explains the extraordinary rise in the price of homes in the past ten years, which has the characteristics of a speculative bubble.

What is the effect of falling house prices on the economy? To answer this question, consider that the value of the homes in which Americans live is about three-quarters of their total wealth. From the start of the financial crisis (summer 2007) until the end of 2009, the value of houses in the USA fell on average by 30%. This means that the wealth of American households has fallen (again on average) by 22.5% (30 × 0.75). What is the effect on consumption? Later (see Chapter 16) you will learn than in normal circumstances a family

Figure 1.3

Oil prices (in 2008 US dollars): January 1947–December 2008

The price of oil reached a historic high in 2008.

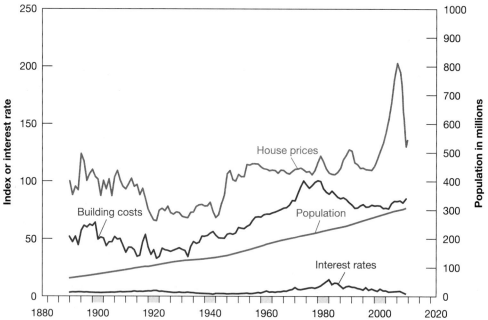

Figure 1.4

US house prices at constant dollars: 1880–2020

House prices in the USA boomed after 2000.

spends each year a share of its wealth equal to the product of the real interest rate multiplied by the value of wealth. Then, with a real interest rate of around 2%, this means that the direct effect (we say direct because there are the indirect effects, such as the fall in the stock market induced by the fall in house prices) of the real estate crisis on household consumption is to reduce spending by about 0.4% (22.5 × 0.02).

After the start of the financial crisis in mid-2007, two other shocks contributed to dampening consumption and aggregate demand in the USA. A fall in the stock market reduced the value of households' wealth invested in equities, and a restriction of credit made it more difficult and expensive to a borrow from banks. We will describe in detail how the crisis erupted and how it triggered a fully-edged recession later (see Chapter 20).

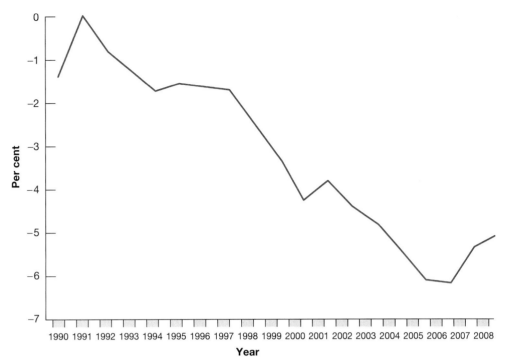

Figure 1.5

The US trade deficit since 1990

The US trade deficit has increased from about 1% of GDP in 1990 to 5% of GDP in 2008.

Here, to complete the outlook for the USA, we should add that, since the mid-1980s, the USA has purchased each year many more goods and services from abroad than those they could sell. In other words, US imports have consistently exceeded US exports to the rest of the world. Moreover, the difference between imports and exports – the trade deficit – has steadily increased and has only slightly reversed during the current recession. Figure 1.5 shows the evolution of the US trade deficit in relation to GDP since 1990.

If you purchase more goods than you are able to sell, it means that your spending exceeds your income, and you must bridge the difference by borrowing. Exactly the same is true for countries. Therefore, to finance the trade deficit, the USA has borrowed from the rest of the world. The increasing trade deficit led to an increase in the amount of money borrowed from abroad. This sounds a little strange: the richest country in the world borrows $720 billion a year from the rest of the world! An obvious question is whether all this can continue. What could happen if the willingness of other nations to lend to the USA stopped?

Think again of your personal situation. As long as people are willing to grant you a loan, you can clearly continue to borrow and thus spend more than your income. However, even if you can borrow, it might not be wise to do so for too long: by borrowing more you will have to repay more and thus spend less in the future. Again, the same logic applies to a country, in this case to the USA.

Can the USA continue to borrow such huge sums of money in the future? So far, foreigners have been prepared – and often eager – to finance the US trade deficit: they have been willing to buy securities issued by the US government or stocks quoted on the US stock exchanges. The question is whether they will be equally willing to do so in the future. In the late 1990s, some Asian countries – Thailand, South Korea and Indonesia, in particular – were borrowing large amounts from the rest of the world. Suddenly the rest of the world changed its mind, and stopped lending to Asia, forcing those countries to cancel their trade deficits suddenly. This 'sudden stop' caused serious economic crises in countries such as Thailand, Indonesia and South Korea. The USA is not Thailand, but some economists fear that it might become increasingly difficult for the USA to continue to borrow huge amounts of money in the future.

Table 1.4 Output growth and inflation in the BRIC countries since 1991

	Output growth rate[a]		Inflation rate[b]	
	1991–2000	2001–2011	1991–2000	2001–2011
Brazil	2.6	4.1	577.3	6.5
China	10.5	10.4	7.2	2.8
India	5.5	7.5	8.1	6.5
Russian Federation	–3.6	4.8	311.8	12.1

[a] Output growth rate: annual rate of growth of output (GDP).
[b] Inflation rate: annual rate of change of the price level (GDP deflator).

Source: IMF *World Economic Outlook* database.

1.3 THE LARGEST EMERGING ECONOMIES

Brazil, China, India and the Russian Federation (which are often called the **BRICs**) have grown rapidly over the past decade and are now the largest economies outside of the group of advanced countries. China, in particular, is in the news every day. It is increasingly seen as one of the major economic powers in the world. China's economy is twice as large as those of the other BRICs combined (and its population is enormous, more than four times that of the United States). China has been growing very fast for more than two decades, and its growth rate is almost twice that of the others.

This is shown in Table 1.4, which gives output growth and inflation for the periods 1991–2000 and 2001–2011 for China and the other three BRIC countries. Note that, compared to the previous tables, this table does not give unemployment rates. Unemployment in poorer countries is much harder to measure, as many workers may decide to stay in agriculture rather than be unemployed. As a result, official unemployment rates are typically not very informative.

Now, focus on the main feature of the table, namely the very high growth rate of output in China since the 1990s, compared to the other three countries considered. Over the past two decades (and also in the 1980s), Chinese output has grown on average at more than 10% a year, and the forecasts are for more of the same. This is a truly astonishing number: compare it to the numbers achieved by Europe or the US economy over the same period. At that rate, output doubles every seven years.

Where does the growth come from? It clearly comes from two sources. The first is very high accumulation of capital. The investment rate (the ratio of investment to output) in China is between 40 and 45% of output, a very high number. For comparison, the investment rate in the USA is only 17%, and 19% in the EU-27. More capital means higher productivity and higher output.

The second is very fast technological progress. The strategy followed by the Chinese government has been to encourage foreign firms to come and produce in China. As foreign firms are typically much more productive than Chinese firms, this has increased productivity and output in China. Another aspect of the strategy has been to encourage joint ventures between foreign and Chinese firms; making Chinese firms work with and learn from foreign firms has made them much more productive. When described in this way, achieving high productivity and high output growth appears easy, with easy recipes that every poor country could and should follow. Unfortunately, things are less obvious.

China is one of many countries which have made the transition from central planning to a market economy. Most of the other countries, from central Europe to the Russian Federation and the other former Soviet republics, have experienced a large decrease in output at the time of transition. Look at the rate of growth of output in the Russian Federation in the 1990s: on average, it was negative during the whole decade (–3.6%). Most still have growth rates far below that of China. In Brazil and the Russian Federation, economic performance over the 1990s was dampened by financial crises and episodes of hyperinflation at the beginning of that decade.

Although rapidly growing, China's output, expressed in dollars by multiplying the number in yuan (the Chinese currency) by the dollar/yuan exchange rate, is only $2.8 trillion,

Acronyms may change fast when they refer to groups of rapidly growing countries. The BRIC countries have recently been put side by side, in an **OECD** study, with two other large and rapidly growing economies, Indonesia and South Africa, and therefore the whole group has become the BRIICS.

There is a very handy way to know approximately how many years it will take for a variable – in this case output – to double. It is called the 'Rule of 70', as it states that in order to know the approximate number of years for a variable to double, take the number 70 and divide it by the growth rate of that variable.

roughly the same as that of Germany, and less than one-fourth that of the USA. Output per person is only $2,100, roughly one-twentieth of output per person in the USA.

In many countries, widespread corruption and poor property rights make firms unwilling to invest. So why has China fared so much better? Economists are not sure. Some believe that this is the result of a slower, better managed, transition: the first Chinese reforms took place in agriculture in 1980 and, even today, many firms remain owned by the state. Others argue that the fact that the communist party has remained in control has actually helped the economic transition; tight political control has allowed for a better protection of property rights, at least for firms, giving them incentives to invest. What about the comparison between China and India? In 1990, the two countries had the same GDP per person; today GDP per person is twice as high in China as it is in India. What explains this difference, and is the superior performance of the Chinese economy sustainable? Getting the answers to these questions, and thus learning what other poor countries can take from the Chinese experience, can clearly make a huge difference, not only for China but for the rest of the world.

Why have we added the BRIC countries to our tour of the world? After two decades of fast growth, the BRIC share of global output is now 15% (compared to 24% of the USA). Therefore, they start to be large enough to be able to make some difference in the world economy. Take, for example, the recent recession which started in 2008. Compared to the negative growth registered by advanced economies in 2009, average weighted real GDP growth in the BRICs was 7–8%.

According to the **IMF**, China added a full percentage point per year to global output growth in 2008–2010 (and thus accounted for 50% of global growth), while the USA 'subtracted' an average of 0.1 percentage points per year from global output during the same period.

1.4 LOOKING AHEAD

This concludes our world tour. There are many other regions of the world we could have looked at:

- Japan, whose growth performance for the 40 years following the Second World War was so impressive that it was referred to as an economic miracle, but is one of the few rich countries which have done very poorly in the past decade. Since a stock market crash in the early 1990s, Japan has been in a prolonged slump, with average output growth of under 1% a year.
- Latin America, which went from very high to low inflation in the 1990s. Some countries, such as Chile, appear to be in good economic shape. Some, such as Argentina, are struggling: a collapse of its exchange rate and a major banking crisis led to a large decline in output in the early 2000s, from which it is now recovering.
- Africa, which has suffered decades of economic stagnation, but where growth has been high since 2000, reaching 6.5% in 2007 (with only a slight decrease to 6% in 2008 and 2009), and reflecting growth in most of the countries of the continent.

There is a limit, however, to how much you can absorb in this first chapter. Think about the questions to which you have been exposed already:

- What determines expansions and recessions? Can government spending or monetary policy be used to help the economy out of a recession, as in the USA, Europe and in other advanced economies in 2008–2009? Why is the euro in big trouble?
- Why is inflation so much lower today than it was in the past? Can Europe reduce its unemployment rate? Should the USA reduce its trade deficit?
- Why do growth rates differ so much across countries, even over long periods? Why is per capita income in Europe lower than in the USA? Can other countries emulate China and grow at the same rate?

The purpose of this book is to give you a way of thinking about these questions. As we develop the tools you need, we shall show you how to use them by returning to these questions and showing you the answers they suggest.

KEY TERMS

EU-27 3

emerging economies 10

BRICs 10

Organisation for Economic
Cooperation and
Development (OECD) 10

International Monetary
Fund (IMF) 11

QUESTIONS AND PROBLEMS

QUICK CHECK

1. *Using the information in this chapter, label each of the following statements true, false or uncertain. Explain briefly.*

a. The unemployment rate in the USA increased considerably at the end of the last decade, but it is still substantially lower than the unemployment rate in Europe.

b. In the 1960s and early 1970s, the USA had a higher rate of unemployment than Europe, but at the time of writing it has a much lower rate of unemployment.

c. After the turn of the millennium, European countries experienced a slowdown in output growth.

d. The BRICs all experienced very high growth rates of output in the past two decades and stable inflation.

e. China's growth has contributed to half of world growth during the recession which started in 2008, and it is likely to become a new engine of world growth in the future.

f. The European 'unemployment miracle' refers to the extremely low rate of unemployment that Europe has been enjoying since the 1980s.

g. Income per capita in the euro area has declined compared to the USA since 1970, and this is true for all the largest member countries.

h. Even though the USA is the richest country in the world, it borrows hundreds of billions of dollars annually from the rest of the world.

2. Macroeconomic policy in Europe

Beware of simplistic answers to complicated macroeconomic questions. Consider each of the following statements and comment on whether there is another side to the story.

a. There is a simple solution to the problem of high European unemployment: reduce labour market rigidities.

b. What can be wrong about joining forces and adopting a common currency? The euro is obviously good for Europe.

3. Productivity growth in China

Productivity growth is at the heart of recent economic developments in China.

a. How has China achieved high rates of productivity growth in recent decades?

b. Has Europe achieved high rates of productivity growth in the past decade?

c. To what degree do you think China's methods of achieving productivity growth are relevant to Europe?

d. Do you think China's experience provides a model for developing countries to follow?

DIG DEEPER

4. Productivity growth in the USA

The average annual growth rate of output per worker in the USA rose from 1.8% during the period 1970–1995 to 2.8% for the years 1996–2006. This has led to talk of a New Economy and of sustained higher growth in the future than in the past.

a. Suppose output per worker grows at 1.8% per year. What will output per worker be – relative to today's level – in 10 years? 20 years? 50 years?

b. Suppose output per worker grows instead at 2.8% per year. What will output per worker be – relative to today's level – in 10 years? 20 years? 50 years?

c. If the USA has really entered a New Economy, and the average annual growth rate of output per worker has increased from 1.8% per year to 2.8%, how much higher will the US standard of living be in 10 years, 20 years and 50 years relative to what it would have been had the USA remained in the Old Economy?

d. Can we be sure the USA has really entered a New Economy, with a permanently higher growth rate? Why or why not?

5. When will Chinese output catch up with US output?

In 2008, US output was $14.3 trillion and Chinese output was $4.4 trillion. Suppose that from now on, the output of China grows at an annual rate of 10% per year (roughly what it has done during the past decade), while the output of the USA grows at an annual rate of 3% per year.

a. Using these assumptions and a spreadsheet, plot US and Chinese output over the next 100 years. How many years will it take for China to have a level of output equal to that of the USA?

b. When China catches up with the USA in total output, will residents of China have the same standard of living as US residents? Explain.

EXPLORE FURTHER

6. Post-war recessions in Europe

This question looks at the recessions of the past 40 years. To handle this problem, first obtain quarterly data on output growth in your country for the period 1970 to the latest year available from the Eurostat website (go to the Economy and Finance Section under Statistics Databases). Copy the data to your favourite spreadsheet program. Plot the quarterly GDP growth rates from 1970 through the more recent available year. Did any quarters have negative growth? Using the standard definition of recessions as two or more consecutive quarters of negative growth, answer the following questions:

a. How many recessions has the economy undergone since 1970?

b. How many quarters has each recession lasted?

c. In terms of length and magnitude, which two recessions have been the most severe?

7. *From problem 6, write down the quarters during which the economy has experienced negative output growth since 1970. Go to the Eurostat web page. Retrieve the monthly data series on the unemployment rate for the period 1970 to the most recent year available. Make sure all data series are seasonally adjusted.*

a. Look at each recession since 1970. What was the unemployment rate in the first month of the first quarter of negative growth? What was the unemployment rate in the last month of the last quarter of negative growth? By how much did the unemployment rate increase?

b. Which recession had the largest increase in the rate of unemployment?

Log on to **MyEconLab** and complete the studyplan exercises for this chapter to see how much you have learnt, and where you need to revise most.

MyEconLab

FURTHER READING

- This text comes with a web page (*www.prenhall.com/ blanchard*), which is updated regularly. For each chapter, the page offers discussions of current events, and includes relevant articles and Internet links. You can also use the page to make comments on the text, and engage in discussions with other readers.

- The best way to follow current economic events and issues is to read *The Economist*, a weekly magazine published in England. The articles in *The Economist* are well informed, well written, witty and opinionated. Make sure to read it regularly. (You may have purchased this book together with a 12-week subscription to the web version of *The Economist*. Take advantage of this.)

APPENDIX

Where to find the numbers?

This appendix will help you find the numbers you are looking for, be it inflation in Hungary last year, or consumption in the UK in 1959, or unemployment in Ireland in the 1980s.

For a quick look at current numbers

- The best source for the most recent numbers on output, unemployment, inflation, exchange rates, interest rates and stock prices for a large number of countries is the last four pages of *The Economist*, published each week (**www.economist.com**). The website, like most of the following websites, contains both information available free to anyone and information available only to subscribers. The 12-week subscription to the web version of *The Economist* which comes with this text gives you access to all the numbers and articles.

- A good source for recent numbers about the European economy is European Economy, the website of the Directorate General on Economic and Financial Affairs of the European Commission (DG ECFIN) and in particular its publication called *Statistical Annex* which contains data back to the 1970s for the main macroeconomic variables.

Numbers for other OECD countries

The OECD (**www.oecd.org**) includes most of the rich countries in the world. The OECD puts out three useful publications, all available electronically on the site:

- The first is the OECD *Economic Outlook*, published twice a year. In addition to describing current macroeconomic issues and evolutions, it includes a data appendix, with data for many macroeconomic variables. The data typically go back to the 1980s, and are reported consistently, both across time and across countries. A more complete data set is available in the form of a CD-ROM, which includes the most important macroeconomic variables for all OECD countries, typically going back to the 1960s. The data are also available on the OECD site.

- The second is the OECD *Employment Outlook*, published annually. It focuses more specifically on labour-market issues and numbers.

- Occasionally, the OECD puts together current and past data, and publishes the OECD *Historical Statistics*. At this point in time, the most recent is *Historical Statistics, 1970–2000*, published in 2001.

- The main strength of the publications of the International Monetary Fund (IMF, located in Washington, DC) is that they cover most of the countries of the world. A particularly useful IMF publication is the *World Economic Outlook*, published twice a year, which describes major evolutions in the world and in specific member countries. Selected series associated with the *Outlook* are available on the IMF site.

- A wealth of data on emerging economies and on the question of what determines an economy's growth can be found on the website of the World Bank (**databank. worldbank.org**), particularly in the section World Development Indicators.

For more detail about European economies

- For data on just about everything, including economic data, a precious source is the Eurostat website, which offers several statistics, databases and publications, amongst which are *Europe in Figures* and *Principal European Economic Indicators*, both published annually.

Current macroeconomic issues

A number of websites offer information and commentaries about the macroeconomic issues of the day. In addition to the *Economist* website mentioned earlier, two useful sites are:

- The Morgan Stanley site, with daily commentaries of macroeconomic events.

- The site maintained by Nouriel Roubini (**www.roubini. com**) offers an extensive set of links to articles and discussions on macroeconomic issues (by subscription).

Chapter 2

A TOUR OF THE BOOK

The words *output*, *unemployment* and *inflation* appear daily in newspapers and on the evening news. So when we used these words earlier (see Chapter 1), you knew roughly what we were talking about. It is now time to define these words more precisely and this is what we do in the first three sections of this chapter.

- Section 2.1 looks at output.

- Section 2.2 looks at the unemployment rate and the inflation rate.

- Section 2.3 introduces two important relations between these three variables: Okun's law and the Phillips curve.

- Section 2.4 then introduces the three central concepts around which the book is organised:

  - The *short run*: What happens to the economy from year to year.

  - The *medium run*: What happens to the economy over a decade or so.

  - The *long run*: What happens to the economy over a half century or longer.

- Building on these three concepts, Section 2.5 gives you the road map to the rest of the book.

2.1 AGGREGATE OUTPUT

Economists studying economic activity in the nineteenth century or during the Great Depression had no measure of aggregate activity (*aggregate* is the word macroeconomists use for total) on which to rely. They had to put together bits and pieces of information, such as the shipments of iron ore, or sales at some department stores, to try to infer what was happening to the economy as a whole.

Two economists, Simon Kuznets, from Harvard University, and Richard Stone, from Cambridge University, were given the Nobel Prize for their contributions to the development of the national income and product accounts – a gigantic intellectual and empirical achievement.

It was not until the end of the Second World War that a **System of National Accounts (SNA)** was put together in a number of European countries. Like any accounting system, the national income accounts first define concepts, and then construct measures corresponding to these concepts. You need only to look at statistics from countries that have not yet developed such accounts to realise how crucial are such precision and consistency. Without them, numbers that should add up do not; trying to understand what is going on feels like trying to balance someone else's personal accounts. We shall not burden you with the details of national income accounting here. But, because you will occasionally need to know the definition of a variable and how variables relate to each other, the Focus 'The circular flow of income' gives you the basic accounting framework used in European countries (and, with minor variations, in most other countries) today. You will find it useful whenever you want to look at economic data on your own.

You may come across another term, **gross national product**, or GNP. There is a subtle difference between 'domestic' and 'national', and thus between GDP and GNP. We examine the distinction later (see Chapter 6). For now, ignore it.

GDP: production, and income

The measure of **aggregate output** in the system of national accounts is called the **gross domestic product**, or **GDP**, for short. To understand how GDP is constructed, it is best to work with a simple example. So consider an economy composed of just two firms:

In reality, not only workers and machines are required for steel production, but also are iron ore, electricity, etc. We shall ignore these to keep the example simple.

- Firm 1 produces steel, employing workers and using machines to produce the steel. It sells the steel for €100 to Firm 2, which produces cars. Firm 1 pays its workers €80, leaving €20 in profit to the firm.
- Firm 2 buys the steel and uses it, together with workers and machines, to produce cars. Revenues from car sales are €200. Of the €200, €100 goes to pay for steel and €70 goes to workers in the firm, leaving €30 in profit to the firm.

We can summarise this information in a table:

Steel company (Firm 1)			Car company (Firm 2)		
Revenues from sales		€100	Revenues from sales		€200
Expenses		€80	Expenses		€170
Wages	€80		Wages	€70	
			Steel purchases	€100	
Profit		€20	Profit		€30

How would you define aggregate output in this economy? As the sum of the values of all goods produced in the economy – the sum of €100 from the production of steel and €200 from the production of cars, so €300? Or as just the value of cars, which is equal to €200?

An intermediate good is a good used in the production of another good. Some goods can be both final goods and intermediate goods. Potatoes sold directly to consumers are final goods. Potatoes used to produce potato chips are intermediate goods. Can you think of other examples?

Some thought suggests that the right answer must be €200. Why? Because steel is an **intermediate good**: it is used up in the production of cars. Once we count the production of cars, we do not want to count the production of the goods that went into the production of these cars.

This motivates the first definition of GDP.

1. *GDP is the value of the final goods and services produced in the economy during a given period.*

The important word here is *final*. We want to count only the production of **final goods**, not intermediate goods. Using our example, we can make this point in another way. Suppose the two firms merged, so that the sale of steel took place inside the new firm and was no longer recorded. The accounts of the new firm would be given by the following table:

Steel and car company	
Revenues from sales	€200
Expenses (wages)	€150
Profit	€50

All we would see would be one firm selling cars for €200, paying workers €80 + €70 = €150, and making €20 + €30 = €50 in profits. The €200 measure would remain unchanged – as it should. We do not want our measure of aggregate output to depend on whether firms decide to merge or not.

This first definition gives us one way to construct GDP: by recording and adding up the production of all final goods – and this is indeed roughly the way actual GDP numbers are put together. But it also suggests a second way of thinking about and constructing GDP.

2. GDP is the sum of value added in the economy during a given period.
The term **value added** means exactly what it suggests. The value added by a firm is defined as the value of its production minus the value of the intermediate goods used in production.

In our two-firm example, the steel company does not use intermediate goods. Its value added is simply equal to the value of the steel it produces, €100. The car company, however, uses steel as an intermediate good. Thus, the value added by the car company is equal to the value of the cars it produces minus the value of the steel it uses in production, €200 – €100 = €100. Total value added in the economy, or GDP, equals €100 + €100 = €200. (Note that aggregate value added would remain the same if the steel and car firms merged and became a single firm. In this case, we would not observe intermediate goods at all – as steel would be produced and then used to produce cars within the single firm – and the value added in the single firm would simply be equal to the value of cars, €200.)

This definition gives us a second way of thinking about GDP. Put together, the two definitions imply that the value of final goods and services – the first definition of GDP – can also be thought of as the sum of the value added by all the firms in the economy – the second definition of GDP.

So far, we have looked at GDP from the *production side*. The other way of looking at GDP is from the *income side*. Go back to our example and think about the revenues left to a firm after it has paid for its intermediate goods. Some of the revenues go to pay workers – this component is called *labour income*. The rest goes to the firm – that component is called *capital income* or *profit income*.

Of the €100 of value added by the steel manufacturer, €80 goes to workers (labour income) and the remaining €20 goes to the firm (capital income). Of the €100 of value added by the car manufacturer, €70 goes to labour income and €30 to capital income. For the economy as a whole, labour income is equal to €150 (€80 + €70), capital income is equal to €50 (€20 + €30). Value added is equal to the sum of labour income, and capital income is equal to €200 (€150 + €50).

This motivates the third definition of GDP.

◄ The labour share in the example is thus 75%. In advanced countries, the share of labour is indeed typically between 65 and 75%.

3. GDP is the sum of incomes in the economy during a given period.
To summarise: you can think about aggregate output – GDP – in three different but equivalent ways.

- From the production side: GDP equals the value of the final goods and services produced in the economy during a given period.
- Also from the production side: GDP is the sum of value added in the economy during a given period.
- From the income side: GDP is the sum of incomes in the economy during a given period.

◄ Two lessons to remember:

- GDP is the measure of aggregate output, which we can look at from the production side (aggregate production), or the income side (aggregate income).
- Aggregate production and aggregate income are always equal.

FOCUS
The circular flow of income

A modern economy comprises a number of actors whose economic decisions are broadly classified into consumption decisions – made by consumers who form the household sector – and production decisions – made by enterprises in the producing sector.

- Consumers buy (durable and non-durable) goods and services produced by firms, so that every euro spent on goods and services becomes income for firms.
- Firms spend this income on factors of production such as capital, labour and raw materials, as well as on purchases of intermediate goods and capital goods, that they need for producing goods and services, and pay a service to factor owners.

These factor payments are what enables expenditure on goods and service. There is a circular flow of money, and the whole amount of money circulating in a given time is aggregate or national income. As every euro spent by consumers becomes a euro of income for firms, it follows that aggregate expenditure in an economy is identical to aggregate income. Parallel to the circular flow of money, there is a circular flow of goods and services between firms and households.

If we consider that a modern economy also includes a government sector that collects taxes, then the amount of income that consumers will have at their disposal for consumption is aggregate income net of taxes, which is defined disposable income. The government sector's earnings are spent on purchases of goods and services, as well as on transfers to households (for example, in the form of subsidies).

The circular flow view shows that national income can be measured in various ways:

- as the income of all the factors of production (wages for workers, rents for land owners, interest payments for capital owners), or
- as the expenditure of the various sectors of the economy (consumption expenditure by households, investment by firms, purchases of goods and services by the government sector).

Therefore, it holds by definition that national income is equal to the sum of all purchases by all sectors in the economy, i.e. consumption, investment and public spending. Later (see Chapter 6) we will consider a more realistic representation of an economy where goods and services produced by domestic firms can also be purchased by foreign consumers (exports), while at the same time domestic consumers can purchase goods and services produced abroad (imports).

Nominal and real GDP

GDP in the EU was around €12,700 billion in 2011, compared to 715 billion in 1970. Was European output really almost 18 times higher in 2011 than in 1970? Obviously not: much of the increase reflected an increase in prices rather than an increase in quantities produced. This leads to the distinction between nominal GDP and real GDP.

Warning! People often use *nominal* to denote small amounts. Economists use *nominal* for variables expressed in current prices. And they surely do not refer to small amounts: the numbers typically run in the billions or trillions of dollars.

Nominal GDP is the sum of the quantities of final goods produced times their current price. This definition makes clear that nominal GDP increases over time for two reasons:

- First, the production of most goods increases over time.
- Second, the prices of most goods also increase over time.

If our goal is to measure production and its change over time, we need to eliminate the effect of increasing prices on our measure of GDP. That's why **real GDP** is constructed as the sum of the quantities of final goods times constant (rather than current) prices.

If the economy produced only one final good, say, a particular car model, constructing real GDP would be easy: we would use the price of the car in a given year, and then use it to multiply the quantity of cars produced in each year. An example will help here. Consider an economy which only produces cars – and, to avoid issues we shall tackle later, assume the same model is produced every year. Suppose the number and the price of cars in three successive years are given by:

Year	Quantity of cars	Price of cars	Nominal GDP	Real GDP (in 2005 prices)
2004	10	€20,000	€200,000	€240,000
2005	12	€24,000	€288,000	€288,000
2006	13	€26,000	€338,000	€312,000

Nominal GDP, which is equal to the quantity of cars times their price, goes up from €200,000 in 2004 to €288,000 in 2005 – a 44% increase – and from €288,000 in 2005 to €338,000 in 2006 – a 16% increase.

- To construct real GDP, we need to multiply the number of cars in each year by a common price. Suppose we use the price of a car in 2005 as the common price. This approach gives us in effect real GDP in 2005 prices.
- Using this approach, real GDP in 2004 (in 2005 prices) equals 10 cars × €24,000 per car = €240,000. Real GDP in 2005 (in 2005 prices) equals 12 cars × €24,000 per car = €288,000, the same as nominal GDP in 2005. Real GDP in 2006 (in 2005 prices) is equal to 13 × €24,000 = €312,000.

    So real GDP goes up from €240,000 in 2004 to €288,000 in 2005 – a 20% increase – and from €288,000 in 2005 to €312,000 in 2006 – an 8% increase.
- How different would our results have been if we had decided to construct real GDP using the price of a car in, say, 2006 rather than 2005? Obviously, the level of real GDP in each year would be different (because the prices are not the same in 2006 as in 2005); but its rate of change from year to year would be the same as above.

 To be sure, compute real GDP in 2006 prices, and compute the rate of growth from 2004 to 2005, and from 2005 to 2006.

The problem in constructing real GDP in practice is that there is obviously more than one final good. Real GDP must be defined as a weighted average of the output of all final goods, and this brings us to what the weights should be.

The relative prices of the goods would appear to be the natural weights. If one good costs twice as much per unit as another, then that good should count for twice as much as the other in the construction of real output. But this raises the question: what if, as is typically the case, relative prices change over time? Should we choose the relative prices of a particular year as weights, or should we change the weights over time? More discussion of these issues, and of the way real GDP is constructed, is left to the appendix to this chapter.

Figure 2.1 plots the evolution of both nominal GDP and real GDP in the EU since 1970. By construction, the two are equal in 2005. The figure shows that real GDP in 2010 was

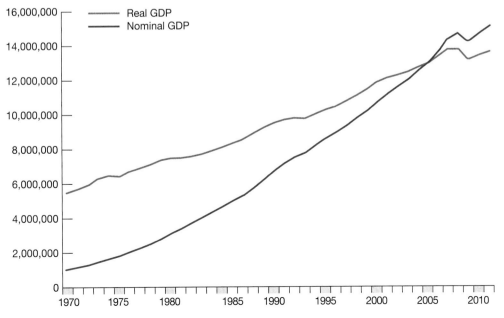

Figure 2.1

Nominal and real GDP in the EU-15 since 1970

Source: http://stats.oecd.org/

Suppose real GDP was measured in ➤ 2006 prices rather than 2005 prices. Where would the nominal GDP and real GDP lines on the graph intersect?

about 2.5 times its level of 1970 – a considerable increase, but clearly much less than the 18-fold increase in nominal GDP over the same period. The difference between the two results comes from the increase in prices over the period.

The terms *nominal GDP* and *real GDP* each have many synonyms, and you are likely to encounter them in your readings:

- Nominal GDP is also called **GDP at current prices**.
- Real GDP is also called **GDP in terms of goods**, **GDP at constant prices**, **GDP adjusted for inflation**.

In the chapters that follow, unless we indicate otherwise:

- GDP will refer to real GDP and Y_t will denote real GDP in year t.
- Nominal GDP, and variables measured in current prices, will be denoted by a euro sign in front of them – for example, $€Y_t$ for nominal GDP in year t.

GDP: level versus growth rate

Warning: One must be careful about ➤ how one does the comparison. More on this in Chapter 13.

We have focused so far on the level of real GDP. This is an important number, which gives the economic size of a country. A country with twice the GDP of another country is economically twice as big as the other country. Equally important is the level of **real GDP per capita**, the ratio of real GDP to the population of the country. It gives us the average standard of living of the country.

In assessing the performance of the economy from year to year, economists focus, however, on the rate of growth of real GDP, on **GDP growth**. Periods of positive GDP growth are called **expansions**. Periods of negative GDP growth are called **recessions**.

The evolution of GDP growth in the EU-15 and the USA since 1970 is given in Figure 2.2. GDP growth in year t is constructed as $(Y_t - Y_{t-1})/Y_{t-1}$. The figure shows how both economies have gone through a series of expansions, interrupted by short recessions. Look in particular at the past 20 years. Note how a recession in the early 1990s gave way to a long expansion from 1992 to 2000. In 2001, growth was positive but very low. It has increased since then,

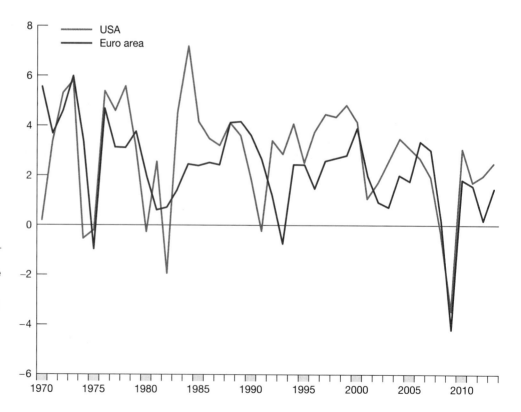

Figure 2.2

Growth rate of GDP in the EU-15 and in the USA since 1970

Since 1970, both the EU-15 and the US economy have gone through a series of expansions, interrupted by short recessions. The recession associated with the current crisis has been particularly deep.

Source: http://stats.oecd.org/

but in 2008 both economies have entered into a severe recession following the financial crisis that has shaken most of the world economy since the summer of 2007. Although there is no official definition of what constitutes a recession, the convention is to refer to a recession if the economy goes through at least two consecutive quarters of negative growth. Sometimes growth is negative in two or more quarters, but positive for a year as a whole. This was the case for the USA in 2001, when growth was negative during each of the first three quarters, but positive for the year as a whole; thus 2001 qualifies as a (mild) recession.

FOCUS
Real GDP, technological progress and the price of computers

A tough problem in computing real GDP is how to deal with changes in quality of existing goods. One of the most difficult cases is computers. It would clearly be absurd to assume that a personal computer in 2010 is the same good as a personal computer produced in 1981 (the year in which the IBM PC was introduced): the same amount of money can clearly buy much more computing in 2010 than it could in 1981. But how much more? Does a 2010 computer provide 10 times, 100 times or 1,000 times the computing services of a 1981 computer? How should we take into account the improvements in internal speed, the size of the RAM or of the hard disk, the fact that computers can access the Internet, and so on?

The approach used by economists to adjust for these improvements is to look at the market for computers and how it values computers with different characteristics in a given year. For example, suppose the evidence from prices of different models on the market show that people are willing to pay 10% more for a computer with a speed of 3 GHz (3,000 MHz) rather than 2 GHz. (The first American edition of this book, published in 1996, compared two computers, with speeds of 50 and 16 MHz respectively. This is a good indication of technological progress. A further indication of technological progress is that, for the past few years, progress has not been made by increasing the speed of processors, but rather by using multi-core processors. We shall leave this aspect aside here, but people in charge of national income accounts cannot; they have to take this change into account as

well.) Suppose new computers this year have a speed of 3 GHz compared to a speed of 2 GHz for new computers last year. And suppose the price of new computers this year is the same as the price of new computers last year. Then, economists in charge of computing the adjusted price of computers will conclude that new computers are in fact 10% cheaper than last year.

This approach, which treats goods as providing a collection of characteristics – here, speed, memory, and so on – each with an implicit price, is called **hedonic pricing** (*hedone* means 'pleasure' in Greek). It is used by Eurostat – which constructs real GDP – to estimate changes in the price of complex and fast changing goods, such as automobiles and computers. Using this approach, Eurostat estimates that, for a given price, the quality of new computers has increased on average by 18% a year since 1981. Put another way, a typical personal computer in 2010 delivers $1.18^{29} = 121$ times the computing services a typical personal computer delivered in 1981.

Not only do computers deliver more services, but they have become cheaper as well: their price has declined by about 10% a year since 1981. Putting this together with the information in the previous paragraph, this implies that their quality-adjusted price has fallen at an average rate of 18% + 10% = 28% per year. Put another way, a pound spent on a computer today buys $1.28^{29} = 1,285$ times more computing services than a pound spent on a computer in 1981.

2.2 OTHER MAJOR MACROECONOMIC VARIABLES

The unemployment rate

Because it is a measure of aggregate activity, GDP is obviously the most important macroeconomic variable. But two other variables, unemployment and inflation, tell us about other important aspects of how an economy is performing. This section focuses on the unemployment rate.

Source: Copyright Universal Press Syndicate.

Let's start with some definitions: **employment** is the number of people who have a job; **unemployment** is the number of people who do not have a job but are looking for one. The **labour force** is the sum of employment and unemployment:

$$L \quad = \quad N \quad + \quad U$$

labour force = employment + unemployment

The **unemployment rate** is the ratio of the number of people who are unemployed to the number of people in the labour force:

$$u = \frac{U}{L}$$

unemployment rate = unemployment/labour force

Constructing the unemployment rate is less obvious than you might have thought. The cartoon notwithstanding, determining whether somebody is employed is straightforward. Determining whether somebody is unemployed is harder. Recall from the definition that, to be classified as unemployed, a person must meet two conditions: that he or she does not have a job, and he or she is looking for one; this second condition is harder to assess.

Until recently, in most European countries, the only available source of data on unemployment was the number of people registered at unemployment offices, and so only those workers who were registered in unemployment offices were counted as unemployed. This system led to a poor measure of unemployment. How many of those looking for jobs actually registered at the unemployment office varied both across countries and across time. Those who had no incentive to register – for example, those who had exhausted their unemployment benefits – were unlikely to take the time to come to the unemployment office, so they were not counted. Countries with less generous benefit systems were likely to have fewer unemployed registering, and therefore smaller measured unemployment rates.

Today, most rich countries rely on large surveys of households to compute the unemployment rate. In Europe, this survey is called the **Labour Force Survey (LFS)**. It relies on interviews to a representative sample of individuals. Each individual is classied as employed if he or she has worked for at least one hour during the week preceding that of the interview in whatever activity. Estimates based on the LFS show that the average unemployment rate in the European Union (EU-15) in 2008 was 7.1%. In the USA, a survey called the Current Population Survey (CPS) relies on interviews of 50,000 households every month. The survey classifies a person as employed if he or she has a job at the time of the interview; it classifies a person as unemployed if he or she does not have a job and has been looking for a job in the past four weeks. Estimates based on the CPS show that, during 2007, an average of 144.4 million people were employed and 7.0 million people were unemployed, so the unemployment rate was 4.6 (7.0/(144.4 + 7.0) × 100).

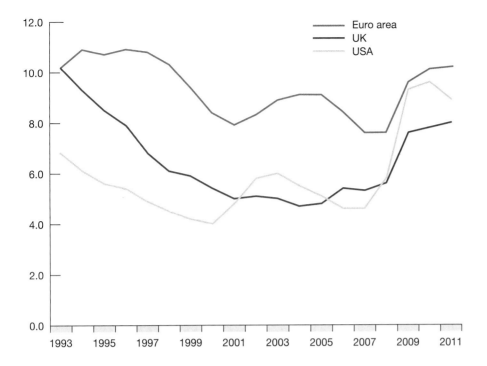

Figure 2.3

Unemployment rate in the euro area, UK and the USA since 1993

Since 1993, the unemployment rate has fluctuated between 4 and 11%, going down during expansions and going up during recessions. The effect of the crisis is highly visible, with the unemployment rate close to 10%.

Source: Eurostat

Note that only those looking for a job are counted as unemployed; those who do not have a job and are not looking for one are counted as **not in the labour force**. When unemployment is high, some of the unemployed give up looking for a job and therefore are no longer counted as unemployed. These people are known as **discouraged workers**. Take an extreme example: if all workers without a job gave up looking for one, the unemployment rate would equal zero. This would make the unemployment rate a very poor indicator of what is happening in the labour market. This example is too extreme; in practice, when the economy slows down, we typically observe both an increase in unemployment and an increase in the number of people who drop out of the labour force. Equivalently, a higher unemployment rate is typically associated with a lower **participation rate**, defined as the ratio of the labour force to the total population of working age.

Figure 2.3 shows the evolution of unemployment in the euro area, the UK and the USA since the early 1990s. At that time, the unemployment rate in the euro area, including the UK, was much higher than in the USA. Since then, it has rapidly gone down in the UK, where now it is similar to the USA, and more slowly in the euro area. In the USA, note in particular how much the unemployment rate decreased during the long expansion of the 1990s, reaching 3.9% in 2000; and how much it increased during the short recession of 2001 and more recently during the recession which began in 2008.

◀ At the start of economic reform in Eastern Europe in the early 1990s, unemployment increased dramatically. But equally dramatic was the fall in the participation rate. In Poland in 1990, 70% of the decrease in employment was reflected in early retirements – by people dropping out of the labour force rather than becoming unemployed.

Why do economists care about unemployment?

Economists care about unemployment for two reasons. They care about unemployment because of its direct effect on the welfare of the unemployed. Although unemployment benefits are more generous today than they were during the Great Depression, unemployment is still often associated with financial and psychological suffering. How much suffering depends on the nature of the unemployment. One image of unemployment is that of a stagnant pool, of people remaining unemployed for long periods of time. As you will see later (in Chapter 8), this image reflects what happens in many European countries, but things are quite different in some other European countries, as well as in the USA where the unemployed typically remain unemployed for a short time, and the image of a stagnant pool is not appropriate. In the USA, for example, each month, many people become unemployed, and many of the unemployed (on average, 25–30% of them) find jobs. However, even there, some groups (often the young, the ethnic minorities and the unskilled) suffer disproportionately from unemployment, remaining chronically unemployed and being more vulnerable to becoming unemployed when the unemployment rate increases.

Economists also care about the unemployment rate because it provides a signal that the economy may not be using some of its resources efficiently. Many workers who want to work do not find jobs; the economy is not utilising efficiently its human resources. From this

> It is probably because of statements like this that economics is known as the 'dismal science'.

viewpoint, can very low unemployment also be a problem? The answer is yes. Like an engine running at too high a speed, an economy in which unemployment is very low may be over-utilising its resources and may run into labour shortages. How low is 'too low'? This is a difficult question, a question we will take up at more length later in the book. The question came up in 2000 in the USA. At the end of 2000, some economists worried that the unemployment rate, 4% at the time, was indeed too low. So, while they did not advocate triggering a recession, they favoured lower (but positive) output growth for some time, so as to allow the unemployment rate to increase to a somewhat higher level. It turned out that they got more than they had asked for: a mild recession, rather than a slowdown.

The inflation rate

Inflation is a sustained rise in the general level of prices – the **price level**. The **inflation rate** is the rate at which the price level increases. Symmetrically, **deflation** is a sustained decline

> Deflation is rare, but it happens. Japan has had deflation, off and on, since the late 1990s.

in the price level. It corresponds to a negative inflation rate.

The practical issue is how to define the price level so the inflation rate can be measured. Macroeconomists typically look at two measures of the price level, at two *price indexes*: the GDP deflator and the consumer price index.

The GDP deflator

We saw earlier how increases in nominal GDP can come either from an increase in real GDP, or from an increase in prices. Put another way, if we see nominal GDP increasing faster than real GDP, the difference must come from an increase in prices.

This remark motivates the definition of the GDP deflator. The **GDP deflator** in year t, P_t, is defined as the ratio of nominal GDP to real GDP in year t:

$$P_t = \frac{Nominal\ GDP_t}{Real\ GDP_t} = \frac{€Y_t}{Y_t}$$

Note that, in the year in which, by construction, real GDP is equal to nominal GDP (which is currently 2005 in official statistics in the EU, as well as the USA), this definition implies that the price level is equal to 1. This is worth emphasising: the GDP deflator is what is

> Index numbers are often set equal to 100 (in the **base year**) rather than to 1.

called an **index number**. Its level is chosen arbitrarily – here it is equal to 1 in 2005 – and has no economic interpretation. But its rate of change, $(P_t - P_{t-1})/P_{t-1}$ (which we shall denote by π_t in the rest of the book), has a clear economic interpretation: it gives the rate at which

> Compute the GDP deflator and the associated rate of inflation from 2004 to 2005 and from 2005 to 2006 in our car example in Section 2.1, when real GDP is constructed using the 2005 price of cars as the common price.

the general level of prices increases over time – the rate of inflation.

One advantage to defining the price level as the GDP deflator is that it implies a simple relation between nominal GDP, real GDP and the GDP deflator. To see this, reorganise the previous equation to get:

$$€Y_t = P_t Y_t$$

> For a refresher, see Appendix 1, Proposition 7.

Nominal GDP is equal to the GDP deflator times real GDP. Or, putting it in terms of rates of change: the rate of growth of nominal GDP is equal to the rate of inflation plus the rate of growth of real GDP.

The consumer price index

The GDP deflator gives the average price of output – the final goods produced in the economy. But consumers care about the average price of consumption – the goods they consume. The two prices need not be the same: the set of goods produced in the economy is not the same as the set of goods purchased by consumers, for two reasons:

- Some of the goods in GDP are sold not to consumers but to firms (machine tools, for example), to the government or to foreigners.
- Some of the goods bought by consumers are not produced domestically but are imported from abroad.

To measure the average price of consumption, or equivalently, the **cost of living**, macroeconomists look at another index, the consumer price index, or CPI. The CPI has been in existence in the USA since 1917, and is published monthly (in contrast, numbers for GDP and the GDP deflator are only constructed and published quarterly). In Europe, the price index which is most frequently used is the **harmonised index of consumer prices**, or **HICP**, measured by Eurostat, the Statistical Office of the European Communities. The HICP gives comparable measures of inflation in different subsets of European countries: the euro area, the EU, the European Economic Area (EEA, which includes Norway, Iceland and Liechtenstein, besides the EU) and for other countries including accession and candidate countries. They provide the official measure of consumer price inflation in the euro area for the purposes of monetary policy. They also allow the assessing of inflation convergence as required under the Maastricht criteria.

◀ Do not confuse the CPI with the PPI, or producer price index, which is an index of prices of domestically produced goods in manufacturing, mining, agriculture, fishing, forestry and electric utility industries.

Like the GDP deflator (the price level associated with aggregate output, GDP), the HICP is an index. It is set equal to 100 in the period chosen as the base period, and so its level has no particular significance. The current base period is 2001, so the value for 2001 is equal to 100. In January 2009, the HICP in the euro area was 117.4; thus, it cost 17.4% more in euros to purchase the same consumption basket than in 2001.

You may wonder how the rate of inflation differs depending on whether the GDP deflator or the HICP is used to measure it. The answer is given in Figure 2.4, which plots the two inflation rates since 1996 for the euro area. The figure yields two conclusions:

- The HICP and the GDP deflator move together most of the time. In most years, the two inflation rates differ by less than 0.5%.
- There are clear exceptions to the first conclusion. In 1998, 2002 and 2009, the increase in the HICP was slightly smaller than the increase in the GDP deflator. That means that the price of goods consumed in the euro area (measured by the HICP) was lower than the price of goods produced in the euro area (measured by the GDP deflator). When the price of imported goods decreases relative to the price of goods produced in the euro area, the HICP increases less than the GDP deflator. This is precisely what

Figure 2.4

Inflation rate, using the HICP and the GDP deflator in the euro area since 1996

The inflation rates, computed using either the HICP or the GDP deflator, are largely similar.

Source: http://stats.oecd.org/

happened in these years. The price of oil plummeted: in 1998 it went to a historic low, only slightly above 10 dollars per barrel, and it recorded a second fall in 2002 and a further fall in 2009. As Europe is a major oil importer, the result was a decrease in the HICP compared to the GDP deflator. Look at what happened in 2008, when oil prices went to very high levels (as described in Chapter 1, Figure 1.3): the HICP increased much more than the GDP deflator.

In what follows, we shall typically assume that the two indexes move together, so we do not need to distinguish between them. We shall simply talk about the price level and denote it by P_t, without indicating whether we have the harmonised index of consumer prices or the GDP deflator in mind.

Why do economists care about inflation?

If a higher inflation rate meant just a faster but proportional increase in all prices and wages – a case called pure inflation – inflation would be only a minor inconvenience, as relative prices would be unaffected.

Take, for example, the workers' real wage – the wage measured in terms of goods rather than in euros. In an economy with 10% inflation, prices would increase by 10% a year. But wages would also increase by 10% a year, so real wages would be unaffected by inflation. Inflation would not be entirely irrelevant; people would have to keep track of the increase in prices and wages when making decisions. But this would be a small burden, hardly justifying making control of the inflation rate one of the major goals of macroeconomic policy.

So, why do economists care about inflation? Precisely because there is no such thing as pure inflation:

- During periods of inflation, not all prices and wages rise proportionately. Because they don't, inflation affects income distribution. For example, retirees in many countries receive pensions that do not keep up with the price level, so they lose in relation to other groups when inflation is high. For example, during the very high inflation that took place in Russia in the 1990s, retirement pensions did not keep up with inflation, and many retirees were pushed to near starvation.
- Inflation leads to other distortions. Some prices, which are fixed by law or by **regulation**, lag behind the others, leading to changes in relative prices. Variations in relative prices also lead to more uncertainty, making it harder for firms to take decisions about the future, such as investment decisions. Taxation interacts with inflation to create more distortions. If tax brackets are not adjusted for inflation, for example, people move into higher and higher tax brackets as their nominal income increases, even if their real income remains the same.

Newspapers sometimes confuse deflation and recession. They may happen together but they are not the same. Deflation is a decrease in the price level. A recession is a decrease in real output. ➤

If inflation is so bad, does this imply that deflation (negative inflation) is good?

The answer is no. First, high deflation (a large negative rate of inflation) would create many of the same problems as high inflation, from distortions to increased uncertainty. Second (as we shall see later in the text), even a low rate of deflation limits the ability of monetary policy to affect output. So what is the 'best' rate of inflation? Most macroeconomists believe that the best rate of inflation is a low and stable rate of inflation, somewhere between 1 and 4%. We shall look at the pros and cons of different rates of inflation later in the text.

2.3 OUTPUT, UNEMPLOYMENT AND THE INFLATION RATE, OKUN'S LAW AND THE PHILLIPS CURVE

We have looked separately at the three main dimensions of aggregate economic activity: output growth, the unemployment rate and the inflation rate. Clearly they are not independent, and much of the text will be spent looking at the relations between them in detail. But it is useful to have a first look now.

Okun's law

Intuition suggests that if output growth is high, unemployment will decrease, and this is indeed true. This relation was first examined by an American economist called Arthur Okun, and for this reason has become known as **Okun's law**. Figure 2.5 plots the change in the unemployment rate on the vertical axis against the rate of growth of output on the horizontal axis, for the USA since 1960. It also draws the line that best fits the cloud of points in the figure. Looking at the figure and the line, two conclusions can be reached:

> Arthur Okun was an adviser to President Kennedy in the 1960s. Okun's law is, of course, not a law, but an empirical regularity.

> Such a graph, plotting one variable against another, is called a scatter plot. The line is called a regression line. For more on regressions, look at the Appendix at the end of the chapter.

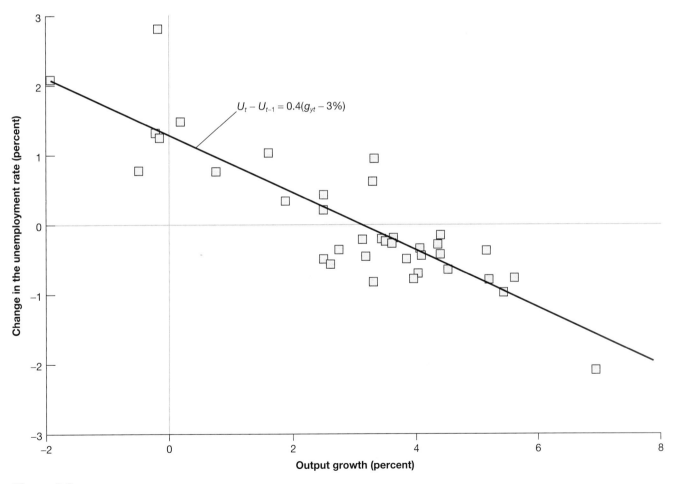

$$U_t - U_{t-1} = 0.4(g_{yt} - 3\%)$$

Figure 2.5

Changes in the unemployment rate versus output growth in the USA, 1960–2010

High output growth leads to a decrease in the unemployment rate, low output growth to an increase in the unemployment rate.

Since 1960, the US unemployment rate has fluctuated between 3% and 10%, going down during expansions and going up during recessions.

- The line is downward sloping and fits the cloud of points quite well. Put in economic terms, there is a tight relation between the two variables: higher output growth leads to a decrease in unemployment. The slope of the line is –0.4. This implies that, on average, an increase in the growth rate of 1% decreases the unemployment rate by roughly –0.4%. This is why unemployment goes up in recessions, and down in expansions. This relation has a simple but important implication: the key to decreasing unemployment is high enough growth.

- The line crosses the horizontal axis at the point where output growth is roughly equal to 3%. In economic terms, it takes a growth rate of about 3% to keep unemployment constant. This is for two reasons. The first is that population, and thus the labour force, increases over time, so employment must grow over time just to keep the unemployment rate constant. The second is that output per worker is also increasing with time, which implies that output growth is higher than employment growth. Suppose, for example, that the labour force grows at 1%, and that output per worker grows at 2%. Then output growth must be equal to 3% (1% + 2%) just to keep the unemployment rate constant.

The Phillips curve

Okun's law implies that, with strong enough growth, one can decrease the unemployment rate to very low levels. But intuition suggests that, when unemployment becomes very low, the economy is likely to overheat, and that this will lead to upward pressure on inflation. And, to a large extent, this is true. This relation was first explored in 1958 by a New Zealand economist, A.W. Phillips, and has become known as the **Phillips curve**. Phillips plotted the rate of inflation against the unemployment rate. Since then, the Phillips curve has been redefined as a relation between the change in the rate of inflation and the unemployment rate. Figure 2.6 plots the change in the inflation rate (measured using the CPI) on the vertical axis against the unemployment rate on the horizontal axis, together with the line that fits the cloud of points best, for the USA since 1960. Looking at the figure, again two conclusions can be reached:

It should probably be known as the *Phillips relation*, but it is too late to change that. ➤

- The line is downward sloping, although the fit is not as tight as it was for Okun's law: Higher unemployment leads, on average, to a decrease in inflation; lower unemployment leads to an increase in inflation. But this is only true on average. Sometimes, high unemployment is associated with an increase in inflation.

- The line crosses the horizontal axis at the point where the unemployment rate is roughly equal to 6%. In economic terms, when unemployment has been below 6%, inflation has typically increased, suggesting that the economy was overheating, operating above its potential. When unemployment has been above 6%, inflation has typically decreased, suggesting that the economy was operating below potential. But, again, here the relation is not tight enough that the unemployment rate at which the economy overheats can be pinned down very precisely. This explains why some economists believe that we should try to maintain a lower unemployment rate, say 4 or 5%, and others believe that it may be dangerous, leading to overheating and increasing inflation.

Clearly, a successful economy is an economy which combines high output growth, low unemployment and low inflation. Can all these objectives be achieved simultaneously? Is low unemployment compatible with low and stable inflation? Do policy makers have the tools to sustain growth, to achieve low unemployment while maintaining low inflation? These are the questions we shall take up as we go through the text. The next two sections give you the road map.

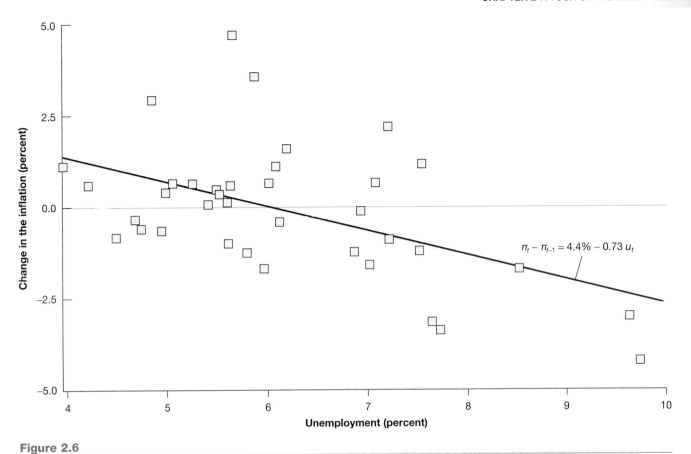

Figure 2.6

Changes in the inflation rate versus the unemployment rate in the USA, 1960–2010

A low unemployment rate leads to an increase in the inflation rate, a high unemployment rate to a decrease in the inflation rate.

2.4 THE SHORT RUN, THE MEDIUM RUN AND THE LONG RUN

What determines the level of aggregate output in an economy?

- One answer is suggested from reading newspapers: movements in output come from movements in the demand for goods. You probably have read news stories that begin like this: 'Production and sales of automobiles were higher last month, due to a surge in consumer confidence, which drove consumers to showrooms in record numbers.' Stories like these highlight the role demand plays in determining aggregate output; they point to factors that affect demand, ranging from consumer confidence to interest rates.
- But, surely, no amount of Indian consumers rushing to Indian showrooms can increase India's output to the level of output in the USA. This suggests a second answer: what matters when it comes to aggregate output is the supply side – how much the economy can produce. How much can be produced depends on how advanced the technology of the country is, how much capital it is using, and the size and the skills of its labour force. These factors – not consumer confidence – are the fundamental determinants of a country's level of output.
- The previous argument can be taken one step further: neither technology, nor capital, nor skills are given. The technological sophistication of a country depends on its ability to innovate and introduce new technologies. The size of its capital stock depends on how much people save. The skills of workers depend on the quality of the country's education

system. Other factors are also important: if firms are to operate efficiently, for example, they need a clear system of laws under which to operate and an honest government to enforce those laws. This suggests a third answer: the true determinants of output are factors like a country's education system, its saving rate, and the quality of its government. If we want to understand what determines the level of output, we must look at these factors.

You might be wondering at this point which of the three answers is right. The fact is all three are right. But each applies over a different time frame:

- In the **short run**, say, 2–3 years, the first answer is the right one. Year-to-year movements in output are primarily driven by movements in demand. Changes in demand, perhaps due to changes in consumer confidence or other factors, can lead to a decrease in output (a recession) or an increase in output (an expansion).
- In the **medium run**, say, a decade, the second answer is the right one. Over the medium run, the economy tends to return to the level of output determined by supply factors: the capital stock, the level of technology and the size of the labour force. And, over a decade or so, these factors move sufficiently slowly that we can take them as given.
- In the **long run**, say, a few decades or more, the third answer is the right one. To understand why China has been able to achieve such a high growth rate since 1980, we must understand why both the capital stock and the level of technology in China are increasing so fast. To do so, we must look at factors like the education system, the saving rate, and the role of the government.

This way of thinking about the determinants of output underlies macroeconomics, and it underlies the organisation of this book.

2.5 A TOUR OF THE BOOK

The book is organised in three parts: a core, extensions, and, finally, an epilogue. This organisation is shown in Figure 2.7. Let us describe it in more detail.

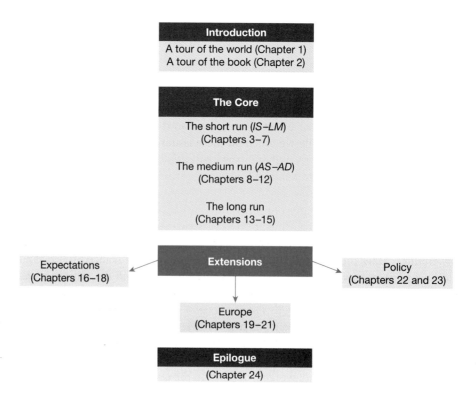

Figure 2.7

The organisation of the book

The core

The core is composed of three parts – the short run, the medium run, and the long run.

- Chapters 3 to 7 look at how output is determined in the short run.

  To focus on the role of demand, we assume that firms are willing to supply any quantity at a given price. In other words, we ignore supply constraints. Chapter 3 looks at the goods market. Chapter 4 focuses on financial markets. Chapter 5 puts the goods and financial markets together. The resulting framework is known as the *IS–LM* model. Developed in the late 1930s, the *IS–LM* model still provides a simple way of thinking about the determination of output in the short run, and it remains a basic building block of macroeconomics. Chapter 6 provides an open economy version of the *IS–LM* model. Chapter 7 describes the joint movement of output, the interest rate and the exchange rate in an open economy.

- Chapters 8 to 12 develop the supply side and look at how output is determined in the medium run.

  Chapter 8 introduces the labour market. Chapter 9 puts together goods, financial and labour markets, and shows you how to think about the determination of output both in the short run and in the medium run. The resulting framework is called the aggregate supply–aggregate demand (*AS–AD*) model, and, together with the *IS–LM* is another workhorse of macroeconomics. Chapter 10 focuses on the relation between unemployment and money growth. Chapter 11 looks at the effects of money growth on output, unemployment and inflation. Chapter 12 provides an open economy version of the *AS–AD* model.

- Chapters 13 to 15 focus on the long run.

  Chapter 13 introduces the relevant facts by looking at the growth of output both across countries and over long periods of time. Chapters 14 and 15 then discuss how both capital accumulation and technological progress determine growth.

Extensions

The core chapters give you a way of thinking about how output (and unemployment and inflation) is determined over the short, medium and long run. However, they leave out several elements, which are explored in two extensions.

- Expectations play an essential role in macroeconomics. Nearly all the economic decisions people and firms make – whether or not to buy a car, whether to buy bonds or to buy stocks, whether or not to build a new plant – depend on their expectations about future income, future profits, future interest rates and so on. Fiscal and monetary policy affect economic activity not only through their direct effects, but also through their effects on people's and firms' expectations. While we touch on these issues in the core, Chapters 16 to 18 offer a more detailed treatment, and draw the implications for fiscal and monetary policy.

- The core chapters on the short run and the medium run focus on fluctuations in output, on expansions and on recessions. Sometimes, however, the word *fluctuations* does not accurately capture what is happening when something goes very wrong such as when, as during the crisis of 2007–2010, the whole world has gone through a prolonged economic slump, or when government debt becomes very high. In Europe, the crisis led to a stockpiling of public debt in all countries, with the result that those who had already accumulated a high debt before the crisis found themselves in trouble, particularly countries within the euro area. How it was that some countries decided to adopt a common currency – the euro – and the origins of the current crisis that has hit the euro area are the topics of Chapter 19. Chapter 20 discusses the origins of the crisis that hit the world economy since 2007, the policy responses to it and the uncomfortable legacies the world has to deal with in these days. Chapter 21 is entirely devoted to the major of such legacies: public debt.

- Monetary policy and fiscal policy are discussed in nearly every chapter of the book. We have seen how economic policy can help a country out of a recession, or slow down an overheating economy, improve its trade position and stimulate capital accumulation. However, there are also arguments in favour of restraining macroeconomic policy. Chapter 22 discusses two possibilities: that policy makers might do more harm than good, and that they might not choose what is the best for the country. Chapter 23 discusses the policy rules that are often introduced by countries to guide or restrain the action of monetary and fiscal policy makers.

Epilogue

Macroeconomics is not a fixed body of knowledge. It evolves over time. The final chapter, Chapter 24, looks at the recent history of macroeconomics and how macroeconomists have come to believe what they believe today. From the outside, macroeconomics sometimes looks like a field divided between schools – 'Keynesians', 'monetarists', 'new classicals', 'supply-siders' and so on – hurling arguments at each other. The actual process of research is more orderly and more productive than this image suggests.

We identify what we see as the main differences among macroeconomists, the set of propositions that define the core of macroeconomics today, and the challenges posed to macroeconomists by the crisis.

SUMMARY

- We can think of GDP, the measure of aggregate output, in three equivalent ways: (1) GDP is the value of the final goods and services produced in the economy during a given period; (2) GDP is the sum of value added in the economy during a given period; and (3) GDP is the sum of incomes in the economy during a given period.

- Nominal GDP is the sum of the quantities of final goods produced multiplied by their current prices. This implies that changes in nominal GDP reflect both changes in quantities and changes in prices. Real GDP is a measure of output. Changes in real GDP reflect changes in quantities only.

- A person is classified as unemployed if he or she does not have a job and is looking for one. The unemployment rate is the ratio of the number of people unemployed to the number of people in the labour force. The labour force is the sum of those employed and those unemployed.

- Economists care about unemployment because of the human cost it represents. They also look at unemployment because it sends a signal about how efficiently the economy is using its resources. High unemployment indicates that the economy is not utilising its human resources efficiently.

- Inflation is a rise in the general level of prices – the price level. The inflation rate is the rate at which the price level increases. Macroeconomists look at two measures of the price level. The first is the GDP deflator, which is the average price of the goods produced in the economy. The second is the consumer price index (CPI), which is the average price of goods consumed in the economy.

- Inflation leads to changes in income distribution, to distortions and to increased uncertainty.

- There are two important relations between output, unemployment and inflation. The first, called Okun's law, is a relation between output growth and the change in unemployment: high output growth typically leads to a decrease in the unemployment rate. The second, called the Phillips curve, is a relation between unemployment and inflation: a low unemployment rate typically leads to an increase in the inflation rate.

- Macroeconomists distinguish between the short run (a few years), the medium run (a decade) and the long run (a few decades or more). They think of output as being determined by demand in the short run. They think of output as being determined by the level of technology, the capital stock and the labour force in the medium run. Finally, they think of output as being determined by factors like education, research, saving and the quality of government in the long run.

KEY TERMS

QUESTIONS AND PROBLEMS

QUICK CHECK

1. *Using the information in this chapter, label each of the following statements true, false or uncertain. Explain briefly.*

a. The share of labour income in GDP is much larger than the share of capital income.

b. GDP in the EU-15 was 14 times higher in 2008 than it was in 1970.

c. When the unemployment rate is high, the participation rate is also likely to be high.

d. The rate of unemployment tends to fall during expansions and rise during recessions.

e. If the Japanese CPI is currently at 108 and the EU-15 HICP is at 104, then the Japanese rate of inflation is higher than the EU-15 rate of inflation.

f. The rate of inflation computed using the CPI is a better index of inflation than the rate of inflation computed using the GDP deflator.

2. *Suppose you are measuring annual GDP by adding up the final value of all goods and services produced in the economy. Determine the effect on GDP of each of the following transactions.*

a. A seafood restaurant buys €100 worth of fish from a fisherman.

b. A family spends €100 on a fish dinner at a seafood restaurant.

c. The Greek national airline buys a new jet from Boeing for €200 million.

d. Airbus sells one of its jets to Denzel Washington for €100 million.

3. During a given year, the following activities occur:

i. A silver-mining company pays its workers €200,000 to mine 75 pounds of silver. The silver is then sold to a jewellery manufacturer for €300,000.

ii. The jewellery manufacturer pays its workers €250,000 to make silver necklaces, which the manufacturer sells directly to consumers for €1,000,000.

a. Using the 'production-of-final-goods' approach, what is GDP in this economy?

b. What is the value added at each stage of production? Using the 'value-added' approach, what is GDP?

c. What are the total wages and profits earned? Using the income approach, what is GDP?

4. *An economy produces three goods: cars, computers and oranges. Quantities and prices per unit for years 2006 and 2007 are as follows:*

	2006		2007	
	Quantity	Price	Quantity	Price
Cars	10	€2,000	12	€3,000
Computers	4	€1,000	6	€500
Oranges	1,000	€1	1,000	€1

a. What is nominal GDP in 2006 and in 2007? By what percentage does nominal GDP change from 2006 to 2007?

b. Using the prices for 2006 as the set of common prices, what is real GDP in 2006 and in 2007? By what percentage does real GDP change from 2006 to 2007?

c. Using the prices for 2007 as the set of common prices, what is real GDP in 2006 and in 2007? By what percentage does real GDP change from 2006 to 2007?

d. Why are the two output growth rates constructed in (b) and (c) different? Which one is correct? Explain your answer.

5. *Consider the economy described in problem 4.*

a. Use the prices for 2006 as the set of common prices to compute real GDP in 2006 and in 2007. Compute the GDP deflator for 2006 and for 2007 and compute the rate of inflation from 2006 to 2007.

b. Use the prices for 2007 as the set of common prices to compute real GDP in 2006 and in 2007. Compute the GDP deflator for 2006 and for 2007 and compute the rate of inflation from 2006 to 2007.

c. Why are the two rates of inflation different? Which one is correct? Explain your answer.

6. *Consider the economy described in problem 4.*

a. Construct real GDP for years 2006 and 2007 by using the average price of each good over the two years.

b. By what percentage does real GDP change from 2006 to 2007?

c. What is the GDP deflator in 2006 and 2007? Using the GDP deflator, what is the rate of inflation from 2006 to 2007?

d. Is this an attractive solution to the problems pointed out in problems 4 and 5 (i.e., two different growth rates and two different inflation rates, depending on which set of prices is used)? (The answer is yes and is the basis for the construction of chained-type deflators. See the appendix to this chapter for more discussion.)

DIG DEEPER

7. Hedonic pricing

As the second Focus box in this chapter explains, it is difficult to measure the true increase in prices of goods whose characteristics change over time. For such goods, part of any price increase can be attributed to an increase in quality. Hedonic pricing offers a method to compute the quality-adjusted increase in prices.

a. Consider the case of a routine medical check-up. Name some reasons you might want to use hedonic pricing to measure the change in the price of this service.

Now consider the case of a medical check-up for a pregnant woman. Suppose that a new ultrasound method is introduced. In the first year that this method is available, half of doctors offer the new method, and half offer the old method. A check-up using the new method costs 10% more than a check-up using the old method.

b. In percentage terms, how much of a quality increase does the new method represent over the old method? (*Hint*: Consider the fact that some women choose to see a doctor offering the new method, when they could have chosen to see a doctor offering the old method.)

Now, in addition, suppose that in the first year the new ultrasound method is available, the price of check-ups using the new method is 15% higher than the price of check-ups in the previous year (when everyone used the old method).

c. How much of the higher price for check-ups using the new method (as compared to check-ups in the previous year) reflects a true price increase of check-ups and how much represents a quality increase? In other words, how much higher is the quality-adjusted price of check-ups using the new method as compared to the price of check-ups in the previous year?

In many cases, the kind of information we used in parts (b) and (c) is not available. For example, suppose that in the year the new ultrasound method is introduced, all doctors adopt the new method, so the old method is no longer used. In addition, continue to assume that the price of check-ups in the year the new method is introduced is 15% higher than the price of check-ups in the previous year (when everyone used the old method). Thus, we observe a 15% price increase in check-ups, but we realise that the quality of check-ups has increased.

d. Under these assumptions, what information required to compute the quality-adjusted price increase of check-ups is lacking? Even without this information, can we say anything about the quality-adjusted price increase of check-ups? Is it more than 15%? Less than 15%? Explain.

8. Measured and true GDP

Suppose that instead of cooking dinner for an hour, you decide to work an extra hour, earning an additional €12. You then purchase some (takeaway) Chinese food, which costs you €10.

a. By how much does measured GDP increase?

b. Do you think the increase in measured GDP accurately reflects the effect on output of your decision to work? Explain.

EXPLORE FURTHER

9. The labour market and the recession of 2007–2012

Go to the Eurostat web page and retrieve the quarterly data at constant prices for your country and for the EU-27.

a. Plot the quarterly GDP growth rates from 2005 to 2012. Did any quarters have negative growth? How did your country differ from the average EU-27?

Now retrieve the monthly data series on the participation rate, employment, the employment-to-population ratio and the unemployment rate for the period 2007–2012. Make sure all data series are seasonally adjusted.

a. How did the unemployment rate change in 2007 and after? Do you think the unemployment rate tells the whole story about the labour market? How did the participation rate evolve? What might explain the change in the participation rate?

b. Some economists prefer to look at employment as opposed to unemployment. How did the growth of employment after 2007 compare to the growth of employment before 2001? How did the employment-to-population ratio change?

c. How did the economic performance in your country compare with the EU-27's?

---

*Log on to **MyEconLab** and complete the studyplan exercises for this chapter to see how much you have learnt, and where you need to revise most.*

MyEconLab

FURTHER READING

- If you want to learn more about the definition and the construction of the many economic indicators that are regularly reported on the news, two easy-to-read references are:
   The Guide to Economic Indicators, by M.E. Sharpe (New York, 7th edn, 2005).
   The Economist Guide to Economic Indicators, by the staff of *The Economist* (New York: Bloomberg, 6th edn, 2007).

- In 1995, the US Senate set up a commission to study the construction of the CPI and make recommendations about potential changes. The commission concluded that the rate of inflation computed using the CPI was on average about 1% too high. If this conclusion is correct, this implies in particular that real wages (nominal wages divided by the CPI) have grown at 1% more per year than is currently being reported. For more on the conclusions of the commission and some of the exchanges that followed, read 'Consumer prices, the consumer price index, and the cost of living', by Michael Boskin et al., *Journal of Economic Perspectives*, 1998, **12**(1), 3–26.

- For a short history of the construction of the National Income Accounts, read 'GDP: one of the great inventions of the 20th century', *Survey of Current Business*, January 2000, 1–9. (***www.bea.gov/bea/articles/beawide/2000/0100od.pdf***).

- For a discussion of some of the problems involved in measuring activity, read 'What we don't know could hurt us; some reflections on the measurement of economic activity', by Katherine Abraham, *Journal of Economic Perspectives*, 2005, **19**(3), 3–18.

- To see why it is hard to measure the price level and output correctly, read 'Viagra and the Wealth of Nations', by Paul Krugman, 1998 (***www.pkarchive.org/theory/viagra.html***). (Paul Krugman is an economist at Princeton University – Nobel prize winner for Economics in 2009 – and a columnist at the *New York Times*. His columns are opinionated, insightful and fun to read.)

APPENDIX

The construction of real GDP and chain-type indexes

The example we used in the chapter had only one final good – cars – so constructing real GDP was easy. But how do we construct real GDP when there is more than one final good? This appendix gives the answer.

To understand how real GDP in an economy with many final goods is constructed, all you need to do is look at an economy where there are just two final goods. What works for two goods works just as well for millions of goods.

So, suppose that an economy produces two final goods, say wine and potatoes:

- In year 0, it produces 10 pounds of potatoes at a price of €1 a pound, and 5 bottles of wine at a price of €2 a bottle.
- In year 1, it produces 15 pounds of potatoes at a price of €1 a pound, and 5 bottles of wine, at a price of €3 a bottle.
- Nominal GDP in year 0 is therefore equal to €20. Nominal GDP in year 1 is equal to €30.

This information is summarised in the following table:

Nominal GDP in Year 0 and in Year 1

	Year 0		
	Quantity	Price (€)	Value (€)
Potatoes (pounds)	10	1	10
Wine (bottles)	5	2	10
Nominal GDP			20

	Year 1		
	Quantity	Price (€)	Value (€)
Potatoes (pounds)	15	1	15
Wine (bottles)	5	3	15
Nominal GDP			30

The rate of growth of nominal GDP from year 0 to year 1 is equal to (€30 − €20)/€20 = 50%. But what is the rate of growth of real GDP?

Answering this question requires consructing real GDP for each of the two years. The basic idea behind constructing real GDP is to evaluate the quantities in each year using the same set of prices.

Suppose we choose, for example, the prices in year 0. Year 0 is then called the base year. In this case, the computation is as follows:

- Real GDP in year 0 is the sum of the quantity in year 0 multiplied by the price in year 0 for both goods: (10 × €1) + (5 × €2) = €20.
- Real GDP in year 1 is the sum of the quantity in year 1 multiplied by the price in year 0 for both goods: (15 × €1) + (5 × €2) = €25.
- The rate of growth of real GDP from year 0 to year 1 is then (€25 − €20)/€20, or 25%.

This answer raises however an obvious issue: instead of using year 0 as the base year, we could have used year 1, or any other year. If, for example, we had used year 1 as the base year, then:

- Real GDP in year 0 would be equal to (10 × €1 + 5 × €3) = €25.
- Real GDP in year 1 would be equal to (15 × €1 + 5 × €3) = €30.
- The rate of growth of real GDP from year 0 to year 1 would be equal to €5/€25, or 20%.

The answer using year 1 as the base year would therefore be different from the answer using year 0 as the base year. So, if the choice of the base year affects the constructed percentage rate of change in output, which base year should one choose?

In most countries today the practice is to choose a base year and change it infrequently, say, every five years or so. This practice was logically unappealing. Every time the base year was changed and a new set of prices was used, all past real GDP numbers – and all past real GDP growth rates – were recomputed. Economic history was, in effect, rewritten every five years! In Europe, Eurostat – the Statistical Office of the European Union – established specific recommendations about the way in which growth rates should be calculated in the System of National Accounts 1993 (SNA 93).

The method requires four steps:

1. Construct the rate of change of real GDP from year t to year $t + 1$ in two different ways. First, use the prices from year t as the set of common prices. Then, use the prices from year $t + 1$ as the set of common prices. For example, the rate of change of GDP from 2006 to 2007 is computed by:

a. Constructing real GDP for 2006 and real GDP for 2007 using 2006 prices as the set of common prices, and computing a first measure of the rate of growth of GDP from 2006 to 2007.

b. Constructing real GDP for 2006 and real GDP for 2007 using 2007 prices as the set of common prices, and computing a second measure of the rate of growth of GDP from 2006 to 2007.

2. Construct the rate of change of real GDP as the average of these two rates of change.

3. Construct an index for the level of real GDP by *linking* – or *chaining* – the constructed rates of change for each year.

The index is set equal to 1 in some arbitrary year. At the time this book was written, the arbitrary year is 2000.

Given that the constructed rate of change from 2000 to 2001 by Eurostat is 0.7%, the index for 2001 equals (1 + 0.07) = 1.007. The index for 2001 is then obtained by multiplying the index for 2000 by the rate of change from 2000 to 2001, and so on.

4. Multiply this index by nominal GDP in 2005 to derive chain-linked GDP at constant prices. As the index is 1 in 2000, this implies that real GDP in 2000 equals nominal GDP in 2000.

Chained refers to the chaining of rates of change described above. '2000' refers to the year where, by construction, real GDP is equal to nominal GDP.

This index is more complicated to construct than the indexes used before 1995. (To make sure you under-stand the steps, construct real GDP in chained (year 0) dollars for year 1 in our example.) But it is clearly better conceptually:

● The prices used to evaluate real GDP in two adjacent years are the right prices, namely the average prices for those two years.

● And, because the rate of change from one year to the next is constructed using the prices in those two years rather than the set of prices in an arbitrary base year, history will not be rewritten every five years – as it used to be when, under the previous method for constructing real GDP, the base year was changed.

THE CORE

" HOW AM I GOING TO LEARN THE VALUE OF A DOLLAR
IF I'M ONLY GETTING 50¢ ALLOWANCE ? "

THE SHORT RUN

In the short run, demand determines output. Many factors affect demand, from consumer confidence to fiscal and monetary policy.

Chapter 3 The goods market

Chapter 3 looks at equilibrium in the goods market and the determination of output. It focuses on the interaction between demand, production and income. It shows how fiscal policy affects output.

Chapter 4 Financial markets

Chapter 4 looks at equilibrium in financial markets and the determination of the interest rate. It shows how monetary policy affects the interest rate.

Chapter 5 Goods and financial markets: the *IS–LM* model

Chapter 5 looks at the goods market and financial markets together. It shows what determines output and the interest rate in the short run. It looks at the roles of fiscal and monetary policies. The model developed in Chapter 5, called the *IS–LM* model, is one of the workhorses of macroeconomics.

Chapter 6 The *IS–LM* model in an open economy

Chapter 6 discusses the implications of openness in goods and financial markets. Openness in goods markets allows people to choose between domestic goods and foreign goods. Openness in financial markets allows people to choose between domestic assets and foreign assets. It then gives an open economy version of the *IS–LM* model.

Chapter 7 Output, the interest rate and the exchange rate

Chapter 7 introduces the difference between flexible and fixed exchange rates and looks at the effects of economic policies in both cases. It shows how, under flexible exchange rates, monetary policy can affect output not only through its effect on the interest rate, but also through its effect on the exchange rate. It also shows how fixing the exchange rate implies giving up the ability to change interest rates.

Chapter 3

THE GOODS MARKET

When economists think about year-to-year movements in economic activity, they focus on the interactions between production, income and demand:

● Changes in the demand for goods lead to changes in production.

● Changes in production lead to changes in income.

● Changes in income lead to changes in the demand for goods.

Nothing makes the point better than the following cartoon:

Source: Universal Press Syndicate.

This chapter looks at these interactions and their implications.

● Section 3.1 looks at the composition of GDP and the different sources of the demand for goods.

- Section 3.2 looks at the determinants of the demand for goods.

- Section 3.3 shows how equilibrium output is determined by the condition that the production of goods must be equal to the demand for goods.

- Section 3.4 gives an alternative way of thinking about the equilibrium, based on the equality of investment and saving.

- Section 3.5 takes a first pass at the effects of fiscal policy on equilibrium output.

3.1 THE COMPOSITION OF GDP

The purchase of a machine by a firm, the decision to go to a restaurant by a consumer and the purchase of aeroplanes by the national government are clearly very different decisions and depend on very different factors. So, if we want to understand what determines the demand for goods, it makes sense to decompose aggregate output (GDP) from the point of view of the different goods being produced, and from the point of view of the different buyers for these goods.

◄ *Output* and *production* are synonymous. There is no rule for using one or the other. Use the one that sounds better.

The decomposition of GDP typically used by macroeconomists is shown in Table 3.1.

1. First comes **consumption** (which we will denote by the letter C when we use algebra below and throughout this text). These are the goods and services purchased by consumers, ranging from food to airline tickets, to new cars and so on. Consumption is by far the largest component of GDP. In 2010, it accounted, on average, for 56% of GDP in the EU (EU-15), ranging from 46.2% in the Netherlands to 71.2% in Greece. In general, consumption is close to 60% or more of national income in the largest European economies (56.3% in Germany, 57.2% in Spain, 56.7% in France, 59.1% in Italy and up to 64.7% in the UK), whereas in smaller countries consumption tends to be closer to 50% of GDP (46.2% in the Netherlands, 46.5% in Sweden, 48.9% in Denmark, 51.4% in Finland and 52.9% in Austria).

2. Second comes **investment** (I), sometimes called **fixed investment** to distinguish it from inventory investment (which we will discuss below). Investment is the sum of **non-residential investment**, the purchase by firms of new plants or new machines (from turbines to computers), and **residential investment**, the purchase by people of new houses or apartments.

   Non-residential investment and residential investment, and the decisions behind them, have more in common than it might first appear. Firms buy machines or plants to produce output in the future. People buy houses or apartments to get housing services in the future. In both cases, the decision to buy depends on the services these goods will yield in the future, so it makes sense to treat them together. Together, non-residential and residential investment accounted, on average, for 18.4% of GDP in EU-15 in 2010, ranging from 14.9% in the UK to 22.9% in Spain.

◄ **Warning!** To most people, *investment* refers to the purchase of assets like gold or shares. Economists use *investment* to refer to the purchase of new capital goods, such as (new) machines, (new) buildings or (new) houses. When economists refer to the purchase of gold, or shares, or other financial assets, they use the term *financial investment*.

◄ This ratio is historically low, and reflects the very low level of residential investment, which itself is the result of the sharp decrease in housing prices since 2007.

Table 3.1 The composition of GDP, EU-15, 2010

	Billion euros	Percentage of GDP
GDP (Y)	11,634	100
1 Consumption (C)	6,735	57.9
2 Investment (I)	1,892	16.3
3 Government spending (G)	2,566	22.1
4 Net exports	136	1.1
Exports (X)	4,890	42
Imports (IM)	−4,754	−40.9
5 Inventory investment	60	0.5

Source: Eurostat.

3. Third comes **government spending (G)**. This represents the purchases of goods and services by the national, regional and local governments. The goods range from aeroplanes to office equipment. The services include services provided by government employees: in effect, the national income accounts treat the government as buying the services provided by government employees – and then providing these services to the public, free of charge.

Note that G does not include **government transfers**, like unemployment benefits and pensions, nor interest payments on the government debt. Although these are clearly government expenditures, they are not purchases of goods and services. That is why the number for government spending on goods and services in Table 3.1 is smaller than the number for total government spending, including transfers and interest payments. In 2010, government spending accounted on average for 22.5% of GDP in EU-15. With the notable exception of Germany, where government expenditure is relatively lower, government spending accounts for particularly high shareas of GDP, both in northern European countries (24.6% in Finland, 24.2% in Belgium, 28.5% in the Netherlands, 26.9% in Sweden and 29.1% in Denmark) and in the largest European countries (France and the UK slightly above with 24.8% and 23.2% respectively).

4. The sum of lines 1, 2 and 3 gives the purchases of goods and services by consumers, firms and the government. To determine the purchases of goods and services, two more steps are needed:

First, we must subtract **imports (IM)**, because these are goods and services that consumers, firms and the government buy from the rest of the world, thus they are not purchased at home.

Second, we must add **exports (X)**, the purchases of domestic goods and services by foreigners.

The difference between exports and imports ($X - IM$) is called **net exports**, or the **trade balance**. If exports exceed imports, the country is said to run a **trade surplus**. If exports are less than imports, the country is said to run a **trade deficit**. In 2010, exports from EU-15 accounted for 39.3% of GDP and imports were equal to 38.4% of GDP, so EU-15 had a trade surplus equal to 0.9% of GDP. Again, this average hides substantial differences across countries: Belgium, Greece, Italy, Spain and the UK were running trade deficits, while most northern European countries, as well as Germany, Denmark and the Netherlands, had considerable trade surpluses.

> Exports > Imports ⇔ Trade surplus
> Exports < Imports ⇔ Trade deficit

5. So far we have looked at various sources of purchases (sales) of goods and services in 2010. To determine production in 2010, we need to take one last step.

In any given year, production and sales need not be equal. Some of the goods produced in a given year are not sold in that year, but in later years. And some of the goods sold in a given year may have been produced in an earlier year. The difference between goods produced and goods sold in a given year – the difference between production and sales, in other words – is called **inventory investment**. If production exceeds sales, and firms accumulate inventories as a result, then inventory investment is said to be positive. If production is less than sales, and firms' inventories fall, then inventory investment is said to be negative. Inventory investment is typically small – positive in some years and negative in others. In 2010, inventory investment was positive, equal to just €26 billion. Put another way, production was higher than sales by an amount equal to €26 billion.

> Make sure you understand each of these three equivalent ways of stating the relation between production, sales and inventory investment:
>
> ● Inventory investment = Production – Sales
> ● Production = Sales + Inventory investment
> ● Sales = Production – Inventory investment

We now have what we need to develop our first model of output determination.

3.2 THE DEMAND FOR GOODS

Denote the total demand for goods by Z. Using the decomposition of GDP we saw in Section 3.1, we can write Z as

$$Z \equiv C + I + G + X - IM$$

> Recall that inventory investment is not part of demand.

This equation is an **identity** (which is why it is written using the symbol $\equiv$ rather than an equals sign). It defines Z as the sum of consumption, plus investment, plus government spending, plus exports, minus imports.

We now need to think about the determinants of Z. To make the task easier, let's first make a number of simplifications:

- Assume that all firms produce the same good, which can then be used by consumers for consumption, by firms for investment, or by the government. With this (big) simplification, we need to look at only one market – the market for 'the' good – and think about what determines supply and demand in that market.

- Assume that firms are willing to supply any amount of the good at a given price level P. This assumption allows us to focus on the role demand plays in the determination of output. As we shall see later in the book, this assumption is valid only in the short run. When we move to the study of the medium run (starting in Chapter 8), we shall abandon it. But for the moment, it will simplify our discussion.

- Assume that the economy is closed – that it does not trade with the rest of the world: both exports and imports are zero. This assumption clearly goes against the facts: modern economies trade with the rest of the world. Later on (starting in Chapter 6), we will abandon this assumption as well and look at what happens when the economy is open. But, for the moment, this assumption will also simplify our discussion because we won't have to think about what determines exports and imports.

◄ A model nearly always starts with 'Assume' (or 'Suppose'). This is an indication that reality is about to be simplified to focus on the issue at hand.

Under the assumption that the economy is closed, $X = IM = 0$, so the demand for goods Z is simply the sum of consumption, investment and government spending:

$$Z = C + I + G$$

Let's discuss each of these three components in turn.

Consumption (C)

Consumption decisions depend on many factors. But the main one is surely income, or more precisely **disposable income (Y_D)**, the income that remains once consumers have received transfers from the government and paid their taxes. When their disposable income goes up, people buy more goods; when it goes down, they buy fewer goods.

Let C denote consumption, and Y_D denote disposable income. We can then write:

$$C = C(Y_D) \qquad [3.1]$$
$$(+)$$

This is a formal way of stating that consumption C is a function of disposable income Y_D. The function $C(Y_D)$ is called the **consumption function**. The positive sign below Y_D reflects the fact that when disposable income increases, so does consumption. Economists call such an equation a **behavioural equation**, to indicate that the equation tries to describe some aspect of behaviour – in this case, the behaviour of consumers.

We will use functions in this text as a way of representing relations between variables. What you need to know about functions – which is very little – is described in the appendix (see Appendix 2 at the end of the text). This appendix develops the mathematics you need to go through this text. Not to worry: we shall always describe a function in words when we introduce it for the first time.

It is often useful to be more specific about the form of the function. Here is such a case. It is reasonable to assume that the relation between consumption and disposable income is given by the simpler relation:

$$C = c_0 + c_1 Y_D \qquad [3.2]$$

In other words, it is reasonable to assume that the function is a **linear relation**. The relation between consumption and disposable income is then characterised by two **parameters**, c_0 and c_1:

- The parameter c_1 is called the propensity to consume. (It is also called the **marginal propensity to consume**. We will drop the word 'marginal' for simplicity.) It gives the effect an additional dollar of disposable income has on consumption. If c_1 is equal to

0.6, then an additional euro of disposable income increases consumption by €1 × 0.6 = 60 cents.

A natural restriction on c_1 is that it must be positive: an increase in disposable income is likely to lead to an increase in consumption. Another natural restriction is that c_1 must be less than 1: people are likely to consume only part of any increase in disposable income and save the rest.

- The parameter c_0 has a simple literal interpretation. It is what people would consume if their disposable income in the current year were equal to zero: if Y_D equals zero in equation (3.2), $C = c_0$. If we use this interpretation, a natural restriction is that, if current income were equal to zero, consumption would still be positive: with or without income, people still need to eat! This implies that c_0 is positive. How can people have positive consumption if their income is equal to zero? Answer: they dissave. They consume either by selling some of their assets, or by borrowing.

Think about your own consumption behaviour. What are your values of c_0 and c_1?

- Changes in c_0 reflect changes in consumption for a given level of disposable income. Increases in c_0 reflect an increase in consumption given income, decreases in c_0 a decrease. There are many reasons why people may decide to consume more or less, given their disposable income. They may, for example, find it easier or more difficult to borrow, or may become more or less optimistic about the future. An example of a decrease in c_0 is given in the Focus box 'The Lehman bankruptcy, fears of another Great Depression, and shifts in the consumption function'.

The relation between consumption and disposable income shown in equation (3.2) is drawn in Figure 3.1. Because it is a linear relation, it is represented by a straight line. Its intercept with the vertical axis is c_0; its slope is c_1. Because c_1 is less than 1, the slope of the line is less than 1: equivalently, the line is flatter than a 45° line. If the value of c_0 increases, then the line shifts up by the same amount. (A refresher on graphs, slopes and intercepts is given in Appendix 2.)

Next we need to define disposable income Y_D. Disposable income is given by

$$Y_D \equiv Y - T$$

In the USA, the two major taxes paid by individuals are income taxes and social security contributions. The main sources of government transfers are social security benefits, Medicare (health care for retirees) and Medicaid (health care for the poor). In 2010, taxes and social contributions paid by individuals were $2,200 billion, and transfers to individuals were $2,300 billion.

where Y is income and T is taxes paid minus government transfers received by consumers. For short, we will refer to T simply as taxes – but remember that it is equal to taxes minus transfers. Note that the equation is an identity, indicated by $\equiv$.

Replacing Y_D in equation (3.2) gives

$$c = c_0 + c_1(Y - T) \qquad [3.3]$$

Equation (3.3) tells us that consumption c is a function of income Y and taxes T. Higher income increases consumption, but less than one for one. Higher taxes decrease consumption, also less than one for one.

Figure 3.1

Consumption and disposable income

Consumption increases with disposable income, but less than one for one. A lower value of c_0 will shift the entire line down.

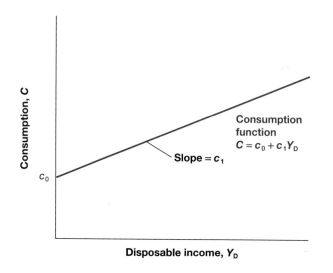

Slope = c_1

Consumption function
$C = c_0 + c_1 Y_D$

Investment (*I*)

Models have two types of variables. Some variables depend on other variables in the model, and are therefore explained within the model. Variables like these are called **endogenous**. This was the case for consumption above. Other variables are not explained within the model but are instead taken as given. Variables like these are called **exogenous**. This is how we will treat investment here. We will take investment as given, and write:

$$I = \bar{I} \qquad\qquad [3.4]$$

Putting a bar on investment is a simple typographical way to remind us that we take investment as given.

We take investment as given to keep our model simple. But the assumption is not innocuous. It implies that, when we later look at the effects of changes in production, we will assume that investment does not respond to changes in production. It is not hard to see that this implication may be a bad description of reality: firms that experience an increase in production might well decide they need more machines and increase their investment as a result. For now, though, we will leave this mechanism out of the model. Later (see Chapter 5) we will introduce a more realistic treatment of investment.

Government spending (*G*)

The third component of demand in our model is government spending, *G*. Together with taxes *T*, *G* describes **fiscal policy** – the choice of taxes and spending by the government. Just as we just did for investment, we will take *G* and *T* as exogenous. But the reason why we assume *G* and *T* are exogenous is different from the reason we assumed investment is exogenous. It is based on two distinct arguments:

- First, governments do not behave with the same regularity as consumers or firms, so there is no reliable rule we could write for *G* or *T* corresponding to the rule we wrote, for example, for consumption. (This argument is not airtight, though. Even if governments do not follow simple behavioural rules as consumers do, a good part of their behaviour is predictable. We will look at these issues later, in particular in Chapters 22 and 23. Until then, we will set them aside.)
- Second, and more importantly, one of the tasks of macroeconomists is to think about the implications of alternative spending and tax decisions. We want to be able to say, 'If the government were to choose these values for *G* and *T*, this is what would happen.' The approach in this text will typically treat *G* and *T* as variables chosen by the government and will not try to explain them within the model.

> Endogenous variables – explained within the model.
> Exogenous variables – taken as given.

> Recall that 'taxes' stand for taxes minus government transfers.

> Because we will (nearly always) take *G* and *T* as exogenous, we won't use a bar to denote their values. This will keep the notation lighter.

3.3 THE DETERMINATION OF EQUILIBRIUM OUTPUT

Let's put together the pieces we have introduced so far.

Assuming that exports and imports are both zero, the demand for goods is the sum of consumption, investment and government spending:

$$Z = C + I + G$$

Replacing *C* and *I* from equations (3.3) and (3.4), we get

$$Z = c_0 + c_1(Y - T) + \bar{I} + G \qquad\qquad [3.5]$$

The demand for goods *Z* depends on income, *Y*, taxes, *T*, investment, $\bar{I}$, and government spending, *G*.

Let's now turn to **equilibrium** in the goods market, and the relation between production and demand. If firms hold inventories, then production need not be equal to demand: for example, firms can satisfy an increase in demand over production by drawing upon their inventories – by having negative inventory investment. They can respond to a decrease in demand over production by continuing to produce and accumulating inventories – by having positive inventory investment. Firms usually have a desired (positive) level of inventory investment. If demand turns out to be higher than production, then firms will accumulate less inventories than desired; if demand turns out to be lower than production, then firms accumulate more inventories than desired. When inventory investment is exactly what firms wanted it to be, then production, Y, is equal to the demand for goods, Z, that is, there is **equilibrium in the goods market**:

$$Y = Z \qquad [3.6]$$

There are three types of equations:
- identities
- behavioural equations
- equilibrium conditions.

➤ This equation is called an **equilibrium condition**. Models include three types of equations: identities, behavioural equations and equilibrium conditions. You have now seen examples of each: the equation defining disposable income is an identity, the consumption function is a behavioural equation, and the condition that production equals demand is an equilibrium condition.

Replacing demand Z in (3.6) by its expression from equation (3.5) gives

$$Y = c_0 + c_1(Y - T) + \bar{I} + G \qquad [3.7]$$

Equation (3.7) represents algebraically what we stated informally at the beginning of this chapter:

> *In equilibrium, production, Y, (the left side of the equation) is equal to demand (the right side).*
Relate this statement to the cartoon at ➤ the start of the chapter.
> *Demand in turn depends on income, Y, which is itself equal to production.*

Note that we are using the same symbol Y for production and income. This is no accident! As you saw earlier (see Chapter 2), we can look at GDP either from the production side or from the income side. Production and income are identically equal.

Having constructed a model, we can solve it to look at what determines the level of output – how output changes in response to, say, a change in government spending. Solving a model means not only solving it algebraically, but also understanding why the results are what they are. In this text, solving a model will also mean characterising the results using graphs – sometimes skipping the algebra altogether – and describing the results and the mechanisms in words. Macroeconomists always use these three tools:

- *algebra* to make sure that the logic is correct
- *graphs* to build the intuition
- *words* to explain the results.

Make it a habit to do the same.

Using algebra

Rewrite the equilibrium equation (3.7):

$$Y = c_0 + c_1 Y - c_1 T + \bar{I} + G$$

Move $c_1 Y$ to the left side and reorganise the right side:

$$(1 - c_1)Y = c_0 + \bar{I} + G - c_1 T$$

Divide both sides by $(1 - c_1)$:

$$Y = \frac{1}{1 - c_1}[c_0 + \bar{I} + G - c_1 T] \qquad [3.8]$$

Equation (3.8) characterises equilibrium output, the level of output such that production equals demand. Let's look at both terms on the right, beginning with the second term.

'Autonomous' means independent – in this case, independent of output. ➤

- The term $[c_0 + \bar{I} + G - c_1 T]$ is that part of the demand for goods that does not depend on output. For this reason, it is called **autonomous spending**.

Can we be sure that autonomous spending is positive? We cannot, but it is very likely to be. The first two terms in brackets, c_0 and $\bar{I}$, are positive. What about the last two, $G - c_1 T$? Suppose the government is running a **balanced budget** – taxes equal government spending. If $T = G$, and the propensity to consume (c_1) is less than one (as we have assumed), then ($G - c_1 T$) is positive and so is autonomous spending. Only if the government were running a very large budget surplus – if taxes were much larger than government spending – could autonomous spending be negative. We can safely ignore that case here.

◀ If $T = G$, then
$(G - c_1 T) = (T - c_1 T) = (1 - c_1)T > 0$

- Turn to the first term, $1/(1 - c_1)$. Because the propensity to consume (c_1) is between zero and one, $1/(1 - c_1)$ is a number greater than one. For this reason, this number, which multiplies autonomous spending, is called the **multiplier**. The closer c_1 is to one, the larger the multiplier.

What does the multiplier imply? Suppose that, for a given level of income, consumers decide to consume more. More precisely, assume that c_0 in equation (3.3) increases by €1 billion. Equation (3.8) tells us that output will increase by more than $1 billion. For example, if c_1 equals 0.6, the multiplier equals $1/(1 - 0.6) = 1/0.4 = 2.5$, so that output increases by $2.5 \times €1$ billion $= €2.5$ billion.

We have looked at an increase in consumption, but equation (3.8) makes it clear that any change in autonomous spending – from a change in investment, to a change in government spending, to a change in taxes – will have the same qualitative effect: it will change output by more than its direct effect on autonomous spending.

Where does the multiplier effect come from? Looking back at equation (3.7) gives us the clue: an increase in c_0 increases demand. The increase in demand then leads to an increase in production. The increase in production leads to an equivalent increase in income (remember the two are identically equal). The increase in income further increases consumption, which further increases demand, and so on. The best way to describe this mechanism is to represent the equilibrium using a graph. Let's do that.

Using a graph

Let's characterise the equilibrium graphically.

- First, plot production as a function of income.
  In Figure 3.2, measure production on the vertical axis. Measure income on the horizontal axis. Plotting production as a function of income is straightforward: recall that

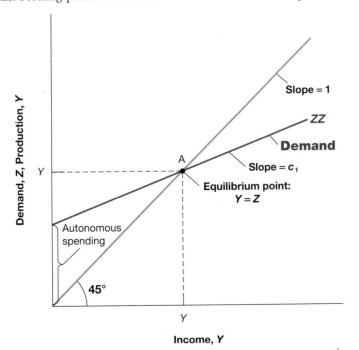

Figure 3.2

Equilibrium in the goods market

Equilibrium output is determined by the condition that production be equal to demand.

production and income are identically equal. Thus, the relation between them is the 45° line, the line with a slope equal to 1.

● Second, plot demand as a function of income.

The relation between demand and income is given by equation (3.5). Let's rewrite it here for convenience, regrouping the terms for autonomous spending together in the term in parentheses:

$$Z = (c_0 + \bar{I} + G - c_1 T) + c_1 Y \qquad [3.9]$$

Demand depends on autonomous spending and on income – via its effect on consumption. The relation between demand and income is drawn as ZZ in the graph. The intercept with the vertical axis – the value of demand when income is equal to zero – equals autonomous spending. The slope of the line is the propensity to consume, c_1: when income increases by 1, demand increases by c_1. Under the restriction that c_1 is positive but less than 1, the line is upward sloping but has a slope of less than 1.

● In equilibrium, production equals demand.

Equilibrium output, Y, therefore occurs at the intersection of the 45° line and the demand function. This is at point A. To the left of A, demand exceeds production; to the right of A, production exceeds demand. Only at A are demand and production equal.

Suppose that the economy is at the initial equilibrium, represented by point A in the graph, with production equal to Y.

Now suppose c_0 increases by €1 billion. At the initial level of income (the level of disposable income associated with point A since T is unchanged in this example), consumers increase their consumption by €1 billion. This makes use of the second interpretation of the value of c_0. What happens is shown in Figure 3.3, which builds on Figure 3.2.

Equation (3.9) tells us that, for any value of income, demand is higher by €1 billion. Before the increase in c_0, the relation between demand and income was given by the line ZZ. After the increase in c_0 by €1 billion, the relation between demand and income is given by the line ZZ′, which is parallel to ZZ but higher by €1 billion. In other words, the demand curve shifts up by €1 billion. The new equilibrium is at the intersection of the 45° line and the new demand relation, at point A′.

Equilibrium output increases from Y to Y′. The increase in output, (Y′ − Y), which we can measure either on the horizontal or the vertical axis, is larger than the initial increase in consumption of €1 billion. This is the multiplier effect.

Look at the vertical axis. The distance ➤ between Y and Y′ on the vertical axis is larger than the distance between A and B – which is equal to €1 billion.

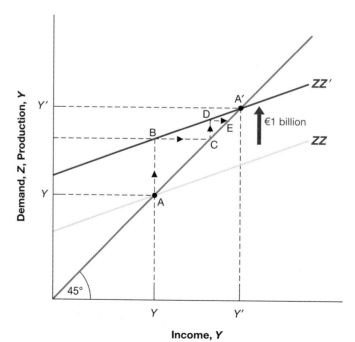

Figure 3.3

The effects of an increase in autonomous spending on output

An increase in autonomous spending has a more than one-for-one effect on equilibrium output.

With the help of the graph, it becomes easier to tell how and why the economy moves from A to A'. The initial increase in consumption leads to an increase in demand of €1 billion. At the initial level of income, Y, the level of demand is shown by point B: demand is €1 billion higher. To satisfy this higher level of demand, firms increase production by €1 billion. This increase in production of €1 billion implies that income increases by €1 billion (recall: income = production), so the economy moves to point C. (In other words, both production and income are higher by €1 billion.) But this is not the end of the story. The increase in income leads to a further increase in demand. Demand is now shown by point D. Point D leads to a higher level of production, and so on, until the economy is at A', where production and demand are again equal. This is therefore the new equilibrium.

We can pursue this line of explanation a bit more, which will give us another way to think about the multiplier.

- The first-round increase in demand, shown by the distance AB in Figure 3.3, equals €1 billion.
- This first-round increase in demand leads to an equal increase in production, or €1 billion, which is also shown by the distance AB.
- This first-round increase in production leads to an equal increase in income, shown by the distance BC, also equal to €1 billion.
- The second-round increase in demand, shown by the distance CD, equals €1 billion (the increase in income in the first round) multiplied by the propensity to consume, c_1 – hence, €c_1 billion.
- This second-round increase in demand leads to an equal increase in production, also shown by the distance CD, and thus an equal increase in income, shown by the distance DE.
- The third-round increase in demand equals €c_1 billion (the increase in income in the second round), multiplied by c_1, the marginal propensity to consume; it is equal to €$c_1 \times c_1 =$ €c_1^2 billion, and so on.

Following this logic, the total increase in production after, say, $n + 1$ rounds equals €1 billion multiplied by the sum:

$$1 + c_1 + c_1^2 + \cdots + c_1^n$$

Such a sum is called a **geometric series**. Geometric series will frequently appear in this text. A refresher is given in the appendix (see Appendix 2 at the end of the text). One property of geometric series is that, when c_1 is less than one (as it is here) and as n gets larger and larger, the sum keeps increasing but approaches a limit. That limit is $1/(1 - c_1)$, making the eventual increase in output €$1/(1 - c_1)$ billion.

The expression $1/(1 - c_1)$ should be familiar: it is the multiplier, derived another way. This gives us an equivalent, but more intuitive way of thinking about the multiplier. We can think of the original increase in demand as triggering successive increases in production, with each increase in production leading to an increase in income, which leads to an increase in demand, which leads to a further increase in production, which leads . . . and so on. The multiplier is the sum of all these successive increases in production.

◄ **Trick question:** think about the multiplier as the result of these successive rounds. What would happen in each successive round if c_1, the propensity to consume, were larger than one?

Using words

How can we summarise our findings in words?

Production depends on demand, which depends on income, which is itself equal to production. An increase in demand, such as an increase in government spending, leads to an increase in production and a corresponding increase in income. This increase in income leads to a further increase in demand, which leads to a further increase in production, and so on. The end result is an increase in output that is larger than the initial shift in demand, by a factor equal to the multiplier.

The size of the multiplier is directly related to the value of the propensity to consume: the higher the propensity to consume, the higher the multiplier. What is the value of the propensity to consume in European countries today? To answer this question, and more generally to estimate behavioural equations and their parameters, economists use **econometrics**, the set of statistical methods used in economics. To give you a sense of what econometrics is and how it is used, read the appendix (see Appendix 2 at the end of this text). This appendix gives you a quick introduction, along with an application estimating the propensity to consume. For example, with a propensity to consume equal to 60% or 0.6, an additional euro of disposable income leads on average to an increase in consumption of 60 cents. This implies that the multiplier is equal to $1/(1 - c_1) = 1/(1 - 0.6) = 2.5$.

How long does it take for output to adjust?

Let's return to our example one last time. Suppose that c_0 increases by €1 billion. We know that output will increase by an amount equal to the multiplier $1/(1 - c_1)$ times €1 billion. But how long will it take for output to reach this higher value?

Under the assumptions we have made so far, the answer is: right away! In writing the equilibrium condition (3.6), we have assumed that production is always equal to demand. In other words, we have assumed that production responds to demand instantaneously. In writing the consumption function (3.2), we have assumed that consumption responds to changes in disposable income instantaneously. Under these two assumptions, the economy goes instantaneously from point A to point A′ in Figure 3.3: the increase in demand leads to an immediate increase in production, the increase in income associated with the increase in production leads to an immediate increase in demand, and so on. There is nothing wrong in thinking about the adjustment in terms of successive rounds as we did earlier, even though the equations indicate that all these rounds happen at once.

This instantaneous adjustment isn't really plausible: a firm that faces an increase in demand might well decide to wait before adjusting its production, meanwhile drawing down its inventories to satisfy demand. A worker who gets a pay raise might not adjust her consumption right away. These delays imply that the adjustment of output will take time.

> In the model we saw earlier, we ruled out this possibility by assuming firms did not hold inventories, and so could not rely on drawing down inventories to satisfy an increase in demand.

Formally describing this adjustment of output over time – that is, writing the equations for what economists call the **dynamics** of adjustment, and solving this more complicated model – would be too hard to do here. But it is easy to do it in words:

- Suppose, for example, that firms make decisions about their production levels at the beginning of each quarter. Once their decisions are made, production cannot be adjusted for the rest of the quarter. If purchases by consumers are higher than production, firms draw down their inventories to satisfy the purchases. On the other hand, if purchases are lower than production, firms accumulate inventories.
- Now suppose consumers decide to spend more, that they increase c_0. During the quarter in which this happens, demand increases, but production – because we assumed it was was set at the beginning of the quarter – doesn't yet change. Therefore, income doesn't change either.
- Having observed an increase in demand, firms are likely to set a higher level of production in the following quarter. This increase in production leads to a corresponding increase in income and a further increase in demand. If purchases still exceed production, firms further increase production in the following quarter, and so on.
- In short, in response to an increase in consumer spending, output does not jump to the new equilibrium, but rather increases over time from Y to Y'.

How long this adjustment takes depends on how and how often firms revise their production schedule. If firms adjust their production schedules more frequently in response to past increases in purchases, the adjustment will occur faster.

We will often do in this text what we just did here. After we have looked at changes in equilibrium output, we will then describe informally how the economy moves from one equilibrium to the other. This will not only make the description of what happens in the economy feel more realistic, but it will often reinforce your intuition about why the equilibrium changes.

We have focused in this section on increases in demand. But the mechanism, of course, works both ways: decreases in demand lead to decreases in output. The recent recession was the result of two of the four components of autonomous spending dropping by a large amount at the same time. To remind you, the expression for autonomous spending is $[c_0 + I + G - c_1 T]$. The Focus box shows how, when the crisis started, worries about the future led consumers to cut on their spending despite the fact that their disposable income had not yet declined, that is, c_0 fell in value. As house prices fell, building new homes became much less desirable. New homes are part of investment spending, I, so the value of I fell sharply. As autonomous spending decreased, the total demand for goods fell, and so did output. We shall return at many points in the text to the factors and the mechanisms behind the crisis, and steadily enrich our storyline. But this effect on autonomous spending will remain a central element of the story.

FOCUS

The Lehman bankruptcy, fears of another Great Depression, and shifts in the consumption function

Why would consumers decrease consumption if their disposable income has not changed? Or, in terms of equation (3.2), why might c_0 decrease – leading in turn to a decrease in demand, output, etc.?

One of the first reasons which comes to mind is that, even if their current income has not changed, they start worrying about the future, and decide to save more. This is precisely what happened at the start of the crisis, in late 2008 and early 2009. The basic facts are shown in Figure 3.4. The figure plots, from the first quarter of 2008 to the last quarter of 2009, the behaviour of three variables – disposable income, total consumption and

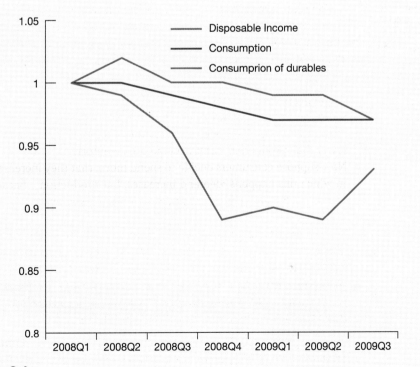

Figure 3.4

Disposable income, consumption and consumption of durables, USA, 2008:1 to 2009:3

Figure 3.5

Google search for 'Great Depression', January 2008 to September 2009

Source: Google trends. 'Great Depression', world search

consumption of durables – that part of consumption which falls on goods such as cars, computers and so on (Appendix 1 at the end of the text gives a more precise definition). To make things visually simple, all three variables are normalised to equal 1 in the first quarter of 2008.

You should note three things about the figure. First, despite the fact that the crisis led to a large fall in GDP, during that period, disposable income did not move much. Second, starting in the third quarter of 2008, consumption declined, by roughly 3% relative to disposable income – the distance between the line for disposable income and the line for consumption. Third, during the third and especially the fourth quarter of 2008, the consumption of durables dropped sharply. By the fourth quarter of 2008, it was down 10% relative to the first quarter, before recovering in early 2009 and decreasing again later.

Why did consumption, and especially consumption of durables, decrease at the end of 2008 despite relatively stable disposable income? A number of factors were at play, but the main one was the psychological fallout of the financial crisis. Recall (from Chapter 1) that, on 15 September Lehman Brothers, a very large bank, went bankrupt and that, in the ensuing weeks, it appeared that many more banks might follow suit and the financial system might collapse. For most people, the main sign of trouble was what they read in newspapers; they still

had their job and received their monthly wages. But, the events reminded them of the stories of the Great Depression, and the pain which came with it. One way to see this is to look at the Google Trends series which gives the number of searches for 'Great Depression', from January 2008 to September 2009, and which is plotted in Figure 3.5. The series is normalised so its average value is 1 over the two years. Note how sharply the series peaked in October 2008, and then slowly decreased over the course of 2009, as it became clear that, while the crisis was a serious one, policy makers were going to do whatever they could do to avoid a repeat of the Great Depression.

If you felt that the economy might go into another Great Depression, what would you do? Worried that you might become unemployed, or that your income might decline in the future, you would probably cut consumption, even if your disposable income had not changed yet. And, given the uncertainty about what was going on, you might also delay the purchases you could afford to delay, for example the purchase of a new car or a new TV. As Figure 3.4 shows, this is exactly what consumers did in late 2008: total consumption decreased, and consumption of durables collapsed. In 2009, as the smoke slowly cleared, and the worse scenarios became increasingly unlikely, consumption of durables picked up. But, by then, many other factors were contributing to the crisis.

3.4 INVESTMENT EQUALS SAVING: AN ALTERNATIVE WAY OF THINKING ABOUT THE GOODS–MARKET EQUILIBRIUM

Thus far, we have been thinking of equilibrium in the goods market in terms of the equality of the production and the demand for goods. An alternative – but equivalent – way of thinking about equilibrium focuses instead on investment and saving. This is how John Maynard Keynes first articulated this model in 1936, in *The General Theory of Employment, Interest and Money*.

Saving: Private saving + Public saving ➤

Let's start by looking at saving. **Saving** is the sum of private saving and public saving.

- By definition, **private saving (S)**, saving by consumers, is equal to their disposable income minus their consumption:

$$S = Y_D - C$$

Using the definition of disposable income, we can rewrite private saving as income minus taxes minus consumption:

$$S = Y - T - C$$

- By definition, **public saving** is equal to taxes (net of transfers) minus government spending, $T - G$. If taxes exceed government spending, the government is running a **budget surplus**, so public saving is positive. If taxes are less than government spending, the government is running a **budget deficit**, so public saving is negative. ◄ Public saving ⇔ Budget surplus
- Now return to the equation for equilibrium in the goods market that we derived earlier. Production must be equal to demand, which in turn is the sum of consumption, investment and government spending:

$$Y = C + \bar{I} + G$$

Subtract taxes (T) from both sides and move consumption to the left side.

$$Y - T - C = \bar{I} + G - T$$

The left side of this equation is simply private saving (S), so

$$S = \bar{I} + G - T$$

Or, equivalently,

$$\bar{I} = S + (T - G) \qquad [3.10]$$

On the left is investment. On the right is saving, the sum of private saving and public saving.

Equation (3.10) gives us another way of thinking about equilibrium in the goods market: it says that equilibrium in the goods market requires that investment equal saving – the sum of private and public saving. This way of looking at equilibrium explains why the equilibrium condition for the goods market is called the *IS* **relation**, which stands for 'investment equals saving': what firms want to invest must be equal to what people and the government want to save.

To understand equation (3.10), imagine an economy with only one person who has to decide how much to consume, invest and save – a 'Robinson Crusoe' economy, for example. For Robinson Crusoe, the saving and the investment decisions are one and the same: what he invests (say, by keeping rabbits for breeding rather than having them for dinner), he automatically saves. In a modern economy, however, investment decisions are made by firms, whereas saving decisions are made by consumers and the government. In equilibrium, equation (3.10) tells us, all these decisions have to be consistent: investment must equal saving.

To summarise: there are two equivalent ways of stating the condition for equilibrium in the goods market:

Production = Demand
Investment = Saving

Earlier, we characterised the equilibrium using the first condition, equation (3.6). We now do the same using the second condition, equation (3.10). The results will be the same, but the derivation will give you another way of thinking about the equilibrium. Note first that consumption and saving decisions are one and the same: given their disposable income, once consumers have chosen consumption, their saving is determined, and vice versa. The way we specified consumption behaviour implies that private saving is given by:

$$S = Y - T - C$$
$$= Y - T - c_0 - c_1(Y - T)$$

Rearranging, we get

$$S = -c_0 + (1 - c_1)(Y - T) \qquad [3.11]$$

In the same way that we called c_1 the propensity to consume, we can call $(1 - c_1)$ the **propensity to save**. The propensity to save tells us how much of an additional unit of income people save. The assumption we made earlier – that the propensity to consume (c_1) is between zero and one implies that the propensity to save ($1 - c_1$) is also between zero and one. Private saving increases with disposable income, but by less than one euro for each additional euro of disposable income.

In equilibrium, investment must be equal to saving, the sum of private and public saving. Replacing private saving in equation (3.10) by its expression from above:

$$\bar{I} = -c_0 + (1 - c_1)(Y - T) + (T - G)$$

Solving for output:

$$Y = \frac{1}{1 - c_1}[c_0 + \bar{I} + G - c_1 T] \qquad [3.12]$$

Equation (3.12) is exactly the same as equation (3.8). This should come as no surprise. We are looking at the same equilibrium condition, just in a different way. This alternative way will prove useful in various applications later in the text. The Focus box looks at such an application, which was first emphasised by Keynes, and is often called the '**paradox of saving**'.

FOCUS
The paradox of saving

As we grow up, we are told about the virtues of thrift. Those who spend all their income are condemned to end up poor. Those who save are promised a happy life. Similarly, governments tell us, an economy that saves is an economy that will grow strong and prosper! The model we have seen in this chapter, however, tells a different and surprising story.

Suppose that, at a given level of disposable income, consumers decide to save more. In other words, suppose consumers decrease c_0, therefore decreasing consumption and increasing saving at a given level of disposable income. What happens to output and to saving?

Equation (3.12) makes it clear that equilibrium output decreases: as people save more at their initial level of income, they decrease their consumption. But this decreased consumption decreases demand, which decreases production.

Can we tell what happens to saving? Let's return to the equation for private saving, equation (3.11) (recall that we assume no change in public saving, so saving and private saving move together):

$$S = -c_0 + (1 - c_1)(Y - T)$$

On the one hand, $-c_0$ is higher (less negative): consumers are saving more at any level of income; this tends to increase saving. On the other hand, their income Y is lower: this decreases saving. The net effect would seem to be ambiguous. In fact, we can tell which way it goes.

To see how, go back to equation (3.10), the equilibrium condition that investment and saving must be equal:

$$\bar{I} = S + (T - G)$$

By assumption, investment does not change: $I = \bar{I}$. Nor do T or G. So, the equilibrium condition tells us, in equilibrium, private saving S cannot change either. Although people want to save more at a given level of income, their income decreases by an amount such that their saving is unchanged.

This means that as people attempt to save more, the result is both a decline in output and unchanged saving. This surprising pair of results is known as the paradox of saving (or the paradox of thrift).

So should you forget the old wisdom? Should the government tell people to be less thrifty? No. The results of this simple model are of much relevance in the short run. The desire of consumers to save more is an important factor in many recessions, in Europe and also in the USA, including, as we saw in the Focus box earlier, the current crisis. But – as we will see later in this text when we look at the medium run and the long run – other mechanisms come into play over time, and an increase in the saving rate is likely to lead over time to higher saving and higher income. A warning remains, however: policies that encourage saving might be good in the medium run and in the long run, but they can lead to a recession in the short run.

3.5 IS THE GOVERNMENT OMNIPOTENT? A WARNING

Equation (3.8) implies that the government, by choosing the level of spending (G) or the level of taxes (T), can choose the level of output it wants. If it wants output to be higher by, say, €1 billion, all it needs to do is to increase G by €$(1 - c_1)$ billion; this increase in government spending, in theory, will lead to an output increase of €$(1 - c_1)$ billion multiplied by the multiplier $1/(1 - c_1)$, or €1 billion.

Can governments really choose the level of output they want? Obviously not: if they could, and it was as easy as it sounds in the previous paragraph, why would the US government have allowed growth to stall in 2008 and output to actually fall in 2009? Why wouldn't it increase the growth rate now, so as to decrease unemployment more rapidly? There are many aspects of reality that we have not yet incorporated in our model, and all of them complicate a government's task. We shall do so in due time. But it is useful to list them briefly here:

- Changing government spending or taxes is not easy. Getting national parliaments to pass bills always takes time, often becoming a premier's nightmare.
- We have assumed that investment remained constant. But investment is also likely to respond in a variety of ways. So are imports: some of the increased demand by consumers and firms will not be for domestic goods but for foreign goods. All these responses are likely to be associated with complex, dynamic effects, making it hard for governments to assess the effects of their policies with much certainty.
- Anticipations are likely to matter. For example, the reaction of consumers to a tax cut is likely to depend very much on whether they think of the tax cut as transitory or permanent. The more they perceive the tax cut as permanent, the larger will be their consumption response.
- Achieving a given level of output can come with unpleasant side effects. Trying to achieve too high a level of output can, for example, lead to increasing inflation and, for that reason, be unsustainable in the medium run.
- Cutting taxes or increasing government spending, as attractive as it may seem in the short run, can lead to large budget deficits and an accumulation of public debt. A large debt has adverse effects in the long run. This is a hot issue in a certain number of countries today, including some highly indebted European countries such as Belgium, Greece and Italy, Japan (the country with the world's highest debt to GDP ratio, well above 150%) and also the USA, where the tax cuts implemented by the Bush administration, together with President Obama's 'stimulus programme' designed to respond to the 2007–2010 crisis, have led to large deficits and to increasing public debt.

In short, the proposition that, by using fiscal policy, the government can affect demand and output in the short run is an important and correct one. But, as we refine our analysis, we will see that the role of the government in general, and the successful use of fiscal policy in particular, become increasingly difficult: governments will never again have it so good as they had it in this chapter.

SUMMARY

Here's what you should remember about the components of GDP:

- GDP is the sum of consumption, investment, government spending, inventory investment, and exports minus imports.

- Consumption (C) is the purchase of goods and services by consumers. Consumption is the largest component of demand.

- Investment (I) is the sum of non-residential investment – the purchase of new plants and new machines by firms – and of residential investment – the purchase of new houses or apartments by people.

- Government spending (G) is the purchase of goods and services by national, regional and local governments.

- Exports (X) are purchases of domestic goods by foreigners. Imports (IM) are purchases of foreign goods by resident consumers, firms and the national government.

- Inventory investment is the difference between production and purchases. It can be positive or negative.

Here's what you should remember about our first model of output determination:

- In the short run, demand determines production. Production is equal to income. Income in turn affects demand.

- The consumption function shows how consumption depends on disposable income. The propensity to consume describes how much consumption increases for a given increase in disposable income.

- Equilibrium output is the level of output at which production equals demand. In equilibrium, output equals autonomous spending multiplied by the multiplier. Autonomous spending is that part of demand that does not depend on income. The multiplier is equal to $1/(1 - c_1)$, where c_1 is the propensity to consume.

- Increases in consumer confidence, investment demand and government spending, as well as decreases in taxes, all increase equilibrium output in the short run.

- An alternative way of stating the goods–market equilibrium condition is that investment must be equal to saving – the sum of private and public saving. For this reason, the equilibrium condition is called the IS relation (I for investment, S for saving).

KEY TERMS

consumption (C) 43	trade balance 44	endogenous variables 47	econometrics 52
investment (I) 43	trade surplus 44	exogenous variables 47	dynamics 52
fixed investment 43	trade deficit 44	fiscal policy 47	saving 54
non-residential investment 43	inventory investment 44	equilibrium 47	private saving (S) 55
residential investment 43	identity 44	equilibrium in the goods market 48	public saving (T – G) 55
government spending (G) 44	disposable income (Y_D) 45		budget surplus 55
	consumption function 45	equilibrium condition 48	budget deficit 55
government transfers 44	behavioural equation 45	autonomous spending 48	IS relation 55
imports (IM) 44	linear relation 45	balanced budget 49	propensity to save
exports (X) 44	parameters 45	multiplier 49	$(1 - c_1)$ 56
net exports (X – IM) 44	propensity to consume (c_1) 45	geometric series 51	paradox of saving 56

QUESTIONS AND PROBLEMS

QUICK CHECK

1. *Using the information in this chapter, label each of the following statements true, false or uncertain. Explain briefly.*

a. The largest component of GDP is consumption.

b. Government spending, including transfers, was equal, on average, to 20.9% of GDP in EU-15 in 2008.

c. The propensity to consume has to be positive, but otherwise it can take on any positive value.

d. *Fiscal policy* describes the choice of government spending and taxes and is treated as exogenous in our goods market model.

e. The equilibrium condition for the goods market states that consumption equals output.

f. An increase of one unit in government spending leads to an increase of one unit in equilibrium output.

g. An increase in the propensity to consume leads to a decrease in output.

2. *Suppose that the economy is characterised by the following behavioural equations:*

$$C = 180 + 0.8Y_D$$
$$I = 160$$
$$G = 160$$
$$T = 120$$

Solve for the following variables.

a. Equilibrium GDP (Y)

b. Disposable income (Y_D)

c. Consumption spending (C)

3. *Use the economy described in problem 2.*

a. Solve for equilibrium output. Compute total demand. Is it equal to production? Explain.

b. Assume that G is now equal to 110. Solve for equilibrium output. Compute total demand. Is it equal to production? Explain.

c. Assume that G is equal to 110, so output is given by your answer to (b). Compute private plus public saving. Is the sum of private and public saving equal to investment? Explain.

DIG DEEPER

4. The balanced budget multiplier

For both political and macroeconomic reasons, governments are often reluctant to run budget deficits. Here, we examine whether policy changes in G and T that maintain a balanced budget are macroeconomically neutral. Put another way, we

examine whether it is possible to affect output through changes in G and T so that the government budget remains balanced.

Start from equation (3.8).

a. By how much does Y increase when G increases by one unit?

b. By how much does Y decrease when T increases by one unit?

c. Why are your answers to (a) and (b) different?

Suppose that the economy starts with a balanced budget: G = T. If the increase in G is equal to the increase in T, then the budget remains in balance. Let us now compute the balanced budget multiplier.

d. Suppose that G and T increase by one unit each. Using your answers to (a) and (b), what is the change in equilibrium GDP? Are balanced budget changes in G and T macroeconomically neutral?

e. How does the specific value of the propensity to consume affect your answer to (a)? Why?

5. Automatic stabilisers

So far in this chapter, we have assumed that the fiscal policy variables G and T are independent of the level of income. In the real world, however, this is not the case. Taxes typically depend on the level of income and so tend to be higher when income is higher. In this problem, we examine how this automatic response of taxes can help reduce the impact of changes in autonomous spending on output.

Consider the following behavioural equations:

$$C = c_0 + c_1 Y_D$$
$$T = t_0 + t_1 Y$$
$$Y_D = Y - T$$

G *and* I *are both constant. Assume that* t_1 *is between 0 and 1.*

a. Solve for equilibrium output.

b. What is the multiplier? Does the economy respond more to changes in autonomous spending when t_1 is 0 or when t_1 is positive? Explain.

c. Why is fiscal policy in this case called an automatic stabiliser?

6. Balanced budget versus automatic stabilisers

It is often argued that a balanced budget amendment would actually be destabilising. To understand this argument, consider the economy of problem 5.

a. Solve for equilibrium output.

b. Solve for taxes in equilibrium.

Suppose that the government starts with a balanced budget and that there is a drop in c_0.

c. What happens to Y? What happens to taxes?

d. Suppose that the government cuts spending in order to keep the budget balanced. What will be the effect on Y? Does the cut in spending required to balance the budget counteract or reinforce the effect of the drop in c_0 on output? (Don't do the algebra. Use your intuition and give the answer in words.)

7. Taxes and transfers

Recall that we define taxes, T, as net of transfers. In other words,

$$T = taxes - transfer\ payments$$

a. Suppose that the government increases transfer payments to private households, but these transfer payments are not financed by tax increases. Instead, the government borrows to pay for the transfer payments. Show in a diagram (similar to Figure 3.2) how this policy affects equilibrium output. Explain.

b. Suppose instead that the government pays for the increase in transfer payments with an equivalent increase in taxes. How does the increase in transfer payments affect equilibrium output in this case?

c. Now suppose that the population includes two kinds of people: those with high propensity to consume and those with low propensity to consume. Suppose the transfer policy increases taxes on those with low propensity to consume to pay for transfers to people with high propensity to consume. How does this policy affect equilibrium output?

d. How do you think the propensity to consume might vary across individuals according to income? In other words, how do you think the propensity to consume compares for people with high incomes and people with low incomes? Explain. Given your answer, do you think tax cuts will be more effective at stimulating output when they are directed toward high-income or toward low-income taxpayers?

8. Investment and income

This problem examines the implications of allowing investment to depend on output. Chapter 5 carries this analysis much further and introduces an essential relation – the effect of the interest rate on investment – not examined in this problem.

a. Suppose the economy is characterised by the following behavioural equations:

$$C = c_0 + c_1 Y_D$$
$$Y_D = Y - T$$
$$I = b_0 + b_1 Y$$

Government spending and taxes are constant. Note that investment now increases with output. (Chapter 5 discusses the reasons for this relation.) Solve for equilibrium output.

b. What is the value of the multiplier? How does the relation between investment and output affect the value of the multiplier? For the multiplier to be positive, what condition must $(c_1 + b_1)$ satisfy? Explain your answers.

c. Suppose that the parameter b_0, sometimes called *business confidence*, increases. How will equilibrium output be affected? Will investment change by more or less than the change in b_0? Why? What will happen to national saving?

EXPLORE FURTHER

9. The paradox of saving revisited

You should be able to complete this question without doing any algebra, although you may find making a diagram helpful for part (a). For this problem, you do not need to calculate the magnitudes of changes in economic variables – only the direction of change.

a. Consider the economy described in problem 8. Suppose that consumers decide to consume less (and therefore to save more) for any given amount of disposable income. Specifically, assume that consumer confidence (c_0) falls. What will happen to output?

b. *As* a result of the effect on output you determined in part (a), what will happen to investment? What will happen to public saving? What will happen to private saving? Explain. (*Hint*: Consider the saving-equals-investment characterisation of equilibrium.) What is the effect on consumption?

c. *Suppose* that consumers had decided to increase consumption expenditure, so that c_0 had increased. What would have been the effect on output, investment and private saving in this case? Explain. What would have been the effect on consumption?

d. Comment on the following logic: 'When output is too low, what is needed is an increase in demand for goods and services. Investment is one component of demand, and saving equals investment. Therefore, if the government could just convince households to attempt to save more, then investment, and output, would increase.'

Log on to **MyEconLab** and complete the studyplan exercises for this chapter to see how much you have learnt, and where you need to revise most.

MyEconLab

Chapter 4

FINANCIAL MARKETS

During the recent financial crisis that hit the USA and most of the world starting in 2007, central banks around the world had a particularly hard time. They were asked to design measures to help economies out of the recession and to enable the financial sector to recover and strengthen in the future. Over these years, central banks were often in the headlines explaining what their strategies and priorities were.

However in tranquil times too, barely a day goes by without the media speculating as to whether the central bank – either the ECB (short for European Central Bank) in the euro area, the Bank of England in the UK, the Riksbank in Sweden or the Fed (short for the Federal Reserve Bank) in the USA – is going to introduce some monetary policy measure, e.g. to change the interest rate, and how that change is likely to affect the economy. The chairmen of these central banks are very influential policy makers in their countries. Among them the chairman of the Fed – Ben Bernanke and his predecessor, Alan Greenspan, chairman of the Fed during 1987–2006 – is widely perceived as the most powerful policy maker in the USA, if not in the world. The President of the ECB – currently Mario Draghi – is probably the single most influential policy maker in the euro area.

The model of economic activity we developed earlier (see Chapter 3) did not include an interest rate, so there was no role for the central bank and its president.

This was an oversimplification, and it is time to relax it. In this chapter, we shall introduce the simplest model needed to think about the determination of the interest rate and the role of the central bank, a model in which people face a simple portfolio choice: whether to hold money or to hold bonds. In that model, we can think of the interest rate as determined by the demand for money and the supply of money. Then, in the next chapter, we shall look at how the interest rate in turn affects demand and output. This simple model does not, however, do justice to the complexity of the financial system. When we focus on the crisis later (see Chapter 20), we shall look at the financial sector in more detail, but it is better to keep things simple until then.

The chapter has four sections:

- Section 4.1 looks at the demand for money.

- Section 4.2 assumes that the central bank directly controls the supply of money and shows how the interest rate is determined by the condition that the demand for money be equal to its supply.

- Section 4.3 introduces banks as suppliers of money, revisits interest rates and how they are determined and describes the role of the central bank in this process.

- Section 4.4, an optional section, presents two alternative ways of looking at the equilibrium. One focuses on the interbank market, the other focuses on the money multiplier.

4.1 THE DEMAND FOR MONEY

This section looks at the determinants of the demand for money. A warning before we start: words such as 'money' or 'wealth' have very specific meanings in economics, often not the same meanings as in everyday conversations. The purpose of the Focus box 'Semantic traps: money, income and wealth' is to help you avoid some of these traps. Read it carefully, and come back to it once in a while.

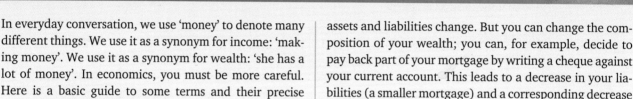

FOCUS
Semantic traps: money, income and wealth

In everyday conversation, we use 'money' to denote many different things. We use it as a synonym for income: 'making money'. We use it as a synonym for wealth: 'she has a lot of money'. In economics, you must be more careful. Here is a basic guide to some terms and their precise meanings in economics.

Income is what you earn from working plus what you receive in interest and dividends. It is a **flow** – something expressed in units of time: weekly income, monthly income or yearly income, for example. J. Paul Getty was once asked what his income was. Getty answered: '$1,000.' He meant but did not say: $1,000 per minute!

Saving is that part of after-tax income that you do not spend. It is also a flow. If you save 10% of your income, and your income is €3,000 per month, then you save €300 per month. **Savings** (plural) is sometimes used as a synonym for wealth – the value of what you have accumulated over time. To avoid confusion, we will not use 'savings' in this book.

Your **financial wealth**, or simply **wealth**, is the value of all your financial assets minus all your financial liabilities. In contrast to income or saving, which are flow variables, financial wealth is a **stock** variable. It is the value of wealth at a given moment in time.

At a given moment in time, you cannot change the total amount of your financial wealth. It can only change over time as you save or dissave, or as the value of your assets and liabilities change. But you can change the composition of your wealth; you can, for example, decide to pay back part of your mortgage by writing a cheque against your current account. This leads to a decrease in your liabilities (a smaller mortgage) and a corresponding decrease in your assets (a smaller deposit account balance); but, at that moment, it does not change your wealth.

Financial assets that can be used directly to buy goods are called *money*. Money includes currency and deposit accounts – deposits against which you can write cheques. Money is also a stock. Someone who is wealthy might have only small money holdings – say, €1,000,000 in stocks but only €500 in a deposit account. It is also possible for a person to have a large income but only small money holdings – say, an income of €10,000 monthly but only €1,000 in a deposit account.

Investment is a term economists reserve for the purchase of new capital goods, from machines to plants to office buildings. When you want to talk about the purchase of shares or other financial assets, you should refer to them as a **financial investment**.

Learn how to be economically correct:

– Do not say 'Mary is making a lot of money'; say 'Mary has a high income.'
– Do not say 'Joe has a lot of money'; say 'Joe is very wealthy.'

Suppose, as a result of having steadily saved part of your income in the past, your financial wealth today is €50,000. You may intend to keep saving in the future and increase your wealth further, but its value today is given. Suppose also that you only have the choice between two assets, money and bonds:

Make sure you see the difference ▶ between the decision about how much to save (a decision that determines how your wealth changes over time) and the decision about how to allocate a given stock of wealth between money and bonds.

● **Money**, which you can use for transactions, pays no interest. In the real world, there are two types of money: **Currency**, coins and bills, and **deposit accounts**, the bank deposits on which you can write cheques. The sum of currency and deposits is called *M1*. The distinction between the two will be important when we look at the supply of money. For the moment, however, the distinction does not matter and we can ignore it.

- **Bonds** pay a positive interest rate, i, but they cannot be used for transactions. In the real world, there are many types of bonds and other financial assets, each associated with a specific interest rate. For the time being, we will also ignore this aspect of reality and assume that there is just one type of bond and that it pays i, the rate of interest.

Assume that buying or selling bonds implies some cost, for example, a phone call to a broker and the payment of a transaction fee. How much of your €50,000 should you hold in money and how much in bonds? On the one hand, holding all your wealth in the form of money is clearly very convenient. You won't ever need to call a broker or pay transaction fees. But it also means you will receive no interest income. On the other hand, if you hold all your wealth in the form of bonds, you will earn interest on the full amount, but you will have to call your broker frequently – whenever you need money to take the bus, pay for a cup of coffee and so on. A rather inconvenient way of going through life.

Therefore, it is clear that you should hold both money and bonds. But in what proportions? This will depend mainly on two variables:

- Your *level of transactions*. You'll want to have enough money on hand to avoid having to sell bonds whenever you need money. Say, for example, that you typically spend €3,000 a month. In this case, you might want to have, on average, say, two months' worth of spending on hand, or €6,000 in money, and the rest, €50,000 – €6,000 = €44,000 in bonds. If, instead, you typically spend €4,000 a month, you might want to have, say, €8,000 in money and only €42,000 in bonds.
- The *interest rate on bonds*. The only reason to hold any of your wealth in bonds is that they pay interest. If bonds paid zero interest, you would want to hold all of your wealth in the form of money because it is more convenient.

  The higher the interest rate, the more you will be willing to deal with the hassle and the costs associated with buying and selling bonds. If the interest rate is very high, you might even decide to squeeze your money holdings to an average of only two weeks' worth of spending, or €1,500 (assuming your monthly spending is €3,000). This way, you will be able to keep, on average, €48,500 in bonds and earn more interest as a result.

Let's make this last point more concrete. Many of you probably do not hold bonds; few of you have a broker. However, many of you probably do hold bonds indirectly if you have a money market account with a financial institution. **Money market funds** (the full name is *money market mutual funds*) pool together the funds of many people. The funds are then used to buy bonds – typically government bonds. Money market funds pay an interest rate close to but slightly below the interest rate on the bonds they hold – the difference coming from the administrative costs of running the funds and from their profit margins.

When the interest rate on these funds reached 14% per year in the early 1980s (a very high interest rate by today's standards), many people who had previously kept all of their wealth in deposit accounts (which paid little or no interest) realised how much interest they could earn by moving some of it into money market accounts instead. As a result, accounts like these became very popular. Since then, however, interest rates have fallen. By the mid-2000s, just before the crisis, the average interest rate paid by money market funds was only around 5%. This was better than zero – the rate paid on many deposit accounts – but is much less attractive than the rate in the early 1980s. Since the crisis, the interest rate has further decreased, and, in 2010, the average interest rate on money market funds was less than 1%. As a result, people are now less careful about putting as much as they can in their money market funds. Put another way, for a given level of transactions, people now keep more of their wealth in money than they did in the early 1980s.

◄ An economy where the interest rate is equal or very close to zero is said to be in a *liquidity trap* (more on this in Chapter 5).

Deriving the demand for money

Let's go from this discussion to an equation describing the demand for money.

Denote the amount of money people want to hold – their demand for money – by M^d (the superscript d stands for *demand*). The demand for money in the economy as a whole is just

Revisit the example of an economy composed of a steel company and a car company (see Chapter 2). Calculate the total value of transactions in that economy. If the steel and the car companies doubled in size, what would happen to transactions and to GDP?

the sum of all the individual demands for money by the people in the economy. Therefore, it depends on the overall level of transactions in the economy and on the interest rate. The overall level of transactions in the economy is hard to measure, but it is likely to be roughly proportional to nominal income (income measured in euros). If nominal income were to increase by 10%, it is reasonable to think that the value of transactions in the economy would also increase by roughly 10%. So we can write the relation between the demand for money, nominal income and the interest rate as:

$$M^d = \text{€}YL(i) \qquad\qquad [4.1]$$
$$(-)$$

where €Y denotes nominal income. Read this equation in the following way: the demand for money M^d is equal to nominal income €Y multiplied by a function of the interest rate i, with the function denoted by $L(i)$. The minus sign under i in $L(i)$ captures the fact that the interest rate has a negative effect on money demand: an increase in the interest rate decreases the demand for money, as people put more of their wealth into bonds.

Equation (4.1) summarises what we have discussed so far:

What matters here is nominal income – income in euros, not real income. If real income does not change but prices double, leading to a doubling of nominal income, people will need to hold twice as much money to buy the same consumption basket.

- First, the demand for money increases in proportion to nominal income. If nominal income doubles, increasing from €Y to €$2Y$, then the demand for money also doubles, increasing from €$YL(i)$ to €$2YL(i)$.
- Second, the demand for money depends negatively on the interest rate. This is captured by the function $L(i)$ and the negative sign underneath: an increase in the interest rate decreases the demand for money.

The relation between the demand for money, nominal income and the interest rate implied by equation (4.1) is shown in Figure 4.1. The interest rate, i, is measured on the vertical axis. Money, M, is measured on the horizontal axis.

The relation between the demand for money and the interest rate for a given level of nominal income €Y is represented by the M^d curve. The curve is downward sloping: the lower the interest rate (the lower i), the higher the amount of money people want to hold (the higher M).

For a given interest rate, an increase in nominal income increases the demand for money. In other words, an increase in nominal income shifts the demand for money to the right, from M^d to $M^{d'}$. For example, at interest rate i, an increase in nominal income from €Y to €Y' increases the demand for money from M to M'.

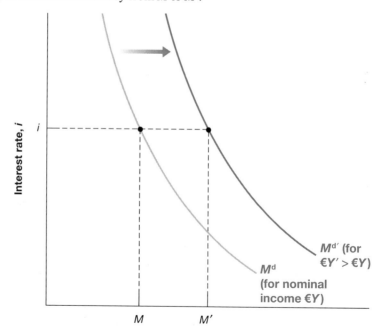

Figure 4.1

The demand for money

For a given level of nominal income, a lower interest rate increases the demand for money. At a given interest rate, an increase in nominal income shifts the demand for money to the right.

FOCUS
Euro vs US dollar as the leading international reserve currency

Of the total amount of US currency in circulation, $750 billion in 2006, around $170 billion was held by US households and around $80 billion by firms (this figure includes an estimate of the amount held by those involved in the underground economy or in illegal activities, such as drug dealers, who often use dollars for their transactions). The remaining $500 billion, or 66% of the total, was held by foreigners.

The dollar is adopted in some countries as a currency for transactions, for example Ecuador and El Salvador. Moreover, in a number of countries that have suffered from high inflation in the past, people have learned that their domestic currency may quickly become worthless, and they see dollars as a safe and convenient asset. This is the case, for example, in Argentina and Russia. Estimates by the US Treasury suggest that Argentina holds more than $50 billion in dollar bills, Russia more than $80 billion, so together they have more than the holdings of US firms.

Besides the private sector's use of the dollar outside of the USA, there is also an important official sector's use of the dollar; central banks and monetary authorities around the world hold foreign exchange reserves in US dollars to safekeep wealth and to intervene in foreign exchange markets. The fact that foreigners hold such a high proportion of the dollar bills in circulation has a major macroeconomic implication. The rest of the world, by holding US currency, is in fact making an interest-free loan to the USA of about $500 billion.

The US dollar has been the leading international reserve currency for more than a century. A leading international currency must have some important features, all of which the USA, unlike any other country in the world, has. The major ones are the following: it must be used as a currency in a large transaction area; it must be the currency of a (strong central) country with stable monetary policy (and therefore stable inflation, otherwise it would not be used as a store of value); it must be free of controls on the part of the government.

Since the turn of the millenium, the birth of the euro has inspired a debate on whether it would ever rival and eventually replace the dollar as the leading international reserve currency. The debate has recently become more lively following an increased willingness of central banks to hold foreign exchange reserves in euros (compared to dollars). Table 4.1 shows how the currency composition of foreign exchange holdings changed since 2001, in both advanced and emerging economies. The euro's share of

Table 4.1 Currency composition of foreign exchange holdings 2001/2010: dollars vs euros

	2001	2005	2010	2011
World	100	100	100	100
US dollars	71.5	66.9	62	61.3
Euros	19.2	24.0	26	25.9
Pound sterling	2.7	3.6	4	3.9
Advanced economies	100	100	100	100
US dollars	71.7	69.7	65	64.8
Euros	18.3	20.7	24	24.1
Pound sterling	2.7	2.8	2.5	2.5
Emerging economies	100	100	100	100
US dollars	72.5	62.1	58	57.5
Euros	21.3	29.7	28	27.9
Pound sterling	2.7	5.0	5.5	5.5

Source: **www.imf.org/external/np/sta/cofer/eng/index.htm**

reserves is higher today than it was prior to the creation of the European monetary union, but it is still well below the US dollar's share. The dollar's share declined since the beginning of the decade (by 7.3 percentage points) largely in favour of the euro (whose share increased by 7.2 percentage points).

So, will the euro ever become a reserve currency? For a currency to achieve international status, it is not enough to be perceived as a store of value by central banks; it must also be used by non-residents as a medium of exchange and unit of account. On these grounds, the euro is lagging behind the dollar. As a medium of exchange, the euro is used in 37% of foreign exchange transactions all over the world compared to 86% for the US dollar. As a unit of account, the euro is still well below the dollar as a currency of choice for invoicing, and also as an exchange rate to which other currencies are pegged (as we will learn in Chapter 12). Even if the euro were ever to challenge the dollar in its role as a store of value, it is unlikely that the same would happen in its roles as a unit of account and medium of exchange.

That being said, we should also remind ourselves that a currency's international status depends on others' use of it as such. Therefore, the more it is used as a medium of exchange, the more convenient and attractive it becomes for new users. That is why international currencies tend to be just a few (or even just one) and also why they tend to change slowly. With the birth of the euro, the dollar now has a potential competitor, but it is still – and is likely to be for a long time – dominant.

4.2 DETERMINING THE INTEREST RATE: PART 1

Having looked at the demand for money, we now look at the supply of money and then at the equilibrium.

In the real world, there are two types of money: deposit accounts, which are supplied by banks, and currency, which is supplied by the central bank. In this section, we will assume that deposit accounts do not exist – that the only money in the economy is currency. In the next section, we will reintroduce deposit accounts and look at the role banks play. Introducing banks makes the discussion more realistic, but it also makes the mechanics of money supply more complicated. It is better to build up the discussion in two steps.

Money demand, money supply and the equilibrium interest rate

Throughout this section, 'money' ➤ stands for 'central bank money' or 'currency'.

Suppose the central bank decides to supply an amount of money equal to M, so

$$M^s = M$$

The superscript s stands for supply. (Let's disregard, for the moment, the issue of how exactly the central bank supplies this amount of money. We shall return to it in a few paragraphs.)

Equilibrium in financial markets requires that money supply be equal to money demand, that $M^s = M^d$. Then, using $M^s = M$, and equation (4.1) for money demand, the equilibrium condition is

$$\text{Money supply} = \text{Money demand}$$
$$M = €YL(i) \qquad [4.2]$$

This equation tells us that the interest rate i must be such that, given their income $€Y$, people are willing to hold an amount of money equal to the existing money supply M. This equilibrium relation is called the **LM relation**. As for the IS relation, the name of the LM relation is more than 50 years old. The letter L stands for **liquidity**: economists use liquidity as a measure of how easily an asset can be exchanged for money. Money is fully liquid; other assets less so.

How liquid depends on the asset: ➤ bonds are typically fairly liquid. Houses are much less so.

We can think of the demand for money as a demand for liquidity. The letter M stands for money. The demand for liquidity must equal the supply of money.

This equilibrium condition is represented graphically in Figure 4.2. As in Figure 4.1, money is measured on the horizontal axis, and the interest rate is measured on the vertical axis. The demand for money, M^d, drawn for a given level of nominal income $€Y$, is downward sloping: a higher interest rate implies a lower demand for money. The supply of money is drawn as the vertical line denoted M^s: the money supply equals M and is independent of the interest rate. Equilibrium occurs at point A, and the equilibrium interest rate is given by i.

Now that we have characterised the equilibrium, we can look at how changes in nominal income or changes in the money supply by the central bank affect the equilibrium interest rate.

- Figure 4.3 shows the effects of an increase in nominal income on the interest rate.

    The figure replicates Figure 4.2, and the initial equilibrium is at point A. An increase in nominal income from $€Y$ to $€Y'$ increases the level of transactions, which increases the demand for money at any interest rate. The money demand curve shifts to the right, from M^d to $M^{d'}$. The equilibrium moves from A up to A', and the equilibrium interest rate increases from i to i'.

    In words: *an increase in nominal income leads to an increase in the interest rate*. The reason: at the initial interest rate, the demand for money exceeds the supply. An increase in the interest rate is needed to decrease the amount of money people want to hold and to re-establish equilibrium.

- Figure 4.4 shows the effects of an increase in the money supply on the interest rate.

    The initial equilibrium is at point A, with interest rate i. An increase in the money supply, from $M^s = M$ to $M^{s'} = M'$, leads to a shift of the money supply curve to the right,

Figure 4.2

The determination of the interest rate

The interest rate must be such that the supply of money (which is independent of the interest rate) is equal to the demand for money (which does depend on the interest rate).

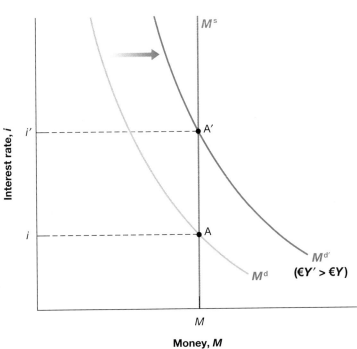

Figure 4.3

The effects of an increase in nominal income on the interest rate

An increase in nominal income leads to an increase in the interest rate.

from M^s to $M^{s'}$. The equilibrium moves from A down to A'; the interest rate decreases from i to i'.

In words: *an increase in the supply of money by the central bank leads to a decrease in the interest rate*. The decrease in the interest rate increases the demand for money so it equals the now larger money supply.

Monetary policy and open market operations

We can get a better understanding of the results in Figures 4.3 and 4.4 by looking more closely at how the central bank actually changes the money supply, and what happens when it does so.

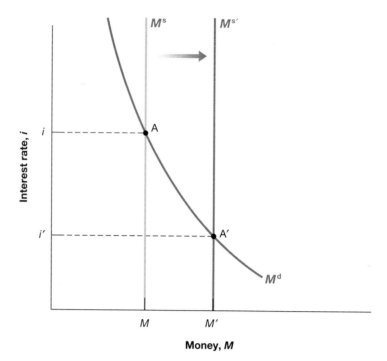

Figure 4.4

The effects of an increase in the money supply on the interest rate

An increase in the supply of money leads to a decrease in the interest rate.

Open market operations

In modern economies, the way central banks change the supply of money is by buying or selling bonds in the bond market. If a central bank wants to increase the amount of money in the economy, it buys bonds and pays for them by creating money. If it wants to decrease the amount of money in the economy, it sells bonds, and removes from circulation the money it receives in exchange for the bonds. These actions are called **open market operations** because they take place in the 'open market' for bonds.

The balance sheet of a bank (or firm, ➤ or individual) is a list of its assets and liabilities at a point in time. The assets are the sum of what the bank owns and what is owed to it by others. The liabilities are what the bank owes to others.

The balance sheet of the central bank is given in Figure 4.5(a). The assets of the central bank are the bonds it holds in its portfolio. Its liabilities are the stock of money in the economy. Open market operations lead to equal changes in assets and liabilities.

If the central bank buys, say, €1 million worth of bonds, the amount of bonds it holds is higher by €1 million, and so is the amount of money in the economy. Such an operation is called an **expansionary open market operation**, because the central bank increases (expands) the supply of money.

If the central bank sells €1 million worth of bonds, both the amount of bonds held by the central bank and the amount of money in the economy are lower by €1 million (Figure 4.5(b)). Such an operation is called a **contractionary open market operation**, because the central bank decreases (contracts) the supply of money.

Figure 4.5

The balance sheet of the central bank and the effects of an expansionary open market operation

The assets of the central bank are the bonds it holds. The liabilities are the stock of money in the economy. An open market operation in which the central bank buys bonds and issues money increases both assets and liabilities by the same amount.

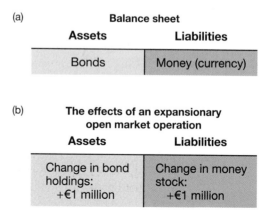

Bond prices and bond yields

We have focused so far on the interest rate on bonds. In fact, what is determined in bonds markets is not interest rates, but bond prices; the interest rate on a bond can then be inferred from the price of the bond. Understanding this relation between the interest rate and bond prices will prove useful both here and later in this text.

- Suppose the bonds in our economy are one-year bonds – bonds that promise a payment of a given number of euros, say €100, a year from now. Let the price of a bond today be €P_B, where the subscript B stands for 'bond'. If you buy the bond today and hold it for a year, the rate of return on holding the bond for a year is (€100 – €P_B)/€P_B. Therefore, the interest rate on the bond is given by:

$$i = \frac{€100 - €P_B}{€P_B}$$

◀ The interest rate is what you get for the bond a year from now (€100) minus what you pay for the bond today (€P_B), divided by the price of the bond today (€P_B).

If €P_B is €95, the interest rate equals €5/€95 = 0.053, or 5.3% per year. If €P_B is €90, the interest rate is 11.1% per year. The higher the price of the bond, the lower the interest rate.
- If we are given the interest rate, we can figure out the price of the bond using the same formula. Reorganising the formula above, the price today of a one-year bond paying €100 a year from today is given by:

$$€P_B = \frac{€100}{1+i}$$

The price of the bond today is equal to the final payment divided by 1 plus the interest rate. If the interest rate is positive, the price of the bond is less than the final payment. The higher the interest rate, the lower the price today. You may read or hear that 'bond markets went up today'. This means that the prices of bonds went up, and therefore that interest rates went down.

We are now ready to return to the effects of an open market operation.

Consider first an expansionary open market operation, in which the central bank buys bonds in the bonds market and pays for them by creating money. As the central bank buys bonds, the demand for bonds goes up, increasing their price. Conversely, the interest rate on bonds goes down.

Consider instead a contractionary open market operation, in which the central bank decreases the supply of money. It sells bonds in the bonds market. This leads to a decrease in their price, and an increase in the interest rate.

Let's summarise what we have learned in the first two sections:

- The interest rate is determined by the equality of the supply of money and the demand for money.
- By changing the supply of money, the central bank can affect the interest rate.
- The central bank changes the supply of money through open market operations, which are purchases or sales of bonds for money.
- Open market operations in which the central bank increases the money supply by buying bonds lead to an increase in the price of bonds and a decrease in the interest rate.
- Open market operations in which the central bank decreases the money supply by selling bonds lead to a decrease in the price of bonds and an increase in the interest rate.

Let us take up two more issues before moving on.

Choosing money or choosing the interest rate?

We have described the central bank as choosing the money supply and letting the interest rate be determined at the point where money supply equals money demand. Instead, we could have described the central bank as choosing the interest rate and then adjusting the money supply so as to achieve the interest rate it has chosen.

To see this, return to Figure 4.4. Figure 4.4, showed the effect of a decision by the central bank to increase the money supply from M^s to $M^{s'}$, causing the interest rate to fall from i to i'. However, we could have described the figure in terms of the central bank decision to lower the interest rate from i to i' by increasing the money supply from M^s to $M^{s'}$.

Why is it useful to think about the central bank as choosing the interest rate? Because this is what modern central banks, including the ECB, the Bank of England and the Fed, typically do. They typically think about the interest rate they want to achieve, and then move the money supply so as to achieve it. This is why, when you listen to the news, you do not hear: 'The central bank decided to increase the money supply today'. Instead you hear: 'The central bank decided to decrease the interest rate today'. The way the central bank did it was by increasing the money supply appropriately.

> Suppose nominal income increases, as in Figure 4.3, and that the central bank wants to keep the interest rate unchanged. How does it need to adjust the money supply?

Money, bonds and other assets

We have been looking at an economy with only two assets: money and bonds. This is obviously a much simplified version of actual economies with their many financial assets and many financial markets. But, as you will see in later chapters, the basic lessons we have just learned apply very generally. The only change we will have to make is replacing 'interest rate' in our conclusions with 'short-term interest rate on government bonds'. You will see that the short-term interest rate is determined by the condition we just discussed – the equilibrium between money supply and money demand. The central bank can, through open market operations, change the short-term interest rate; and open market operations are indeed the basic tool used by most modern central banks to affect interest rates.

> The complication: the short-term interest rate – the rate directly controlled by the central bank – is not the only interest rate that affects spending. (We return to this issue first in Chapter 6.)

There is one dimension, however, to which our model must be extended. We have assumed that all money in the economy consisted of currency, supplied by the central bank. In the real world, money includes not only currency but also deposit accounts. Deposit accounts are supplied not by the central bank but by (private) banks. How the presence of banks and checkable deposits changes our conclusions is the topic of the next section.

4.3 DETERMINING THE INTEREST RATE: PART 2

To understand what determines the interest rate in an economy with both currency and deposit accounts, we must first look at what banks do.

> But let us give you the bottom line in case you want to skip the section: even in this more complicated case, the central bank can, by changing the amount of central bank money, control the short-term interest rate.

What banks do

Modern economies are characterised by the existence of many types of **financial intermediaries** – institutions which receive funds from people and firms, and use these funds to buy financial assets or to make loans to other people and firms. The assets of these institutions are the financial assets they own and the loans they have made. Their liabilities are what they owe to the people and firms from whom they have received funds.

Banks are one type of financial intermediaries. What makes banks special – and the reason we focus on banks here rather than on financial intermediaries in general – is that their liabilities are money: people can pay for transactions by writing cheques up to the amount of their account balance. Let's look at what they do more closely.

> Banks have other types of liabilities in addition to deposit accounts, and they are engaged in more activities than just holding bonds or making loans. Ignore these complications for the moment.

Their balance sheet is shown in Figure 4.6(b).

● Banks receive funds from people and firms who either deposit funds directly or have funds sent to their deposit accounts (via direct deposit of their pay cheques, for example.) At any point in time, people and firms can write cheques or withdraw up to the full amount of their account balances. The liabilities of the banks are therefore equal to the value of these deposit accounts.

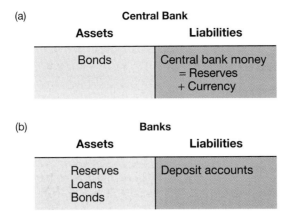

Figure 4.6

The balance sheet of banks and the balance sheet of the central bank, revisited

- Banks keep as **reserves** some of the funds they receive. They are held partly in cash and partly in an account the banks have at the central bank, which they can draw on when they need to. Banks hold reserves for three reasons:
  1. On any given day, some depositors withdraw cash from their deposit accounts while others deposit cash into their accounts. There is no reason for the inflows and outflows of cash to be equal, so the bank must keep some cash on hand.
  2. In the same way, on any given day, people with accounts at the bank write cheques to people with accounts at other banks, and people with accounts at other banks write cheques to people with accounts at the bank. What the bank, as a result of these transactions, owes the other banks can be larger or smaller than what the other banks owe to it. For this reason also, the bank needs to keep reserves.

     The first two reasons imply that the banks would want to keep some reserves even if they were not required to do so. But, in addition, banks are subject to reserve requirements, which require them to hold reserves in some proportion of their deposit accounts.
  3. In Europe, there are special reserve requirements applied to banks in the euro area according to which each institution must keep reserves in relation to the composition of their liabilities. In particular, the **reserve ratio** is equal to 1% on sight and overnight deposits, on term deposits up to two years and on debt securities with short maturity up to two years.
  4. Loans represent roughly 70% of banks' non-reserve assets. Bonds account for the rest, 30%. The distinction between bonds and loans is unimportant for our purposes in this chapter – which is to understand how the money supply is determined. For this reason, to keep the discussion simple, we will assume that banks do not make loans, that they hold only reserves and bonds as assets. But the distinction between loans and bonds is important for other purposes, from the possibility of 'bank runs' to the role of federal deposit insurance. These topics are explored in the Focus box 'Bank runs, deposit insurance and wholesale funding'.

Figure 4.6(a) returns to the balance sheet of the central bank, in an economy in which there are banks. It is very similar to the balance sheet of the central bank we saw in Figure 4.5. The asset side is the same as before: the assets of the central bank are the bonds it holds. The liabilities of the central bank are the money it has issued, **central bank money**. The new feature is that not all of central bank money is held as currency by the public. Some of it is held as reserves by banks.

FOCUS
Bank runs, deposit insurance and wholesale funding

Is bank money (deposit accounts) just as good as central bank money (currency)? To answer this question, we must look at what banks do with their funds, and at the distinction between making loans or holding bonds.

Making a loan to a firm or buying a government bond are more similar than they may seem. In one case, the bank lends to a firm. In the other, the bank lends to the government. This is why, for simplicity, we assumed in the text that banks held only bonds.

But, in one respect, making a loan is very different from buying a bond. Bonds, especially government bonds, are very liquid: if need be, they can be sold easily in the bond market. Loans, on the other hand, are often not liquid at all. Calling them back may be impossible. Firms have probably already used their loans to buy inventories or new machines, so they no longer have the cash on hand. Likewise, individuals are likely to have used their loans to purchase cars, houses or other things. The bank could in principle sell the loans to a third party to get cash. However, selling them might be very difficult because potential buyers would know little about how reliable the borrowers are.

This fact has one important implication: take a healthy bank, a bank with a portfolio of good loans. Suppose rumours start that the bank is not doing well and some loans will not be repaid. Believing that the bank may fail, people with deposits at the bank will want to close their accounts and withdraw cash. If enough people do so, the bank will run out of reserves. Given that the loans cannot be called back, the bank will not be able to satisfy the demand for cash, and it will have to close.

Conclusion: fear that a bank will close can actually cause it to close – even if all its loans are good. The financial history of the USA up to the 1930s is full of such **bank runs**. One bank fails for the right reason (because it has made bad loans). This causes depositors at other banks to panic and withdraw money from their banks, forcing them to close. In an old movie with James Stewart, *It's a Wonderful Life*, after another bank in Stewart's town fails, depositors at the savings and loan he manages get scared and want to withdraw their money, too. Stewart successfully persuades them this is not a good idea. *It's a Wonderful Life* has a happy ending. But in real life, most bank runs didn't.

What can be done to avoid bank runs? One solution is called **narrow banking**. Narrow banking would restrict banks to holding liquid and safe government bonds, like T-bills. Loans would have to be made by financial intermediaries other than banks. This would eliminate bank runs, as well as the need for **deposit insurance**. Some recent changes in US regulation have gone in that direction, restricting banks which rely on deposits from engaging in some financial operations, but they stop far short of imposing narrow banking.

Another solution, and one which has been adopted by governments in most advanced countries, is deposit insurance. The USA, for example, introduced federal deposit insurance in 1934. The US government now insures each account up to a ceiling, which, since 2008, is $250,000 (In response to the crisis, all accounts are currently fully insured, regardless of the amount, but this is scheduled to end in December 2012). As a result, there is no reason for depositors to run and withdraw their money.

The EU Directive 94/19/EC of the European Parliament on deposit-guarantee schemes requires all member states to have a deposit guarantee scheme for at least 90% of the deposited amount, up to at least €20,000 per person. On 7 October 2008, the Ecofin (the Economic and Financial Affairs Council comprising the Economics and Financial Affairs Ministers of the 27 EU member states) agreed to increase the minimum amount to €50,000. The increased amount followed Ireland's move, in September 2008, to increase its deposit insurance to an unlimited amount. Many other EU countries, starting with the UK reacted by increasing their own limits to discourage people from transferring deposits to Irish banks.

Deposit insurance leads, however, to problems of its own: depositors, who do not have to worry about their deposits, no longer look at the activities of the banks in which they have their accounts. Banks may then misbehave, by making loans they wouldn't have made in the absence of deposit insurance. And, as the crisis has unfortunately shown, deposit insurance is no longer enough. The reason is that banks have increasingly relied on other sources of funds, often borrowing overnight from other financial institutions and investors, a method of financing known as *wholesale funding*. Wholesale funding, just before the crisis, accounted for close to 30% of total funding for banks. These funds were not insured, and when, in late 2008, doubts increased about the quality of the assets held by banks, there was in effect a bank run on many banks, this time not from the traditional depositors, but from wholesale funders. To avoid more bank collapses in the USA, the Fed had no choice than to provide funds to banks on a very large scale.

Since then, banks have reduced their reliance on wholesale funding, which is down to roughly 25% in the USA. In parallel, regulation is being considered which would force banks to hold enough liquid assets to be able to withstand a large decrease in their wholesale funding. This is one of the main challenges facing bank regulators today.

The supply and the demand for central bank money

The easiest way to think about how the interest rate in this economy is determined is by thinking in terms of the supply and the demand for central bank money:

● The demand for central bank money is equal to the demand for currency by people plus the demand for reserves by banks.
● The supply of central bank money is under the direct control of the central bank.
● The equilibrium interest rate is such that the demand and the supply for central bank money are equal.

Figure 4.7 shows the structure of the demand and the supply of central bank money in more detail. (Ignore the equations for the time being. Just look at the boxes.) Start on the left side. The demand for money by people is for both deposit accounts and currency. Because banks have to hold reserves against deposit accounts, the demand for deposit accounts leads to a demand for reserves by banks. Consequently, the demand for central bank money is equal to the demand for reserves by banks plus the demand for currency. Go to the right side: the supply of central bank money is determined by the central bank. Look at the equal sign: the interest rate must be such that the demand and the supply of central bank money are equal.

We now go through each of the boxes in Figure 4.7 and ask:

● What determines the demand for deposit accounts and the demand for currency?
● What determines the demand for reserves by banks?
● What determines the demand for central bank money?
● How does the condition that the demand and the supply of central money be equal determine the interest rate?

◀ Be careful to distinguish among:

● demand for money (demand for currency and deposit accounts)
● demand for bank money (demand for deposit accounts)
● demand for central bank money (demand for currency by people and demand for reserves by banks).

The demand for money

When people can hold both currency and deposit accounts, the demand for money involves two decisions. First, people must decide how much money to hold. Second, they must

Demand for money

Demand for money
$M^d = €YL(i)$

Demand for deposit accounts
$D^d = (1 - c)M^d$

Demand for reserves by banks
$R^d = \theta(1 - c)M^d$

Demand for central bank money
$H^d = CU^d + R^d = [c + \theta(1 - c)]M^d =$

Supply of central bank money

Demand for currency
$CU^d = cM^d$

$[c + \theta(1 - c)]€YL(i)$ = H

Figure 4.7

Determinants of the demand and supply of central bank money

decide how much of this money to hold in currency and how much to hold in deposit accounts.

It is reasonable to assume that the overall demand for money (currency plus deposit accounts) is given by the same factors as before. People will hold more money the higher the level of transactions and the lower the interest rate on bonds. So we can assume that overall money demand is given by the same equation as before (equation (4.1)):

$$M^d = €YL(i) \qquad [4.3]$$
$$(-)$$

That brings us to the second decision. How do people decide how much to hold in currency, and how much in deposit accounts? Currency is more convenient for small transactions (it is also more convenient for illegal transactions). Checks are more convenient for large transactions. Holding money in your deposit account is safer than holding cash.

Let's assume people hold a fixed proportion of their money in currency – call this proportion c – and, by implication, hold a fixed proportion $(1 - c)$ in deposit accounts. Call the demand for currency CU^d (CU for currency, and d for demand). Call the demand for deposit accounts D^d (D for deposits, and d for demand). The two demands are given by:

$$CU^d = cM^d \qquad [4.4]$$

$$D^d = (1 - c)M^d \qquad [4.5]$$

Equation (4.4) shows the first component of the demand for central bank money – the demand for currency by the public. Equation (4.5) shows the demand for deposit accounts.

We now have a description of the first box, 'Demand for money', on the left side of Figure 4.7: equation (4.3) shows the overall demand for money. Equations (4.4) and (4.5) show the demand for deposit accounts and the demand for currency respectively.

The demand for deposit accounts leads to a demand by banks for reserves, the second component of the demand for central bank money. To see how, let's turn to the behaviour of banks.

The demand for reserves

The larger the amount of deposit accounts, the larger the amount of reserves the banks must hold, both for precautionary and for regulatory reasons. Let θ (the Greek lower case letter theta) be the reserve ratio, the amount of reserves banks hold per euro of deposit accounts. Let R denote the reserves of banks. Let D denote the amount of deposit accounts. Then, by the definition of θ, the following relation holds between R and D:

$$R = \theta D \qquad [4.6]$$

If people want to hold D^d in deposits, then, from equation (4.6) banks must hold θD^d in reserves. Combining equations (4.5) and (4.6), the second component of the demand for central bank money – the demand for reserves by banks – is given by:

$$R^d = \theta(1 - c)M^d \qquad [4.7]$$

We now have the equation corresponding to the second box, 'Demand for reserves by banks', on the left side of Figure 4.7.

The demand for central bank money

Call H^d the demand for central bank money. This demand is equal to the sum of the demand for currency and the demand for reserves:

$$H^d = CU^d + R^d \qquad [4.8]$$

Replace CU^d and R^d by their expressions from equations (4.4) and (4.7) to get:

$$H^d = cM^d + \theta(1 - c)M^d = [c + \theta(1 - c)]M^d$$

Finally, replace the overall demand for money, M^d, by its expression from equation (4.3) to get:

$$H^d = [c + \theta(1 - c)]€YL(i) \qquad [4.9]$$

This gives us the equation corresponding to the third box, 'Demand for central bank money', on the left side of Figure 4.7.

◄ Suppose banks doubled the number of locations of ATM machines, making them more convenient to use for their customers. What would happen to the demand for central bank money?

The determination of the interest rate

We are now ready to characterise the equilibrium. Let H be the supply of central bank money; H is directly controlled by the central bank; just like in the previous section, the central bank can change the amount of H through open market operations. The equilibrium condition is that the supply of central bank money be equal to the demand for central bank money:

$$H = H^d \qquad [4.10]$$

Or, using equation (4.9):

$$H = [c + \theta(1 - c)]€YL(i) \qquad [4.11]$$

The supply of central bank money (the left side of equation (4.11)) is equal to the demand for central bank money (the right side of equation (4.11)), which is equal to the term in brackets multiplied by the overall demand for money.

Look at the term in brackets more closely. Suppose that people held only currency, so $c = 1$. Then, the term in brackets would be equal to 1, and the equation would be exactly the same as equation (4.2) in section 4.2 (with the letter H replacing the letter M on the left side, but H and M both stand for the supply of central bank money). In this case, people would hold only currency, and banks would play no role in the supply of money. We would be back to the case we looked at in section 4.2.

Assume instead that people did not hold currency at all, but held only deposit accounts, so $c = 0$. Then, the term in brackets would be equal to θ. Suppose for example that $\theta = 0.1$, so that the term in brackets was equal to 0.1. Then, the demand for central bank money would be equal to one-tenth of the overall demand for money. This is easy to understand: people would hold only deposit accounts. For every euro they wanted to hold, banks would need to have 10 cents in reserves. In other words, the demand for reserves would be one-tenth of the overall demand for money.

Leaving aside these two extreme cases, note that, as long as people hold some deposit accounts (so that $c < 1$), the term in brackets is less than 1. This means the demand for central bank money is less than the overall demand for money. This is due to the fact that the demand for reserves by banks is only a fraction of the demand for deposit accounts.

We can represent the equilibrium condition, equation (4.11), graphically, and we do this in Figure 4.8. The figure looks the same as Figure 4.2, but with central bank money rather than money on the horizontal axis. The interest rate is measured on the vertical axis. The demand for central bank money, $CU^d + R^d$, is drawn for a given level of nominal income. A higher interest rate implies a lower demand for central bank money for two reasons: (1) the demand for currency by people goes down; (2) the demand for deposit accounts by people also goes down. This leads to lower demand for reserves by banks. The supply of money is fixed and is represented by a vertical line at H. Equilibrium is at point A, with interest rate i.

The effects of either changes in nominal income or changes in the supply of central bank money are qualitatively the same as in the previous section. In particular, an increase in the supply of central bank money leads to a shift in the vertical supply line to the right. This leads to a lower interest rate. As before, an increase in central bank money leads to a decrease in the interest rate. Conversely, a decrease in central bank money leads to an increase in the interest rate.

◄ Suppose people get worried about the possibility of bank runs and decide to hold a higher proportion of money in the form of currency. If the central bank keeps the money supply constant, what will happen to the interest rate?

Figure 4.8

Equilibrium in the market for central bank money and the determination of the interest rate

The equilibrium interest rate is such that the supply of central bank money is equal to the demand for central bank money.

4.4 TWO ALTERNATIVE WAYS OF LOOKING AT THE EQUILIBRIUM

In Section 4.3, we looked at the equilibrium through the condition that the supply and the demand of central bank money be equal. There are two other ways of looking at the equilibrium. While they are all equivalent, each provides a different way of thinking about the equilibrium, and going through each one will strengthen your understanding of how monetary policy affects the interest rate.

The interbank market and the overnight interest rate

Instead of thinking in terms of the supply and the demand for central bank money, we can think in terms of the supply and the demand for bank reserves.

The supply of reserves is equal to the supply of central bank money H, minus the demand for currency by the public, CU^d. The demand for reserves by banks is R^d. So the equilibrium condition that the supply and the demand for bank reserves be equal is given by:

$$H - CU^d = R^d$$

Notice that, if we move CU^d from the left side to the right side, and use the fact that the demand for central bank money H^d is given by $H^d = CU^d + R^d$, then this equation becomes $H = H^d$. In other words, looking at the equilibrium in terms of the supply and the demand for reserves is equivalent to looking at the equilibrium in terms of the supply and the demand for central bank money – the approach we followed in section 4.3.

The market for bank reserves, where the interest rate moves up and down to balance the supply and demand for reserves, is not free: most central banks intervene to inuence the interest rate, because all interest rates in the economy are linked to the interest rate on reserves. The central bank can influence the **interbank market**, and thus the interest rate, in different ways. By conducting open market operations, it can influence the supply of reserves. For example, it can buy bonds from banks, thereby increasing their reserves, which (other things being equal) should push the interbank interest rate down.

In the USA and Europe, the central bank (the Fed and the ECB, respectively) controls the interest rate on bank reserves in slightly different ways. The Fed controls the interest rate on bank reserves (which is called the Federal Funds Rate) trying to keep it close to the target (the Federal Funds Target). The ECB keeps the interest rate on bank reserves in the euro area (which is called **EONIA**, short for Euro Overnight Index Average), the rate at which banks lend reserves to one another, within a corridor.

Whether banks buy reserves from one another or directly from the central bank normally makes little difference. The rate at which banks lend money to each other (the EONIA rate in the Euro area, the SONIA rate in the UK) is usually very close to the interest rate at which banks can borrow reserves from the ECB using the so-called *Marginal Lending Facility*, or from the Bank of England or any other central bank. EONIA typically exceeds the interest on overnight loans from the ECB through the Marginal Lending Facility by around 20 basis points or 0.2%. This slightly higher cost reflects an important difference. When a bank borrows reserves from the ECB, it must post securities as a guarantee; however, no guarantee is required for loans between commercial banks. From 9 August 2007 (the outbreak of the recent financial crisis), the difference between EONIA and the interest on the ECB Facility literally exploded, reaching, in 2008, 350 basis points. The same happened in the USA and in the UK. This is because banks considered lending to each other without guarantees much more risky. When the market in which banks lend reserves to each other effectively froze, it was only the central bank that could provide banks with reserves. But the problem remained that a bank still needed to post a guarantee when it borrowed from the central bank. Both the Fed and the ECB tried to solve this problem by widening the type of securities they would accept as guarantee. Before the crisis they would only accept government bonds. Since 2008 they also accept loans to private firms and in some cases even household mortgages. This reduced banks' demand for interbank loans and normalised the interest rate on that market.

◁ During the financial crisis, however, even interbank loans in the euro area required the borrower to offer a guarantee by depositing some securities with the lender.

The supply of money, the demand for money and the money multiplier

We have seen how we can think of the equilibrium in terms of the equality of the supply and demand of central bank money, or in terms of the equality of the supply and demand of reserves. There is yet another way of thinking about the equilibrium, which is sometimes very useful. We can think about the equilibrium in terms of the equality of the overall supply and the overall demand for money (currency and deposit accounts).

To derive an equilibrium condition in terms of the overall supply and the overall demand for money, start with the equilibrium condition (4.11) (which states that the supply of central bank money must equal the demand for central bank money) and divide both sides by $[c + \theta(1 - c)]$:

◁ Remember: all three ways are equivalent in the sense that they yield the same answer. But each gives us a different way of thinking about the answer and strengthens our intuition.

$$\frac{1}{[c + \theta(1 - c)]} H = \text{€} Y L(i) \qquad [4.12]$$

Supply of money = Demand for money

The right side of equation (4.12) is the overall demand for money (currency plus deposit accounts). The left side is the overall supply of money (currency plus deposit accounts). Basically the equation says that, in equilibrium, the overall supply and the overall demand of money must be equal.

- If you compare equation (4.12) with equation (4.2), the equation characterising the equilibrium in an economy without banks, you will see that the only difference is that the overall supply of money is equal not just to central bank money but to central bank money multiplied by a constant term $1/(c + \theta(1 - c))$.

Notice also that, because $(c + \theta(1 - c))$ is less than one, its inverse – the constant term on the left of the equation – is greater than one. For this reason, this constant term is called the **money multiplier**. The overall supply of money is therefore equal to central bank money multiplied by the money multiplier. If the money multiplier is 4, for example, then the overall supply of money is equal to four times the supply of central bank money.

● To reflect the fact that the overall supply of money depends in the end on the amount of central bank money, central bank money is sometimes called **high-powered money** (this is where the letter H we used to denote central bank money comes from), or the **monetary base**. The term *high powered* reflects the fact that increases in H lead to more than one-for-one increases in the overall money supply, and are therefore high powered. In the same way, the term *monetary base* reflects the fact that the overall money supply depends ultimately on a 'base' – the amount of central bank money in the economy.

The presence of a multiplier in equation (4.12) implies that a given change in central bank money has a larger effect on the money supply – and in turn a larger effect on the interest rate – in an economy with banks than in an economy without banks. To understand why, it is useful to return to the description of open market operations, this time in an economy with banks.

Understanding the money multiplier

To make the arithmetic easier, let's consider a special case where people hold only deposit accounts, so $c = 0$. In this case, the multiplier is $1/\theta$. In other words, an increase of a euro of high-powered money leads to an increase of $1/\theta$ euros in the money supply. Assume further that $\theta = 0.1$, so that the multiplier equals $1/0.1 = 10$. The purpose of what follows is to help you understand where this multiplier comes from, and, more generally, how the initial increase in central bank money leads to a ten-fold increase in the overall money supply.

Suppose the central bank buys €100 worth of bonds in an open market operation. It pays the seller – call him seller 1 – €100. To pay the seller, the central bank creates €100 in central bank money. The increase in central bank money is €100. When we looked earlier at the effects of an open market operation in an economy in which there were no banks, this was the end of the story. Here, it is just the beginning:

● Seller 1 (who, we have assumed, does not want to hold any currency) deposits the €100 in a deposit account at his bank – call it bank A. This leads to an increase in deposit accounts of €100.
● Bank A keeps €100 times $0.1 = €10$ in reserves, and buys bonds with the rest, €100 times $0.9 = €90$. It pays €90 to the seller of those bonds – call her seller 2.
● Seller 2 deposits €90 in a deposit account in her bank – call it bank B. This leads to an increase in deposit accounts of €90.
● Bank B keeps €90 times $0.1 = €9$ in reserves and buys bonds with the rest, €90 times $0.9 = €81$. It pays €81 to the seller of those bonds – call him seller 3.
● Seller 3 deposits €81 in a deposit account in his bank – call it bank C.
● And so on.

By now, the chain of events should be clear. What is the eventual increase in the money supply? The increase in deposit accounts is €100 when seller 1 deposits the proceeds of his sale of bonds in bank A, plus €90 when seller 2 deposits the proceeds of her sale of bonds in bank B, plus €81 when seller 3 does the same, and so on. Let's write the sum as:

$$€100 \,(1 + 0.9 + 0.9^2 + \cdots)$$

The series in parentheses is a geometric series, so its sum is equal to $1/(1 - 0.9) = 10$ (see Appendix 1 at the end of this text for a refresher on geometric series). The money supply increases by €1,000 – 10 times the initial increase in central bank money.

This derivation gives us another way of thinking about the money multiplier: we can think of the ultimate increase in the money supply as the result of successive rounds of purchases of bonds – the first started by the central bank in its open market operation, the following rounds by banks. Each successive round leads to an increase in the money supply, and eventually the increase in the money supply is equal to ten times the initial increase in the central bank money. Note the parallel between our interpretation of the money multiplier as the result of successive purchases of bonds and the interpretation of the goods market multiplier (Chapter 3) as the result of successive rounds of spending. Multipliers can often be interpreted as the result of successive rounds of decisions, and derived as the sum of a geometric series. This interpretation often gives a better understanding of how the process works.

SUMMARY

- The demand for money depends positively on the level of transactions in the economy and negatively on the interest rate.

- The interest rate is determined by the equilibrium condition that the supply of money be equal to the demand for money.

- For a given supply of money, an increase in income leads to an increase in the demand for money and an increase in the interest rate. An increase in the supply of money leads to a decrease in the interest rate.

- The way the central bank changes the supply of money is through open market operations.

- Expansionary open market operations, in which the central bank increases the money supply by buying bonds, lead to an increase in the price of bonds and a decrease in the interest rate.

- Contractionary open market operations, in which the central bank decreases the money supply by selling bonds, lead to a decrease in the price of bonds and an increase in the interest rate.

- When money includes both currency and deposit accounts, we can think of the interest rate as being determined by the condition that the supply of central bank money be equal to the demand for central bank money.

- The supply of central bank money is under the control of the central bank. The demand for central bank money depends on the overall demand for money, the proportion of money people keep in currency, and the ratio of reserves to deposit accounts chosen by banks.

- Another, but equivalent, way to think about the determination of the interest rate is in terms of the equality of the supply and demand for bank reserves. The market for bank reserves is called the interbank market. The interest rate determined in that market is called the overnight interest rate, EONIA in the euro area.

- Yet another way to think about the determination of the interest rate is in terms of the equality of the overall supply and the overall demand of money. The overall supply of money is equal to central bank money times the money multiplier.

KEY TERMS

QUESTIONS AND PROBLEMS

QUICK CHECK

1. *Using the information in this chapter, label each of the following statements true, false or uncertain. Explain briefly.*

a. Income and financial wealth are both examples of stock variables.

b. The term *investment*, as used by economists, refers to the purchase of bonds and shares of stock.

c. The demand for money does not depend on the interest rate because only bonds earn interest.

d. About two-thirds of US currency is held outside the USA.

e. The central bank can increase the supply of money by selling bonds in the bonds market.

f. The central bank can determine the money supply, but it cannot determine interest rates because interest rates are determined in the private sector.

g. Bond prices and interest rates always move in opposite directions.

h. Since the Great Depression, the USA has used federal deposit insurance to deal with bank runs.

2. *Suppose that a person's yearly income is €60,000. Also suppose that this person's money demand function is given by*

$$M^d = €Y(0.30 - i)$$

a. What is this person's demand for money when the interest rate is 5%? 10%?

b. Explain how the interest rate affects money demand.

c. Suppose that the interest rate is 10%. In percentage terms, what happens to this person's demand for money if her yearly income is reduced by 50%?

d. Suppose that the interest rate is 5%. In percentage terms, what happens to this person's demand for money if her yearly income is reduced by 50%?

e. Summarise the effect of income on money demand. In percentage terms, how does this effect depend on the interest rate?

3. *Consider a bond that promises to pay €100 in one year.*

a. What is the interest rate on the bond if its price today is €75? €85? €95?

b. What is the relation between the price of the bond and the interest rate?

c. If the interest rate is 8%, what is the price of the bond today?

4. *Suppose that money demand is given by*

$$M^d = €Y(0.25 - i)$$

where €Y is €100. Also, suppose that the supply of money is €20.

a. What is the equilibrium interest rate?

b. If the central bank wants to increase i by 10 percentage points (e.g., from 2% to 12%), at what level should it set the supply of money?

DIG DEEPER

5. *Suppose that a person's wealth is €50,000 and that her yearly income is €60,000. Also suppose that her money demand function is given by*

$$M^d = €Y(0.35 - i)$$

a. Derive the demand for bonds. Suppose the interest rate increases by 10 percentage points. What is the effect on the demand for bonds?

b. What are the effects of an increase in wealth on the demand for money and the demand for bonds? Explain in words.

c. What are the effects of an increase in income on the demand for money and the demand for bonds? Explain in words.

d. Consider the statement 'When people earn more money, they obviously will hold more bonds.' What is wrong with this statement?

6. The demand for bonds

In this chapter, you learned that an increase in the interest rate makes bonds more attractive, so it leads people to hold more of their wealth in bonds, as opposed to money. However, you also learned that an increase in the interest rate reduces the price of bonds.

How can an increase in the interest rate make bonds more attractive and reduce their price?

7. ATMs and credit cards

This problem examines the effect of the introduction of ATMs and credit cards on money demand. For simplicity, let's examine a person's demand for money over a period of four days.

Suppose that before ATMs and credit cards, this person goes to the bank once at the beginning of each four-day period and withdraws from her savings account all the money she needs for four days. Assume that she spends €4 per day.

a. How much does this person withdraw each time she goes to the bank? Compute this person's money holdings for days 1 through 4 (in the morning, before she spends any of the money she withdraws).

b. What is the amount of money this person holds, on average?

Suppose now that with the advent of ATMs, this person withdraws money once every two days.

c. Recompute your answer to part (a).

d. Recompute your answer to part (b).

Finally, with the advent of credit cards, this person pays for all her purchases using her card. She withdraws no money until the fourth day, when she withdraws the whole amount necessary to pay for her credit card purchases over the previous four days.

e. Recompute your answer to part (a).

f. Recompute your answer to part (b).

g. Based on your previous answers, what do you think has been the effect of ATMs and credit cards on money demand?

8. The money multiplier

The money multiplier is described in Section 4.4. Assume the following:

i. The public holds no currency.

ii. The ratio of reserves to deposits is 0.1.

iii. The demand for money is given by

$$M^d = €Y(0.8 - 4i)$$

Initially, the monetary base is €100 billion, and nominal income is €5 trillion.

a. What is the demand for central bank money?

b. Find the equilibrium interest rate by setting the demand for central bank money equal to the supply of central bank money.

c. What is the overall supply of money? Is it equal to the overall demand for money at the interest rate you found in part (b)?

d. What is the impact on the interest rate if central bank money is increased to €300 billion?

e. If the overall money supply increases to €3000 billion, what will be the impact on *i*? [*Hint*: Use what you learned in part (c).]

9. Bank runs and the money multiplier

During the Great Depression, the US economy experienced many bank runs, to the point where people became unwilling to keep their money in banks, preferring to keep it in cash.

How would you expect such a shift away from deposit accounts toward currency to affect the size of the money multiplier?

EXPLORE FURTHER

10. Current monetary policy

*Go to the website of the European Central Bank (**www.ecb.int/home/html/index.en.html**) and download the most recent monetary policy decisions press release of the Governing Council. Make sure you get the most recent GC press release and not simply the most recent ECB press release.*

a. What is the current stance of monetary policy? (Note that policy will be described in terms of increasing or decreasing interest rates as opposed to increasing or decreasing the money supply.)

b. If the interest rate on the main refinancing operations has changed recently, what does the change imply about the bond holdings of the ECB? Has the ECB been increasing or decreasing its bond holdings?

Log on to **MyEconLab** and complete the studyplan exercises for this chapter to see how much you have learnt, and where you need to revise most.

MyEconLab

FURTHER READING

- While we shall return to many aspects of the financial system throughout the text, you may want to dig deeper and read a textbook on money and banking. Here are four of them: *Money, Banking, and Financial Markets*, by Laurence Ball (Worth, 2010); *Money, Banking, and Financial Markets*, by Stephen Cecchetti and Kermit Schoenholtz (McGraw-Hill/Irwin, 2010); *Money, the Financial System and the Economy*, by R. Glenn Hubbard (Reading, MA: Addison-Wesley, 2007); *The Economics of Money, Banking, and the Financial System*, by Frederic Mishkin (Pearson, 9th edn, 2010).

- The ECB maintains a useful website that contains not only data on financial markets, but also information on what the ECB does (*www.ecb.int/*).

Chapter 5

GOODS AND FINANCIAL MARKETS: THE *IS–LM* MODEL

Earlier we looked at the goods market (see Chapter 3) and financial markets (see Chapter 4). We now look at goods and financial markets together. By the end of this chapter you will have a framework to think about how output and the interest rate are determined in the short run.

In developing this framework, we follow a path first traced by two economists, John Hicks and Alvin Hansen, in the late 1930s and the early 1940s. When the economist John Maynard Keynes published his *General Theory* in 1936, there was much agreement that his book was both fundamental and nearly impenetrable. (Try to read it, and you will agree.) There were (and still are) many debates about what Keynes 'really meant'. In 1937, John Hicks summarised what he saw as one of Keynes's main contributions: the joint description of goods and financial markets. His analysis was later extended by Alvin Hansen. Hicks and Hansen called their formalisation the *IS–LM* model.

Macroeconomics has made substantial progress since the early 1940s. This is why the *IS–LM* model is treated in this and the next chapter rather than later. (If you had taken this course 40 years ago, you would be nearly done!) But to most economists, the *IS–LM* model still represents an essential building block – one that, despite its simplicity, captures much of what happens in the economy in the short run. This is why the *IS–LM* model is still taught and used today.

This chapter develops the basic version of the *IS–LM*. It has six sections:

- Section 5.1 looks at equilibrium in the goods market, and derives the *IS* relation.

- Section 5.2 looks at equilibrium in financial markets, and derives the *LM* relation.

- Sections 5.3 and 5.4 put the *IS* and the *LM* relations together and use the resulting *IS–LM* model to study the effects of fiscal and monetary policy – first separately, then together.

- Section 5.5 shows how the *IS–LM* model must be modified to take into account of the possibility of a liquidity trap.

- Section 5.6 introduces dynamics and explores how the *IS-LM* model captures what happens in the economy in the short run.

5.1 THE GOODS MARKET AND THE *IS* RELATION

Let's first summarise what we learned earlier (see Chapter 3):

- We characterised equilibrium in the goods market as the condition that production, Y, be equal to the demand for goods, Z. We called this condition the *IS* relation.
- We defined demand as the sum of consumption, investment and government spending. We assumed that consumption was a function of disposable income (income minus taxes) and took investment spending, government spending and taxes as given:

$$Z = C(Y - \bar{T}) + \bar{I} + \bar{G}$$

(In Chapter 3, we assumed, to simplify the algebra, that the relation between consumption C and disposable income, $Y - \bar{T}$, was linear. Here, we shall not make this assumption, and use the more general form $C = C(Y - \bar{T})$ instead.)

- The equilibrium condition was thus given by

$$Y = C(Y - \bar{T}) + \bar{I} + \bar{G}$$

- Using this equilibrium condition, we then looked at the factors that moved equilibrium output. We looked in particular at the effects of changes in government spending and of shifts in consumption demand.

The main simplification of this first model was that the interest rate did not affect the demand for goods. Our first task in this chapter is to abandon this simplification and introduce the interest rate in our model of equilibrium in the goods market. For the time being, we focus only on the effect of the interest rate on investment and leave a discussion of its effects on the other components of demand until later.

◀ (Much) more on the effects of interest rates on both consumption and investment later (see Chapter 17).

Investment, sales and the interest rate

Earlier (see Chapter 3), investment was assumed to be constant. This was for simplicity. Investment is in fact far from constant, and depends primarily on two factors:

- *The level of sales.* Consider a firm facing an increase in sales, and needing to increase production. To do so, it may need to buy additional machines or build an additional plant. In other words, it needs to invest. A firm facing low sales will feel no such need and will spend little, if anything, on investment.
- *The interest rate.* Consider a firm deciding whether or not to buy a new machine. Suppose that to buy the new machine, the firm must borrow. The higher the interest rate, the less attractive it is to borrow and buy the machine.

    At a high enough interest rate, the additional profits from using the new machine will not cover interest payments, and the new machine will not be worth buying.

For the moment, and to keep things simple, we leave aside the distinction between the nominal interest rate – the interest rate in terms of euros – and the real interest rate – the interest rate in terms of goods. The distinction, however, is important (and we return to it ◀ in Chapter 11).

To capture these two effects, we write the investment relation as follows:

$$I = I(Y, i) \qquad [5.1]$$
$$(+, -)$$

◀ The argument still holds if the firm uses its own funds: the higher the interest rate, the more attractive it is to lend the funds rather than to use them to buy the new machine.

Equation (5.1) states that investment I depends on production Y, and the interest rate i. (We continue to assume that inventory investment is equal to zero, so sales and production are always equal. As a result, Y denotes sales, and it also denotes production.) The positive sign under Y indicates that an increase in production (equivalently, an increase in sales) leads to an increase in investment. The negative sign under the interest rate i indicates that an increase in the interest rate leads to a decrease in investment.

◀ An increase in output leads to an increase in investment. An increase in the interest rate leads to a decrease in investment.

Determining output

Taking into account the investment relation (5.1), the condition for equilibrium in the goods market becomes:

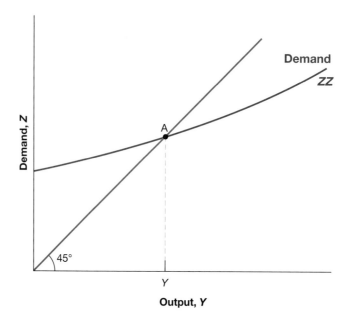

Figure 5.1

Equilibrium in the goods market

The demand for goods is an increasing function of output. Equilibrium requires that the demand for goods be equal to output.

$$Y = C(Y - \bar{T}) + I(Y, i) + \bar{G} \tag{5.2}$$

Production (the left side of the equation) must be equal to the demand for goods (the right side). Equation (5.2) is our expanded *IS* relation. We can now look at what happens to output when the interest rate changes.

Start with Figure 5.1. Measure the demand for goods on the vertical axis. Measure output on the horizontal axis. For a given value of the interest rate *i*, demand is an increasing function of output, for two reasons:

● An increase in output leads to an increase in income and thus to an increase in disposable income. The increase in disposable income leads to an increase in consumption. We studied this relation earlier (see Chapter 3).
● An increase in output also leads to an increase in investment. This is the relation between investment and production that we have introduced in this chapter.

In short, an increase in output leads, through its effects on both consumption and investment, to an increase in the demand for goods. This relation between demand and output, for a given interest rate, is represented by the upward-sloping curve *ZZ*.

Note two characteristics of *ZZ* in Figure 5.1:

● Since we have not assumed that the consumption and investment relations in equation (5.2) are linear, *ZZ* is in general a curve rather than a line. Thus, we have drawn it as a curve in Figure 5.1. All the arguments that follow would apply if we assumed that the consumption and investment relations were linear, and that *ZZ* were a straight line.
● We have drawn *ZZ* so that it is flatter than the 45° line. Put another way, we have assumed that an increase in output leads to a less than one-for-one increase in demand.

> Make sure you understand why the two statements mean the same thing.

We saw earlier (in Chapter 3), that where investment was constant, this restriction naturally followed from the assumption that consumers spend only part of their additional income on consumption. But now that we allow investment to respond to production, this restriction may no longer hold. When output increases, the sum of the increase in consumption and the increase in investment could exceed the initial increase in output. Although this is a theoretical possibility, the empirical evidence suggests that it is not the case in reality. That's why we will assume the response of demand to output is less than one-for-one and draw *ZZ* flatter than the 45° line.

Equilibrium in the goods market is reached at the point where the demand for goods equals output, that is, at point A, the intersection of *ZZ* and the 45° line. The equilibrium level of output is given by *Y*.

So far, what we have done is extend, in straightforward fashion, the analysis developed earlier (see Chapter 3). But we are now ready to derive the *IS* curve.

Deriving the *IS* curve

We have drawn the demand relation, *ZZ*, in Figure 5.1 for a given value of the interest rate. Let's now derive in Figure 5.2 what happens if the interest rate changes.

Suppose that, in Figure 5.2(a), the demand curve is given by *ZZ*, and the initial equilibrium is at point A. Suppose now that the interest rate increases from its initial value *i* to a new higher value *i'*. At any level of output, the higher interest rate leads to lower investment and lower demand. The demand curve *ZZ* shifts down to *ZZ'*: At a given level of output, demand is lower. The new equilibrium is at the intersection of the lower demand curve *ZZ'* and the 45° line, at point *A'*. The equilibrium level of output is now equal to *Y'*.

In words: the increase in the interest rate decreases investment. The decrease in investment leads to a decrease in output, which further decreases consumption and investment, through the multiplier effect.

Can you show graphically what the size of the multiplier is? (Hint: Look at the ratio of the decrease in equilibrium output to the initial decrease in investment.) ◄

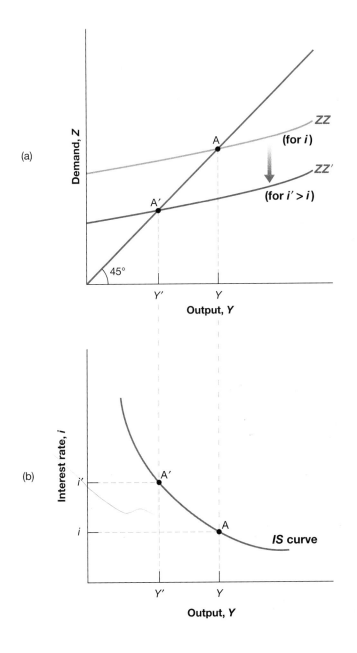

(a)

(b)

Figure 5.2
_____

The derivation of the *IS* curve

(a) An increase in the interest rate decreases the demand for goods at any level of output, leading to a decrease in the equilibrium level of output.

(b) Equilibrium in the goods market implies that an increase in the interest rate leads to a decrease in output. The *IS* curve is therefore downward sloping.

Using Figure 5.2(a), we can find the equilibrium value of output associated with *any* value of the interest rate. The resulting relation between equilibrium output and the interest rate is drawn in Figure 5.2(b).

Figure 5.2(b) plots equilibrium output Y on the horizontal axis against the interest rate on the vertical axis. Point A in Figure 5.2(b) corresponds to point A in Figure 5.2(a), and point A′ in Figure 5.2(b) corresponds to A′ in Figure 5.2(a). The higher interest rate is associated with a lower level of output.

> Equilibrium in the goods market implies that an increase in the interest rate leads to a decrease in output. This relation is represented by the downward-sloping *IS* curve.

This relation between the interest rate and output is represented by the downward-sloping curve in Figure 5.2(b). This curve is called the **IS curve**.

Shifts of the *IS* curve

We have drawn the *IS* curve in Figure 5.2 taking as given the values of taxes, $\bar{T}$, and government spending, $\bar{G}$. Changes in either $\bar{T}$ or $\bar{G}$ will shift the *IS* curve.

To see how, consider Figure 5.3. The *IS* curve gives the equilibrium level of output as a function of the interest rate. It is drawn for given values of taxes and spending. Now consider an increase in taxes, from $\bar{T}$ to $\bar{T}'$. At a given interest rate, say i, disposable income decreases, leading to a decrease in consumption, leading in turn to a decrease in the demand for goods and a decrease in equilibrium output. The equilibrium level of output decreases from Y to Y'. Put another way, the *IS* curve shifts to the left: at a given interest rate, the equilibrium level of output is lower than it was before the increase in taxes.

> For a given interest rate, an increase in taxes leads to a decrease in output. In graphic terms: an increase in taxes shifts the *IS* curve to the left.

More generally, any factor that, for a given interest rate, decreases the equilibrium level of output, causes the *IS* curve to shift to the left. We have looked at an increase in taxes. But the same would hold for a decrease in government spending, or a decrease in consumer confidence (which decreases consumption, given disposable income). Symmetrically, any factor that, for a given interest rate, increases the equilibrium level of output – a decrease in taxes, an increase in government spending, an increase in consumer confidence – causes the *IS* curve to shift to the right.

> Suppose that the government announces that the social security system is in trouble, and it may have to cut retirement benefits in the future. How are consumers likely to react? What is then likely to happen to demand and output today?

Let's summarise:

● Equilibrium in the goods market implies that an increase in the interest rate leads to a decrease in output. This relation is represented by the downward-sloping *IS* curve.

● Changes in factors that decrease the demand for goods, given the interest rate, shift the *IS* curve to the left. Changes in factors that increase the demand for goods, given the interest rate, shift the *IS* curve to the right.

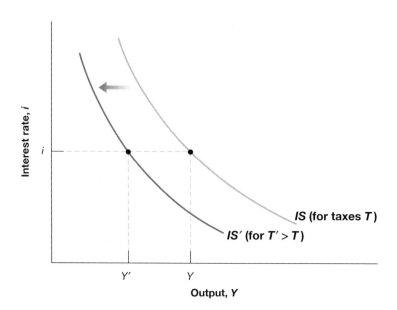

Figure 5.3

Shifts in the *IS* curve

An increase in taxes shifts the *IS* curve to the left.

5.2 FINANCIAL MARKETS AND THE *LM* RELATION

Let's now turn to financial markets. We saw earlier (see Chapter 4) that the interest rate is determined by the equality of the supply of and the demand for money:

$$M = €YL(i)$$

The variable M on the left side is the nominal money stock. We will ignore here the details of the money supply process that we saw in sections 4.3 and 4.4, and simply think of the central bank as controlling M directly.

The right side gives the demand for money, which is a function of nominal income, $€Y$, and of the nominal interest rate, i. As we saw in section 4.1, an increase in nominal income increases the demand for money; an increase in the interest rate decreases the demand for money. Equilibrium requires that money supply (the left side of the equation) be equal to money demand (the right side of the equation).

Real money, real income and the interest rate

The equation $M = €YL(i)$ gives a relation between money, nominal income and the interest rate. It will be more convenient here to rewrite it as a relation between real money (that is, money in terms of goods), real income (that is, income in terms of goods) and the interest rate.

Recall that nominal income divided by the price level equals real income, Y. Dividing both sides of the equation by the price level P gives

$$\frac{M}{P} = YL(i) \qquad [5.3]$$

◀ (From Chapter 2)

Nominal GDP = Real GDP multiplied by the GDP deflator: $€Y = Y \times P$.

Equivalently: Real GDP = Nominal GDP divided by the GDP deflator: $Y = €Y/P$.

Hence, we can restate our equilibrium condition as the condition that the *real money* supply – that is, the money stock in terms of goods, not euros – be equal to the *real money demand*, which depends on real income Y and the interest rate i.

The notion of a 'real' demand for money may feel a bit abstract, so an example will help. Think not of your demand for money in general but just of your demand for coins. Suppose you like to have coins in your pocket to buy two cups of coffee during the day. If a cup costs €1.20, you will want to keep about €2.40 in coins: this is your nominal demand for coins. Equivalently, you want to keep enough coins in your pocket to buy two cups of coffee. This is your demand for coins in terms of goods – here in terms of cups of coffee.

From now on, we shall refer to equation (5.3) as the *LM relation*. The advantage of writing things this way is that *real income*, Y, appears on the right side of the equation instead of *nominal income* $€Y$. And real income (equivalently real output) is the variable we focus on when looking at equilibrium in the goods market. To make the reading lighter, we will refer to the left and right sides of equation (5.3) simply as 'money supply' and 'money demand' rather than the more accurate but heavier 'real money supply' and 'real money demand'. Similarly, we will refer to 'income' rather than 'real income'.

Also recall that so far we have been assuming that prices are constant, and can thus be set equal to 1 (remember that P is an index that can be set equal to 1 in any 'base' year). So $€Y = PY = Y$. ◀

Deriving the *LM* curve

To see the relation between output and the interest rate implied by equation (5.3), let's use Figure 5.4. Look first at Figure 5.4(a). Let the interest rate be measured on the vertical axis, and (real) money be measured on the horizontal axis. (Real) money supply is given by the vertical line at M/P, and is denoted M^s. For a given level of (real) income, Y, (real) money demand is a decreasing function of the interest rate. It is drawn as the downward-sloping curve denoted M^d. Except for the fact that we measure real rather than nominal money on the horizontal axis, the figure is similar to Figure 4.3 (in Chapter 4). The equilibrium is at point A, where money supply is equal to money demand, and the interest rate is equal to i.

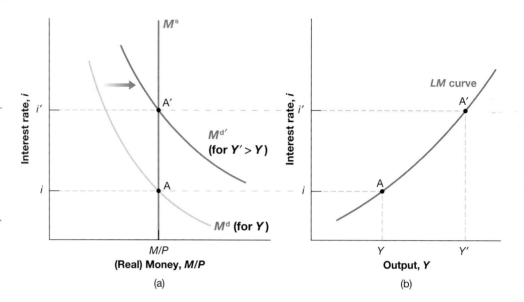

Figure 5.4

The derivation of the *LM* curve

(a) An increase in income leads, at a given interest rate, to an increase in the demand for money. Given the money supply, this increase in the demand for money leads to an increase in the equilibrium interest rate.

(b) Equilibrium in the financial markets implies that an increase in income leads to an increase in the interest rate. The *LM* curve is therefore upward sloping.

Now consider an increase in income from Y to Y', which leads people to increase their demand for money at any given interest rate. Money demand shifts to the right, to $M^{d'}$. The new equilibrium is at A', with a higher interest rate, i'. Why does an increase in income lead to an increase in the interest rate? When income increases, money demand increases; but the money supply is given. Thus, the interest rate must go up until the two opposite effects on the demand for money – the increase in income that leads people to want to hold more money and the increase in the interest rate that leads people to want to hold less money – cancel each other. At that point, the demand for money is equal to the unchanged money supply, and financial markets are again in equilibrium.

Using Figure 5.4(a), we can find the value of the interest rate associated with *any* value of income for a given money stock. The relation is derived in Figure 5.4(b).

> Equilibrium in financial markets implies that, for a given money stock, the interest rate is an increasing function of the level of income. This relation is represented by the upward-sloping *LM* curve.

Figure 5.4(b) plots the equilibrium interest rate i on the vertical axis against income on the horizontal axis. Point A in Figure 5.4(b) corresponds to point A in Figure 5.4(a), and point A′ in Figure 5.4(b) corresponds to point A′ in Figure 5.4(a). More generally, equilibrium in financial markets implies that the higher the level of output, the higher the demand for money, and therefore the higher the equilibrium interest rate.

> Why do we think about shifts of the *IS* curve to the left or to the right, but about shifts of the *LM* curve up or down? The reason:
>
> ● We think of the goods market as determining Y given i, so we want to know what happens to Y when an exogenous variable changes. Y is on the horizontal axis, and moves right or left.
>
> ● We think of financial markets as determining i given Y, so we want to know what happens to i when an exogenous variable changes. i is on the vertical axis, and moves up or down.

This relation between output and the interest rate is represented by the upward-sloping curve in Figure 5.4(b). This curve is called the ***LM* curve**. Economists sometimes characterise this relation by saying 'higher economic activity puts pressure on interest rates'. Make sure you understand the steps behind this statement.

Shifts of the *LM* curve

We have derived the *LM* curve in Figure 5.4 taking both the nominal money stock, M, and the price level, P – and, by implication, their ratio, the real money stock, M/P – as given. Changes in M/P, whether they come from changes in the nominal money stock, M, or from changes in the price level, P, will shift the *LM* curve.

To see how, let us look at Figure 5.5, and consider an increase in the nominal money supply, from M to M'. Given the fixed price level, the real money supply increases from M/P to M'/P. Then, at any level of income, say Y, the interest rate consistent with equilibrium in financial markets is lower, going down from i to, say, i'. The *LM* curve shifts down, from LM to LM'. By the same reasoning, at any level of income, a decrease in the money supply leads to an increase in the interest rate. It causes the *LM* curve to shift up.

Let's summarise:

> For a given level of output, an increase in the money supply leads to a decrease in the interest rate. In graphic terms: an increase in the money supply shifts the *LM* curve down.

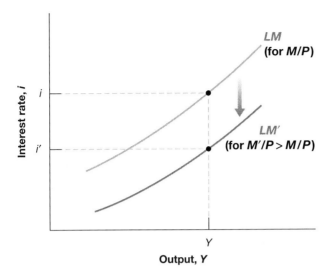

Figure 5.5

Shifts in the *LM* curve

An increase in money causes the *LM* curve to shift down.

- Equilibrium in financial markets implies that, for a given real money supply, an increase in the level of income, which increases the demand for money, leads to an increase in the interest rate. This relation is represented by the upward-sloping *LM* curve.
- An increase in the money supply shifts the *LM* curve down; a decrease in the money supply shifts the *LM* curve up.

FOCUS

An alternative derivation of the *LM* relation as an interest rate rule

We have derived the *LM* relation under the assumption that the *money stock remained constant*. This gave us the positive relation between the interest rate and income shown for example in Figure 5.4(b).

As we discussed earlier (see Chapter 4), however, the assumption that the central bank keeps the money stock constant and lets the interest rate adjust when income changes is not a good description of what modern central banks do. Most central banks think instead in terms of setting the interest rate, i.e. adjusting the money supply so as to achieve the interest rate they want. Thus, we may want to derive the *LM* relation under the alternative assumption that the central bank sets the interest rate, and adjusts the money supply as needed to achieve that goal.

To see what this implies, turn to Figure 5.6(a). Like Figure 5.4(a), the panel plots money supply and money demand, with the interest rate on the vertical axis, and money on the horizontal axis. The money supply is given by the vertical line M^s, money demand by the downward-sloping curve M^d. The initial equilibrium is at point A, with interest rate i_A.

Now consider an increase in income which shifts money demand from M^d to $M^{d'}$. If the central bank does

not change the money supply, then the equilibrium will move from A to B, and the interest rate will increase from i_A to i_B. The implied *LM* curve, *LM*, the relation between the interest rate and income, is drawn in Figure 5.6(b). It is exactly the same as in Figure 5.4(a).

Suppose, however, that the central bank wants to keep the interest rate constant in the face of the increase in income. Can it do it? Yes. How can it do it? By increasing the money supply in response to the increase in income, from M^s to $M^{s'}$ If it does so, the interest rate will remain constant. The equilibrium will move from A to D, and the interest rate will remain constant at i_A. The resulting *LM* curve, denoted by *LM'* in Figure 5.6(b), will be horizontal: in response to the increase in income, the central bank will adjust the money supply so as to keep the interest rate constant.

This may be too extreme a policy. Perhaps the central bank wants to allow the interest rate to increase, but by less than it would if the central bank kept the money supply constant. For example, in response to the increase in income, the central bank may choose to increase the money supply by $M^{s''} < M^{s'}$. In this case, the equilibrium will move from A to C, and the interest rate will increase

Figure 5.6

The *LM* relation as an interest rate rule

(a) Depending on whether and by how much the central bank increases the money supply in response to a shift in money demand coming from changes in income, the interest rate may remain constant, increase a little or increase a lot.

(b) We can think of the *LM* curve as showing whether and by how much the central bank allows the interest rate to increase in response to increases in income.

from i_A to i_C. The resulting *LM* curve, denoted by *LM"* in Figure 5.6(b) will be upward sloping, but flatter than *LM*.

To summarise: the *LM* relation we derived in the text gave us the relation between the interest rate and income for a *given money supply*. The *LM* relation derived in the appendix (at the end of the chapter) gives us the relation between the interest rate and income when the central bank follows a given **interest rate rule**, and lets the money supply adjust as needed. Its slope then depends on how much the central bank increases the interest rate in response to increases in income.

Which *LM* relation should you use? It depends on the question at hand. Take, for example, the case of an increase in the budget deficit, shifting the *IS* curve to the right. You may want to know what would happen to output and the interest rate if the central bank money supply remained constant, in which case you will use the *LM* relation derived in the text. However, you might know, for example, that the central bank is likely to keep the interest rate constant, in which case you would use the *LM* relation we derived here – in this particular case, a horizontal *LM* curve.

Under which of the two assumptions will fiscal policy have the strongest effect on output?

5.3 PUTTING THE *IS* AND THE *LM* RELATIONS TOGETHER

The *IS* relation follows from the condition that the supply of goods must be equal to the demand for goods. It tells us how the interest rate affects output. The *LM* relation follows from the condition that the supply of money must be equal to the demand for money. It tells us how output in turn affects the interest rate. We now put the *IS* and *LM* relations together. At any point in time, the supply of goods must be equal to the demand for goods, and the supply of money must be equal to the demand for money. Both the *IS* and *LM* relations must hold. Together, they determine both output and the interest rate.

$$\text{IS relation:} \quad Y = C(Y - T) + I(Y, i) + G$$

$$\text{LM relation:} \quad \frac{M}{P} = YL(i)$$

Figure 5.7 plots both the *IS* curve and the *LM* curve on one graph. Output – equivalently, production or income – is measured on the horizontal axis. The interest rate is measured on the vertical axis.

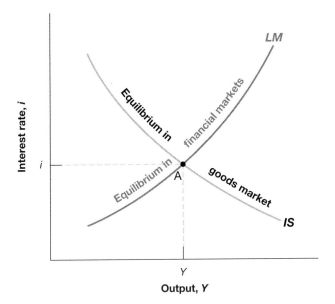

Figure 5.7

The *IS–LM* model

Equilibrium in the goods market implies that an increase in the interest rate leads to a decrease in output. This is represented by the *IS* curve. Equilibrium in financial markets implies that an increase in output leads to an increase in the interest rate. This is represented by the *LM* curve. Only at point A, which is on both curves, are both goods and financial markets in equilibrium.

Any point on the downward-sloping *IS* curve corresponds to equilibrium in the goods market. *Any point* on the upward-sloping *LM* curve corresponds to equilibrium in financial markets. *Only at point* A are both equilibrium conditions satisfied. That means point A, with the associated level of output *Y* and interest rate *i*, is the overall equilibrium – the point at which there is equilibrium in both the goods market and the financial markets.

The *IS* and *LM* relations that underlie Figure 5.7 contain a lot of information about consumption, investment, money demand and equilibrium conditions. But you may ask: so what if the equilibrium is at point A? How does this fact translate into anything directly useful about the world? Don't despair: Figure 5.7 holds the answer to many questions in macroeconomics. Used properly, it allows us to study what happens to output and the interest rate when the central bank decides to increase the money stock, or when the government decides to increase taxes, or when consumers become more pessimistic about the future and so on.

Let's now see what the *IS–LM* model can do.

Fiscal policy, activity and the interest rate

Suppose the government decides to reduce the budget deficit and does so by increasing taxes while keeping government spending unchanged. Such a change in fiscal policy is often called a **fiscal contraction** or a **fiscal consolidation**. (An increase in the deficit, either due to an increase in government spending or to a decrease in taxes, is called a **fiscal expansion**.) What are the effects of this fiscal contraction on output, on its composition and on the interest rate?

◄ Decrease in *G* – *T* ⇔ Fiscal contraction ⇔ Fiscal consolidation.

Increase in *G* – *T* ⇔ Fiscal expansion.

When you answer this or any question about the effects of changes in policy, always go through the following three steps:

1. Ask how the change affects equilibrium in the goods market and how it affects equilibrium in the financial markets. Put another way: how does it shift the *IS* and/or the *LM* curves?
2. Characterise the effects of these shifts on the intersection of the *IS* and the *LM* curve. What does this do to equilibrium output and the equilibrium interest rate?
3. Describe the effects in words.

With time and experience, you will often be able to go directly to step 3. By then you will be ready to give an instant commentary on the economic events of the day. But until you get to that level of expertise, go step by step:

- Start with step 1. The first question is how the increase in taxes affects equilibrium in the goods market – that is, how it affects the *IS* curve.

  Let's draw, in Figure 5.8(a), the *IS* curve corresponding to equilibrium in the goods market before the increase in taxes. Now take an arbitrary point, B, on this *IS* curve. By construction of the *IS* curve, output Y_B and the corresponding interest rate i_B are such that the supply of goods is equal to the demand for goods.

  At the interest rate i_B, ask what happens to output if taxes increase from T to T'. We saw the answer in section 5.1. Because people have less disposable income, the increase in taxes decreases consumption, and, through the multiplier, decreases output. At interest rate i_B, output decreases from Y_B to Y_C. More generally, at *any* interest rate, higher taxes lead to lower output. Consequently, the *IS* curve shifts to the left, from *IS* to *IS'*.

Taxes appear in the *IS* relation ⇔ Taxes shift the *IS* curve. ➤

  Next, let's see if anything happens to the *LM* curve. Figure 5.8(b) draws the *LM* curve corresponding to equilibrium in the financial markets before the increase in taxes. Take an arbitrary point, F, on this *LM* curve. By construction of the *LM* curve, the interest rate, i_F, and income, Y_F, are such that the supply of money is equal to the demand for money.

  What happens to the *LM* curve when taxes are increased? The answer: nothing. At the given level of income, Y_F, the interest rate at which the supply of money is equal to the demand for money is the same as before, namely i_F. In other words, because taxes do not appear in the *LM* relation, they do not affect the equilibrium condition. They do not affect the *LM* curve.

Taxes do not appear in the *LM* relation ⇔ Taxes do not shift the *LM* curve. ➤

  Note the general principle here: a curve shifts in response to a change in an exogenous variable only if this variable appears directly in the equation represented by that curve. Taxes enter in equation (5.2), so, when they change, the *IS* curve shifts. But taxes do not enter in equation (5.3), so the *LM* curve does not shift.

A reminder: an exogenous variable is a ➤ variable we take as given, unexplained within the model: here, taxes.

- Now consider step 2, the determination of the equilibrium.

  Let the initial equilibrium in Figure 5.8(c) be at point A, at the intersection between the initial *IS* curve and the *LM* curve. The *IS* curve is the same as the *IS* curve in Figure 5.8(a), and the *LM* curve is the same as the *LM* curve in Figure 5.8(b).

  After the increase in taxes, the *IS* curve shifts to the left – from *IS* to *IS'*. The new equilibrium is at the intersection of the new *IS* curve and the unchanged *LM* curve, or point *A'*. Output decreases from Y to Y'. The interest rate decreases from i to i'. Thus, as the *IS* curve *shifts*, the economy *moves along* the *LM* curve, from A to A'. The reason these words are italicised is that it is important to always distinguish between the shift of a curve (here the shift of the *IS* curve) and the *movement along* a curve (here the movement along the *LM* curve). Many mistakes come from not distinguishing between the two.

The increase in taxes shifts the *IS* ➤ curve. The *LM* curve does not shift. The economy moves along the *LM* curve.

- Step 3 is to tell the story in words. The increase in taxes leads to lower disposable income, which causes people to decrease their consumption. This decrease in demand leads, in turn, to a decrease in output and income. At the same time, the decrease in income reduces the demand for money, leading to a decrease in the interest rate. The decline in the interest rate reduces but does not completely offset the effect of higher taxes on the demand for goods.

If the interest rate did not decline, the ➤ economy would go from point A to point D in Figure 5.8(c), and output would be directly below point D. Because of the decline in the interest rate – which stimulates investment – the decline in activity is only to point A'.

What happens to the components of demand? By assumption, government spending remains unchanged (we have assumed that the reduction in the budget deficit takes place through an increase in taxes.) Consumption surely goes down: taxes go up and income goes down, so disposable income goes down on both counts. The last question is, what happens to investment? On the one hand, lower output means lower sales and lower investment. On the other, a lower interest rate leads to higher investment. Without knowing more about the exact form of the investment relation, equation (5.1), we cannot tell which effect dominates.

If investment depended only on the interest rate, then investment would surely increase; if investment depended only on sales, then investment would surely decrease. In general, investment depends on both the interest rate and on sales, so we cannot tell. Contrary to what is often stated by politicians, a reduction in the budget deficit does not necessarily lead

(a)

(b)

(c)

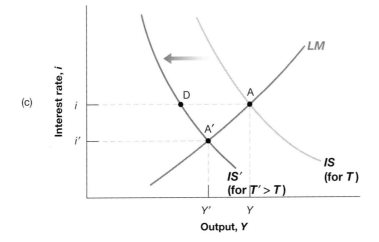

Figure 5.8

The effects of an increase in taxes

An increase in taxes shifts the *IS* curve to the left and leads to a decrease in the equilibrium level of output and the equilibrium interest rate.

to an increase in investment. (The Focus box, 'Deficit reduction: good or bad for investment?' discusses this in more detail.)

We shall return to the relation between fiscal policy and investment many times in this text and we shall qualify this first answer in many ways.

But the result that, in the short run, a reduction of the budget deficit may decrease investment, will remain.

FOCUS
Deficit reduction: good or bad for investment?

You may have heard this argument in some form before: 'Private saving goes either towards financing the budget deficit or financing investment. It does not take a genius to conclude that reducing the budget deficit leaves more saving available for investment, so investment increases.'

This argument sounds simple and convincing. How do we reconcile it with what we just saw, namely that a deficit reduction may decrease rather than increase investment?

To make progress, first go back to equation (3.10) (in Chapter 3). There we learned that we can also think of the goods–market equilibrium condition as:

$$\text{Investment} = \text{Private saving} + \text{Public saving}$$
$$I = S + (\bar{T} - \bar{G})$$

In equilibrium, investment is indeed equal to private saving plus public saving. If public saving is positive, the government is said to be running a budget surplus; if public saving is negative, the government is said to be running a budget deficit. So it is true that, given private saving, if the government reduces its deficit – either by increasing taxes or reducing government spending so that $\bar{T} - \bar{G}$ goes up – investment must go up: given S, $\bar{T} - \bar{G}$ going up implies that I goes up.

The crucial part of this statement, however, is 'given private saving'. The point is that a fiscal contraction affects private saving as well: the contraction leads to lower output and therefore to lower income. As consumption goes down by less than income, private saving also goes down. And it may go down by more than the reduction in the budget deficit, leading to a decrease rather than an increase in investment. In terms of the equation above: if S decreases by more than $\bar{T} - \bar{G}$ increases, then I will decrease, not increase.

To sum up, a fiscal contraction may decrease investment. Or, looking at the reverse policy, a fiscal expansion – a decrease in taxes or an increase in spending – may actually increase investment.

Monetary policy, activity and the interest rate

Increase in M ⇔ monetary expansion. Decrease in M ⇔ Monetary contraction ⇔ Monetary tightening.

> An increase in the money supply is called a **monetary expansion**. A decrease in the money supply is called a **monetary contraction** or **monetary tightening**.

Let's take the case of a monetary expansion. Suppose that the central bank increases nominal money, M, through an open market operation. Given our assumption that the price level is fixed in the short run, this increase in nominal money leads to a one-for-one increase in real money, M/P. Let us denote the initial real money supply by M/P, the new higher one by M'/P, and trace in Figure 5.9 the effects of the money supply increase on output and the interest rate.

For a given price level P: M increases by 10% ⇒ M/P increases by 10%.

- Again, step 1 is to see whether and how the IS and the LM curves shift.

    Let's look at the IS curve first. The money supply does not *directly* affect either the supply of or the demand for goods. In other words, M does not appear in the IS relation. Thus, a change in M does not shift the IS curve.

Money does not appear in the IS relation ⇔ Money does not shift the IS curve.

    Money enters the LM relation, however, so the LM curve shifts when the money supply changes. As we saw in section 5.2, an increase in the money supply shifts the LM curve down, from LM to LM': at a given level of income, an increase in money leads to a decrease in the interest rate.

Money appears in the LM relation ⇔ Money shifts the LM curve.

- Step 2 is to see how these shifts affect the equilibrium. The monetary expansion shifts the LM curve. It does not shift the IS curve. The economy moves along the IS curve, and the equilibrium moves from point A to point A'. Output increases from Y to Y', and the interest rate decreases from i to i'.

The increase in M shifts the LM curve down. It does not shift the IS curve. The economy moves along the IS curve.

- Step 3 is to say it in words: the increase in money leads to a lower interest rate. The lower interest rate leads to an increase in investment and, in turn, to an increase in demand and output.

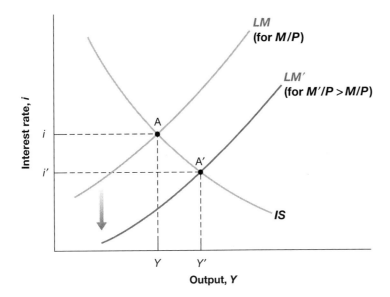

Figure 5.9

The effects of a monetary expansion

A monetary expansion leads to higher output and a lower interest rate.

In contrast to the case of fiscal contraction, we can tell exactly what happens to the different components of demand after a monetary expansion. Because income is higher and taxes are unchanged, disposable income goes up, and so does consumption. Because sales are higher, and the interest rate is lower, investment also unambiguously goes up. So a monetary expansion is more investment-friendly than a fiscal expansion.

Let's summarise:

- You should remember the three-step approach (characterise the shifts, show the effect on the equilibrium, tell the story in words) we have developed in this section to look at the effects of changes in policy on activity and the interest rate. We shall use it throughout the text.
- Table 5.1 summarises what we have learned about the effects of fiscal and monetary policy. Use the same method to look at changes other than changes in policy. For example, trace the effects of a decrease in consumer confidence through its effect on consumption demand, or, say, the introduction of new, more convenient credit cards through their effect on the demand for money.

Table 5.1 **The effects of fiscal and monetary policy**

	Shift of *IS*	Shift of *LM*	Movement in output	Movement in interest rate
Increase in taxes	Left	None	Down	Down
Decrease in taxes	Right	None	Up	Up
Increase in spending	Right	None	Up	Up
Decrease in spending	Left	None	Down	Down
Increase in money	None	Down	Up	Down
Decrease in money	None	Up	Down	Up

5.4 USING A POLICY MIX

We have looked so far at fiscal policy and monetary policy in isolation. Our purpose was to show how each worked. In practice, the two are often used together. The combination of monetary and fiscal policies is known as the **monetary–fiscal policy mix**, or simply the **policy mix**.

Sometimes, the right mix is to use fiscal and monetary policy in the same direction. This was the case, for example, during the recession of 2007–2010 in Europe and in the USA, as well as in many other countries, when both monetary and scal policies were used to fight the recession.

Sometimes, the right mix is to use the two policies in opposite directions, for example, combining a fiscal contraction with a monetary expansion. This was the case in the early 1990s in the USA. When Bill Clinton was elected President in 1992, one of his priorities was to reduce the budget deficit using a combination of cuts in spending and increases in taxes. Clinton was worried, however, that, by itself, such a fiscal contraction would lead to a decrease in demand and trigger another recession. The right strategy was to combine a fiscal contraction (so as to get rid of the deficit) with a monetary expansion (to make sure that demand and output remained high). This was the strategy adopted and carried out by Bill Clinton (who was in charge of fiscal policy) and Alan Greenspan (who was in charge of monetary policy). The result of this strategy – and a bit of economic luck – was a steady reduction of the budget deficit (which turned into a budget surplus at the end of the 1990s) and a steady increase in output throughout the rest of the decade.

Make sure you can tell the story using the *IS–LM* diagram. Which curves shifted? What was the effect on the equilibrium?

5.5 *IS–LM* AND THE LIQUIDITY TRAP

Earlier (see Chapter 4), we assumed that the central bank could always affect the interest rate, by changing the money supply. However, there is a limit to what the central bank can do: it cannot decrease the interest rate below zero.

Go back first to our characterisation of the demand and the supply of money in section 4.1. There we drew the demand for money, for a given level of income, as a decreasing function of the interest rate. The lower the interest rate, the larger the demand for money (equivalently, the smaller the demand for bonds). What we did not ask is what happens when the interest rate goes down to zero. The answer: once people hold enough money for transaction purposes, they are then indifferent between holding the rest of their financial wealth in the form of money or in the form of bonds. The reason they are indifferent: both money and bonds pay the same interest rate: zero. Thus, the demand for money is as shown in Figure 5.10.

Look at Figure 5.10. Note how we avoided the issue by not drawing the demand for money for interest rates close to zero.

- As the interest rate decreases, people want to hold more money (and thus fewer bonds): the demand for money therefore increases.
- As the interest rate becomes equal to zero, people want to hold an amount of money at least equal to the distance OB. This is what they need for transaction purposes, but they are willing to hold even more money (and therefore hold fewer bonds) because they are

Figure 5.10

Money demand, money supply and the liquidity trap

When the interest rate is equal to zero, and once people have enough money for transaction purposes, they become indifferent between holding money and holding bonds. The demand for money becomes horizontal. This implies that, when the interest rate is equal to zero, further increases in the money supply have no effect on the interest rate.

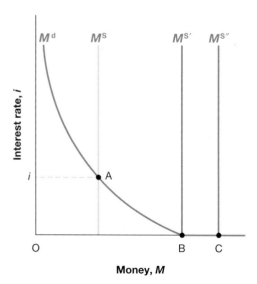

indifferent between money and bonds. Therefore, the demand for money beyond point B becomes horizontal.

Now consider the effects of an increase in the money supply:

- Consider a case in which the money supply is M^s, so the interest rate consistent with financial market equilibrium is positive and equal to i. (This is the case we considered in section 4.1.) Starting from that equilibrium in Figure 5.10, an increase in the money supply – a shift of the M^s line to the right – leads to a decrease in the interest rate.
- Now consider a case in which the money supply is $M^{s'}$, so the equilibrium is at point B; or the case where the money supply is $M^{s''}$, so the equilibrium is given at point C. In either case, the initial interest rate is zero; and, in either case, an increase in the money supply has no effect on the interest rate. Think of it this way. Suppose the central bank increases the money supply. It does so through an open market operation in which it buys bonds and pays for them by creating money. Because the interest rate is zero, people are indifferent to how much money or how many bonds they hold, so they are willing to hold fewer bonds and more money at the same interest rate: zero. The money supply increases but with no effect on the nominal interest rate – which remains equal to zero.

What can a central bank do to expand the money supply if the economy is stuck in a liquidity trap? How can the central bank put more money into the economy in order to boost spending and increase output? And, most importantly, does it make sense to increase the money supply, if such an increase has no effect on the interest rate because it is stuck at zero? These questions became central to monetary policy during the 2007–2010 crisis because interest rates fell to zero. What happens if the interest rate is equal to zero, and the central bank further increases the supply of money?

In short: once the interest rate is equal to zero, expansionary monetary policy becomes powerless. Or, to use the words of Keynes who was the first to point out the problem, the increase in money falls into a *liquidity trap*: people are willing to hold more money (more *liquidity*) at the same interest rate.

The derivation of the *LM* curve when one takes into account the possibility of a liquidity trap is shown in the two panels of Figure 5.11. Recall that the *LM* curve gives, for a given real money stock, the relation between the interest rate and the level of income implied by equilibrium in financial markets. To derive the *LM* curve, Figure 5.11(a) looks at equilibrium in the financial markets for a given value of the real money stock and draws three money demand curves, each corresponding to a different level of income:

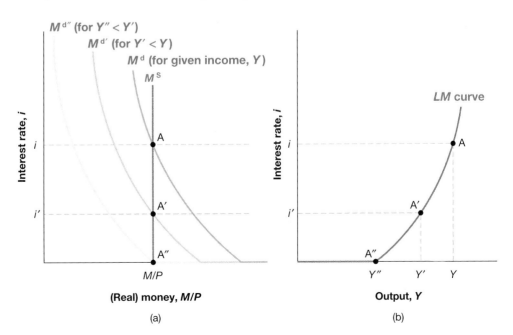

Figure 5.11

The derivation of the *LM* curve in the presence of a liquidity trap

For low levels of output, the *LM* curve is a flat segment, with an interest rate equal to zero. For higher levels of output, it is upward sloping: an increase in income leads to an increase in the interest rate.

- M^d shows the demand for money for a given level of income Y. The equilibrium is given by point A, with interest rate equal to i. This combination of income Y and interest rate i gives us the first point on the LM curve, point A' in Figure 5.11(b)
- $M^{d'}$ shows the demand for money for a lower level of income, $Y' < Y$. Lower income means less transactions, and, therefore, a lower demand for money at any interest rate. In this case, the equilibrium is given by point A', with interest rate equal to i'.This combination of income Y' and interest rate i' gives us the second point on the LM curve, point A' in Figure 5.11(b).

So far, the derivation of the *LM* curve is exactly the same as we saw earlier (in Chapter 4). It is only when income is lower than Y'' that things become different.

- $M^{d''}$ gives the demand for money for a still lower level of income $Y'' < Y'$. In this case, the equilibrium is given by point A'' in Figure 5.11(a), with interest rate equal to zero. Point A'' in Figure 5.11(b) corresponds to A'' in Figure 5.11(a).

What happens if income decreases below Y'', shifting the demand for money further to the left in Figure 5.11(a)? The intersection between the money supply curve and the money demand curve takes place on the horizontal portion of the money demand curve. The equilibrium remains at A'', and the interest rate remains equal to zero.

Let's summarise: in the presence of a liquidity trap, the LM curve is given by Figure 5.11(b). For values of income greater than Y'', it is upward sloping – just as it was (in Chapter 4) when we first characterised the LM curve. For values of income less than Y'', it is flat at $i = 0$. Intuitively, the interest rate cannot go below zero.

Having derived the LM curve in the presence of a liquidity trap, we can look at the properties of the IS–LM model modified in this way. Suppose the economy is initially at point A in Figure 5.12. Equilibrium is at point A, at the intersection of the IS curve and the LM curve, with output Y and interest rate i. And suppose that this level of output is very low. The question is: can monetary policy help the economy return to a higher level of output?

Suppose the central bank increases the money supply, shifting the LM curve from LM to LM'. The equilibrium moves from point A down to point B. The interest rate decreases from i to zero, and output increases from Y to Y'. Thus, to this extent, expansionary monetary policy can indeed increase output.

What happens, however, if, starting from point B, the central bank increases the money supply further, shifting the LM curve from LM' to, say, LM''? The intersection of IS and LM'' remains at point B, and output remains equal to Y'. Expansionary monetary policy no longer has an effect on output; it cannot therefore help output increase to Y_n.

In words: when the interest rate is equal to zero, the economy falls in a *liquidity trap*. The central bank can increase *liquidity* – that is, increase the money supply. But this *liquidity* falls into a *trap*: the additional money is willingly held by people at an unchanged interest rate, namely zero. If, at this zero interest rate, the demand for goods is still too low, then there is nothing further conventional monetary policy can do to increase output.

Figure 5.12

The *IS–LM* model and the liquidity trap

In the presence of a liquidity trap, there is a limit to how much monetary policy can increase output. Monetary policy may not be able to increase output back to its natural level.

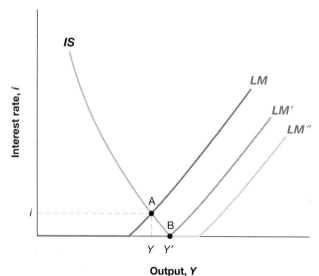

5.6 HOW DOES THE *IS–LM* MODEL FIT THE FACTS?

We have so far ignored dynamics. For example, when looking at the effects of an increase in taxes in Figure 5.8 – or the effects of a monetary expansion in Figure 5.9 – we made it look as if the economy moved instantaneously from A to A′, as if output went instantaneously from Y to Y′. This is clearly not realistic: the adjustment of output clearly takes time. To capture this time dimension, we need to introduce dynamics.

Introducing dynamics formally would be difficult. But, as we did in an earlier chapter (see Chapter 3), we can describe the basic mechanisms in words. Some of the mechanisms will be familiar from that chapter, some are new:

- Consumers are likely to take some time to adjust their consumption following a change in disposable income.
- Firms are likely to take some time to adjust investment spending following a change in their sales.
- Firms are likely to take some time to adjust investment spending following a change in the interest rate.
- Firms are likely to take some time to adjust production following a change in their sales.

So, in response to an increase in taxes, it takes some time for consumption spending to respond to the decrease in disposable income, some more time for production to decrease in response to the decrease in consumption spending, yet more time for investment to decrease in response to lower sales, for consumption to decrease in response to the decrease in income and so on.

In response to a monetary expansion, it takes some time for investment spending to respond to the decrease in the interest rate, some more time for production to increase in response to the increase in demand, yet more time for consumption and investment to increase in response to the induced change in output and so on.

Describing precisely the adjustment process implied by all these sources of dynamics is obviously complicated. But the basic implication is straightforward: time is needed for output to adjust to changes in fiscal and monetary policy. How much time? This question can only be answered by looking at the data and using econometrics. Figure 5.13 shows the results of such an econometric study, which uses data for the euro area and the USA from 1980 to 1998. The study compares the effects of an increase in the interest rate in the euro area and in the USA. It describes the typical effects of such an increase on macroeconomic variables.

Each box in Figure 5.13 represents the effects of a change in the interest rate on a given variable. Each box contains three lines. The purple line at the centre represents the best estimate of the effect of a change in the interest rate on the variable considered in that frame. The green and blue lines and the space between them represent a confidence interval, an interval within which the true value lies with a probability of 90%.

Figure 5.13(a) shows the effects of an increase in the interest rate, respectively on production and prices in the euro area (the last box at the bottom shows the evolution of the interest rate itself). The percentage change of variables is shown on the vertical axis and the time, measured in quarters, is shown on the horizontal axis.

Looking the best estimate – the purple line – we can see that increasing the interest rate leads to a reduction in output. In the euro area, the greatest decline in production is reached in the second and third quarters after the increase in the interest rate, compared to five quarters in the USA.

The second panel from top shows the evolution of the price level. Remember that one of the assumptions of the *IS–LM* model is that the price level is fixed, and thus does not vary when demand changes. The figure shows that this assumption is not a bad representation of reality, at least in the short term. In the euro area the price level remains almost unchanged approximately for the first five quarters (compared to two quarters in the USA). It is only after the first five quarters that the price level begins to decline. This suggests that the

◄ The size of a change in the interest rate, whose effects are studied in Figure 5.13, is equal to a typical monetary policy decision in the two areas under consideration, measured as one standard deviation (equal to 30 basis points in the euro area and 45 basis points in the USA).

Figure 5.13

The empirical effects of an increase in the interest rate in (a) the euro area and (b) the USA

In the short run, an increase in the interest rate leads to a decrease in output and to an increase in unemployment, but it also has little effect on the price level.

Source: G. Peersman and F. Smets, 'The monetary transmission mechanism in the euro area: more evidence from Var analysis', European Central Bank, working paper No. 91, December 2001.

IS–LM model becomes less reliable when we look at the medium run: in the medium run we can no longer assume that the price level is fixed, and changes in prices become signicant.

Comparing the euro area and the USA we observe that prices react more rapidly in the USA, although the size of the responses are eventually the same.

Figure 5.13 provides two important lessons.

- First, it gives us a sense of the dynamic adjustment of output and other variables to monetary policy.
- Second, and more fundamentally, it shows that what we observe in the economy is consistent with the implications of the *IS–LM* model. This does not prove that the *IS–LM* model is the right model. It may be that what we observe in the economy is the result of a completely different mechanism, and the fact that the *IS–LM* model fits well is only a coincidence. But this seems unlikely. The *IS–LM* model looks like a solid basis on which to build when looking at movements in activity in the short run.

We are now ready to extend the *IS–LM* model making it more realistic. Later (see Chapters 16–18) we shall extend the model to look at the role of expectations. Before doing that, however, we must understand the implications of openness to the rest of the world (Chapter 6), how the economy moves from the short run to the medium run and what determines output in the medium run (Chapters 8 to 12).

SUMMARY

- The *IS–LM* model characterises the implications of equilibrium in both the goods and the financial markets.

- The *IS* relation and the *IS* curve show the combinations of the interest rate and the level of output that are consistent with equilibrium in the goods market. An increase in the interest rate leads to a decline in output. Consequently, the *IS* curve is downward sloping.

- The *LM* relation and the *LM* curve show the combinations of the interest rate and the level of output consistent with equilibrium in financial markets. Given the real money supply, an increase in output leads to an increase in the interest rate. Consequently, the *LM* curve is upward sloping.

- A fiscal expansion shifts the *IS* curve to the right, leading to an increase in output and an increase in the interest rate. A fiscal contraction shifts the *IS* curve to the left, leading to a decrease in output and a decrease in the interest rate.

- A monetary expansion shifts the *LM* curve down, leading to an increase in output and a decrease in the interest rate.

A monetary contraction shifts the *LM* curve up, leading to a decrease in output and an increase in the interest rate.

- The combination of monetary and fiscal policies is known as the monetary–fiscal policy mix, or simply the policy mix. Sometimes monetary and fiscal policy are used in the same direction. This was the case during the 2001 US recession. Sometimes, they are used in opposite directions. Fiscal contraction and monetary expansion can, for example, achieve a decrease in the budget deficit while avoiding a decrease in output.

- The *IS–LM* model appears to describe well the behaviour of the economy in the short run. In particular, the effects of monetary policy that one observes in the data appear to be similar to those implied by the *IS–LM* model once dynamics are introduced into the model. An increase in the interest rate due to a monetary contraction leads to a steady decrease in output, with the maximum effect taking place after about five quarters in the USA and after two to three quarters in the euro area.

KEY TERMS

IS curve 86

LM curve 88

interest rate rule 90

fiscal contraction, fiscal consolidation 91

fiscal expansion 91

monetary expansion 94

monetary contraction, monetary tightening 94

monetary–fiscal policy mix, or policy mix 95

fiscal policy multiplier 104

QUESTIONS AND PROBLEMS

QUICK CHECK

1. *Using the information in this chapter, label each of the following statements true, false or uncertain. Explain briefly.*

a. The main determinants of investment are the level of sales and the interest rate. $\top$

b. If all the exogenous variables in the *IS* relation are constant, then a higher level of output can be achieved only by lowering the interest rate.

c. The *IS* curve is downward sloping because goods market equilibrium implies that an increase in taxes leads to a lower level of output. $\vdash$ $i\uparrow$ $y\uparrow$

d. If government spending and taxes increase by the same amount, the *IS* curve does not shift. f

e. The *LM* curve is upward sloping because a higher level of the money supply is needed to increase output.

f. An increase in government spending leads to a decrease in investment.

g. Government policy can increase output without changing the interest rate only if both monetary and fiscal policy variables change.

2. *Consider first the goods market model with constant investment that we saw in Chapter 3. Consumption is given by*

$$C = c_0 + c_1(Y - T)$$

and I, G and T are given.

a. Solve for equilibrium output. What is the value of the multiplier?

Now let investment depend on both sales and the interest rate:

$$I = b_0 + b_1Y - b_2i$$

b. Solve for equilibrium output. At a given interest rate, is the effect of a change in autonomous spending bigger than what it was in part (a)? Why? (Assume $c_1 + b_1 < 1$.)

Next, write the LM relation as

$$M/P = d_1Y - d_2i$$

c. Solve for equilibrium output. (*Hint*: Eliminate the interest rate from the *IS* and *LM* relations.) Derive the multiplier (the effect of a change of one unit in autonomous spending on output).

d. Is the multiplier you obtained in part (c) smaller or larger than the multiplier you derived in part (a)? Explain how your answer depends on the parameters in the behavioural equations for consumption, investment and money demand.

3. The response of investment to fiscal policy

a. Using the *IS–LM* diagram, show the effects on output and the interest rate of a decrease in government spending. Can you tell what happens to investment? Why?

Now consider the following IS–LM model:

$$C = c_0 + c_1(Y - T)$$
$$I = b_0 + b_1Y - b_2i$$
$$M/P = d_1Y - d_2i$$

b. Solve for equilibrium output. Assume $c_1 + b_1 < 1$. (*Hint*: You may want to work through problem 2 if you are having trouble with this step.)

c. Solve for the equilibrium interest rate. (*Hint*: Use the *LM* relation.)

d. Solve for investment.

e. Under what conditions on the parameters of the model (i.e., c_0, c_1, and so on) will investment increase when *G* decreases? (*Hint*: If *G* decreases by one unit, by how much does *I* increase? Be careful: you want the change in *I* to be positive when the change in *G* is negative.)

f. Explain the condition you derived in part (e).

4. *Consider the following IS–LM model:*

$$C = 400 + 0.25Y_D$$
$$I = 300 + 0.25Y - 1{,}500i$$
$$G = 600$$
$$T = 400$$
$$(M/P)^d = 2Y - 12{,}000i$$
$$M/P = 3{,}000$$

a. Derive the *IS* relation. (*Hint*: You want an equation with *Y* on the left side and everything else on the right.)

b. Derive the *LM* relation. (*Hint*: It will be convenient for later use to rewrite this equation with *i* on the left side and everything else on the right.)

c. Solve for equilibrium real output. (*Hint*: Substitute the expression for the interest rate given by the *LM* equation into the *IS* equation and solve for output.)

d. Solve for the equilibrium interest rate. (*Hint*: Substitute the value you obtained for *Y* in part (c) into either the *IS* or *LM* equations and solve for *i*. If your algebra is correct, you should get the same answer from both equations.)

e. Solve for the equilibrium values of *C* and *I*, and verify the value you obtained for *Y* by adding *C, I* and *G*.

f. Now suppose that the money supply increases to $M/P = 4{,}320$. Solve for *Y, i, C* and *I*, and describe in words the effects of an expansionary monetary policy.

g. Set M/P equal to its initial value of 3,000. Now suppose that government spending increases to $G = 840$. Summarise the effects of an expansionary fiscal policy on *Y, i* and *C*.

DIG DEEPER

5. Investment and the interest rate

The chapter argues that investment depends negatively on the interest rate because an increase in the cost of borrowing discourages investment. However, firms often finance their investment projects using their own funds.

If a firm is considering using its own funds (rather than borrowing) to finance investment projects, will higher interest rates discourage the firm from undertaking these projects? Explain. (*Hint*: Think of yourself as the owner of a firm that has earned profits and imagine that you are going to use the profits either to finance new investment projects or to buy bonds. Will your decision to invest in new projects in your firm be affected by the interest rate?)

6. The liquidity trap

a. Suppose the interest rate on bonds is negative. Will people want to hold bonds or to hold money? Explain.

b. Draw the demand for money as a function of the interest rate for a given level of real income. How does your answer to part (a) affect your answer? (*Hint*: Show that the demand for money becomes very flat as the interest rate gets very close to zero.)

c. Derive the *LM* curve. What happens to the *LM* curve as the interest rate gets very close to zero? (*Hint*: It becomes very flat.)

d. Consider your *LM* curve. Suppose that the interest rate is very close to zero, and the central bank increases the supply of money. What happens to the interest rate at a given level of income?

e. Can an expansionary monetary policy increase output when the interest rate is already very close to zero?

The inability of the central bank to reduce the interest rate when it is already very close to zero is known as the liquidity trap and was first mentioned by Keynes in 1936 in his General Theory – which laid the foundations of the IS–LM model.

7. Policy mixes

Suggest a policy mix to achieve each of the following objectives.

a. Increase *Y* while keeping *i* constant.

b. Decrease the fiscal deficit while keeping *Y* constant. What happens to *i*? to investment?

8. The (less paradoxical) paradox of saving

A chapter problem at the end of Chapter 3 considered the effect of a drop in consumer confidence on private saving and investment, when investment depended on output but not the interest rate. Here, we consider the same experiment in the context of the IS–LM framework, in which investment depends on the interest rate and output.

a. Suppose households attempt to save more, so that consumer confidence falls. In an *IS–LM* diagram, show the effect of the fall in consumer confidence on output and the interest rate.

b. How will the fall in consumer confidence affect consumption, investment and private saving? Will the attempt to save more necessarily lead to more saving? Will this attempt necessarily lead to less saving?

EXPLORE FURTHER

9. Consumption, investment and the recession of 2007–2010

*This question asks you to examine the movements of investment and consumption before, during and after the recession of 2007–2010. Go to the Eurostat website (**http://epp.eurostat. ec.europa.eu/portal/page/portal/eurostat/home/**). Find the data on the percentage change in real GDP and its components and on the contribution of the components of GDP to the overall percentage change in GDP. Investment is more variable than consumption, but consumption is much bigger than investment, so smaller percentage changes in consumption can have the same impact on GDP as much larger percentage changes in investment. Note that the quarterly percentage changes are annualised (i.e. expressed as annual rates). Get quarterly data on real GDP, consumption, gross private domestic investment and non-residential fixed investment for the years 2005–2010.*

a. Identify the quarters of negative growth in 2009 and 2010.

b. Track consumption and investment around 2009 and 2010. Which variable had the bigger percentage change around this time? Compare non-residential fixed investment with overall investment. Which variable had the bigger percentage change?

c. Get the contribution to GDP growth of consumption and investment for 2008–2010. Calculate the average of the quarterly contributions for each variable for each year. Now calculate the change in the contribution of each variable for 2009 and 2010 (i.e. subtract the average contribution of consumption in 2009 from the average contribution of consumption in 2010, subtract the average contribution of consumption in 2009 from the average contribution of consumption in 2010, and do the same for investment for both years). Which variable had the bigger fall in contribution to growth? What do you think was the proximate cause of the recession of 2007–2010? (Was it a fall in investment demand or a fall in consumption demand?)

> *Log on to **MyEconLab** and complete the studyplan exercises for this chapter to see how much you have learnt, and where you need to revise most.*
>
> MyEconLab

FURTHER READING

- For a discussion of the 'liquidity trap', see 'Krugman Liquidity Trap vs Roche BSR' on YouTube.

APPENDIX

An analytical version of the *IS–LM* model

In this appendix we use algebra to derive equations for the *IS* and *LM* curves, and use them to derive and discuss equilibrium in goods and financial markets as well as monetary and **fiscal policy multipliers**.

The *IS* curve

The *IS* curve graphically represents all the combinations of output and interest rate for which the goods market is in equilibrium, that is, the demand for goods equals the supply of goods. To derive explicitly the *IS* curve, we must choose a functional form for the relation (5.2) that we rewrite for convenience:

$$Y = C(Y - \bar{T}) + I(Y, i) + \bar{G} \qquad [5A.1]$$

More precisely, we must choose a functional form for consumption, $C(Y - \bar{T})$, and for investment demand, $I(Y, i)$. For consumption we use the linear function used earlier (in Chapter 3):

$$C = c_0 + c_1(Y - \bar{T}) \quad c_0 > 0, \ 0 < c_1 < 1 \qquad [5A.2]$$

For investment we use a linear function of the type:

$$I = \bar{I} + d_1 Y - d_2 i \qquad d_1, d_2 > 0 \qquad [5A.3]$$

where $\bar{I}$ is the independent (or exogenous) component of investment, while d_1 and d_2 measure, respectively, the sensitivity of investment to income and to the interest rate.

According to equation (5A.3), investment depends positively on the level of production and negatively on the interest rate. The positive relationship between investment and income is due to the fact that, faced with an increase in sales, companies increase production and then buy new machinery, thereby increasing investment. The negative relationship between investment and the interest rate is determined by the fact that the higher the interest rate, the lower the incentive for a company to borrow to invest.

To derive the *IS* curve, just replace the consumption function (5A.2) and the investment function (5A.3) in equation (5A.1):

$$Y = [c_0 + c_1(Y - \bar{T})] + \bar{I} + d_1 Y - d_2 i + \bar{G} \qquad [5A.4]$$

and solve this equation for Y in order to derive the equilibrium level of output as a function of the interest rate:

$$Y = \frac{1}{1 - c_1 - d_1} A - \frac{d_2}{1 - c_1 - d_1} i \qquad [5A.5]$$

where $A = [c_0 + \bar{I} + \bar{G} - c_1\bar{T}]$ is autonomous spending and $c_1 + d_1 < 1$ is the marginal propensity to spend (consumption *plus* investment). To represent the *IS* curve in a graph (Y, i), we rewrite equation (5A.5) as:

$$i = \frac{1}{d_2} A - \frac{1 - c_1 - d_1}{d_2} Y \qquad [5A.6]$$

Equation (5A.6) is a straight line with intercept $(1/d_2)A$ and slope $-(1 - c_1 - d_1)/d_2$.

The position of the *IS* curve

The position of the *IS* curve is determined by the intercept $(1d_2)A$, i.e. the level of the autonomous component of aggregate demand. This means that changes in autonomous spending cause *movements* of the *IS* curve. In other words, the *IS* moves when one of the following varies:

1. the exogenous component of consumption demand, Δc_0
2. the autonomous investment spending, $\Delta \bar{I}$
3. public spending, ΔG
4. taxes, T, which, by changing the disposable income, change aggregate demand by $-c_1\Delta T$.

Given equation (5A.5), and *for a given interest rate, i,* a variation of A, ΔA, in autonomous spending increases production by:

$$\Delta y = \frac{1}{1 - c_1 - d_1} \Delta A \qquad [5A.7]$$

In equation (5A.7), the term $1/(1 - c_1 - d_1)$ is the multiplier of autonomous demand in the case where investment and not only consumption depends on income.

Graphically, as shown in Figure 5.14, a ΔA increase in autonomous spending moves the *IS* curve horizontally to the right, and the size of displacement is given by $1/(1 - c_1 - d_1)\Delta A$. Conversely, a reduction in autonomous spending

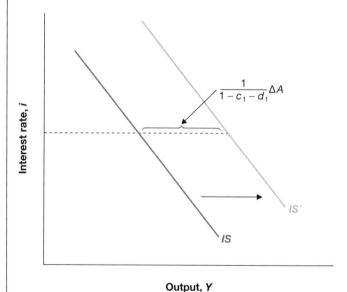

Figure 5.14

Shifts of the *IS* curve

An increase in autonomous spending by ΔA shifts the *IS* curve horizontally to the right by $1/(1 - c_1 - d_1)\Delta A$.

by ΔA moves the *IS* curve horizontally to the left. It is important to note that following a change in autonomous demand only a shift in the *IS* curve occurs and not a movement along the curve itself. Furthermore, since changes in autonomous spending will not change the slope of the *IS* curve, the shift of the latter occurs parallel to itself.

Slope of the *IS* curve

At the beginning of this chapter we saw that the *IS* curve is downward sloping because a higher interest rate reduces investment and consumption and thus the equilibrium level of output. But what determines the slope of the *IS* curve? Intuitively, the slope of the curve depends on the extent to which the equilibrium level of production varies following a change in the interest rate. If, following a small change in the interest rate, production has to change much to restore equilibrium in the goods market, the *IS* curve will be slightly sloped. This result is illustrated in Figure 5.15.

To give a more rigorous answer to our question, we can use equation (5A.5). Given A, a Δi change in the interest rate changes income by:

$$\Delta y = -\frac{d_2}{1 - c_1 - d_1}\Delta i \qquad [5A.8]$$

The larger d_2 – the sensitivity of investment demand to the interest rate – the greater Δy. Graphically, if d_2 is high and the multiplier is large, the *IS* curve is flat, and the greater the response of output to changes in the interest rate. Conversely, if d_2 is small and the multiplier is low, the

IS curve will have a greater slope. Similarly, the variation of Y is large if c_1 and d_1 are high, that is to say the multiplier $1/(1 - c_1 - d_1)$ is large. From an economic point of view, the greater the sensitivity of investment to the interest rate $- d_2$ is high – the greater will be the direct effect of the interest rate on demand. This direct effect is then amplified through the multiplier. The total effect of a change in the interest rate on production depends, therefore, on the sensitivity of investment to the interest rate and on the demand multiplier.

The *LM* curve

Graphically the *LM* curve represents all the combinations of output and interest rate for which the money market is in equilibrium, i.e. the demand for money equals the supply of money (or demand for bonds equals the supply of bonds). To develop the analytical version of the *LM* curve, we have to choose a functional form for equation (5.3) which we rewrite for convenience:

$$\frac{M}{P} = L(Y, i) \qquad [5A.9]$$

Similarly to the derivation of the *IS* curve, we consider the following *linear* relationship between money, output and the interest rate:

$$\frac{M}{P} = f_1 Y - f_2 i \qquad f_1, f_2 > 0 \qquad [5A.10]$$

In equation (5A.10), parameters f_1 and f_2 measure, respectively, the response of demand for (real) money to changes in income and interest rate. An increase in income raises the demand for money; an increase in the interest rate decreases the demand for money. Solving for Y, we derive the equilibrium level of Y as a function of i:

$$Y = \frac{1}{f_1}\frac{M}{P} + \frac{f_2}{f_1}i \qquad [5A.11]$$

This equation, with intercept $(1/f_1)(M/P)$ and slope f_2/f_1, is the *LM* curve in the space (Y, i).

The position of the *LM* curve

The position of the *LM* curve depends on the intercept $(1/f_1)(M/P)$, that is on the real money supply. What happens if the central bank varies the nominal supply of money by ΔM? Given the assumption of constant prices, real money supply will also change by $\Delta M/P$. So, according to equation (5A.11), and *for a given interest rate i*, the change in M/P will change production by:

$$\Delta Y = \frac{1}{f_1}\frac{\Delta M}{P} \qquad [5A.12]$$

In other words, if the nominal money supply increases by ΔM, the *LM* curve *moves horizontally to the right* by

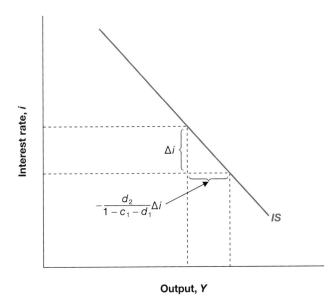

Figure 5.15

Movements along the *IS* curve

The *IS* curve is flat if, following a small change in the interest rate, output has to change a lot to restore equilibrium in the goods market, that is if $d_2/(1 - c_1 - d_1)$ is high.

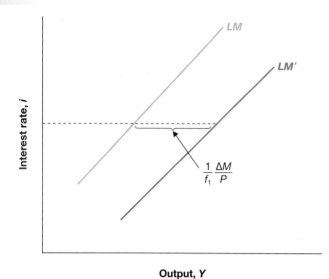

Figure 5.16

Shifts of the *LM* curve

An increase in the nominal money supply by ΔM shifts the *LM* curve horizontally to the right by $(1/f_1)\Delta M/P$.

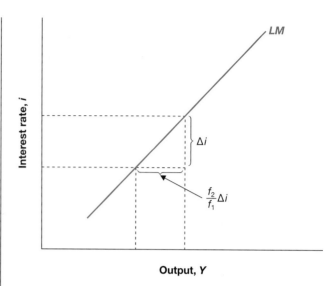

Figure 5.17

Movements along the *LM* curve

The *LM* curve is flat if, following a small change in the interest rate, output has to increase a lot to restore equilibrium in the money market, that is if f_2/f_1 is high.

$(1/f_1)\Delta M/P$ (see Figure 5.16). Indeed, for a given interest rate, the level of income must increase in order to raise the demand for money to the new (increased) level of money supply. Conversely, if the nominal money supply decreases by ΔM, the *LM* curve *moves horizontally to the left*. Notice that the lower the sensitivity of money demand to income – f_1 is small – the larger must be the change in income for any given change in M. The reason is simple. If f_1 is small, the response of money demand to a change in income is low. Then income must grow enough to increase the demand for money and balance the money market.

Slope of the *LM* curve

Now consider the slope of the *LM* curve. Figure 5.17 shows that when the *LM* curve is flat, a small change in the interest rate implies that output must grow enough to restore equilibrium in the money market. According to equation (5A.11), the relationship between the change in output and the change in the interest rate is given by:

$$\Delta y = \frac{f_2}{f_1}\Delta i \qquad [5A.13]$$

Therefore the total effect of a change in the interest rate on output depends on the ratio f_2/f_1. If this ratio is high, the curve will flatten. For example, if the demand for money is very sensitive to the interest rate – f_2 is high – a small increase in the interest rate is sufcient to cause a sharp drop in demand for money. In turn, if the demand for money is not very sensitive to changes in income – f_1 is small – production must increase enough to ensure sufficient growth in demand for money necessary to balance the money market.

Equilibrium

In Section 5.3 we said that the simultaneous equilibrium in goods and financial markets is represented by the intersection of *IS* and *LM* curves (see Figure 5.7). The intersection corresponds to the unique combination of production and interest rate that ensures equilibrium in *both* markets. To compute the values of Y and i we have to jointly solve the equations *IS* and *LM*, which we rewrite for convenience:

$$Y = [c_0 + c_1(Y - \bar{T})] + \bar{I} + d_1 Y - d_2 i + \bar{G} \qquad [5A.4]$$

$$\frac{M}{P} = f_1 Y - f_2 i \qquad [5A.10]$$

One way to find the combination of Y and i that guarantees equilibrium in both the goods and financial markets is to solve for the interest rate in equation (5A.10) and replace it in equation (5A.4) in order to derive the equilibrium value of output:

$$Y = \frac{1}{(1 - c_1 - d_1)\dfrac{f_2}{d_2} + f_1}\frac{M}{P} + \frac{1}{(1 - c_1 - d_1) + d_2\dfrac{f_1}{f_2}}A \qquad [5A.14]$$

Subsequently, to calculate the equilibrium value of the interest rate, we can replace the equilibrium value of Y in equation (5A.10), which is the *LM* curve:

$$i = -\frac{1}{f_2 + \dfrac{d_2 f_1}{1 - c_1 - d_1}}\frac{M}{P} + \frac{1}{(1 - c_1 - d_1)\dfrac{f_2}{f_1} + d_2}A \qquad [5A.15]$$

Equations [5A.14] and [5A.15] show that:

● The equilibrium values of Y and i are *functions of exogenous variables*: the real money supply M/P and autonomous spending A. An increase in autonomous spending increases both production and the interest rate. Instead, an increase in real money supply raises output, but decreases the interest rate.

- Both Y and i are linear functions of the exogenous variables. This result derives from our assumption of linearity of the *IS* and *LM* functions.

- The coefficients of money supply and autonomous spending are complex functions of all the parameters that appear in the *IS* and *LM* equations. These expressions are the result of the interaction between the goods market and the money market and allow us to derive the so-called multiplier of fiscal policy and monetary policy.

Fiscal policy multiplier

From equations (5A.14) and (5A.15) we can calculate the effect on the equilibrium levels of Y and i of a change in autonomous spending, where the real money supply is constant:

$$\Delta Y = \frac{1}{(1 - c_1 - d_1) + d_2 \frac{f_1}{f_2}} \Delta A \qquad [5A.16]$$

$$\Delta i = \frac{1}{(1 - c_1 - d_1) \frac{f_2}{f_1} + d_2} \Delta A \qquad [5A.17]$$

Since we assumed that $c_1 + d_1 < 1$, the effect on output and the interest rate of an increase in autonomous spending is unambiguously positive. An increase in autonomous spending moves the *IS* curve up and to the right, along the *LM* curve, causing an increase in both the interest rate and production.

If we use equation (5A.16) and divide Δy by ΔA, we obtain the **fiscal policy multiplier**:

$$\frac{\Delta y}{\Delta A} = \frac{1}{(1 - c_1 - d_1) + d_2 \frac{f_1}{f_2}} \qquad [5A.18]$$

which measures by how much the equilibrium level of output changes following a change in autonomous spending. It should be noted that the fiscal policy multiplier resembles the demand multiplier $1/(1 - c_1 - d_1)$, which is actually a special case of (5A.18) when $d_2 = 0$. The latter, however, was obtained by looking only at the goods market, while the fiscal policy multiplier has been obtained taking into account the interactions between the goods market and the money market. The fiscal policy multiplier allows us to make the following observations:

- The higher the demand multiplier, that is, the smaller $(1 - c_1 - d_1)$, the greater $\Delta y/\Delta A$, given the other para-

meters. A high value of $1/(1 - c_1 - d_1)$ implies that the multiplicative effect on demand and thus on Δy is stronger. In turn, the stronger the response of production to an increase in autonomous spending, the greater the effect of income on the demand for money and the greater will be the increase in the interest rate necessary to restore equilibrium in the money market (see equation (5A.16)).

- The response of y to A is strong if d_2 and f_1 are small and f_2 is big. Because the sensitivity of investment demand to the interest rate is relatively low – d_2 is small – the negative effect of a higher interest rate on investment demand is limited. Also, if the sensitivity of money demand to income is low – f_1 is small – the demand for money grows only a little when production increases. Consequently, the increase in the interest rate needed to reduce money demand is small and so is the crowding-out effect on investment. Finally, if the demand for money is very sensitive to the interest rate – f_2 is high – a small adjustment of the interest rate is sufficient to restore equilibrium in the money market.

This can be confirmed by calculating $\Delta i/\Delta A$:

$$\frac{\Delta i}{\Delta A} = \frac{1}{(1 - c_1 - d_1) \frac{f_2}{f_1} + d_2} \qquad [5A.19]$$

where the interest rate varies little when f_2 is large and/or f_1 is small. Also, if d_2 is high, the change in the interest rate for any given change in A will be smaller.

Monetary policy multiplier

Consider now what happens to Y and i when the real money supply changes. From equation (5A.12), we can calculate the size of Δi following a change in $\Delta M/P$ for a given level of A:

$$\frac{\Delta i}{\Delta M/P} = -\frac{1}{f_2 + \frac{d_2 f_1}{1 - c_1 - d_1}} \qquad [5A.20]$$

Using equation (5A.11), we can calculate the **monetary policy multiplier**, namely the response of production *to a change in the money supply*:

$$\frac{\Delta y}{\Delta M/P} = -\frac{1}{(1 - c_1 - d_1) \frac{f_2}{d_2} + f_1} \qquad [5A.21]$$

Notice that in both cases, changes in Y and i depend on $(1 - c_1 - d_1)$, f_1, f_2 and d_2. We leave it up to you to figure out the interpretation of equations (5A.20) and (5A.21) following a change in these parameters.

Chapter 6

THE *IS–LM* MODEL IN AN OPEN ECONOMY

We have assumed until now that the economy was closed – that it did not interact with the rest of the world. We started this way to keep things simple and build up your intuition for the basic macroeconomic mechanisms. In fact, most economies, and all European economies in particular, are very open – they trade both goods and assets with the rest of the world (and also, actually mostly, with each other).

'Openness' has three distinct dimensions:

1. **Openness in goods markets** – The ability of consumers and firms to choose between domestic goods and foreign goods.

2. **Openness in financial markets** – The ability of financial investors to choose between domestic assets and foreign assets.

3. **Openness in factor markets** – The ability of firms to choose where to locate production, and of workers to choose where to work.

Some empires, the British empire for instance, had created bigger markets, at least for their times, but the countries forming such empires were not sovereign nations which had freely decided to join the empire. ➤ The EU is the biggest ever common market among sovereign countries, with 27 member states. Within the EU, goods, services and factors (capital and labour) are free to circulate without **tariffs** or other barriers. Since the Schengen Agreement in 1995, citizens from any member state can freely circulate inside the EU.

In financial markets, openness is much higher than in goods markets. Most world financial markets are closely integrated, although some countries still forbid the free movement of financial assets. China, for example, has long prohibited its citizens from buying foreign financial assets.

Factors markets are also increasingly integrated. Multinational companies operate plants in many countries and move their operations around the world to take advantage of lower production costs. Much of the debate about the accession to the EU of countries in Central and Eastern Europe centred on the extent to which this would induce European firms to relocate there. And immigration from low-wage countries is a hot political issue in many EU countries.

This chapter has five sections:

● Section 6.1 looks at openness in goods markets, and the determinants of the choice between domestic and foreign assets.

- Section 6.2 looks at openness in financial markets, the determinants of the choice between domestic goods and foreign goods and the role of the real exchange rate.

- Section 6.3 studies equilibrium in the goods market in an open economy.

- Section 6.4 studies equilibrium in financial markets, including the foreign exchange market.

- Section 6.5 puts the two equilibrium conditions together and looks at the joint determination of output, the interest rate and the exchange rate.

6.1 OPENNESS IN GOODS MARKETS

Let us start by looking at how much an open economy, such as the UK, sells to and buys from the rest of the world. Then we will be better able to think about the choice between domestic goods and foreign goods and the role of the relative price of domestic goods in terms of foreign goods – the real exchange rate.

Exports and imports

Figure 6.1 plots the evolution of UK exports and UK imports, as ratios to GDP, since 1960. ('UK exports' means exports *from* the UK; 'UK imports' means imports *into* the UK.) The figure suggests two main conclusions:

- The UK economy has become more open over time. Exports and imports, which were around 20% of GDP in 1960, are now equal to about 30% of GDP (29% for exports, 32% for imports). In other words, the UK trades much more (relative to its GDP) with the rest of the world than it did just 50 years ago. Notice the large increase in both exports and

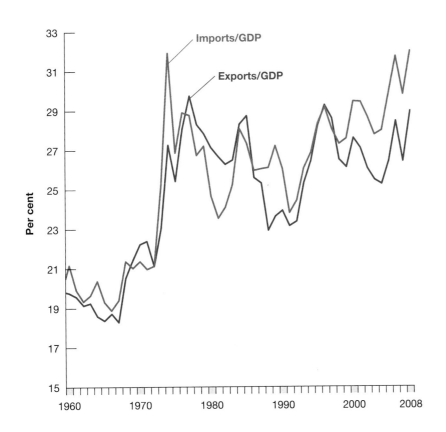

Figure 6.1

UK exports and imports as ratios to GDP since 1960

Since 1960, exports and imports have increased by around 10 percentage points in relation to GDP.

Source: UK Office for National Statistics.

imports in the early 1970s, which corresponds to the time the UK joined the European Union.

- Although imports and exports have broadly followed the same upward trend, they have also diverged for long periods of time, generating sustained trade surpluses and trade deficits. Three episodes stand out:
  - The large trade surplus in the early 1980s – The ratio of the trade surplus to GDP reached 3.1% in 1981.
  - The large trade deficits at the end of the 1980s – The ratio of the trade deficit to GDP reached 3.6% in 1989 and then decreased to less than 1% in the early 1990s.
  - The large and increasing trade deficits since the mid-1990s – The ratio of the trade deficit to GDP reached 3.4% in 2005 and has remained relatively high in the following years.

> The trade balance is the difference between exports and imports. If exports exceed imports, there is a trade surplus (equivalently, a positive trade balance). If imports exceed exports, there is a trade deficit (equivalently, a negative trade balance). (See Chapter 3.)

Understanding the sources and implications of these trade imbalances is a central issue in macroeconomics today, and one to which we shall return later.

Given all the talk in the media about *globalisation*, a volume of trade (measured by the average of the ratios of exports and imports to GDP) around 30% of GDP might strike you as small. However, the volume of trade is not necessarily a good measure of openness. Many firms are exposed to foreign competition but, by being competitive and keeping their prices low enough, these firms are able to retain their domestic market share and limit imports. This suggests that a better index of openness than export or import ratios is the proportion of aggregate output composed of **tradable goods** – goods that compete with foreign goods in either domestic markets or foreign markets.

> - Tradable goods: cars, computers, and so on.
> - Non-tradable goods: most medical services, haircuts, meals at restaurants, and so on.

With exports around 30% of GDP, it is true that the UK has one of the smallest ratios of exports to GDP among the high-income countries of the world. Table 6.1 gives ratios for a number of OECD countries.

The USA is at the low end of the range of export ratios, with 13%, followed by Japan with 15%. In Europe, most of the largest economies have export ratios close to or around 50%, including Germany, Denmark, Finland, Norway and Sweden. The UK has a relatively small ratio of exports to GDP, at least compared to other EU countries. The smaller European economies have the highest ratios: 80% in Belgium, 78% in the Netherlands. Ireland's 101% ratio of exports to GDP raises an odd possibility: can a country have exports larger than its GDP? In other words, can a country have an export ratio greater than 1? The answer is yes. The reason is given in the Focus box 'Can exports exceed GDP?'

Do these numbers mean that the UK has more trade barriers than, say, Germany or Belgium? No. The main factors behind these differences are geography and size. Distance from other markets explains a good part of the low ratio for Japan. Size also matters: the smaller the country, the more it must specialise in producing and exporting only a few products and rely on imports for other products. Belgium can hardly afford to produce the range of goods produced by Germany, a country roughly seven times bigger.

The choice between domestic goods and foreign goods

How does openness in goods markets force us to rethink the way we look at equilibrium in the goods market?

Table 6.1 Ratios of exports to GDP (%) for selected OECD countries, 2010

Country	Export ratio (%)	Country	Export ratio (%)
Ireland	101	Norway	41
Belgium	80	Finland	40
Netherlands	78	UK	30
Sweden	50	Spain	27
Germany	47	Japan	15
Italy	27	USA	13

Source: Eurostat.

Until now, when we were thinking about consumers' decisions in the goods market we focused on their decision to save or to consume. When goods can be traded internationally, domestic consumers face a second decision: whether to buy domestic goods or to buy foreign goods. Indeed, all buyers – including domestic and foreign firms and governments – face a similar decision. This decision has a direct effect on domestic output: if buyers decide to buy more domestic goods, the demand for domestic goods increases, and so does domestic output. If they decide to buy more foreign goods, then foreign output increases instead of domestic output.

> In a closed economy, people face one decision:
> ● Save or buy (consume).
> In an open economy, they face two decisions:
> ● Save or buy.
> ● Buy domestic or buy foreign.

FOCUS
Can exports exceed GDP?

Can a country have exports larger than its GDP that is, can it have an export ratio greater than 1?

It would seem that the answer must be no: a country cannot export more than it produces, so the export ratio must be at most 1. Not so. The key to the answer is to realise that exports and imports may include exports and imports of intermediate goods.

Take, for example, a country that imports intermediate goods for €1 billion. Suppose it then transforms them into final goods using only labour. Say labour is paid €200 million and that there are no profits. The value of these final goods is thus equal to €1,200 million. Assume that €1 billion worth of final goods is exported and the rest, €200 million, is consumed domestically.

Exports and imports therefore both equal €1 billion. What is GDP in this economy? Remember that GDP is value added in the economy (see Chapter 2). So, in this example, GDP equals €200 million, and the ratio of exports to GDP equals €1000/€200 = 5.

Hence, exports can exceed GDP. This is actually the case for a number of small countries where most economic activity is organised around a harbour and import–export activities, such as the Netherlands, where the ratio of exports to GDP in 2010 was 78%. This is also the case for small countries such as Malaysia, where the ratio of exports to GDP exceeds 100%. In 2010, the ratio of exports to GDP in Singapore was 229%!

Central to the decision of whether to buy domestic goods or foreign goods is the price of domestic goods relative to foreign goods. We call this relative price the **real exchange rate**. The real exchange rate is not directly observable, and you will not find it in newspapers. What you will find in newspapers are nominal exchange rates, the relative prices of currencies. We start by looking at *nominal exchange rates* and then see how we can use them to construct real exchange rates.

Nominal exchange rates

The nominal exchange rate between two currencies can be quoted in one of two ways:

● As the price of the domestic currency in terms of the foreign currency. If, for example, we look at the UK and the euro area and think of the pound as the domestic currency and the euro as the foreign currency, we can express the nominal exchange rate as the price of a pound in terms of euros. In December 2012, the exchange rate defined this way (pound-euro nominal exchange rate) was 1.23. In other words, with £1 you could buy €1.23.

● As the price of the foreign currency in terms of the domestic currency. Continuing with the same example, we can express the nominal exchange rate as the price of a euro in terms of pounds (euro-pound nominal exchange rate). In December 2012, the price of a euro in terms of pounds was 0.81 (1/1.23).

Either definition is fine; the important thing is to remain consistent. In this book, we adopt the first denition: we define the **nominal exchange rate** as *the price of the domestic currency in terms of foreign currency* and denote it by E. When looking, for example, at the

> **Warning:** There is no agreed-upon rule among economists or among newspapers as to which of the two definitions to use. You will encounter both. Usually, the first definition is preferred in the UK, the second definition is preferred in the rest of Europe. Always check which definition is used.

E: Nominal exchange rate – price of domestic currency in terms of foreign currency. (From the point of view of the UK looking at the euro area, the price of a pound in terms of euros.)

exchange rate between the UK and the euro (from the viewpoint of the UK, so the pound is the domestic currency), *E* denotes the price of a pound in terms of euros (so, for example, *E* was 1.23 in December 2012).

Exchange rates between most foreign currencies change every day and every minute of the day. These changes are called *nominal appreciations* or *nominal depreciations* – *appreciations* or *depreciations* for short:

Appreciation of the domestic currency ⇔ Increase in the price of the domestic currency in terms of foreign currency ⇔ Increase in the exchange rate.

Depreciation of the domestic currency ⇔ Decrease in the price of the domestic currency in terms of foreign currency ⇔ Decrease in the exchange rate.

● An **appreciation** of the domestic currency is an increase in the price of the domestic currency in terms of a foreign currency. Given our definition of the exchange rate, an appreciation corresponds to an increase in the exchange rate, *E*.
● A **depreciation** of the domestic currency is a decrease in the price of the domestic currency in terms of a foreign currency. So, given our definition of the exchange rate, a depreciation of the domestic currency corresponds to a decrease in the exchange rate, *E*.

We shall discuss fixed exchange rates later (see Chapter 12).

You may have encountered two other words to denote movements in exchange rates: 'revaluations' and 'devaluations'. These two terms are used when countries operate under **fixed exchange rates** – a system in which two or more countries maintain a constant exchange rate between their currencies. Under such a system, increases in the exchange rate – which are infrequent by definition – are called **revaluations** (rather than appreciations). Decreases in the exchange rate are called **devaluations** (rather than depreciations).

Figure 6.2 plots the nominal exchange rate between the pound and the euro since 1999. Note the two main characteristics of the figure:

● *The trend decrease in the exchange rate* – In 1999, £1 was worth €1.4. In 2012, £1 was worth €1.23. Put another way, there was a depreciation of the pound vis-à-vis the euro over the period.
● *The large fluctuations in the exchange rate* – In the space of a few years, from 1999 to 2003, the value of the pound increased from €1.4 in 1999 to €1.75 in 2000, back down to €1.5 in mid-2001 and to €1.23 in 2012. Put another way, there was a very large appre-

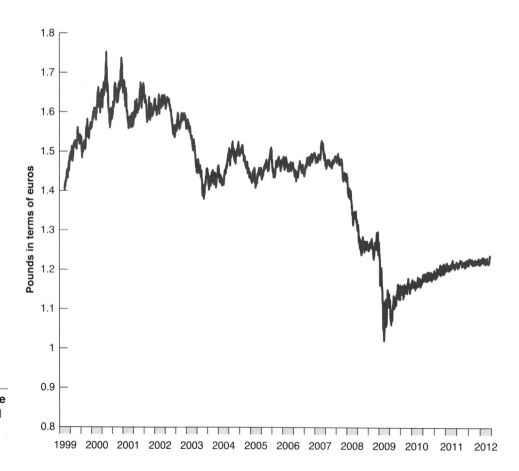

Figure 6.2

The nominal exchange rate between the British pound and the euro since 1999

Source: European Central Bank.

ciation of the pound at the end of the 1990s, followed by a large depreciation in the following decade.

If we are interested, however, in the choice between domestic goods and foreign goods, the nominal exchange rate gives us only part of the information we need. Figure 6.2, for example, tells us only about movements in the relative price of the two currencies, the pound and the euro. To British tourists thinking of visiting Italy, France or Greece the question is not only how many euos they will get in exchange for their pounds, but also how many Italian, French or Greek goods they will be able to buy with their pounds. This takes us to our next step – the construction of real exchange rates.

From nominal to real exchange rates

How can we construct the real exchange rate between the UK and the euro area – the price of UK goods in terms of European goods?

Suppose the UK produced only one good, a Jaguar, and the euro area also produced only one good, a Mercedes. (This is one of those 'suppose' statements that run completely against the facts, but we shall become more realistic shortly.) Constructing the real exchange rate, the price of the UK goods (Jaguars) in terms of European goods (Mercedes), would be straightforward. We would express both goods in terms of the same currency and then compute their relative price.

Suppose, for example, we expressed both goods in terms of pounds. Then:

> Expressing both in terms of euros would make no difference: we would get the same result for the real exchange rate.

- One way would be to express both Jaguars and Mercedes in pounds. The price of a Jaguar in pounds is, say, 30,000 pounds. The price of a Mercedes is, say, 50,000 euros. Since E = 1.23 (it takes 1.23 euros to buy one pound) the price of a Mercedes in pounds is 50,000/1.23 = 40,650 pounds approximately. The real exchange rate is the price of UK goods in terms of euro area goods, that is, how many Mercedes it takes to buy one Jaguar. It is 30,000/40,650 = 0.738. It takes less than a full Mercedes (73.8 per cent of a Mercedes) to buy one Jaguar.
- Alternatively you could express both Jaguars and Mercedes in euros. The price of a Jaguar in euros is 30,000 × 1.23 = 36,900 euros. Thus the real exchange rate – how many Mercedes it takes to buy one Jaguar – is, again, 36,900/50,000 = 0.738.

The example is straightforward, but how do we generalise it? The UK and the euro area produce more than Jaguars and Mercedes, and we want to construct a real exchange rate that reflects the relative price of *all* the goods produced in the UK in terms of *all* the goods produced in the euro area.

The computation we just went through tells us how to proceed. Rather than use the price of a Jaguar and the price of a Mercedes, we must use a price index for all goods produced in the UK and a price index for all goods produced in the euro area. This is exactly what the GDP deflators we introduced earlier (see Chapter 2) do: they are, by definition, price indexes for all final goods and services produced in the economy.

Let P be the GDP deflator for the UK, P^* be the GDP deflator for the euro area (as a rule, we shall denote foreign variables with an asterisk) and E be the pound–euro nominal exchange rate. Figure 6.3 goes through the steps needed to construct the real exchange rate:

1. The price of UK goods in pounds is P. Multiplying it by the exchange rate, E – the price of pounds in terms of euros – gives us the price of UK goods in euros, EP.
2. The price of European goods in euros is P^*. The *real exchange rate*, the price of UK goods in terms of European goods, which we shall call ε (the Greek lowercase epsilon), is thus given by

$$\varepsilon = \frac{EP}{P^*} = \frac{[\text{€}/\text{£}] \cdot [\text{£/units of UK goods}]}{[\text{€/unit of euro area goods}]} = \frac{\text{units of euro area goods}}{\text{units of UK goods}} \quad [6.1]$$

The real exchange rate is constructed by multiplying the domestic price level by the nominal exchange rate and then dividing by the foreign price level – a straightforward extension of the computation we made in our Jaguar/Mercedes example.

Figure 6.3

The construction of the real exchange rate

Note, however, an important difference between our Jaguar/Mercedes example and this more general computation. Unlike the price of Jaguars in terms of Mercedes, the real exchange rate is an index number: that is, its level is arbitrary and, therefore, uninformative. It is uninformative because the GDP deflators used to construct the real exchange rate are themselves index numbers; as we saw earlier (in Chapter 2), they are equal to 1 (or 100) in whatever year is chosen as the base year.

But all is not lost. Although the level of the real exchange rate is uninformative, the rate of change of the real exchange rate is informative. If, for example, the real exchange rate between the UK and the euro area increases by 10%, this tells us UK goods are now 10% more expensive relative to European goods than they were before.

Like nominal exchange rates, real exchange rates move over time. These changes are called *real appreciations* or *real depreciations*:

- An increase in the real exchange rate – that is, an increase in the relative price of domestic goods in terms of foreign goods – is called a **real appreciation**.
- A decrease in the real exchange rate – that is, a decrease in the relative price of domestic goods in terms of foreign goods – is called a **real depreciation**.

Figure 6.4 plots the evolution of the real exchange rate between the UK and the euro area since 1999, constructed using equation (6.1). For convenience, it also reproduces the evolution of the nominal exchange rate from Figure 6.2.

Two aspects stand out in Figure 6.4. The large nominal and real appreciation of the pound at the end of the 1990s and the collapse of the pound in 2008–2009.

The large fluctuations in the nominal exchange rate we saw in Figure 6.2 also show up in the real exchange rate. This not surprising: year-to-year movements in the price ratio, P/P^*, are typically small compared to the often sharp movements in the nominal exchange rate, E. Thus, from year to year, or even over the course of a few years, movements in the real exchange rate, ε, tend to be driven mostly by movements in the nominal exchange rate, E. Note that, since 1999, the nominal exchange rate and the real exchange rate have moved nearly together. This reflects the fact that, since then, inflation rates have been very similar – and low – in both areas.

> If inflation rates were exactly equal, P/P^* would be constant, and ε and E would move together exactly.

From bilateral to multilateral exchange rates

We need to take one last step. We have so far concentrated on the exchange rate between the UK and the euro area, but the euro area is just one of many partners the UK trades with.

Table 6.2 shows the geographic composition of UK trade for both exports and imports. The main message of the table is that the UK does most of its trade with two countries: the USA and Germany (which together account for 25% of UK exports and 21% of UK imports). The second largest group of export partners includes the closest countries of the EU, such as Ireland, the Netherlands, France and Belgium.

How do we go from **bilateral exchange rates**, like the real exchange rate between the UK and the euro area we focused on earlier, to **multilateral exchange rates** that reflect this composition of trade? The principle we want to use is simple, even if the details of construction are complicated: we weigh each country by how much each country trades with

Figure 6.4

Real and nominal exchange rates in the UK since 1999

The nominal and the real exchange rates in the UK have moved largely together since 1999.

Source: ECB, Eurostat, Bank of England.

Table 6.2 The country composition of UK exports and imports, 2010

	Proportion of exports to (%)	Proportion of imports from (%)
USA	14	8
Germany	11	13
Netherlands	8	8
Ireland	8	4
France	7	7
Belgium	5	5
Spain	4	3
Italy	4	4
Sweden	2	2
China	2	7
Russia	2	2
India	2	1
Japan	2	3
Hong Kong	2	2
Norway	1	6
TOTAL	74	75

Source: UK Office for National Statistics.

the UK and how much it competes with the UK in other countries. The variable constructed in this way is called the **multilateral real exchange rate**, or the real exchange rate for short.

Figure 6.5 shows the evolution of this multilateral real exchange rate, the price of domestic goods in terms of foreign goods for the UK, since 1980. Like the bilateral real exchange rate we saw in Figure 6.4, it is an index number. So its level is arbitrary; here it is set equal to 100 in January 2005. The most striking aspect of the figure is the large swing in the real exchange rate in the 1980s and 1990s, compared to the relative stability between the mid-1990s and 2007. The second remarkable aspect of the figure is the collapse of the real exchange rate in 2009.

◀ These are all equivalent names for the relative price of domestic goods in terms of foreign goods:

● The real multilateral exchange rate.
● The trade-weighted real exchange rate.
● The effective real exchange rate.

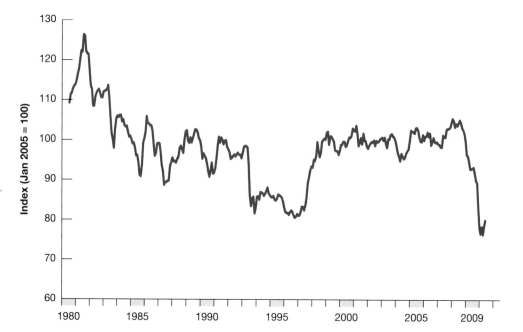

Figure 6.5

The UK multilateral real exchange rate since 1980

The 1980s and 1990s were characterised by large swings in the real exchange rate. The real exchange rate was much more stable since the end of the 1990s, until the large real depreciation in 2009.

Source: Bank of England.

6.2 OPENNESS IN FINANCIAL MARKETS

Openness in financial markets allows financial investors to hold both domestic assets and foreign assets, to diversify their portfolios, to speculate on movements in foreign interest rates versus domestic interest rates, to speculate on movements in exchange rates, and so on.

Diversify and speculate they do. Given that buying or selling foreign assets implies buying or selling foreign currency – sometimes called **foreign exchange** – the volume of transactions in foreign exchange markets gives us a sense of the importance of international financial transactions. In 2005, for example, the recorded daily volume of foreign exchange transactions in the world was €4 trillion, of which 37% – about €1.6 trillion – involved euros on one side of the transaction (and 86% involved dollars on the other side of the transation).

To get a sense of the magnitude of these numbers, the sum of exports and imports of the euro area with the rest of the world in 2007 totalled €3 trillion for the year, or about €8 billion per day. Suppose the only euro transactions in foreign exchange markets had been, on one side, by euro area exporters selling their foreign currency earnings, and on the other side by euro area importers buying the foreign currency they needed to buy foreign goods. Then, the volume of transactions involving euros in foreign exchange markets would have been €8 billion per day, or about 0.5% of the actual daily total volume of transactions (€1.6 trillion) involving euros in foreign exchange markets. This computation tells us that most of the foreign exchange transactions are associated not with trade but with purchases and sales of financial assets. Moreover, the volume of transactions in foreign exchange markets is not only high but also rapidly increasing. The volume of foreign exchange transactions has more than doubled since 2001. Again, this increase in activity reflects mostly an increase in financial transactions rather than an increase in trade.

For a country as a whole, openness in financial markets has another important implication. It allows the country to run trade surpluses and trade deficits. Recall that a country running a trade deficit is buying more from the rest of the world than it is selling to the rest of the world. In order to pay for the difference between what it buys and what it sells, the country must borrow from the rest of the world. It borrows by making it attractive for foreign financial investors to increase their holdings of domestic assets – in effect, to lend to the country.

Table 6.3 The UK balance of payments, 2008 (in billions of pounds)

Current account		
Exports	422	
Inports	459	
Trade balance (deficit = –) (1)		–37
Investment income	263	
Investment income paid	236	
Net investment income (2)		27
Net transfers received (3)		–14
Current account balance (deficit = –) (1) + (2) + (3)		–24
Capital account		
Increase in foreign holdings of UK assets (4)	650	
Increase in UK holdings of foreign assets (5)	620	
Capital account balance (deficit = –) (4) – (5)		30
Statistical discrepancy		–6

Source: UK Office of National Statistics.

Let us start by looking more closely at the relation between trade flows and financial flows. When this is done, we shall look at the determinants of these financial flows.

The balance of payments

A country's transactions with the rest of the world, including both trade flows and financial flows, are summarised in a set of accounts called the **balance of payments**. Table 6.3 presents the UK balance of payments for 2008. The table has two parts, separated by a line. Transactions are referred to as being either **above the line** or **below the line**.

The current account

The transactions above the line record payments to and from the rest of the world. They are called **current account** transactions:

- The first two lines record the exports and imports of goods and services. Exports lead to payments from the rest of the world, and imports lead to payments to the rest of the world. In 2008, imports exceeded exports, leading to a UK trade deficit of £37 billion, roughly 8.4% of UK GDP.
- Exports and imports are not the only sources of payments to and from the rest of the world. UK residents receive **investment income** on their holdings of foreign assets, and foreign residents receive investment income from the UK on their holdings of UK assets. In 2008, UK investment income received from the rest of the world was £263 billion, and investment income paid to foreigners was £236 billion, for a net positive balance of £27 billion.
- Finally, countries give and receive foreign aid; the net value of these payments is recorded as **net transfers received**. These net transfers amounted in 2008 to –£14 billion. This negative amount reflects the fact that, in 2008, the UK was – as it has traditionally been – a net donor of foreign aid.

The sum of net payments to and from the rest of the world is called the **current account balance**. If net payments from the rest of the world are positive, the country is running a **current account surplus**; if they are negative, the country is running a **current account deficit**. Adding all payments to and from the rest of the world, net payments from the UK to the rest of the world were equal in 2008 to –£37 + £27 – £14 = –£24 billion. Put another way, in 2008, the UK ran a current account deficit of £24 billion – roughly 5.4% of its GDP.

◄ Can a country have:
- A trade deficit and no current account deficit?
- A current account deficit and no trade deficit?

(The answer to both questions: yes.)

The capital account

The fact that the UK had a current account deficit of £24 billion in 2008 implies that it had to borrow £24 billion from the rest of the world or, equivalently, that net foreign holdings of UK assets had to increase by £24 billion. The numbers below the line describe how this was achieved. Transactions below the line are called capital account transactions.

The increase in foreign holdings of UK assets was £650 billion: foreign investors, be they foreign private investors, foreign governments or foreign central banks, bought £650 billion worth of UK stocks, UK bonds and other UK assets. At the same time, there was an increase in UK holdings of foreign assets of £620 billion: UK investors, private and public, bought £620 billion worth of foreign stocks, bonds and other assets. The result was an increase in net UK foreign indebtedness (the increase in foreign holdings of UK assets minus the increase in UK holdings of foreign assets), also called **net capital flows**, to the UK of £(−650) − £(−620) = £30 billion. Another name for net capital flows is the **capital account balance**: positive net capital flows are called a **capital account surplus**; negative net capital flows are called a **capital account deficit**. So, put another way, in 2008, the UK ran a capital account surplus of £30 billion.

> A country that runs a current account deficit must finance it through positive net capital flows. Equivalently, it must run a capital account surplus.

Shouldn't net capital flows (equivalently, the capital account surplus) be exactly equal to the current account deficit (which we saw earlier was equal to £24 billion in 2008)? In principle, yes; in practice, no.

The numbers for current and capital account transactions are constructed using different sources; although they should give the same answers, typically they do not. In 2008, the difference between the two – the **statistical discrepancy** – was £6 billion, about 25% of the current account balance. This is yet another reminder that, even for a rich country such as the UK, economic data are far from perfect. (This problem of measurement manifests itself in another way as well. The sum of the current account deficits of all the countries in the world should be equal to 0: one country's deficit should show up as a surplus for the other countries taken as a whole. However, this is not the case in the data: if we just add the published current account deficits of all the countries in the world, it would appear that the world is running a large current account deficit and the answer cannot be that we are exporting to Mars less than we are importing!)

Now that we have looked at the current account, we can return to an issue we touched on earlier (see Chapter 2): the difference between GDP, the measure of output we have used so far, and GNP, another measure of aggregate output. This is done in the Focus box 'GDP versus GNP: the example of Ireland'.

The choice between domestic and foreign assets

Openness in financial markets implies that people (or financial institutions, for example investment trusts, that act on their behalf) face a new financial decision: whether to hold domestic assets or foreign assets.

Remembering what we learned earlier (in Chapter 5), it would appear that we actually have to think about at least two new decisions. The choice of holding domestic money versus foreign money, and the choice of holding domestic interest-paying assets versus foreign interest-paying assets. But remember why people hold money: to engage in transactions. For someone who lives in the UK and whose transactions are mostly or fully in pounds, there is little point in holding foreign currency, say, euros, because euros cannot be used for transactions in the UK. If the goal is to hold foreign assets, holding foreign currency is clearly less desirable than holding foreign bonds, which pay interest. This leaves us with only one new choice to think about, the choice between domestic interest-paying assets and foreign interest-paying assets.

Let us think of these assets for now as domestic one-year bonds and foreign one-year bonds. Consider, for example, the choice between US one-year bonds and UK one-year bonds, from your point of view, as a UK investor:

- Suppose you decide to hold UK bonds.

    Let i_t be the one-year UK nominal interest rate in year t (the subscript t refers to the year). Then, as Figure 6.6 shows, for every £1 you put in UK bonds, you will get £1$(1 + i_t)$ next year. (This is represented by the arrow pointing to the right at the top of the figure.)

FOCUS
GDP versus GNP: the example of Ireland

Should value added in an open economy be defined as:

● the value added domestically (that is, within the country), or
● the value added by domestically owned factors of production?

The two definitions are not the same: some domestic output is produced with capital owned by foreigners, while some foreign output is produced with capital owned by domestic residents.

The answer is that either definition is fine, and economists use both. **Gross domestic product (GDP)**, the measure we have used so far, corresponds to value added domestically. **Gross national product (GNP)** corresponds to the value added by domestically owned factors of production. To go from GDP to GNP, one must start from GDP, add factor payments received from the rest of the world, and subtract factor payments paid to the rest of the world. Put another way, GNP is equal to GDP plus net factor payments from the rest of the world. While GDP is now the measure most commonly mentioned, GNP was widely used until the early 1990s, and you will still encounter it in newspapers and academic publications.

For most countries, the difference between GNP and GDP is very small because factor payments to and from the rest of the world roughly cancel one another. There are a few exceptions. Among them is Ireland. Ireland has received a great amount of foreign direct investment during the last two decades. Therefore, the country now pays substantial factor income to the rest of the world. Table 6.4 gives GDP, GNP and net factor payments for Ireland from 2002 to 2008. Note how much larger GDP is compared to GNP throughout the period. Net factor payments now exceed 15% of GDP.

Table 6.4 GDP, GNP and net factor income in Ireland, 2002–2008

Year	GDP	GNP	Net factor income
2002	130,258	106,562	−23,696
2003	139,763	118,039	−21,724
2004	149,098	126,219	−22,879
2005	162,091	137,188	−24,903
2006	176,759	152,529	−24,230
2007	189,751	161,244	−28,507
2008	181,815	154,596	−27,218

Note: numbers are in millions of euros.

Source: Central Statistics Office Ireland.

Figure 6.6

Expected returns from holding one-year UK bonds or one-year US bonds

● Suppose you decide instead to hold US bonds.

To buy US bonds, you must first buy dollars. Let E_t be the nominal exchange rate between the pound and the dollar at the start of year t. For every £1, you get $\$E_t$. (This is represented by the arrow pointing downward in the figure.)

Let i_t^* denote the one-year nominal interest rate on US bonds (in dollars) in year t. When next year comes, you will have $\$E_t(1 + i_t^*)$. (This is represented by the arrow pointing to the right at the bottom of the figure.)

You will then have to convert your dollars back into pounds. If you expect the nominal exchange rate next year to be E_{t+1}^e (the superscript e indicates that it is an expectation: you do not yet know what the pound–dollar exchange rate will be in year $t + 1$), each dollar will be worth £$(1/E_{t+1}^e)$. So you can expect to have £$E_t(1 + i_t^*)(1/E_{t+1}^e)$ next year for every pound you invest now. (This is represented by the arrow pointing upward in the figure.) We shall look at the expression we just derived in more detail soon, but note its basic implication already: in assessing the attractiveness of US versus UK bonds, you cannot look just at the US interest rate and the UK interest rate; you must also assess what you think will happen to the pound–dollar exchange rate between this year and next. As a matter of fact, the decision about whether to invest abroad or at home depends on more than interest rates. It also depends on the expected movements in the exchange rate in the future. We will study exchange rates later (in Chapter 7).

Let's now assume that you and other financial investors care only about the expected rate of return and therefore want to hold only the asset with the highest expected rate of return. In that case, if both US bonds and UK bonds are to be held, they must have the same expected rate of return. In other words the following relation must hold:

$$(1 + i_t) = (E_t)(1 + i_t^*)\left(\frac{1}{E_{t+1}^e}\right)$$

Reorganising, we have

$$(1 + i_t) = (1 + i_t^*)\left(\frac{E_t}{E_{t+1}^e}\right) \qquad [6.2]$$

The word 'uncovered' is to distinguish this relation from another relation called the *covered interest parity* condition. The covered interest parity condition is derived by looking at the following choice:

- Buy and hold UK bonds for one year.
- Or buy dollars today, buy one-year US bonds with the proceeds and agree to sell the dollars for pounds a year ahead at a predetermined price, called the *forward exchange rate*.

The rate of return on these two alternatives, which can both be realised at no risk today, must be the same. The covered interest parity condition is a *riskless arbitrage* condition.

Equation (6.2) is called the **uncovered interest parity** (UIP) relation, or simply the **interest parity condition**.

The assumption that financial investors will hold only the bonds with the highest expected rate of return is obviously too strong, for two reasons:

- It ignores transaction costs. Going into and out of US bonds requires three separate transactions, each with a transaction cost.
- It ignores risk. The exchange rate a year from now is uncertain; holding US bonds is therefore more risky, in terms of pounds, than holding UK bonds.

Whether holding US bonds or UK bonds is more risky actually depends on which investors we are looking at. Holding UK bonds is more risky from the point of view of US investors. Holding US bonds is more risky from the point of view of UK investors. (Why?)

However, as a characterisation of capital movements among the major world financial markets (New York, Frankfurt, London and Tokyo), the assumption is not far off. Small changes in interest rates and rumours of impending appreciation or depreciation can lead to movements of billions of dollars within minutes. For the rich countries of the world, the assumption in equation (6.2) is a good approximation of reality. Other countries whose capital markets are smaller and less developed, or countries that have various forms of **capital controls**, have more leeway in choosing their domestic interest rate than is implied by equation (6.2). We shall return to this issue later (at the end of Chapter 7).

Interest rates and exchange rates

Let us get a better sense of what the interest parity condition implies. First, rewrite E_t/E^e as $1/[1 + (E_{t+1}^e - E_t)/E_t]$. Replacing in equation (6.2) gives

$$(1 + i_t) = \frac{(1 + i_t^*)}{[1 + (E_{t+1}^e - E_t)/E_t]} \qquad [6.3]$$

This gives us a relation between the domestic nominal interest rate, i_t, the foreign nominal interest rate, i_t^*, and the expected rate of appreciation of the domestic currency, $(E_{t+1}^e - E_t)/E_t$. As long as interest rates and the expected rate of appreciation are not too large – say below 20% per year – a good approximation to this equation is given by

$$i_t \approx i_t^* - \frac{E_{t+1}^e - E_t}{E_t} \qquad [6.4]$$

This is the form of the interest parity condition you must remember: arbitrage by investors implies that the domestic interest rate must be equal to the foreign interest rate minus the expected appreciation rate of the domestic currency.

Note that the expected appreciation rate of the domestic currency is also the expected depreciation rate of the foreign currency. So equation (6.4) can be equivalently stated as saying that the domestic interest rate must be equal to the foreign interest rate minus the expected depreciation rate of the foreign currency.

If the pound is expected to depreciate by 3% vis-à-vis the dollar, then the dollar is expected to appreciate by 3% vis-à-vis the pound.

Let us apply this equation to US bonds versus UK bonds. Suppose the one-year nominal interest rate is 1.0% in the USA, and it is 2.0% in the UK. Should you hold UK bonds or US bonds? The answer:

- It depends whether you expect the pound to depreciate vis-à-vis the dollar over the coming year by more or less than the difference between the US interest rate and the UK interest rate, 1.0% in this case (2.0% − 1.0%).
- If you expect the pound to depreciate by more than 1.0%, then, despite the fact that the interest rate is higher in the UK than in the USA, investing in UK bonds is less attractive than investing in US bonds. By holding UK bonds, you will get higher interest payments next year, but the pound will be worth less in terms of dollars next year, making investing in UK bonds less attractive than investing in US bonds.
- If you expect the pound to depreciate by less than 1.0% or even to appreciate, then the reverse holds, and UK bonds are more attractive than US bonds.

Looking at it another way: if the uncovered interest parity condition holds, and the US one-year interest rate is 1% lower than the UK interest rate, it must be that financial investors are expecting on average an appreciation of the dollar vis-à-vis the pound over the coming year of about 1%, and this is why they are willing to hold US bonds despite their lower interest rate. (Another application of the uncovered interest parity condition is provided in the Focus box 'Buying Brazilian bonds'.)

FOCUS
Buying Brazilian bonds

Let us go back to September 1993 because the very high interest rate in Brazil at the time helps make the point we want to get across here. Brazilian bonds are paying a monthly interest rate of 36.9%. This seems very attractive compared to the annual rate of 3% on US bonds corresponding to a monthly interest rate of about 0.2%. Shouldn't you buy Brazilian bonds?

The discussion in this chapter tells you that, in order to decide, you need one more crucial element: the expected rate of depreciation of the *cruzeiro* (the name of the Brazilian currency at the time; the currency is now called the *real*) in terms of dollars.

You need this information because, as we saw in equation (6.3), the return in dollars from investing in Brazilian bonds for a month is equal to 1 plus the Brazilian interest rate, i_t^*, divided by 1 plus the expected rate of depreciation of the cruzeiro relative to the dollar (E here is cruzeiros per \$1):

$$\frac{1 + i_1^*}{[1 + (E_{t+1}^e - E_t)/E_t]}$$

What rate of depreciation of the cruzeiro should you expect over the coming month? A reasonable assumption is to expect the rate of depreciation during the coming month to be equal to the rate of depreciation during last month. The dollar was worth 100,000 cruzeiros at the end of July 1993, and it was worth 134,600 cruzeiros at the end of August 1993, so the rate of appreciation of the dollar vis-à-vis the cruzeiro – equivalently, the rate of depreciation of the cruzeiro vis-à-vis the dollar – in August was 34.6%. If depreciation is expected to continue at the same rate in September as it did in August, the expected return from investing in Brazilian bonds for a month is

$$\frac{1.369}{1.346} = 1.017$$

The expected rate of return in dollars from holding Brazilian bonds is only (1.017 − 1) = 1.7% per month, not the 36.9% per month that initially looked so attractive. Note that 1.7% per month is still much higher than the monthly interest rate on US bonds (about 0.2%). But think of the risk and the transaction costs – all the elements we ignored when we wrote the arbitrage condition. When these are taken into account, you may well decide to keep your funds out of Brazil.

Figure 6.7

**Three-months' nominal
interest rates in the USA
and in the UK since 1970**

UK and US nominal interest rates
have largely moved together over
the past 40 years.

The arbitrage relation between interest rates and exchange rates, either in the form of equation (6.2) or equation (6.4), will play a central role in the following chapters. It suggests that, unless countries are willing to tolerate large movements in their exchange rates, domestic and foreign interest rates are likely to move very much together. Take the extreme case of two countries that commit to maintaining their bilateral exchange rates at a fixed value. If markets have faith in this commitment, they will expect the exchange rate to remain constant: the expected depreciation will then be equal to zero. In this case, the arbitrage condition implies that interest rates in the two countries will have to move exactly together. Most of the time, as we shall see, governments do not make such absolute commitments to maintain the exchange rate, but they often do try to avoid large movements in the exchange rate. This puts sharp limits on how much they can allow their interest rates to

If $E^e_{t+1} = E_t$, then the interest parity ➤ deviate from interest rates elsewhere in the world.
condition implies that $i_t = i^*_t$.

How much do nominal interest rates actually move together in major countries? Figure 6.7 plots the three-month nominal interest rate in the USA and the three-month nominal interest rate in the UK (both expressed at annual rates) since 1970. The figure shows that the movements are related but not identical. Interest rates were very high in both countries in the early 1980s, and they were high again – although much more so in the UK than in the

Meanwhile, do the following. Look at the back pages of a recent issue of *The Economist* for short-term interest rates in different countries relative to the currency of your country. Assume that uncovered interest parity holds. Which currencies are expected to appreciate against your currency?

USA – in the late 1990s. They have been low in both countries since the mid-1990s. At the same time, differences between the two have sometimes been quite large: in 1990, for example, the UK interest rate was nearly 7% higher than the US interest rate. In the coming chapters we shall return to why such differences emerge and what their implications may be. For the time being all you have studied so far in this chapter allows us to describe
➤ equilibrium in the goods market in an open economy.

6.3 THE *IS* RELATION IN AN OPEN ECONOMY

The domestic demand for goods and the demand for domestic goods sound close but are not the same. Part of domestic demand falls on foreign goods. Part of foreign demand falls on domestic goods.

When we were assuming that the economy was closed to trade, there was no need to distinguish between the domestic demand for goods and the demand for domestic goods: they were clearly the same thing. Now, we must distinguish between the two. Some domestic demand falls on foreign goods, and some of the demand for domestic goods comes from foreigners. Let's look at this distinction more closely.

The demand for domestic goods

In an open economy, the **demand for domestic goods** is given by

$$Z = C + I + G - \frac{IM}{\varepsilon} + X \qquad [6.5]$$

The first three terms – consumption, C, investment, I, and government spending, G – constitute the **domestic demand for goods**. If the economy were closed, $C + I + G$ would also be the demand for domestic goods. This is why, until now, we have only looked at $C + I + G$, but now we have to make two adjustments:

- First, we must subtract imports – that part of the domestic demand that falls on foreign goods rather than on domestic goods.

  Earlier (in Chapter 3), we ignored the real exchange rate and subtracted IM, not IM/ε. But that was a cheat; we did not want to have to talk about the real exchange rate – and complicate matters – so early in the text.

  We must be careful here: foreign goods are different from domestic goods, so we cannot just subtract the quantity of imports, IM. If we were to do so, we would be subtracting apples (foreign goods) from oranges (domestic goods). We must first express the value of imports in terms of domestic goods. This is what IM/ε in equation (6.5) stands for: recall from section 6.1 that ε, the real exchange rate, is defined as the price of domestic goods in terms of foreign goods. Equivalently, $1/\varepsilon$ is the price of foreign goods in terms of domestic goods. So $IM(1/\varepsilon)$ – or, equivalently, IM/ε – is the value of imports in terms of domestic goods.

  As an example, let us use the real exchange rate to express euro area goods in terms of UK goods. Assume that the importing country, the domestic economy, is the UK and it imports from the euro area (EA). Then

$$\frac{IM}{\varepsilon} = \frac{\text{EA goods}}{\dfrac{EP}{P^*}} = \text{EA goods}\frac{P^*}{EP} = \text{EA goods}\frac{\dfrac{\text{€}}{\text{units of EA goods}}}{\left(\dfrac{\text{€}}{\text{£}}\right)\dfrac{\text{£}}{\text{units of UK goods}}}$$

$$= \text{EA goods}\frac{\text{units of UK goods}}{\text{units of EA goods}} = [\text{EA goods}] \text{ expressed in units of UK goods} \qquad [6.6]$$

- Second, we must add exports – that part of the demand for domestic goods that comes from abroad. This is captured by the term X in equation (6.5). Note that exports are in units of domestic goods, like Z, C, I and G, thus you do not need to use the real exchange rate.

◀ Domestic demand for goods, $C + I + G$

Minus domestic demand for foreign goods (imports), IM/ε

Plus foreign demand for domestic goods (exports), X

Equals demand for domestic goods,

$C + I + G - IM/\varepsilon + X$

The determinants of *C*, *I* and *G*

Having listed the five components of demand, our next task is to specify their determinants. Let us start with the first three: C, I and G. Now that we are assuming that the economy is open, how should we modify our earlier descriptions of consumption, investment and government spending? The answer: not very much, if at all. How much consumers decide to spend still depends on their disposable income. While the real exchange rate surely affects the composition of consumption spending between domestic goods and foreign goods, there is no obvious reason why it should affect the overall level of consumption. The same is true of investment: the real exchange rate may affect whether firms buy domestic machines or foreign machines, but it should not affect total investment.

This is good news because it implies that we can use the descriptions of consumption, investment and government spending that we developed earlier. Therefore,

$$\text{Domestic demand: } C + I + G = C(Y - T) + I(Y, i) + G$$
$$\phantom{\text{Domestic demand: } C + I + G =} (+) \qquad (+, -)$$

We assume that consumption depends positively on disposable income, $Y - T$, and that investment depends positively on production, Y, and negatively on the interest rate, i. We continue to take government spending, G, as given.

The determinants of imports

Imports are the part of domestic demand that falls on foreign goods. What do they depend on? They clearly depend on domestic income: higher domestic income leads to a higher domestic demand for all goods, both domestic and foreign. So a higher domestic income leads to higher imports. Imports also clearly depend on the real exchange rate – the price of domestic goods in terms of foreign goods. The more expensive domestic goods are relative to foreign goods – equivalently, the cheaper foreign goods are relative to domestic goods – the higher the domestic demand for foreign goods. So a higher real exchange rate leads to higher imports. Thus, we write imports as

$$IM = IM(Y, \varepsilon) \qquad [6.7]$$
$$(+, +)$$

- An increase in domestic income, Y (equivalently, an increase in domestic output-income and output are still equal in an open economy), leads to an increase in imports. This positive effect of income on imports is captured by the positive sign under Y in equation (6.7).
- An increase in the real exchange rate, ε, leads to an increase in imports, IM. This positive effect of the real exchange rate on imports is captured by the positive sign under ε in equation (6.7). Remember from equation (6.6) that ε = units of EA goods for one unit of UK goods. Thus as ε goes up, consumers in the UK get more EA goods for each unit of UK goods. This means that EA goods have become cheaper and demand in the UK will shift towards imported goods.

The determinants of exports

Exports are the part of foreign demand that falls on domestic goods. What do they depend on? They depend on foreign income: higher foreign income means higher foreign demand for all goods, both foreign and domestic. So higher foreign income leads to higher exports. Exports also depend on the real exchange rate: the higher the price of domestic goods in terms of foreign goods, the lower the foreign demand for domestic goods. In other words, the higher the real exchange rate, the lower the exports.

Recall that asterisks refer to foreign ➤ variables.

Let Y^* denote foreign income (equivalently, foreign output). We therefore write exports as

$$X = X(Y^*, \varepsilon) \qquad [6.8]$$
$$(+, -)$$

- An increase in foreign income, Y^*, leads to an increase in exports.
- An increase in the real exchange rate, ε leads to a decrease in exports.

Putting the components together

Figure 6.8 puts together what we have learned so far. It plots the various components of demand against output, keeping constant all other variables (the interest rate, taxes, government spending, foreign output and the real exchange rate) that affect demand.

In Figure 6.8(a), the line DD plots domestic demand, $C + I + G$, as a function of output, Y. We have seen this relation between demand and output (from Chapter 3). The slope of the relation between demand and output is positive but less than 1. An increase in output – equivalently, an increase in income – increases demand but less than one-for-one. (In the absence of good reasons to the contrary, we draw the relation between demand and output, and the other relations in this chapter, as lines rather than curves. This is purely for convenience, and none of the discussions that follow depends on this assumption.)

For a given real exchange rate ε, IM/ε – the value of imports in terms of ➤ domestic goods – moves exactly with IM – the quantity of imports.

To arrive at the demand for domestic goods, we must first subtract imports. This is done in Figure 6.8(b), and it gives us the line AA. The line AA represents the domestic demand for

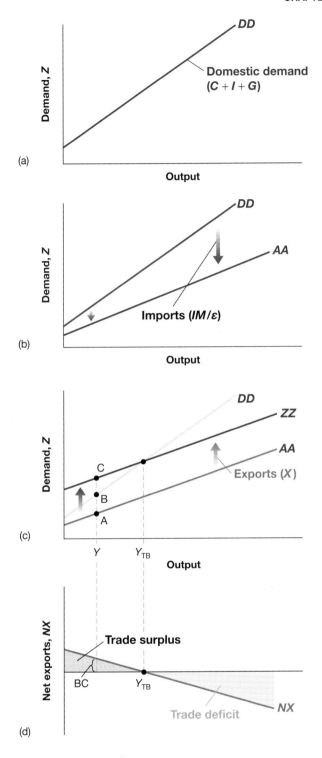

Figure 6.8

The demand for domestic goods and net exports

(a) The domestic demand for goods is an increasing function of income (output).

(b) and (c) The demand for domestic goods is obtained by subtracting the value of imports from domestic demand and then adding exports.

(d) The trade balance is a decreasing function of output.

domestic goods. The distance between *DD* and *AA* equals the value of imports, *IM/ε*. Because the quantity of imports increases with income, the distance between the two lines increases with income. We can establish two facts about line *AA*, which will be useful later in the chapter:

- *AA* is flatter than *DD*: as income increases, some of the additional domestic demand falls on foreign goods rather than on domestic goods. In other words, as income increases, the domestic demand for domestic goods increases less than total domestic demand.
- As long as some of the additional demand falls on domestic goods, *AA* has a positive slope: an increase in income leads to some increase in the demand for domestic goods.

Finally, we must add exports. This is done in Figure 6.8(c), and it gives us the line *ZZ*, which is above *AA*. The line *ZZ* represents the demand for domestic goods. The distance between *ZZ* and *AA* equals exports. Because exports do not depend on domestic income (they depend on foreign income), the distance between *ZZ* and *AA* is constant, which is why the two lines are parallel. Because *AA* is flatter than *DD*, *ZZ* is also flatter than *DD*.

From the information in Figure 6.8(c), we can characterise the behaviour of net exports – the difference between exports and imports – as a function of output. At output level *Y*, for example, exports are given by the distance AC and imports by the distance AB, so net exports ($X - IM/\varepsilon$) are given by the distance BC.

This relation between net exports and output is represented as the line *NX* (for net exports) in Figure 6.8(d). Net exports are a decreasing function of output: as output increases, imports increase, and exports are unaffected, so net exports decrease. Call Y_{TB} (TB for trade balance) the level of output at which the value of imports equals the value of exports, so that net exports are equal to 0. Levels of output above Y_{TB} lead to higher imports and to a trade deficit. Levels of output below Y_{TB} lead to lower imports and to a trade surplus.

> Recall that net exports is synonymous with trade balance. Positive net exports correspond to a trade surplus, whereas negative net exports correspond to a trade deficit.

To determine the equilibrium output in an open economy, you just have to recall what you learned earlier (see Chapter 5). The goods market is in equilibrium when domestic output equals the demand – both domestic and foreign – for domestic goods:

$$Y = Z$$

Collecting the relations we derived for the components of the demand for domestic goods, *Z*, we get

$$Y = C(Y - T) + I(Y, i) + G - IM(Y, \varepsilon)/\varepsilon + X(Y^*, \varepsilon) \qquad [6.9]$$
$$ (+) \qquad (+, -) \qquad (+, +) \qquad (+, -)$$

For the goods market to be in equilibrium, output (the left side of the equation) must be equal to the demand for domestic goods (the right side of the equation). The demand for domestic goods is equal to consumption, *C*, plus investment, *I*, plus government spending, *G*, minus the value of imports, IM/ε, plus exports, *X*:

- Consumption, *C*, depends positively on disposable income, $Y - T$.
- Investment, *I*, depends positively on output, *Y*, and negatively on the interest rate, *i*.
- Government spending, *G*, is taken as given.
- The quantity of imports, *IM*, depends positively on both output, *Y*, and the real exchange rate, ε. The value of imports in terms of domestic goods is equal to the quantity of imports divided by the real exchange rate.
- Exports, *X*, depend positively on foreign output, Y^*, and negatively on the real exchange rate, ε.

This equilibrium condition determines output as a function of all the variables we take as given, from taxes to the real exchange rate to foreign output. This is not a simple relation; Figure 6.9 represents it graphically, in a more user-friendly way.

In Figure 6.9(a), demand is measured on the vertical axis, and output (equivalently, production or income) is measured on the horizontal axis. The line *ZZ* plots demand as a function of output; this line simply replicates the line *ZZ* in Figure 6.8; *ZZ* is upward sloping but with slope less than 1.

Equilibrium output is at the point where demand equals output, at the intersection of the line *ZZ* and the 45° line: point A in the figure, with associated output level *Y*.

Figure 6.9(b) replicates Figure 6.8(d), drawing net exports as a decreasing function of output. There is, in general, no reason why the equilibrium level of output, *Y*, should be the same as the level of output at which trade is balanced, Y_{TB}. As we have drawn the figure, equilibrium output is associated with a trade deficit, equal to the distance BC. Note that we could have drawn it differently, so equilibrium output was associated instead with a trade surplus. The equilibrium level of output is given by the condition $Y = Z$. The level of output at which there is trade balance is given by the condition $X = IM/\varepsilon$. These are two different conditions.

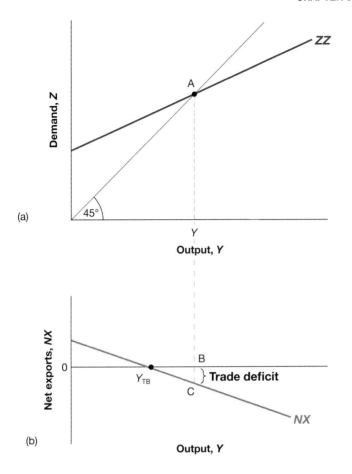

Figure 6.9

Equilibrium output and net exports

The goods market is in equilibrium when domestic output is equal to the demand for domestic goods. At the equilibrium level of output, the trade balance may show a deficit or a surplus.

It will be convenient, in what follows, to regroup the last two terms under 'net exports', defined as exports minus the value of imports:

$$NX(Y, Y^*, \varepsilon) \equiv X(Y^*, \varepsilon) - IM(Y, \varepsilon)/\varepsilon$$

It follows from our assumptions about imports and exports that net exports, *NX*, depend on domestic output, *Y*, foreign output, *Y**, and the real exchange rate, *ε*. An increase in domestic output increases imports, thus decreasing net exports. An increase in foreign output increases exports, thus increasing net exports. An increase in the real exchange rate leads to a decrease in net exports.

We shall assume, throughout the chapter, that an increase in the real exchange rate – a real appreciation – leads to a decrease in net exports (this condition is called the Marshall–Lerner condition, as we will learn in Chapter 7).

Using this definition of net exports, we can rewrite the equilibrium condition as

$$Y = C(Y - T) + I(Y, i) + G + NX(Y, Y^*, \varepsilon) \qquad [6.10]$$
$$ (+) \qquad (+, -) \qquad (-, +, -)$$

For our purposes, the main implication of equation (6.10) is that both the interest rate and the real exchange rate affect demand and, in turn, equilibrium output:

- An increase in the interest rate leads to a decrease in investment spending and, as a result, to a decrease in the demand for domestic goods. This leads, through the multiplier, to a decrease in output.
- An increase in the exchange rate leads to a shift in demand toward foreign goods and, as a result, to a decrease in net exports. The decrease in net exports decreases the demand for domestic goods. This leads, through the multiplier, to a decrease in output.

For the remainder of the chapter, we shall make a simplification to equation (6.10):

- As we are still studying the short run, when prices are assumed to be constant, the real exchange rate, $\varepsilon = EP/P^*$, and the nominal exchange rate, E, move together. If P and P^* are fixed, a decrease in the nominal exchange rate – a nominal depreciation – leads, one-for-one, to a decrease in the real exchange rate – a real depreciation. Conversely, an increase in the nominal exchange rate – a nominal appreciation – leads, one-for-one, to an increase in the real exchange rate – a real appreciation. If, for notational convenience, we choose P and P^* so that $P/P^* = 1$ (and we can do so because both are index numbers), then $\varepsilon = E$, and we can replace ε by E in equation (6.10).

$P = P^* = I$, so $\varepsilon = E$

With this simplification, equation (6.10) becomes

$$Y = C(Y - T) + I(Y, i) + G + NX(Y, Y^*, E)$$

In words: goods market equilibrium implies that output depends negatively on both the interest rate and the exchange rate.

6.4 THE *LM* RELATION IN AN OPEN ECONOMY

When we looked at financial markets in the IS–LM model for a closed economy, we assumed that people choose between two financial assets only, money and bonds. Now that we are looking at a financially open economy, we must also take into account the fact that people have a choice between domestic bonds and foreign bonds. Let us consider each choice in turn.

Money versus bonds

When we looked at the determination of the interest rate in the *IS–LM* model earlier (see Chapter 5), we wrote the condition that the supply of money be equal to the demand for money as

$$\frac{M}{P} = YL(i) \qquad [6.11]$$

We took the real supply of money (the left side of equation (6.11)) as given. We assumed that the real demand for money (the right side of equation (6.11)) depended on the level of transactions in the economy, measured by real output, Y, and on the opportunity cost of holding money rather than bonds – that is, the interest rate on bonds, i.

How should we change this characterisation now that the economy is open? You will like the answer: not very much, if at all.

In an open economy, the demand for domestic money is still mostly a demand by domestic residents. There is not much reason for, say, the residents of the UK to hold euros as currency or demand deposits. Transactions in the UK require payment in pounds, not in euros. If residents of the UK want to hold euro-denominated assets, they are better off holding euro bonds, which have the advantage of paying a positive interest rate. Thus the demand for money by domestic residents in any country still depends on the same factors as before: their level of transactions, which we measure by domestic real output, and the opportunity cost of holding money, the interest rate on bonds.

Therefore, we can still use equation (6.11) to think about the determination of the interest rate in an open economy. The interest rate must be such that the supply of money and the demand for money are equal. An increase in the money supply leads to a decrease in the interest rate. An increase in money demand, say, as a result of an increase in output, leads to an increase in the interest rate.

Domestic bonds versus foreign bonds

As we look at the choice between domestic bonds and foreign bonds, we shall rely on the assumption we introduced in section 6.2: financial investors, domestic or foreign, go for the highest expected rate of return. This implies that, in equilibrium, both domestic bonds and foreign bonds must have the same expected rate of return; otherwise, investors would be willing to hold only one or the other, but not both, and this could not be an equilibrium. (Like most other economic relations, this relation is only an approximation to reality and does not always hold. More on this in the Focus box 'Sudden stops, the strong dollar and limits to the interest parity condition' in section 6.5.)

As we saw earlier (equation (6.2)), this assumption implies that the following arbitrage relation – the interest parity condition – must hold:

$$(1 + i_t) = (1 + i_t^*)\left(\frac{E_t}{E_{t+1}^e}\right)$$

where i_t is the domestic interest rate, i_t^* is the foreign interest rate, E_t is the current exchange rate and E_{t+1}^e is the future expected exchange rate. The left side gives the return, in terms of domestic currency, from holding domestic bonds. The right side gives the expected return, also in terms of domestic currency, from holding foreign bonds. In equilibrium, the two expected returns must be equal.

Multiply both sides by E_{t+1}^e and reorganise, to get

$$E_t = \frac{1 + i_t}{1 + i_t^*} E_{t+1}^e \qquad [6.12]$$

For now, we shall take the expected future exchange rate as given and denote it as $\bar{E}^e$ (we shall relax this assumption in Chapter 7). Under this assumption, and dropping time indexes, the interest parity condition becomes

$$E = \frac{1 + i}{1 + i^*} \bar{E}^e \qquad [6.13]$$

> ◄ The presence of E_t comes from the fact that, in order to buy the foreign bond, you must first exchange domestic currency for foreign currency. The presence of E_{t+1}^e comes from the fact that, in order to bring the funds back next period, you will have to exchange foreign currency for domestic currency.

This relation tells us that the current exchange rate depends on the domestic interest rate, on the foreign interest rate and on the expected future exchange rate:

- An increase in the domestic interest rate leads to an increase in the exchange rate (an appreciation).
- An increase in the foreign interest rate leads to a decrease in the exchange rate (a depreciation).
- An increase in the expected future exchange rate leads to an increase in the current exchange rate (an appreciation).

This relation plays a central role in the real world and will play a central role in this chapter. To understand the relation further, consider the following example.

Consider financial investors – investors, for short – choosing between UK bonds and Japanese bonds. Suppose that the one-year interest rate on UK bonds is 5% and the one-year interest rate on Japanese bonds is also 5%. Suppose that the current exchange rate is 100 (£1 is worth 100 yen), and the expected exchange rate a year from now is also 100. Under these assumptions, both UK and Japanese bonds have the same expected return in pounds, and the interest parity condition holds.

Suppose that investors now expect the exchange rate to be 10% higher a year from now, so E^e is now equal to 110. At an unchanged current exchange rate, UK bonds are now much more attractive than Japanese bonds: UK bonds offer an interest rate of 5% in pounds. Japanese bonds still offer an interest rate of 5% in yen, but yen a year from today are now expected to be worth 10% less in terms of pounds. In terms of pounds, the return on Japanese bonds is therefore 5% (the interest rate) – 10%.

So what will happen? At the initial exchange rate of 100, investors want to shift out of Japanese bonds into UK bonds. To do so, they must first sell Japanese bonds for yen, then sell yen for pounds, and then use the pounds to buy UK bonds. As investors sell yen and buy pounds, the pound appreciates. By how much? Equation (6.13) gives us the answer: $E = (1.05/1.05)110 = 110$. The current exchange rate must increase in the same proportion as the expected future exchange rate. Put another way, the pound must appreciate today by

10%. When it has appreciated by 10%, so that $E = \bar{E}^e = 110$, the expected returns on UK and Japanese bonds are again equal, and there is equilibrium in the foreign exchange market.

Suppose instead that, as a result of a UK monetary contraction, the UK interest rate increases from 5% to 8%. Assume that the Japanese interest rate remains unchanged at 5%, and that the expected future exchange rate remains unchanged at 100. At an unchanged current exchange rate, UK bonds are now again much more attractive than Japanese bonds. UK bonds yield a return of 8% in pounds. Japanese bonds give a return of 5% in yen and – because the exchange rate is expected to be the same next year as it is today – an expected return of 5% in pounds as well.

So what will happen? Again, at the initial exchange rate of 100, investors want to shift out of Japanese bonds into UK bonds. As they do so, they sell yen for pounds, and the pound appreciates. By how much? Equation (6.13) gives the answer: $E = (1.08/1.05)100 \approx 103$. The current exchange rate increases by approximately 3%. Why 3%? Think of what happens when the pound appreciates. If, as we have assumed, investors do not change their expectation of the future exchange rate, then the more the pound appreciates today, the more investors expect it to depreciate in the future (as it is expected to return to the same value in the future). When the pound has appreciated by 3% today, investors expect it to depreciate by 3% during the coming year. Equivalently, they expect the yen to appreciate vis-à-vis the pound by 3% over the coming year. The expected rate of return in pounds from holding Japanese bonds is therefore 5% (the yen interest rate) + 3% (the expected yen appreciation), or 8%. This expected rate of return is the same as the rate of return on holding UK bonds, so there is equilibrium in the foreign exchange market.

Note that our argument relies heavily on the assumption that, when the interest rate changes, the expected exchange rate remains unchanged. This implies that an appreciation today leads to an expected depreciation in the future – because the exchange rate is expected to return to the same, unchanged, value. Later (see Chapter 7) we shall relax the assumption that the future exchange rate is fixed. But the basic conclusion will remain: an increase in the domestic interest rate relative to the foreign interest rate leads to an appreciation.

Figure 6.10 plots the relation between the domestic interest rate, i, and the exchange rate, E, implied by equation (6.13) – the interest parity relation. The relation is drawn for a given expected future exchange rate, $\bar{E}^e$, and a given foreign interest rate, i^*, and is represented by an upward-sloping line: the higher the domestic interest rate, the higher the exchange rate. Equation (6.13) also implies that when the domestic interest rate is equal to the foreign interest rate ($i = i^*$), the exchange rate is equal to the expected future exchange rate ($E = \bar{E}^e$). This implies that the line corresponding to the interest parity condition goes through point A in the figure.

> Make sure you understand the argument. Why doesnt the pound appreciate by, say, 20%?

> What happens to the line if i^* increases? What happens to the line if $\bar{E}^e$ increases?

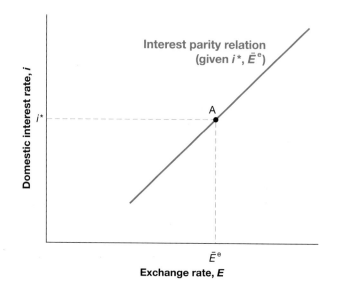

Figure 6.10

The relation between the interest rate and exchange rate implied by interest parity

A higher domestic interest rate leads to a higher exchange rate – an appreciation.

6.5 PUTTING GOODS AND FINANCIAL MARKETS TOGETHER IN AN OPEN ECONOMY

We now have the elements we need to understand the movements of output, the interest rate and the exchange rate.

Goods market equilibrium implies that output depends, among other factors, on the interest rate and the exchange rate:

$$Y = C(Y - T) + I(Y, i) + G + NX(Y, Y^*, E)$$

The interest rate, in turn, is determined by the equality of money supply and money demand:

$$\frac{M}{P} = YL(i)$$

And the interest parity condition implies a positive relation between the domestic interest rate and the exchange rate:

$$E = \frac{1 + i}{1 + i^*} \bar{E}^e$$

Together, these three relations determine output, the interest rate and the exchange rate. Working with three relations is not very easy, but we can easily reduce them to two by using the interest parity condition to eliminate the exchange rate in the goods market equilibrium relation. Doing this gives us the following two equations, the open-economy versions of our familiar *IS* and *LM* relations:

$$IS: \quad Y = C(Y - T) + I(Y, i) + G + NX\left(Y, Y^*, \frac{1 + i}{1 + i^*} \bar{E}^e \right)$$

$$LM: \frac{M}{P} = YL(i)$$

Take the *IS* relation first and consider the effects of an increase in the interest rate on output. An increase in the interest rate now has two effects:

- The first effect, which was already present in a closed economy, is the direct effect on investment: a higher interest rate leads to a decrease in investment, a decrease in the demand for domestic goods and a decrease in output.
- The second effect, which is present only in the open economy, is the effect through the exchange rate: an increase in the domestic interest rate leads to an increase in the exchange rate – an appreciation. The appreciation, which makes domestic goods more expensive relative to foreign goods, leads to a decrease in net exports and, therefore, to a decrease in the demand for domestic goods and a decrease in output.

Both effects work in the same direction: an increase in the interest rate decreases demand directly and indirectly – through the adverse effect of the exchange rate appreciation on demand.

The *IS* relation between the interest rate and output is drawn in Figure 6.11(a), for given values of all the other variables in the relation – namely T, G, Y^*, i^* and E^e_{t+1}. The *IS* curve is downward sloping: an increase in the interest rate leads to lower output. The curve looks very much the same in an open economy as in a closed economy, but it hides a more complex relation than before: the interest rate affects output not only directly but also indirectly through the exchange rate.

◄ An increase in the interest rate leads, both directly and indirectly (through the exchange rate), to a decrease in output.

The *LM* relation is exactly the same in an open economy as in a closed economy. The *LM* curve is upward sloping. For a given value of the real money stock, M/P, an increase in output leads to an increase in the demand for money and to an increase in the equilibrium interest rate.

Equilibrium in the goods and financial markets is attained at point A in Figure 6.11(a), with output level Y and interest rate i. The equilibrium value of the exchange rate cannot be read directly from the graph, but it is easily obtained from Figure 6.11(b), which replicates Figure 6.10, and gives the exchange rate associated with a given interest rate. The exchange rate associated with the equilibrium interest rate, i, is equal to E.

FOCUS
Sudden stops, the strong dollar and the limits to the interest parity condition

The interest parity condition assumes that financial investors care only about expected returns. As we discussed in section 6.2, investors care not only about returns but also about risk and about liquidity – how easy it is to buy or sell an asset.

Much of the time, we can ignore these other factors. Sometimes, however, these factors play a big role in investors' decisions and in determining exchange rate movements.

Perceptions of risk often play an important role in the decisions of large financial investors – for example, pension funds – to invest or not to invest at all in a country. Sometimes the perception that risk has decreased leads many foreign investors to simultaneously buy assets in a country, leading to a large increase in demand for the assets of that country. Sometimes the perception that risk has increased leads the same investors to want to sell all the assets they have in that country, no matter what the interest rate. These episodes, which have affected many Latin American and Asian emerging economies, are known as sudden stops. During these episodes, the interest parity

condition fails, and the exchange rate may decrease a lot, without any change in domestic or foreign interest rates.

Large countries can also be affected. For example, the appreciation of the dollar in the 1990s came not so much from an increase in US interest rates over foreign interest rates, as from an increased foreign demand for dollar assets at a given interest rate. Many private foreign investors wanted to have some proportion of their wealth in US assets: they perceived US assets as being relatively safe. Many foreign central banks wanted to hold a large proportion of their reserves in US T-bills. The reason they did so is because the T-bill market is very liquid, so they could buy and sell T-bills without affecting the price. This very high demand for US assets, at a given interest rate, was behind the strong dollar in the 1990s. Even while US interest rates are relatively low, foreign investors are still eager to increase their holdings of US assets, and thus to finance the large US trade deficit. How long they are willing to do so will determine what happens to the dollar and to the US trade balance.

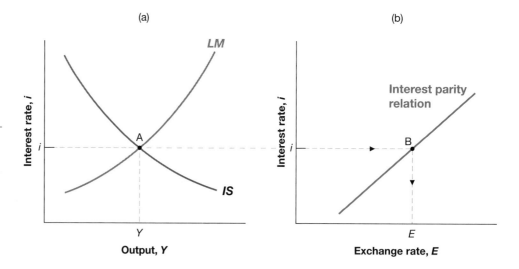

Figure 6.11

The *IS–LM* model in an open economy

An increase in the interest rate reduces output both directly and indirectly (through the exchange rate): the *IS* curve is downward sloping. Given the real money stock, an increase in output increases the interest rate: the *LM* curve is upward sloping.

Equilibrium output and the equilibrium interest rate are given by the intersection of the *IS* and the *LM* curves. Given the foreign interest rate and the expected future exchange rate, the equilibrium interest rate determines the equilibrium exchange rate.

Let us summarise: we have derived the *IS* and the *LM* relations for an open economy.

- The *IS* curve is downward sloping – An increase in the interest rate leads directly and indirectly (through the exchange rate) to a decrease in demand and a decrease in output.
- The *LM* curve is upward sloping – An increase in income increases the demand for money, leading to an increase in the equilibrium interest rate.

SUMMARY

- Openness in goods markets allows people and firms to choose between domestic goods and foreign goods. Openness in financial markets allows financial investors to hold domestic financial assets or foreign financial assets.

- The nominal exchange rate is the price of the domestic currency in terms of foreign currency. From the viewpoint of the UK, the nominal exchange rate between the UK and the euro area is the price of a pound in terms of euros.

- A nominal appreciation (an appreciation, for short) is an increase in the price of the domestic currency in terms of foreign currency. In other words, it corresponds to an increase in the exchange rate. A nominal depreciation (a depreciation, for short) is a decrease in the price of the domestic currency in terms of foreign currency. It corresponds to a decrease in the exchange rate.

- The real exchange rate is the relative price of domestic goods in terms of foreign goods. It is equal to the nominal exchange rate multiplied by the domestic price level divided by the foreign price level.

- A real appreciation is an increase in the relative price of domestic goods in terms of foreign goods – i.e. an increase in the real exchange rate. A real depreciation is a decrease in the relative price of domestic goods in terms of foreign goods – i.e. a decrease in the real exchange rate.

- The multilateral real exchange rate, or real exchange rate for short, is a weighted average of bilateral real exchange rates, with the weight for each foreign country equal to its share in trade.

- In an open economy, the demand for domestic goods is equal to the domestic demand for goods (consumption plus investment plus government spending) minus the value of imports (in terms of domestic goods) plus exports.

- In an open economy, an increase in domestic demand leads to a smaller increase in output than it would in a closed economy because some of the additional demand falls on imports. For the same reason, an increase in domestic demand also leads to a deterioration of the trade balance.

KEY TERMS

openness in goods markets 108

openness in financial markets 108

openness in factor markets 108

tariffs 108

tradable goods 110

real exchange rate 111

nominal exchange rate 111

appreciation (nominal) 112

depreciation (nominal) 112

fixed exchange rate 112

revaluation 112

devaluation 112

real appreciation 114

real depreciation 114

bilateral exchange rate 114

multilateral exchange rate 114

multilateral real exchange rate 115

foreign exchange 116

balance of payments 117

above the line, below the line 117

current account 117

investment income 117

net transfers received 117

current account balance 117

current account surplus 117

current account deficit 117

capital account transactions 118

net capital flows 118

capital account balance 118

capital account surplus 118

capital account deficit 118

statistical discrepancy 118

gross domestic product (GDP) 119

gross national product (GNP) 119

uncovered interest parity 120

interest parity condition 120

capital controls 120

demand for domestic goods 123

domestic demand for goods 123

QUESTIONS AND PROBLEMS

QUICK CHECK

1. *Using the information in this chapter, label each of the following statements true, false or uncertain. Explain briefly.*

a. The national income identity implies that budget deficits cause trade deficits.

b. Opening the economy to trade tends to increase the multiplier because an increase in expenditure leads to more exports.

c. If the trade deficit is equal to zero, then the domestic demand for goods and the demand for domestic goods are equal.

d. A real depreciation leads to an immediate improvement in the trade balance.

e. A small open economy can reduce its trade deficit through fiscal contraction at a smaller cost in output than can a large open economy.

f. While the export ratio can be larger than one – as it is in Singapore – the same cannot be true of the ratio of imports to GDP.

g. That a rich country like Japan has such a small ratio of imports to GDP is clear evidence of an unfair playing field for European exporters to Japan.

h. Given the definition of the exchange rate adopted in this chapter, if the euro is the domestic currency and the dollar the foreign currency, a nominal exchange rate of 0.75 means that €1 is worth $0.75.

i. A real appreciation means that domestic goods become less expensive relative to foreign goods.

2. Real and nominal exchange rates and inflation

Using the definition of the real exchange rate (and Propositions 7 and 8 in Appendix 1 at the end of the book), you can show that

$$\frac{\varepsilon_t - \varepsilon_{t-1}}{\varepsilon_{t-1}} = \frac{E_t - E_{t-1}}{E_{t-1}} + \pi_t - \pi_t^*$$

In words: the percentage real appreciation equals the percentage nominal appreciation plus the difference between domestic and foreign inflation.

a. If domestic inflation is higher than foreign inflation, but the domestic country has a fixed exchange rate, what happens to the real exchange rate over time? Assume that the Marshall–Lerner condition holds. What happens to the trade balance over time? Explain in words.

b. Suppose the real exchange rate is constant – say, at the level required for net exports (or the current account) to equal zero. In this case, if domestic inflation is higher than foreign inflation, what must happen to the nominal exchange rate over time?

DIG DEEPER

3. *Consider a world with three equal-sized economies (A, B and C) and three goods (clothes, cars and computers). Assume that consumers in all three economies want to spend an equal amount on all three goods.*

The value of production of each good in the three economies is given below.

	A	B	C
Clothes	10	0	5
Cars	5	10	0
Computers	0	5	10

a. What is GDP in each economy? If the total value of GDP is consumed and no country borrows from abroad, how much will consumers in each economy spend on each of the goods?

b. If no country borrows from abroad, what will be the trade balance in each country? What will be the pattern of trade in this world (i.e., which good will each country export and to whom)?

c. Given your answer to part (b), will country A have a zero trade balance with country B? With country C? Will any country have a zero trade balance with any other country?

d. The USA has a large trade deficit. It has a trade deficit with each of its major trading partners, but the deficit is much larger with some countries (e.g. China) than with others. Suppose the USA eliminates its overall trade deficit (with the world as a whole). Do you expect it to have a zero trade balance with every one of its trading partners? Does the especially large trade deficit with China necessarily indicate that China does not allow US goods to compete on an equal basis with Chinese goods?

4. Net exports and foreign demand

a. Suppose there is an increase in foreign output. Show the effect on the domestic economy (i.e. replicate Figure 6.4). What is the effect on domestic output? On domestic net exports?

b. If the interest rate remains constant, what will happen to domestic investment? If taxes are fixed, what will happen to the domestic budget deficit?

c. Using equation (6.5), what must happen to private saving? Explain.

d. Foreign output does not appear in equation (6.5), yet it evidently affects net exports. Explain how this is possible.

5. Eliminating a trade deficit

a. Consider an economy with a trade deficit (*NX* < 0) and with output equal to its natural level. Suppose that, even though output may deviate from its natural level in the short run, it returns to its natural level in the medium run. Assume that the natural level is unaffected by the real exchange rate. What must happen to the real exchange rate over the medium run to eliminate the trade deficit (i.e., to increase *NX* to 0)?

b. Now write down the national income identity. Assume again that output returns to its natural level in the medium run. If *NX* increases to 0, what must happen to domestic demand (*C* + *I* + *G*) in the medium run? What government policies are available to reduce domestic demand in the medium run? Identify which components of domestic demand each of these policies affect.

EXPLORE FURTHER

6. *Retrieve the nominal exchange rates between Japan and the USA from the Internet. A useful and free Canadian site that allows you to construct graphs online is the Pacific Exchange Rate Service (http://fx.sauder.ubc.ca), provided by Werner Antweiler at the Sauder School of Business, University of British Columbia.*

a. Plot the yen versus the dollar since 1979. During which time period(s) did the yen appreciate? During which period(s) did the yen depreciate?

b. Given the current Japanese slump (although there are some encouraging signs at the time of writing), one way of increasing demand would be to make Japanese goods more attractive. Does this require an appreciation or a depreciation of the yen?

c. What has happened to the yen during the past few years? Has it appreciated or depreciated? Is this good or bad for Japan?

7. Saving and investment throughout the world

Retrieve the most recent World Economic Outlook (WEO) from the website of the International Monetary Fund (www.imf.org). In the Statistical Appendix, find the table titled 'Summary of Sources and Uses of World Saving', which lists saving and investment (as a percentage of GDP) around the world. Use the data for the most recent year available to answer parts (a) and (b).

a. Does world saving equal investment? (You may ignore small statistical discrepancies.) Offer some intuition for your answer.

b. How does US saving compare to US investment? How is the USA able to finance its investment? (We explain this explicitly in the next chapter, but your intuition should help you figure it out now.)

Log on to **MyEconLab** and complete the studyplan exercises for this chapter to see how much you have learnt, and where you need to revise most.

MyEconLab

FURTHER READING

- If you want to learn more about international trade and international economics, read the very good textbook by Paul Krugman and Maurice Obstfeld, *International Economics, Theory and Policy* (New York: Pearson Addison-Wesley, 7th edn, 2007).

- If you want to know current exchange rates between nearly any pair of currencies in the world, look at the currency converter at *www.oanda.com*.

- A good discussion of the relation among trade deficits, budget deficits, private saving and investment is given in Barry Bosworth, *Saving and Investment in a Global Economy* (Washington, DC: Brookings Institution, 1993).

- A good discussion of the US trade deficit and its implications for the future is given in William Cline, *The United States as a Debtor Nation* (Washington, DC: Peterson Institute, 2005).

Chapter 7

OUTPUT, THE INTEREST RATE AND THE EXCHANGE RATE

Earlier (see Chapter 5), we introduced the *IS–LM* model to understand the movements of output and the interest rate in a closed economy. There, we also saw how policy makers can affect the equilibrium levels of output and the interest rate, through fiscal policy, monetary policy or a mix of the two. We also introduced an open economy version of the *IS–LM* model (see Chapter 6). That model allows us to characterise the joint movements of output, the interest rate and the exchange rate in an open economy. In this chapter we ask what the effects of fiscal and monetary policies are on economic activity, when both goods and financial markets are open to the rest of the world.

This chapter has six sections:

- Section 7.1 shows the effects of domestic shocks and foreign shocks on the domestic economy's output and trade balance.

- Sections 7.2 and 7.3 look at the effects of a real depreciation on output and the trade balance.

- Section 7.4 gives an alternative description of the equilibrium, which shows the close connection between saving, investment and the trade balance.

- Section 7.5 looks at the role of policy under flexible exchange rates.

- Section 7.6 looks at the role of policy under fixed exchange rates.

7.1 INCREASES IN DEMAND, DOMESTIC OR FOREIGN

How do changes in demand affect output in an open economy? Let's start with an old favorite – an increase in government spending – then turn to a new exercise, the effects of an increase in foreign demand.

Increases in domestic demand

Suppose the economy is in a recession and the government decides to increase government spending in order to increase domestic demand and output. What will be the effects on output and on the trade balance?

The answer is given in Figure 7.1. Before the increase in government spending, demand is given by ZZ in Figure 7.1(a), and the equilibrium is at point A, where output equals Y. Let's assume that trade is initially balanced – even though, as we have seen, there is no reason why this should be true in general. So, in Figure 7.1(b), $Y = Y_{TB}$

What happens if the government increases spending by ΔG? At any level of output, demand is higher by ΔG, shifting the demand relation up by ΔG from ZZ to ZZ'. The equilibrium point moves from A to A', and output increases from Y to Y'. The increase in output is larger than the increase in government spending: there is a multiplier effect.

So far, the story sounds the same as the story for a closed economy (see Chapter 3). However, there are two important differences:

- There is now an effect on the trade balance. Because government spending enters neither the exports relation nor the imports relation directly, the relation between net exports and output in Figure 7.1(b) does not shift. So the increase in output from Y to Y' leads to a trade deficit equal to BC: imports go up, and exports do not change.
- Not only does government spending now generate a trade deficit, but also the effect of government spending on output is smaller than it would be in a closed economy. Recall

◄ We start with the goods market; the conclusions we derive here will still largely be correct when we introduce financial markets and labour markets later on.

◄ Starting from trade balance, an increase in government spending leads to a trade deficit.

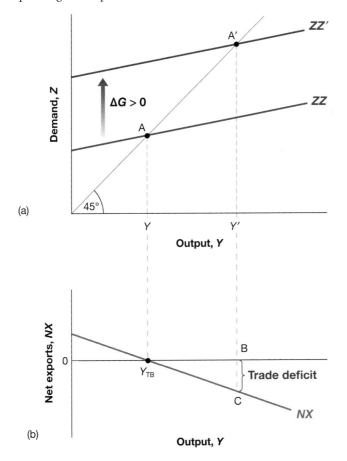

(a)

(b)

Figure 7.1

The effects of an increase in government spending (1)

An increase in government spending leads to an increase in output and to a trade deficit.

(from Chapter 3) that the smaller the slope of the demand relation, the smaller the multiplier (for example, if ZZ were horizontal, the multiplier would be 1). And recall (from Chapter 6) that the demand relation, ZZ, is flatter than the demand relation in the closed economy, DD. This means the muitiplier is smaller in the open economy.

An increase in government spending ➤ increases output. The multiplier is smaller than in a closed economy.

The trade deficit and the smaller multiplier have the same cause: because the economy is open, an increase in demand now falls not only on domestic goods, but also on foreign goods. So, when income increases, the effect on the **demand for domestic goods** is smaller than it would be in a closed economy, leading to a smaller multiplier. And, because some of the increase in demand falls on imports – and exports are unchanged – the result is a trade deficit.

The smaller multiplier and the trade ➤ deficit have the same cause: some domestic demand falls on foreign goods.

These two implications are important. In an open economy, an increase in domestic demand has a smaller effect on output than in a closed economy, and an adverse effect on the trade balance. Indeed, the more open the economy, the smaller the effect on output and the larger the adverse effect on the trade balance. Take Belgium, for example. As we saw earlier (in Chapter 6), Belgium's ratio of exports to GDP is very high. It is also true that Belgium's ratio of imports to GDP is very high. When domestic demand increases in Belgium, much of the increase in demand is likely to result in an increase in the demand for foreign goods rather than an increase in the demand for domestic goods. The effect of an increase in government spending is therefore likely to be a large increase in Belgium's trade deficit and only a small increase in its output, making domestic demand expansion a rather unattractive policy for Belgium. Even for the USA, which has a much lower import ratio, an increase in demand will be associated with a worsening of the trade balance.

Increases in foreign demand

Consider now an increase in foreign output, that is, an increase in Y^*. This could be due to an increase in foreign government spending, G^* – the policy change we just analysed, but now taking place abroad. But we do not need to know where the increase in Y^* comes from to analyse its effects on the domestic economy.

Figure 7.2 shows the effects of an increase in foreign activity on domestic output and the trade balance. The initial demand for domestic goods is given by ZZ in Figure 7.2(a). The equilibrium is at point A, with output level Y. Let us again assume trade is balanced, so that in Figure 7.2(b) the net exports associated with Y are equal to zero so that $Y = Y_{TB}$.

It will be useful here to refer to the line which shows the **domestic demand for goods** $C + I + G$ as a function of income. This line is drawn as DD. Recall (from Chapter 6) that DD is steeper than ZZ. The difference between ZZ and DD equal net exports, so that if trade is balanced at point A, then ZZ and DD intersect at point A.

DD is the domestic demand for goods. ➤ ZZ is the demand for domestic goods. The difference between the two is equal to the trade deficit.

Now consider the effects of an increase in foreign output, ΔY^* (for the moment, ignore the line DD; we only need it later). Higher foreign output means higher foreign demand, including higher foreign demand for domestic goods. So the direct effect of the increase in foreign output is an increase in US exports by some amount, which we shall denote by ΔX.

- For a given level of output, this increase in exports leads to an increase in the demand for US goods by ΔX, so the line showing the demand for domestic goods as a function of output shifts up by ΔX, from ZZ to ZZ′.
- For a given level of output, net exports go up by ΔX. So the line showing net exports as a function of output in Figure 7.2(b) also shifts up by ΔX, from NX to NX′.

The new equilibrium is at point A′ in Figure 7.2(a), with output level Y′. The increase in foreign output leads to an increase in domestic output. The channel is clear: higher foreign output leads to higher exports of domestic goods, which increases domestic output and the domestic demand for goods through the multiplier.

What happens to the trade balance? We know that exports go up. But could it be that the increase in domestic output leads to such a large increase in imports that the trade balance actually deteriorates? No: the trade balance must improve. To see why, note that, when foreign demand increases, the demand for domestic goods shifts up from ZZ to ZZ′; but the line DD,

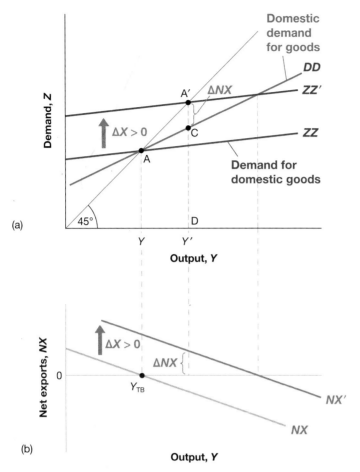

Figure 7.2

The effects of an increase in foreign demand (1)

An increase in foreign demand leads to an increase in output and to a trade surplus.

which gives the domestic demand for goods as a function of output, does not shift. At the new equilibrium level of output Y, domestic demand is given by the distance DC, and the demand for domestic goods is given by DA. Net exports are therefore given by the distance CA′ – which, because *DD* is necessarily below *ZZ′*, is necessarily positive. Thus, while imports increase, the increase does not offset the increase in exports, and the trade balance improves.

◄ *Y** directly affects exports and so enters the relation between the demand for domestic goods and output. An increase in *Y** shifts *ZZ* up.

*Y** does not affect either domestic consumption, domestic investment or domestic government spending directly, and so it does not enter the relation between the domestic demand for goods and output. An increase in *Y** does not shift *DD*.

Fiscal policy revisited

We have derived two basic results so far:

● An increase in domestic demand leads to an increase in domestic output, but leads also to a deterioration of the trade balance. (We looked at an increase in government spending, but the results would have been the same for a decrease in taxes, an increase in consumer spending, and so on.)

◄ An increase in foreign output increases domestic output and improves the trade balance.

● An increase in foreign demand (which could come from the same types of changes taking place abroad) leads to an increase in domestic output and an improvement in the trade balance.

These results, in turn, have two important implications.

First, and most obviously, they imply that shocks to demand in one country affect all other countries. The stronger the trade links between countries, the stronger the interactions, and the more countries will move together.

Second, these interactions complicate the task of policy makers, especially in the case of fiscal policy. Let us explore this argument more closely.

Start with the following observation: governments do not like to run trade deficits, and for good reasons. The main reason: a country that consistently runs a trade deficit accumulates debt vis-à-vis the rest of the world, and therefore has to pay steadily higher interest payments to the rest of the world. Thus, it is no wonder that countries prefer increases in foreign demand (which improve the trade balance) to increases in domestic demand (which worsen the trade balance).

But these preferences can have disastrous implications. Consider a group of countries, all doing a large amount of trade with each other, so that an increase in demand in any one country falls largely on the goods produced in the other countries. Suppose all these countries are in recession and each has roughly balanced trade to start. In this case, each country might be very reluctant to take measures to increase domestic demand. Were it to do so, the result might be a small increase in output but also a large trade deficit. Instead, each country might just wait for the other countries to increase their demand. This way, it gets the best of both worlds, higher output and an improvement in its trade balance. But if all the countries wait, nothing will happen and the recession may last a long time. (To learn more about the relationship between fiscal multipliers and import propensities across countries, read the Focus box 'Fiscal multipliers in an open economy'.)

Is there a way out? There is – at least in theory. If all countries coordinate their macro-economic policies so as to increase domestic demand simultaneously, each can increase demand and output without increasing its trade deficit (vis-à-vis the others; their combined

FOCUS
Fiscal multipliers in an open economy

In this chapter we have shown how an increase in domestic or foreign demand leads to an increase in domestic output. One of the most important implications of these interactions is the impact of fiscal policy, at home and abroad, when countries trade a lot with each other. This is very much the case of European countries that are very open to trade, especially with each other. To understand this, consider a world of two countries, namely Home (a small open economy) and Foreign. Let us write down the components of domestic demand in both countries, based on equation (6.9):

$$Y = C + I + G - \frac{IM}{\varepsilon} + X \qquad [7.1]$$

$$Y^* = C^* + I^* + G^* - IM^*\varepsilon + X^* \qquad [7.2]$$

where $X = IM^* = m^*Y^*$, with m^* being the proportion of foreign income, Y^*, spent on imports (or the foreign propensity to import), i.e. Home's exports are identically equal to Foreign's imports (by definition, as we are describing a world of just two countries), and $X^* = IM = mY$, i.e. Foreign's exports are identically equal to Home's imports. By substituting the latter into (1) we get:

$$Y = C + I + G - m\frac{Y}{\varepsilon} + m^*Y^*$$

And, by replacing consumption, C, with a linear function (as in Chapter 5), we get:

$$Y = c_0 + c_1Y + I + G - m\frac{Y}{\varepsilon} + m^*Y^* = A + \left(c_1 - \frac{m}{\varepsilon}\right)Y + m^*Y^*$$

where $A = (c_0 + I + G)$ is autonomous spending.

If we solve for the level of real income, Y, we obtain:

$$Y = \frac{1}{1 - c_1 + \dfrac{m}{\varepsilon}}(A + m^*Y^*)$$

Let us now compute the fiscal multiplier, that is the impact on income, Y, of an increase in public spending, G.

The multiplier of Home's fiscal policy

$$\frac{\Delta Y}{\Delta G} = \frac{1}{1 - c_1 + \dfrac{m}{\varepsilon}} \qquad [7.3]$$

Equation (7.3) shows us two important things.

First, in an open economy (that is, an economy that consumes both domestic goods and imported goods, therefore the propensity to import, m, is positive), the fiscal multiplier is lower than in a closed economy (remember that the fiscal multiplier in a closed economy was equal to $1/(1 - c_1)$).

Second, countries with higher import propensities have lower fiscal multipliers. That is, in countries that demand a relatively high amount of foreign goods (compared to domestic goods), the impact of fiscal policy will be relatively low (compared to countries with a lower import propensity). This is clearly shown in Figure 7.3. Economies with high import propensities such as Belgium, the Czech Republic, Hungary and Ireland have low fiscal multipliers, whereas countries such as France, Italy and the UK have much higher fiscal multipliers.

trade deficit with respect to the rest of the world will still increase). The reason is clear: the coordinated increase in demand leads to increases in both exports and imports in each country. It is still true that domestic demand expansion leads to larger imports; but this increase in imports is offset by the increase in exports, which comes from the foreign demand expansions.

In practice, however, coordination is not so easy to achieve:

- Some countries might have to do more than others and may not want to do so. Suppose that only some countries are in recession. Countries that are not in a recession will be reluctant to increase their own demand; but if they do not, the countries that expand will run a trade deficit vis-à-vis countries that do not. Or suppose some countries are already running a large budget deficit. These countries will not want to cut taxes nor increase spending further, as this would further increase their deficits. They will ask other countries to take on more of the adjustment. Those other countries may be reluctant to do so.
- Countries have a strong incentive to promise to coordinate, and then not deliver on that promise. Once all countries have agreed, say, to an increase in spending, each country has an incentive not to deliver, so as to benefit from the increase in demand elsewhere

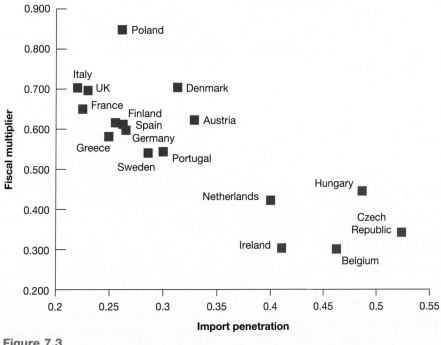

Figure 7.3

Fiscal multipliers and import penetration

Source: Ali Al-Eyd, Ray Barrell and Dawn Holland (2006), *The Role of Financial Markets' Openness in the Transmission of Shocks in Europe*, National Institute of Economic and Social Research, Discussion Paper No. 271, p. 18.

The multiplier of Foreign's fiscal policy

$$\frac{\Delta Y}{\Delta G^*} = \frac{m^*}{1 - c_1 + \frac{m}{\varepsilon}} \qquad [7.4]$$

Equation (7.4) shows another important implication of openness. Fiscal stimuli abroad have expansionary effects also at home. The increase in domestic output following a fiscal expansion abroad is higher the higher the foreign propensity to import, m^*, and the lower the domestic propensity to import, m. In times of widespread recessions, countries with low m may be tempted to just wait for other countries to increase their demand. On the other hand, countries with high m have little incentive to increase demand through public spending because their fiscal multipliers are low. This is very much what happened in 2009, when European countries were largely reluctant to increase public spending to sustain demand. (For more on the 2009 fiscal stimulus see the next Focus box.)

and thereby improve its trade position. But if each country cheats, or does not do everything it promised, there will be insufficient demand expansion to get out of the recession.

These reasons are far from abstract concerns. Countries in the EU, which are highly integrated with one another, have in the past 30 years often suffered from such coordination problems. In the late 1970s, a bungled attempt at coordination left most countries wary of trying again. In the early 1980s, an attempt by France to go at it alone led to a large French trade deficit and eventually to a change in policy. Thereafter, most countries decided that it was better to wait for an increase in foreign demand than to increase their own demand. There has been very little coordination of fiscal policy since then in Europe.

Only when things are really bad does coordination appear to take hold. This was the case in 2009, and is explored in the Focus box 'The G20 and the 2009 fiscal stimulus'.

FOCUS
The G20 and the 2009 fiscal stimulus

In November 2008, the leaders of the G20 met in an emergency meeting in Washington. The G20, a group of ministers of finance and central bank governors from 20 countries, including both the major advanced and the major emerging countries in the world, had been created in 1999, but had not played a major role until the crisis. With mounting evidence that the crisis was going to be deep and wide, the group met to coordinate their responses, in terms of both macroeconomic and financial policies.

On the macroeconomic front, it had become clear that monetary policy would not be enough, and so the focus turned to fiscal policy. The decrease in output was going to lead to a decrease in revenues, and thus an increase in budget deficits. Dominique Strauss-Kahn, then the managing director of the International Monetary Fund, argued that further fiscal actions were needed, and suggested taking additional discretionary measures – either decreases in taxes or increases in spending – adding up to roughly 2% of GDP. He said: 'The fiscal stimulus is now essential to restore global growth. Each country's fiscal stimulus can be twice as effective in raising domestic output growth if its major trading partners also have a stimulus package.'

He noted that some countries had more room for manoeuvre than others. 'We believe that those countries – advanced and emerging economies – with the strongest fiscal policy frameworks, the best ability to finance fiscal expansion, and the most clearly sustainable debt should take the lead.'

Over the next few months, most countries indeed adopted discretionary measures, aimed at increasing either private or public spending. For the G20 as a whole, discretionary measures added up to about 2.3% of GDP in 2009. Some countries, with less fiscal room, such as Italy, did less. Some countries, such as the USA and France, did more.

Was this fiscal stimulus successful? Some have argued that it was not: after all, the world economy had large negative growth in 2009. The issue here is one of counterfactuals. What would have happened in the absence of the stimulus? Many believe that, absent the fiscal stimulus, growth would have been even more negative, perhaps catastrophically so. Counterfactuals are hard to prove or disprove, and thus the controversy is likely to go on. (On the issue of counterfactuals, and the difference between economists and politicians, here's a very nice quote from Barney Frank, a US congressman: 'Not for the first time, as an elected official, I envy economists. Economists have available to them, in an analytical approach, the counterfactual. Economists can explain that a given decision was the best one that could be made, because they can show what would have happened in the counterfactual situation. They can contrast what happened to what would have happened. No one has ever gotten re-elected where the bumper sticker said, "It would have been worse without me." You probably can get tenure with that. But you can't win office.')

Was this fiscal stimulus dangerous? Some have argued that it has led to a large increase in debt, which is now forcing governments to adjust, leading to a fiscal contraction and making recovery more difficult (we shall discuss these issues in Chapter 21). That argument is largely misplaced. Most of the increase in debt in 2008–2009 did not come from the discretionary measures that were taken, but from the decrease in revenues which came from the decrease in output during the crisis. It remains true, however, that this large increase in debt is now making it more difficult to use fiscal policy to help the recovery.

For more discussion at the time, see 'Financial crisis response: IMF spells out need for global fiscal stimulus', in *IMF Survey Magazine*, 29 December, 2008. (*www.imf.org/external/pubs/ft/survey/so/2008/INT122908A.htm*)

7.2 DEPRECIATION, THE TRADE BALANCE AND OUTPUT

Suppose the UK government takes policy measures that lead to a depreciation of the pound – a decrease in the nominal exchange rate. (We shall see in Chapter 12 how it can do this by using monetary policy. For the moment we will assume the government can simply choose the exchange rate.)

Recall that the real exchange rate is given by

$$\varepsilon = \frac{EP}{P^*}$$

The real exchange rate, ε (the price of domestic goods in terms of foreign goods) is equal to the nominal exchange rate, E (the price of domestic currency in terms of foreign currency) multiplied by the domestic price level, P, divided by the foreign price level, P^*. In the short run, we can take the two price levels P and P^* as given. This implies that the nominal depreciation is reflected one-for-one in a real depreciation. More concretely, if the pound depreciates vis-à-vis the euro by 10% (a 10% nominal depreciation), and if the price levels in the UK and the euro area do not change, UK goods will be 10% cheaper compared to euro area goods (a 10% real depreciation).

◄ Given P and P^*, E falls $\Rightarrow$ $\varepsilon - EP/P^*$ falls.

Le us now ask how this real depreciation will affect the UK trade balance and UK output.

◄ A look ahead: later (see Chapter 12), we shall look at the effects of a nominal depreciation when we allow the price level to adjust over time. You will see that a nominal depreciation leads to a real depreciation in the short run, but not in the medium run.

Depreciation and the trade balance: the Marshall–Lerner condition

Return to the definition of net exports earlier (see Chapter 6):

$$NX = X - IM/\varepsilon$$

Replace X and IM by their expressions from equations (6.7) and (6.8):

$$NX = X(Y^*, \varepsilon) - IM(Y, \varepsilon)/\varepsilon$$

As the real exchange rate ε enters the right side of the equation in three places, this makes it clear that the real depreciation affects the trade balance through three separate channels:

◄ More concretely, if the pound depreciates vis-à-vis the euro by 10%:

- Exports, X, increase. The real depreciation makes UK goods relatively less expensive abroad. This leads to an increase in foreign demand for UK goods – an increase in UK exports.
- Imports, IM, decrease. The real depreciation makes foreign goods relatively more expensive in the UK. This leads to a shift in domestic demand towards domestic goods, and to a decrease in the quantity of imports.
- The relative price of foreign goods in terms of domestic goods, $1/\varepsilon$, increases. This increases the import bill, IM/ε. The same quantity of imports now costs more to buy (in terms of domestic goods).

  - UK goods will be cheaper in the euro area, leading to a larger quantity of UK exports to the euro area.
  - Euro area goods will be more expensive in the UK, leading to a smaller quantity of imports of euro area goods to the UK.
  - Euro area goods will be more expensive, leading to a higher import bill for a given quantity of imports of euro area goods to the UK.

For the trade balance to improve following a depreciation, exports must increase enough and imports must decrease enough to compensate for the increase in the price of imports. The condition under which a real depreciation leads to an increase in net exports is known as the **Marshall–Lerner condition**. (It is derived formally in the appendix, called 'Derivation of the Marshall–Lerner condition' at the end of the chapter.) It turns out – with a complication we will state when we introduce dynamics later in this chapter – that this condition is satisfied in reality. So, for the rest of this text, we shall assume that a real depreciation – a decrease in ε – leads to an increase in net exports – an increase in NX.

◄ It is named after the two economists, the Londoner Alfred Marshall and Abba Lerner (a Russian economist who emigrated first to the UK and later to the USA) who were the first to derive it.

The effects of a depreciation

We have looked so far at the direct effects of a depreciation on the trade balance – that is, the effects given UK and foreign output. But the effects do not end there. The change in net exports changes domestic output, which affects net exports further.

Because the effects of a real depreciation are very much like those of an increase in foreign output, we can use Figure 7.2, the same figure that we used to show the effects of an increase in foreign output earlier.

Just like an increase in foreign output, a depreciation leads to an increase in net exports (assuming, as we do, that the Marshall–Lerner condition holds), at any level of output. Both the demand relation (ZZ in Figure 7.2(a)) and the net exports relation (NX in Figure 7.2(b)) shift up. The equilibrium moves from A to A′, and output increases from Y to Y'. By the same argument we used earlier, the trade balance improves: the increase in imports induced by the increase in output is smaller than the direct improvement in the trade balance induced by the depreciation.

> Marshall–Lerner condition: given output, a real depreciation leads to an increase in net exports.

Let us summarise. The depreciation leads to a shift in demand, both foreign and domestic, toward domestic goods. This shift in demand leads in turn to both an increase in domestic output and an improvement in the trade balance.

Although a depreciation and an increase in foreign output have the same effect on domestic output and the trade balance, there is a subtle but important difference between the two. A depreciation works by making foreign goods relatively more expensive. But this means that, given their income, people – who now have to pay more to buy foreign goods because of the depreciation – are poorer. This mechanism is strongly felt in countries that go through a large depreciation. Governments trying to achieve a large depreciation often find themselves with strikes and riots in the streets, as people react to the much higher prices of imported goods. This was, for example, the case in Mexico, where the large depreciation of the peso in 1994–1995 – from 29 US cents per peso in November 1994 to 17 cents per peso in May 1995 – led to a large decline in workers' living standards and to social unrest.

> There is an alternative to riots – asking for and obtaining an increase in wages. But, if wages increase, the prices of domestic goods will follow and increase as well, leading to a smaller real depreciation. To discuss this mechanism, we need to look at the supply side in more detail than we have done so far. We return to the dynamics of depreciation, wage and price movements later (in Chapter 12).

Combining exchange rate and fiscal policies

Suppose output is at its natural level, but the economy is running a large trade deficit. The government would like to reduce the trade deficit while leaving output unchanged. What should it do?

A depreciation alone will not do: it will reduce the trade deficit, but it will also increase output. Nor will a fiscal contraction: it will reduce the trade deficit, but it will decrease output. What should the government do? The answer: use the right combination of depreciation and fiscal contraction. Figure 7.4 shows what this combination should be.

Suppose the initial equilibrium in Figure 7.4(a) is at A, associated with output Y. At this level of output, there is a trade deficit, given by the distance BC in Figure 7.4(b). If the government wants to eliminate the trade deficit without changing output, it must do two things:

- It must achieve a depreciation sufficient to eliminate the trade deficit at the initial level of output. So the depreciation must be such as to shift the net exports relation from NX to NX' in Figure 7.4(b).

  The problem is that this depreciation, and the associated increase in net exports, also shifts the demand relation in Figure 7.4(a) from ZZ to ZZ'. In the absence of other measures, the equilibrium would move from A to A′, and output would increase from Y to Y'.

- In order to avoid the increase in output, the government must reduce government spending so as to shift ZZ' back to ZZ. This combination of a depreciation and a fiscal contraction leads to the same level of output and an improved trade balance.

> A general lesson: if you want to achieve two targets (here, output and trade balance), you had better have two instruments (here, fiscal policy and the exchange rate).

There is a general point behind this example. To the extent that governments care about both the level of output and the trade balance, they have to use both fiscal policy and exchange-rate policies. We just saw one such combination. Table 7.1 gives you others, depending on the initial output and trade situation. Take, for example, the situation in the top right corner of the table: initial output is too low (put another way, unemployment is

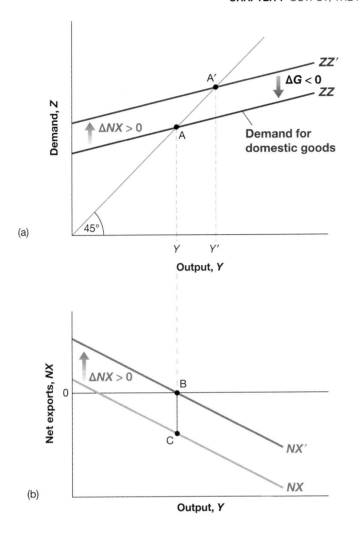

(a)

(b)

Figure 7.4

The effects of an increase in foreign demand (2)

An increase in foreign demand leads to an increase in output and to a trade surplus.

Table 7.1 Exchange rate and fiscal policy combinations

Initial condition	Trade surplus	Trade deficit
Low output	ε? G $\uparrow$	$\varepsilon \downarrow$ G?
High output	$\varepsilon \uparrow$ G?	ε? G $\downarrow$

too high), and the economy has a trade deficit. A depreciation will help on both the trade and the output fronts: it reduces the trade deficit and increases output. But there is no reason for the depreciation to achieve both the correct increase in output and the elimination of the trade deficit. Depending on the initial situation and the relative effects of the depreciation on output and the trade balance, the government may need to complement the depreciation with either an increase or a decrease in government spending. This ambiguity is captured by the question mark in the box. Make sure that you understand the logic behind each of the other three boxes.

7.3 LOOKING AT DYNAMICS: THE J-CURVE

We have ignored dynamics so far in this chapter. It is time to reintroduce them. The dynamics of consumption, investment, sales and production we discussed earlier (in Chapter 3) are as relevant to the open economy as they are to the closed economy. But there are additional dynamic effects as well, which come from the dynamics of exports and imports. We focus on these effects here.

Return to the effects of the exchange rate on the trade balance. We argued earlier that a depreciation leads to an increase in exports and to a decrease in imports. But this does not happen overnight. Think of the dynamic effects of, say, a 10% pound depreciation.

And even these prices may adjust ➤ slowly: consider a pound depreciation. If you are an exporter to the UK, you may want to increase your price less than implied by the exchange rate, in order to remain competitive with your UK competitors. If you are a UK exporter, you may decrease your price abroad by less than implied by the exchange rate. In other words, you may increase your profits.

In the first few months following the depreciation, the effect of the depreciation is likely to be reflected much more in prices than in quantities. The price of imports in the UK goes up, and the price of UK exports abroad goes down. But the quantity of imports and exports is likely to adjust only slowly: it takes a while for consumers to realise that relative prices have changed, it takes a while for firms to shift to cheaper suppliers, and so on. So a depreciation may well lead to an initial deterioration of the trade balance because quantities (the volume of export and imports) adjust slowly, but the UK immediately starts paying more for whatever it imports. In other words, ε decreases, but neither X nor IM adjusts very much initially, leading to a decline in net exports $(X - IM/\varepsilon)$.

As time passes, the effects of the change in the relative prices of both exports and imports become stronger. Cheaper UK goods cause UK consumers and firms to decrease their demand for foreign goods: UK imports decrease. Cheaper UK goods abroad lead foreign consumers and firms to increase their demand for UK goods: UK exports increase. If the Marshall–Lerner condition eventually holds – and we have argued that it does – the response of exports and imports eventually becomes stronger than the adverse price effect, and the

The response of the trade balance to ➤ the real exchange rate:

● Initially:
  X, IM unchanged, ε decreases
  $\Rightarrow (X - IM/\varepsilon)$ decreases.
● Eventually:
  X increases, *IM* decreases, ε
  decreases
  $\Rightarrow (X - IM/\varepsilon)$ increases.

eventual effect of the depreciation is an improvement of the trade balance.

Figure 7.5 captures this adjustment by plotting the evolution of the trade balance against time in response to a real depreciation. The pre-depreciation trade deficit is 0A. The depreciation initially increases the trade deficit to 0B: ε decreases, but neither IM nor X changes right away. Over time, however, exports increase and imports decrease, reducing the trade deficit.

Eventually (if the Marshall–Lerner condition is satisfied), the trade balance improves beyond its initial level; this is what happens from point C on in the figure. Economists refer to this adjustment process as the **J-curve**, because – admittedly, with a bit of imagination – the curve in the figure resembles a 'J': first down, then up.

In general, the econometric evidence on the dynamic relation between exports, imports and the real exchange rate suggests that in all OECD countries, a real depreciation eventually leads to a trade balance improvement. But it also suggests that this process takes some time, typically between six months and a year. These lags have implications not only for the effects of a depreciation on the trade balance but also for the effects of a depreciation on output. If a depreciation initially decreases net exports, it also initially exerts a contractionary effect on output. Thus, if a government relies on a depreciation both to improve the trade balance and to expand domestic output, the effects will go the 'wrong' way for a while. For example, Sterling depreciation in 1992 initially led to a worsening of the trade balance. By mid-1993, however, the trade balance had improved. The opposite happened when Sterling appreciated in 1997 (Figure 7.6).

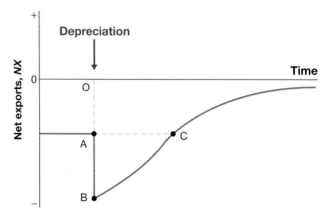

Figure 7.5

The J-curve

A real depreciation leads initially to a deterioration and then to an improvement of the trade balance.

Figure 7.6

Sterling exchange and the balance of trade in goods

Source: Hughes Hallett, Andrew J. and Wren-Lewis, S., 1997. 'Is there life outside the ERM? *ttp://ideas.repec.org/a/ijf/ijfiec/ v2y1997i3p199-216.html*

7.4 SAVING, INVESTMENT AND THE TRADE BALANCE

We now shift to a different topic, also related to how what we learned so far needs to be adapted when the economy is open to trade with the rest of the world. Remember (from Chapter 3) how we could rewrite the condition for equilibrium in the goods market as the condition that investment was equal to saving – the sum of private saving and public saving. We can now derive the corresponding condition for the open economy, and show how useful this alternative way of looking at the equilibrium can be.

Start from our equilibrium condition in the goods market:

$$Y = C + I + G - IM/\varepsilon + X$$

Private saving is equal to $S = Y - C - T$. Subtract $C + T$ from both sides, to get:

$$S = I + G - T - IM/\varepsilon + X$$

Use the definition of net exports $NX = X - IM/\varepsilon$, and reorganise to get

$$NX = S + (T - G) - I \qquad [7.5]$$

So, in equilibrium, the trade balance (NX) must be equal to total saving – private saving (S) and public saving ($T - G$) – minus investment (I). It follows that a trade surplus must correspond to an excess of saving over investment; a trade deficit must correspond to an excess of investment over saving.

One way of getting more intuition for this relation is to go back to the discussion of the current account and the capital account (in Chapter 6). There we saw that a trade surplus means that the country is lending to the rest of the world, and a trade deficit implies that it is borrowing from the rest of the world. So, consider a country that invests more than it saves, so that $S + (T - G) - I$ is negative. That country must be borrowing the difference from the rest of the world; it must therefore be running a trade deficit.

Note some of the things that equation (7.5) says:

◄ Recall our earlier simplification that net investment income and net transfers from abroad were both equal to zero, so the trade balance and the current account balance are identical. If we relaxed this assumption and went through the same derivation taking net investment income and transfers into account, equation (7.5) would relate the current account balance, not the trade balance, to saving and investment.

- An increase in investment must be reflected either in an increase in private saving or public saving, or in a deterioration of the trade balance (a smaller trade surplus, or a larger trade deficit).

- An increase in the budget deficit must be reflected in either an increase in private saving, or a decrease in investment, or a deterioration of the trade balance.
- A country with a high saving rate (private plus public) must have either a high investment rate or a large trade surplus.

Note also what equation (7.5) does not say. It does not say, for example, whether a budget deficit will lead to a trade deficit, or, instead, to an increase in private saving, or to a decrease in investment. To find out what happens in response to a budget deficit, we must explicitly solve for what happens to output and its components using the assumptions that we have made about consumption, investment, exports and imports. We can do so using either equation (6.9) – as we have done throughout this chapter – or equation (7.5), as the two are equivalent. However, let us recommend that you start by using equation (6.9). Using (7.5) can, if you are not careful, be very misleading. To see how misleading, consider, for example, the following argument (which is so common that you may have read something similar in newspapers).

It is clear the United Kingdom cannot reduce its trade deficit (currently around 2.5% of GDP) through a depreciation. Look at equation (7.5). It shows that the trade deficit is equal

FOCUS
The US trade deficit: origins and implications

Since 1996, the ratio of exports to GDP has remained flat, while the ratio of imports to GDP in the USA has rapidly increased. As a result, the trade deficit increased from $104 billion, or 1.2% of US GDP in 1996, to $681 billion, or 4.7% of US GDP in 2008.

The current account deficit (which is equal to the trade deficit minus net income from abroad) was $673 billion in 2008. Put another way, the USA borrowed $673 billion from the rest of the world in 2008. This is a very large amount. It represents about 50% of the world's net saving (saving net of depreciation). And the notion that the world's richest economy is borrowing so much from the rest of the world is quite surprising. It raises two main questions: Where do these deficits come from? And what do they imply for the future? Let's take up each question in turn.

Where does the trade deficit and, by implication, the current account deficit come from?

Three factors appear to have played roughly equal roles in the increase in the current account deficit since the mid-1990s.

The first has been the high US growth rate since the mid-1990s, relative to the growth rates of some of its main trading partners. Table 7.2 gives the average annual growth rate for the USA, the EU and Japan for three periods: 1991–1995, 1996–2000 and 2001–2006. Since 1996, US growth has been much higher than growth in

Table 7.2 Average annual growth rates in the USA, the EU and Japan since 1991 (per cent per year)

	1991–1995	1996–2000	2001–2006
USA	2.5	4.1	3.4
EU	2.1	2.6	1.6
Japan	1.5	1.5	1.6

Europe and Japan. The US performance from 1996–2000 reflects the technology boom, which we have discussed at many points in the book. US growth has decreased since 2001, but it has remained higher than growth in Europe and Japan.

Higher growth does not necessarily lead to a higher trade deficit. If the main source of the increase in demand and growth in a country is an increase in foreign demand, the country can grow fast and maintain trade balance, or even sustain a trade surplus. In the case of the USA since the mid-1990s, however, the main source of increased demand has been domestic demand, with high consumption demand as the main factor behind the sustained expansion. Thus, higher growth has come with an increasing trade deficit.

The second factor is shifts in the export and import functions – that is, changes in exports or in imports due neither to changes in activity nor to changes in the exchange rate. The evidence is that these shifts have played an important role as well, explaining up to one-third of the to investment minus saving. Why should a depreciation affect either saving or investment? So, how can a depreciation affect the trade deficit?

The argument might sound convincing, but we know it is wrong. We showed earlier that a depreciation leads to an improvement in a country's trade position. So what is wrong with the argument? A depreciation actually affects saving and investment: it does so by affecting the demand for domestic goods, thereby increasing output. Higher output leads to an increase in saving over investment, or equivalently to a decrease in the trade deficit.

A good way of making sure that you understand the material in this section is to go back and look at the various cases we have considered, from changes in government spending, to changes in foreign output, to combinations of depreciation and fiscal contraction, and so on. Trace what happens in each case to each of the four components of equation (7.5): private saving, public saving (equivalently, the budget surplus), investment and the trade balance. Make sure, as always, that you can tell the story in words.

A good way of making sure you understand the material in this chapter is to read the Focus box on the US trade deficit. It will show you how the concepts we have developed in the chapter can be used to understand the origins and implications of one of the main issues facing US policy makers today.

◀ Suppose, for example that the government wants to reduce the trade deficit without changing the level of output, so it uses a combination of depreciation and fiscal contraction. What happens to private saving, public saving, and investment?

increase in the trade deficit. At a given level of income and a given exchange rate, US consumers, for example, buy a higher proportion of foreign goods – say, more foreign cars and fewer domestic cars.

The third factor has been the evolution of the exchange rate. Even if, at a given real exchange rate, growth leads to an increase in the trade deficit, a real depreciation can help maintain trade balance by making domestic goods more competitive. But just the opposite has happened to the US real exchange rate: from 1996–2002, the USA experienced a large real appreciation, not a real depreciation.

Why was the dollar so strong until 2002, in the face of a large current account deficit? The answer is that there was a very high demand for US assets on the part of foreign investors. This demand was enough to drive the dollar up and, in doing so, to increase the trade and the current account deficits. Since the beginning of 2002, the dollar has depreciated but, because of the two other factors listed – growth differentials and shifts in relative demand for domestic and foreign goods – and because of the lags in the adjustment of exports and imports to the real ex-change rate – the J curve – the trade deficit has continued to increase.

This is a good place to make sure we can tell the story in terms of saving and investment. Figure 7.7 gives the evolution of US net saving (that is, US saving net of depreciation) and US net investment (US investment net of depreciation) as ratios to GDP, since 1996, and it tells a clear story: the increase in the trade deficit (which, as you will recall, is equal to the difference between investment and saving) has come primarily from a decrease in the ratio of saving to GDP. And, if one looks closely, it is clear

that this decrease in saving has come mostly from a decrease in private saving, S, rather than an increase in the budget deficit, $G - T$: the ratio of the budget deficit to GDP is roughly the same in 2006 as it was in 1996, and the ratio of private saving to GDP is more than 3 percentage points lower in 2006 than it was in 1996. Thus, another way of describing what lies behind the trade deficit is that US consumers are saving substantially less than they were ten years ago. Should they be saving more? (We discuss this in Chapter 17.) The answer: most of them appear to be saving enough.

What happens next?

Should we expect the large trade deficit and current account deficit to naturally disappear in the future? At an unchanged real exchange rate, the answer is probably no.

If there were good reasons to expect US trading partners to experience much higher growth than the USA over the coming decade, then we could expect to see the same process we saw in the past ten years but this time in reverse: lower growth in the USA than in the rest of the world would lead to a steady reduction in the trade deficit. There are few reasons, however, to expect such a scenario. Although the USA cannot expect to replicate the growth rates of the late 1990s, there is also no reason to expect much lower growth than average over the coming decade. And, while growth has increased in Europe and Japan, sustained higher growth in Europe and Japan than in the USA seems unlikely.

Can we expect the shifts in exports and imports to reverse themselves, leading to an improvement in the trade balance without the need for a depreciation? The

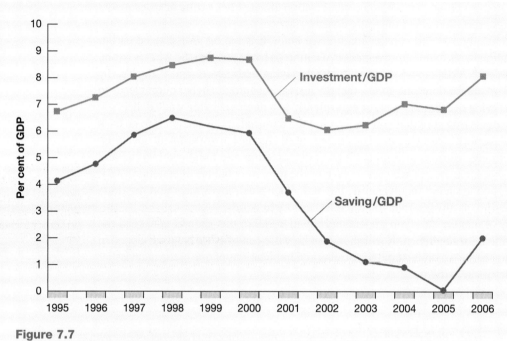

Figure 7.7

US net saving and net investment since 1996 (% of GDP)

source of the shifts is poorly understood, so one must be careful in predicting what might happen. But there does not appear to be any particular reason to think that, for example, US consumers will shift back from foreign cars to US cars. Put another way, there is no particular reason to expect that the trade deficit will narrow by itself, without a depreciation of the dollar.

Will the dollar depreciate further, leading eventually to a reduction in the trade and current account deficits? The answer is: probably. While financial investors have been willing to lend to the USA until now, there are many reasons to think that they will be reluctant to lend at the current levels of $800 billion or so per year.

These arguments have three implications:

- The US trade and current account deficits will decline in the future.
- This decline is unlikely to happen without a real depreciation. How large a depreciation? Estimates range from 20% to 40% from where we are today – in short, a substantial further real depreciation.
- When will this depreciation take place? This is a hard question to answer. It will take place when foreign investors become reluctant to lend to the USA at the rate of $800 billion or so per year.

Let's go back to the issues discussed in Table 7.1: a depreciation on such a scale will have major effects on the demand for goods both in the USA and abroad.

The depreciation will increase the demand for US goods. If, when the depreciation takes place, US output is already close to its natural level, the risk is that the depreciation will lead to too high a level of demand and too high a level of output. If this happens, it will require a decrease in domestic demand. This may come either from a decrease in spending by consumers or firms or from a reduction in government spending. If the US government succeeds in achieving a smooth depreciation and the decrease in domestic spending, the outcome can be sustained US growth and a reduction of the US trade deficit.

The depreciation will decrease the demand for foreign goods. By the same argument, this may require foreign governments to implement policies to sustain their own demand and output. This would ordinarily call for a fiscal expansion, but it might not be the right solution in this case. A number of countries, such as France and Japan, are already running large budget deficits. As we shall see later (Chapter 18), increasing these deficits further may be difficult and even dangerous. If fiscal policy cannot be used to sustain demand and output, a strong dollar depreciation might therefore trigger a recession in those countries.

In short, a smooth reduction of the US trade deficit will require the combination of a dollar depreciation and spending changes both in the USA and abroad. This can be achieved, but it may not be easy.

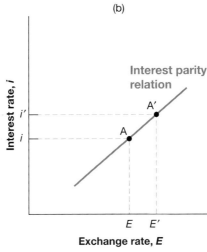

Figure 7.8

The effects of an increase in government spending (2)

An increase in government spending leads to an increase in output, an increase in the interest rate and an appreciation.

7.5 THE EFFECTS OF POLICY IN AN OPEN ECONOMY

Having derived, in section 6.5, the *IS–LM* model for the open economy, we now put it to use and look at the effects of policy.

The effects of fiscal policy in an open economy

Let us look again at a change in government spending. Suppose that, starting from a balanced budget, the government decides to increase defence spending without raising taxes and so runs a budget deficit. What happens to the level of output? To the composition of output? To the interest rate? To the exchange rate?

The answers are given in Figure 7.8. The economy is initially at point A. The increase in government spending increases output at a given interest rate, shifting the *IS* curve to the right, from *IS* to *IS'* in Figure 7.8(a). Because government spending does not enter the *LM* relation, the *LM* curve does not shift. The new equilibrium is at point A', with a higher level of output and a higher interest rate. In Figure 7.8(b), the higher interest rate leads to an increase in the exchange rate – an appreciation. So an increase in government spending leads to an increase in output, an increase in the interest rate and an appreciation.

In words: an increase in government spending leads to an increase in demand, leading to an increase in output. As output increases, so does the demand for money, leading to upward pressure on the interest rate. The increase in the interest rate, which makes domestic bonds more attractive, leads to an appreciation. The higher interest rate and the appreciation both decrease the domestic demand for goods, offsetting some of the effect of government spending on demand and output.

Can we tell what happens to the various components of demand?

◄ An increase in government spending shifts the *IS* curve to the right. It shifts neither the *LM* curve nor the interest-parity line.

- Clearly, consumption and government spending both go up. Consumption goes up because of the increase in income, and government spending goes up by assumption.
- What happens to investment is ambiguous. Recall that investment depends on both output and the interest rate. On the one hand, output goes up, leading to an increase in investment. But on the other, the interest rate also goes up, leading to a decrease in investment. Depending on which of these two effects dominates, investment can go up or down. In short: the effect of government spending on investment is ambiguous in a closed economy; it remains ambiguous in an open economy.
- Recall that net exports depend on domestic output, foreign output and the exchange rate. Thus, both the increase in output and the appreciation combine to decrease net exports: the increase in output increases imports, and the appreciation decreases exports

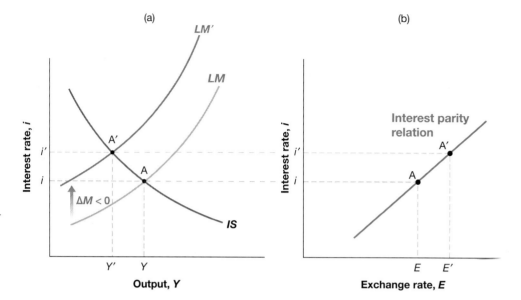

Figure 7.9

The effects of a monetary contraction

A monetary contraction leads to a decrease in output, an increase in the interest rate and an appreciation.

and increases imports. As a result, the budget deficit leads to a deterioration of the trade balance. If trade is balanced to start, then the budget deficit leads to a trade deficit. Note that, while an increase in the budget deficit increases the trade deficit, the effect is far from mechanical. It works through the effect of the budget deficit on output and on the exchange rate, and, in turn, on the trade deficit.

The effects of monetary policy in an open economy

Now that we have looked at fiscal policy, we look at our other favourite policy experiment, a monetary contraction. Look at Figure 7.9(a). At a given level of output, a decrease in the money stock leads to an increase in the interest rate: the LM curve shifts up, from LM to LM′. Because money does not directly enter the IS relation, the IS curve does not shift. The equilibrium moves from point A to point A′. In Figure 7.9(b), the increase in the interest rate leads to an appreciation. (Can you tell what happens to consumption, to investment and to net exports?)

A monetary contraction shifts the *LM* ➤ curve up. It shifts neither the *IS* curve nor the interest-parity curve.

So a monetary contraction leads to a decrease in output, an increase in the interest rate and an appreciation. The story is easy to tell. A monetary contraction leads to an increase in the interest rate, making domestic bonds more attractive and triggering an appreciation. The higher interest rate and the appreciation both decrease demand and output.

This version of the *IS–LM* model for the open economy was first put together in the 1960s by two economists, Robert Mundell at Columbia University and Marcus Fleming at the International Monetary Fund and is known as the Mundell–Fleming model. Robert Mundell was awarded the Nobel Prize in Economics in 1999. As an example, the sharp monetary and fiscal policy changes the US economy went through in the late 1970s and early 1980s produced exactly the same results as predicted by the Mundell–Fleming model.

7.6 FIXED EXCHANGE RATES

We have assumed so far that the central bank chooses the money supply and lets the exchange rate freely adjust in whatever manner is implied by equilibrium in the foreign exchange market. In many countries, this assumption does not reflect reality: central banks act under implicit or explicit exchange rate targets and use monetary policy to achieve those targets. The targets are sometimes implicit, sometimes explicit; they are sometimes specific values, sometimes bands or ranges. These exchange rate arrangements (or regimes, as they are called) have many names. Let us first see what the names mean.

For a list of all possible – sometimes esoteric – exchange rate arrangements, go to the IMF website at *www.imf.org/ external/NP/mfd/er/index.aspx* ➤

Pegs, crawling pegs, bands, the EMS and the euro

At one end of the spectrum are countries with **flexible exchange rates**, such as the USA, the UK, Sweden or Japan. These countries do not have explicit exchange rate targets. Although their central banks probably do not ignore movements in the exchange rate, they have shown themselves to be quite willing to let their exchange rates fluctuate considerably.

At the other end are countries that operate under **fixed exchange rates**. These countries maintain a fixed exchange rate in terms of some foreign currency. Some peg their currency to the dollar. For example, from 1991 to 2001, Argentina pegged its currency, the peso, at the highly symbolic exchange rate of 1 dollar for 1 peso (more on this in Chapter 12). Other countries used to peg their currency to the French franc (most of these are former French colonies in Africa); as the French franc has been replaced by the euro, they are now pegged to the euro. Still other countries peg their currency to a basket of foreign currencies, with the weights reflecting the composition of their trade.

The label 'fixed' is a bit misleading: it is not the case that the exchange rate in countries with fixed exchange rates never actually changes. But changes are rare. An extreme case involves the African countries pegged to the French franc. When their exchange rates were readjusted in January 1994, it was the first adjustment in 45 years! Because these changes are rare, economists use specific words to distinguish them from the daily changes that occur under flexible exchange rates. A decrease in the exchange rate under a regime of fixed exchange rates is called a **devaluation** rather than a **depreciation**, and an increase in the exchange rate under a regime of fixed exchange rates is called a **revaluation** rather than an **appreciation**.

Between these extremes (flexible and fixed) are countries with various degrees of commitment to an exchange rate target. For example, some countries operate under a crawling peg. The name describes it well: these countries typically have inflation rates that exceed the inflation rate in the countries with which they trade. If they were to peg their nominal exchange rate against the currencies of these countries (that is if they pegged their exchange rate to a basket), the more rapid increase in their domestic price level above the price level in such countries would lead to a steady real appreciation and rapidly make their goods uncompetitive. To avoid this effect, these countries choose a predetermined rate of depreciation against the basket. They choose to crawl (move slowly) vis-à-vis the basket.

> Recall the definition of the real exchange rate, $\varepsilon = EP/P^*$.
>
> If domestic inflation is higher than foreign inflation:
>
> - P increases faster than P^*
> - If E is fixed, EP/P^* steadily increases
>
> Equivalently: there is a steady real appreciation. Domestic goods become steadily more expensive relative to foreign goods.

Yet another arrangement is for a group of countries to maintain their bilateral exchange rates (the exchange rate between each pair of countries) within some **bands**. Perhaps the most prominent example was the **Bretton Woods system** which was established just after the Second World War and for a quarter of a century kept most world currencies within a small band relative to the US dollar. Another example was the **European Monetary System (EMS),** which determined the movements of exchange rates within the EU from 1978 to 1998. Under the EMS rules, EU countries agreed to maintain their exchange rate vis-à-vis each other within narrow bands, around a central parity – a given value for the exchange rate. Changes in the central parity and devaluations or revaluations of specic currencies could occur, but only by common agreement among member countries. After a major crisis in 1992, which led a number of countries, including the UK, to drop out of the EMS altogether, changes in central parities became more and more infrequent, leading a number of countries to move one step further and adopt a common currency, the euro. The conversion from domestic currencies to the euro began on 1 January 1999, and was completed in early 2002. We shall return to the implications of the move to the euro later (in Chapter 19).

> We will also study the 1992 crisis later (in Chapter 12).

We shall discuss the pros and cons of different exchange regimes later (in Chapter 12). But first, we must understand how pegging the exchange rate affects monetary policy and fiscal policy. This is what we do in the rest of this section. You can think of countries adopting a common currency as adopting an extreme form of fixed exchange rates: their exchange rate is fixed at one-to-one between any pair of countries.

Pegging the exchange rate and monetary control

Suppose a country decides to peg its exchange rate at some chosen value, call it $\bar{E}$. How does it actually achieve this? The government cannot just announce the value of the exchange rate and stand there. Rather, it must take measures so that its chosen exchange rate will prevail in the foreign exchange market. Let us look at the implications and mechanics of pegging.

Pegging or no pegging, the exchange rate and the nominal interest rate must satisfy the interest parity condition:

$$(1 + i_t) = (1 + i_t^*)\frac{E_t}{E_{t+1}^e}$$

Now suppose a country pegs the exchange rate at E_t, so the current exchange rate is $\bar{E}$. If financial and foreign exchange markets believe that the exchange rate will remain pegged at this value, then their expectation of the future exchange rate, E_{t+1}, is also equal to $\bar{E}$, and the interest parity relation becomes

$$(1 + i_t) = (1 + i_t^*) \Rightarrow i_t = i_t^*$$

In words: if financial investors expect the exchange rate to remain unchanged, they will require the same nominal interest rate in both countries. Under a fixed exchange rate and perfect capital mobility, the domestic interest rate must be equal to the foreign interest rate.

This condition has one further important implication. Return to the equilibrium condition that the supply of money and demand for money be equal. Now that $i_t = i_t^*$, this condition becomes

$$\frac{M}{P} = YL(i_t^*) \tag{7.6}$$

FOCUS
German unification, interest rates and the EMS

Under a fixed exchange rate regime such as the European Monetary System (EMS) (let's ignore here the degree of flexibility that was afforded by the bands), no individual country can change its interest rate if the other countries do not change theirs as well. So how do interest rates actually change? Two arrangements are possible. One is for all the member countries to coordinate changes in their interest rates. Another is for one of the countries to take the lead and for the other countries to follow – this is, in effect, what happened in the EMS, with Germany as the leader.

During the 1980s, most European central banks shared similar goals and were happy to let the Bundesbank (the German central bank) take the lead. But in 1990, German unification led to a sharp divergence in goals between the Bundesbank and the central banks of the other EMS countries. Large budget deficits, triggered by government transfers to people and firms in Eastern Germany, together with an investment boom (most Eastern Germany had obsolete capital which needed to be replaced), led to a large increase in demand in Germany. The Bundesbank's fear that this shift would generate too strong an increase in activity led it to adopt a restrictive monetary policy. The result was strong growth in Germany together with a large increase in interest rates.

This may have been the right policy mix for Germany, but for the other European countries this policy mix was much less appealing. They were not experiencing the same increase in domestic demand, but to stay in the EMS they had to match German interest rates. The net result was a sharp decrease in demand and output in the other countries. These results are presented in Table 7.3, which gives nominal interest rates, real interest rates, inflation rates and GDP growth from 1990 to 1992 for Germany and for two of its EMS partners, France and Belgium.

Note first how the high German nominal interest rates were matched by those of France and Belgium. In fact, nominal interest rates were actually higher in France than in Germany in all three years! Why did France need higher interest rates than Germany to maintain the

Suppose an increase in domestic output increases the demand for money. In a closed economy, the central bank could leave the money stock unchanged, leading to an increase in the equilibrium interest rate. In an open economy, and under flexible exchange rates, the central bank can still do the same: the result will be both an increase in the interest rate and an appreciation. But under fixed exchange rates, the central bank cannot keep the money stock unchanged. If it did, the domestic interest rate would increase above the foreign interest rate, leading to an appreciation. To maintain the exchange rate, the central bank must increase the supply of money in line with the increase in the demand for money so the equilibrium interest rate does not change. Given the price level, P, nominal money, M, must adjust so that equation (7.6) holds.

Let us summarise. Under fixed exchange rates, the central bank gives up monetary policy as a policy instrument. With a fixed exchange rate, the domestic interest rate must be equal to the foreign interest rate. And the money supply must adjust so as to maintain the interest rate.

Fiscal policy under fixed exchange rates

If monetary policy can no longer be used under fixed exchange rates, what about fiscal policy? To answer this question, we use Figure 7.10.

Figure 7.10 starts by replicating Figure 7.9(a), which we used earlier to analyse the effects of fiscal policy under flexible exchange rates. In that case, we saw that a fiscal expansion shifted the IS curve to the right. Under flexible exchange rates, the money stock remained unchanged, leading to a movement in the equilibrium from point A to point B, with an increase in output from Y_A to Y_B, an increase in the interest rate and an appreciation.

However, under fixed exchange rates, the central bank cannot let the currency appreciate. Because the increase in output leads to an increase in the demand for money, the central

Deutschmark/franc parity? The reason is that financial markets were not sure that France would actually keep the parity of the franc vis-à-vis the Deutschmark. Worried about a possible devaluation of the franc, financial investors asked for a higher interest rate on French bonds than on German bonds.

In both France and Belgium, the period 1990–1992 was characterised by slow growth and rising unemployment. Unemployment in France in 1992 was 10.4%, up from 8.9% in 1990. The corresponding numbers for Belgium were 12.1% and 8.7%.

A similar story was unfolding in the other EMS countries. By 1992, average unemployment in the EU, which had been 8.7% in 1990, had increased to 10.3%. The effects of high real interest rates on spending were not the only source of this slowdown, but they were the main one.

By 1992, an increasing number of countries were wondering whether to keep defending their EMS exchange rate parity or to give it up and lower their interest rates. Worried about the risk of devaluations, financial markets started to ask for higher interest rates in countries where they thought devaluations were more likely. The result was two major exchange rate crises, one in the fall of 1992 and the other in the summer of 1993. By the end of these two crises, five countries, Finland, Ireland, Italy, Sweden and the UK, had left the EMS. We shall look at these crises, their origins and their implications later (in Chapter 12).

Table 7.3 Interest rates and output growth: Germany, France and Belgium, 1990–1992

	Nominal interest rates (%)			GDP growth		
	1990	**1991**	**1992**	**1990**	**1991**	**1992**
Germany	8.05	9.02	9.05	5.07	4.05	2.01
France	10.03	9.06	10.03	2.05	0.07	1.04
Belgium	9.06	9.04	9.04	3.03	2.01	0.08

Note: the nominal interest rate is the short-term nominal interest rate. All rates are annual.

Source: OECD *Economic Outlook* database.

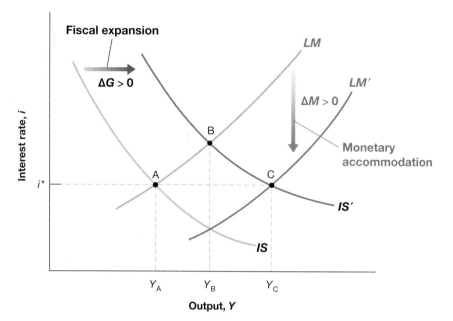

Figure 7.10

The effects of a fiscal expansion under fixed exchange rates

Under flexible exchange rates, a fiscal expansion increases output from Y_A to Y_B. Under fixed exchange rates, output increases from Y_A to Y_C.

bank must accommodate this increased demand for money by increasing the money supply. In terms of Figure 7.10, the central bank must shift the *LM* curve down as the *IS* curve shifts to the right so as to maintain the same interest rate and, thus, the same exchange rate. The equilibrium therefore moves from A to C, with higher output, Y_0, and unchanged interest and exchange rates. So, under fixed exchange rates, fiscal policy is more powerful than it is under flexible exchange rates. This is because fiscal policy triggers monetary accommodation.

As this chapter comes to an end, a question should have started to form in your mind: why would a country choose to fix its exchange rate? You have seen a number of reasons why this appears to be a bad idea:

- By fixing the exchange rate, a country gives up a powerful tool for correcting trade imbalances or changing the level of economic activity.
- By committing to a particular exchange rate, a country also gives up control of its interest rate. Not only that, but the country must also match movements in the foreign interest rate, at the risk of unwanted effects on its own activity. As we learn in the Focus box 'German unication, interest rates and the EMS', this is what happened in the early 1990s in Europe. Because of the increase in demand due to the reunication of West and East Germany, Germany felt it had to increase its interest rate. To maintain their parity with the Deutschmark, other countries in the European Monetary System were forced to also increase their interest rates, something that they would rather have avoided.
- Although the country retains control of fiscal policy, one policy instrument may not be enough. As you saw earlier (in section 7.1), a fiscal expansion can help the economy get out of a recession, but only at the cost of a larger trade deficit. And a country that wants, for example, to decrease its budget deficit cannot, under fixed exchange rates, use monetary policy to offset the contractionary effect of its fiscal policy on output.

So why do some countries fix their exchange rate? Why have 17 European countries – with more to come – adopted a common currency? To answer these questions, we must do some more work. We must look at what happens not only in the short run – which is what we did in this chapter – but also in the medium run, when the price level can adjust. We must look at the nature of exchange rate crises. Once we have done this, we shall then be able to assess the pros and cons of different exchange rate regimes. (These are the topics we take up in Chapter 12.)

SUMMARY

- In an open economy, the demand for domestic goods is equal to the domestic demand for goods (consumption, plus investment, plus government spending) minus the value of imports (in terms of domestic goods), plus exports.

- In an open economy, an increase in domestic demand leads to a smaller increase in output than it would in a closed economy because some of the additional demand falls on imports. For the same reason, an increase in domestic demand also leads to a deterioration of the trade balance.

- An increase in foreign demand leads, as a result of increased exports, to both an increase in domestic output and an improvement of the trade balance.

- Because increases in foreign demand improve the trade balance and increases in domestic demand worsen the

trade balance, countries might be tempted to wait for increases in foreign demand to move them out of a recession. When a group of countries is in recession, coordination can, in principle, help them get out of it.

- If the Marshall–Lerner condition is satisfied – and the empirical evidence indicates that it is – a real depreciation leads to an improvement in net exports.

- A real depreciation leads first to a deterioration of the trade balance, and then to an improvement. This adjustment process is known as the J-curve.

- The condition for equilibrium in the goods market can be rewritten as the condition that saving (public and private) minus investment must be equal to the trade balance. A trade surplus corresponds to an excess of saving over investment. A trade deficit corresponds to an excess of investment over saving.

KEY TERMS

demand for domestic goods 138

domestic demand for goods 138

Marshall–Lerner condition 143

J-curve 146

flexible exchange rates 153

fixed exchange rates 153

devaluation 153

depreciation 153

revaluation 153

appreciation 153

QUESTIONS AND PROBLEMS

QUICK CHECK

1. *Using the information in this chapter, label each of the following statements true, false or uncertain. Explain briefly.*

a. The current US trade deficit is the result of unusually high investment, not the result of a decline in national saving.

b. The national income identity implies that budget deficits cause trade deficits.

c. Opening the economy to trade tends to increase the multiplier because an increase in expenditure leads to more exports.

d. If the trade deficit is equal to zero, then the domestic demand for goods and the demand for domestic goods are equal.

e. A real depreciation leads to an immediate improvement in the trade balance.

f. A small open economy can reduce its trade deficit through fiscal contraction at a smaller cost in output than can a large open economy.

g. The current high US trade deficit is solely the result of a real appreciation of US goods between 1995 and 2002.

2. Real and nominal exchange rates and inflation

Using the definition of the real exchange rate (and Propositions 7 and 8 in Appendix 1 at the end of the book), you can show that

$$\frac{(\varepsilon_t - \varepsilon_{t-1})}{\varepsilon_{t-1}} = \frac{(E_t - E_{t-1})}{E_{t-1}} + \pi_t - \pi_t^*$$

In words: the percentage real appreciation equals the percentage nominal appreciation plus the difference between domestic and foreign inflation.

a. If domestic inflation is higher than foreign inflation, but the domestic country has a fixed exchange rate, what happens to the real exchange rate over time? Assume that the Marshall–Lerner condition holds. What happens to the trade balance over time? Explain in words.

b. Suppose the real exchange rate is constant – say, at the level required for net exports (or the current account) to equal zero. In this case, if domestic inflation is higher than foreign inflation, what must happen to the nominal exchange rate over time?

3. *In this chapter, we showed that a monetary expansion in an economy operating under flexible exchange rates leads to an increase in output and a depreciation of the domestic currency.*

a. How does a monetary expansion (in an economy with flexible exchange rates) affect consumption and investment?

b. How does a monetary expansion (in an economy with flexible exchange rates) affect net exports?

4. *Consider an open economy with flexible exchange rates. Suppose output is at the natural level, but there is a trade deficit. What is the appropriate fiscal-monetary policy mix?*

5. Flexible exchange rates and foreign macroeconomic policy

Consider an open economy with flexible exchange rates. Let UIP stand for the uncovered interest parity condition.

a. In an *IS–LM–UIP* diagram, show the effect of an increase in foreign output, Y^*, on domestic output, Y. Explain in words.

b. In an *IS–LM–UIP* diagram, show the effect of an increase in the foreign interest rate, i^*, on domestic output, Y. Explain in words.

c. Given the discussion of the effects of fiscal policy in this chapter, what effect is a foreign fiscal expansion likely to have on foreign output, Y^*, and on the foreign interest rate, i^*? Given the discussion of the effects of monetary policy in this chapter, what effect is a foreign monetary expansion likely to have on Y^* and i^*?

d. Given your answers to parts (a), (b) and (c), how does a foreign fiscal expansion affect domestic output? How does a foreign monetary expansion affect domestic output? (*Hint*: one of these policies has an ambiguous effect on output.)

DIG DEEPER

6. Fixed exchange rates and foreign macroeconomic policy

Consider a fixed exchange rate system, in which a group of countries (called follower countries) peg their currencies to the currency of one country (called the leader country). Since the currency of the leader country is not fixed against the currencies of countries outside the fixed exchange rate system, the leader country can conduct monetary policy as it wishes. For this problem, consider the domestic country to be a follower country and the foreign country to be the leader country.

a. Redo the analysis of problem 5(a).

b. Redo the analysis of problem 5(b).

c. Using your answers to parts (a) and (b) and problem 5(c), how does a foreign monetary expansion (by the leader country) affect domestic output? How does a foreign fiscal expansion (by the leader country) affect

domestic output? (You may assume that the effect of Y^* on domestic output is small.) How do your answers differ from those in 5(d)?

7. Net exports and foreign demand

a. Suppose there is an increase in foreign output. Show the effect on the domestic economy (i.e. replicate Figure 7.2). What is the effect on domestic output? On domestic net exports?

b. If the interest rate remains constant, what will happen to domestic investment? If taxes are fixed, what will happen to the domestic budget deficit?

c. Using equation (7.1), what must happen to private saving? Explain.

d. Foreign output does not appear in equation (7.1), yet it evidently affects net exports. Explain how this is possible.

8. The exchange rate and the labour market

Suppose the domestic currency depreciates (E falls). Assume that P and P* remain constant.

a. How does the nominal depreciation affect the relative price of domestic goods (i.e. the real exchange rate)? Given your answer, what effect would a nominal depreciation likely have on (world) demand for domestic goods? on the domestic unemployment rate?

b. Given the foreign price level, P^*, what is the price of foreign goods in terms of domestic currency? How does a nominal depreciation affect the price of foreign goods in terms of domestic currency? How does a nominal depreciation affect the domestic consumer price index? (*Hint*: remember that domestic consumers buy foreign goods (imports) as well as domestic goods.)

c. If the nominal wage remains constant, how does a nominal depreciation affect the real wage?

d. Comment on the following statement: 'A depreciating currency puts domestic labour on sale.'

9. Eliminating a trade deficit

a. Consider an economy with a trade deficit ($NX < 0$) and with output equal to its natural level. Suppose that, even though output may deviate from its natural level in the short run, it returns to its natural level in the medium run. Assume that the natural level is unaffected by the real exchange rate. What must happen to the real exchange rate over the medium run to eliminate the trade deficit (i.e. to increase NX to 0)?

b. Now write down the national income identity. Assume again that output returns to its natural level in the medium run. If NX increases to 0, what must happen to domestic demand ($C + I + G$) in the medium run? What government policies are available to reduce domestic demand in the medium run? Identify which components of domestic demand each of these policies affect.

10. Multipliers, openness and fiscal policy

Consider an open economy characterised by the equations below:

$$C = c_0 + c_1(Y - T)$$
$$I = d_0 + d_1 Y$$
$$IM = m_1 Y$$
$$X = x_1 Y^*$$

The parameters m_1 and x_1 are the propensities to import and export. Assume that the real exchange rate is fixed at a value of 1 and treat foreign income, Y^*, as fixed. Also, assume that taxes are fixed and that government purchases are exogenous (i.e. decided by the government). We explore the effectiveness of changes in G under alternative assumptions about the propensity to import.

a. Write the equilibrium condition in the market for domestic goods and solve for Y.

b. Suppose government purchases increase by one unit. What is the effect on output? (Assume that $0 < m_1 < c_1 + < 1$. Explain why.)

c. How do net exports change when government purchases increase by one unit?

Now consider two economies, one with $m_1 = 0.5$ and the other with $m_1 = 0.1$. Each economy is characterised by $(c_1 + d_1) = 0.6$.

d. Suppose one of the economies is much larger than the other. Which economy do you expect to have the larger value of m_1? Explain.

e. Calculate your answers to parts (b) and (c) for each economy by substituting the appropriate parameter values.

f. In which economy will fiscal policy have a larger effect on output? In which economy will fiscal policy have a larger effect on net exports?

11. Policy coordination and the world economy

Consider an open economy in which the real exchange rate is fixed and equal to one. Consumption, investment, government spending, and taxes are given by

$$C = 10 + 0.8(Y - T), I = 10, G = 10 \text{ and } T = 10$$

Imports and exports are given by

$$IM = 0.3Y \text{ and } X = 0.3Y^*$$

where Y^* denotes foreign output.

a. Solve for equilibrium output in the domestic economy, given Y^*. What is the multiplier in this economy? If we were to close the economy – so exports and imports were identically equal to zero – what would the multiplier be? Why would the multiplier be different in a closed economy?

b. Assume that the foreign economy is characterised by the same equations as the domestic economy (with asterisks reversed). Use the two sets of equations to solve for the equilibrium output of each country.

(Hint: use the equations for the foreign economy to solve for Y^* as a function of Y and substitute this solution for Y^* in part (a).) What is the multiplier for each country now? Why is it different from the open economy multiplier in part (a)?

c. Assume that the domestic government, G, has a target level of output of 125. Assuming that the foreign government does not change G^*, what is the increase in G necessary to achieve the target output in the domestic economy? Solve for net exports and the budget deficit in each country.

d. Suppose each government has a target level of output of 125 and that each government increases government spending by the same amount. What is the common increase in G and G^* necessary to achieve the target output in both countries? Solve for net exports and the budget deficit in each country.

e. Why is fiscal coordination, such as the common increase in G and G^* in part (d), difficult to achieve in practice?

EXPLORE FURTHER

12. The exchange rate as an automatic stabiliser

Consider an economy that suffers a fall in business confidence (which tends to reduce investment). Let UIP stand for the uncovered interest parity condition.

a. Suppose the economy has a flexible exchange rate. In an *IS–LM–UIP* diagram, show the short-run effect of the fall in business confidence on output, the interest rate and the exchange rate. How does the change in the exchange rate, by itself, tend to affect output? Does the change in the exchange rate dampen (make smaller) or amplify (make larger) the effect of the fall in business confidence on output?

b. Suppose, instead, the economy has a fixed exchange rate. In an *IS–LM–UIP* diagram, show how the economy responds to the fall in business confidence. What must happen to the money supply in order to maintain the fixed exchange rate? How does the effect on output in this economy, with fixed exchange rates, compare to the effect you found for the economy in part (a), with flexible exchange rates?

c. Explain how the exchange rate acts as an automatic stabiliser in an economy with flexible exchange rates.

13. Demand for US assets, the dollar and the trade deficit

This question explores how an increase in demand for US assets may have slowed the depreciation of the dollar that many economists believe is warranted by the large US trade deficit. Here, we modify the IS–LM–UIP framework (where UIP stands for uncovered interest parity) to analyse the effects of an increase in demand for US assets. Write the uncovered interest parity condition as

$$(1 + i_t) = (1 + i_t^*)E_t/E_{t+1}^e - x$$

where the parameter x represents factors affecting the relative demand for domestic assets. An increase in x means that investors are willing to hold domestic assets at a lower interest rate (given the foreign interest rate, and the current and expected exchange rates).

a. Solve the *UIP* condition for the current exchange rate, E_t.

b. Substitute the result from part (a) in the *IS* curve and construct the *UIP* diagram. As in the text, you may assume that *P* and *P** are constant and equal to one.

c. Suppose that as a result of a large trade deficit in the domestic economy, financial market participants believe that the domestic currency must depreciate in the future. Therefore, the expected exchange rate, E_{t+1}^e, falls. Show the effect of the fall in the expected exchange rate in the *IS–LM–UIP* diagram. What are the effects on the exchange rate and the trade balance? (*Hint*: in analysing the effect on the trade balance, remember why the *IS* curve shifted in the first place.)

d. Now suppose that the relative demand for domestic assets, *x*, increases. As a benchmark, suppose that the increase in *x* is exactly enough to return the *IS* curve to its original position, before the fall in the expected exchange rate. Show the combined effects of the fall in E_{t+1}^e and the increase in *x* in your *IS–LM–UIP* diagram. What are the ultimate effects on the exchange rate and the trade balance?

e. Based on your analysis, is it possible that an increase in demand for US assets could prevent the dollar from depreciating? Is it possible than an increase in demand for US assets could worsen the US trade balance. Explain your answers.

By the time you read this book, it is possible that relative demand for US assets could be weaker than it is at the time of this writing and that the dollar could be depreciating. Think about how you would use the framework of this problem to assess the current situation.

Log on to **MyEconLab** and complete the studyplan exercises for this chapter to see how much you have learnt, and where you need to revise most.

MyEconLab

FURTHER READING

- A good discussion of the relation among trade deficits, current account deficits, budget deficits, private saving and investment is given in Barry Bosworth's *Saving and Investment in a Global Economy* (Washington, DC: Brookings Institution, 1993).

- One view on the dollar's likely future is found in Martin Feldstein, 'Why the dollar will weaken further', *The International Economy*, Summer 2011.

APPENDIX

Derivation of the Marshall–Lerner condition

Start from the definition of net exports

$$NX = X - IM/\varepsilon$$

Assume trade to be initially balanced, so that $NX = 0$ and $X = IM/\varepsilon$, or equivalently $\varepsilon X = IM$. The Marshall–Lerner condition is the condition under which a real depreciation, a decrease in ε, leads to an increase in net exports.

To derive this condition, first multiply both sides of the equation above by ε to get

$$\varepsilon NX = \varepsilon X - IM$$

Now consider a change in the real exchange rate of $\Delta \varepsilon$. The effect of the change in the real exchange rate on the left side of the equation is given by $(\Delta \varepsilon) NX + \varepsilon (\Delta NX)$. Note that, if trade is initially balanced, $NX = 0$, so the first term in this expression is equal to zero, and the effect of the change on the left side is simply given by $\varepsilon(\Delta NX)$. The effect of the change in the real exchange rate on the right side of the equation is given by $(\Delta \varepsilon) X + \varepsilon(\Delta X) - (\Delta IM)$. Putting the two sides together gives

$$\varepsilon(\Delta NX) = (\Delta \varepsilon) X + \varepsilon(\Delta X) - (\Delta IM)$$

Divide both sides by εX to get:

$$\frac{\varepsilon(\Delta NX)}{\varepsilon X} = \frac{(\Delta \varepsilon) X}{\varepsilon X} + \frac{\varepsilon(\Delta X)}{\varepsilon X} - \frac{\Delta (IM)}{\varepsilon X}$$

Simplify, and use the fact that, if trade is initially balanced, $\varepsilon X = IM$ to replace εX by IM in the last term on the right. This gives

$$\frac{\Delta NX}{X} = \frac{\Delta \varepsilon}{\varepsilon} + \frac{\Delta X}{X} - \frac{\Delta IM}{IM}$$

The change in the trade balance (as a ratio to exports) in response to a real depreciation is equal to the sum of three terms:

- The first term is equal to the proportional change in the real exchange rate. It is negative if there is a real depreciation.
- The second term is equal to the proportional change in exports. It is positive if there is a real depreciation.
- The third term is equal to minus the proportional change in the imports. It is positive if there is a real depreciation.

The Marshall–Lerner condition is the condition that the sum of these three terms be positive. If it is satisfied, a real depreciation leads to an improvement in the trade balance.

A numerical example will help here. Suppose that a 1% depreciation leads to a proportional increase in exports of 0.9% and to a proportional decrease in imports of 0.8%. (Econometric evidence on the relation of exports and imports to the real exchange rate suggest that these are indeed reasonable numbers.) In that case, the right-hand side of the equation is equal to $-1\% + 0.9\% - (-0.8\%) = 0.7\%$. Thus, the trade balance improves: the Marshall–Lerner condition is satisfied.

THE MEDIUM RUN

In the medium run, the economy returns to a level of output associated with the natural rate of unemployment.

Chapter 8 The labour market

Chapter 8 looks at equilibrium in the labour market. It derives the natural rate of unemployment – the unemployment rate to which the economy tends to return in the medium run. Associated with the natural rate of unemployment is a natural level of output.

Chapter 9 Putting all markets together: the *AS–AD* model

Chapter 9 looks at equilibrium in all three markets – goods, financial and labour – together. It shows that, while output typically deviates from the natural level of output in the short run, it returns to the natural level in the medium run. The model developed in Chapter 9 is called the *AS–AD* model and, together with the *IS–LM* model, is one of the workhorses of macroeconomics.

Chapter 10 The Phillips curve, the natural rate of unemployment and inflation

Chapter 10 looks more closely at the relation between inflation and unemployment, a relation known as the Phillips curve. It shows that low unemployment leads to an increase in inflation; high unemployment leads to a decrease in inflation.

Chapter 11 Inflation, money growth and the real rate of interest

Chapter 11 looks at the determination of output, unemployment and inflation, and the effects of money growth. In the short run, decreases in money growth can trigger a recession. In the medium run, however, they are neutral; they have no effect on unemployment or output but are reflected one-for-one in changes in the rate of inflation.

Chapter 12 The medium run in an open economy

Chapter 12 extends the *AS–AD* model to an open economy. It first shows how, in the medium run, the real exchange rate can adjust even under a fixed exchange rate regime. It then studies the effects of exchange rate devaluations and revaluations under fixed exchange rates. It ends by discussing the pros and cons of various exchange rate regimes, including the adoption of a common currency such as the euro.

Chapter 8

THE LABOUR MARKET

Think about what happens when firms respond to an increase in demand by increasing production: higher production leads to higher employment. Higher employment leads to lower unemployment. Lower unemployment leads to higher wages. Higher wages increase production costs, leading firms to increase prices. Higher prices lead workers to ask for higher wages. Higher wages lead to further increases in prices, and so on.

So far, we have simply ignored this sequence of events: by assuming a constant price level in the *IS–LM* model, we in effect assumed that firms were able and willing to supply any amount of output at a given price level. So long as our focus was on the short run, this assumption was acceptable. But, as our attention turns to the medium run, we must now abandon this assumption, explore how prices and wages adjust over time, and how this, in turn, affects output. This will be our task in this and the next three chapters.

At the centre of the sequence of events described in the first paragraph is the labour market, the market in which wages are determined. This chapter focuses on the labour market. It has five sections:

- Section 8.1 provides an overview of the labour market in Europe.

- Sections 8.2 and 8.3 look at wage and price determination.

- Section 8.4 then looks at equilibrium in the labour market. It characterises the natural rate of unemployment, the rate of unemployment to which the economy tends to return in the medium run.

- Section 8.5 gives the map of where we will be going next.

8.1 A TOUR OF THE LABOUR MARKET

The total EU-27 population in 2011 was 495 million (Figure 8.1). Excluding those who were either under working age (under 15), or above the retirement age (which is currently around 65, although it is increasing in all countries because expected lifetime is increasing), the number of people potentially available for employment, the **population in working age**, was 331 million.

The **labour force** – the sum of those either working or looking for work – was only 240 million. The other 91 million people were **out of the labour force**, i.e. neither working in the marketplace nor looking for work. The **participation rate**, defined as the ratio of the labour force to the population in working age, was therefore 240/331, or 73%. Conversely, the non-participation rate, defined as the number of people out of the labour force divided by the population in working age, was 91/331, or 27%. In Europe, as in most of the other OECD countries, the participation rate has steadily increased over time, reflecting mostly the increasing participation rate of women: in Western Europe, like in the USA, only one woman out of three was in the labour force in 1950; now the number is close to two out of three and not far from the participation rate of men (three out of four). However, this is not true in all European countries. Figure 8.2 shows the participation rates of men and

◁ Work in the home, such as cooking or raising children, is not classified as work in the official statistics. This is a reflection of the difficulty of measuring these activities – not a value judgement about what constitutes work and what doesn't.

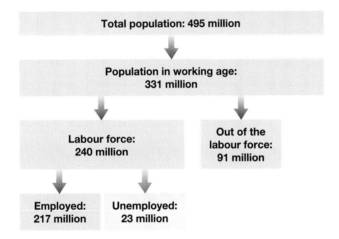

Figure 8.1

Population, labour force, employment and unemployment in the EU-27 (in millions), 2011

Source: Eurostat.

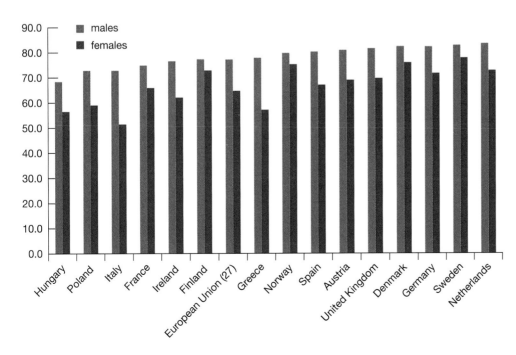

Figure 8.2

The participation rate of men and women in Europe, 2010

Source: Eurostat.
Table: population activity and inactivity, annual averages
http://epp.eurostat.ec.europa.eu/portal/ page/portal/statistics/search_database

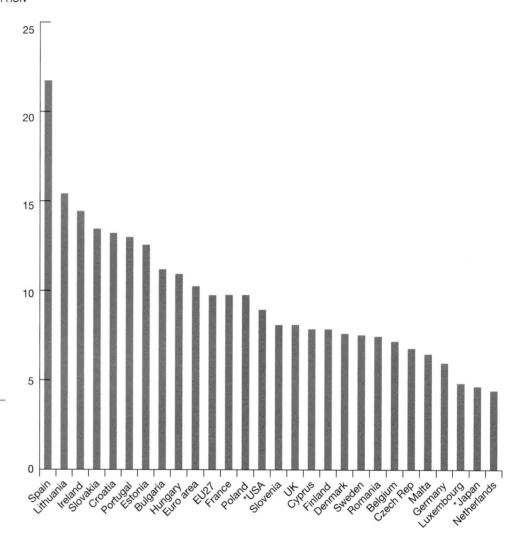

Figure 8.3

Unemployment rate in European countries, 2011

The average unemployment rate in Europe hides big differences among countries.

Source: Labour market statistics. Labour force statistics by sex and age: indicators. OECD Employment and Labour Market Statistics *http://stats.oecd.rog/*

women in Europe in 2010 (where countries are ranked from left to right in terms of the participation rate of women): in Northern European countries, the participation rates of men and women are pretty high and close to each other, whereas in Southern Europe, Central and Eastern Europe, and also in Ireland, the participation rate of women is much lower, just about 50%.

Of those in the labour force, 217 million were employed, and 23 million were unemployed – looking for work. The **unemployment rate**, defined as the ratio of the unemployed to the labour force, was therefore 23/240 = 9.7%.

Unemployment in Europe has not always been so high. Between the end of the Second World War and the end of the 1970s, European unemployment was very low, around 2%. It started to rise during the 1970s; it hit 8% in the 1980s and reached a peak of 10% in the 1990s. Today it is still rather high (9.7% in 2011), but the average unemployment rate actually hides a lot of differences among European countries. Figure 8.3 shows unemployment rates in European countries together with the EU-27 as a whole, the USA and Japan in 2011. In many of them unemployment is quite low: Austria, Belgium, Denmark, Finland, Germany, the Netherlands, Romania, Slovakia, Sweden and the UK have unemployment rates lower than the USA (8.9% in 2011). The high average unemployment rate in Europe reflects high unemployment rates in Spain (21.7% in 2011, further up to around 24% in the spring of 2012), as well as in smaller economies such as Bulgaria, Ireland and Portugal. In Spain, the unemployment rate had already gone well above 20% in the early 1990s, then it decreased, and then it increased again in the last few years following the financial crisis which began in 2007.

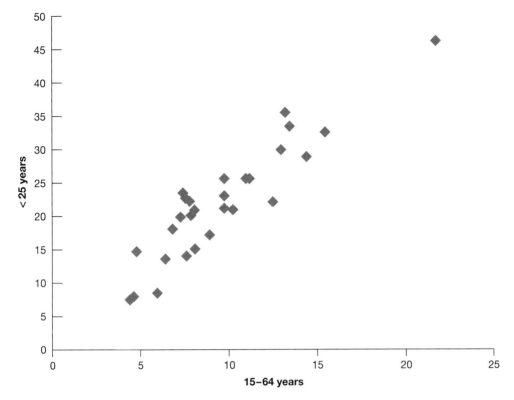

Figure 8.4

Youth unemployment in European countries, 2011

The incidence of unemployment is usually higher among young workers (less than 25 years).

Source: Unemployment rate, annual average, by sex and age groups (%)
http://epp.eurostat.ec.europa.eu/ portal/page/portal/statistics/ search_database

The average unemployment rate also hides large differences among different groups of workers within the same country. The most notable one is the higher incidence of unemployment among young workers. Figure 8.4 shows the total unemployment rate (i.e. the unemployment rate computed for the total labour force) and the youth unemployment rate (i.e. the unemployment rate among workers younger than 25 years) in European countries in 2011. The figure shows a dramatic incidence of unemployment among young workers compared to the average incidence of unemployment, and this is true in all European countries, especially in countries with higher than average unemployment rates (such as Greece, Italy and Spain), but also where the total unemployment rate is very low (such as the Netherlands and Norway).

Flows of workers between employment, unemployment and non-participation

To get a sense of what a given unemployment rate implies for individual workers, consider the following analogy. Take an airport full of passengers. It may be crowded because many planes are coming and going, and many passengers are quickly moving in and out of the airport or from one flight to another. Or it may be crowded because bad weather is delaying flights and passengers are stuck, waiting for the weather to improve. The number of passengers in the airport will be high in both cases, but their plights are quite different. Passengers in the second scenario are likely to be much less happy.

In the same way, a given unemployment rate may reflect two very different realities. It may reflect an active labour market, with many **separations** (i.e. workers who are leaving for another job or losing their jobs) and many **hires** (i.e. workers newly employed by firms), and so with many workers entering and exiting unemployment; or it may reflect a sclerotic labour market, with few separations, few hires and a stagnant unemployment pool.

Finding out which reality hides behind the aggregate unemployment rate requires data on the movements of workers. These data are available in Europe from a quarterly survey called the **Labour Force Survey (LFS)**. If you want to know more about how the LFS is conducted, see the Focus box 'The European Union Labour Force Survey' later in this chapter.

◄ *Sclerosis*, a medical term, means hardening of tissue. By analogy, it is used in economics to describe markets that function poorly and have few transactions.

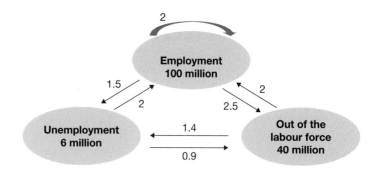

Figure 8.5

Average flows between employment, unemployment and non-participation in a hypothetical country

To keep things simple, imagine that, out of an employment pool of 100 million, in a given month 2 million workers move directly from one job to another (shown by the circular arrow at the top of Figure 8.5). Another 1.5 million move from employment to unemployment (shown by the arrow from employment to unemployment). This means that, on average, there are 6 (2 + 1.5 + 2.5) million **separations** each month in this country.

1.5 out of 4 million of all separations are **leavers** – workers leaving their jobs for a better alternative. The remaining half are **layoffs**. Layoffs are the effect of changes in employment levels across firms. At any given time, some firms are suffering decreases in demand and decreasing their employment; other firms are enjoying increases in demand and increasing employment. Even if aggregate employment numbers are stable, this does not mean nothing happens in the labour market: a high number of layoffs suggests a reality of continual job destruction and job creation across firms.

In reality, the flows in and out of the labour force are large. This fact has an important implication. The sharp focus on the unemployment rate by economists, policy makers and the news media is partly misdirected. Some of the people classified as out of the labour force are very much like the unemployed. They are in effect **discouraged workers**. And while they are not actively looking for a job, they would take one if they found one. This is why economists sometimes focus on the **non-employment rate**, the ratio of working age population, minus employment, to population, rather than the unemployment rate. We will follow tradition in this book and focus on the unemployment rate, but you should keep in mind that the unemployment rate is not the best estimate of the number of people available for work.

> Working in the opposite direction: some of the unemployed may be unwilling to accept any job offered to them and should probably not be counted as unemployed because they are not really looking for a job.

The average proportion of unemployed leaving unemployment each month is a very useful piece of information, as it allows computing the average **duration of unemployment**, which is the average length of time people spend unemployed. To see why, consider an example. Suppose the number of unemployed is constant and equal to 100, and each unemployed person remains unemployed for two months. So, at any given time, there are 50 people who have been unemployed for one month and 50 who have been unemployed for two months. Each month, the 50 unemployed who have been unemployed for two months leave unemployment. In this example, the proportion of unemployed leaving unemployment each month is 50/100, or 50%. The duration of unemployment is two months – the inverse of 1/50%. The average duration of unemployment equals the inverse of the proportion of unemployed leaving unemployment each month. Now, suppose·that each unemployed person remains unemployed for five months. In this case, at any given time, there are 20 people who have been unemployed for one month, 20 who have been unemployed for two months, 20 who have been unemployed for three months, 20 who have been unemployed for four months and 20 who have been unemployed for five months. Each month, the 20 unemployed who have been unemployed for five months leave unemployment. In this case, the proportion of unemployed leaving unemployment each month is 20/100, or 20%. The duration of unemployment is five months – the inverse of 1/20%.

The longer it takes for unemployed people to find a job, the higher is the average duration of unemployment. Countries with a high percentage of long-term unemployment (usually defined as unemployment for more than 12 months) have high average duration, and vice versa.

The average duration of unemployment has an important implication. In a country where the average duration is high, unemployment can be described as a stagnant pool of workers waiting indefinitely for jobs. In a country where the average duration is low, as in our example, for most (but obviously not all) of the unemployed, being unemployed is more a quick transition than a long wait between jobs. Among rich countries, the USA has one of the lowest average duration of unemployment of all (and one of the lowest percentage of long-term unemployment on the labour force, 2.8% in 2010). The average duration of unemployment has comparatively been much longer in Europe, but recently the picture has slightly changed. Although the average incidence of long-term unemployment in the EU-27 is still higher (3.9%) than in the USA, many European countries now have the lowest percentages among high-income countries, ranging from 0.7% in Norway, to 1.5% in Sweden and UK, to 6.3% in Portugal, up to a dramatic 9.2% in the Slovak Republic. Figure 8.6 shows the average duration of unemployment in some European countries, compared to the USA, since 2000.

The most striking feature of Figure 8.6 is the large difference between Europe and the USA: the average duration of unemployment is now slightly more than one year in Europe compared to around seven months in the USA. Unemployment is still a very different phenomenon in Europe, on average, than in the USA: being unemployed in Europe is often not a transitory condition as it is, on average, in the USA.

The second feature of Figure 8.6 is the divergent trends within Europe, where Northern European countries (Norway and to a minor extent Finland) are quite similar to the USA, while other Central or Southern European countries have much higher average duration of unemployment.

The duration of unemployment is also useful as it allows to think about the unemployment rate in a different way, as the flows of workers becoming unemployed each month multiplied by the average time they stay unemployed:

$$u = \text{flows} \times \text{duration}$$

For example, an unemployment rate, u, of 24 million can describe an economy where 8 million workers lose their jobs each month and stay unemployed for 3 months on average

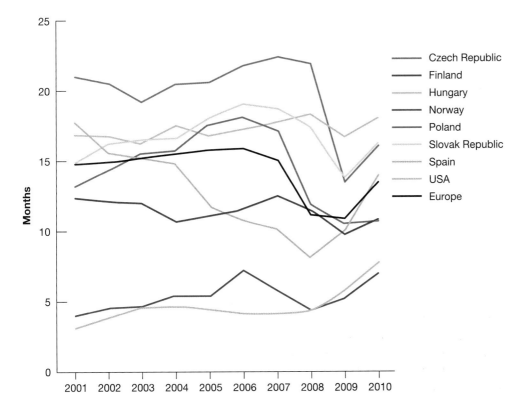

Figure 8.6

Average duration of unemployment in Europe and in the USA, 2000–2010

Source: OECD
Table: Average duration of unemployment
(yearly data) *http://stats.oecd.org*

FOCUS
The European Union Labour Force Survey

The European Union Labour Force Survey (EU LFS) is a quarterly sample survey covering households in the EU, EFTA (except Liechtenstein) and Candidate Countries. It provides annual and quarterly information on labour participation of people aged 15 and over as well as persons outside the labour force. The EU LFS sample size amounts approximately to 1.5 million individuals each quarter. The quarterly sampling rates vary between 0.2% and 3.3% in each country. The data range is from 1983 to 2010.

In providing data on employment, unemployment and inactivity, the EU LFS is an important source of information about the situation and trends in the labour market in the EU. Various breakdowns are available by age, sex, educational attainment, temporary employment, full-time/part-time distinction and many other dimensions.

The quarterly EU LFS also forms the basis for Eurostat's calculation of monthly unemployment figures, complemented by either monthly LFS estimates for the unemployment rates or additional sources such as unemployment registers. The resulting monthly harmonised unemployment rate – one of Eurostat's key short-term indicators – is published in a news release and in the online database.

$(8 \times 3 = 24)$, or an economy where 2 million workers lose their jobs each month and stay unemployed for one year on average $(2 \times 12 = 24)$. The same unemployment rate therefore can describe very different realities, with very different human costs. In the first, more workers lose theirs jobs each month, but quickly find another job. In the second, it is less likely to lose one's job, but unemployment may last a long time.

8.2 WAGE DETERMINATION

Having looked at unemployment, let's turn to wage determination, and to the relation between wages and unemployment.

Wages are set in many ways. Sometimes they are set by **collective bargaining**, that is, bargaining between firms and unions. Unlike in the USA, where collective bargaining plays a limited role, especially outside the manufacturing sector.

In most of the countries in Europe, collective bargaining is the predominant mean by which wages are agreed. The percentage of workers covered by collective bargaining is as high as 98% in Austria, 95% in Finland and higher than 90% in Belgium, Germany and France. In the rest of Europe, it is slightly lower, generally between 60 and 80%, but still much higher than in the USA or in Japan, where the percentage of workers covered by collective bargaining is around 20%. In Europe, however, the UK stands out as an exception, as collective bargaining plays a limited role, especially outside the manufacturing sector. Today, just around one-third of UK workers have their wages set by collective bargaining agreements. For the rest, wages are either set by employers or by bargaining between the employer and individual employee. The higher the skills needed to do the job, the more likely there is going to be bargaining. Wages offered for entry-level jobs at McDonald's are on a take-it-or-leave-it basis. New college graduates, on the other hand, can typically negotiate a few aspects of their compensation. Football stars can negotiate a lot more.

Given these differences across workers and across countries, can we hope to formulate anything like a general theory of wage determination? Yes. Although institutional differences influence wage determination, there are common forces at work in all countries. Two sets of facts stand out:

Collective bargaining: bargaining between a union (or a group of unions) and a firm (or a group of firms).

● Workers are typically paid a wage that exceeds their **reservation wage**, the wage that would make them indifferent between working or being unemployed. In other words, most workers are paid a high enough wage that they prefer being employed to being unemployed.

- Wages typically depend on labour-market conditions. The lower the unemployment rate, the higher the wages. (We will state this more precisely in the next section.)

To think about these facts, economists have focused on two broad lines of explanation. The first is that even in the absence of collective bargaining, workers have some bargaining power, which they can and do use to obtain wages above their reservation wages. The second is that firms themselves may, for a number of reasons, want to pay wages higher than the reservation wage. Let's look at each explanation in turn.

Bargaining

How much **bargaining power** a worker has depends on two factors. The first is how costly it would be for the firm to replace him or her, were he or she to leave the firm. The second is how hard it would be for him or her to find another job, were he or she to leave the firm. The more costly it is for the firm to replace the worker, and the easier it is for him or her to find another job, the more bargaining power he or she will have. This has two implications:

- How much bargaining power a worker has depends first on the nature of the job. Replacing a worker at McDonald's is not very costly: the required skills can be taught quickly, and typically a large number of willing applicants have already filled out job application forms. In this situation, the worker is unlikely to have much bargaining power. If he or she asks for a higher wage, the firm can lay him or her off and easily find a replacement. In contrast, a highly skilled worker who knows in detail how the firm operates may be very difficult and costly to replace. This gives him or her more bargaining power. If he or she asks for a higher wage, the firm may decide that it is best to give it to him or her.
- How much bargaining power a worker has also depends on labour market conditions. When the unemployment rate is low, it is more difficult for firms to find acceptable replacement workers. At the same time, it is easier for workers to find other jobs. Under these conditions, workers are in a stronger bargaining position and may be able to obtain a higher wage. Conversely, when the unemployment rate is high, finding good replacement workers is easier for firms, while finding another job is harder for workers. Being in a weak bargaining position, workers may have no choice but to accept a lower wage.

◀ Peter Diamond, Dale Mortensen and Christopher Pissarides received the 2010 Nobel Prize in economics precisely for working out the characteristics of a labour market with large flows and wage bargaining.

Efficiency wages

Regardless of workers' bargaining power, firms may want to pay more than the reservation wage. They may want their workers to be productive, and a higher wage can help them achieve that goal. If, for example, it takes a while for workers to learn how to do a job correctly, firms will want their workers to stay for some time. But if workers are paid only their reservation wage, they will be indifferent between staying or leaving. In this case, many of them will quit, and the turnover rate will be high. Paying a wage above the reservation wage makes it more attractive for workers to stay. It decreases turnover and increases productivity.

Behind this example lies a more general proposition: most firms want their workers to feel good about their jobs. Feeling good promotes good work, which leads to higher productivity. Paying a high wage is one instrument the firm can use to achieve these goals. (See the Focus box on 'Henry Ford and efficiency wages'.) Economists call the theories which link the productivity or the efficiency of workers to the wage they are paid **efficiency wage theories**.

Like theories based on bargaining, efficiency wage theories suggest that wages depend on both the nature of the job and on labour-market conditions:

◀ Before 11 September 2001, the approach to airport security was to hire workers at low wages and accept the resulting high turnover. Now that airport security has become a much higher priority, the approach is to make the jobs more attractive and higher paid so as to get more motivated and more competent workers, and reduce turnover.

- Firms – such as high-tech firms – that see employee morale and commitment as essential to the quality of their work will pay more than firms in sectors where workers' activities are more routine.

FOCUS
Henry Ford and efficiency wages

In 1914, Henry Ford – the builder of the most popular car in the world at the time, the Model T – made a stunning announcement. His company would pay all employees a minimum of $5 a day for an eight-hour day. This was a very large salary increase for most employees, who had been earning an average $2.30 for a nine-hour day. From the point of view of the Ford company, this increase in pay was far from negligible – it represented about half of the company's profits at the time.

What Ford's motivations were is not entirely clear. Ford himself gave too many reasons for us to know which ones he actually believed. The reason was not that the company had a hard time finding workers at the previous wage. But the company clearly had a hard time retaining workers. There was a very high turnover rate, as well as high dissatisfaction among workers.

Whatever the reasons behind Ford's decision, the results of the wage increase were astounding, as Table 8.1 shows.

The annual turnover rate (the ratio of separations to employment) plunged from a high of 370% in 1913 to a

low of 16% in 1915 (An annual turnover rate of 370% means that, on average, 31% of the company's workers left each month, so that over the course of a year the ratio of separations to employment was 31% × 12 = 370%.). The layoff rate collapsed from 62% to nearly 0%. The average rate of absenteeism (not shown in the table), which ran at close to 10% in 1913, was down to 2.5% one year later. There is little question that higher wages were the main source of these changes.

Did productivity at the Ford plant increase enough to offset the cost of increased wages? The answer to this question is less clear. Productivity was much higher in 1914 than in 1913. Estimates of the productivity increases range from 30% to 50%. Despite higher wages, profits were also higher in 1914 than in 1913. But how much of this increase in profits was due to changes in workers' behaviour and how much was due to the increasing success of Model T cars is harder to establish.

While the effects support efficiency wage theories, it may be that the increase in wages to $5 a day was excessive, at least from the point of view of profit maximisation. But Henry Ford probably had other objectives as well, from keeping the unions out – which he did – to generating publicity for himself and the company – which he surely did.

Table 8.1 Annual turnover and layoff rates (%) at Ford 1913–1915

	1913	1914	1915
Turnover rate	370	54	16
Layoff rate	62	7	0.1

Source: Dan Raff and Lawrence Summers, 'Did Henry Ford pay efficiency wages?', *Journal of Labour Economics*, 1987, **5**(4), 557–586.

- Labour-market conditions will affect the wage. A low unemployment rate makes it more attractive for employed workers to quit: when unemployment is low, it is easy to find another job. That means, when unemployment decreases, a firm that wants to avoid an increase in quits will have to increase wages to induce workers to stay with the firm. When this happens, lower unemployment will again lead to higher wages. Conversely, higher unemployment will lead to lower wages.

Wages, prices, and unemployment

We capture our discussion of wage determination by using the following equation:

$$W = P^e F(u, z) \qquad [8.1]$$
$$(-, +)$$

The aggregate nominal wage W depends on three factors:

- The expected price level, P^e.
- The actual unemployment rate, u.
- A catchall variable, z, that stands for all other variables that may affect the outcome of wage setting.

Let's look at each factor.

The expected price level

First, ignore the difference between the expected and the actual price level and ask: why does the price level affect nominal wages? The answer: because both workers and firms care about real wages, not nominal wages.

- Workers do not care about how many euros or pounds they receive but about how many goods they can buy with that wage. In other words, they do not care about the nominal wages they receive, but about the nominal wages (W) they receive relative to the price of the goods they buy (P). They care about W/P, the real wage.
- In the same way, firms do not care about the nominal wages they pay but about the nominal wages (W) they pay relative to the price of the goods they sell (P). So they also care about W/P.

Think of it another way: if workers expect the price level – the price of the goods they buy – to double, they will ask for a doubling of their nominal wage. If firms expect the price level – the price of the goods they sell – to double, they will be willing to double the nominal wage. So, if both workers and firms expect the price level to double, they will agree to double the nominal wage, keeping the real wage constant. This is captured in equation (8.1): a doubling in the expected price level leads to a doubling of the nominal wage chosen when wages are set.

◄ An increase in the expected price level leads to an increase in the nominal wage, in the same proportion.

Return now to the distinction we set aside at the start of the paragraph: why do wages depend on the expected price level, P^e, rather than the actual price level, P? Because wages are set in nominal terms, and when they are set, the relevant price level is not yet known. For example, in many union contracts in Europe, nominal wages are set in advance for one or more years. (Typically for one year in the UK, for three years in Germany.) Unions and firms have to decide what nominal wages will be over the following years based on what they expect the price level to be over those years. Even when wages are set by firms, or by bargaining between the firm and each worker, nominal wages are typically set for a year. If the price level rises unexpectedly during the year, nominal wages are typically not readjusted. The adjustment only happens when a new contract is signed. (How workers and firms form expectations of the price level will occupy us for much of the next three chapters; we will leave this issue aside for the moment.)

The unemployment rate

Also affecting the aggregate wage in equation (8.1) is the unemployment rate, u. The minus sign under u indicates that an increase in the unemployment rate decreases wages.

The fact that wages depend on the unemployment rate was one of the main conclusions of our earlier discussion. If we think of wages as being determined by bargaining, then higher unemployment weakens workers' bargaining power, forcing them to accept lower wages. If we think of wages as being determined by efficiency wage considerations, then higher unemployment allows firms to pay lower wages and still keep workers willing to work.

◄ An increase in unemployment leads to a decrease in the nominal wage.

The other factors

The third variable in equation (8.1), z, is a catchall variable that stands for all the factors that affect wages, given the expected price level and the unemployment rate. By convention, we will define z so that an increase in z implies an increase in the wage (thus, the positive sign under z in the equation). Our earlier discussion suggests a long list of potential factors here.

◄ By the definition of z, an increase in z leads to an increase in the nominal wage.

Take, for example, unemployment insurance – the payment of unemployment benefits to workers who lose their jobs. There are very good reasons why society should provide some insurance to workers who lose their job and have a hard time finding another. But there is little question that, by making the prospects of unemployment less distressing, more generous unemployment benefits do increase wages at a given unemployment rate. To take an extreme example, suppose unemployment insurance did not exist. Some workers would have little to live on and would be willing to accept very low wages to avoid remaining

Table 8.2 Net replacement rates in Europe, 2010

	Initial phase of unemployment		Long-term unemployment	
	No children Single person	Two children One-earner married couple	No children Single person	Two children One-earner married couple
Austria	55	69	51	65
Belgium	66	60	52	58
Czech Republic	65	69	36	57
Denmark	57	64	57	64
Estonia	54	59	24	41
Finland	53	61	43	74
France	66	67	33	52
Germany	62	72	34	62
Greece	34	43	0	4
Hungary	56	64	22	34
Ireland	38	70	58	85
Italy	56	69	0	0
Luxembourg	84	88	46	72
Netherlands	74	80	52	72
Poland	36	44	23	45
Portugal	75	76	17	50
Slovak Republic	64	57	19	42
Slovenia	73	77	32	72
Spain	60	75	23	33
Sweden	47	52	43	63
UK	13	44	38	71
USA	48	45	7	37

Source: OECD, Tax-Benefit Models.
www.oecd.org/els/benefitsandwagesstatistics

unemployed. But unemployment insurance does exist, and it allows unemployed workers to hold out for higher wages. In this case, we can think of z as representing the level of unemployment benefits: at a given unemployment rate, higher unemployment benefits increase the wage.

In Europe, the replacement rate – which is computed as the fraction of the last wage which the social security administration provides to a person if he or she no longer works (and are called net replacement rates) – varies across countries and, within each country, vary basically according to the type of household (single person or couple with children) and the sector of industry. Table 8.2 shows the replacement rates for an average production worker in the initial phase of unemployment and after five years he or she has been out of work (the data refer to the year 2010). In practically all countries, the replacement rate at the beginning of a spell of unemployment is usually higher for a couple with two children than for someone who is single. For instance in Finland, where the initial replacement rate is 82%, the unemployed have little incentive to seek regular work. The replacement rates for long-term unemployed are lowest in Italy, Greece and the USA and highest in the Scandinavian countries (except Norway), the Slovak Republic, the Netherlands, Austria and Germany.

Another aspect of unemployment insurance that is likely to affect wages is the duration of unemployment benefits – that is, the number of months they are provided for by the social security administration. At a given unemployment rate, a longer duration of unemployment benefits increases the wage. In Europe, the duration of unemployment insurance varies a lot across countries, much more than the level of the benefits provided. Figure 8.7 shows the duration of unemployment insurance in European countries in 2010. In most of the countries, unemployment benefits are granted for less than one year, with the noteworthy exceptions of Belgium, where the benefits are unlimited, and of Denmark and the Netherlands where benefits are paid for 30 to 36 months maximum.

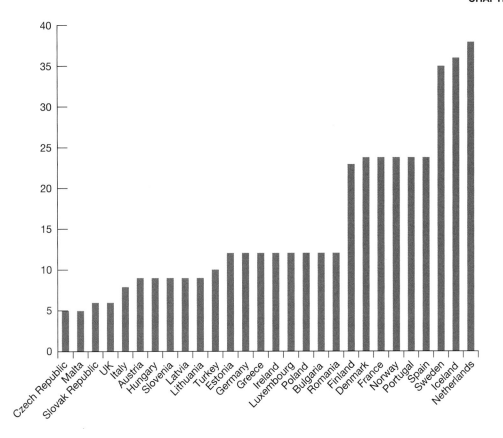

Figure 8.7

Duration of unemployment insurance in Europe, 2010 (in months)

Source: Benefits and Wages, OECD indicators
www.oecd.org/els/social/workincentives

Another factor that affects wages, given the expected price level and the unemployment rate, is the level of **employment protection**. The higher the legal protection for workers, the more expensive it is for firms to lay off workers. Higher employment protection is likely to lead to higher wages. This is because high employment protection is likely to increase the bargaining power of workers covered by this protection (laying them off and hiring other workers is now more costly for firms), increasing the wage for a given unemployment rate.

In Europe, the level of legal protection for workers is on average higher than in the USA. However, there are also wide variations within Europe itself: most notably, the UK has signicantly reduced the level of employment protection since the 1980s and is now rather different from the so-called European social model which prevails in continental Europe. Figure 8.8 shows the level of employment protection in Europe, compared to other OECD countries. The indicator of employment protection ranges between 0 and 2 and it increases with the strictness of employment protection (that is, the higher the indicator, the higher the employment protection). In Europe, the UK ranks very low, followed by Ireland and the Scandinavian countries, while countries in Southern Europe – France, Spain, Italy and Portugal – have the highest level of employment protection of all.

A further factor that is likely to affect wages, given the expected price level and unemployment, is the presence of a **minimum wage** set by the law. The presence of a minimum wage can cause wage rigidity, as it prevents wages from falling below the legal minimum to restore equilibrium in the labour market. Although most workers earn well above the minimum wage, for some groups of workers, especially for the unskilled, the presence of a minimum wage is likely to reduce firms' demand for unskilled labour. This is the reason why many economists argue that the presence of a minimum wage is largely responsible for high youth unemployment. In fact, an increase in the minimum wage may increase not only the minimum wage itself but also wages just above the minimum wage, leading to an increase in the average wage, W, at a given unemployment rate.

European countries, including the UK since April 1999 (and with the notable exception of Germany), as well as the USA, have a mandatory minimum wage. Figure 8.9 shows the

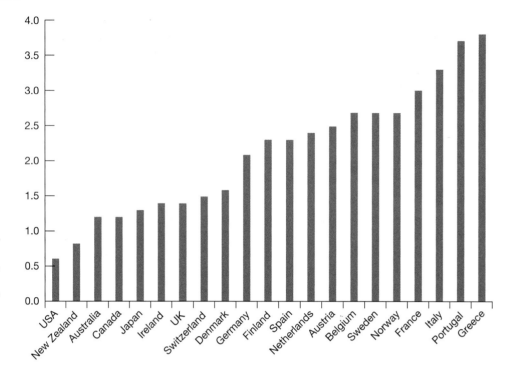

Figure 8.8

Employment protection across European countries, 2003

Source: Allard, Gayle, 'Measuring job security over time: in search of a historical indicator for EPL', IE Working Paper, WP05-17, Madrid 2005. CESifo, DICE database **www.cesifo-group.de/portal/page/portal/ifoHome/a-winfo/d3iiv**

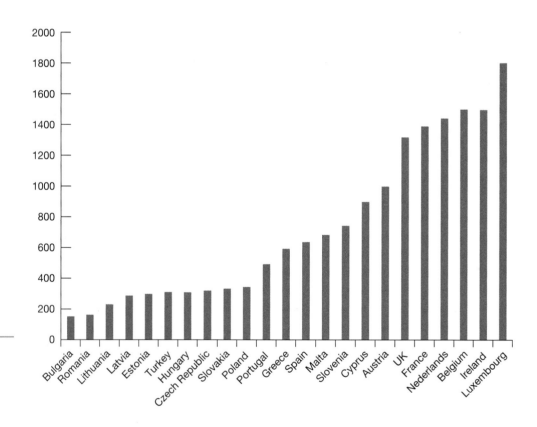

Figure 8.9

Gross minimum wages, euro per month, 2012

Source: The Federation of European Employers **www.fedee.com/pay-job-evaluation/minimum-wage-rates/**

gross minimum wage in euro per month in each European country in 2012. The striking feature of Figure 8.9 is the very low level of minimum wages in Central and Eastern European countries, where the statutory gross minimum wage per month is around €200. The size of the minimum wage in absolute terms varies a lot across countries, ranging from very low levels in Portugal and Spain (where the minimum wage is significantly lower than in the USA), to high levels such as in the Netherlands or in Ireland. (In the USA, the Federal minimum wage is $7.25 per hour, but individual states can and often do apply different minimum wages.)

It has been widely debated whether the European social model should be considered one of the sources of the higher unemployment rates in continental Europe, compared to the UK or the USA. According to some labour economists, there is no doubt that high levels of unemployment insurance, employment protection and high minimum wages are partly responsible for the high unemployment rates in many European countries. Yet, it has also been argued that labour market rigidities need not necessarily be associated with high unemployment. Although it is true that, on average, countries with higher labour market rigidities have higher unemployment rates, it is also true that some countries with low unemployment rates do have high levels of workers' protection in the form of generous unemployment insurance and high minimum wages. The most notable case in Europe is Denmark. The peculiarity of the Danish system is that, since the early 1980s, it combines generous unemployment benefits with an effective system for helping workers find a job: the result is a low unemployment rate, one of the lowest in Europe.

8.3 PRICE DETERMINATION

Having looked at wage determination, let's now turn to price determination.

The prices set by firms depend on the costs they face. These costs depend, in turn, on the nature of the **production function** – the relation between the inputs used in production and the quantity of output produced – and on the prices of these inputs.

For the moment, we will assume that firms produce goods using labour as the only factor of production. We will write the production function as follows:

$$Y = AN \qquad [8.2]$$

where Y is output, N is employment, and A is labour productivity. This way of writing the production function implies that **labour productivity** – output per worker – is constant and equal to A.

It should be clear that this is an oversimplification. In reality, firms use other factors of production in addition to labour. They use capital – machines and factories. They use raw materials – oil, for example. Moreover, there is technological progress, so that labour productivity, A, is not constant but steadily increases over time. We shall introduce these complications later: we will introduce raw materials (in Chapter 9) when we discuss changes in the price of oil; we will focus on the role of capital and technological progress when we turn to the determination of output in the long run (in Chapters 13–15). For the moment, though, this simple relation between output and employment will make our lives easier and still serve our purposes.

◁ Using a term from microeconomics: this assumption implies constant returns to labour in production. If firms double the number of workers they employ, they double the amount of output they produce.

If there were perfect competition in the goods market, the price of a unit of output would be equal to marginal cost: P would be equal to W. But many markets for goods and services are not competitive, and firms charge a price higher than their marginal cost. A simple way of capturing this fact is to assume that firms set their price according to

$$P = (1 + \mu)W \qquad [8.3]$$

where μ is the **mark-up** of the price over the cost. If goods markets were perfectly competitive, μ would be equal to zero, and the price, P, would simply equal the cost, W, the marginal cost. To the extent they are not competitive and firms have market power, μ is positive, and the price, P, will exceed the cost, W, by a factor equal to $(1 + \mu)$.

8.4 THE NATURAL RATE OF UNEMPLOYMENT

Let's now look at the implications of wage and price determination for unemployment.

The wage-setting relation

Let's go back to equation (8.1), which characterises wage determination:

$$W = P^e F(u, z)$$

Dividing both sides by the expected price level:

$$\frac{W}{P^e} = F(u, z) \qquad [8.4]$$
$$(-, +)$$

Wage determination implies a negative relation between the expected real wage, W/P^e, and the unemployment rate, u: the higher the unemployment rate, the lower the real wage that wage setters expect to get. The intuition is straightforward: the higher the unemployment rate, the weaker workers are in a position to bargain and the lower the real wage will be.

This relation between the expected real wage and the rate of unemployment – let's call it the **wage-setting relation** – is drawn in Figure 8.10. The expected real wage is measured on the vertical axis. The unemployment rate is measured on the horizontal axis. The wage-setting relation is drawn as the downward-sloping curve WS (for wage setting): the higher the unemployment rate, the lower the expected real wage.

> Wage setters: unions and firms, if wages are set by collective bargaining; individual workers and firms, if wages are set on a case-by-case basis; firms, if wages are set on a take-it-or-leave-it basis.

The price-setting relation

Let's now look at the implications of price determination. If we divide both sides of the price-determination equation (8.3), by the nominal wage, we get

$$\frac{P}{W} = 1 + \mu \qquad [8.5]$$

The ratio of the price level to the wage implied by the price-setting behaviour of firms equals 1 plus the mark-up. Now invert both sides of this equation to get the implied real wage:

$$\frac{W}{P} = \frac{1}{1 + \mu} \qquad [8.6]$$

Figure 8.10

Wages, prices, and the natural rate of unemployment

The natural rate of unemployment is the unemployment rate such that the real wage expected by wage setters is equal to the real wage paid by firms.

Note what this equation says: price-setting decisions determine the real wage paid by firms. An increase in the mark-up leads firms to increase their prices, given the wage they have to pay; equivalently, it leads to a decrease in the real wage.

The step from equation (8.5) to equation (8.6) is algebraically straightforward. But how price setting actually determines the real wage paid by firms may not be intuitively obvious. Think of it this way: suppose the firm you work for increases its mark-up and therefore increases the price of its product. Your real wage does not change very much: you are still paid the same nominal wage, and the product produced by the firm is at most a small part of your consumption basket.

Now suppose that not only the firm you work for, but also all the firms in the economy increase their mark-up. All the prices go up. Even if you are paid the same nominal wage, your real wage goes down. So, the higher the mark-up set by firms, the lower your (and everyone else's) real wage will be. This is what equation (8.6) says.

The **price-setting relation** in equation (8.6) is drawn as the horizontal line *PS* (for price setting) in Figure 8.10. The real wage implied by price setting is $1/(1 + \mu)$; it does not depend on the unemployment rate.

Equilibrium real wages and unemployment

Equilibrium in the labour market requires that the real wage expected by wage setting be equal to the effective real wage paid by firms. The expected real wage and the effective real wage are equal when the expected price level is equal to the effective price level. In Figure 8.10, equilibrium is given by point A, and the equilibrium unemployment rate is given by u_n.

Algebraically, when $P^e = P$, equations (8.4) and (8.6) give

$$F(u_n, z) = \frac{1}{1 + \mu} \tag{8.7}$$

The equilibrium unemployment rate, u_n, is such that the expected real wage chosen in wage setting – the left side of equation (8.7) – is equal to the effective real wage implied by price setting – the right side of equation (8.7).

The equilibrium unemployment rate (u_n) is called the **natural rate of unemployment** (which is why we have used the subscript n to denote it). The terminology has become standard, so we will adopt it, but this is actually a bad choice of words. The word 'natural' suggests a constant of nature, one that is unaffected by institutions and policy. As its derivation makes clear, however, the 'natural' rate of unemployment is anything but natural. The positions of the wage-setting and price-setting curves, and thus the equilibrium unemployment rate, depend on both z and u. Consider two examples:

◀ *Natural*, in Webster's dictionary, means 'in a state provided by nature, without man-made changes'.

● An increase in unemployment benefits – An increase in unemployment benefits can be represented by an increase in z: since an increase in benefits makes the prospect of unemployment less painful, it increases the reservation wage (i.e. the wage below which workers prefer to stay at home and get the unemployment benefits instead of working for that wage), and therefore the nominal wage desired by wage setters for a given expected price level (i.e. the real wage they expect to get), at any given unemployment rate. So it shifts the wage-setting relation up, from *WS* to *WS'* in Figure 8.11. At the initial equilibrium rate of unemployment, u_n, the expected real wage turns out to be higher than the effective real wage. For the labour market to return to equilibrium, a higher unemployment rate is needed to bring the expected real wage back to what firms are willing to pay. The natural rate of unemployment increases from u_n to u_n'.

● A less stringent enforcement of existing anti-trust legislation – To the extent that this allows firms to collude more easily and increase their market power, it will lead to an increase in their mark-up – an increase in μ. The increase in μ implies a decrease in the effective real wage firms are willing to pay, and so it shifts the price-setting relation down, from *PS* to *PS'* in Figure 8.12. At the initial equilibrium rate of unemployment, u_n, wage setters still expect the real wage they were getting before, which now turns out to

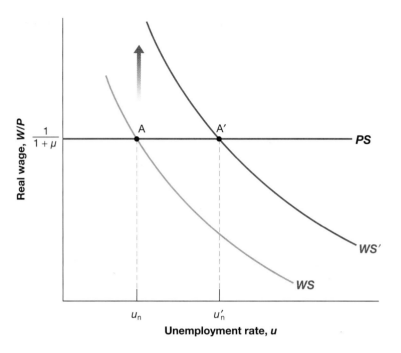

Figure 8.11

Unemployment benefits and the natural rate of unemployment

An increase in unemployment benefits leads to an increase in the natural rate of unemployment.

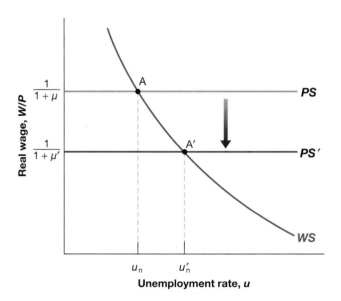

Figure 8.12

Mark-ups and the natural rate of unemployment

An increase in mark-ups decreases the real wage and leads to an increase in the natural rate of unemployment.

Unions often overlook competition and think that anti-trust legislation is none of their business because it has nothing to do with real wages and unemployment. What you have just learned indicates, instead, that they should bargain for a strong anti-trust legislation at least as much as they do for high real wages.

This name has been suggested by Edmund Phelps, from Columbia University. Phelps was awarded the Nobel Prize in 2006. (For more on some of his contributions, see Chapters 11 and 24.)

be higher than what firms are now willing to pay. The new equilibrium rate of unemployment, u'_n, must be higher to force workers to expect a comparatively lower real wage. The equilibrium moves from A to A', and the natural rate of unemployment increases from u_n to u'_n. Higher unemployment is required to make workers accept this lower real wage, leading to an increase in the natural rate of unemployment.

Factors like the generosity of unemployment benefits or anti-trust legislation can hardly be thought of as the result of nature. Rather, they reflect various characteristics of the structure of the economy. For that reason, a better name for the equilibrium rate of unemployment would be the **structural rate of unemployment**, but so far the name has not caught on.

From unemployment to employment

Associated with the natural rate of unemployment is a **natural level of employment**, the level of employment that prevails when unemployment is equal to its natural rate.

Let's review the relation between unemployment, employment, and the labour force. Let U denote unemployment, N denote employment, and L the labour force. Then:

$$u = \frac{U}{L} = \frac{L-N}{L} = 1 - \frac{N}{L}$$

The first step follows from the definition of the unemployment rate, u. The second follows from the fact that, from the definition of the labour force, the level of unemployment, U, equals the labour force, L, minus employment, N. The third step follows from simplifying $\blacktriangleleft\ L = N + U\ \Rightarrow\ U = L - N$ the fraction. Putting all three steps together: the unemployment rate, u, equals 1 minus the ratio of employment, N, to the labour force, L.

Rearranging to get employment in terms of the labour force and the unemployment rate gives:

$$N = L(1-u)$$

Employment, N, is equal to the labour force, L, multiplied by 1 minus the unemployment rate, u.

So, if the natural rate of unemployment is u_n, and the labour force is equal to L, the natural level of employment, N_n, is given by

$$N_n = L(1 - u_n)$$

For example, if the labour force is 150 million and the natural rate of unemployment is, say, 5%, then the natural level of employment is $150 \times (1 - 0.05) = 142.5$ million.

From employment to output

Finally, associated with the natural level of employment is the **natural level of output**, the level of production when employment is equal to the natural level of employment. Given the production function we have used in this chapter ($Y = AN$), the natural level of output, Y_n, is easy to derive. It is given by

$$Y_n = AN_n = AL(1 - u_n)$$

Using equation (8.7) and the relations between the unemployment rate, employment and output we just derived, the natural level of output satisfies the following equation:

$$F\left(1 - \frac{Y_n}{AL}, z\right) = \frac{1}{1+\mu} \tag{8.8}$$

The natural level of output, Y_n, is such that, at the associated rate of unemployment ($u_n = 1 - Y_n/AL$), the real wage expected in wage setting – the left side of equation (8.8) – is equal to the effective real wage implied by price setting – the right side of equation (8.8). As you will see, equation (8.8) will turn out to be very useful in the next chapter. Make sure you understand it.

We have gone through many steps in this section. Let's summarise:

- The expected real wage targeted by wage setters is a decreasing function of the unemployment rate.
- The effective real wage firms are willing to pay is constant as the mark-up is constant, as implied by the price-setting relation.
- Equilibrium in the labour market requires that the expected real wage in wage setting be equal to the effective real wage. This determines the equilibrium unemployment rate.
- This equilibrium unemployment rate is known as the natural rate of unemployment.
- Associated with the natural rate of unemployment is a natural level of employment and a natural level of output.

FOCUS
Labour market regulation and unemployment across European countries

In this chapter we have looked at two ways of thinking about the rate of unemployment. In terms of stocks, the unemployment rate is defined as the ratio of the unemployed over the total work force ($u = U/L$). In terms of flows, the unemployment rate can be thought of as the number of workers who become unemployed during a given time, multiplied by the average duration of unemployment.

This way of looking at the unemployment rate helps understand how differences across countries in labour market regulation can affect the rate of unemployment. Labour market regulation affects wage setting by setting minimum wages, unemployment benefits, bargaining rules and employment protection legislation. How does labour market regulation affect the unemployment rate?

Labour market regulation affects the unemployment rate because it has an impact on both the flows of workers who become unemployed, and the duration of unemployment. On the one hand, it decreases the flows, as the more regulated the labour market is, the lower the number of workers who become unemployed each period. On the other hand, it increases the duration of unemployment, as firms will be more reluctant to hire new workers in a highly regulated labour market. So labour market regulation may increase or decrease the unemployment rate, depending on which effect is stronger. As we have learned in this chapter, at any given unemployment rate, the pain of unemployment will be higher the longer it takes, on average, for unemployed workers to find a job – that is, on the duration of unemployment. This is why labour market regulation, by increasing the bargaining power of workers, needs to be offset, in equilibrium, by a longer duration of unemployment.

We just saw that employment protection increases the duration of unemployment, and may therefore increase or decrease unemployment rate. What happens, however, if only one group of workers has employment protection, and not the rest. This is indeed the direction that many countries have gone in, during the last decade. Some European countries with high unemployment rates introduced major labour market reforms with the aim to increase employment, particularly among the youth. Following the examples of some Northern European countries where employment protection is low and unemployment rates are also low, the way these reforms were designed, for example in Italy, was by reducing the bargaining power and the degree of employment protection of newly hired workers. This has created a dual labour market: standard (permanent) workers – still the vast majority of the labour force – keep enjoying high employment protection, so that the separation rate, s, is low. At the same time, newly hired workers, in particular younger workers, are hired on short-term contracts with high separation rates. Their jobs are often of poor quality, since, being temporary, firms lack the incentive to train them. Moreover, due to the flexibility of temporary contracts, these workers absorb a large fraction of the employment fluctuations associated with short-run fluctuations in output. Therefore, unemployment is still high, especially among younger workers. A different type of reform was introduced in Germany through the 2003 Hartz laws, named after Peter Hartz, the Volkswage's personnel director who led the commission which drafted them. These reforms increased the incentives for unemployed workers to find a job and improve job matching, similar to the so-called Danish system of flex-security, which combines low employment protection with unemployment benefits that are relatively generous, but elapse the moment the employment office offers an unemployed worker a job he or she refuses. These countries show that high social protection can be consistent with a low unemployment rate. All these examples show that a reduction in the levels of employment protection will not automatically bring unemployment rates down, unless it is accompanied by measures that increase the probability that the unemployed find a job. What should we conclude? Employment protection can be consistent with both low and high unemployment rates, the difference depending on how efficiently the whole labour market regulations are designed.

8.5 WHERE WE GO FROM HERE

We have just seen how equilibrium in the labour market determines the equilibrium unemployment rate (we have called it the natural rate of unemployment), which in turn determines the level of output (we have called it the natural level of output).

So, you may ask, what did we do in the previous four chapters? If equilibrium in the labour market determines the unemployment rate, and by implication, the level of output, why did we spend so much time looking at the goods and financial markets? What about our earlier conclusions that the level of output was determined by factors such as monetary policy, fiscal policy, consumer confidence and so on – all factors which do not enter equation (8.8) and therefore do not affect the natural level of output?

The key to the answer is simple:

- We have derived the natural rate of unemployment as the rate at which the expected real wage by wage setters equals the effective real wage firms are willing to pay.
- However, there is no reason for which the expected price level should be equal to the effective price level in the short run. The price level may well turn out to be different from what was expected when nominal wages were set. Therefore, the wage rate expected by workers need not be equal to the effective real wage they get. This implies that employment will different from its natural level, N_n. Hence, in the short run, there is no reason for unemployment to be equal to the natural rate or for output to be equal to its natural level. For example, if the expected price level, P^e, is higher than the effective price level, P, then the real wage they expect to get is lower than what they effectively receive. This will induce a number of workers not to accept jobs and therefore the effective rate of unemployment will be higher than the natural rate of unemployment.

  As we will see in the next chapter, the factors that determine movements in output in the short run are indeed the factors we focused on in the preceding three chapters: monetary policy, fiscal policy and so on. Your time (and ours) was not wasted.

> In the short run, the factors that determine movements in output are the factors we focused on in the preceding three chapters: monetary policy, fiscal policy and so on.

- But expectations are unlikely to be systematically wrong (say, too high or too low) forever. That is why, in the medium run, unemployment tends to return to the natural rate, and output tends to return to the natural level. In the medium run, the factors that determine unemployment and output are the factors that appear in equations (8.7) and (8.8).

> In the medium run, output tends to return to the natural level, and the factors that determine output are the factors we have focused on in this chapter.

These, in short, are the answers to the questions asked in the first paragraph of this chapter. Developing these answers in detail will be our task in the next two chapters.

SUMMARY

- The labour force consists of those who are working (employed) or looking for work (unemployed). The unemployment rate is equal to the ratio of the number of unemployed to the number in the labour force. The participation rate is equal to the ratio of the labour force to the working-age population.

- The European labour market is characterised by large differences across countries, in terms of employment, of participation rate among men and women and the incidence of unemployment across different groups of workers, the young in particular.

- Wages are set unilaterally by firms or by bargaining between workers and firms. They depend negatively on the unemployment rate and positively on the expected price level. The reason why wages depend on the expected price level is that they are typically set in nominal terms for some period of time. During that time, even if the price level turns out to be different from what was expected, wages are typically not readjusted.

- The price set by firms depends on the wage and on the mark-up of prices over wages. The higher the mark-up chosen by firms, the higher the price given the wage, and thus the lower the real wage implied by price-setting decisions.

- Equilibrium in the labour market requires that the expected real wage by wage setters be equal to the effective real wage that firms are willing to pay. The equilibrium unemployment rate is known as the natural rate of unemployment.

- In general, the actual price level may turn out to be different from the price level expected by wage setters. Therefore the unemployment rate need not be equal to the natural rate.

- The coming chapters will show that, in the short run, unemployment and output are determined by the factors we focused on in the previous three chapters, but, in the medium run, unemployment tends to return to the natural rate, and output tends to return to its natural level.

KEY TERMS

QUESTIONS AND PROBLEMS

QUICK CHECK

1. *Using the information in this chapter, label each of the following statements true, false or uncertain. Explain briefly.*

a. Since 1950, the participation rate in Europe has remained roughly constant at 60%.

b. In Europe, the average duration of unemployment is small compared to the USA.

c. The incidence of unemployment among different groups of workers is similar.

d. The unemployment rate tends to be high in recessions and low in expansions.

e. Most workers are typically paid their reservation wage.

f. Workers who do not belong to unions have no bargaining power.

g. It may be in the best interest of employers to pay wages higher than their workers' reservation wage.

h. The natural rate of unemployment is unaffected by policy changes.

2. *Answer the following questions using the information provided in this chapter.*

a. Is it true that European countries have very different participation rates, regardless of the gender of workers?

b. Is it true that countries with lower participation rates among women also have lower participation rates among men?

c. Is it true that countries with lower participation rates (on the total population in working age) also have lower participation rates of older workers?

d. Which are the countries with the lowest and the highest total unemployment?

e. Which are the countries with the lowest and the highest youth unemployment? Are they the same countries in your answer at part (d)?

3. The natural rate of unemployment

Suppose that the mark-up of goods prices over marginal cost is 5%, and that the wage-setting equation is $W = P(1 - u)$, where u is the unemployment rate.

a. What is the real wage, as determined by the price-setting equation?

b. What is the natural rate of unemployment?

c. Suppose that the mark-up of prices over costs increases to 10%. What happens to the natural rate of unemployment? Explain the logic behind your answer.

DIG DEEPER

4. Reservation wages

In the mid-1980s, a famous supermodel once said that she would not get out of bed for less than $10,000 (presumably per day).

a. What is your own reservation wage?

b. Did your first job pay more than your reservation wage at the time?

c. Relative to your reservation wage at the time you accept each job, which job pays more: your first one or the one you expect to have in ten years' time?

d. Explain your answers to parts (a) through (c) in terms of the efficiency wage theory.

5. Bargaining power and wage determination

Even in the absence of collective bargaining, workers do have some bargaining power that allows them to receive wages higher than their reservation wage. Each worker's bargaining power depends both on the nature of the job and on the economy-wide labour market conditions. Let's consider each factor in turn.

a. Compare the job of a delivery person and a computer network administrator. In which of these jobs does a worker have more bargaining power? Why?

b. For any given job, how do labour market conditions affect a worker's bargaining power? Which labour market variable would you look at to assess labour market conditions?

c. Suppose that for given labour market conditions (the variable you identified in part (b)), worker bargaining power throughout the economy increases. What effect would this have on the real wage in the medium run? In the short run? What determines the real wage in the model described in this chapter?

6. The existence of unemployment

a. Suppose the unemployment rate is very low. How easy is it for firms to find workers to hire? How easy is it for workers to find jobs? What do your answers imply about the relative bargaining power of workers and firms when the unemployment rate is very low? What do your answers imply about what happens to the wage as the unemployment rate gets very low?

b. Given your answer to part (a), why is there unemployment in the economy? (What would happen to real wages if the unemployment rate were equal to zero?)

7. The informal labour market

You learned in Chapter 2 that informal work at home (e.g. preparing meals, taking care of children) is not counted as part of GDP. Such work also does not constitute employment in labour market statistics. With these observations in mind, consider two economies, each with 100 people, divided into 25 households, each composed of four people. In each household, one person stays at home and prepares the food, two people work in the non-food sector, and one person is unemployed. Assume that the workers outside food preparation produce the same actual and measured output in both economies.

In the first economy, EatIn, the 25 food-preparation workers (one per household) cook for their families at home and do not work outside the house. All meals are prepared and eaten at home. The 25 food-preparation workers in this economy do not seek work in the formal labour market (and, when asked, they say they are not looking for work). In the second economy, EatOut, the 25 food-preparation workers are employed by restaurants. All meals are purchased in restaurants.

a. Calculate measured employment and unemployment and the measured labour force for each economy. Calculate the measured unemployment rate and participation rate for each economy. In which economy is measured GDP higher?

b. Suppose now that EatIn's economy changes. A few restaurants open, and the food-preparation workers in the restaurants. The members of these ten households now eat all of their meals in restaurants. The food-preparation workers in the remaining 15 households continue to work at home and do not seek jobs in the formal sector. The members of these 15 households continue to eat all of their meals at home. Without calculating the numbers, what will happen to measured employment and unemployment and to the measured labour force, unemployment rate and participation rate in EatIn? What will happen to measured GDP in EatIn?

c. Suppose that you want to include work at home in GDP and the employment statistics. How would you measure the value of work at home in GDP? How would you alter the definitions of *employment*, *unemployment* and *out of the labour force*?

d. Given your new definitions in part (c), would the labour market statistics differ for EatIn and EatOut? Assuming that the food produced by these economies has the same value, would measured GDP in these economies differ? Under your new definitions, would the experiment in part (b) have any effect on the labour market or GDP statistics for EatIn?

EXPLORE FURTHER

8. Unemployment spells and long-term unemployment

In the example presented in this chapter, about 47% of unemployed workers leave unemployment each month.

a. What is the probability that an unemployed worker will still be unemployed after one month? Two months? Six months?

Now consider the composition of the unemployment pool. We will use a simple experiment to determine the proportion of the unemployed who have been unemployed for six months or more. Suppose the number of unemployed workers is constant and equal to x (where x is some constant). Each month, 47% of the unemployed find jobs, and an equivalent number of previously employed workers become unemployed.

b. Consider the group of x workers who are unemployed this month. After a month, what percentage of this group will still be unemployed? (*Hint*: if 47% of unemployed workers find jobs every month, what percentage of the original x unemployed workers did not find jobs in the first month?)

c. After a second month, what percentage of the original x unemployed workers has been unemployed for at least two months? (*Hint*: given your answer to part (b), what percentage of those unemployed for at least one month do not find jobs in the second month?) After the sixth month, what percentage of the original x unemployed workers has been unemployed for at least six months? *This percentage applies to the economy at any time (remember that we started with an arbitrary month). Under our assumptions, the percentage of the unemployed who have been unemployed six months or more is constant.*

9. *Go to the Eurostat website (http://epp.eurostat.ec. europa.eu/portal/page/portal/eurostat/home/). Find the labour market data for your country.*

a. What are the latest monthly data on the size of the labour force, on the number of unemployed and on the unemployment rate in your country?

b. How many people are employed?

c. Compute the change in the number of unemployed from the first number in the table to the most recent month in the table. Do the same for the number of employed workers. Is the decline in unemployment equal to the increase in employment? Explain in words.

10. *Go to the Eurostat website (http://epp.eurostat.ec. europa.eu/portal/page/portal/eurostat/home/). Find the data on harmonised unemployment in the statistics portal.*

a. What are the latest monthly data on the unemployment rate in your country, by gender?

b. What are the latest monthly data on the unemployment rate in your country, by age groups?

c. Compute the change in the unemployment rate from the first number in the table to the most recent month in the table. Do the same for men, women and different age groups. Is the change in unemployment equal for all groups of workers? Explain in words.

Log on to **MyEconLab** and complete the studyplan exercises for this chapter to see how much you have learnt, and where you need to revise most.

MyEconLab

FURTHER READING

● A further discussion of unemployment along the lines of this chapter is given by Richard Layard, Stephen Nickell and Richard Jackman, in *The Unemployment Crisis* (Oxford: Oxford University Press, 1994).

APPENDIX

Wage and price setting relations versus labour supply and labour demand

If you have taken a microeconomics course, you probably saw a representation of labour market equilibrium in terms of labour supply and labour demand. You may therefore be asking yourself: how does the representation in terms of wage setting and price setting relate to the representation of the labour market I saw in that course?

In an important sense, the two representations are similar. To see why, let's redraw Figure 8.10 in terms of the real wage on the vertical axis, and the level of employment (rather than the unemployment rate) on the horizontal axis. We do this in Figure 8.13.

Employment, N, is measured on the horizontal axis. The level of employment must be somewhere between zero and L, the labour force: employment cannot exceed the number of people available for work, i.e. the labour force. For any employment level N, unemployment is given by $U = L - N$. Knowing that, we can measure unemployment by starting from L and moving to the left on the horizontal axis: unemployment is given by the distance between L and N. The lower is employment, N, the higher is unemployment, and by implication the higher is the unemployment rate, u.

Let's now draw the wage-setting and price-setting relations, and characterise the equilibrium:

● An increase in employment (a movement to the right along the horizontal axis) implies a decrease in unemployment and therefore an increase in the real wage chosen in wage setting. Thus, the wage-setting relation is now upward sloping: higher employment implies a higher real wage.

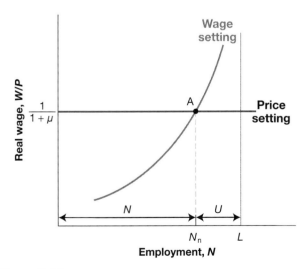

Figure 8.13

Wage and price setting and the natural level of employment

● The price-setting relation is still a horizontal line at $W/P = 1/(1 + \mu)$.
● The equilibrium is given by point A, with 'natural' employment level N_n (and an implied natural unemployment rate equal to $u_n = (L - N_n)/L$).

In this figure the wage-setting relation looks like a labour-supply relation. As the level of employment increases, the real wage paid to workers increases as well. For that reason, the wage-setting relation is sometimes called the 'labour supply' relation (in quotes).

What we have called the price-setting relation looks like a flat labour–demand relation. The reason it is flat rather than downward sloping has to do with our simplifying assumption of constant returns to labour in production. Had we assumed, more conventionally, that there were decreasing returns to labour in production, our price-setting curve would, like the standard labour-demand curve, be downward sloping: as employment increased, the marginal cost of production would increase, forcing firms to increase their prices, given the wages they pay. In other words, the real wage implied by price setting would decrease as employment increased.

But, in a number of ways, the two approaches are different:

● The standard labour-supply relation gives the wage at which a given number of workers are willing to work: The higher the wage, the larger the number of workers who are willing to work.

In contrast, the wage corresponding to a given level of employment in the wage-setting relation is the result of a process of bargaining between workers and firms, or unilateral wage setting by firms. Factors like the structure of collective bargaining or the use of wages to deter quits affect the wage-setting relation. In the real world, they seem to play an important role. Yet they play no role in the standard labour-supply relation.

● The standard labour-demand relation gives the level of employment chosen by firms at a given real wage. It is derived under the assumption that firms operate in competitive goods and labour markets and therefore take wages and prices – and by implication the real wage – as given.

In contrast, the price-setting relation takes into account the fact that in most markets firms actually set prices. Factors such as the degree of competition in the goods market affect the price-setting relation by affecting the mark-up. But these factors aren't considered in the standard labour-demand relation.

● In the labour supply–labour demand framework, those unemployed are willingly unemployed: at the equilibrium real wage, they prefer to be unemployed rather than work.

In contrast, in the wage setting–price setting framework, unemployment is likely to be involuntary. For example, if firms pay an efficiency wage – a wage above the reservation wage – workers would rather be employed than unemployed. Yet, in equilibrium, there is still involuntary unemployment. This also seems to capture reality better than does the labour supply–labour demand framework.

These are the three reasons why we have relied on the wage-setting and the price-setting relations rather than on the labour supply–labour demand approach to characterise equilibrium in this chapter.

Chapter 9

PUTTING ALL MARKETS TOGETHER: THE *AS–AD* MODEL

Earlier (in Chapter 5) we looked at the determination of output in a closed economy in the short run. Then we looked at the determination of output in a closed economy in the medium run (see Chapter 8). We are now ready to put the two together and look at the determination of output in a closed economy in both the short run and the medium run.

To do so, we use the equilibrium conditions for all the markets we have looked at so far – the goods and financial markets (in Chapter 5), and the labour market (in Chapter 8).

Then, using these equilibrium conditions, we derive two relations:

The first relation, which we call the *aggregate supply relation*, captures the implications of equilibrium in the labour market (it builds on what you saw in Chapter 8).

The second relation, which we call the *aggregate demand relation*, captures the implications of equilibrium in both the goods market and financial markets (it builds on what you saw in Chapter 5).

Combining these two relations gives us the *AS–AD* model (for aggregate supply–aggregate demand). This chapter presents the basic version of the model. When confronted with a macroeconomic question, this is the version we typically use to organise our thoughts. For some questions, if we want to focus on the behaviour of inflation, for example, or understand the role of the financial system in the current crisis, the basic *AS–AD* model must be extended. But it provides a base from which one can start, and this is what we shall do in the next two chapters.

This chapter is organised as follows:

- Section 9.1 derives the aggregate supply relation, and Section 9.2 derives the aggregate demand relation.

- Section 9.3 combines the two to characterise equilibrium output in the short run and in the medium run.

- Section 9.4 looks at the dynamic effects of monetary policy.

- Section 9.5 looks at the dynamic effects of fiscal policy.

- Section 9.6 looks at the effects of an increase in the price of oil.

- Section 9.7 summarises.

9.1 AGGREGATE SUPPLY

The **aggregate supply relation** captures the effects of output on the price level. It is derived from the behaviour of wages and prices we described earlier (in Chapter 8).

Then, we had derived the following equation for wage determination (equation (8.1)):

$$W = P^e F(u, z)$$

The nominal wage, W, set by wage setters, depends on the expected price level, P^e; on the unemployment rate, u; and on the catchall variable, z, for all the other factors that affect wage determination, from unemployment benefits to the form of collective bargaining.

We also derived the following equation for price determination (equation (8.3)):

$$P = (1 + \mu)W$$

The price, P, set by firms (equivalently, the price level) is equal to the nominal wage, W, times 1 plus the markup, μ.

We then used these two relations together to derive the natural rate of unemployment – that is, the unemployment rate when the actual price level is equal to the expected price level. In this chapter we will start by considering that the price level is equal to the expected price level in the medium run but will typically not be equal to the expected price level in the short run. Therefore, the price-setting relation and the wage-setting relation give us a relation, which we now derive, between the price level, the output level and the expected price level.

The first step is to eliminate the nominal wage, W, between the two equations. Replacing the nominal wage in the second equation above by its expression from the first gives

$$P = P^e(1 + \mu)F(u, z) \tag{9.1}$$

The price level, P, depends on the expected price level, P^e, on the unemployment rate, u, (as well as on the markup, μ, and on the catchall variable, z; but we will assume both u and z are constant here).

The second step is to replace the unemployment rate u with its expression in terms of output. To replace u, recall the relation between the unemployment rate, employment, and output we derived earlier (in Chapter 8):

$$u = \frac{U}{L} = \frac{L - N}{L} = 1 - \frac{N}{L} = 1 - \frac{Y}{AL}$$

The first equality follows from the definition of the unemployment rate. The second equality follows from the definition of unemployment ($U \equiv L - N$). The third equality just simplifies the fraction. The fourth equality follows from the specification of the production function, so that $Y = AN$. What we get then is

$$u = 1 - \frac{Y}{AL}$$

In words: for a given labour force, and a given productivity, the higher the output, the lower the the unemployment rate.

A better name would be 'the labour market relation'. But because the relation looks graphically like a supply curve (there is a positive relation between output and the price), it is called 'the aggregate supply relation'. We follow this tradition.

Replacing u by $1 - (Y/AL)$ in equation (9.1) gives us the *aggregate supply relation*, or *AS relation* for short:

$$P = P^e(1 + \mu)F\left(1 - \frac{Y}{AL}, z\right) \tag{9.2}$$

The price level, P, depends on the expected price level, P^e, and on the level of output, Y (and also on the markup, μ, the catchall variable, z, the labour force, L, and productivity, A, which we all take as constant here). The AS relation has two important properties.

An increase in Y leads to an increase in P.

The first property is that, given the expected price level, an increase in output leads to an increase in the price level. This is the result of four underlying steps:

1. An increase in output leads to an increase in employment.
2. The increase in employment leads to a decrease in unemployment and therefore to a decrease in the unemployment rate.
3. The lower unemployment rate leads to an increase in the nominal wage.
4. The increase in the nominal wage leads to an increase in the prices set by firms and therefore to an increase in the price level.

The second property is that, given unemployment, an increase in the expected price level leads, one-for-one, to an increase in the actual price level. For example, if the expected price level doubles, then the price level will also double. This effect works through wages:

◄ An increase in P^e leads to an increase in P.

1. If wage setters expect the price level to be higher, they set a higher nominal wage.
2. The increase in the nominal wage leads to an increase in costs, which leads to an increase in the prices set by firms and a higher price level.

The relation between the price level P and output Y, for a given value of the expected price level P^e, is represented by the curve *AS* in Figure 9.1. The *AS* curve has three properties which will prove useful in what follows:

- The aggregate supply curve is upward sloping. Put another way, an increase in output Y leads to an increase in the price level P. You saw why earlier.

◄ Put informally, high economic activity puts pressure on prices.

- The aggregate supply curve goes through point A, where $Y = Y_n$ and $P = P^e$. Put another way: when output Y is equal to the natural level of output Y_n, the price level P turns out to be exactly equal to the expected price level P^e.

  How do we know this? From the definition of the natural level of output given earlier (in Chapter 8). Recall that we defined the natural rate of unemployment (and by implication the natural level of output) as the rate of unemployment (and by implication the level of output) that prevails if the price level and the expected price level are equal. This property – that the price level equals the expected price level when output is equal to the natural level of output – has two straightforward implications.

  When output is above the natural level of output, the price level turns out to be higher than expected. In Figure 9.1: if Y is to the right of Y_n, P is higher than P^e. In words: a higher expected price level reduces the real wage workers expect to get and hence reduces the labour supply. With a lower employment N, output is also lower as $Y = AN$. Conversely, when output is below the natural level of output, the price level turns to be lower than expected. In Figure 9.1: if Y is to the left of Y_n, P is lower than P^e.

- An increase in the expected price level P^e shifts the aggregate supply curve up. Conversely, a decrease in the expected price level shifts the aggregate supply curve down.

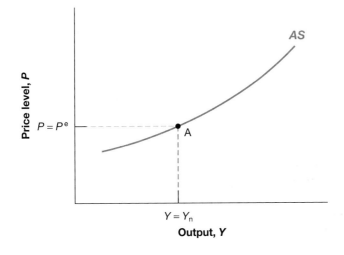

Figure 9.1

The aggregate supply curve

Given the expected price level, an increase in output leads to an increase in the price level. When output is equal to the natural level of output, the price level is equal to the expected price level.

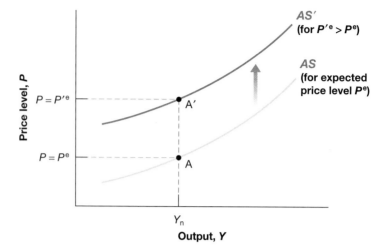

Figure 9.2

The effect of an increase in the expected price level on the aggregate supply curve

An increase in the expected price level shifts the aggregate supply curve up.

This third property is shown in Figure 9.2. Suppose the expected price level increases from P^e to P'^e. At a given level of output, and, correspondingly, at a given unemployment rate, the increase in the expected price level leads to an increase in wages, which leads in turn to an increase in prices. So, at any level of output, the price level is higher: the aggregate supply curve shifts up. In particular, instead of going through point A (where $Y = Y_n$ and $P = P^e$), the aggregate supply curve now goes through point A' (where $Y = Y_n$, $P = P'^e$).

> Recall that when output equals the natural level of output, the price level turns out to be equal to the expected price level.

Let's summarise:

- Starting from wage determination and price determination in the labour market, we have derived the *aggregate supply relation*.
- This relation implies that for a given expected price level, the price level is an increasing function of the level of output. It is represented by an upward-sloping curve, called the *aggregate supply curve*.
- Increases in the expected price level shift the aggregate supply curve up; decreases in the expected price level shift the aggregate supply curve down.

9.2 AGGREGATE DEMAND

The **aggregate demand relation** captures the effect of the price level on output. It is derived from the equilibrium conditions in the goods and financial markets we described earlier (in Chapter 5).

There, we derived the following equation for goods market equilibrium (equation (5.2)):

$$Y = C(Y - T) + I(Y, i) + G$$

Equilibrium in the goods market requires that output equal the demand for goods – the sum of consumption, investment and government spending. This is the *IS* relation.

We also derived the following equation for equilibrium in financial markets (equation (5.3)):

$$\frac{M}{P} = Y L(i)$$

Equilibrium in financial markets requires that the supply of money equal the demand for money. This is the *LM* relation.

Recall that what appears on the left side of the *LM* equation is the real money stock, M/P. We focused earlier (in Chapters 5 and 6) on changes in the real money stock that came from changes in nominal money, M, by the central bank. But changes in the real money stock, M/P, can also come from changes in the price level, P. A 10% increase in the price level, P, has the same effect on the real money stock as a 10% decrease in the stock of nominal money, M: either leads to a 10% decrease in the real money stock.

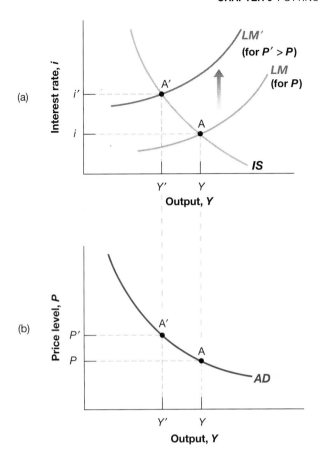

Figure 9.3

The derivation of the aggregate demand curve

An increase in the price level leads to a decrease in output.

Using the *IS* and *LM* relations, we can derive the relation between the price level and the level of output implied by equilibrium in the goods and financial markets. We do this in Figure 9.3.

- Figure 9.3(a) draws the *IS* curve and the *LM* curve. The *IS* curve is drawn for given values of *G* and *T*. It is downward sloping: an increase in the interest rate leads to a decrease in output. The *LM* curve is drawn for a given value of *M/P*. It is upward sloping: an increase in output increases the demand for money, and the interest rate increases so as to maintain equality of money demand and the (unchanged) money supply. The point at which the goods market and the financial markets are both in equilibrium is at the inter-section of the *IS* curve and the *LM* curve, at point A.

  Now consider the effects of an increase in the price level from *P* to *P′*. Given the stock of nominal money, *M*, the increase in the price level, *P*, decreases the real money stock, *M/P*. This implies that the *LM* curve shifts up: at a given level of output, the lower real money stock leads to an increase in the interest rate. The economy moves along the *IS* curve, and the equilibrium moves from A to A′. The interest rate increases from *i* to *i′*, and output decreases from *Y* to *Y′*. In short, the increase in the price level leads to a decrease in output.

  In words: the increase in the price level leads to a decrease in the real money stock. This monetary contraction leads to an increase in the interest rate, which leads in turn to a lower demand for goods and lower output.

- The negative relation between output and the price level is drawn as the downward-sloping curve *AD* in Figure 9.3(b). Points A and A′ in Figure 9.3(b) correspond to points A and A′ in Figure 9.3(a). An increase in the price level from *P* to *P′* leads to a decrease in output from *Y* to *Y′*. This curve is called the *aggregate demand curve*. The underlying negative relation between output and the price level is called the *aggregate demand relation*.

Any variable other than the price level that shifts either the *IS* curve or the *LM* curve also shifts the aggregate demand relation.

A better name would be 'the goods market and financial markets relation'. But, because it is a long name, and because the relation looks graphically ◀ like a demand curve (that is, a negative relation between output and the price), it is called the 'aggregate demand rela-tion'. We will, again, follow tradition.

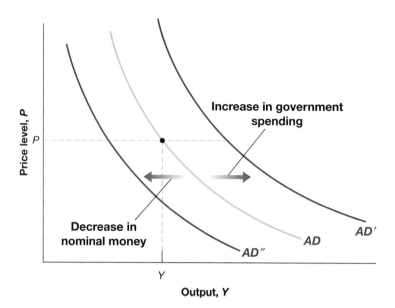

Figure 9.4

Shifts of the aggregate demand curve

At a given price level, an increase in government spending increases output, shifting the aggregate demand curve to the right. At a given price level, a decrease in nominal money decreases output, shifting the aggregate demand curve to the left.

Take, for example, an increase in government spending, G. At a given price level, the level of output implied by equilibrium in the goods and the financial markets is higher: in Figure 9.4, the aggregate demand curve shifts to the right, from AD to AD'.

Or take a contractionary, open-market operation – a decrease in M. At a given price level, the level of output implied by equilibrium in the goods and the financial markets is lower. In Figure 9.4, the aggregate demand curve shifts to the left, from AD to AD''.

Let's represent what we have just derived by the following aggregate demand relation:

$$Y = Y\left(\frac{M}{P}, G, T\right)$$ [9.3]
$$(+, \ +, \ -)$$

Output Y is an increasing function of the real money stock M/P, an increasing function of government spending G, and a decreasing function of taxes, T.

Given monetary and fiscal policy – that is, given M, G, and T – an increase in the price level P leads to a decrease in the real money stock, M/P, which leads to a decrease in output. This is the relation captured by the AD curve back in Figure 9.3(b).

Let's summarise:

- Starting from the equilibrium conditions for the goods and financial markets, we have derived the *aggregate demand relation*.
- This relation implies that the level of output is a decreasing function of the price level. It is represented by a downward-sloping curve, called the *aggregate demand curve*.
- Changes in monetary or fiscal policy – or more generally in any variable, other than the price level, that shifts the IS or the LM curves – shift the aggregate demand curve.

> Recall that open-market operations are the means through which the central bank changes the nominal money stock.

9.3 EQUILIBRIUM IN THE SHORT RUN AND IN THE MEDIUM RUN

The next step is to put the AS and the AD relations together. From sections 9.1 and 9.2, the two relations are given by

$$AS \text{ relation:} \quad P = P^e(1 + \mu)F\left(1 - \frac{Y}{AL}, z\right)$$

$$AD \text{ relation:} \quad Y = Y\left(\frac{M}{P}, G, T\right)$$

For a given value of the expected price level, P^e, (which enters the aggregate supply relation), and for given values of the monetary and fiscal policy variables M, G and T (which enter the aggregate demand relation), these two relations determine the equilibrium values of output, Y, and the price level, P.

Note that the equilibrium depends on the value of P^e. The value of P^e determines the position of the aggregate supply curve (go back to Figure 9.2), and the position of the aggregate supply curve affects the equilibrium. In the short run, we can take P^e, the price level expected by wage setters when they last set wages, as given. But, over time, P^e is likely to change, shifting the aggregate supply curve, and changing the equilibrium. With this in mind, we first characterise equilibrium in the short run – that is, taking P^e as given. We then look at how P^e changes over time, and how that change affects the equilibrium.

Equilibrium in the short run

The short-run equilibrium is characterised in Figure 9.5:

- The aggregate supply curve *AS* is drawn for a given value of P^e. It is upward sloping: the higher the level of output, the higher the price level. The position of the curve depends on P^e. Recall from section 9.1 that, when output is equal to the natural level of output, the price level is equal to the expected price level. This means that, in Figure 9.5, the aggregate supply curve goes through point B: if $Y = Y_n$, then $P = P^e$.
- The aggregate demand curve *AD* is drawn for given values of M, G and T. It is downward sloping: the higher the price level, the lower the level of output.

The equilibrium is given by the intersection of the *AS* and *AD* curves at point A. By construction, at point A, the goods market, the financial markets and the labour market are all in equilibrium. The fact that the labour market is in equilibrium is because point A is on the aggregate supply curve. That fact that the goods and financial markets are in equilibrium is because point A is on the aggregate demand curve. The equilibrium level of output and price level are given by Y and P.

There is no reason why, in general, equilibrium output, Y, should be equal to the natural level of output, Y_n. Equilibrium output depends both on the position of the aggregate supply curve (and therefore on the value of P^e) and on the position of the aggregate demand curve (and therefore on the values of M, G and T). As we have drawn the two curves, Y is greater than Y_n: in other words, the equilibrium level of output exceeds the natural level of output. But we could clearly have drawn the *AS* and the *AD* curves so equilibrium output, Y, was smaller than the natural level of output, Y_n.

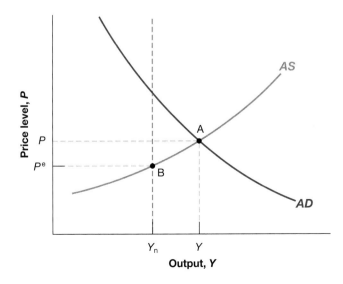

Figure 9.5

The short-run equilibrium

The equilibrium is given by the intersection of the aggregate supply curve and the aggregate demand curve. At point A, the labour market, the goods market and financial markets are all in equilibrium.

Figure 9.5 gives us our first important conclusion: in the short run, there is no reason why output should equal the natural level of output. Whether it does depends on the specific values of the expected price level and the values of the variables affecting the position of aggregate demand.

We must now ask, what happens over time? More precisely, suppose that in the short run, output is above the natural level of output – as is the case in Figure 9.5. What will happen over time? Will output eventually return to the natural level of output? If so, how? These are the questions we take up in the rest of the section.

From the short run to the medium run

To think about what happens over time, consider Figure 9.6. The curves denoted AS and AD are the same as in Figure 9.5, and so the short-run equilibrium is at point A – which corresponds to point A in Figure 9.5. Output is equal to Y, and is higher than the natural level of output, Y_n.

At point A, output exceeds the natural level of output. So we know from section 9.1 that the price level is higher than the expected price level – higher than the price level wage setters expected when they set nominal wages.

The fact that the price level is higher than wage setters expected is likely to lead them to revise upward their expectations of what the price level will be in the future. So, next time they set nominal wages, they are likely to make that decision based on a higher expected price level, say, based on $P^{e'}$, where $P^{e'} > P^e$.

This increase in the expected price level implies that in the next period, the aggregate supply curve shifts up, from AS to AS': at a given level of output, wage setters expect a higher price level. They set a higher nominal wage, which in turn leads firms to set a higher price. The price level therefore increases.

This upward shift in the AS curve implies that the economy moves up along the AD curve. The equilibrium moves from A to A'. Equilibrium output decreases from Y to Y'.

The adjustment does not end at point A'. At A', output, Y', still exceeds the natural level of output, Y_n, so the price level is still higher than the expected price level. Because of this, wage setters are likely to continue to revise upward their expectation of the price level.

This means that as long as equilibrium output exceeds the natural level of output, Y_n, the expected price level increases, shifting the AS curve upward. As the AS curve shifts upward and the economy moves up along the AD curve, equilibrium output continues to decrease.

Does this adjustment eventually come to an end? Yes. It ends when the AS curve has shifted all the way to AS'', when the equilibrium has moved all the way to A", and the equilibrium level of output is equal to Y_n. At A", equilibrium output is equal to the natural level of output, so the price level is equal to the expected price level. At this point, wage setters have no reason to change their expectations; the AS curve no longer shifts, and the economy stays at A".

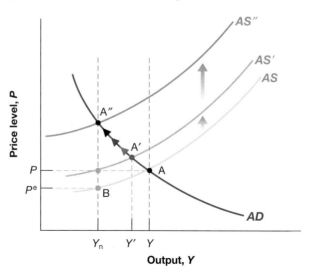

Figure 9.6

The adjustment of output over time

If output is above the natural level of output, the AS curve shifts up over time until output has fallen back to the natural level of output.

In words: as long as output exceeds the natural level of output, the price level turns out to be higher than expected. This leads wage setters to revise their expectations of the price level upward, leading to an increase in the price level. The increase in the price level leads to a decrease in the real money stock, which leads to an increase in the interest rate, which leads to a decrease in output. The adjustment stops when output is equal to the natural level of output. At that point, the price level is equal to the expected price level, expectations no longer change and output remains at the natural level of output. Put another way, in the medium run, output returns to the natural level of output.

We have looked at the dynamics of adjustment starting from a case in which initial output was higher than the natural level of output. Clearly, a symmetric argument holds when initial output is below the natural level of output. In this case, the price level is lower than the expected price level, leading wage setters to lower their expectations of the price level. Lower expectations of the price level cause the *AS* curve to shift down and the economy to move down the *AD* curve until output has increased back to the natural level of output.

Let's summarise:

- In the short run, output can be above or below the natural level of output. Changes in any of the variables that enter either the aggregate supply relation or the aggregate demand relation lead to changes in output and to changes in the price level. ◀ In formal terms, in the short run, $Y \neq Y_n$.

- In the medium run, output eventually returns to the natural level of output. The adjustment works through changes in the price level. When output is above the natural level of output, the price level increases. The higher price level decreases demand and output. When output is below the natural level of output, the price level decreases, increasing demand and output. ◀ In formal terms, in the medium run, $Y = Y_n$.

- The best way to understand more fully the *AS–AD* model is to use it to look at the dynamic effects of changes in policy or in the economic environment. In the next three sections, we focus on three such changes. The first two are our two favourite policy changes: a change in the stock of nominal money and a change in the budget deficit. The third, which we could not examine before we had developed a theory of wage and price determination, is an increase in the oil price.

9.4 THE EFFECTS OF A MONETARY EXPANSION

What are the short-run and medium-run effects of an expansionary monetary policy, say, of a one-time increase in the level of nominal money from M to M'?

The dynamics of adjustment

Look at Figure 9.7. Assume that before the change in nominal money, output is at its natural level. Aggregate demand and aggregate supply cross at point A, the level of output at A equals Y_n, and the price level equals P.

Now consider an increase in nominal money. Recall the specification of aggregate demand from equation (9.3):

$$Y = Y\left(\frac{M}{P}, G, T\right)$$

For a given price level, P, the increase in nominal money, M, leads to an increase in the real money stock, M/P, leading to an increase in output. The aggregate demand curve shifts to the right, from *AD* to *AD'*. In the short run, the economy goes from point A to A'. Output ◀ increases from Y_n to Y', and the price level increases from P to P'.

Over time, the adjustment of price level expectations comes into play. As output is higher than the natural level of output, the price level is higher than wage setters expected. They then revise their expectations, which causes the aggregate supply curve to shift up over time. The economy moves up along the aggregate demand curve *AD'*. The adjustment

We think of shifts in the *AD* curve as shifts to the right or to the left because we think of the *AD* relation as telling us what output is for a given price level. We then ask: at a given price level, does output increase (a shift to the right) or decrease (a shift to the left)?

We think of shifts in the *AS* curve as shifts up or down because we think of the *AS* relation as telling us what the price level is for a given level of output. We then ask: at a given output level, does the price level increase (a shift up) or decrease (a shift down)?

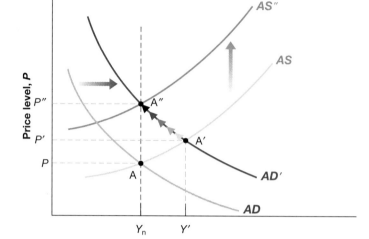

Figure 9.7

The dynamic effects of a monetary expansion

A monetary expansion leads to an increase in output in the short run but has no effect on output in the medium run.

Go back to equation (9.3): if *Y* is unchanged (and *G* and *T* are also unchanged), then *M/P* must also be unchanged.

If *M/P* is unchanged, it must be that *M* and *P* each increase in the same proportion.

process stops when output has returned to the natural level of output. At that point, the price level is equal to the expected price level. In the medium run, the aggregate supply curve is given by AS″, and the economy is at point A″: output is back to Y_n, and the price level is equal to P″.

We can actually pin down the exact size of the eventual increase in the price level. If output is back to the natural level of output, the real money stock must also be back to its initial value. In other words, the proportional increase in prices must be equal to the proportional increase in the nominal money stock: if the initial increase in nominal money is equal to 10%, then the price level ends up 10% higher.

Going behind the scenes

To get a better sense of what is going on, it is useful to go behind the scenes to see what happens not only to output and to the price level, but also what happens to the interest rate. We can do this by looking at what happens in terms of the *IS–LM* model.

Figure 9.8(a) reproduces Figure 9.7 (leaving out the AS″ curve to keep things simple), and shows the adjustment of output and the price level in response to the increase in nominal money. Figure 9.8(b) shows the adjustment of output and the interest rate by looking at the same adjustment process, but in terms of the *IS–LM* model.

Look first at Figure 9.8(b). Before the change in nominal money, the equilibrium is given by the intersection of the *IS* and *LM* curves, that is, at point A – which corresponds to point A in Figure 9.8(a). Output is equal to the natural level of output, Y_n, and the interest rate is given by *i*.

The short-run effect of the monetary expansion is to shift the *LM* curve down from *LM* to *LM′*, moving the equilibrium from point A to point A′ – which corresponds to point A′ in Figure 9.8(a). The interest rate is lower, and output is higher.

Note that there are two effects at work behind the shift from *LM* to *LM′*: one is due to the increase in nominal money. The other, which partly offsets the first, is due to the increase in the price level. Let's look at these two effects more closely:

- If the price level did not change, the increase in nominal money would shift the *LM* curve down to *LM″*. So, if the price level did not change – as was our assumption earlier (in Chapter 5) – the equilibrium would be at the intersection of *IS* and *LM″*, or point B.

Why only partially? Suppose the price level increased in the same proportion as the increase in nominal money, leaving the real money stock unchanged. If the real money stock were unchanged, output would remain unchanged as well. But if output were unchanged, the price level would not increase, contradicting our premise.

- However, the price level increases – from P to P′ in Figure 9.8(a). This increase in the price level shifts the *LM* curve upward from *LM″* to *LM′*, partially offsetting the effect of the increase in nominal money.
- The net effect of these two shifts – down from *LM* to *LM″* in response to the increase in nominal money, and up from *LM″* to *LM′* in response to the increase in the price level – is a shift of the *LM* curve from *LM* to *LM′*, and the equilibrium is given by A′.

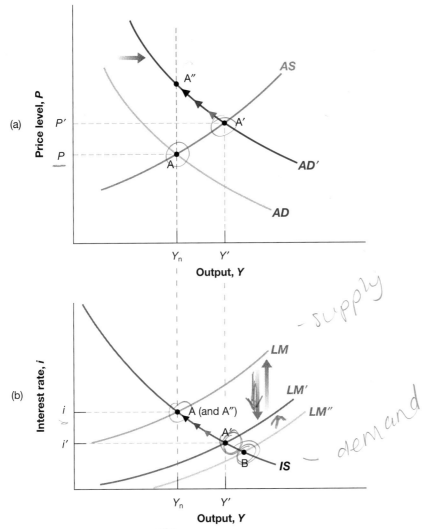

- supply

- demand

Figure 9.8

The dynamic effects of a monetary expansion on output and the interest rate

The increase in nominal money initially shifts the *LM* curve down, decreasing the interest rate and increasing output. Over time, the price level increases, shifting the *LM* curve back up until output is back at the natural level of output.

① total of monetary
value of
assets available
on economy

Over time, the fact that output is above its natural level implies that the price level continues to increase. As the price level increases, it further reduces the real money stock and shifts the *LM* curve back up. The economy moves along the *IS* curve: the interest rate increases and output declines. Eventually, the *LM* curve returns to where it was before the increase in nominal money.

The economy ends up at point A, which corresponds to point A″ in Figure 9.8(a): the increase in nominal money is exactly offset by a proportional increase in the price level. The real money stock is therefore unchanged. With the real money stock unchanged, output is back to its initial value, Y_n, which is the natural level of output, and the interest rate is also back to its initial value, i.

The neutrality of money

Let us summarise what we have just learned about the effects of monetary policy:

- In the short run, a monetary expansion leads to an increase in output, a decrease in the interest rate and an increase in the price level.

  How much of the effect of a monetary expansion falls initially on output and how much on the price level depends on the slope of the aggregate supply curve. Earlier (in Chapter 5), we assumed the price level did not respond at all to an increase in output – we assumed in effect that the aggregate supply curve was flat. Although we intended this as a simplification, empirical evidence does show that the initial effect of changes in output on the price level is indeed quite small. We saw this when we looked at estimated responses to changes in the interest rate in Figure 5.13: despite the change in output, the price level remained practically unchanged for nearly a year.

● Over time, the price level increases, and the effects of the monetary expansion on output and on the interest rate disappear. In the medium run, the increase in nominal money is reflected entirely in a proportional increase in the price level. The increase in nominal money has no effect on output or on the interest rate. (How long it takes in reality for the effects of money on output to disappear is the topic of the Focus box 'How long lasting are the real effects of money?') Economists refer to the absence of a medium-run effect of money on output and on the interest rate by saying that money is neutral in the medium run.

Actually, the way the proposition is ➤ typically stated is that money is neutral in the long run. This is because many economists use 'long run' to refer to what we call in this book the 'medium run'.

The **neutrality of money** in the medium run does not mean that monetary policy cannot or should not be used to affect output. An expansionary monetary policy can, for example, help the economy move out of a recession and return more quickly to the natural level of output. But it is a warning that monetary policy cannot sustain higher output forever.

9.5 A DECREASE IN THE BUDGET DEFICIT

The policy we just looked at – a monetary expansion – led to a shift in aggregate demand coming from a shift in the *LM* curve. Let's now look at the effects of a shift in aggregate demand coming from a shift in the *IS* curve.

Suppose the government is running a budget deficit and decides to reduce it by decreasing its spending from G to G' while leaving taxes, T, unchanged. How will this affect the economy in the short run and in the medium run?

Recall (from Chapter 5) that a reduction ➤ in the budget deficit is also called a fiscal contraction, or a fiscal consolidation.

Assume that output is initially at the natural level of output, so that the economy is at point A in Figure 9.9: output equals Y_n. The decrease in government spending from G to G' shifts the aggregate demand curve to the left, from AD to AD': for a given price level, output is lower. In the short run, the equilibrium moves from A to A'; output decreases from Y_n to Y' and the price level decreases from P to P'.

The initial effect of the deficit reduction triggers lower output. (We first derived this result in Chapter 3, then in Chapter 5, and it holds here as well.)

What happens over time? As long as output is below the natural level of output, we know that the aggregate supply curve keeps shifting down. The economy moves down along the aggregate demand curve AD' until the aggregate supply curve is given by AS'' and the economy reaches point A''. By then, the recession is over, and output is back at Y_n.

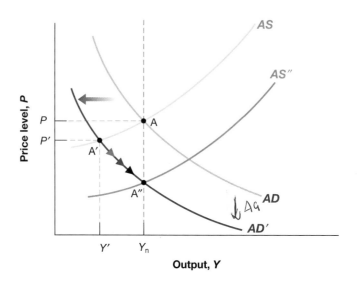

Figure 9.9

The dynamic effects of a decrease in the budget deficit

A decrease in the budget deficit leads initially to a decrease in output. Over time, however, output returns to the natural level of output.

FOCUS
How long lasting are the real effects of money?

To determine how long lasting the real effects of money are, economists use macroeconometric models. These models are larger-scale versions of the aggregate supply and aggregate demand model in this chapter.

The model we examine in this box was built in the early 1990s by John Taylor at Stanford University.

The Taylor model is substantially larger than the model we studied in this chapter. On the aggregate supply side, it has separate equations for price and for wage setting. On the demand side, it has separate equations for consumption, for investment, for exports and for imports. (Recall that, so far, we have assumed the economy is closed, so we have ignored exports and imports altogether.) In addition, instead of looking at just one country as we have done here, it looks at eight countries (the USA and seven major OECD countries) and solves for equilibrium in all eight countries simultaneously. Each equation, for each country, is estimated using econometrics, and allows for a richer dynamic structure than the equations we have relied on in this chapter.

The implications of the model for the effects of money on output are shown in Figure 9.10. The simulation looks at the effects of an increase in nominal money of 3%, taking place over four quarters – 0.1% in the first quarter, 0.6% in the second, 1.2% in the third, and 1.1% in the fourth. After these four step increases, nominal money remains at its new higher level forever.

The effects of money on output reach a maximum after three quarters. By then, output is 1.8% higher than it would have been without the increase in nominal money. Over time, however, the price level increases and output returns to the natural level of output. In year 4, the price level is up by 2.5%, while output is up by only 0.3%. Therefore, the Taylor model suggests, it takes roughly four years for output to return to its natural level, or put another way, four years for changes in nominal money to become neutral.

Do all macroeconometric models give the same answer? No. Because they differ in the way they are constructed, in the way variables are chosen, in the way equations are estimated, their answers are different. But most of them have the following implications in common: the effects of an increase in money on output build up for one to two years, and then decline over time. (For a sense of how the answers differ across models, see the Focus Box 'Four macroeconometric models', in Chapter 22.)

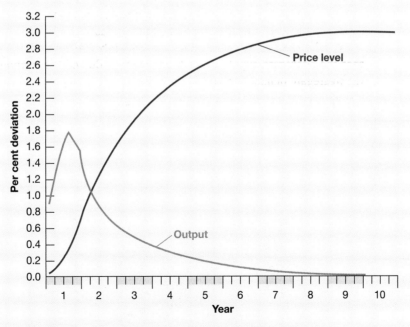

Figure 9.10

The effects of an expansion in nominal money in the Taylor model

Source: Reproduced from John Taylor, *Macroeconomic Policy in a World Economy*, W. W. Norton, New York, 1993, Figure 5.1A, p. 138.

Like an increase in nominal money, a reduction in the budget deficit does not affect output forever. Eventually, output returns to its natural level. But there is an important difference between the effects of a change in money and the effects of a change in the deficit. At point A″, not everything is the same as before: output is back to the natural level of output, but the price level and the interest rate are lower than before the shift. The best way to see these specific effects is again to look at the adjustment in terms of the underlying *IS–LM* model.

The fact that the price level decreases ➤ feels strange. This result comes from the fact that we are looking at an economy in which money growth is zero (we are assuming that *M* is constant, not growing), and there is no sustained inflation. If we were to allow for money growth and thus for inflation, then the result would be that the price level decreases relative to what it would have been, or, in other words, that inflation goes down for a while. (More on money growth and inflation in Chapter 11.)

Deficit reduction, output, and the interest rate

Figure 9.11(a) reproduces Figure 9.9, showing the adjustment of output and the price level in response to the increase in the budget deficit (but leaving out *AS″* to keep things visually simple). Figure 9.11(b) shows the adjustment of output and the interest rate by looking at the same adjustment process, but in terms of the *IS–LM* model.

Look first at Figure 9.11(b). Before the change in fiscal policy, the equilibrium is given by the intersection of the *IS* curve and the *LM* curve, at point A – which corresponds to point A in Figure 9.11(a). Output is equal to the natural level of output, Y_n, and the interest rate is given by i.

As the government reduces the budget deficit, the *IS* curve shifts to the left, to *IS′*. If the price level did not change (the assumption we made in Chapter 5), the economy would

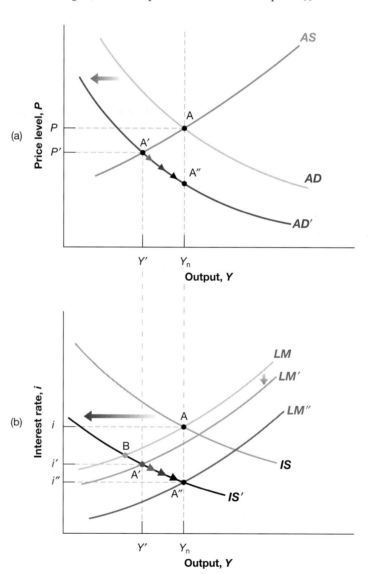

Figure 9.11

The dynamic effects of a decrease in the budget deficit on output and the interest rate

A deficit reduction leads in the short run to a decrease in output and to a decrease in the interest rate. In the medium run, output returns to its natural level, while the interest rate declines further.

move from point A to point B. But, because the price level declines in response to the decrease in output, the real money stock increases, leading to a partially offsetting shift of the *LM* curve, down to *LM′*. So, the initial effect of deficit reduction is to move the economy from point A to point A′. (Point A′ in Figure 9.11(b) corresponds to point A′ in Figure 9.11(a).) Both output and the interest rate are lower than before the fiscal contraction. Note that (just as was the case in Chapter 5) we cannot tell whether or not investment increases or decreases in the short run: lower output decreases investment, but the lower interest rate increases investment.

So long as output remains below the natural level of output, the price level continues to decline, leading to a further increase in the real money stock. The *LM* curve continues to shift down. In Figure 9.11(b), the economy moves down from point A′ along *IS′*, and eventually reaches A″ (which corresponds to A″ in Figure 9.11(a)). At A″, the *LM* curve is given by *LM″*.

At A″, output is back at the natural level of output. But the interest rate is lower than it was before deficit reduction, down from *i* to *i″*. The composition of output is also different: to see how and why, let's rewrite the *IS* relation, taking into account that at A″, output is back at the natural level of output, so that $Y = Y_n$:

$$Y_n = C(Y_n - T) + I(Y_n, i) + G$$

Because income, Y_n, and taxes, T, are unchanged, consumption, C, is the same as before deficit reduction. By assumption, government spending, G, is lower than before. Therefore investment, I, must be higher than before the deficit reduction – higher by an amount exactly equal to the decrease in G. Put another way, in the medium run, a reduction in the budget deficit unambiguously leads to a decrease in the interest rate and an increase in investment.

Budget deficits, output and investment

Let's summarise what you have just learned about the effects of fiscal policy:

- In the short run, a budget deficit reduction, if implemented alone – that is, without an accompanying change in monetary policy – leads to a decrease in output and may lead to a decrease in investment.

  Note the qualification 'without an accompanying change in monetary policy': in principle, these adverse short-run effects on output can be avoided by using the right monetary–fiscal mix. What is needed is for the central bank to increase the money supply enough to offset the adverse effects of the decrease in government spending on aggregate demand. This is what happened in the USA in the 1990s. As the Clinton administration reduced budget deficits, the Fed made sure that, even in the short run, the deficit reduction did not lead to a recession and lower output.

◀ Recall the discussion of the policy mix earlier (in Chapter 5).

- In the medium run, output returns to the natural level of output, and the interest rate is lower. In the medium run, a deficit reduction leads unambiguously to an increase in investment.

  We have not taken into account so far the effects of investment on capital accumulation and the effects of capital on production (we will do so in Chapters 13 to 15 when we look at the long run). But it is easy to see how our conclusions would be modified if we did take into account the effects on capital accumulation. In the long run, the level of output depends on the capital stock in the economy. So if a lower government budget deficit leads to more investment, it will lead to a higher capital stock, and the higher capital stock will lead to higher output.

◀ Effects of a deficit reduction:

- Short run: *Y* decreases, *I* increases or decreases.
- Medium run: *Y* unchanged, *I* increases.
- Long run: *Y* increases, *I* increases.

Everything we have just said about the effects of deficit reduction through a fiscal consolidation would apply equally to policy measures aimed at increasing private saving. An increase in the private saving rate – that is, lower consumption at the same level of disposable income – decreases demand and output in the short run, leaves output unchanged in the medium run, and, through increases in the capital stock from increased investment, increases output in the long run.

Disagreements among economists about the effects of measures aimed at increasing either public saving or private saving often come from differences in timeframes. Those who are concerned with short-run effects worry that measures to increase saving, public or private, might create a recession and decrease saving and investment for some time. Those who look beyond the short run see the eventual increase in saving and investment and emphasise the favourable medium-run and long-run effects on output.

9.6 AN INCREASE IN THE PRICE OF OIL

We have looked so far at the effects of variables that shift the aggregate demand curve: an increase in the money supply and a reduction in the budget deficit. Now that we have formalised the supply side, we can look at the effects of variables that shift the aggregate supply curve. One of the most interesting candidates is the price of oil.

Increases in the price of oil have often made the news in the recent past, and for good reasons: the price of oil, which stood around $7.5 per barrel at the end of 1998, in the summer of 2008 went above $128, and then declined to $45 to return to $90 in the spring of 2012. What effects such an increase is likely to have on the economy is clearly of much current concern to policy makers.

This is not the first time the world economy has experienced a sharp increase in the price of oil. In the 1970s, the formation of **OPEC (the Organization of Petroleum Exporting Countries)**, a cartel of oil producers, together with disruptions due to wars and revolutions in the Middle East, led to two sharp increases in the price of oil, the first one in 1973–1975, the second in 1979–1981. Figure 9.12 plots the real price of oil, defined as the ratio of the price of crude petroleum to the United States Consumer Price Index, since 1970 (the ratio is set to 100 in 1970). As the figure shows, by 1981, the real price of oil reached 2.5 times its level in 1970. This high price did not last very long. From 1982 until the late 1990s, the OPEC cartel became steadily weaker, unable to enforce the production quotas it had set for its members. By 1998, the real price of oil was less than half its 1970 level. Since then, however, the combination of the Iraq war and a steady increase in the demand for oil by fast-growing countries such as China and India, has led to large increases in prices, to levels higher than those of the early 1980s. Note that the recent hike in oil prices led the nominal price of oil to levels that are almost triple compared to 1981 (around $94 per barrel in 2008

Figure 9.12

The real price of oil since 1970

There were two sharp increases in the relative price of oil in the 1970s, followed by a decrease until the 1990s, and a large increase since then.

Source: Energy Information Administration (EIA) – Official Energy Statistics from the US Government, Eurostat.

Figure 9.13

The real price of oil in Europe and in the USA

Since 2003, the real price of oil in Europe increased less rapidly than in the USA.

Source: Dow Jones & Company and US Department of Labor: Bureau of Labor Statistics for the USA, Eurostat for Europe.

compared to $32 per barrel in 1981) but, in real terms, the price today is not three times higher than in 1981 (around $87 per barrel in 2008 compared to $71 per barrel in 1981). This is due to the fact that, since 1981, the general price level also increased.

Moreover, in real terms, oil prices in Europe increased less than in the USA. Figure 9.13 compares the real price of oil in Europe and in the USA since 1996. Until 2002, the real price of oil was similar in the two areas but, beginning in 2003, the depreciation of the dollar vis-à-vis the euro led to a much more limited increase in the real price of oil in Europe: in 2012 the real price of oil stood around $90 in Europe, while it exceeded $100 in the USA.

Each of the two large price increases of the 1970s was associated with a sharp recession and a large increase in inflation – a combination macroeconomists call **stagflation**, to capture the combination of stagnation and inflation that characterised these episodes. The obvious worry is that the recent price of oil may trigger another such episode. So far, it has not happened, and we shall re-examine the issue shortly. First, we must understand the effects of the price of oil in our model.

Note that we face a serious problem in using the model to think about the macroeconomic effects of an increase in the price of oil: the price of oil appears neither in our aggregate supply relation nor in our aggregate demand relation! The reason is that, until now, we have assumed that output was produced using only labour. One way to extend our model would be to recognise explicitly that output is produced using labour and other inputs (including energy) and then figure out what effect an increase in the price of oil has on the price set by firms and on the relation between output and employment. An easier way, and the way we will go, is simply to describe the increase in the price of oil by a shift of the price-setting relation upwards. It has the same effects of an increase in the mark-up of the price over the nominal wage. The justification is straightforward: given wages, an increase in the price of oil increases the cost of production, forcing firms to increase prices.

Having made this assumption, we can then track the dynamic effects of an increase in the mark-up on output and the price level. It will be easiest here to work backward in time, first asking what happens in the medium run, and then working out the dynamics of adjustment from the short run to the medium run.

Effects on the natural rate of unemployment

Let's start by asking what happens to the natural rate of unemployment when the real price of oil increases (for simplicity, we shall drop 'real' in what follows). Figure 9.14 reproduces the characterisation of labour market equilibrium from Figure 8.10 (in Chapter 8).

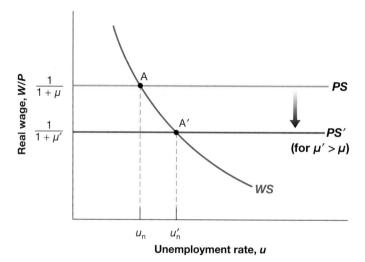

Figure 9.14

The effects of an increase in the price of oil on the natural rate of unemployment

An increase in the price of oil leads to a lower real wage and a higher natural rate of unemployment.

Careful: u and μ are not the same; u is the unemployment rate, μ is the markup.

The wage-setting curve is downward sloping. The price-setting relation is represented by the horizontal line at $W/P = 1/(1 + \mu)$. The initial equilibrium is at point A, and the initial natural unemployment rate is u_n. An increase in the mark-up leads to a downward shift of the price-setting line, from PS to PS′: the higher the mark-up, the lower the real wage implied by price setting. The equilibrium moves from A to A′. The real wage is lower. The natural unemployment rate is higher: getting workers to accept the lower real wage requires an increase in unemployment.

The increase in the natural rate of unemployment leads in turn to a decrease in the natural level of employment. If we assume that the relation between employment and output is unchanged – that is, that each unit of output still requires one worker in addition to the energy input – then the decrease in the natural level of employment leads to an identical decrease in the natural level of output. Putting things together: an increase in the price of oil leads to a decrease in the natural level of output.

This assumes that the increase in the price of oil is permanent. If, in the medium run, the price of oil goes back to its initial value, then the natural rate is clearly unaffected.

The dynamics of adjustment

Let's now turn to dynamics. Suppose that before the increase in the price of oil, the aggregate demand curve and the aggregate supply curve are given by AD and AS respectively, so the economy is at point A in Figure 9.15, with output at the natural level of output, Y_n, and by implication $P = P^e$.

Figure 9.15

The dynamic effects of an increase in the price of oil

An increase in the price of oil leads, in the short run, to a decrease in output and an increase in the price level. Over time, output decreases further and the price level increases further.

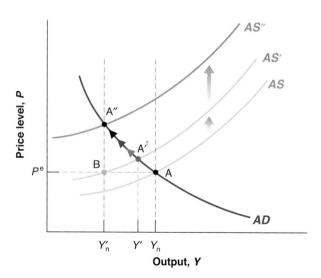

We have just established that the increase in the price of oil decreases the natural level of output. Call this lower level Y'_n. We now want to know what happens in the short run and how the economy moves from Y_n to Y'_n.

To know what happens in the short run, recall the aggregate supply relation is given by

$$P = P^e(1 + \mu)F\left(1 - \frac{Y}{L}, z\right)$$

Given P^e, the increase in the price of oil has the same effects as an increase in the markup, μ. It leads firms to increase their prices, leading to an increase in the price level, P, at any level of output, Y. The aggregate supply curve shifts up.

Does the aggregate demand curve shift as a result of the increase in the price of oil? The answer is: maybe. There are many channels through which demand might be affected at a given price level: the higher price of oil may lead firms to change their investment plans, cancelling some investment projects and/or shifting to less energy-intensive equipment. ◀ The increase in the price of oil also redistributes income from oil buyers to oil producers. Oil producers may spend less than than oil buyers, leading to a decrease in consumption demand. Let us take the easy way out: because some of the effects shift the aggregate demand curve to the right and others shift the aggregate demand curve to the left, let us ◀ simply assume that the effects cancel each other out and that aggregate demand does not shift.

Under this assumption, in the short run, only the *AS* shifts. The economy therefore moves along the *AD* curve, from A to A′. Output decreases from Y_n to Y'. The increase in the price of oil leads firms to increase their prices. This increase in the price level then decreases demand and output.

Does this fit what we have observed in response to increases in the price of oil, both in the 1970s and recently? The answer is given by Figure 9.16, which plots the evolution of the real price of oil and inflation – using the UK CPI – and Figure 9.17, which plots the evolution of the real price of oil and the unemployment rate in the UK since 1970.

First, the good news (for our model, although not for the UK economy): note how both the first and the second large increases in the price of oil were followed by major increases in inflation and in unemployment. This fits our analysis perfectly. Then, the bad news (for our model): note how the increase in the price of oil since the late 1990s has not been associated – at least so far – with either an increase in inflation or an increase in unemployment. In light of what happened in the 1970s, this lack of an effect has come as a surprise to macroeconomists. The state of research and the various hypotheses being explored are discussed in the Focus box 'Oil price increases: why are the 2000s so different from the 1970s?'

> Higher petrol prices may lead you to shift to more fuel-efficient means of transportation, such as the train or the bicycle.

> This is indeed typically the case. Oil producers realise that high oil revenues might not last forever. This leads them to save a large proportion of the income from oil revenues.

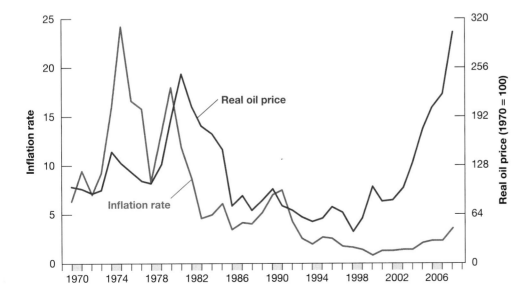

Figure 9.16

Oil price increases and inflation in the UK since 1970

The oil price increases of the 1970s were associated with large increases in inflation, but this has not been the case for the recent oil price increases.

Source: Energy Information Administration (EIA) – Official Energy Statistics from the US Government, Eurostat.

Figure 9.17

Oil price increases and unemployment in the UK since 1970

The oil price increases of the 1970s were associated with large increases in unemployment, but this has not been the case for the recent oil price increases.

Source: Energy Information Administration (EIA) – Official Energy Statistics from the US Government, Eurostat.

FOCUS
Oil price increases: why are the 2000s so different from the 1970s?

The question triggered by Figures 9.16 and 9.17 is an obvious one: why is it that oil price increases were associated with stagation in the 1970s but have had so little apparent effect on the economy in the 2000s?

A first line of explanation is that other shocks besides just the increase in the price of oil were at work in the 1970s and in the 2000s. In the 1970s, not only did the price of oil increase, but so did the prices of many other raw materials. This implies that the aggregate supply relation shifted up by more than implied by just the increase in the price of oil. In the 2000s, many economists believe that, partly because of globalisation and foreign competition, workers in advanced countries became weaker in bargaining. If true, this implies that, while the increase in oil prices shifted the aggregate supply curve up, the decrease in bargaining power of workers shifted it down, dampening or even eliminating the adverse effects of the oil price increase on output and the price level.

Econometric studies suggest, however, that more was at work, and that, even after controlling for the presence of these other factors, the effects of the price of oil have changed since the 1970s. Figure 9.18 shows the effects of a 100% increase in the price of oil on output and the price level, estimated using data from two different periods. The black and brown lines show the effects of an increase in the price of oil on the CPI and on GDP, based on data from 1970:1 to 1986:4; the blue and pink lines do the same, but based on data from 1987:1 to 2006:4 (the time

scale on the horizontal axis is in quarters). The figure suggests two main conclusions. First, in both periods, as predicted by our model, the increase in the price of oil leads to an increase in the CPI and a decrease in GDP. Second, the effects of the increase in the price of oil on both the CPI and GDP have become smaller, roughly half of what they were earlier.

Why have the adverse effects of the increase in the price of oil become smaller? This is still very much a topic of research but, at this stage, three hypotheses appear plausible.

The first hypothesis is that, today, US workers are less powerful in bargaining than they were in the 1970s. Thus, as the price of oil has increased, workers have been more willing to accept a reduction in wages, limiting the upward shift in the aggregate supply curve and thus limiting the adverse effect on the price level and on output.

The second hypothesis concerns monetary policy. When the price of oil increased in the 1970s, people started expecting much higher prices, and P^e increased a lot. The result was a further shift of the aggregate supply curve, leading to a larger increase in the price level and a larger decrease in output. Today, monetary policy is very different from what it was in the 1970s, and expectations are that central banks will not let the increase in the price of oil lead to a higher price level. Thus, P^e has barely increased, leading to a smaller shift of the aggregate supply curve, and thus a smaller effect on output and the price level, than in the 1970s.

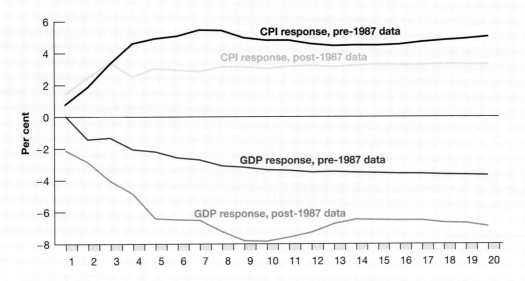

Figure 9.18

The effects of 100% increase in the price of oil on the CPI and on GDP

The effects of an increase in the price of oil on output and the price level are much smaller than they used to be.

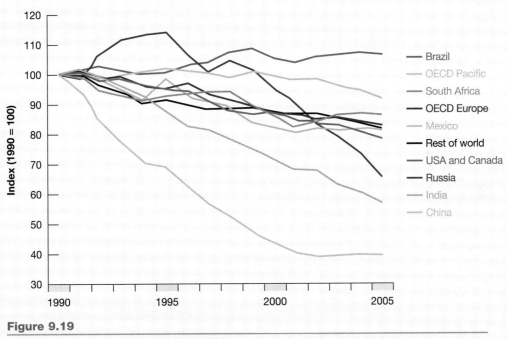

Figure 9.19

Energy intensity of GDP from 1990–2005

From 1990 to 2005 the use of energy per unit of output declined in many countries of the world, both among the OECD countries and among the emerging countries, with the exception of Brazil.

Source: International Energy Agency (2008), Worldwide Trends in Energy Use and Efficiency.

The third hypothesis regards the evolution of energy use in the last three decades. Figure 9.19 shows the trend in energy intensity of GDP (which measures how much energy is needed to produce one unit of product) in a number of countries and regions from 1990 to 2005. All countries have seen a decrease, with the exception of Brazil. This means that for every unit of output, the power requirements have decreased in almost every country in the world and hence the impact of an increase in the price of oil is lower today than it was in the 1970s, when the degree of intensity was much higher. In general, in the OECD countries the reduction was less rapid than in non-OECD countries. In many cases, these reductions can be attributed to strong improvements in energy efficiency following the introduction of technology and modern production processes. For example, in the case of China, the sharp decline in energy intensity of GDP during the 1990s was caused mainly by an improvement in energy efficiency. However, in addition to the degree of energy efficiency, there are other factors that explain why the levels of energy are so different between countries: these are the climate, geographical conditions, the size of the economic system and the productive structure.

For example, changes in production structure may decrease or increase the overall energy intensity of GDP of a country. In the case of Brazil, for example, the increase in energy intensity of GDP between 1990 and 2005 is due to the sharp increase of energy in manufacturing and the transport sector, accompanied by a modest economic growth.

9.7 CONCLUSIONS

This chapter has covered a lot of ground. Let us repeat some key ideas and develop some of the earlier conclusions.

The short run versus the medium run

One key message of this chapter is that changes in policy typically have different effects in the short run and in the medium run. The main results of this chapter are summarised in Table 9.1. A monetary expansion, for example, affects output in the short run but not in the medium run. In the short run, a reduction in the budget deficit decreases output and decreases the interest rate, and may decrease investment. But in the medium run, the interest rate decreases and output returns to the natural level of output, and investment unambiguously increases.

Disagreements among economists about the effects of various policies often come from differences in the time frame they have in mind. If you are worried about output and investment in the short run, you might be reluctant to proceed with fiscal consolidation. But if your focus is on the medium or the long run, you will see the consolidation as helping investment, and, eventually, through higher capital accumulation, increasing output. One implication is that where you stand depends in particular on how fast you think the economy adjusts to shocks. If you believe that it takes a long time for output to return to its natural level, you will naturally focus more on the short run, and be willing to use policies which increase output in the short run, even if medium-run effects are nil or negative. If you believe instead that output returns to its natural level quickly, you will put more emphasis on the medium-run implications, and will, by implication, be more reluctant to use those policies.

Shocks and propagation mechanisms

This chapter also gives you a general way of thinking about **output fluctuations** (sometimes called **business cycles**) – movements in output around its trend.

You can think of the economy as being constantly hit by **shocks**. These shocks may be shifts in consumption coming from changes in consumer confidence, shifts in investment, shifts in the demand for money and so on. Or they may come from changes in policy – from

Table 9.1 Short-run effects and medium-run effects of a monetary expansion, a budget deficit reduction and an increase in oil price

	Short run			Medium run		
	Output level	**Interest rate**	**Price level**	**Output level**	**Interest rate**	**Price level**
Monetary expansion	Increase	Decrease	Increase (small)	No change	No change	Increase
Deficit reduction	Decrease	Decrease	Decrease (small)	No change	Decrease	Decrease
Increase in oil price	Decrease	Increase	Increase	Decrease	Increase	Increase

the introduction of a new tax law, to a new program of infrastructure investment, to a decision by the central bank to fight inflation through by tightening the money supply.

Each shock has dynamic effects on output and its components. These dynamic effects are called the **propagation mechanism** of the shock. Propagation mechanisms are different for different shocks. The effects of a shock on activity may build up over time, affecting output in the medium run. Or the effects may build up for a while and then decrease and disappear. We saw, for example, that the effects of an increase in money on output reach a peak after six to nine months and then slowly decline afterward as the price level eventually increases in proportion to the increase in nominal money. At times, some shocks are sufficiently large, or come in sufficiently bad combinations that they create a recession. The two recessions of the 1970s were due largely to increases in the price of oil; the recession of the early 1980s was due to a sharp contraction in money; the recession of the early 1990s was due primarily to a sudden decline in consumer confidence; the recession of 2001 was due to a sharp drop in investment spending. The current crisis and the sharp decrease in output in 2010 had its origins in the problems of the housing market, which then led to a major financial shock, and in turn to a sharp reduction in output. What we call economic fluctuations are the result of these shocks and their dynamic effects on output.

◀ How to define *shocks* is harder than it looks. Suppose a failed economic program in an Eastern European country leads to political chaos in that country, which leads to increased risk of nuclear war in the region, which leads to a fall in consumer confidence in the USA, which leads to a recession in the USA. What is the 'shock'? The failed program? The fall of democracy? The increased risk of nuclear war? Or the decrease in consumer confidence? In practice, we have to cut the chain of causation somewhere. Thus, we may refer to the drop in consumer confidence as 'the shock', ignoring its underlying causes.

Where we go from here

- We assumed in this chapter that the nominal money stock was constant, that there was no nominal money growth. This led to a constant price level in the medium run. What we observe most of the time, however, is positive inflation, namely a steady increase in the price level. This in turn requires us to extend our analysis to the case where money growth is positive, and to revisit the relation between output, unemployment, inflation and money growth. We take this up in the next chapter.

- The *AS–AD* model we constructed in this chapter has a reassuring property. While shocks move output away from its natural level in the short run, there are forces which tend to take it back to its natural level over time. Output below its natural level leads to a decrease in the price level, which leads in turn to an increase in the real money stock, a decrease in the interest rate, and an increase in demand and in output. This process takes place until output has returned to its natural level and there is no longer pressure on the price level to adjust further. And, if this process is too slow, fiscal and monetary policies can help accelerate the return to the natural rate. The 2007 crisis, and the very slow recovery (recall the facts presented in Chapter 1) we are experiencing force us to reconsider these conclusions. (This is what we will do in Chapter 20.)

SUMMARY

- The model of aggregate supply and aggregate demand describes the movements in output and the price level when account is taken of equilibrium in the goods market, the financial markets and the labour market.

- The aggregate supply relation captures the effects of output on the price level. It is derived from equilibrium in the labour market. It is a relation between the price level, the expected price level and the level of output. An increase in output decreases unemployment; the decrease in unemployment increases wages and, in turn, increases the price level. An increase in the expected price level leads, one-for-one, to an increase in the actual price level.

- The aggregate demand relation captures the effects of the price level on output. It is derived from equilibrium in goods and financial markets. An increase in the price level

decreases the real money stock, increasing the interest rate and decreasing output.

- In the short run, movements in output come from shifts in either aggregate demand or aggregate supply. In the medium run, output returns to the natural level of output, which is determined by equilibrium in the labour market.

- An expansionary monetary policy leads in the short run to an increase in the real money stock, a decrease in the interest rate and an increase in output. Over time, the price level increases, and the real money stock decreases until output has returned to its natural level. In the medium run, money does not affect output, and changes in money are reflected in proportional increases in the price level. Economists refer to this fact by saying that, in the medium run, money is neutral.

- A reduction in the budget deficit leads in the short run to a decrease in the demand for goods and therefore to a decrease in output. Over time, the price level decreases, leading to an increase in the real money stock and a decrease in the interest rate. In the medium run, output increases back to the natural level of output, but the interest rate is lower and investment is higher.

- An increase in the price of oil leads, in the short run, to an increase in the price level, which decreases the real money stock and leads to a contraction of demand and output. In the medium run, an increase in the price of oil decreases the real wage paid by firms, increases the natural rate of unemployment and, therefore, decreases the natural level of output.

- An increase in productivity leads, in the short run, to an increase in output at any given level of employment.

- The difference between short-run effects and medium-run effects of policies is one of the reasons economists disagree in their policy recommendations. Some economists believe the economy adjusts quickly to its medium-run equilibrium, so they emphasise medium-run implications of policy. Others believe the adjustment mechanism through which output returns to the natural level of output is a slow process at best, and so they put more emphasis on the short-run effects of policy.

- Economic fluctuations are the result of a continual stream of shocks to aggregate supply or to aggregate demand and of the dynamic effects of each of these shocks on output. Sometimes the shocks are sufficiently adverse, alone or in combination, that they lead to a recession.

KEY TERMS

aggregate supply relation 190

aggregate demand relation 192

neutrality of money 200

Organization of Petroleum Exporting Countries (OPEC) 204

stagflation 205

output fluctuations 210

business cycles 210

shocks 210

propagation mechanism 211

QUESTIONS AND PROBLEMS

QUICK CHECK

1. *Using the information in this chapter, label each of the following statements true, false or uncertain. Explain briefly.*

a. The aggregate supply relation implies that an increase in output leads to an increase in the price level.

b. The natural level of output can be determined by looking at the aggregate supply relation alone.

c. The aggregate demand relation slopes down because, at a higher price level, consumers wish to purchase fewer goods.

d. In the absence of changes in fiscal or monetary policy, the economy will always remain at the natural level of output.

e. Expansionary monetary policy has no effect on the level of output in the medium run.

f. Fiscal policy cannot affect investment in the medium run because output always returns to its natural level.

g. In the medium run, output and the price level always return to the same value.

2. Spending shocks and the medium run

Suppose the economy begins with output equal to its natural level. Then, there is a reduction in income taxes.

a. Using the *AS–AD* model developed in this chapter, show the effects of a reduction in income taxes on the position of the *AD*, *AS*, *IS* and *LM* curves in the medium run.

b. What happens to output, the interest rate, and the price level in the medium run? What happens to consumption and investment in the medium run?

3. Supply shocks and the medium run

Consider an economy with output equal to the natural level of output. Now suppose there is an increase in unemployment benefits.

a. Using the model developed in this chapter, show the effects of an increase in unemployment benefits on the position of the *AD* and *AS* curves in the short run and in the medium run.

b. How will the increase in unemployment benefits affect output and the price level in the short run and in the medium run?

4. The neutrality of money

a. In what sense is money neutral? How is monetary policy useful if money is neutral?

b. Fiscal policy, like monetary policy, cannot change the natural level of output. Why then is monetary policy considered neutral but fiscal policy is not?

c. Discuss the statement: 'Because neither fiscal nor monetary policy can affect the natural level of output, it follows that, in the medium run, the natural level of output is independent of all government policies.'

DIG DEEPER

5. The paradox of saving, one last time

In the chapter problems at the end of Chapters 3 and 5, we examined the paradox of saving in the short run, under different assumptions about the response of investment to output and the interest rate. Here we consider the issue one last time in the context of the AS–AD model.

a. Suppose the economy begins with output equal to its natural level. Then there is a decrease in consumer confidence, as households attempt to increase their saving, for a given level of disposable income. In *AS–AD* and *IS–LM* diagrams, show the effects of the decline in consumer confidence in the short run and the medium run. Explain why curves shift in your diagrams.

c. What happens to output, the interest rate and the price level in the short run? What happens to consumption, investment and private saving in the short run? Is it possible that the decline in consumer confidence will actually lead to a fall in private saving in the short run?

d. Repeat part (b) for the medium run. Is there any paradox of saving in the medium run?

6. Suppose that the interest rate has no effect on investment

a. Can you think of a situation in which this may happen?

b. What does this imply for the slope of the *IS* curve?

c. What does this imply for the slope of the *LM* curve?

d. What does this imply for the slope of the *AD* curve?

Continue to assume that the interest rate has no effect on investment. Assume that the economy starts at the natural level of output. Suppose there is a shock to the variable z, so that the AS curve shifts up.

e. What is the short-run effect on output and the price level? Explain in words.

f. What happens to output and the price level over time? Explain in words.

7. You learned in problem 6 (on the liquidity trap) in Chapter 5 that money demand becomes very flat at low interest rates. For this problem, consider the money demand function to be horizontal at a zero nominal interest rate.

a. Draw the *LM* curve. How does the slope of the curve change when the interest rate rises above zero?

b. Draw the *IS* curve. Does the shape of the curve change (necessarily) when the interest rate falls below zero?

c. Draw the *AD* curve? (*Hint:* from the *IS–LM* diagram, think about the price level at which the interest rate is zero. How does the *AD* curve look above this price level? How does the *AD* curve look below this price level?)

d. Draw the *AD* and *AS* curves and assume that equilibrium is at a point where output is below the natural level of output and where the interest rate is zero. Suppose the central bank increases the money supply. What will be the effects on output in the short run and in the medium run? Explain in words.

8. Demand shocks and demand management

Assume that the economy starts at the natural level of output. Now suppose there is a decline in business confidence, so that investment demand falls for any interest rate.

a. In an *AD–AS* diagram, show what happens to output and the price level in the short run and the medium run.

b. What happens to the unemployment rate in the short run? in the medium run?

Suppose that the European Central Bank decides to respond immediately to the decline in business confidence in the short run. In particular, suppose that the European Central Bank wants to prevent the unemployment rate from changing in the short run after the decline in business confidence.

c. What should the European Central Bank do? Show how the European Central Bank's action, combined with the decline in business confidence, affects the *AD–AS* diagram in the short run and the medium run.

d. How do short-run output and the short-run price level compare to your answers from part (a)?

e. How do the short-run and medium-run unemployment rates compare to your answers from part (b)?

9. Supply shocks and demand management

Assume that the economy starts at the natural level of output. Now suppose there is an increase in the price of oil.

a. In an *AS–AD* diagram, show what happens to output and the price level in the short run and the medium run.

b. What happens to the unemployment rate in the short run? in the medium run?

Suppose that the European Central Bank decides to respond immediately to the increase in the price of oil. In particular, suppose that the European Central Bank wants to prevent the unemployment rate from changing in the short run, after the increase in the price of oil. Assume that the European Central Bank changes the money supply once – immediately after the increase in the price of oil – and then does not change the money supply again.

c. What should the European Central Bank do to prevent the unemployment rate from changing in the short run? Show how the European Central Bank's action, combined with the decline in business confidence, affects the *AD–AS* diagram in the short run and the medium run.

d. How do output and the price level in the short run and the medium run compare to your answers from part (a)?

e. How do the short-run and medium-run unemployment rates compare to your answers from part (b)?

10. Based on your answers to problems 8 and 9 and the material from the chapter, comment on the following statement:

The European Central Bank has the easiest job in the world. All it has to do is conduct expansionary monetary

policy when the unemployment rate increases and contractionary monetary policy when the unemployment
rate falls.

11. Taxes, oil prices and workers

*Everyone in the labour force is concerned with two things:
whether they have a job and, if so, their after-tax income from
the job (i.e. their after-tax real wage). An unemployed worker
may also be concerned with the availability and amount of
unemployment benefits, but we will leave that issue aside for
this problem.*

a. Suppose there is an increase in oil prices. How will this
   affect the unemployment rate in the short run and the
   medium run? How about the real wage (W/P)?

b. Suppose there is a reduction in income taxes. How will
   this affect the unemployment rate in the short run and
   the medium run? How about the real wage? For a given
   worker, how will after-tax income be affected?

c. According to our model, what policy tools does the government have available to increase the real wage?

d. During 2003 and 2004, oil prices increased more or less
   at the same time that income taxes were reduced. A popular joke at the time was that people could use their tax
   refunds to pay for the higher petrol prices. How do your
   answers to this problem make sense of this joke?

EXPLORE FURTHER

12. Adding energy prices to the AS curve

*In this problem, we incorporate the price of energy inputs
(e.g. oil) explicitly into the AS curve.*

Suppose the price-setting equation is given by

$$P = (1 + \mu)W^a P_E^{1-a}$$

*where P_E is the price of energy resources and $0 < a < 1$. Ignoring
a multiplicative constant, $W^a P_E^{1-a}$ is the marginal cost function
that would result from the production technology, $Y = N^a E^{1-a}$,
where N is employed labour and E represents units of energy
resources used in production.*

As in the text, the wage-setting relation is given by

$$W = P^e F(u, z)$$

*Make sure to distinguish between P_E, the price of energy
resources, and P^e, the expected price level for the economy as a
whole.*

a. Substitute the wage-setting relation into the price-setting
   relation to obtain the aggregate supply relation.

b. Let $x \equiv P_E/P$, the real price of energy. Observe that $P \times x =
   P_E$ and substitute for P_E in the AS relation you derived in
   part (a). Solve for P to obtain

$$P = P^e(1 + m)^{1/a}F(u, z)x^{(1-a)/a}$$

c. Graph the AS relation from part (b) for a given P^e and a
   given x.

d. Suppose that $P = P^e$. How will the natural rate of unemployment change if x, the real price of energy, increases?
   (*Hint:* you can solve the AS equation for x to obtain
   the answer, or you can reason it out. If $P = P^e$, how must
   $F(u, z)$ change when x increases to maintain the equality
   in part (b)? How must u change to have the required
   effect on $F(u, z)$?)

e. Suppose that the economy begins with output equal to
   the natural level of output. Then the real price of energy
   increases. Show the short-run and medium-run effects
   of the increase in the real price of energy in an *AD–AS*
   diagram.

*The text suggests that a change in expectations about monet-
ary policy may help explain why increases in oil prices over
the past few years have had less of an adverse effect on the
economy than the oil price shocks of the 1970s. Let us examine
how such a change in expectations would alter the effect of an
oil price shock.*

f. Suppose there is an increase in the real price of energy. In
   addition, despite the increase in the real price of energy,
   suppose that the expected price level (i.e. P^e) does not
   change. After the short-run effect of the increase in the
   real price of energy, will there be any further adjustment
   of the economy over the medium run? In order for the
   expected price level not to change, what monetary action
   must wage setters be expecting after an increase in the
   real price of energy?

13. Growth and fluctuations: some economic history

*When economists think about history, fluctuations often stand
out – oil shocks and stagflation in the 1970s, a recession
followed by a long expansion in the 1980s, a recession followed
by an extraordinary low-unemployment, low-inflation boom
in the 1990s. This question puts these fluctuations into some
perspective. Go to the website of the OECD Economic Outlook
Database and and retrieve the quarterly data on real GDP at
constant prices. Get real GDP for the fourth quarter of 1959,
1969, 1979, 1989 and 1999 and for the fourth quarter of the
most recent year available.*

a. Using the real GDP numbers for 1959 and 1969, calculate
   the decadal growth rate of real GDP for the 1960s. Do the
   same for the 1970s, 1980s and 1990s and for the available years of the most recent decade.

b. How does growth in the 1970s compare to growth in the
   later decades? How does growth in the 1960s compare to
   the later decades? Which decade looks most unusual?

---

*Log on to **MyEconLab** and complete the studyplan exercises for this chapter to see
how much you have learnt, and where you need to revise most.*

MyEconLab

Chapter 10

THE PHILLIPS CURVE, THE NATURAL RATE OF UNEMPLOYMENT AND INFLATION

In 1958, A. W. Phillips drew a diagram plotting the rate of inflation against the rate of unemployment in the UK for each year from 1861 to 1957. He found clear evidence of a negative relation between inflation and unemployment: when unemployment was low, inflation was high, and when unemployment was high, inflation was low, often even negative.

Two years later, Paul Samuelson and Robert Solow replicated Phillips's exercise for the USA, using data from 1900 to 1960. Figure 10.1 reproduces their findings, using CPI inflation as a measure of the inflation rate. Apart from the period of very high unemployment during the 1930s (the years from 1931 to 1939 are denoted by triangles and are clearly to the right of the other points in the figure), there also appeared to be a negative relation between inflation and unemployment in the USA.

This relation, which Samuelson and Solow labelled the **Phillips curve**, rapidly became central to macroeconomic thinking and policy. It appeared to imply that countries could choose between different combinations of unemployment and inflation. A country could achieve low unemployment if it were willing to tolerate higher inflation, or it could achieve price-level stability – zero inflation – if it were willing to tolerate higher unemployment. Much of the discussion about macroeconomic policy became a discussion about which point to choose on the Phillips curve.

In the 1970s, however, the relation broke down. In the USA and most OECD countries, there was both high inflation and high unemployment, clearly contradicting the original Phillips curve. A relation reappeared, but it reappeared as a relation between the unemployment rate and the change in the inflation rate. Today in the USA, high unemployment typically leads not to low inflation, but to a decrease in inflation over time. Conversely, low unemployment doesn't lead to high inflation but to an increase in inflation over time.

The purpose of this chapter is to explore the mutations of the Phillips curve and, more generally, to understand the relation between inflation and unemployment. You will see that what Phillips discovered was the aggregate supply relation and that the mutations of the Phillips curve came from changes in the way people and firms formed expectations.

The chapter has three sections:

● Section 10.1 shows how we can think of the aggregate supply relation as a relation between inflation, expected inflation and unemployment.

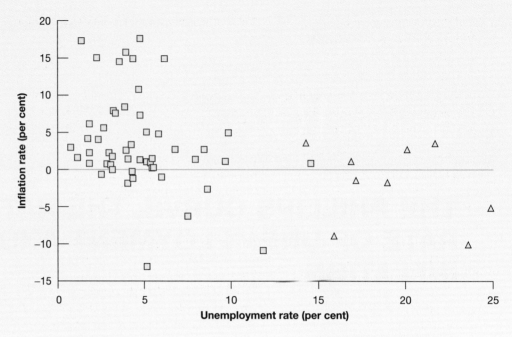

Figure 10.1

Inflation versus unemployment in the USA, 1900–1960

During the period 1900–1960 in the USA, a low unemployment rate was typically associated with a high inflation rate, and a high unemployment rate was typically associated with a low or negative inflation rate.

- Section 10.2 uses this relation to interpret the mutations in the Phillips curve over time. It shows the relation between the actual unemployment rate, the natural unemployment rate and inflation. It then draws two central implications of the Phillips curve for the medium run: in the medium run, unemployment returns to the natural rate, independent of inflation. The inflation rate is determined by the rate of money growth.

- Section 10.3 further discusses the relation between unemployment and inflation in Europe.

10.1 INFLATION, EXPECTED INFLATION AND UNEMPLOYMENT

Our first step will be to show that the aggregate supply relation we derived earlier (in Chapter 9) can be rewritten as a relation between inflation, expected inflation and the unemployment rate.

To rewrite, go back to the aggregate supply relation between the price level, the expected price level and the unemployment rate we derived in equation (9.1):

$$P = P^e(1 + \mu)F(u, z)$$

We then replaced the unemployment rate by its expression in terms of output to obtain a relation between the price level, the expected price level and output. As our focus is on the relation between unemployment (rather than output) and inflation, we do not need to take this step here.

Recall that the function F captures the effects on the wage of the unemployment rate, u, and of the other factors that affect wage setting represented by the catchall variable z. It will be convenient here to assume a specific form for this function:

$$F(u, z) = 1 - \alpha u + z$$

The function F comes from the wage setting relation, equation (9.1):
$W = P^e F(u, z)$.

This captures the notion that the higher the unemployment rate, the lower the wage; and the higher z (for example, the more generous unemployment benefits are), the higher the wage. The parameter α (the Greek lowercase letter alpha) captures the strength of the effect of unemployment on the wage.

Replace the function F by this specific form in the aggregate supply relation above:

$$P = P^e(1 + \mu)(1 - \alpha u + z) \qquad [10.1]$$

Finally, let π denote the inflation rate, and π^e denote the expected inflation rate. Then, equation (10.1) can be rewritten as

$$\pi = \pi^e + (\mu + z) - \alpha u \qquad [10.2]$$

Deriving equation (10.2) from equation (10.1) is not difficult, but it is tedious, so it is left to an appendix at the end of this chapter. What is important is that you understand each of the effects at work in equation (10.2):

- An increase in expected inflation, π^e, leads to an increase in actual inflation, π.

  To see why, start from equation (10.1). An increase in the expected price level, P^e, leads, one-for-one, to an increase in the actual price level, P: if wage setters expect a higher price level, they set a higher nominal wage, which leads to an increase in the price level.

  Now note that, given last period's price level, a higher price level this period implies a higher rate of increase in the price level from last period to this period – that is, higher inflation. Similarly, given last period's price level, a higher expected price level this period implies a higher expected rate of increase in the price level from last period to this period – that is, higher expected inflation. So the fact that an increase in the expected price level leads to an increase in the actual price level can be restated as: an increase in expected inflation leads to an increase in inflation.

▷ *From now on, to lighten your reading, we shall often refer to the inflation rate simply as inflation, and to the unemployment rate simply as unemployment.*

▷ Increase in $\pi^e \Rightarrow$ Increase in π.

- Given expected inflation, π^e, an increase in the mark-up μ, or an increase in the factors that affect wage determination – an increase in z – lead to an increase in inflation, π.

  From equation (10.1): given the expected price level, P^e, an increase in either μ or z increases the price level, P. Using the same argument as in the previous point to restate this proposition in terms of inflation and expected inflation: given expected inflation, π^e, an increase in either μ or z lead to an increase in inflation, π.

▷ Increase in μ or $z \Rightarrow$ Increase in π.

- Given expected inflation, π^e, an increase in the actual unemployment rate, u, leads to a decrease in inflation, π.

  From equation (10.1): given the expected price level, P^e, an increase in the unemployment rate, u, leads to a lower nominal wage, which leads to a lower price level, P. Restating this in terms of inflation and expected inflation: given expected inflation, π^e, an increase in the unemployment rate, u, leads to a decrease in inflation, π.

▷ Increase in $u \Rightarrow$ Decrease in π.

- Given expected inflation, π^e, an increase in the parameter α leads to a decrease in inflation, π.

  From equation (10.1): given the expected price level, P^e, an increase in the strength of the effect of unemployment on the wage leads to a decrease in inflation, π.

▷ Increase in $\alpha \Rightarrow$ Decrease in π.

We need one more step before we return to a discussion of the Phillips curve: when we look at movements in inflation and unemployment in the rest of the chapter, it will often be convenient to use time indexes so that we can refer to variables like inflation, or expected inflation, or unemployment, in a specific year. So we rewrite equation (10.2) as:

$$\pi_t = \pi_t^e + (\mu + z) - \alpha u_t \qquad [10.3]$$

The variables π_t, π_t^e and u_t refer to inflation, expected inflation and unemployment in year t. Be sure you see that there are no time indexes on μ and z. This is because we shall typically think of both μ and z as constant while we look at movements in inflation, expected inflation and unemployment over time.

10.2 THE PHILLIPS CURVE

Let's start with the relation between unemployment and inflation as it was first discovered by Phillips, Samuelson and Solow around 1960.

The early incarnation

Imagine an economy where inflation is positive in some years, negative in others, and is on average equal to zero. This is not the way things have been for some time. Since 1960, world inflation has been positive in all years but one, 2009, when it was negative, but small. But as we shall see later in this chapter, average inflation was close to zero during much of the period Phillips, Samuelson and Solow were looking at.

In such an environment, how will wage setters choose nominal wages for the coming year? With the average inflation rate equal to zero in the past, it is reasonable for wage setters to expect that inflation will be equal to zero over the next year as well. So, let's assume that expected inflation is equal to zero – that $\pi_t^e = 0$. Equation (10.3) then becomes

$$\pi_t = (\mu + z) - \alpha u_t \qquad [10.4]$$

This is precisely the negative relation between unemployment and inflation that Phillips found for the UK, and Solow and Samuelson found for the USA. The story behind it is simple: given the expected price level, which workers simply take to be last year's price level, lower unemployment leads to a higher nominal wage. A higher nominal wage leads to a higher price level. Putting the steps together, lower unemployment leads to a higher price level this year relative to last year's price level – that is, to higher inflation. This mechanism has sometimes been called the **wage–price spiral**, an expression that captures well the basic mechanism at work:

- Low unemployment leads to a higher nominal wage.
- In response to the higher nominal wage, firms increase their prices. The price level increases.
- In response to the higher price level, workers ask for a higher nominal wage the next time the wage is set.
- The higher nominal wage leads firms to further increase their prices. As a result, the price level increases further.
- In response to this further increase in the price level, workers, when they set the wage again, ask for a further increase in the nominal wage.
- And so the race between prices and wages results in steady wage and price inflation.

Mutations

The combination of an apparently reliable empirical relation, together with a plausible story to explain it, led to the adoption of the Phillips curve by macroeconomists and policy makers. During the 1960s, US macroeconomic policy was aimed at maintaining unemployment in the range that appeared consistent with moderate inflation. And, throughout the 1960s, the negative relation between unemployment and inflation provided a reliable guide to the joint movements in unemployment and inflation.

Figure 10.2 plots the combinations of the inflation rate and the unemployment rate in the USA for each year from 1948 to 1969. Note how well the Phillips relation held during the long economic expansion that lasted during most of the 1960s. During the years 1961 to 1969, denoted by black diamonds in the figure, the unemployment rate declined steadily from 6.8% to 3.4%, and the inflation rate steadily increased, from 1.0% to 5.5%. Put informally, from 1961 to 1969, the US economy moved up along the Phillips curve.

Around 1970, however, the relation between the inflation rate and the unemployment rate, so visible in Figure 10.2, broke down. Figure 10.3 shows the combination of the inflation rate and the unemployment rate in the USA for each year since 1970. The points are scattered in a roughly symmetric cloud: there is no visible relation between the unemployment rate and the inflation rate.

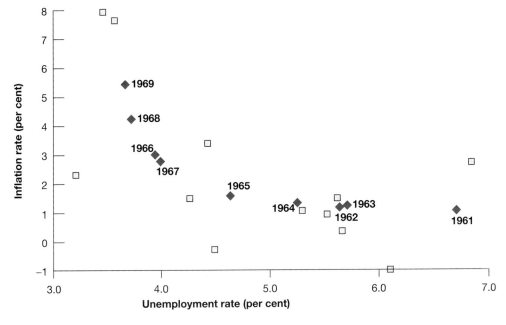

Figure 10.2

Inflation versus unemployment in the USA, 1948–1969

The steady decline in the US unemployment rate throughout the 1960s was associated with a steady increase in the inflation rate.

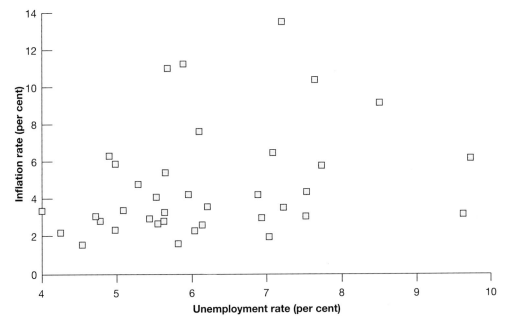

Figure 10.3

Inflation versus unemployment in the USA since 1970

Beginning in 1970, the relation between the unemployment rate and the inflation rate disappeared in the USA.

Why did the original Phillips curve vanish? There are two main reasons:

● The USA was hit twice in the 1970s by a large increase in the price of oil (see Chapter 7). The effect of this increase in non-labour costs was to force firms to increase their prices relative to the wages they were paying – in other words, to increase the mark-up, μ. As shown in equation (10.3), an increase in μ leads to an increase in inflation, even at a given rate of unemployment, and this happened twice in the 1970s. The main reason for the breakdown of the Phillips curve relation, however, lay elsewhere:

● Wage setters changed the way they formed their expectations. This change came, in turn, from a change in the behaviour of inflation. Look at Figure 10.4, which shows the US inflation rate since 1900. Starting in the 1960s (the decade shaded in the figure), you can see a clear change in the behaviour of the rate of inflation. First, rather than being sometimes positive and sometimes negative, as it had for the first part of the century, the rate of inflation became consistently positive. Second, inflation became more persistent: high inflation in one year became more likely to be followed by high inflation the next year.

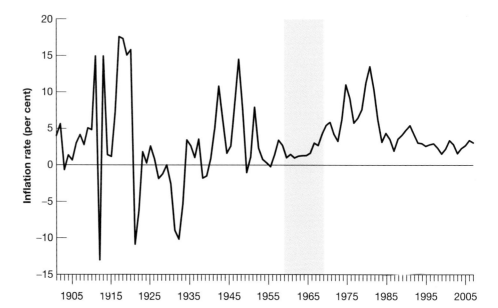

Figure 10.4

US inflation since 1900

Since the 1960s, the US inflation rate has been consistently positive. Inflation has also become more persistent: a high inflation rate this year is more likely to be followed by a high inflation rate next year.

The persistence of inflation led workers and firms to revise the way they formed their expectations. When inflation is consistently positive year after year, expecting that the price level this year will be the same as the price level last year – which is the same as expecting zero inflation – becomes systematically incorrect; worse, it becomes foolish. People do not like to make the same mistake repeatedly. So, as inflation became consistently positive and more persistent, people, when forming expectations, started to take into account the presence and the persistence of inflation. This change in expectation formation changed the nature of the relation between unemployment and inflation.

Let's look at the argument in the previous paragraph more closely. First, suppose expectations of inflation are formed according to

$$\pi_t^e = \theta \pi_{t-1} \qquad\qquad [10.5]$$

The value of the parameter θ (the Greek lowercase theta) captures the effect of last year's inflation rate, π_{t-1}, on this year's expected inflation rate, π_t^e. The higher the value of θ, the more last year's inflation leads workers and firms to revise their expectations of what inflation will be this year, and so the higher the expected inflation rate is. We can think of what happened in the 1970s as an increase in the value of θ over time:

- As long as inflation was low and not very persistent, it was reasonable for workers and firms to ignore past inflation and to assume that the price level this year would be roughly the same as price level last year. For the period that Samuelson and Solow had looked at, θ was close to zero, and expectations were roughly given by $\pi_t^e = 0$.
- But, as inflation became more persistent, workers and firms started changing the way they formed expectations. They started assuming that if inflation had been high last year, inflation was likely to be high this year as well. The parameter θ, the effect of last year's inflation rate on this year's expected inflation rate, increased. The evidence suggests that, by the mid-1970s, people formed expectations by expecting this year's inflation rate to be the same as last year's inflation rate – in other words, that θ was now equal to 1.

> Think about how *you* form expectations. What do you expect inflation to be next year? How did you come to this conclusion?

Now turn to the implications of different values of θ for the relation between inflation and unemployment. To do so, replace equation (10.5) in equation (10.3):

$$\pi_t = \overbrace{\theta \pi_{t-1}}^{\pi_t^e} + (\mu + z) - \alpha u_t$$

- When θ equals zero, we get the original Phillips curve, a relation between the inflation rate and the unemployment rate:

$$\pi_t = (\mu + z) - \alpha u_t$$

- When θ is positive, the inflation rate depends not only on the unemployment rate but also on last year's inflation rate:

$$\pi_t = \theta \pi_{t-1} + (\mu + z) - \alpha u_t$$

- When θ equals 1, the relation becomes (moving last year's inflation rate to the left side of the equation)

$$\pi_t - \pi_{t-1} = (\mu + z) - \alpha u_t \qquad [10.6]$$

So, when $\theta = 1$, the unemployment rate affects not the inflation rate, but rather the change in the inflation rate: high unemployment leads to decreasing inflation; low unemployment leads to increasing inflation.

This discussion is the key to what happened from 1970 onward. As θ increased from 0 to 1, the simple relation between the unemployment rate and the inflation rate disappeared. This disappearance is what we saw in Figure 10.3. But a new relation emerged, this time between the unemployment rate and the change in the inflation rate – as predicted by equation (10.6). This relation is shown in Figure 10.5, which plots the change in the inflation rate versus the unemployment rate observed for each year since 1970. The figure shows a negative relation between the unemployment rate and the change in the inflation rate. The line that best fits the scatter of points for the period 1970–2010 is given by

$$\pi_t - \pi_{t-1} = 3.3\% - 0.55 u_t \qquad [10.7]$$

◀ This line, called a regression line, is obtained using econometrics. (See Appendix 2 at the end of the text.) Note the line does not fit the cloud of points very tightly. There are years when the change in inflation is much larger than implied by the line and years when the change in inflation is much smaller than implied by the line. We return to this point later.

The line is drawn in Figure 10.5. For low unemployment, the change in inflation is positive. For high unemployment, the change in inflation is negative. This is the form the Phillips curve relation between unemployment and inflation takes today.

To distinguish it from the original Phillips curve (equation (10.4)), equation (10.6) (or its empirical counterpart, equation (10.7)) is often called the **modified Phillips curve**, or the **expectations-augmented Phillips curve** (to indicate that π_{t-1} stands for expected inflation), or the **accelerationist Phillips curve** (to indicate that a low unemployment rate

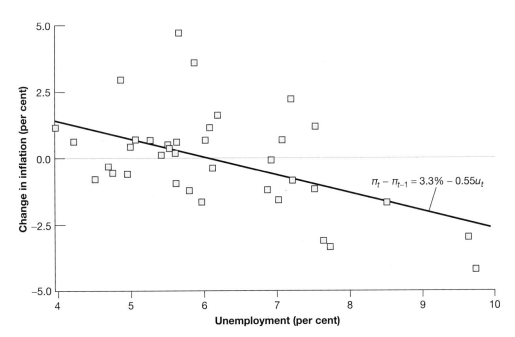

Figure 10.5

Change in inflation versus unemployment in the USA since 1970

Since 1970, there has been a negative relation between the unemployment rate and the change in the inflation rate in the USA.

● Original Phillips curve: Increase in ➤
u_t ⇒ Lower inflation.
● (Modified) Phillips curve: Increase in
u_t ⇒ Decreasing inflation.

leads to an increase in the inflation rate and thus an acceleration of the price level). We will simply call equation (10.6) the Phillips curve and refer to the earlier incarnation, equation (10.4), as the original Phillips curve.

The Phillips curve and the natural rate of unemployment

The history of the Phillips curve is closely related to the discovery of the concept of the natural unemployment rate that we introduced earlier (in Chapter 8).

The original Phillips curve implied that there was no such thing as a natural unemployment rate: if policy makers were willing to tolerate a higher inflation rate, they could maintain a lower unemployment rate forever.

In the late 1960s, while the original Phillips curve still gave a good description of the data, two economists, Milton Friedman and Edmund Phelps, questioned the existence of such a trade-off between unemployment and inflation. They questioned it on logical grounds, arguing that such a trade-off could exist only if wage setters systematically underpredicted inflation, and that they were unlikely to make the same mistake forever. Friedman and Phelps also argued that if the government attempted to sustain lower unemployment by accepting higher inflation, the trade-off would ultimately disappear; the unemployment rate could not be sustained below a certain level, a level they called the 'natural rate of unemployment'. Events proved them right, and the trade-off between the unemployment rate and the inflation rate indeed disappeared. (See the Focus box 'Theory

Friedman was awarded the Nobel Prize ➤
in 1976. Phelps was awarded the Nobel
Prize in 2006.

ahead of facts: Milton Friedman and Edmund Phelps'.) Today, most economists accept the notion of a natural rate of unemployment – subject to the many caveats we will see in the next section.

Let's make explicit the connection between the Phillips curve and the natural rate of unemployment.

By definition (see Chapter 8), the natural rate of unemployment is the unemployment rate such that the actual price level is equal to the expected price level. Equivalently, and more conveniently here, the natural rate of unemployment is the unemployment rate such that the actual inflation rate is equal to the expected inflation rate. Denote the natural unemployment rate by u_n (where the index 'n' stands for 'natural'). Then, imposing the condition that actual inflation and expected inflation be the same ($\pi_t = \pi_t^e$) in equation (8.3) gives

$$0 = (\mu + z) - \alpha u_n$$

Solving for the natural rate u_n:

$$u_n = \frac{\mu + z}{\alpha} \qquad [10.8]$$

The higher the mark-up, μ, or the higher the factors that affect wage setting, z, the higher the natural rate of unemployment.

Now rewrite equation (10.3) as

$$\pi_t - \pi_t^e = -\alpha\left(u_t - \frac{\mu + z}{\alpha}\right)$$

Note from equation (10.8) that the fraction on the right side is equal to u_n, so we can rewrite the equation as

$$\pi_t - \pi_t^e = -\alpha(u_t - u_n) \qquad [10.9]$$

If the expected rate of inflation (π_t^e) is well approximated by last year's inflation rate (π_{t-1}), the equation finally becomes

$$\pi_t - \pi_{t-1} = -\alpha(u_t - u_n) \qquad [10.10]$$

Equation (10.10) is an important relation, for two reasons:

- It gives us another way of thinking about the Phillips curve, as a relation between the actual unemployment rate, u_t, the natural unemployment rate, u_n, and the change in the inflation rate, $\pi_t - \pi_{t-1}$:

  The change in the inflation rate depends on the difference between the actual and the natural unemployment rates. When the actual unemployment rate is higher than the natural unemployment rate, the inflation rate decreases; when the actual unemployment rate is lower than the natural unemployment rate, the inflation rate increases.

$u_t < u_n \Rightarrow \pi_t > \pi_{t-1}$
$u_t > u_n \Rightarrow \pi_t < \pi_{t-1}$

- It also gives us another way of thinking about the natural rate of unemployment: the natural rate of unemployment is the rate of unemployment required to keep the inflation rate constant. This is why the natural rate is also called the **non-accelerating inflation rate of unemployment (NAIRU).**

◀ Calling the natural rate 'the non-accelerating inflation rate of unemployment' is actually wrong: it should be called 'the non-increasing inflation rate of unemployment', or NIIRU. But NAIRU has now become so standard that it is too late to change it.

What has been the natural rate of unemployment since 1970? Put another way: what has been the unemployment rate that, on average, has led to constant inflation?

To answer this question for the USA, all we need to do is to return to equation (10.7), the estimated relation between the change in inflation and the unemployment rate since 1970. Setting the change in inflation equal to zero in that equation implies a value for the natural unemployment rate of $3.3\%/0.55 = 6\%$. In words: the evidence suggests that, since 1970 in the USA, the average rate of unemployment required to keep inflation constant has been equal to 6%.

We will turn to the natural rate of unemployment in Europe in the next section.

FOCUS
Theory ahead of facts: Milton Friedman and Edmund Phelps

Economists are usually not very good at predicting major changes before they happen, and most of their insights are derived after the fact. Here is an exception.

In the late 1960s – precisely as the original Phillips curve relation was working like a charm – two economists, Milton Friedman and Edmund Phelps, argued that the appearance of a trade-off between inflation and unemployment was an illusion.

Here are a few quotes from Milton Friedman. About the Phillips curve, he said:

> Implicitly, Phillips wrote his article for a world in which everyone anticipated that nominal prices would be stable and in which this anticipation remained unshaken and immutable whatever happened to actual prices and wages. Suppose, by contrast, that everyone anticipates that prices will rise at a rate of more than 75% a year – as, for example, Brazilians did a few years ago. Then, wages must rise at that rate simply to keep real wages unchanged. An excess supply of labor [by this, Friedman means high unemployment] will be reflected in a less rapid rise in nominal wages than in anticipated prices, not in an absolute decline in wages.

He went on:

> To state [my] conclusion differently, there is always a temporary trade-off between inflation and unemployment; there is no permanent trade-off. The temporary trade-off comes not from inflation per se, but from a rising rate of inflation.

He then tried to guess how much longer the apparent trade-off between inflation and unemployment would last in the USA:

> But how long, you will say, is 'temporary'? . . . We can at most venture a personal judgment, based on some examination of the historical evidence, that the initial effect of a higher and unanticipated rate of inflation lasts for something like two to five years; that this initial effect then begins to be reversed; and that a full adjustment to the new rate of inflation takes as long for employment as for interest rates, say, a couple of decades.

Friedman could not have been more right. A few years later, the original Phillips curve started to disappear, in exactly the way Friedman had predicted.

Source: Milton Friedman, 'The role of monetary policy', *American Economic Review*, 1968, **58**(1), 1–17. (The article by Phelps, 'Money–wage dynamics and labor–market equilibrium', *Journal of Political Economy*, 1968, **76**, 678–711, made many of the same points more formally.)

The neutrality of money, revisited

Earlier (in Chapter 9), we looked at the effects of a change in the level of nominal money on output and on the price level in the medium run. We derived two propositions. First, output returned to its natural level, unaffected by the level of nominal money. Second, the price level moved in proportion to the nominal money stock, leaving the real money stock unchanged. We are now ready to extend these results, and look at the effects of changes in the rate of growth of nominal money on unemployment and on inflation in the medium run.

Take unemployment first, and go back to equation (10.9). In the medium run, expected inflation must be equal to actual inflation. Thus the unemployment rate must be equal to the natural rate, which is clearly independent of the rate of growth of money.

Recall the derivation of the natural rate (in Chapter 8). The natural rate depends on such factors as the mark-up of firms and the nature of bargaining in the labour market. Nowhere does the growth rate of money appear in the determination of the natural rate.

Turn to inflation, and go back to the aggregate demand relation we derived in, equation (9.3):

$$Y = Y\left(\frac{M}{P}, G, T\right)$$

If unemployment returns to the natural rate, u_n, it follows that output must return to its natural level, Y_n. So the relation becomes

As we have done in previous chapters, we continue to ignore output growth, and thus assume that output is constant in the medium run.

$$Y_n = Y\left(\frac{M}{P}, G, T\right)$$

If Y_n is constant, for this equality to hold – that is, for aggregate demand to be equal to the natural level of output – the right side of the equation must be constant. If we assume unchanged fiscal policy – that is, constant G and constant T – this implies that the real money stock must also be constant. This implies in turn that the rate of inflation must be equal to the rate of money growth:

See Proposition 8 in Appendix 1.

$$\pi = g_m$$

This is an important result: in the medium run, the rate of inflation is determined by the rate of money growth. Milton Friedman put it this way: inflation is always and everywhere a monetary phenomenon. As we have seen, factors such as the monopoly power of firms, strong unions, strikes, fiscal deficits, increases in the price of oil, do affect the price level and, by implication, do affect inflation in the short run. But, unless they affect the rate of money growth, they have no effect on inflation in the medium run.

The 'unless' is important here. It could be, for example, that some of these shocks lead to a change in the rate of money growth. For example, a wage explosion, or a large budget deficit, may lead to higher money creation (more on deficits and inflation in Chapter 21). If this is the case, these shocks will, indirectly, affect inflation even in the medium run.

10.3 THE PHILLIPS CURVE AND THE NATURAL RATE OF UNEMPLOYMENT IN EUROPE

In the previous section we showed how the relation between inflation and unemployment has held quite well in the USA since 1970. But evidence from its earlier history, as well as evidence from other countries, suggests that the relation between inflation and unemployment can and does vary across countries and time. What has been the natural rate of unemployment in European countries since 1970? And has it changed over time?

Variations in the natural rate across European countries

Recall from equation (10.8) that the natural rate of unemployment depends on all the factors that affect wage setting, represented by the catchall variable, z; the mark-up set by firms, μ; and the response of inflation to unemployment, represented by α, $(u_n = \mu + z/\alpha)$. If these factors differ across countries, there is no reason to expect all countries to have the same natural rate of unemployment. And natural rates indeed differ across countries, sometimes considerably. The first column in Table 10.1 reports the value for the natural rate of unemployment in some European countries since 1970.

Table 10.1 The natural rate of unemployment in some European countries

Country	1970–2012	1970–1990	1991–2012
Denmark	5.40%	5.20%	5.70%
Finland	7.50%	5.30%	9.75%
France	7.60%	6.10%	9%
Germany	7.50%	6.10%	7.50%
Ireland	9.80%	13.70%	9.60%
Netherlands	4.60%	4.80%	4.50%
Sweden	5.40%	3.50%	7.30%
UK	7.10%	7.50%	6.85%

Source: Based on data from OECD *Economic Outlook* database (***http://stats.oecd.org***). *Economic Outlook*, 90, Dec 2011, OECD Annual Projections, © OECD, 2011.

Some European countries have natural rates of unemployment that are very low by international standards, even compared to the USA. Denmark, the Netherlands and Norway are such cases. Other countries such as Finland, France and Spain have higher natural rates of unemployment. Where should we look for explanations? To understand why the natural rate of unemployment has varied across European countries since 1970, we need to return again to equation (10.8). The natural rate of unemployment depends on the factors determining the wage-setting and the price-setting relations. On the wage-setting side, the natural rate of unemployment depends on labour market institutions: the higher the factors that increase workers' bargaining power (z), the higher the natural rate of unemployment will be. On the price-setting side, the higher the mark-up (u) set by firms, the higher the natural rate of unemployment will be. Moreover, the natural rate of uneployment depends on how strong the effect of unemployment is on the wage, i.e. on the parameter a. We will explain these factors in more detail in the next section.

Labour market rigidities

One often hears the statement that one of the main problems of Europe is its *labour market rigidities*. These rigidities, the argument goes, are responsible for its high natural rate of unemployment. What do critics have in mind when they talk about the labour market rigidities afficting Europe? They have in mind all the labour market institutions that are likely to affect wage setting, and go under the name of social protection, in particular:

- A generous system of **unemployment insurance** – The replacement rate (that is, the ratio of unemployment benefits to the after-tax wage) is often high in Europe, and the duration of benefits – the period of time for which the unemployed are entitled to receive benefits – often runs in years.

  Some unemployment insurance is clearly desirable, but generous benefits may increase unemployment in at least two ways: they decrease the incentives the unemployed have to search for jobs. They may also increase the wage that firms have to pay. Recall our discussion of efficiency wages earlier (in Chapter 8): the higher unemployment benefits are, the higher the wages firms have to pay in order to motivate and keep workers.

- A high degree of **employment protection** – By employment protection, economists have in mind the set of rules that increase the cost of layoffs for firms. These range from high severance payments to the need for firms to justify layoffs, to the possibility for workers to appeal the decision in court and have it reversed. The purpose of employment protection is to decrease layoffs and thus to protect workers from the risk of unemployment. What it does, however, is also increase the cost of labour for firms, thus reducing those hired and making it harder for the unemployed to get jobs. The evidence suggests that, while employment protection does not necessarily increase unemployment, it changes its nature: the flows in and out of unemployment decrease, but the average duration of unemployment increases. Such long duration increases the risk that the unemployed lose skills and morale, decreasing their employability.

- Minimum wages – Most European countries have national **minimum wages**. In some countries, the ratio of the minimum wage to the median wage can be quite high. As we discussed earlier (in Chapter 8), high minimum wages clearly run the risk of decreasing employment for the least skilled workers, thus increasing their unemployment rate.
- Bargaining rules – In most European countries, labour contracts are subject to 'extension agreements'. A contract agreed to by a subset of firms and unions can be automatically extended to all firms in the same sector. This considerably reinforces the bargaining power of unions because it reduces the scope for competition by non-unionised firms. As we saw earlier (in Chapter 8), stronger bargaining power on the part of the unions may result in higher unemployment: higher unemployment is needed to reconcile the demands of workers with the wages paid by firms.

All these forms of social protection give more bargaining power to workers, who can succeed in bargaining for higher nominal wages (W) at a given expected price level (P^e), for any given unemployment rate. This is why countries with higher social protection end up with higher natural rates of unemployment for any given price setting behaviour by firms. This is what happens, on average, in Europe, where social protection is higher than in the USA and the average natural unemployment rate is also higher.

However, the rate of unemployment differs widely across Europe: some countries have much higher natural rates of unemployment than some other countries, despite social protection being largely similar across countries. What is even more puzzling is that some Northern European countries with the lowest unemployment rates in Europe rank pretty high in terms of degree of social protection. How can we explain the lower natural unemployment rate in those countries? Do labour market institutions really explain the high natural rates of unemployment in Europe? Not quite. Here it is important to recall two important facts.

Fact 1: as we saw earlier (in Chapter 1), unemployment was not always high in Europe. Recall the evolution of unemployment shown in Figure 1.2: in the 1970s, the unemployment rate in the four major continental European countries was lower than that in the USA, around 2–3% (compared to 5% in the USA). The natural rate in these countries has increased since 1970 and today is around 8–9%. Let us return to Table 10.1. The second and third columns in the table compare the natural unemployment rate in 1970–1990 with the same rate in 1991–2012. In most cases, with the exceptions of the Netherlands, Ireland and the UK, the natural rate of unemployment increased. How do we explain this increase?

One hypothesis is that institutions were different then and that labour market rigidities have increased in the past 40 years. This turns out not to be the case, however. It is true that, in response to the adverse shocks of the 1970s (in particular the two recessions following the increases in the price of oil), many European governments increased the generosity of unemployment insurance and the degree of employment protection. But, even in the 1960s, European labour market institutions looked nothing like US labour market institutions. Social protection was higher in Europe, yet unemployment was lower.

Fact 2: until the current crisis started, many European countries actually had low natural rates of unemployment (see Table 10.1). The natural unemployment rate is high in the four large continental countries. But note how low the natural rates of unemployment is in some other countries – in particular, Denmark, Ireland and the Netherlands.

Is it the case that these low-natural-unemployment countries have low benefits, low employment protection and weak unions? Things are unfortunately not so simple: countries such as Ireland and the UK indeed have labour market institutions that resemble those of the USA: limited benefits, low employment protection and weak unions. But countries such as Denmark and the Netherlands have a high degree of social protection – in particular, high unemployment benefits and strong unions.

During the last decade, some European countries with high unemployment rates introduced major labour market reforms with the aim of increasing employment. The way it was done is by reducing the bargaining power and the degree of social protection of newly hired workers. This has created a dual labour market: standard (permanent) workers – still the vast majority of the labour force – still have high bargaining power and enjoy high social protection, so that the natural rate of unemployment has barely changed. At the same time, newly hired workers face short-term contracts with high separation rates. The uneployment rate among these workers – the majority of young workers – is still high, they have almost no social protection and their jobs are poor-quality jobs. These examples show that low social protection can hardly improve labour market conditions without measures to increase the probability that unemployed find a job.

So what is one to conclude? An emerging consensus among economists is that the devil is in the detail: generous social protection is consistent with low unemployment, but it has to be provided efficiently. For example, unemployment benefits can be generous, as long as the unemployed are, at the same time, forced to take jobs if such jobs are available. Some employment protection – for example, in the form of generous severance payments – may not prevent low unemployment as long as firms do not face the prospect of long adminis-trative or judicial uncertainty when they lay off workers. Countries such as Denmark – whose system is called 'Danish flex-security' to underline that it combines security for workers with flexibility for firms – appear to have been more successful in achieving these goals. Creating incentives for the unemployed to take jobs and simplifying the rules of employment protection are on the reform agenda of many European governments. One may hope they will lead to a decrease in the natural rate in the future.

Product market regulation

Besides labour market rigidities, another factor that can explain the high natural rates of unemployment in some European countries is the price-setting behaviour of firms, i.e. the level of mark-up (μ). We can think of the mark-up as depending on the degree of competition in the goods market. The higher the degree of competition, the lower the mark-up and, vice versa, the lower the degree of competition, the higher the mark-up. To keep things simple, we can assume that the degree of competition is higher the higher the number of compet-ing products in a market; because a high number of competing products in a market forces producers to keep prices down in order not to lose market share. Moreover, the mark-up also depends on the degree of regulation of the goods market. To see this, imagine a highly regulated goods market with a lot of trade barriers: trade barriers will limit the number of foreign products that can be sold in that market, and therefore will reduce the degree of market competition. Therefore, the higher the degree of product market regulation, the lower the degree of competition. Therefore, the mark-up, u, which depends negatively on the level of competition in the market, will depend positively on product market regulation.

In the context of European integration, for example, decreases in product market regula-tion may reflect the elimination of tariff barriers, or standardisation measures, making it easier to sell domestic products in other EU countries. Suppose the government increases competition in the product market for a given number of firms. Higher competition means that firms face a more elastic demand for their products (as consumers can more easily switch to other suppliers if they want to). Hence, to maintain their market share, they have to decrease their mark-up, leading in turn to both an increase in real wages and a decrease in unemployment. Therefore, lower product market regulation should be associated with higher real wages and lower natural rates of unemployment.

In Europe the completion of the internal market has increased both competition and real wages. Since 1998, product market regulation has decreased everywhere, even more so in countries which started from higher levels, such as France, Italy and Spain. Today, the differences in the levels of product market regulation across European countries are very small compared to the end of the 1990s. Scandinavian countries show slightly lower levels – that is, higher internal competition. Over the same decade, increased competition has been associated with higher wages. Wages increased all over Europe, more so in Scandinavian countries, Germany and the UK and much less in Southern Europe (Figure 10.6).

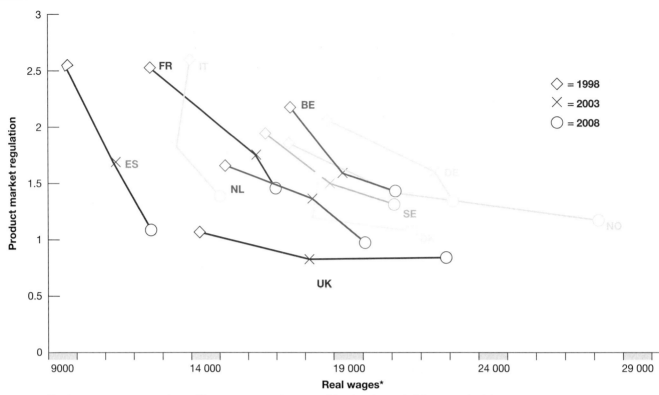

*Real wages are computed net of income taxes and corrected for the change in labour productivity over the period considered.

Figure 10.6

Relationship between trends in product market regulation and wages in Europe (1998, 2003, 2008)

Source: OECD, Eurostat.

Variations in the natural rate over time

In writing equation (10.6) and estimating equation (10.7), we treated $\mu + z$ as a constant, but there are good reasons to believe that μ and z vary over time. The degree of monopoly power of firms, the structure of wage bargaining, the system of unemployment benefits and so on are likely to change over time, leading to changes in either μ or z and, by implication, changes in the natural rate of unemployment.

Changes in the natural unemployment rate over time are hard to measure. The reason is, again, that we do not observe the natural rate, only the actual rate. But broad evolutions can be established by comparing average unemployment rates, say, across decades. Using this approach, we just saw how the natural rate of unemployment had increased in Europe since the 1970s, and discussed some reasons why this might be. In the USA, the natural rate has moved much less than that in Europe. Nevertheless, it is also far from constant. From the 1950s to the 1980s, the US unemployment rate fluctuated around a slowly increasing trend: average unemployment was 4.5% in the 1950s, and it was 7.3% in the 1980s. Since 1990, the trend appears to have been reversed, with an average unemployment rate of 5.7% in the 1990s and an average unemployment rate of 5.0% from 2000 to 2007. In 2007, the unemployment rate was 4.6%, and inflation was roughly constant, suggesting that unemployment was close to the natural rate.

Disinflation, credibility and unemployment

In 1979, US unemployment was 5.8%, roughly equal to the natural rate at the time. But the inflation rate, measured using the CPI, was running above 13%. Some of it was due to the large increase in oil prices, but, leaving this effect aside, underlying inflation was running at close to 10%. The question the Federal Reserve faced was no longer whether or not it should reduce inflation, but how fast it should reduce it. In August 1979, President Carter appointed Paul Volcker as Chairman of the Federal Reserve Board. Volcker, who had served in the Nixon administration, was considered an extremely qualified chairman who would and could lead the fight against inflation.

Fighting inflation implied tightening monetary policy, decreasing output growth, and thus accepting higher unemployment for some time. The question arose as to how much unemployment, and for how long, would likely be needed to achieve a lower level of inflation, say, 4% – which is the rate Volcker wanted to achieve.

- Some economists argued that such a **disinflation** would likely be very costly. Their starting point was equation (8.10):

$$\pi_t - \pi_{t-1} = -\alpha(u_t - u_n)$$

  ▹ Make sure to distinguish between deflation: decrease in the price level, (equivalently, negative inflation), and disinflation: a decrease in the inflation rate.

  According to this equation, the only way to bring down inflation is to accept unemployment above the natural rate for some time. We saw earlier that α is estimated to be equal to 0.55. The equation therefore implies that, to decrease inflation by one percentage point, the unemployment rate has to be higher than the natural unemployment rate by 1/0.55, or about 1.8 percentage points for a year. Or, to decrease inflation from 10% to 4%, the unemployment rate has to be higher than the natural rate by about 10 ((10 – 4)/0.55) percentage points for a year, or more realistically, if inflation was decreased from 10% to 6% in five years, by about 2 (10/5) percentage points for five years. The natural conclusion was that it would make sense to go slowly, so as not to increase unemployment too much in a given year.

- Some economists argued that disinflation might in fact be much less costly. In what has become known as the *Lucas critique*, Lucas pointed out that when trying to predict the effects of a major policy change – like the change considered by the Fed at the time – it could be very misleading to take as given the relations estimated from past data. In the case of the Phillips curve, taking equation (8.10) as given was equivalent to assuming that wage setters would keep expecting inflation in the future to be the same as it was in the past, that the way wage setters formed their expectations would not change in response to the change in policy. This was an unwarranted assumption, Lucas argued: why shouldn't wage setters take policy changes directly into account? If wage setters believed that the Fed was committed to lower inflation, they might well expect inflation to be lower in the future than in the past. They argued that the relevant equation was not equation (8.10) but equation (8.9). And equation (8.9) implied that, if the Fed was fully credible, the decrease in inflation might not require any increase in the unemployment rate. If wage setters expected inflation to now be 4%, then actual inflation would decrease to 4%, with unemployment remaining at the natural rate:

  ▹ Robert Lucas was awarded the Nobel Prize in 1995, and teaches at the University of Chicago.

$$\pi_t - \pi_t^e = \alpha(u_t - u_n)$$
$$4\% - 4\% = 0\%$$

Lucas did not believe that disinflation could really take place without some increase in unemployment. But Thomas Sargent, looking at the historical evidence on the end of several very high inflations, concluded that the increase in unemployment could be small. The essential ingredient of successful disinflation, he argued, was **credibility** of monetary policy – the belief by wage setters that the central bank was truly committed to reducing inflation. Only credibility would cause wage setters to change the way they formed their expectations. Furthermore, he argued, a clear and quick disinflation program was more likely to be credible than a protracted one that offered plenty of opportunities for reversal and political infighting along the way.

▹ Thomas Sargent was awarded the Nobel Prize in 2011, and now teaches at New York University.

Who turned out to be right? In September 1979, Paul Volcker started increasing the interest rate, so as to slow down the economy and reduce inflation. From 9% in 1979, the

Table 10.2 Inflation and unemployment, 1979–1985

	1979	1980	1981	1982	1983	1984	1985
CPI inflation (%)	13.3	12.5	8.9	3.8	3.8	3.9	3.8
GDP growth (%)	2.5	−0.5	1.8	−2.2	3.9	6.2	3.2
Unemployment rate (%)	5.8	7.1	7.6	9.7	9.6	7.5	7.2

3-month Treasury bill rate was increased to 15% in August 1981. The effects on inflation, output growth and unemployment are shown in Table 10.2. The table makes clear that there was no credibility miracle: disinflation was associated with a sharp recession, negative growth in both 1980 and 1982, and with a large and long-lasting increase in unemployment. The average unemployment rate was above 9% in both 1982 and 1983, peaking at 10.8% in the month of December 1982. If we assume a natural rate of 6%, and add the excess of unemployment above the natural rate (so 7.1% − 6.0% = 1.1% for 1980, 7.6% − 6.0% = 1.6% for 1981, etc.), total excess unemployment from 1979 to 1985 was 12.7%, a number no better than what equation (8.10) predicted.

Does this settle the issue of how much credibility matters? Not really. Those who argued before the fact that credibility would help, argued after the fact that Volcker had not been fully credible. After increasing the interest rate from September 1979 to April 1980 and inducing a sharp decrease in growth, he appeared to have second thoughts, reversing course and sharply decreasing the interest rate from April to September, only to increase it again in 1981. This lack of consistency, some argued, reduced his credibility, and increased the unemployment cost of the disinflation. A larger lesson still stands. The behaviour of inflation depends very much on how people and firms form expectations. The Lucas critique still stands: the past relation between unemployment and inflation may be a poor guide to what happens when policy changes.

High inflation and the Phillips curve relation

Recall how, in the 1970s, the US Phillips curve changed as inflation became more persistent and wage setters changed the way they formed inflation expectations. The lesson is a general one: the relation between unemployment and inflation is likely to change with the level and the persistence of inflation. Evidence from countries with high inflation confirms this lesson. Not only does the way workers and firms form their expectations change, but so do institutional arrangements.

When the inflation rate becomes high, inflation also tends to become more variable. As a result, workers and firms become more reluctant to enter into labour contracts that set nominal wages for a long period of time: if inflation turns out higher than expected, real wages may plunge and workers will suffer a large cut in their living standard. If inflation turns out lower than expected, real wages may go up sharply. Firms may not be able to pay their workers. Some may go bankrupt.

For this reason, the terms of wage agreements change with the level of inflation. Nominal wages are set for shorter periods of time, down from a year to a month or even less. **Wage indexation**, a provision that automatically increases wages in line with inflation, becomes more prevalent.

These changes lead in turn to a stronger response of inflation to unemployment. To see this, an example based on wage indexation will help. Imagine an economy that has two types of labour contracts. A proportion, λ (the Greek lowercase letter lambda), of labour contracts is indexed: nominal wages in those contracts move one-for-one with variations in the actual price level. A proportion, $1 - \lambda$, of labour contracts is not indexed: nominal wages are set on the basis of expected inflation.

Under this assumption, equation (10.9) becomes

$$\pi_t = [\lambda \pi_t + (1 - \lambda)\pi_t^e] - \alpha(u_t - u_n)$$

> More concretely: when inflation runs on average at 3% a year, wage setters can be reasonably confident inflation will be between 1% and 5%. When inflation runs on average at 30% a year, wage setters can be confident inflation will be between 20% and 40%. In the first case, the real wage may end up 2% higher or lower than they expected when they set the nominal wage. In the second case, it may end up 10% higher or lower than they expected. There is much more uncertainty in the second case.

The term in brackets on the right reflects the fact that a proportion, λ, of contracts is indexed and thus responds to actual inflation, π_t, and a proportion, $1 - \lambda$, responds to expected inflation, π_t^e. If we assume that this year's expected inflation is equal to last year's actual inflation, $\pi_t^e = \pi_{t-1}$, we get

$$\pi_t = [\lambda\pi_t + (1 - \lambda)\pi_{t-1}] - \alpha(u_t - u_n) \qquad [10.11]$$

When $\lambda = 0$, all wages are set on the basis of expected inflation – which is equal to last year's inflation, π_{t-1} – and the equation reduces to equation (10.10):

$$\pi_t - \pi_{t-1} = -\alpha(u_t - u_n)$$

When λ is positive, however, a proportion, λ, of wages is set on the basis of actual inflation rather than expected inflation. To see what this implies, reorganise equation (10.11): move the term in brackets to the left, factor $(1 - \lambda)$ on the left of the equation, and divide both sides by $(1 - \lambda)$, to get

$$\pi_t - \pi_{t-1} = -\frac{\alpha}{(1 - \lambda)}(u_t - u_n)$$

Wage indexation increases the effect of unemployment on inflation. The higher the proportion of wage contracts that are indexed – the higher λ – the larger the effect the unemployment rate has on the change in inflation and the higher the coefficient $\alpha/(1 - \lambda)$.

The intuition is as follows: without wage indexation, lower unemployment increases wages, which in turn increases prices. But because wages do not respond to prices right away, there is no further increase in prices within the year. With wage indexation, however, an increase in prices leads to a further increase in wages within the year, which leads to a further increase in prices, and so on, so that the effect of unemployment on inflation within the year is higher.

If, and when, λ gets close to 1 – which is when most labour contracts allow for wage indexation – small changes in unemployment can lead to very large changes in inflation. Put another way, there can be large changes in inflation with nearly no change in unemployment. This is what happens in countries where inflation is very high: the relation between inflation and unemployment becomes more and more tenuous and eventually disappears altogether.

Deflation and the Phillips curve relation

We have just looked at what happens to the Phillips curve when inflation is very high. Another issue is what happens when inflation is low, and possibly negative–when there is deflation.

The motivation for asking the question is given by an aspect of Figure 10.1 we mentioned at the start of the chapter but then left aside. In that figure, note how the points corresponding to the 1930s (they are denoted by triangles) lie to the right of the others. Not only is unemployment unusually high – this is no surprise because we are looking at the years corresponding to the Great Depression – but, given the high unemployment rate, the inflation rate is surprisingly high. In other words, given the very high unemployment rate, we would have expected not merely deflation, but a large rate of deflation. In fact, deflation was limited, and from 1934 to 1937, despite still very high unemployment, inflation actually turned positive.

How do we interpret this fact? There are two potential explanations.

One is that the Great Depression was associated with an increase not only in the actual unemployment rate, but also in the natural unemployment rate. This seems unlikely. Most economic historians see the depression primarily as the result of a large adverse shift in aggregate demand leading to an increase in the actual unemployment rate over the natural rate of unemployment, rather than an increase in the natural rate of unemployment itself.

Consider two scenarios. In one, inflation is 4%, and your nominal wage goes up by 2%. In the other, inflation is 0%, and your nominal wage is cut by 2%. Which do you dislike most? You should be indifferent between the two: in both cases, your real wage goes down by 2%. There is some evidence, however, that most people find the first scenario less painful, and thus suffer from money illusion. (More on this in Chapter 23.)

Why deflation is potentially dangerous, and why policy makers want to avoid it, will have to wait until we introduce the distinction between nominal and real interest rates. We shall do this and return to this issue later (in Chapter 14).

The other is that, when the economy starts experiencing deflation, the Phillips curve relation breaks down. One possible reason is the reluctance of workers to accept decreases in their nominal wages. Workers will unwittingly accept a cut in their real wages that occurs when their nominal wages increase more slowly than inflation. However, they are likely to fight the same cut in their real wages if it results from an overt cut in their nominal wages. If this argument is correct, this implies that the Phillips curve relation between the change in inflation and unemployment may disappear or at least become weaker when the economy is close to zero inflation.

This issue is not just of historical interest: in many countries today, unemployment is very high, and inflation is low. Whether inflation will turn into deflation is one of the developments closely watched by macroeconomists today.

SUMMARY

- The aggregate supply relation can be expressed as a relation between inflation, expected inflation and unemployment. Given unemployment, higher expected inflation leads to higher inflation. Given expected inflation, higher unemployment leads to lower inflation.

- When inflation is not very persistent, expected inflation does not depend very much on past inflation. Thus, the aggregate supply relation becomes a relation between inflation and unemployment. This is what Phillips in the UK, and Solow and Samuelson in the USA, discovered when they looked, in the late 1950s, at the joint behaviour of unemployment and inflation.

- As inflation became more persistent in the 1970s and 1980s, expectations of inflation became based more and more on past inflation. In the USA today, the aggregate supply relation takes the form of a relation between unemployment and the change in inflation. High unemployment leads to decreasing inflation; low unemployment leads to increasing inflation.

- The natural unemployment rate is the unemployment rate at which the inflation rate remains constant. When the actual unemployment rate exceeds the natural rate of unemployment, the inflation rate typically decreases; when the actual unemployment rate is less than the natural unemployment rate, the inflation rate typically increases.

- The natural rate of unemployment depends on many factors that differ across countries and can change over time. This is why the natural rate of unemployment varies across countries: it is higher in Europe than in the USA. Also, the natural unemployment rate varies over time: in Europe, the natural unemployment rate has increased a lot since the 1960s. In the USA, the natural unemployment rate increased from the 1960s to the 1980s, and appears to have decreased since then.

- Changes in the way the inflation rate varies over time affect the way wage setters form expectations and also affects how much they use wage indexation. When wage indexation is widespread, small changes in unemployment can lead to very large changes in inflation. At high rates of inflation, the relation between inflation and unemployment disappears altogether.

- At very low or negative rates of inflation, the Phillips curve relation appears to become weaker. During the Great Depression, even very high unemployment led only to limited deflation. The issue is important because many countries have both high unemployment and low inflation today.

KEY TERMS

Phillips curve 215

wage–price spiral 218

modified, or expectations-augmented, or

accelerationist Phillips curve 221

non-accelerating inflation rate of unemployment (NAIRU) 223

unemployment insurance 225

employment protection 225

extension agreements 226

disinflation 229

credibility 229

wage indexation 230

QUESTIONS AND PROBLEMS

QUICK CHECK

1. *Using the information in this chapter, label each of the following statements true, false or uncertain. Explain briefly.*

a. The original Phillips curve is the negative relation between unemployment and inflation first observed in the UK.

b. The original Phillips curve relation has proven to be very stable across countries and over time.

c. The aggregate supply relation is consistent with the Phillips curve as observed before the 1970s, but not since.

d. Policy makers can exploit the inflation–unemployment trade-off only temporarily.

e. In the late 1960s, the economists Milton Friedman and Edmund Phelps said that policy makers could achieve as low a rate of unemployment as they wanted.

f. The expectations-augmented Phillips curve is consistent with workers and firms adapting their expectations after the macroeconomic experience of the 1960s.

2. *Discuss the following statements.*

a. The Phillips curve implies that when unemployment is high, inflation is low, and vice versa. Therefore, we may experience either high inflation or high unemployment, but we will never experience both together.

b. As long as we do not mind having high inflation, we can achieve as low a level of unemployment as we want. All we have to do is increase the demand for goods and services by using, for example, expansionary fiscal policy.

3. Mutations of the Phillips curve

Suppose that the Phillips curve is given by

$$\pi_t = \pi_t^e + 0.1 - 2u_t$$

a. What is the natural rate of unemployment?

Assume,

$$\pi_t^e = \theta\pi_{t-1}$$

and suppose that θ is initially equal to 0. Suppose that the rate of unemployment is initially equal to the natural rate. In year t, the authorities decide to bring the unemployment rate down to 3% and hold it there for ever.

b. Determine the rate of inflation in years t, $t + 1$, $t + 2$ and $t + 5$.

c. Do you believe the answer given in (b)? Why or why not? (*Hint*: think about how people are likely to form expectations of inflation.)

Now suppose that in year $t + 5$, θ increases from 0 to 1. Suppose that the government is still determined to keep u at 3% for ever.

d. Why might θ increase in this way?

e. What will the inflation rate be in years $t + 5$, $t + 6$ and $t + 7$?

f. Do you believe the answer given in (e)? Why or why not?

4. Oil shocks, inflation and unemployment

Suppose that the Phillips curve is given by

$$\pi_t - \pi_t^e = 0.08 + 0.1\mu_t - 2u_t$$

where μ is the mark-up of prices over wages. Suppose that μ is initially equal to 20%, but that as a result of a sharp increase in oil prices, μ increases to 40% in year t and after.

a. Why would an increase in oil prices result in an increase in μ?

b. What is the effect of the increase in μ on the natural rate of unemployment? Explain in words.

DIG DEEPER

5. The macroeconomic effects of the indexation of wages

Suppose that the Phillips curve is given by

$$\pi_t - \pi_t^e = 0.1 - 2u_t$$

where

$$\pi_t^e = \pi_{t-1}$$

Suppose that inflation in year $t - 1$ is zero. In year t, the authorities decide to keep the unemployment rate at 4% for ever.

a. Compute the rate of inflation for years t, $t + 1$, $t + 2$ and $t + 3$.

Now suppose that half the workers have indexed labour contracts.

b. What is the new equation for the Phillips curve?

c. Re-compute your answer to part (a).

d. What is the effect of wage indexation on the relation between π and u?

6. The price of oil declined substantially in the 1990s

a. Can the fall in the price of oil help explain the evidence (presented in this chapter) on inflation and unemployment in the 1990s?

b. What was the likely effect of the fall in the price of oil on the natural rate of unemployment?

7. Supply shocks and wage flexibility

Suppose that the Phillips curve is given by

$$\pi_t - \pi_{t-1} = -\alpha(u_t - u_n)$$

where

$$u_n = (\mu + z)/\alpha$$

Recall that this Phillips curve was derived in this chapter under the assumption that the wage-bargaining equation took the form

$$W - P^e(1 - \alpha u_t + z)$$

We can think of α as a measure of wage flexibility – the higher is α, the greater is the response of the wage to a change in the unemployment rate, αu_t.

a. Suppose $\mu = 0.03$ and $z = 0.03$. What is the natural rate of unemployment if $\alpha = 1$? if $\alpha = 2$? What is the relation between α and the natural rate of unemployment? Interpret your answer.

In Chapter 10, the text suggested that a reduction in the bargaining power of workers may have something to do with the economy's relatively mild response to the increases in oil prices in the past few years as compared to the economy's response to increases in oil prices in the 1970s. One manifestation of a reduction in worker-bargaining power could be an overall increase in wage flexibility, i.e., an increase in π.

b. Suppose that as a result of an oil price increase, μ increases to 0.06. What is the new natural rate of unemployment if $\alpha = 1$? if $\alpha = 2$? Would an increase in wage flexibility tend to weaken the adverse effect of an oil price increase?

EXPLORE FURTHER

8. Estimating the natural rate of unemployment

*To answer this question, you will need data on the annual unemployment and inflation rates since 1970, which can be obtained from the website of the Organization for Economic Cooperation and Development (OECD) (**www.oecd.org**).*

Retrieve the data for the unemployment rate. In addition, retrieve the data for the consumer price index (CPI), all urban consumers.

a. Define the inflation rate in year t as the percentage change in the CPI between year $t - 1$ and year t. Compute the inflation rate for each year and the change in the inflation rate from one year to the next.

b. Plot the data for all the years since 1970 on a diagram, with the change in inflation on the vertical axis and the rate of unemployment on the horizontal axis. Is your graph similar to Figure 10.5?

c. Using a ruler, draw the line that appears to fit best the points in the figure. Approximately what is the slope of the line? What is the intercept? Write down the corresponding equation.

d. According to your analysis in (b), what has been the natural rate of unemployment since 1970?

9. Changes in the natural rate of unemployment

a. Repeat problem 8, but now draw separate graphs for the period 1970 to 1990 and the period since 1990.

b. Do you find that the relation between inflation and unemployment is different in the two periods? If so, how has the natural rate of unemployment changed?

*Log on to **MyEconLab** and complete the studyplan exercises for this chapter to see how much you have learnt, and where you need to revise most.*

MyEconLab

FURTHER READING

- For more, read Olivier Blanchard, 'European unemployment. The evolution of facts and ideas', *Economic Policy*, **1**, 2006, 1–54, and Gilles Saint-Paul, 'Why are European Countries Diverging in Their Unemployment Experience?', *Journal of Economic Perspectives*, **18**, 4, 2004, 49–58.

APPENDIX

From the aggregate supply relation to a relation between inflation, expected inflation and unemployment

This appendix shows how to go from the relation between the price level, the expected price level, and the unemployment rate given by equation (10.1):

$$P = P^e(1 + \mu)(1 - \alpha u + z)$$

to the relation between inflation, expected inflation and the unemployment rate given by equation (10.2):

$$\pi = \pi^e + (\mu + z) - \alpha u$$

First, introduce time subscripts for the price level, the expected price level and the unemployment rate, so P_t, P_t^e and u_t refer to the price level, the expected price level and the unemployment rate in year t. Equation (10.1) becomes

$$P_t = P_t^e(1 + \mu)(1 - \alpha u_t + z)$$

Next, go from an expression in terms of price levels to an expression in terms of inflation rates. Divide both sides by last year's price level, P_{t-1}^e:

$$\frac{P_t}{P_{t-1}} = \frac{P_t^e}{P_{t-1}}(1 + \mu)(1 - \alpha u_t + z) \qquad [10A.1]$$

Take the fraction P_t/P_{t-1} on the left side and rewrite it as

$$\frac{P_t}{P_{t-1}} = \frac{P_t - P_{t-1} + P_{t-1}}{P_{t-1}} = 1 + \frac{P_t - P_{t-1}}{P_{t-1}} = 1 + \pi_t$$

where the first equality follows from adding and subtracting P_{t-1} in the numerator of the fraction, the second equality follows from the fact that $P_{t-1}/P_{t-1} = 1$, and the third follows from the definition of the inflation rate ($\pi_t \equiv (P_t - P_{t-1})/P_{t-1}$).

Do the same for the fraction P_t^e/P_{t-1} on the right side, using the definition of the expected inflation rate ($\pi_t^e \equiv (P_t^e - P_{t-1})/P_{t-1}$):

$$\frac{P_t^e}{P_{t-1}} = \frac{P_t^e - P_{t-1} + P_{t-1}}{P_{t-1}} = 1 + \frac{P_t^e - P_{t-1}}{P_{t-1}} = 1 + \pi_t^e$$

Replacing P_t/P_{t-1} and P_t^e/P_{t-1} in equation (10A.1) by the expressions we have just derived:

$$(1 + \pi_t) = (1 + \pi_t^e)(1 + \mu)(1 - \alpha u_t + z)$$

This gives us a relation between inflation, π_t, expected inflation, π_t^e, and the unemployment rate, u_t. The remaining steps make the relation look more friendly:

Divide both sides by $(1 + \pi_t^e)(1 + \mu)$:

$$\frac{(1 + \pi_t)}{(1 + \pi_t^e)(1 + \mu)} = 1 - \alpha u_t + z$$

So long as inflation, expected inflation and the mark-up are not too large, a good approximation to the left side of this equation is given by $1 + \pi_t - \pi_t^e - \mu$ (see Propositions 3 and 6 in Appendix 1 at the end of the text). Replacing in the equation above and rearranging gives

$$\pi_t = \pi_t^e + (\mu + z) - \alpha u_t$$

Dropping the time indexes, this is equation (10.2) in the text. With the time indexes kept, this is equation (10.3) in the text.

The inflation rate, π_t, depends on the expected inflation rate, π_t^e, and the unemployment rate, u_t. The relation also depends on the mark-up, μ, on the factors that affect wage setting, z, and on the effect of the unemployment rate on wages, α.

Chapter 11

INFLATION, MONEY GROWTH AND THE REAL RATE OF INTEREST

At the end of the 1970s, inflation reached very high levels in most industrialised countries: 14% per year in the USA and over 13% in the UK. In 1979, the Fed in the USA and the first government led by Margaret Thatcher in the UK decided to reduce inflation and, to do so, embarked on a major monetary contraction. Five years later, and after a deep recession, inflation was down to 3% per year in the USA and below 6% in the UK.

Why did the government decide to reduce inflation in both countries? How did it do it? Why was there a recession? More generally, what are the effects of nominal money growth on inflation and output? Our treatment of expectations (in Chapter 9) was too simple to allow us to take up these questions. But, with our discussion of expectations and the introduction of the Phillips curve relation (in Chapter 10), we now have the tools we need to answer them. This is what we do in this chapter:

● Section 11.1 extends the earlier model (see Chapter 10) and looks at the three relations between output, unemployment and inflation: Okun's law, the Phillips curve and the aggregate demand relation.

● Sections 11.2 and 11.3 introduce the distinction between nominal and real interest rates and how that distinction can be included in the *IS–LM* model.

● Sections 11.4 and 11.5 look at the effects of money growth on output, unemployment and inflation, in both the short and medium run.

● Section 11.6 revisits disinflation, looking at the trade-off between unemployment and inflation and at how credibility of the central bank affects the adjustment of the economy to a decrease in nominal money growth.

11.1 OUTPUT, UNEMPLOYMENT AND INFLATION

Earlier (in Chapter 10), we examined the behaviour of two variables: output and the price level. We characterised the economy by two relations: an aggregate supply relation and an aggregate demand relation. In this chapter, we extend the earlier model (of Chapter 10) to examine three variables: output, unemployment and inflation. We characterise the economy by three relations:

- A relation between output growth and the change in unemployment, called Okun's law.
- A relation between unemployment, inflation and expected inflation. This is the Phillips curve relation we developed earlier (in Chapter 9).
- An aggregate demand relation between output growth, money growth and inflation. This relation follows from the aggregate demand relation we derived earlier (in Chapter 10).

In this section, we look at each of these relations on its own. In section 11.2, we put them together and show their implications for movements in output, unemployment and inflation.

Okun's law

We discussed the relation between output and unemployment in an earlier chapter (see Chapter 8). We did so, however, under two convenient but restrictive assumptions. We assumed that, given productivity, output moved with employment, so changes in output led to equal changes in employment. We also assumed that the labour force was constant, so changes in employment were reflected one-for-one in opposite changes in unemployment.

◄ We assumed that $Y = AN$ and that L (the labour force) was constant.

We must now move beyond these assumptions. To see why, let's see what they imply for the relation between the rate of output growth and the unemployment rate. If output and employment moved together, a 1% increase in output would lead to a 1% increase in employment. And if movements in employment were reflected in opposite movements in unemployment, the 1% increase in employment would lead to a decrease of 1% in the unemployment rate. Let u_t denote the unemployment rate in year t, u_{t-1} the unemployment rate in year $t - 1$, and g_{yt} the growth rate of output from year $t - 1$ to year t. Then, under these two assumptions, the following relation would hold:

$$u_t - u_{t-1} = -g_{yt}$$ [11.1]

In words: the change in the unemployment rate would be equal to the negative of the growth rate of output. If output growth is, say, 4% for a year, then the unemployment rate should decline by 4% in that year.

Contrast this with the actual relation between output growth and the change in the unemployment rate, a relation called **Okun's law**. Figure 11.1 plots the change in the unemployment rate against the rate of output growth in the USA for each year since 1970. It also plots the regression line that best fits the scatter of points. The equation corresponding to the line is given by

◄ The relation is named after Arthur Okun, an economist and an adviser to President Kennedy, who first characterised and interpreted this relation.

$$u_t - u_{t-1} = -0.4(g_{yt} - 3\%)$$ [11.2]

◄ If $g_{yt} > 3\%$ then $u_t < u_{t-1}$
If $g_{yt} < 3\%$ then $u_t > u_{t-1}$
If $g_{yt} = 3\%$ then $u_t = u_{t-1}$

Like equation (11.1), equation (11.2) shows a negative relation between the change in unemployment and output growth. But it differs from equation (11.1) in two ways:

- Annual output growth has to be at least 3% to prevent the unemployment rate from rising. This is because of two factors we have neglected so far: labour force growth and labour productivity growth.

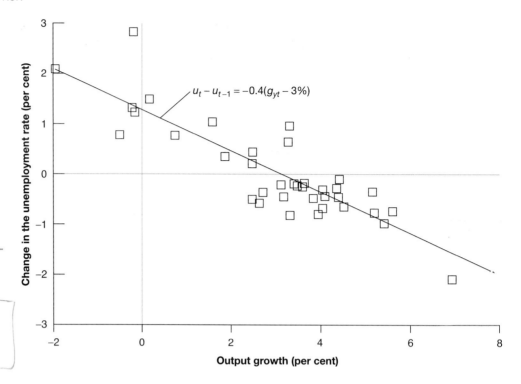

$$u_t - u_{t-1} = -0.4(g_{yt} - 3\%)$$

Figure 11.1

Changes in the unemployment rate versus output growth in the USA since 1970

High output growth is associated with a reduction in the unemployment rate; low output growth is associated with an increase in the unemployment rate.

Suppose productivity growth increases ➤ from 1.3% to 2.3%. What is now the growth rate of output required to maintain a constant unemployment rate?

To maintain a constant unemployment rate, employment must grow at the same rate as the labour force. Suppose the labour force grows at 1.7% per year: then employment must grow at 1.7% per year. If, in addition, labour productivity – output per worker – grows at 1.3% per year, this implies that output must grow at 1.7% + 1.3% = 3% per year. In other words, just to maintain a constant unemployment rate, output growth must be equal to the sum of labour force growth and labour productivity growth.

In the USA, the sum of the rate of labour force growth and of labour productivity growth has been roughly equal to 3% per year on average since 1960, and this is why the number 3% appears on the right side of equation (11.2). We shall call the rate of output growth needed to maintain a constant unemployment rate the **normal growth rate** in the following text.

- The coefficient on the right side of equation (11.2) is 0.4, compared to 1.0 in equation (11.1). Put another way, output growth 1% above normal leads only to a 0.4% reduction in the unemployment rate in equation (11.2) rather than a 1% reduction in equation (11.1). There are two reasons:
  - Firms adjust employment less than one-for-one in response to deviations of output growth from normal. More specifically, output growth 1% above normal for one year leads to only a 0.6% increase in the employment rate.

Employment responds less than one- ➤ for-one to movements in output.

    One reason is that some workers are needed, no matter what the level of output. The accounting department of a firm, for example, needs roughly the same number of employees whether the firm is selling more or less than normal.

    Another reason is that training new employees is costly; for this reason, firms prefer to keep current employees rather than lay them off when output is lower than normal and to ask them to work overtime rather than hire new employees when output is higher than normal. In bad times, firms in effect hoard labour – the labour they will need when times are better; this behaviour of firms is therefore called **labour hoarding**.

  - An increase in the employment rate does not lead to a one-for-one decrease in the unemployment rate. More specifically, a 0.6% increase in the employment rate leads to only a 0.4% decrease in the unemployment rate. The reason is that labour force participation increases. When employment increases, not all the new jobs are filled by the unemployed. Some of the jobs go to people who were classified as out of the labour force, meaning were not actively looking for jobs. Also, as labour market prospects improve for the unemployed, some discouraged workers – who were previously classified as out of the labour force – decide to start actively looking for jobs and become classified as unemployed. For both reasons, unemployment decreases less than employment increases.

Let us write equation (11.2) using letters rather than numbers. Let $\bar{g}_y$ denote the normal growth rate (about 3% per year for the USA). Let the coefficient β (the Greek lowercase beta) measure the effect of output growth above normal on the change in the unemployment rate. As you saw in equation (11.2), in the USA, β equals 0.4. We will give the evidence for European countries in the next section. We can then write:

$$u_t - u_{t-1} = -\beta(g_{yt} - \bar{g}_y) \qquad [11.3]$$

Output growth above normal leads to a decrease in the unemployment rate; output growth below normal leads to an increase in the unemployment rate.

The operation of Okun's law in several different countries is described in the Focus box 'Okun's law across European and non-European countries'.

> ◁ Employment responds less than one-for-one to movements in output. Putting the two steps together: unemployment responds less than one-for-one to movements in employment, which itself responds less than one-for-one to movements in output.

The Phillips curve

Earlier we saw (in Chapter 10) that the aggregate supply relation can be expressed as a relation between inflation, expected inflation and unemployment (equation (10.10)), the *Phillips curve*:

$$\pi_t = \pi_t^e - \alpha(u_t - u_n) \qquad [11.4]$$

Inflation depends on expected inflation and on the deviation of unemployment from the natural rate of unemployment.

We then argued that in the USA today, expected inflation is reasonably well approximated by last year's inflation. This means we can replace π_t^e with π_{t-1}. With this assumption, the relation between inflation and unemployment takes the form

$$\pi_t - \pi_{t-1} = -\alpha(u_t - u_n) \qquad [11.5]$$

Unemployment below the natural rate leads to an increase in inflation; unemployment above the natural rate leads to a decrease in inflation. The parameter α gives the effect of unemployment on the change in inflation. Earlier we saw (in Chapter 10) that, since 1970 in the USA, the natural unemployment rate has been on average equal to 6%, and α has been equal to 0.73. This value of α means that an unemployment rate of 1% above the natural rate for one year leads to a decrease in the inflation rate of about 0.73%.

The aggregate demand relation

The third relation we will need is a relation between output growth, money growth and inflation. We will now see that it follows from the aggregate demand relation we derived earlier (in Chapter 9).

There (in Chapter 9), we derived the aggregate demand relation as a relation between the level of output and the real money stock, government spending and taxes (equation 9.3), based on equilibrium in both goods and financial markets:

$$Y_t = Y\left(\frac{M_t}{P_t}, G_t, T_t\right)$$

Note that we have added time indexes, which we did not need then but will need in this chapter. To simplify things, we will make two further assumptions here.

First, to focus on the relation between the real money stock and output, we will ignore changes in factors other than real money here and write the aggregate demand relation simply as

$$Y_t = Y\left(\frac{M_t}{P_t}\right)$$

Second, we shall assume a linear relation between real money balances and output and rewrite the aggregate demand relation further as

$$Y_t = \gamma\left(\frac{M_t}{P_t}\right) \qquad [11.6]$$

where γ (the Greek lowercase gamma) is a positive parameter. This equation states that the demand for goods, and thus output, is proportional to the real money stock. You should

FOCUS
Okun's law across European and non-European countries

The coefficient β in Okun's law describes the effect on the unemployment rate of deviations of output growth from normal. A value of β of 0.4 tells us that output growth 1% above the normal growth rate for one year decreases the unemployment rate by 0.4%.

The coefficient β depends in part on how firms adjust their employment in response to fluctuations in production. This adjustment of employment depends in turn on such factors as the internal organisation of firms and the legal and social constraints on hiring and firing. As these differ across countries, we would therefore expect the coefficient β to differ across countries, and indeed it does. Table 11.1 gives the estimated coefficient β for a number of countries.

The first column gives estimates of β based on data from 1960–1980. Germany has the highest coefficient among European countries, 0.20, followed by Denmark, 0.18. The UK, 0.11, France, 0.14 and the Netherlands,

0.13, have slightly lower coefficients. The lowest coefficients are in Italy, 0.08 and Sweden, 0.09. The table also reports Okun's coefficients for three non-European countries, the USA, with the highest coefficient of all, 0.39, Australia, which also has a rather high coefficient, 0.26 and Japan, with the lowest coefficient of all, 0.02.

The ranking in the 1960–1980 column fits well with what we know about the behaviour of firms and the structure of firing/hiring regulations across countries. Italian firms – somehow like Japanese firms, although to a lesser extent – have traditionally offered a high degree of job security to their workers, so fluctuations in Italy's output have little effect on employment and, by implication, little effect on unemployment. So it is no surprise that β is very small in Italy (and is the smallest in Japan). A high degree of employment protection (see Chapter 9) explains why the coefficients estimated for most European countries are in between those of Japan and the USA. Restrictions to firings mitigate the adverse effect on employment of a fall in output. They also reduce the positive employment effects of an increase in output because firing restrictions make firms very cautious when it comes to hiring new workers.

The last column gives estimates based on data from 1981 to 2007. The coefficient is nearly unchanged for the USA, but it becomes higher for all the other countries. This again fits with what we know about firms and regulations. Increased competition in goods markets since the early 1980s has led firms in these countries to reconsider and reduce their commitment to job security. And, at the urging of firms, legal restrictions on hiring and firing have been weakened in many countries. Both factors have led to a larger response of employment to fluctuations in output, thus to a larger value of β.

Table 11.1 Okun's law coefficients across countries and time

Country	1960–1980	1981–2007
Germany	0.20	0.29
Denmark	0.18	0.72
UK	0.15	0.48
France	0.14	0.41
Netherlands	0.13	0.50
Sweden	0.09	0.49
Italy	0.08	0.11
Non-European countries:		
USA	0.39	0.41
Australia	0.26	0.47
Japan	0.02	0.11

keep in mind, however, that behind this simple relation lies the mechanism you saw in the *IS–LM* model:

- An increase in the real money stock leads to a decrease in the interest rate.
- The decrease in the interest rate leads to an increase in the demand for goods and, therefore, to an increase in output.

Equation (11.6) gives a relation between levels – the output level, the level of money and the price level. We need to go from this relation to a relation between growth rates – the growth rate of output, the growth rate of money and the inflation rate (the growth rate of the price level). Fortunately, this is easy.

Let g_{yt} be the growth rate of output. Let π_t be the growth rate of the price level – the rate of inflation – and g_{mt} be the growth rate of nominal money.

Then, from equation (11.6), it follows that

$$g_{yt} = g_{mt} - \pi_t \qquad [11.7]$$

If nominal money growth exceeds inflation, real money growth is positive, and so is output growth. If nominal money growth is less than inflation, real money growth is negative, and so is output growth. In other words, given inflation, expansionary monetary policy (high nominal money growth) leads to high output growth; contractionary monetary policy (low nominal money growth) leads to low, possibly negative, output growth.

The three relations we have just derived between inflation, unemployment and output growth are the tools we need to understand the effects of money growth. We will see that they differ in the short and medium run. In the medium run, output returns to its natural level. To understand the short run effects of money growth and how the economy gets to the medium run equilibrium, we have to take one step back and introduce the distinction between nominal and real interest rates. This is what we do in the next section.

11.2 NOMINAL VERSUS REAL INTEREST RATES

In 1980, the interest rate in the UK was 16.3%. In 2008, the same rate was only 4.7%. It was much cheaper to borrow in 2008 than it was in 1980.

Or was it? In 1980, inflation was around 18%. In 2008, inflation was around 3.6%. This would seem relevant: the interest rate tells us how many pounds we shall have to pay in the future in exchange for having 1 more pound today.

But we do not consume pounds. We consume goods. When we borrow, what we really want to know is how many goods we will have to give up in the future in exchange for the goods we get today. Likewise, when we lend, we want to know how many goods – not how many pounds – we will get in the future for the goods we give up today. The presence of inflation makes the distinction important. What is the point of receiving high interest payments in the future if inflation between now and then is so high that we are unable to buy more goods then?

This is where the distinction between nominal interest rates and real interest rates comes in:

- Interest rates expressed in terms of units of the national currency are called **nominal interest rates**. The interest rates printed in the financial pages of newspapers are nominal interest rates. For example, when we say that the one-year rate on government bonds is 4.36%, we mean that for every euro an individual borrows from a bank, he or she will have to pay €1.0436 in one year. More generally, if the nominal interest rate for year t is i_t, borrowing 1 this year requires you to pay €$(1 + i_t)$ next year. (We use interchangeably this year for today and next year for one year from today.)

  ◄ Nominal interest rate: the interest rate in terms of units of national currency.

- Interest rates expressed in terms of a basket of goods are called **real interest rates**. If we denote the real interest rate for year t by r_t, then, by definition, borrowing the equivalent of one basket of goods this year requires you to pay the equivalent of $1 + r_t$ baskets of goods next year.

  ◄ Real interest rate: the interest rate in terms of a basket of goods.

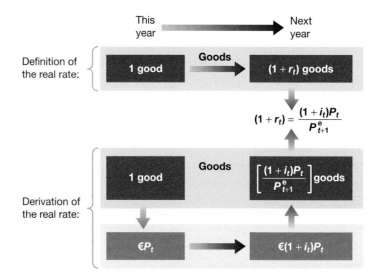

Figure 11.2

Definition and derivation of the real interest rate

What is the relation between nominal and real interest rates? How do we go from nominal interest rates – which we do observe – to real interest rates – which we typically do not observe? The intuitive answer: we must adjust the nominal interest rate to take into account expected inflation.

Let us go through the step-by-step derivation. Assume that there is only one good in the economy, bread (we shall add jam and other goods later). Denote the one-year nominal interest rate, in terms of euros, by i_t: if you borrow €1 this year, you will have to repay €$(1 + i_t)$ next year. But you are not interested in euros. What you really want to know is: if you borrow enough to eat 1 more kilo of bread this year, how much will you have to repay, in terms of kilos of bread, next year?

Figure 11.2 helps us derive the answer. The top part repeats the definition of the one-year real interest rate. The bottom part shows how we can derive the one-year real interest rate from information about the one-year nominal interest rate and the price of bread:

1. Start with the arrow pointing down in the lower left of Figure 11.2. Suppose you want to eat 1 more kilo of bread this year. If the price of a kilo of bread this year is €P_t, to eat 1 more kilo of bread, you must borrow €P_t.
2. If i_t is the one-year nominal interest rate – the interest rate in terms of euros – and if you borrow €P_t, you will have to repay €$(1 + i_t)P_t$ next year. This is represented by the arrow from left to right at the bottom of Figure 11.2.
3. What you care about, however, is not euros but kilos of bread. Thus, the last step involves converting euros back to kilos of bread next year. Let P_{t+1}^e be the price of bread you expect for next year. (The superscript e indicates that this is an expectation: you do not know yet what the price of bread will be next year.) How much you expect to repay next year, in terms of kilos of bread, is therefore equal to $(1 + i_t)P_t$ (the number of euros you have to repay next year) divided by P_{t+1}^e (the price of bread in terms of euros expected for next year), so $(1 + i_t)P_t/P_{t+1}^e$. This is represented by the arrow pointing up in the lower right of Figure 11.2.

Putting together what you see in the top part and what you see in the bottom part of Figure 11.2, it follows that the one-year real interest rate, r_t, is given by

If you have to pay €10 next year, and you expect the price of bread next year to be €2 per kilo, you expect to have to repay the equivalent of 10/2 = 5 kilos of bread next year. This is why we divide the euro amount $(1 + i_t)P_t$ by the expected price of bread next year, P_{t+1}^e.

$$1 + r_t = (1 + i_t)\frac{P_t}{P_{t+1}^e}$$ [11.8]

This relation looks intimidating. Two simple manipulations make it look friendlier:

- Denote expected inflation between t and $t + 1$ by π_{t+1}^e. Given that there is only one good – bread – the expected rate of inflation equals the expected change in the euro price of bread between this year and next year, divided by the euro price of bread this year:

$$\pi_{t+1}^e = \frac{(P_{t+1}^e - P_t)}{P_t} \qquad [11.9]$$

Using equation (11.9), rewrite P_t/P_{t+1}^e in equation (11.8) as $1/(1 + \pi_{t+1}^e)$. Replace in (11.8) to get

$$(1 + r_t) = \frac{1 + i_t}{1 + \pi_{t+1}^e} \qquad [11.10]$$

1 plus the real interest rate equals the ratio of 1 plus the nominal interest rate, divided by 1 plus the expected rate of inflation.

- Equation (11.10) gives us the exact relation between the real interest rate, the nominal interest rate and expected inflation. However, when the nominal interest rate and expected inflation are not too large – say, less than 20% per year – a close approximation to this equation is given by the simpler relation

$$r_t \approx i_t - \pi_{t+1}^e \qquad [11.11]$$

Equation (11.11) is simple. Remember it. It says that the real interest rate is (approximately) equal to the nominal interest rate minus expected inflation. (In the rest of the text, we often treat the relation (11.11) as if it were an equality. Remember, however, that it is only an approximation.)

Note some of the implications of equation (11.11):

- When expected inflation equals 0, the nominal and the real interest rates are equal.
- Because expected inflation is typically positive, the real interest rate is typically lower than the nominal interest rate.
- For a given nominal interest rate, the higher the expected rate of inflation, the lower the real interest rate.

The case where expected inflation happens to be equal to the nominal interest rate is worth looking at more closely. Suppose the nominal interest rate and expected inflation both equal 10%, and you are the borrower. For every euro you borrow this year, you will have to repay €1.10 next year, but euros will be worth 10% less in terms of bread next year. So, if you borrow the equivalent of €1 of bread, you will have to repay the equivalent of €1 of bread next year: the real cost of borrowing – the real interest rate – is equal to 0. Now suppose you are the lender: for every euro you lend this year, you will receive €1.10 next year. This looks attractive, but euros next year will be worth 10% less in terms of bread. If you lend the equivalent of €1 of bread this year, you will get the equivalent of €1 of bread next year: despite the 10% nominal interest rate, the real interest rate is equal to 0.

We have assumed so far that there is only one good – bread. But what we have done generalises easily to many goods. All we need to do is to substitute the price level – the price of a basket of goods – for the price of bread in equation (11.8) or equation (11.10). If we use the consumer price index (CPI) to measure the price level, the real interest rate tells us how much consumption we must give up next year to consume more today.

Nominal and real interest rates in the UK since 1980

Let us return to the question at the start of this section. We can now restate it as follows: was the real interest rate lower in 2008 than it was in 1985? More generally, what has happened to the real interest rate in the UK since the early 1980s?

The answer is shown in Figure 11.3, which plots both nominal and real interest rates since 1980. To construct the real interest rate, we need a measure of expected inflation – more precisely, the rate of inflation expected as of the beginning of each year. Figure 11.3 uses, for each year, the forecast of inflation for that year published at the end of the previous year by the OECD. For example, the forecast of inflation used to construct the real interest rate for 2008 is the forecast of inflation published by the OECD in December 2007 – 1.98%.

◄ Add 1 to both sides in (11.9):

$$1 + \pi_{t+1}^e = 1 + \frac{(P_{t+1}^e - P_t)}{P_t}$$

◄ Reorganise:

$$1 + \pi_{t+1}^e = \frac{P_{t+1}^e}{P_t}$$

Take the inverse on both sides:

$$\frac{1}{1 + \pi_{t+1}^e} = \frac{P_t}{P_{t+1}^e}$$

Replace in (11.8).

◄ See Proposition 6 in Appendix 1 at the end of the text. Suppose $i = 10\%$ and $\pi^e = 5\%$. The exact relation gives $r_t = 4.8\%$. The approximation given by equation (A1.6) gives 5% – close enough. The approximation can be quite poor, however, when i and π^e are high. If $i = 100\%$ and $\pi^e = 80\%$, the exact relation gives $r_t = 11\%$, but the approximation gives $r_t = 20\%$, a big difference.

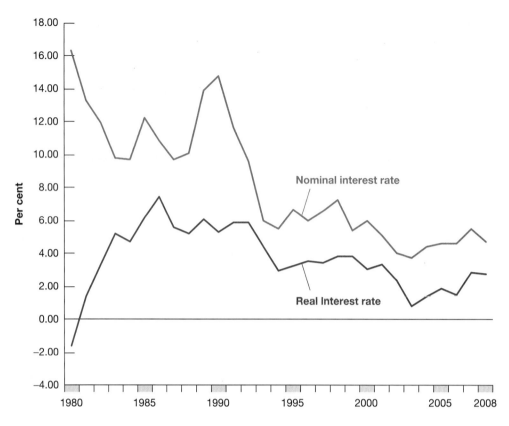

Figure 11.3

Nominal and real interest rates in the UK since 1980

Although the nominal interest rate has declined considerably since the early 1980s, the real interest rate was actually higher in 2008 than in 1980.

(To know more about how inflation expectations can be measured, read the Focus box 'How can inflation expectations be measured?', in Chapter 16.)

Note that the real interest rate $(i - \pi^e)$ is based on expected inflation. If actual inflation turns out to be different from expected inflation, the realised real interest rate $(i - \pi)$ will be different from the real interest rate. For this reason, the real interest rate is sometimes called the *ex-ante* real interest rate. (*Ex-ante* means 'before the fact'. Here it means before inflation is known.) The realised real interest rate is called the *ex-post* real interest rate. (*Ex-post* means 'after the fact'. Here it means after inflation is known.)

> The real interest rate can be negative when inflation is higher than the nominal interest rate. But remember that the same is not true for the nominal interest rate, which cannot be negative!

Figure 11.3 shows the importance of adjusting for inflation. Although the nominal interest was much lower in 2008 than it was in 1980, the real interest rate was actually higher in 2008 than it was in 1980: 2.7% in 2008 versus −1.6% in 1980. Put another way, despite the large decline in nominal interest rates, borrowing was actually more expensive in 2008 than it was in 1980. This is due to the fact that inflation (and, with it, expected inflation) was lower in 2008 with respect to 1980.

11.3 NOMINAL AND REAL INTEREST RATES AND THE *IS–LM* MODEL

In the *IS–LM* model we developed earlier (in Chapter 5), the interest rate came into play in two places: it affected investment in the *IS* relation, and it affected the choice between money and bonds in the *LM* relation. Which interest rate – nominal or real – were we talking about in each case?

> We shall ignore time subscripts here; they are not needed for this and the next section.

● Take the *IS* relation first. Our discussion in section 11.2 makes it clear that firms, in deciding how much investment to undertake, care about the real interest rate: firms produce goods. They want to know how much they will have to repay, not in terms of money but in terms of goods. So what belongs in the *IS* relation is the real interest rate. Let r denote the real interest rate. The *IS* relation must therefore be modified as follows:

$$Y = C(Y - T) + I(Y, r) + G$$

Investment spending, and thus the demand for goods, depends on the real interest rate.

● Now turn to the *LM* relation. When we derived the *LM* relation, we assumed that the demand for money depended on the interest rate, but were we referring to the nominal interest rate or the real interest rate? The answer is: to the nominal interest rate. Remember why the interest rate affects the demand for money. When people decide whether to hold money or bonds, they take into account the opportunity cost of holding money rather than bonds – the opportunity cost is what they give up by holding money rather than bonds. Money pays a zero nominal interest rate. Bonds pay a nominal interest rate of i. Hence, the opportunity cost of holding money is equal to the difference between the interest rate from holding bonds minus the interest from holding money, so $i - 0 = i$, which is just the nominal interest rate. Therefore, the *LM* relation is still given by

$$\frac{M}{P} = YL(i)$$

◁ For the time being, we shall focus only on how the interest rate affects investment. Later (in Chapters 17 and 18), you will see how the real interest rate affects both investment and consumption decisions.

Putting together the *IS* relation above with this equation and the relation between the real interest rate and the nominal interest rate, the extended *IS–LM* model is given by

$$IS \text{ relation: } Y = C(Y - T) + I(Y, r) + G$$

$$LM \text{ relation: } \frac{M}{P} = YL(i)$$

$$\text{Real interest rate: } r = i - \pi^e$$

Note the immediate implications of these three relations:

● The interest rate directly affected by monetary policy (the interest rate that enters the *LM* equation) is the nominal interest rate.

● The interest rate that affects spending and output (the rate that enters the *IS* relation) is ◁ the real interest rate.

◁ Interest rate in the *LM* relation: nominal interest rate, *i*.

● The effects of monetary policy on output therefore depend on how movements in the ◁ nominal interest rate translate into movements in the real interest rate. To explore this question further, the next section looks at how an increase in money growth affects the nominal interest rate and the real interest rate, both in the short run and in the medium run.

◁ Interest rate in the *IS* relation: real interest rate, *r*.

11.4 THE EFFECTS OF MONEY GROWTH

Let's collect the three relations between inflation, unemployment and output growth we have derived in section 11.1:

● Okun's law relates the change in the unemployment rate to the deviation of output growth from normal (equation (11.3)):

$$u_t - u_{t-1} = -\beta(g_{gt} - \bar{g}_y)$$

● The Phillips curve – equivalently the aggregate supply relation – relates the change in inflation to the deviation of the unemployment rate from the natural rate (equation (11.5)):

$$\pi_t - \pi_{t-1} = -\alpha(u_t - u_n)$$

● The aggregate demand relation relates output growth to the difference between nominal money growth and inflation (equation (11.7)):

$$g_{yt} = g_{mt} - \pi_t$$

These three relations are shown in Figure 11.4. Start on the left and follow the arrows. Through aggregate demand, nominal money growth and inflation determine output growth. Through Okun's law, output growth determines the change in unemployment. And through the Phillips curve relation, unemployment determines the change in inflation.

Our task now is to see what these three relations imply for the effects of nominal money growth on output, unemployment and inflation. The easiest way to proceed is to work backward in time – that is, to start by looking at the medium run (by looking at where the

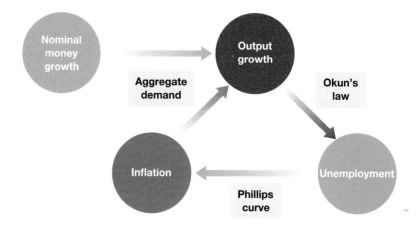

Figure 11.4

Output growth, unemployment, inflation and nominal money growth

economy ends up when all the dynamics have worked themselves out) and then to turn to the dynamics themselves (that is, to see how the economy gets there).

The medium run

Assume that the central bank maintains a constant growth rate of nominal money, call it $\bar{g}_m$. In this case, what will be the values of output growth, unemployment and inflation in the medium run?

- In the medium run, the unemployment rate must be constant: the unemployment rate cannot increase or decrease forever. Putting $u_t = u_{t-1}$ in Okun's law implies that $g_{yt} = \bar{g}_y$. In the medium run, output must grow at its normal rate of growth, $\bar{g}_y$.
- With nominal money growth equal to $\bar{g}_m$ and output growth equal to $\bar{g}_y$, the aggregate demand relation implies that inflation is constant and satisfies

$$\bar{g}_y = \bar{g}_m - \pi$$

Moving π to the left and $\bar{g}_y$ to the right gives an expression for inflation:

$$\pi = \bar{g}_m - \bar{g}_y \qquad [11.12]$$

In the medium run, inflation must be equal to nominal money growth minus normal output growth. If we define **adjusted nominal money growth** as equal to nominal money growth minus normal output growth, equation (11.12) can be stated as: in the medium run, inflation equals adjusted nominal money growth.

The way to think about this result is as follows: a growing level of output implies a growing level of transactions and thus a growing demand for real money. So, if output is growing at 3%, the real money stock must also grow at 3% per year. If the nominal money stock grows at a rate different from 3% per year, the difference must show up in inflation (or deflation). For example, if nominal money growth is 8% per year, then inflation must be equal to 5% per year.

- If inflation is constant, then inflation this year is equal to inflation last year: $\pi_t = \pi_{t-1}$. Putting $\pi_t = \pi_{t-1}$ in the Phillips curve implies that $u_t = u_n$. In the medium run, the unemployment rate must be equal to the natural rate of unemployment.

Let us summarise: in the medium run, output growth is equal to the normal growth rate. Unemployment is equal to the natural rate. And both are independent of nominal money growth. Nominal money growth affects only inflation.

These results are the natural extension of the results we derived earlier (in Chapter 9). There, we saw that changes in the level of nominal money were neutral in the medium run: they had no effect on either output or unemployment but were reflected one-for-one in changes in the price level. We see here that a similar neutrality result applies to changes in the growth rate of nominal money: changes in nominal money growth have no effect on output or unemployment in the medium run but are reflected one-for-one in changes in the rate of inflation.

Another way to state this last result is that the only determinant of inflation in the medium run is nominal money growth. Milton Friedman put it this way: inflation is always and everywhere a monetary phenomenon. Unless they lead to higher nominal money growth, factors such as the monopoly power of firms, strong unions, strikes, fiscal deficits, the price of oil and so on have no effect on inflation in the medium run.

The word 'unless' is important. During episodes of very high inflation, fiscal deficits often lead to nominal money creation and to higher nominal money growth.

Nominal and real interest rates in the medium run

What will happen to output and to nominal and real interest rates in the medium run?

To answer that question, we can rely on an important proposition we derived earlier (in Chapter 8): in the medium run, output returns to the natural level of output, Y_n.

This has a straightforward implication for what happens to the real interest rate. To see why, return to the *IS* equation:

$$Y = C(Y - T) + I(Y, r) + G$$

One way of thinking about the *IS* relation is that it tells us, for given values of G and T, what real interest rate, r, is needed to sustain a given level of spending and so a given level of output, Y. If, for example, output is equal to the natural level of output, Y_n, then, for given values of G and T, the real interest rate must be such that

$$Y_n = C(Y_n - T) + I(Y_n, r) + G$$

Since we used the word 'natural' to denote the level of output in the medium run, let us similarly call this value of the real interest rate the *natural real interest rate* and denote it by r_n. Then, our earlier proposition that, in the medium run, output returns to its natural level, Y_n, has a direct implication for the real interest rate.

◄ This is what the rate was called by Wicksell, a Swedish economist, at the turn of the twentieth century.

In the medium run, the real interest rate returns to the natural interest rate, r_n. It is independent of the rate of money growth.

In this chapter we have learned that the rate of inflation is equal to the rate of money growth minus the rate of growth of output (equation (11.8)).

If we assume, as we have done here, that output growth, g_y is equal to zero, this proposition takes an even simpler form: in the medium run, the rate of inflation, π, is equal to the rate of nominal money growth, g_m.

This proposition, together with the previous result about the real interest rate, has a straightforward implication for what happens to the nominal interest rate in the medium run. To see why, recall the relation between the nominal interest rate and the real interest rate:

$$i = r + \pi^e$$

We saw that in the medium run, the real interest rate equals the natural interest rate, r_n. Also in the medium run, expected inflation is equal to actual inflation (people cannot have incorrect expectations of inflation forever). It follows that

$$i = r_n + \pi$$

Now, because, in the medium run, inflation is equal to money growth, g_m, we get

$$i = r_n + g_m$$

In the medium run, the nominal interest rate is equal to the natural real interest rate plus the rate of money growth. So an increase in money growth leads to an equal increase in the nominal interest rate.

Let us summarise: in the medium run, money growth does not affect the real interest rate, but it affects both inflation and the nominal interest rate one-for-one.

A permanent increase in nominal money growth of, say, 10%, is eventually reflected in a 10% increase in the inflation rate and a 10% increase in the nominal interest rate, leaving the real interest rate unchanged. This result – that, in the medium run, the nominal interest rate increases one-for-one with inflation – is known as the **Fisher effect**, or the **Fisher hypothesis**, after Irving Fisher, an economist at Yale University who first stated it and its logic at the beginning of the twentieth century.

The short run

Let's now turn to dynamics. Suppose that the economy is initially at its medium-run equilibrium: unemployment is equal to the natural rate. Output growth is equal to the normal growth rate. The inflation rate is equal to adjusted nominal money growth.

Suppose that the central bank decides to decrease nominal money growth. We saw earlier that, in the medium run, lower money growth will lead to lower inflation and unchanged output growth and unemployment. The question now is: what will happen in the short run?

Just by looking at our three relations, we can tell the beginning of the story:

- Look at the aggregate demand relation – Given the initial rate of inflation, lower nominal money growth leads to lower real nominal money growth and thus to a decrease in output growth.
- Now, look at Okun's law – Output growth below normal leads to an increase in unemployment.
- Now, look at the Phillips curve relation – Unemployment above the natural rate leads to a decrease in inflation.

So we have our first result: tighter monetary policy leads initially to lower output growth and lower inflation. If tight enough, it may lead to negative output growth and thus to a recession. What happens between this initial response and the medium run (when unemployment returns to the natural rate)? The answer depends on the path of monetary policy, and the best way to show what happens is to work out a simple example.

Suppose the economy starts in year 0 in medium-run equilibrium. Assume that normal output growth is 3%, the natural unemployment rate is 6% and nominal money growth is 8%. Inflation is therefore equal to nominal money growth minus output growth, $8\% - 3\% = 5\%$. Real money growth is equal to nominal money growth minus inflation, $8\% - 5\% = 3\%$.

Suppose that the central bank decides to tighten monetary policy in the following way: it decides to decrease real money growth relative to trend by 2.5% in year 1 and to increase it relative to trend by 2.5% in year 2. (Why 2.5%? To make the arithmetic simple, as will be clear later on.) The path of the relevant macroeconomic variables is given in ➤ Table 11.2:

> It would be more natural to describe monetary policy in terms of what happens to nominal money growth. The algebra would get more complicated, however. For our purposes, it is easier to describe it in terms of what happens to real money growth. We can do so without loss of generality: given the inflation rate, the central bank can always choose nominal money growth to achieve the real money growth it wants.

Table 11.2 The effects of a monetary tightening

		Year 0	Year 1	Year 2	Year 3
1 Real money growth %	$(g_m - \pi)$	3.0	0.05	5.05	3.0
2 Output growth %	(g_y)	3.0	0.05	5.05	3.0
3 Unemployment rate %	(u)	6.0	7.00	6.00	6.0
4 Inflation rate %	(π)	5.0	4.00	4.00	4.0
5 (Nominal money growth) %	(g_m)	8.0	4.05	9.05	7.0

- Row 1 shows the path of real money growth. In year 0 (before the change in policy), real money growth is equal to 3%. Under the assumptions we have just made, the change in monetary policy leads to real money growth of 0.5% (2.5% below normal) in year 1, 5.5% (2.5% above normal) in year 2 and 3% thereafter.
- Row 2 shows the path of output growth. From the aggregate demand relation, real money growth of 0.5% in year 1 leads to output growth of 0.5% (2.5% below normal); real money growth of 5.5% in year 2 leads to output growth of 5.5% (2.5% above normal); thereafter, output growth is equal to the normal growth rate, 3%.
- Row 3 shows the path of the unemployment rate. Okun's law implies that output growth of 2.5% below normal for one year leads to an increase in the unemployment rate of 1 percentage point (2.5% multiplied by 0.4, the coefficient in Okun's law). So, in year 1, the unemployment rate increases from 6% to 7%. In year 2, output growth of 2.5% above normal for one year leads to a decrease in the unemployment rate of 1 percentage point. So, in year 2, the unemployment rate decreases from 7% back to 6%. The unemployment rate remains equal to 6% thereafter.
- Row 4 shows the path of the inflation rate. For this computation, let's assume that α is equal to 1.0 rather than its estimated value of 0.73 that we saw earlier (in Chapter 10). This assumption will simplify our computations. From the Phillips curve relation, an unemployment rate of 7%, which is 1% above the natural rate, leads to a decrease in inflation from 5% to 4% in year 1. In year 2 and thereafter, the unemployment rate is equal to the natural rate and, therefore, inflation remains constant at 4%.
- For completeness, row 5 shows the behaviour of nominal money growth consistent with the path of real money growth we assumed in row 1. Nominal money growth is equal to real money growth plus inflation. Adding the numbers for real money growth in row 1 and for inflation in row 4 gives the numbers in row 5. This implies a decrease in the rate of nominal money growth from 8% to 4.5% in year 1, an increase to 9.5% in year 2 and a decrease to 7% thereafter.

In words: in the short run, monetary tightening leads to a slowdown in growth and a temporary increase in unemployment. In the medium run, output growth returns to normal and the unemployment rate returns to the natural rate. Money growth and inflation are both permanently lower.

◁ Put less formally: the temporary increase in unemployment buys a permanent decrease in inflation.

From the short run to the medium run

We are now able to explain what happens to nominal and real interest rates from the short run to the medium run. In the short run, the real interest rate and the nominal interest rate both go down. Why don't they stay down forever? Let us first state the answer in short: low interest rates lead to higher demand, which leads to higher output, which eventually leads to higher inflation; higher inflation leads in turn to a decrease in the real money stock and an increase in interest rates.

Now, here is the answer step-by-step:

1. As long as the real interest rate is below the natural real interest rate – that is, the value corresponding to the natural level of output – output is higher than the natural level of output, and unemployment is below its natural rate.
2. From the Phillips curve relation, we know that, as long as unemployment is below the natural rate of unemployment, inflation increases.
3. As inflation increases, it eventually becomes higher than nominal money growth, leading to negative real money growth. When real money growth turns negative, the nominal interest rate starts increasing. And, given expected inflation, so does the real interest rate.
4. In the medium run, the real interest rate increases back to its initial value. Output is then back to the natural level of output, unemployment is back to the natural rate of unemployment, and inflation is no longer changing. As the real interest rate converges back to its initial value, the nominal interest rate converges to a new higher value, equal to the real interest rate plus the new, higher, rate of nominal money growth.

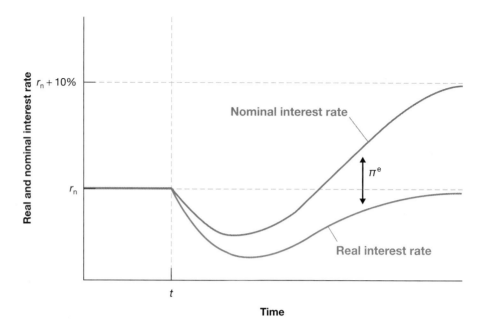

Figure 11.5

The adjustment of the real and the nominal interest rates to an increase in money growth

An increase in money growth leads initially to decreases in both the real and the nominal interest rates. Over time, however, the real interest rate returns to its initial value, and the nominal interest rate converges to a new higher value, equal to the initial value plus the increase in money growth.

Figure 11.5 summarises these results by showing the adjustment over time of the real interest rate and the nominal interest rate to an increase in nominal money growth from, say, 0% to 10%, starting at time t. Before time t, both interest rates are constant and equal to each other. The real interest rate is equal to r_n. The nominal interest rate is also equal to r_n (as inflation and expected inflation are equal to zero).

At time t, the rate of money growth increases from 0% to 10%. The increase in the rate of nominal money growth leads, for some time, to an increase in the real money stock and to a decrease in the nominal interest rate. As expected inflation increases, the decrease in the real interest rate is larger than the decrease of the nominal interest rate.

Eventually, the nominal interest rate and the real interest rate start increasing. In the medium run, the real interest rate returns to its initial value. Inflation and expected inflation converge to the new rate of money growth in this case, 10%. The result is that the nominal interest rate converges to a value equal to the real interest rate plus 10%.

Evidence for the Fisher hypothesis

There is plenty of evidence that a monetary expansion decreases nominal interest rates in the short run (see, for example, Chapter 5, section 5.5). But how much evidence is there for the Fisher hypothesis, the proposition that, in the medium run, increases in inflation lead to one-for-one increases in nominal interest rates?

Economists have tried to answer this question by looking at two types of evidence. One is the relation between nominal interest rates and inflation across countries. Because the relation holds only in the medium run, we should not expect inflation and nominal interest rates to be close to each other in any one country at any one time, but the relation should hold on average. This approach is explored further in the Focus box 'Nominal interest rates and inflation across Latin America in the early 1990s', which looks at Latin American countries during a period when they had high inflation and finds substantial support for the Fisher hypothesis.

The other type of evidence is the relation between the nominal interest rate and inflation over time in a given country. Again, the Fisher hypothesis does not imply that the two should move together from year to year, but it does suggest that the long swings in inflation should eventually be reflected in similar swings in the nominal interest rate. To see these

FOCUS
Nominal interest rates and inflation across Latin America in the early 1990s

Figure 11.6 plots nominal interest rate–inflation pairs for eight Latin American countries (Argentina, Bolivia, Chile, Ecuador, Mexico, Peru, Uruguay and Venezuela) for 1992 and 1993 – a period of high inflation in Latin America. Because the Brazilian numbers would dwarf those from other countries, they are not included in the figure. (In 1992, Brazil's annual inflation rate was 1,008%, and its nominal interest rate was 1,560%. In 1993, its inflation was 2,140%, and its nominal interest rate was 3,240%!) The numbers for inflation refer to the rate of change of the consumer price index. The numbers for nominal interest rates refer to the lending rate. The exact definition of the lending rate varies with each country, but you can think of it as corresponding to the prime interest rate in the USA – the rate charged to borrowers with the best credit rating.

Note the wide range of inflation rates, from 10% to about 100%. This is precisely why we have chosen to present numbers from Latin America in the early 1990s. With this much variation in inflation, we can learn a lot about the relation between nominal interest rates and inflation. And the figure indeed shows a clear relation between inflation and nominal interest rates. The line drawn in the figure plots what the nominal interest rate should be under the Fisher hypothesis, assuming an underlying real interest rate of 5%, so that $i = 5\% + \pi$. The slope of the line is 1: under the Fisher hypothesis, a 1% increase in inflation should be reflected in a 1% increase in the nominal interest rate.

As you can see, the line fits reasonably well, and roughly half of the points are above the line, and the other half are below. The Fisher hypothesis appears roughly consistent with the cross-country evidence from Latin America in the early 1990s.

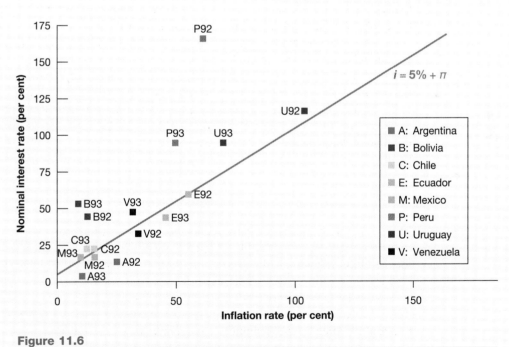

Figure 11.6

Nominal interest rates and inflation in Latin America, 1992–1993

long swings, we need to look at as long a period of time as we can. Figure 11.7 looks at the nominal interest rate and inflation in the USA since 1927. The nominal interest rate is the three-month Treasury bill rate, and inflation is the rate of change of the CPI.

Figure 11.7 has at least three interesting features:

Figure 11.7

The three-month US treasury bill rate and inflation since 1927

The increase in inflation from the early 1960s to the early 1980s was associated with an increase in the nominal interest rate. The decrease in inflation since the mid-1980s has been associated with a decrease in the nominal interest rate.

- The steady increase in inflation from the early 1960s to the early 1980s was associated with a roughly parallel increase in the nominal interest rate. The decrease in inflation since the mid-1980s has been associated with a decrease in the nominal interest rate. This evidence supports the Fisher hypothesis.
- Evidence of the short-run effects that we discussed earlier is also easy to see. The nominal interest rate lagged behind the increase in inflation in the 1970s, while the disinflation of the early 1980s was associated with an initial increase in the nominal interest rate, followed by a much slower decline in the nominal interest rate than in inflation.
- The other episode of inflation, during and after the Second World War, underscores the importance of the medium-run qualifier in the Fisher hypothesis. During that period, inflation was high but short-lived. And it was gone before it had time to be reflected in a higher nominal interest rate. The nominal interest rate remained very low throughout the 1940s.

More careful studies confirm our basic conclusion. The Fisher hypothesis that, in the medium run, increases in inflation are reflected in a higher nominal interest rate, appears to fit the data quite well, but the adjustment takes a long time. The data confirm the conclusion reached by Milton Friedman, which we quoted in the Focus box 'Theory ahead of facts' (in Chapter 10), that it typically takes a couple of decades for nominal interest rates to reflect the higher inflation rate.

11.5 MONEY GROWTH, INFLATION AND NOMINAL AND REAL INTEREST RATES

When reading the economy pages in any newspaper you will find apparently conflicting comments about the reaction of financial markets to possible decisions by the central bank (be it the Bank of England or the European Central Bank or the Riksbank, Sweden's central bank) on the growth rate of money. You might read both that higher money growth will lead to a decline in interest rates and that it will cause higher interest rates in the future.

Which one is right? Does higher money growth lead to lower interest rates, or does higher money growth lead to higher interest rates? The answer: both!

There are two keys to the answer: one is the distinction we just introduced between the real and the nominal interest rate. The other is the distinction we developed in the core between the short run and the medium run. As you will see, the full answer is:

- Higher money growth leads to lower nominal interest rates in the short run but to higher nominal interest rates in the medium run.
- Higher money growth leads to lower real interest rates in the short run but has no effect on real interest rates in the medium run.

The purpose of this section is to develop this answer and explore its implications.

Revisiting the *IS–LM* model

We have derived three equations – the *IS* relation, the *LM* relation and the relation between the real and the nominal interest rates. It will be more convenient to reduce them to two equations. To do so, replace the real interest rate in the *IS* relation with the nominal interest rate minus expected inflation: $r = i - \pi^e$. This gives:

$$IS = Y = C(Y - T) + I(Y, i - \pi^e) + G$$

$$LM = \frac{M}{P} = YL(i)$$

(These two equations are the same as in Chapter 5, with just one difference: investment spending in the *IS* relation depends on the real interest rate, which is equal to the nominal interest rate minus expected inflation.)

The associated *IS* and *LM* curves are drawn in Figure 11.8, for given values of P, M, G and T, and for a given expected rate of inflation, π^e:

- The *IS* curve is still downward sloping. For a given expected rate of inflation, π^e, the nominal interest rate and the real interest rate move together. So, a decrease in the nominal interest rate leads to an equal decrease in the real interest rate, leading to an increase in spending and in output.
- The *LM* curve is upward sloping. Given the money stock, an increase in output, which leads to an increase in the demand for money, requires an increase in the nominal interest rate.

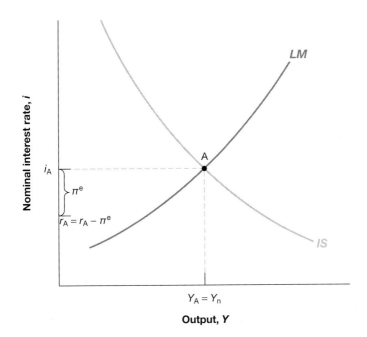

Figure 11.8

Equilibrium output and interest rates

The equilibrium level of output and the equilibrium nominal interest rate are given by the intersection of the *IS* curve and the *LM* curve. The real interest rate equals the nominal interest rate minus expected inflation.

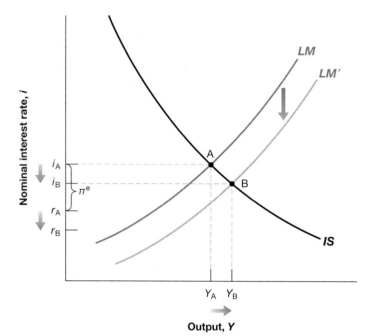

Figure 11.9

The short-run effects of an increase in money growth

An increase in money growth increases the real money stock in the short run. This increase in real money leads to an increase in output and decreases in both the nominal and real interest rates.

- The equilibrium is at the intersection of the *IS* curve and the *LM* curve, point A, with output level, Y_A, and nominal interest rate, i_A. Given the nominal interest rate, the real interest rate, r_A, is given by $r_A = i_A - \pi^e$.

Nominal and real interest rates in the short run

Assume that the economy is initially at the natural rate of output, so $Y_A = Y_n$. Now suppose the central bank increases the rate of growth of money. What happens to output, to the nominal interest rate and to the real interest rate in the short run?

One of the lessons from our analysis of monetary policy (in Chapter 9) is that, in the short run, the faster increase in nominal money will not be matched by an equal increase in the price level. In other words, the higher rate of growth of nominal money will lead, in the short run, to an increase in the real money stock, M/P. This is all we need to know for our purposes. What happens to output and to interest rates in the short run is shown in Figure 11.9.

The increase in the real money stock causes a shift in the *LM* curve down, from *LM* to *LM''*: for a given level of output, the increase in the real money stock leads to a decrease in the nominal interest rate. If we assume – as seems reasonable – that people and firms do not revise their expectations of inflation immediately, the *IS* curve does not shift: given expected inflation, a given nominal interest rate corresponds to the same real interest rate and to the same level of spending and output.

The economy moves down the *IS* curve, and the equilibrium moves from A to B. Output is higher: the nominal interest rate is lower and, given expected inflation, so is the real interest rate.

Let's summarise: in the short run, the increase in nominal money growth leads to an increase in the real money stock. This increase in real money leads to a decrease in both the nominal and the real interest rates and to an increase in output.

11.6 DISINFLATION

To better understand the mechanics and the implications of our model, let's imagine a situation in which the economy is in medium-run equilibrium: unemployment is at the natural rate of unemployment; output growth is equal to the normal growth rate. The inflation rate is equal to adjusted nominal money growth. The rate of nominal money growth and, by implication, the inflation rate, are high, however, and there is a consensus among policy makers that inflation must be reduced.

At this point, you might ask: what is so bad about high inflation if growth is proceeding at a normal rate and unemployment is at the natural rate of unemployment? To answer, we need to discuss the costs of inflation. (We shall do so in Chapter 22.)

We know from the previous section that lower inflation requires lower money growth. We also know that lower money growth implies an increase in unemployment for some time. For the central bank, the question now is: having decided to act, at what pace should it proceed?

This was the result of a deliberate policy by the Fed to maintain a very low nominal interest rate, to reduce interest payments on the large government debt created during the Second World War.

A first pass

A first pass at the answer can be given by using the Phillips curve relation (equation (11.5)):

$$\pi_t - \pi_{t-1} = -\alpha(u_t - u_n)$$

The relation makes it clear that **disinflation** – the decrease in inflation – can only be obtained at the cost of higher unemployment: for the left side of the equation to be negative – that is, for inflation to decrease – the term $(u_t - u_n)$ must be positive. In other words, the unemployment rate must exceed the natural rate.

The equation, however, has a stronger and more striking implication: the total amount of unemployment required for a given decrease in inflation does not depend on the speed at which disinflation is achieved. In other words, disinflation can be achieved quickly, at the cost of high unemployment for a few years. Or, alternatively, it can be achieved more slowly, with a smaller increase in unemployment spread over many years. In both cases, the total amount of unemployment, summed over the years, will be the same.

Let's see why. First, define a **point-year of excess unemployment** as the difference between the actual and the natural unemployment rates of 1 percentage point for one year. While the expression may sound a bit strange, the concept is simple: for example, if the natural rate of unemployment is 6%, an unemployment rate of 8% four years in a row corresponds to 4 times (8 – 6) = 8 point-years of excess unemployment.

Now look at a central bank that wants to reduce inflation by x percentage points. To make things simpler, let's use specific numbers: assume that the central bank wants to reduce inflation from 14% to 4%, so that x is equal to 10. Let's also make the convenient, if not quite correct, assumption that α equals 1; again, this will simplify computations:

Make sure to distinguish between:
- Deflation: decrease in the price level (equivalently, negative inflation).
- Disinflation: decrease in the inflation rate.

- Suppose the central bank wants to achieve the reduction in inflation in one year. Equation (11.5) tells us that what is required is one year of unemployment at 10% above the natural rate. In this case, the right side of the equation is equal to –10%, and the inflation rate decreases by 10% within a year.
- Suppose the central bank wants to achieve the reduction in inflation over two years. Equation (11.5) tells us that what is required is two years of unemployment at 5% above the natural rate. During each of the two years, the right side of the equation is equal to –5%, so the inflation rate decreases by 5% each year, thus by 2 × 5% = 10% over two years.
- By the same reasoning, reducing inflation over five years requires five years of unemployment at 2% above the natural rate (5 × 2% = 10); reducing inflation over ten years requires ten years of unemployment at 1% above the natural rate (10 × 1% = 10%); and so on.

Note that in each case the number of point-years of excess unemployment required to decrease inflation is the same, namely ten: one year times 10% excess unemployment in the first scenario, two years times 5% in the second, ten years times 1% in the last. The implication is straightforward: the central bank can choose the distribution of excess unemployment over time, but it cannot change the total number of point-years of excess unemployment.

We can state this conclusion another way: define the **sacrifice ratio** as the number of point-years of excess unemployment needed to achieve a decrease in inflation of 1%:

$$\text{Sacrifice ratio} = \frac{\text{Point} - \text{Years of excess unemployment}}{\text{Decrease in inflation}}$$

From equation (11.5), excess unemployment of 1% for one year decreases the inflation rate by α times 1%. Put the other way, to reduce the inflation rate by 1%, excess unemployment must be equal to $1/\alpha$ for one year.

Equation (11.5) then implies that this ratio is independent of policy and simply equal to $(1/\alpha)$.

If the sacrifice ratio is constant, does this mean that the speed of disinflation is irrelevant? No. Suppose that the central bank tried to achieve the decrease in inflation in one year. As you have just seen, this would require an unemployment rate of 10% above the natural rate for one year. With a natural unemployment rate of 6%, this would require increasing the actual unemployment rate to 16% for one year. From Okun's law, using a value of 0.4 for β and a normal output growth rate of 3%, output growth would have to satisfy

$$u_t - u_{t-1} = -\beta(g_{yt} - \bar{g}_y)$$
$$16\% - 6\% = -0.4(g_{yt} - 3\%)$$

This implies a value for $g_{yt} = -(10\%)/0.4 + 3\% = -22\%$. In words, output growth would have to equal −22% for a year! In comparison, the largest negative growth rate ever in the USA in the twentieth century was −15%. It occurred in 1931, during the Great Depression. During the recent recession of 2007–2010, the worst after the Great Depression, the lowest growth rate registered by the USA was −6.4% in the first quarter of 2009. It is fair to say that macroeconomists do not know with great confidence what would happen if monetary policy were aimed at inducing such a large negative growth rate, but they would surely be unwilling to try. The increase in the overall unemployment rate would lead to extremely high unemployment rates for some groups – specifically the young and the unskilled, whose unemployment typically increases more than the average unemployment rate. The associated sharp drop in output would most probably also lead to a large number of bankruptcies. This suggests that the central bank will want to go more slowly and to achieve disinflation over a number of years rather than do it all in one year.

The analysis we have just developed is close to the type of analysis economists at the Fed were conducting in the late 1970s. The econometric model they used, as well as most econometric models in use at the time, shared our simple model's property that policy could change the timing but not the number of point-years of excess unemployment. We shall call this the traditional approach in the following text. The traditional approach was challenged, however, by two separate groups of macroeconomists. The focus of both groups was the role of expectations and how changes in expectation formation might affect the unemployment cost of disinflation but, despite this common focus, they reached quite different conclusions.

Expectations and credibility: the Lucas critique

Robert Lucas was awarded the Nobel Prize in 1995 and is still at the University of Chicago. Thomas Sargent is now at New York.

The conclusions of the first group were based on the work of Robert Lucas and Thomas Sargent, then at the University of Chicago. In what has become known as the **Lucas critique**, Lucas pointed out that when trying to predict the effects of a major policy change – such as the change considered by the Fed at the time – it could be very misleading to take as given the relations estimated from past data.

In the case of the Phillips curve, taking equation (11.5) as given was equivalent to assuming that wage setters would keep expecting inflation in the future to be the same as it was in the past, that the way wage setters formed their expectations would not change in response to the change in policy. This was an unwarranted assumption, Lucas argued: why shouldn't wage setters take policy changes directly into account? If wage setters believed that the central bank was committed to lowering inflation, they might well expect inflation to be lower in the future than in the past. If they lowered their expectations of inflation, then actual inflation would decline without the need for a protracted recession.

The logic of Lucas's argument can be seen by returning to equation (11.4), the Phillips curve with expected inflation on the right:

$$\pi_t = \pi_t^e - \alpha(u_t - u_n)$$

◄ If $\pi_t^e = \pi_{t-1}$, the Phillips curve is given by

$$\pi_t - \pi_{t-1} = \alpha(u_t - u_n)$$

To achieve $\pi_t < \pi_{t-1}$, it must be that

$$u_t > u_n.$$

If wage setters kept forming expectations of inflation by looking at the previous year's inflation (if $P_t^e = P_{t-1}$), then the only way to decrease inflation would be to accept higher unemployment for some time; we explored the implications of this assumption in the preceding subsection.

But if wage setters could be convinced that inflation was indeed going to be lower than in the past, they would decrease their expectations of inflation. This would in turn reduce actual inflation, without any change in the unemployment rate. For example, if wage setters were convinced that inflation, which had been running at 14% in the past, would be only 4% in the future, and if they formed their expectations accordingly, then inflation would fall to 4% even if unemployment remained at the natural rate of unemployment.

Nominal money growth, inflation and expected inflation could all be reduced without the need for a recession. Put another way, decreases in nominal money growth could be neutral not only in the medium run but also in the short run.

Lucas and Sargent did not believe that disinflation could really take place without some increase in unemployment. But Sargent, looking at the historical evidence on the end of several very high inflations, concluded that the increase in unemployment could be small. The sacrifice ratio – the amount of excess unemployment needed to achieve disinflation – might be much lower than suggested by the traditional approach. The essential ingredient of successful disinflation, he argued, was **credibility** of monetary policy – the belief by wage setters that the central bank was truly committed to reducing inflation. Only credibility would cause wage setters to change the way they formed their expectations. Furthermore, he argued, a clear and quick disinflation programme was much more likely to be credible than a protracted one that offered plenty of opportunities for reversal and political infighting along the way.

◄ The credibility view is that fast disinflation is likely to be more credible than slow disinflation. Credibility decreases the unemployment cost of disinflation. So the central bank should go for fast disinflation.

Nominal rigidities and contracts

A contrary view was taken by Stanley Fisher, then from MIT, and John Taylor, then at Columbia University. Both emphasised the presence of **nominal rigidities**, meaning that, in modern economies, many wages and prices are set in nominal terms for some time and are typically not readjusted when there is a change in policy.

◄ Fisher is now the Governor of the Central Bank of Israel. Taylor was under-secretary for international affairs in the G. W. Bush administration and is now a professor at Stanford University.

Fisher argued that, even with credibility, too rapid a decrease in nominal money growth would lead to higher unemployment. Even if the central bank fully convinced workers and firms that nominal money growth was going to be lower, the wages set before the change in policy would still reflect the expectations of inflation prior to the policy change. In effect, inflation would already be built into existing wage agreements and could not be reduced instantaneously and without cost. At the very least, Fisher said, a policy of disinflation should be announced sufficiently in advance of its actual implementation to allow wage setters to take it into account when setting wages.

Taylor's argument went one step further. An important characteristic of wage contracts, he argued, is that they are not all signed at the same time. Instead, they are staggered over time. He showed that this **staggering of wage decisions** imposed strong limits on how fast disinflation could proceed without triggering higher unemployment, even if the central bank's commitment to inflation was fully credible. Why the limits? If workers cared about their wage relative to the wages of other workers, each wage contract would choose a wage not very different from the wages in the other contracts in force at the time. Too rapid a decrease in nominal money growth would therefore not lead to a proportional decrease in

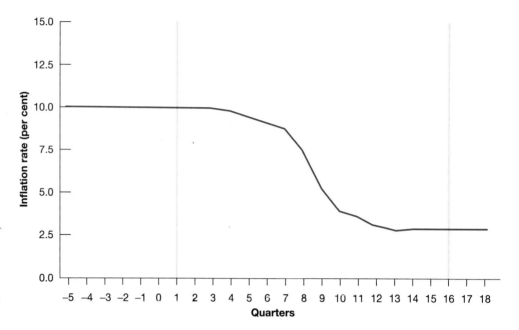

Figure 11.10

Disinflation without unemployment in the Taylor model

If wage decisions are staggered, disinflation must be phased in slowly to avoid an increase in unemployment.

inflation. As a result, the real money stock would decrease, triggering a recession and an increase in the unemployment rate.

Taking into account the time pattern of wage contracts in the USA, Taylor then showed that, under full credibility of monetary policy, there was a path of disinflation consistent with no increase in unemployment. This path is shown in Figure 11.10.

In Figure 11.10, disinflation starts in quarter 1 and lasts for 16 quarters. Once it is achieved, the inflation rate, which started at 10%, is 3%. The striking feature is how slowly disinflation proceeds at the beginning. One year (four quarters) after the announcement of the change in policy, inflation is still 9.9%. But then disinflation proceeds more quickly. By the end of the third year, inflation is down to 4%, and by the end of the fourth year, the desired disinflation is achieved.

The reason for the slow decrease in inflation at the beginning – and, behind the scenes, for the slow decrease in nominal money growth – is straightforward: wages in force at the time of the policy change are the result of decisions made before the policy change occurred. Because of this, the path of inflation in the near future is largely predetermined. If nominal money growth were to decrease sharply, inflation could not fall very much right away, and the result would be a decrease in real money and a recession. So the best policy is for the central bank to proceed slowly at the beginning of the process while announcing it will proceed faster in the future. This announcement leads new wage settlements to take into account the new policy. When most wage decisions in the economy are based on decisions made after the change in policy, disinflation can proceed much more quickly. This is what happens in the third year following the policy change.

Like Lucas and Sargent, Taylor did not believe that disinflation could really be implemented without an increase in unemployment. For one thing, he realised that the path of disinflation drawn in Figure 11.10 might not be credible. Announcing this year that the central bank will decrease nominal money growth two years from now is likely to cause a serious credibility problem. Wage setters are likely to ask: if the decision has been made to disinflate, why does the central bank want to wait two years? Without credibility, inflation expectations might not change, defeating the hope of disinflation without an increase in the unemployment rate. But Taylor's analysis had two clear messages. First, like Lucas and Sargent, Taylor's analysis emphasised the role of expectations. Second, it suggested that a slow but credible disinflation might have a cost lower than the one implied by the traditional approach.

Whose approach is right? The traditional approach, the Sargent–Lucas approach, or the Fisher–Taylor approach? The answer in the case of the disinflation experience in the UK in

FOCUS
Mrs Thatcher's disinflation, 1979–1985

In 1979, at the start of Margaret Thatcher's government, the economic performance of the UK was rather poor. The inflation rate was higher than 13% and the immediate objective was to reduce it using monetary policy. To this end the government instituted a Medium Term Financial Strategy (MTFS) that envisaged a steady reduction in nominal GDP growth through a gradual reduction in the rate of growth of the money stock, accompanied by a reduction in public sector borrowing requirements (PSBR). Targets for the money stock were not new, having been first introduced by the Labour government in 1977. The MTFS, however, was different in providing target ranges for a number of years ahead. The rate of growth of the monetary base slowed from 12.1% in 1979 to 2.6% in 1981. The reduction in inflation is indeed one of the most conspicuous economic successes of the Thatcher years.

The most obvious failure was the level of unemployment. Let us compare the UK's unemployment experience with those of most industrialised countries that went through a short period of disinflation during the first half of the 1980s. Has disinflation been more costly in the UK than elsewhere? Table 11.3 reports inflation and unemployment rates in 1980 and 1985 in the UK and a number of other countries.

Economic policies in the USA and the UK after 1979 provide good laboratories to test the credibility hypothesis, which states that credible policies to reduce inflation would lead to a more rapid and less costly reduction in inflation than would traditional approaches. Charlie Bean and James Symons calculate 'sacrifice ratios' for the UK and other countries in Table 11.3.

The 'sacrifice ratio', as discussed in this chapter, is the ratio of the cumulated excess of the unemployment rate over its 1980 level during the disinflation period. Compared to Japan, Sweden and the USA – three countries with very different economic and institutional structures – the UK performance was rather poor. However, its performance is better when compared to the rest of the EU; Germany, for instance, fared especially badly under the sacrifice ratio criterion. However, the most obvious comparison, in terms of similarity of initial conditions (inflation was close to 20% in both countries in 1980), is with Italy: the sacrifice ratio was 2.5 times higher in the UK compared to Italy.

The results suggest that there was no credibility miracle. The UK sacrifice ratio ranks third out of seven even though most would agree that the UK had the most draconian anti-inflation policies of any of the countries. It is interesting to note as well that the country with the most deeply embedded hostility to inflation, Germany, has the highest sacrifice ratio.

If one also looks at the evolution of inflation and unemployment in the second half of the 1980s, in the UK as well as continental Europe, one can see that rising trends in unemployment have gone along with a persistence of inflation. The experience is in contrast with the conventional Phillips curve theory, which cannot explain why inflation does not continue to decline with rates of unemployment that are presumably well above the natural rates.

The Phillips curve theory has great difficulties in explaining wage–price movements over the 1980s in the UK and in much of Europe. Attempts to find stable Phillips curves have proven elusive, except perhaps for Japan and the USA.

Source: Charlie Bean and James Symons, 1989, 'Ten years of Mrs T', *NBER Macroeconomics Annual*, Volume 4, NBER, Cambridge, MA, 13–72.

Table 11.3 Comparative inflation and unemployment performance

| | Inflation | | Unemployment | | 'Sacrifice |
	1980	1985	1980	1985	ratio'
Germany	4.9	2.3	3.0	7.2	6.8
France	11.6	5.9	6.3	10.2	2.1
Italy	21.5	9.2	7.5	10.1	0.7
Japan	3.9	1.5	2.0	2.6	1.0
Sweden	11.9	6.9	2.0	2.8	0.4
UK	19.1	5.8	6.4	11.2	1.8
United States	9.1	3.0	7.0	7.1	1.0

Source: Charles Bean and James Symons, 'Ten years of Mrs T', in *NBER Macroeconomics Annual*, Volume 4, 13–61, Table 3, p. 23. NBER, Cambridge, MA, 1989.

the early 1980s is given in the Focus box 'Mrs Thatcher's disinflation, 1979–1985', and is easy to summarise: the disinflation of about 10% triggered a deep recession and about 12 point-years of excess unemployment. In other words, there were no obvious credibility gains, and the sacrifice ratio turned out to be roughly what was predicted by the traditional approach.

The nominal rigidities view is that many wages are set in nominal terms, sometimes for many years. The way to decrease the unemployment cost of disinflation is to give wage setters time to take into account the change in policy, so the central bank should go for slow disinflation.

Was this outcome due to a lack of credibility of the change in monetary policy or to the fact that credibility is not enough to substantially reduce the cost of disinflation? One way of learning more is to look at other disinflation episodes. This is the approach followed by Laurence Ball, from the Johns Hopkins University in the USA, who estimated sacrifice ratios for 65 disinflation episodes in 19 OECD countries over the past 30 years. He reached three main conclusions:

- Disinflations typically lead to a period of higher unemployment. Put another way, even if a decrease in nominal money growth is neutral in the medium run, unemployment increases for some time before returning to the natural rate of unemployment.
- Faster disinflations are associated with smaller sacrifice ratios. This conclusion provides some evidence to support the expectation and credibility effects emphasised by Lucas and Sargent.
- Sacrifice ratios are smaller in countries that have shorter wage contracts. This provides some evidence to support Fisher and Taylor's emphasis on the structure of wage settlements.

Let's summarise: policy makers face a trade-off between unemployment and inflation. In particular, to permanently lower inflation requires higher unemployment for some time. One might have hoped that, with credible policies, the trade-off would be much more favourable. The evidence can be read as saying that credibility gains may be present, but they are small.

SUMMARY

- Three relations link inflation, output and unemployment:
  - Okun's law, which relates the change in the unemployment rate to the deviation of the rate of growth of output from the normal growth rate. In the USA today, output growth of 1% above normal for a year leads to a decrease in the unemployment rate of about 0.4%.
  - The aggregate supply relation – the Phillips curve – which relates the change in the inflation rate to the deviation of the actual unemployment rate from the natural rate of unemployment. In the USA today, an unemployment rate 1% below the natural rate of unemployment for a year leads to an increase in inflation of about 1%.
  - The aggregate demand relation, which relates the rate of growth of output to the rate of growth of real money. The growth rate of output is equal to the growth rate of nominal money minus the rate of inflation. Given nominal money growth, higher inflation leads to a decrease in output growth.
- In the medium run, the unemployment rate is equal to the natural rate of unemployment, and output grows at its normal growth rate. Nominal money growth determines the inflation rate: a 1% increase in nominal money growth leads to a 1% increase in the inflation rate. As Milton Friedman put it: inflation is always and everywhere a monetary phenomenon.

- In the short run, a decrease in nominal money growth leads to a slowdown in growth and an increase in unemployment for some time.

- The proposition that, in the medium run, changes in inflation are reflected one-for-one in changes in the nominal interest rate is known as the Fisher effect or the Fisher hypothesis. The empirical evidence suggests that, while it takes a long time, changes in inflation are eventually reflected in changes in the nominal interest rate.

- Disinflation (a decrease in the inflation rate) can be achieved only at the cost of more unemployment. How much unemployment is required is a controversial issue. The traditional approach assumes that people do not change the way they form expectations when monetary policy changes, so the relation between inflation and unemployment is unaffected by the change in policy. This approach implies that disinflation can be achieved by a short but large increase in unemployment or by a longer and smaller increase in unemployment. But policy cannot affect the total number of point-years of excess unemployment.

- An alternative view is that, if the change in monetary policy is credible, expectation formation may change, leading to a smaller increase in unemployment than predicted by the traditional approach. In its extreme form, this alternative view implies that if policy is fully credible, it can achieve disinflation at no cost in unemployment. A less extreme form recognises that, while expectation formation may change, the presence of nominal rigidities is likely to result in some increase in unemployment, but less than that implied by the traditional approach.

KEY TERMS

Okun's law 237

normal growth rate 238

labour hoarding 238

nominal interest rates 241

real interest rates 241

adjusted nominal money growth 246

Fisher effect, Fisher hypothesis 248

disinflation 255

point-year of excess unemployment 255

sacrifice ratio 256

Lucas critique 256

credibility 257

nominal rigidities 257

staggering of wage decisions 257

QUESTIONS AND PROBLEMS

QUICK CHECK

1. *Using the information in this chapter, label each of the following statements true, false or uncertain. Explain briefly.*

a. The unemployment rate will remain constant as long as there is positive output growth.

b. Many firms prefer to keep workers around when demand is low (rather than lay them off) even if the workers are underutilised.

c. The behaviour of Okun's law across countries and across decades is consistent with our knowledge of firms' behaviour and labour market regulations.

d. There is a reliable negative relation between the rate of inflation and the growth rate of output.

e. In the medium run, the rate of inflation is equal to the rate of nominal money growth.

f. In the medium run, the real interest rate is not affected by money growth.

g. The Fisher effect states that in the medium run, the nominal interest rate is not affected by money growth.

h. The experience of Latin American countries in the early 1990s supports the Fisher hypothesis.

i. According to the Phillips curve relation, the sacrifice ratio is independent of the speed of disinflation.

j. If Lucas and Sargent were right, and if monetary policy was fully credible, there would be no relation between inflation and unemployment – i.e. no Phillips curve relation.

k. Contrary to the traditional Phillips curve analysis, Taylor's analysis of staggered wage contracts makes the case for a slow approach to disinflation.

l. Ball's analysis of disinflation episodes provides some support for both the credibility effects of Lucas and Sargent and the wage-contract effects of Fischer and Taylor.

m. As long as inflation remains roughly constant, the movements in the real interest rate are roughly equal to the movements in the nominal interest rate.

n. If inflation turns out to be higher than expected, the realised real cost of borrowing turns out to be lower than the real interest rate.

o. Looking across countries, the real interest rate is likely to vary much less than the nominal interest rate.

p. The real interest rate is equal to the nominal interest rate divided by the price level.

2. *As shown by equation (11.2), the estimated Okun's law for the USA is given by*

$$u_t - u_{t-1} = -0.4(g_{yt} - 3\%)$$

a. What growth rate of output leads to an increase in the unemployment rate of 1% per year? How can the unemployment rate increase even though the growth rate of output is positive?

b. Suppose output growth is constant for the next four years. What growth rate would reduce the unemployment rate by 2 percentage points over the next four years?

c. How would you expect Okun's law to change if the rate of growth of the labour force was higher by 2 percentage points? How do you expect Okun's law to change if the rate of growth of the labour force increases by 2 percentage points?

3. *Suppose that an economy can be described by the following three equations:*

$$u_t - u_{t-1} = -0.4(g_{yt} - 3\%) \quad \text{Okun's law}$$

$$\pi_t - \pi_{t-1} = -(u_t - 5\%) \qquad \text{Phillips curve}$$

$$g_{yt} = g_{mt} - \pi_t \qquad \qquad \text{Aggregate demand}$$

a. What is the natural rate of unemployment for this economy?

b. Suppose that the unemployment rate is equal to the natural rate and that the inflation rate is 8%. What is the growth rate of output? What is the growth rate of the money supply?

c. Suppose that conditions are as in (b), when, in year t, the authorities use monetary policy to reduce the inflation rate to 4% in year t and keep it there. Given this inflation rate and using the Phillips curve, what must happen to the unemployment rate in years t, $t + 1$, $t + 2$ and so on? Given the unemployment rate and using Okun's law, what must happen to the rate of growth of output in years t, $t + 1$, $t + 2$ and so on? Given the rate of growth of output and using the aggregate demand equation, what must be the rate of nominal money growth in years t, $t + 1$, $t + 2$ and so on?

4. *Suppose that you are advising a government that wants to reduce the inflation rate. It is considering two options: a gradual reduction over several years or an immediate reduction.*

a. Lay out the arguments for and against each option.

b. Considering only the sacrifice ratio, which option is preferable? Why might you want to consider criteria other than the sacrifice ratio?

c. What particular features of the economy would you want to consider before giving your advice?

5. Mark-ups, unemployment and inflation

Suppose that the Phillips curve is given by

$$\pi_t - \pi_{t-1} = -(u_t - 5\%) + 0.1\mu$$

where μ is the mark-up.

Suppose that unemployment is initially at its natural rate. Suppose now that μ increases as a result of an oil price shock, but that the monetary authority continues to keep the unemployment rate at its previous value.

a. What will happen to inflation?

b. What should the monetary authority do instead of trying to keep the unemployment rate at its previous value?

6. The Fisher hypothesis

a. What is the Fisher hypothesis?

b. Does the experience of Latin American countries in the 1990s support or refute the Fisher hypothesis? Explain.

c. Look at the figure in the Focus box on Latin America. Note that the line drawn through the scatter of points does not go through the origin. Does the 'Fisher effect' suggest that it should go through the origin? Explain.

d. Consider this statement: 'If the Fisher hypothesis is true, then changes in the growth rate of the money stock translate one-for-one into changes in i, and the real interest rate is left unchanged. Thus, there is no room for monetary policy to affect real economic activity.' Discuss.

7. *For which of the problems listed in (a)–(c) would you want to use real payments and real interest rates, and for which would you want to use nominal payments and nominal interest rates, to compute the expected present discounted value? In each case, explain why.*

a. Estimating the present discounted value of the profits from an investment in a new machine.

b. Estimating the present value of a ten-year British government security.

c. Deciding whether to lease or buy a car.

8. *Compute the real interest rate using the exact formula and the approximation formula for each set of assumptions listed in (a)–(c).*

a. $i = 4\%$; $\pi^e = 2\%$

b. $i = 15\%$; $\pi^e = 11\%$

c. $i = 54\%$; $\pi^e = 46\%$

9. *Nominal and real interest rates around the world*

a. Can the nominal interest rate ever be negative? Explain.

b. Can the real interest rate ever be negative? Under what circumstances can it be negative? If so, why not just hold cash instead of bonds?

c. What are the effects of a negative real interest rate on borrowing and lending?

d. Find a recent issue of *The Economist* and look at the tables in the back (titled 'Economic Indicators and Financial Indicators'). Use the three-month money market rate as the nominal interest rate and the most recent three-month rate of change in consumer prices as the expected rate of inflation (both are in annual terms). Which countries have the lowest nominal interest rates? Which countries have the lowest real interest rates? Are these real interest rates close to being negative?

DIG DEEPER

10. Credibility and disinflation

Suppose that the Phillips curve is given by

$$\pi_t = \pi_t^e - (u_t - 5\%)$$

and expected inflation is given by

$$\pi_t^e = \pi_{t-1}$$

a. What is the sacrifice ratio in this economy?

Suppose that unemployment is initially equal to the natural rate and $\pi = 12\%$. The central bank decides that 12% inflation is too high and that, starting in year t, it will maintain the unemployment rate 1 percentage point above the natural rate of unemployment until the inflation rate has decreased to 2%.

b. Compute the rate of inflation for years t, $t + 1$, $t + 2$ and so on.

c. For how many years must the central bank keep the unemployment rate above the natural rate of unemployment? Is the implied sacrifice ratio consistent with your answer to (a)?

Now suppose that people know that the central bank wants to lower inflation to 2%, but they are not sure about the central bank's willingness to accept an unemployment rate above the natural rate of unemployment. As a result, their expectation of inflation is a weighted average of the target of 2% and last year's inflation – i.e.

$$\pi_t^e = \lambda 2\% + (1 - \lambda)\pi_{t-1}$$

where λ is the weight they put on the central bank's target of 2%.

d. Let $\lambda = 0.25$. How long will it take before the inflation rate is equal to 2%? What is the sacrifice ratio? Why is it different from the answer in (c)?

Suppose that after the policy has been in effect for one year, people believe that the central bank is indeed committed to reducing inflation to 2%. As a result, they now set their expectations according to

$$\pi_t^e = 2\%$$

e. From what year onward can the central bank let the unemployment rate return to the natural rate? What is the sacrifice ratio now?

f. What advice would you give to a central bank that wants to lower the rate of inflation by increasing the rate of unemployment as little and for as short a time period as possible?

11. The effects of a permanent decrease in the rate of nominal money growth

Suppose that the economy can be described by the following three equations:

$$u_t - u_{t-1} = -0.4(g_{yt} - 3\%) \quad \text{Okun's law}$$
$$\pi_t - \pi_{t-1} = -(u_t - 5\%) \quad \text{Phillips curve}$$
$$g_{yt} = g_{mt} - \pi_t \quad \text{Aggregate demand}$$

a. Reduce the three equations to two by substituting g_{yt} from the aggregate demand equation into Okun's law.

Assume initially that $u_t = u_{t-1} = 5\%$, $g_{mt} = 13\%$ and $\pi_t = 10\%$. Now suppose that money growth is permanently reduced from 13% to 3%, starting in year t.

b. Compute (using a calculator or a spreadsheet program) unemployment and inflation in year t, $t + 1$, . . . , $t + 10$.

c. Does inflation decline smoothly from 10% to 3%? Why or why not?

d. Compute the values of the unemployment rate and the inflation rate in the medium run.

12. *When looking at the short run in Section 11.2, we showed how an increase in nominal money growth led to higher output, a lower nominal interest rate and a lower real interest rate.*

The analysis in the text (as summarised in Figure 11.9) assumed that expected inflation, π^e, did not change in the short run. Let us now relax this assumption and assume that, in the short run, both money growth and expected inflation increase.

a. Show the effect on the *IS* curve. Explain in words.

b. Show the effect on the *LM* curve. Explain in words.

c. Show the effect on output and on the nominal interest rate. Could the nominal interest rate end up higher – not lower – than before the change in money growth? Why?

d. Even if what happens to the nominal interest rate is ambiguous, can you tell what happens to the real interest rate? (*Hint*: What happens to output relative to Figure 11.9? What does this imply about what happens to the real interest rate?)

EXPLORE FURTHER

13. *Go to the Eurostat website and retrieve quarterly data on gross domestic product at constant prices for 2011 and 2012 and on monthly unemployment rates and monthly employment levels for 2011 and 2012, for your country.*

a. Was output growth positive throughout 2011 and 2012?

b. What happened to the unemployment rate over the period January 2011–June 2012?

c. How do you reconcile your answers to parts (a) and (b)?

d. Now consider the employment level. Compare the monthly employment levels from September 2011 and December 2011. What happened to employment over the last quarter of 2011?

e. Was output growth positive in the last quarter of 2011?

f. How do you reconcile your answers to parts (d) and (e)?

14. *Go to the Eurostat website and retrieve monthly data on the level of employment and unemployment for 2011. You will notice that the level of unemployment rose in every month of 2011.*

a. Did the level of employment rise in any month(s) in 2011?

b. How is it possible that both employment and unemployment could rise in the same month?

Chapter 12

THE MEDIUM RUN IN AN OPEN ECONOMY

This chapter repeats what we did earlier (in Chapter 6), where we extended the model to the case of an open economy in the short run. Here we study the medium run of an economy that trades both in goods and financial assets with the rest of the world.

To do this, however, we need to recognise that what happens in the medium run in an open economy depends on the exchange rate regime the country has adopted: whether the exchange rate between the country's currency and that of its neighbours is fixed or flexible, i.e. it is kept constant by central banks, or it can fluctuate depending on demand and supply of the different currencies. Let us start from some history.

In July 1944, representatives of 44 countries met in Bretton Woods, a mountain resort in New Hampshire, to design a new international monetary and exchange rate system. The system they adopted was based on fixed exchange rates, with all member countries other than the USA fixing the price of their currency in terms of dollars. In 1973, a series of exchange rate crises brought an abrupt end to the system – and an end to what is now called 'the Bretton Woods period'. Since then, the world has been characterised by many exchange rate arrangements. Some countries operate under flexible exchange rates, some operate under fixed exchange rates and some go back and forth between regimes. At the end of the 1990s, a group of European countries decided to permanently fix their exchange rates by adopting a single currency, the euro. A few other countries have since joined the euro area, while others, most notably the UK and Denmark, did not. Which exchange rate regime to choose is one of the most debated issues in macroeconomics, a decision facing every country in the world.

This chapter discusses these issues:

- Section 12.1 looks at the medium run. It shows that, in sharp contrast to the results we derived for the short run (in Chapter 7), an economy ends up with the same real exchange rate and output level in the medium run, regardless of whether it operates under fixed exchange rates or flexible exchange rates. This obviously does not make the exchange rate regime irrelevant – the short run matters very much – but it is an important extension and qualification to our previous analysis.

- Section 12.2 takes another look at fixed exchange rates and focuses on exchange rate crises. During a typical exchange rate crisis, a country operating under a fixed exchange rate is forced, often under dramatic conditions, to abandon its parity and to devalue. Such crises were behind the breakdown of the Bretton Woods system. They rocked the European

Monetary System in the early 1990s and were a major element of the Asian Crisis of the late 1990s. It is important to understand why they happen and what they imply.

- Section 12.3 takes another look at flexible exchange rates and focuses on the behaviour of exchange rates under a flexible exchange rate regime. It shows that the behaviour of exchange rates and the relation of the exchange rate to monetary policy are, in fact, more complex than we assumed (in Chapter 7). Large fluctuations in the exchange rate, and the difficulty of using monetary policy to affect the exchange rate, make a flexible exchange rate regime less attractive than it appeared to be.

- Section 12.4 puts all these conclusions together and reviews the case for flexible or fixed rates. It discusses two recent and important developments: the move toward a common currency in Europe, and the move toward strong forms of fixed exchange rate regimes, from currency boards to dollarisation.

12.1 THE MEDIUM RUN

When we focused on the short run (in Chapter 7), we drew a sharp contrast between the behaviour of an economy with flexible exchange rates (in sections 7.1 to 7.4) and an economy with fixed exchange rates (in section 7.5):

- Under flexible exchange rates, a country that needed to achieve a real depreciation – for example, to reduce its trade deficit or to get out of a recession – could do so by relying on an expansionary monetary policy to achieve both lower interest and a decrease in the exchange rate – a depreciation.
- Under fixed exchange rates, a country lost both of these instruments: by definition, its nominal exchange rate was fixed and thus could not be adjusted. Moreover, the fixed exchange rate and the interest parity condition implied that the country could not adjust its interest rate; the domestic interest rate had to remain equal to the foreign interest rate.

This appeared to make a flexible exchange rate regime much more attractive than a fixed exchange rate regime: why should a country give up two macroeconomic instruments? As we now shift focus from the short run to the medium run, you shall see that this earlier conclusion needs to be qualied. Although our conclusions about the short run were valid, we shall see that, in the medium run, the difference between the two regimes fades away. More specically, in the medium run, the economy reaches the same real exchange rate and the same level of output, whether it operates under fixed or under flexible exchange rates.

The intuition for this result is actually easy to give. Recall the definition of the real exchange rate:

$$\varepsilon = \frac{EP}{P^*}$$

The real exchange rate, ε, is equal to the nominal exchange rate, E (the price of domestic currency in terms of foreign currency), times the domestic price level, P, divided by the foreign price level, P^*. There are, therefore, two ways in which the real exchange rate can adjust:

● Through a change in the nominal exchange rate, E – this can be done only under flexible exchange rates. And if we assume that the domestic price level, P, and the foreign price level, P^*, do not change in the short run, it is the only way to adjust the real exchange rate in the short run.

There are three ways in which a UK car ➤ can become cheaper relative to a German car: first, through a decrease in the pound price of the UK car. Second, through an increase in the euro price of the German car. Third, through a decrease in the nominal exchange rate – a decrease in the value of the pound in terms of euros.

● Through a change in the domestic price level, P, relative to the foreign price level P^* – in the medium run, this option is open even to a country operating under a fixed (nominal) exchange rate. And this is indeed what happens under fixed exchange rates: the adjustment takes place through the price level rather than through the nominal exchange rate.

Let us go through this argument step by step. To begin, let's derive the aggregate demand and aggregate supply relations for an open economy under a fixed exchange rate.

Aggregate demand under fixed exchange rates

In an open economy with fixed exchange rates, we can write the aggregate demand relation as

$$Y = Y\left(\frac{\bar{E}P}{P^*}, G, T\right) \qquad [12.1]$$

Output, Y, depends on the real exchange rate, $\bar{E}P/P^*$ ($\bar{E}$ denotes the fixed nominal exchange rate, and P and P^* denote the domestic and foreign price levels, respectively), government spending, G, and taxes, T. An increase in the real exchange rate – a real appreciation – leads to a decrease in output. An increase in government spending leads to an increase in output; an increase in taxes leads to a decrease in output.

Recall that the aggregate demand relation captures the effects of the price level on output. It is derived from equilibrium in goods and financial markets.

See equation (9.3).

Recall that, in a closed economy, the aggregate demand relation took the same form as equation (12.1), except for the presence of the real money stock, M/P, instead of the real exchange rate, ε.

● The reason for the presence of M/P in a closed economy was the following: by controlling the money supply, the central bank could change the interest rate and affect output. In an open economy, and under fixed exchange rates and perfect capital mobility, the central bank can no longer change the interest rate – which is pinned down by the foreign interest rate. Put another way, under fixed exchange rates, the central bank gives up monetary policy as a policy instrument. This is why the money stock no longer appears in the aggregate demand relation.

● At the same time, the fact that the economy is open implies that we must include a variable that we did not include when we looked at the closed economy earlier: the real exchange rate, ε. As we saw earlier (in Chapter 7), an increase in the real exchange rate leads to a decrease in the demand for domestic goods and thus a decrease in output. Conversely, a decrease in the real exchange rate leads to an increase in output.

Note that, just as in a closed economy, the aggregate demand relation (12.1) implies a negative relation between the price level and output. But, while the sign of the effect of the price level on output remains the same, the channel is very different:

● In a closed economy, the price level affects output through its effect on the real money stock and, in turn, its effect on the interest rate.

● In an open economy under fixed exchange rates, the price level affects output through its effect on the real exchange rate. Given the fixed nominal exchange rate, E, and the foreign price level, P^*, an increase in the domestic price level, P, leads to an increase in the real exchange rate – a real appreciation. This real appreciation leads to a decrease in the demand for domestic goods and, in turn, to a decrease in output. Put simply: an increase in the price level makes domestic goods more expensive, thus decreasing the demand for domestic goods and, in turn, decreasing output.

Aggregate demand relation in the open economy under fixed exchange rates: P increases $\Rightarrow$ $\bar{E}P/P^*$ increases $\Rightarrow$ Y decreases.

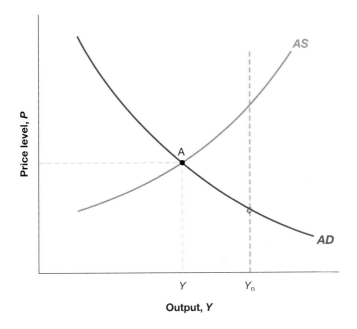

Figure 12.1

Aggregate demand and aggregate supply in an open economy under fixed exchange rates

An increase in the price level leads to a real appreciation and a decrease in output: the aggregate demand curve is downward sloping. An increase in output leads to an increase in the price level: the aggregate supply curve is upward sloping.

Equilibrium in the short run and in the medium run

The aggregate demand curve associated with equation (12.1) is drawn as the *AD* curve in Figure 12.1. It is downward sloping: an increase in the price level decreases output. As always, the relation is drawn for given values of the other variables, in this case for given values of $\bar{E}$, P^*, G and T.

For the aggregate supply curve, we rely on the relation we derived in the core. Going back to the aggregate supply relation we derived earlier (in Chapter 9), equation (9.2).

$$P = P^e(1 + \mu)\left(1 - \frac{Y}{L}, z\right)$$ [12.2]

> Recall that the aggregate supply relation captures the effects of output on the price level. It is derived from equilibrium in labour markets.

The price level, P, depends on the expected price level, P^e, and on the level of output, Y. Recall the two mechanisms at work:

- The expected price level matters because it affects nominal wages, which in turn affect the price level.
- Higher output matters because it leads to higher employment, which leads to lower unemployment, which leads to higher wages, which leads to a higher price level.

> Aggregate supply relation: Y increases $\Rightarrow P$ increases.

The aggregate supply curve is drawn as the *AS* curve in Figure 12.1 for a given value of the expected price level. It is upward sloping: higher output leads to a higher price level.

The short-run equilibrium is given by the intersection of the aggregate demand curve and the aggregate supply curve, point A in Figure 12.1. As is the case in a closed economy, there is no reason why the short-run equilibrium level of output, Y, should be equal to the natural level of output, Y_n. As the figure is drawn, Y is smaller than Y_n, so output is below the natural level of output.

What happens over time? The basic answer is familiar from our earlier look at adjustment in a closed economy, and is shown in Figure 12.2. As long as output remains below the natural level of output, the aggregate supply shifts down. The reason: when output is below the natural level of output, the price level turns out to be lower than was expected. This leads wage setters to revise their expectation of the price level downward, leading to a lower price level at a given level of output – hence, the downward shift of the aggregate supply curve. So, starting from A, the economy moves over time along the aggregate demand curve until it reaches B. At B, output is equal to the natural level of output. The price level is lower than it was at A; by implication, the real exchange rate is lower than it was at A.

> Make sure you understand this step. If you need a refresher, return to section 9.1.

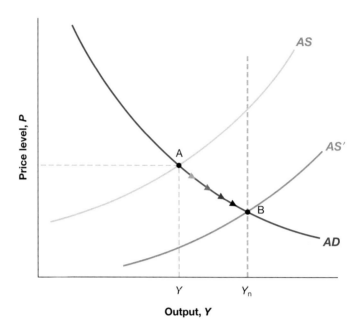

Figure 12.2

Adjustment under fixed exchange rates

The aggregate supply curve shifts down over time, leading to a decrease in the price level, to a real depreciation and to an increase in output. The process ends when output has returned to its natural level.

In words: as long as output is below the natural level of output, the price level decreases. The decrease in the price level over time leads to a steady real depreciation. This real depreciation then leads to an increase in output until output has returned to its natural level.

In the medium run, despite the fact that the nominal exchange rate is fixed, the economy still achieves the real depreciation needed to return output to its natural level. This is an important qualification to the conclusions we reached in the previous chapter – where we were focusing only on the short run.

The result that the price level decreases along the path of adjustment comes from our assumption that the foreign price level is constant. If we had assumed instead that the foreign price level was increasing over time, what would be needed would be for the domestic price level to increase less than the foreign price level or, put another way, for domestic inflation to be lower than foreign inflation for some time.

- In the short run, a fixed nominal exchange rate implies a fixed real exchange rate.
- In the medium run, the real exchange rate can adjust even if the nominal exchange rate is fixed. This adjustment is achieved through movements in the price level.

The case for and against a devaluation

The result that, even under fixed exchange rates, the economy returns to the natural level of output in the medium run is important. But it does not eliminate the fact that the process of adjustment may be long and painful. Output may remain too low and unemployment may remain too high for a long time.

Are there faster and better ways to return output to normal? The answer, within the model we have just developed, is a clear yes.

Suppose that the government decides, while keeping the fixed exchange rate regime, to allow for a one-time devaluation. For a given price level, a devaluation (a decrease in the nominal exchange rate) leads to a real depreciation (a decrease in the real exchange rate) and, therefore, to an increase in output. In other words, a devaluation shifts the aggregate demand curve to the right: output is higher at a given price level.

This has a straightforward implication: a devaluation of the right size can take the economy directly from Y to Y_n. This is shown in Figure 12.3. Suppose the economy is initially at A, the same point A as in Figure 12.2. The right size depreciation shifts the aggregate demand curve from AD to AD'', moving the equilibrium from A to C. At C, output is equal to the natural level of output, Y_n, and the real exchange rate is the same as at B. (We know this

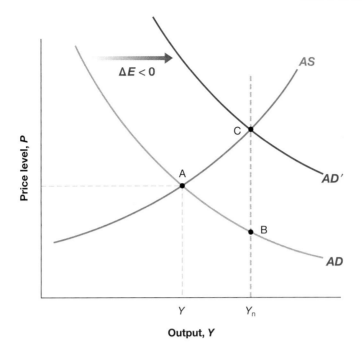

Figure 12.3

Adjustment with a devaluation

A devaluation of the right size can shift aggregate demand to the right, moving the economy to point C. At point C, output is back to the natural level of output.

because output is the same at points B and C. From equation (12.1), and without changes in G or T, this implies that the real exchange rate must also be the same.)

That a devaluation of the 'right size' can return output to the natural level of output right away sounds too good to be true – and, in reality, it is. Achieving the 'right size' devaluation – the devaluation that takes output to Y_n right away – is easier to achieve in a graph than in reality:

- In contrast to our simple aggregate demand relation (see equation (12.1)), the effects of the depreciation on output do not happen right away: as you saw earlier (in Chapter 7), the initial effects of a depreciation on output can be contractionary, as people pay more for imports, and the quantities of imports and exports have not adjusted yet.
- Also, in contrast to our simple aggregate supply relation (see equation (12.2)), there is likely to be a direct effect of the devaluation on the price level. As the price of imported goods increases, the price of a consumption basket increases. This increase is likely to lead workers to ask for higher nominal wages, forcing firms to increase their prices as well.

◀ See section 7.3 on the J-curve.

But these complications do not affect the basic conclusion: a devaluation can hasten the return of output to its natural level. And so, whenever a country under fixed exchange rates faces either a large trade deficit or a severe recession, there is a lot of political pressure either to give up the fixed exchange rate regime altogether, or, at least, to have a one-time devaluation. Perhaps the most forceful presentation of this view was made more than 80 years ago by Keynes, who argued against Winston Churchill's decision to return the British pound in 1925 to its pre-First World War parity with gold. His arguments are presented in the Focus box 'The return of Britain to the gold standard: Keynes versus Churchill'. Most economic historians believe that history proved Keynes right, and that overvaluation of the pound was one of the main reasons for Britain's poor economic performance after the First World War.

Those who oppose a shift to flexible exchange rates or who oppose a devaluation argue that there are good reasons to choose fixed exchange rates and that too much willingness to devalue defeats the purpose of adopting a fixed exchange rate regime in the first place. They argue that too much willingness on the part of governments to consider devaluations actually leads to an increased likelihood of exchange rate crises. To understand their arguments, we now turn to these crises, what triggers them and what their implications might be.

12.2 EXCHANGE RATE CRISES UNDER FIXED EXCHANGE RATES

Suppose a country has chosen to operate under a fixed exchange rate. Suppose also that financial investors start believing that there may soon be an exchange rate adjustment – either a devaluation or a shift to a flexible exchange rate regime accompanied by a depreciation.

We just saw why this might be the case:

- The real exchange rate may be too high. Or, put another way, the domestic currency may be overvalued. In this case, a real depreciation is called for. Although this could be achieved in the medium run without a devaluation, financial investors might conclude that the government will take the quickest way out – and devalue.

FOCUS
The return of Britain to the gold standard: Keynes versus Churchill

In 1925, Britain decided to return to the **gold standard**. The gold standard was a system in which each country fixed the price of its currency in terms of gold and stood ready to exchange gold for currency at the stated parity. This system implied fixed exchange rates between countries.

The gold standard had been in place from 1870 until the First World War. Because of the need to finance the war, and to do so in part by money creation, Britain suspended the gold standard in 1914. In 1925, Winston Churchill, then Britain's Chancellor of the Exchequer (the English equivalent of Secretary of the Treasury in the USA), decided to return to the gold standard and to return to it at the pre-war parity – that is, at the pre-war value of the pound in terms of gold. But because prices had increased faster in Britain than in many of its trading partners, returning to the pre-war parity implied a large real appreciation: at the same nominal exchange rate as before the war, British goods were now relatively more expensive relative to foreign goods. (Go back to the definition of the real exchange rate, $\varepsilon = EP/P^*$: the price level in Britain, P, had increased more than the foreign price level, P^*. At a given nominal exchange rate, E, this implied that ε was higher and that Britain suffered from a real appreciation.)

Keynes severely criticised the decision to return to the pre-war parity. In *The Economic Consequences of Mr Churchill*, a book he published in 1925, Keynes argued that if Britain were going to return to the gold standard, it should have done so at a lower price of currency in terms of gold – that is, at a lower nominal exchange rate than the pre-war nominal exchange rate. In a newspaper article, he articulated his views as follows:

There remains, however, the objection to which I have never ceased to attach importance, against the return to gold in actual present conditions in view of the possible consequences on the state of trade and employment. I believe that our price level is too high, if it is converted to gold at the par of exchange, in relation to gold prices elsewhere; and if we consider the prices of those articles only which are not the subject of international trade, and of services, i.e. wages, we shall find that these are materially too high – not less than 5 per cent, and probably 10 per cent. Thus, unless the situation is saved by a rise of prices elsewhere, the Chancellor is committing us to a policy of forcing down money wages by perhaps 2 shillings in the Pound.

I do not believe that this can be achieved without the gravest danger to industrial profits and industrial peace. I would much rather leave the gold value of our currency where it was some months ago than embark on a struggle with every trade union in the country to reduce money wages. It seems wiser and simpler and saner to leave the currency to find its own level for some time longer rather than force a situation where employers are faced with the alternative of closing down or of lowering wages, cost what the struggle may.

For this reason, I remain of the opinion that the Chancellor of the Exchequer has done an ill-judged thing – ill-judged because we are running the risk for no adequate reward if all goes well.

Keynes's prediction turned out to be right. While other countries were growing, Britain remained in recession for the rest of the decade. Most economic historians attribute a good part of the blame to the initial overvaluation.

Source: *The Nation and Athenaeum*, 2 May 1925.

Such an overvaluation is likely to happen in a country that pegs its nominal exchange rate to the currency of a country with lower inflation. Higher relative inflation implies a steadily increasing price of domestic goods relative to foreign goods, a steady real appreciation, and so a steady worsening of the trade position. As time passes, the need for an adjustment of the real exchange rate increases, and financial investors become more and more nervous. They start thinking that a devaluation might be coming.

- Internal conditions may call for a decrease in the domestic interest rate. As we have seen, a decrease in the domestic interest rate cannot be achieved under fixed exchange rates, but it can be achieved if the country is willing to shift to a flexible exchange rate regime. If a country lets the exchange rate float and then decreases its domestic interest rate, we know (from Chapter 7) that this will trigger a decrease in the nominal exchange rate – a nominal depreciation. Because it is more convenient, we use the approximation, equation (6.4), rather than the original interest parity condition, equation (6.2).

As soon as financial markets believe a devaluation may be coming, maintaining the exchange rate requires an increase – often a large one – in the domestic interest rate. To see this, return to the interest parity condition we derived earlier (in Chapter 6):

$$i_t = i_t^* - \frac{(E_{t+1}^e - E_t)}{E_t} \qquad [12.3]$$

There, we interpreted this equation as a relation between the one-year domestic and foreign nominal interest rates, the current exchange rate and the expected exchange rate a year hence, but the choice of one year as the period was arbitrary. The relation holds over a day, a week or a month. If financial markets expect the exchange rate to be 2% lower one month from now, they will hold domestic bonds only if the one-month domestic interest rate exceeds the one-month foreign interest rate by 2% (or, if we express interest rates at an annual rate, if the annual domestic interest rate exceeds the annual foreign interest rate by $2\% \times 12 = 24\%$).

Under fixed exchange rates, the current exchange rate, E_t, is set at some level, $E_t = \bar{E}$. If markets expect that the parity will be maintained over the period, then $E_{t+1}^e = \bar{E}$, and the interest parity condition simply states that the domestic and the foreign interest rates must be equal.

Suppose, however, that participants in financial markets start anticipating a devaluation a decrease in the exchange rate. Suppose they believe that, over the coming month, there is a 75% chance the parity will be maintained and a 25% chance there will be a 20% devaluation. The term in the interest parity equation (12.3), which we assumed equal to 0 earlier, now equals $0.75 \times 0\% + 0.25 \times 20\% = 5\%$ (that is, a 75% chance of no change plus a 25% chance of a devaluation of 20%).

This implies that, if the central bank wants to maintain the existing parity, it must now set a monthly interest rate 5% higher than before – 60% higher at an annual rate (12 months × 5% per month) is the interest differential needed to convince investors to hold domestic bonds rather than foreign bonds! Any smaller interest differential, and investors will not want to hold domestic bonds.

What choices, then, do the government and the central bank have?

- First, the government and the central bank can try to convince markets that they have no intention of devaluing. This is always the first line of defence: communiqués are issued and prime ministers go on TV to reiterate their absolute commitment to the existing parity. But words are cheap, and they rarely convince financial investors.
- Second, the central bank can increase the interest rate but by less than would be needed to satisfy equation (12.3) – in our example, by less than 60%. Although domestic interest rates are high, they are not high enough to fully compensate for the perceived risk of devaluation. This action typically leads to a large capital outflow because financial investors still prefer to get out of domestic bonds into foreign bonds. They sell domestic bonds, getting the proceeds in domestic currency. They then go to the foreign exchange

In most countries, the government is formally in charge of choosing the parity, and the central bank is formally in charge of maintaining it. In practice, choosing and maintaining the parity are joint responsibilities of the government and the central bank.

FOCUS
The 1992 EMS crisis

An example of the problems we are discussing in section 12.2 is the exchange rate crisis that shook the European Monetary System (EMS) in the early 1990s.

At the start of the 1990s, the EMS appeared to work well. The EMS, which had started in 1979, was an exchange rate system based on fixed parities with bands: each member country (among them, France, Germany, Italy and, beginning in 1990, the UK) had to maintain its exchange rate vis-à-vis all other member countries within narrow bands. The first few years had been rocky, with many realignments – adjustment of parities – among member countries. From 1987 to 1992, however, there were only two realignments, and there was increasing talk about narrowing the bands further and even moving to the next stage – to the adoption of a common currency.

In 1992, however, financial markets became increasingly convinced that more realignments were soon to come. The reason was one we have already seen (in Chapter 7) – namely, the macroeconomic implications of Germany's reunication. Because of the pressure on demand coming from reunication, the Bundesbank (the German central bank) was maintaining high interest rates to avoid too large an increase in output and an increase in inflation in Germany. While Germany's EMS partners needed lower interest rates to reduce the growing unemployment problem, they had to match the German interest rates to maintain their EMS parities. To financial markets, the position of Germany's EMS partners looked increasingly untenable. Lower interest rates outside Germany, and thus devaluations of many currencies vis-à-vis the Deutschmark, appeared increasingly likely.

Throughout 1992, the perceived probability of a devaluation forced a number of EMS countries to maintain higher nominal interest rates than even those in Germany.

Still, the first major crisis did not come until September 1992.

In early September 1992, the belief that a number of countries were soon going to devalue led to speculative attacks on a number of currencies, with financial investors selling in anticipation of an oncoming devaluation. All the lines of defence described earlier were used by the monetary authorities and the governments of the countries under attack. First, solemn communiqués were issued, but with no discernible effect. Then, interest rates were increased. For example, Sweden's overnight interest rate (the rate for lending and borrowing overnight) increased to 500% (expressed at an annual rate)! But interest rates were not increased by enough to prevent capital outflows and large losses of foreign exchange reserves by the central banks under pressure.

At that point, different countries took different courses of action: Spain devalued its exchange rate. Italy and the UK suspended their participation in the EMS. France decided to tough it out through higher interest rates until the storm was over. Figure 12.4 shows the evolution of the exchange rates vis-à-vis the Deutschmark for a number of European countries from January 1992 to December 1993: you can clearly see the effects of the September 1992 crisis and the ensuing depreciations/devaluations.

By the end of September, investors, by and large, believed that no further devaluations were imminent. Some countries were no longer in the EMS. Others had devalued but remained in the EMS, and those that had maintained their parity had shown their determination to stay in the EMS, even if it meant very high interest rates. But the underlying problem – the high German interest rates – was still present, and it was only a matter of time before the next crisis started. In November 1992, further

market to sell domestic currency for foreign currency in order to buy foreign bonds. If the central bank did not intervene in the foreign exchange market, the large sales of domestic currency for foreign currency would lead to a depreciation. If it wants to maintain the exchange rate, the central bank must therefore stand ready to buy domestic currency and sell foreign currency at the current exchange rate. In doing so, it often loses most of its reserves of foreign currency.

● Eventually – after a few hours or a few weeks – the choice for the central bank becomes either to increase the interest rate enough to satisfy equation (12.3), or to validate the market's expectations and devalue. Setting a very high short-term domestic interest rate can have a devastating effect on demand and on output – no firm wants to invest and no consumer wants to borrow when interest rates are very high. This course of action makes sense only if (1) the perceived probability of a devaluation is small, so the interest rate

> In the summer of 1998, Boris Yeltsin announced that the Russian government had no intention of devaluing the rouble. Two weeks later, the rouble collapsed.

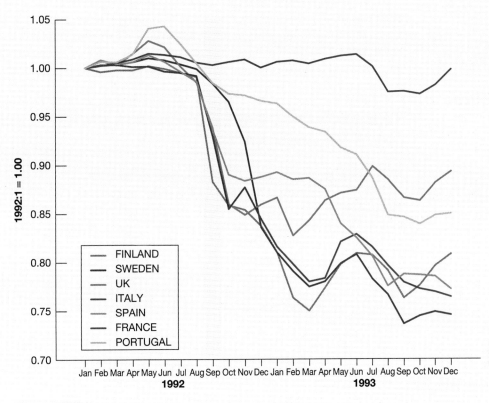

Figure 12.4

Exchange rates of selected European countries relative to the Deutschmark, January 1992–December 1993

speculation forced a devaluation of the Spanish peseta, the Portuguese escudo and the Swedish krona. The peseta and the escudo were further devalued in May 1993. In July 1993, after yet another large speculative attack, EMS countries decided to adopt large fluctuation bands (±15%) around central parities, in effect moving to a system that allowed for very large exchange rate fluctuations. This system with wider bands was kept until the adoption of a common currency, the euro, in January 1999.

To summarise: the 1992 EMS crisis resulted from the perception by financial markets that the high interest rates forced by Germany upon its partners under the rules of the EMS were becoming very costly. The belief that some countries might want to devalue or get out of the EMS led investors to ask for even higher interest rates, making it even more costly for those countries to maintain their parity. In the end, some countries could not bear the cost; some devalued and some dropped out. Others remained in the system but at a substantial cost in terms of output. (For example, average growth in France from 1990 to 1996 was 1.2%, compared to 2.3% for Germany over the same period.)

does not have to be too high, and (2) the government believes markets will soon become convinced that no devaluation is coming, allowing domestic interest rates to decrease. Otherwise, the only option is to devalue. (All these steps were very much in evidence during the exchange rate crisis that affected much of Western Europe in 1992. See the Focus box 'The 1992 EMS crisis'.)

To summarise, expectations that a devaluation may be coming can trigger an exchange rate crisis. Faced with such expectations, the government has two options:

- Give in and devalue.
- Fight and maintain the parity, at the cost of very high interest rates and a potential recession. Fighting may not work anyway: the recession may force the government to change policy later on or force the government out of office.

An interesting twist here is that a devaluation can occur even if the belief that a devaluation was coming was initially groundless. In other words, even if the government initially has no intention of devaluing, it might be forced to do so if financial markets believe that it will devalue: the cost of maintaining the parity would be a long period of high interest rates and a recession; the government might prefer to devalue instead.

12.3 EXCHANGE RATE MOVEMENTS UNDER FLEXIBLE EXCHANGE RATES

In the model we developed earlier (in Chapter 7), there was a simple relation between the interest rate and the exchange rate: the lower the interest rate, the lower the exchange rate. This implied that a country that wanted to maintain a stable exchange rate just had to maintain its interest rate close to the foreign interest rate. A country that wanted to achieve a given depreciation just had to decrease its interest rate by the right amount.

In reality, the relation between the interest rate and the exchange rate is not so simple. Exchange rates often move even in the absence of movements in interest rates. Furthermore, the size of the effect of a given change in the interest rate on the exchange rate is hard to predict. This makes it much harder for monetary policy to achieve its desired outcome.

To see why things are more complicated, we must return once again to the interest parity condition we derived earlier (in Chapter 6):

$$(1 + i_t) = (1 + i_t^*)\left(\frac{E_t}{E_{t+1}^e}\right)$$

As we did in equation (8.11), we multiply both sides by E_{t+1}^e, and reorganise to get

$$E_t = \frac{1 + i_t}{1 + i_t^*} E_{t+1}^e \qquad [12.4]$$

Think of the time period (from t to $t + 1$) as one year. The exchange rate this year depends on the one-year domestic interest rate, the one-year foreign interest rate and the exchange rate expected for next year.

We assumed (in Chapter 7) that the expected exchange rate next year was constant, but that was a simplification. The exchange rate expected one year hence is not constant. Using equation (12.4), but now for next year, it is clear that the exchange rate next year will depend on next year's one-year domestic interest rate, the one-year foreign interest rate, the exchange rate expected for the year after and so on. So, any change in expectations of current and future domestic and foreign interest rates, as well as changes in the expected exchange rate in the far future, will affect the exchange rate today.

Let's explore this more closely. Write equation (12.4) for year $t + 1$ rather than for year t:

$$E_{t+1} = \frac{1 + i_{t+1}}{1 + i_{t+1}^*} E_{t+2}^e$$

The exchange rate in year $t + 1$ depends on the domestic interest rate and the foreign interest rate for year $t + 1$, as well as on the expected future exchange rate in year $t + 2$. So, the expectation of the exchange rate in year $t + 1$, held as of year t, is given by

$$E_{t+1}^e = \frac{1 + i_{t+1}^e}{1 + i_{t+1}^{*e}} E_{t+2}^e$$

Replacing E_{t+1}^e in equation (12.4) with this expression gives

$$E_t = \frac{(1 + i_t)(1 + i_{t+1}^e)}{(1 + i_t^*)(1 + i_{t+1}^{*e})} E_{t+2}^e$$

The current exchange rate depends on this year's domestic and foreign interest rates, on next year's expected domestic and foreign interest rates, and on the expected exchange rate two years from now. Continuing to solve forward in time in the same way (by replacing E^e_{t+2}, E^e_{t+3} and so on until, say, year $t+n$) we get

$$E_t = \frac{(1+i_t)(1+i^e_{t+1}) \cdots (1+i^e_{t+n})}{(1+i^*_t)(1+i^{*e}_{t+1}) \cdots (1+i^{*e}_{t+1})} E^e_{t+n+1} \qquad [12.5]$$

Suppose we take n to be large, say, ten years (equation (12.5) holds for any value of n). This relation tells us that the current exchange rate depends on two sets of factors:

● Current and expected domestic and foreign interest rates for each year over the next ten years.
● The expected exchange rate ten years from now.

For some purposes, it is useful to go further and derive a relation between current and expected future domestic and foreign real interest rates, the current real exchange rate and the expected future real exchange rate. (The derivation is not much fun, but it is a useful way of brushing up on the relations between real and nominal interest rates and between real and nominal exchange rates.) Equation (12.5) is sufficient, however, to make the three points we want to make here.

Exchange rates and the current account

Any factor that moves the expected future exchange rate, E^e_{t+1}, moves the current exchange rate, E_t. Indeed, if the domestic interest rate and the foreign interest rate are expected to be the same in both countries from t to $t+n$, the fraction on the right in equation (12.5) is equal to 1, so the relation reduces to $E_t = E^e_{t+n}$. In words: the effect of any change in the expected future exchange rate on the current exchange rate is one-for-one.

If we think of n as large (say, ten years or more), we can think of E^e_{t+n} as the exchange rate required to achieve current account balance in the medium or long run: countries cannot borrow – run a current account deficit – forever and will not want to lend – run a current account surplus – forever either. Thus, any news that affects forecasts of the current account balance in the future is likely to have an effect on the expected future exchange rate and, in turn, on the exchange rate today. For example, the announcement of a larger-than-expected trade deficit may lead investors to conclude that a depreciation will eventually be needed to reestablish trade balance. Thus, E^e_{t+n} will decrease, leading in turn to a decrease in E_t today.

◄ News about the current account is likely to affect the exchange rate.

Exchange rates and current and future interest rates

Any factor that moves current or expected future domestic or foreign interest rates between year t and year $t+n$ moves the current exchange rate, too. For example, given foreign interest rates, an increase in current or expected future domestic interest rates leads to an increase in E_t – an appreciation.

◄ News about current and future domestic and foreign interest rates is likely to affect the exchange rate.

This implies that any variable which causes investors to change their expectations of future interest rates will lead to a change in the exchange rate today. For example, the dance of the dollar in the 1980s we discussed in earlier chapters – the sharp appreciation of the dollar in the first half of the decade, followed by an equally sharp depreciation later – can be largely explained by the movement in current and expected future US interest rates relative to interest rates in the rest of the world during that period. During the first half of the 1980s, tight monetary policy and expansionary fiscal policy combined to increase US short-term and long-term interest rates, with the increase in long-term rates reflecting anticipations of high short-term interest rates in the future. This increase in both current and expected future interest rates was, in turn, the main cause of the dollar appreciation. Both fiscal and monetary policy were reversed in the second half of the decade, leading to lower US interest rates and a depreciation of the dollar. (For more on the relation between long-term interest rates and current and expected future short-term interest rates, go to Chapter 16.)

Exchange rate volatility

The third implication follows from the first two. In reality, and in contrast to our analysis earlier (in Chapter 7), the relation between the interest rate, i_t, and the exchange rate, E_t, is all but mechanical. When the central bank cuts the interest rate, financial markets have to assess whether this action signals a major shift in monetary policy and the cut in the interest rate is just the first of many such cuts, or whether this cut is just a temporary movement in interest rates. Announcements by the central bank may not be very useful: the central bank itself may not even know what it will do in the future. Typically, it will be reacting to early signals, which may be reversed later. Investors also have to assess how foreign central banks will react – whether they will stay put or follow suit and cut their own interest rates. All this makes it difficult to predict what the effect of the change in the interest rate will be on the exchange rate.

Let us be more concrete. Go back to equation (12.5). Assume that $E^e_{t+n} = 1$. Assume that current and expected future domestic interest rates and current and expected future foreign interest rates are all equal to 5%. The current exchange rate is then given by

$$E_t = \frac{1.05^n}{1.05^n} 1 = 1$$

Now consider a monetary expansion that decreases the current domestic interest rate, it, from 5% to 3%. Will this lead to a decrease in E_t – to a depreciation – and if so by how much? The answer: it depends.

Suppose the interest rate is expected to be lower for just one year, so the $n - 1$ expected future interest rates remain unchanged. The current exchange rate then decreases to

$$E_t = \frac{(1.03)(1.05)^{n-1}}{(1.05)^n} = \frac{1.03}{1.05} = 0.98$$

The expansionary monetary policy leads to a decrease in the exchange rate – a depreciation – of only 2%.

Suppose instead that, when the current interest rate declines from 5% to 3%, investors expect the decline to last for five years (so $i_{t+4} = \cdots = i_{t+1} = i_t = 3\%$). The exchange rate then decreases to

$$E_t = \frac{(1.03)^5(1.05)^{n+5}}{(1.05)^n} = \frac{(1.03)^5}{(1.05)^5} = 0.90$$

The expansionary monetary policy now leads to a decrease in the exchange rate – a depreciation – of 10%, a much larger effect.

You can surely think of yet other outcomes. Suppose investors anticipated that the central bank was going to decrease interest rates, and the actual decrease turns out to be smaller than they anticipated. In this case, the investors will revise their expectations of future nominal interest rates upward, leading to an appreciation rather than a depreciation of the currency.

When, at the end of the Bretton Woods period, countries moved from fixed exchange rates to flexible exchange rates, most economists had expected that exchange rates would be stable. The large fluctuations in exchange rates that followed – and have continued to this day – came as a surprise. For some time, these fluctuations were thought to be the result of irrational speculation in foreign exchange markets. It was not until the mid-1970s that economists realised that these large movements could be explained, as we have explained them here, by the rational reaction of financial markets to news about future interest rates and the future exchange rate. This has an important implication: a country that decides to operate under flexible exchange rates must accept the fact that it will be exposed to substantial exchange rate fluctuations over time.

12.4 CHOOSING BETWEEN EXCHANGE RATE REGIMES

Let us now return to the question that motivates this chapter: should countries choose flexible exchange rates or fixed exchange rates? Are there circumstances under which flexible rates dominate and others under which fixed rates dominate?

Much of what we have seen in this chapter and earlier (Chapter 7) would seem to favour flexible exchange rates:

- Section 12.1 argues that the exchange rate regime may not matter in the medium run. But it does still matter in the short run. In the short run, countries that operate under fixed exchange rates and perfect capital mobility give up two macroeconomic instruments: the interest rate and the exchange rate. This not only reduces their ability to respond to shocks, but can also lead to exchange rate crises.
- Section 12.2 argues that, in a country with fixed exchange rates, the anticipation of a devaluation leads investors to ask for very high interest rates. This in turn makes the economic situation worse and puts more pressure on the country to devalue. This is another argument against fixed exchange rates.
- Section 12.3 introduces one argument against flexible exchange rates – namely that, under flexible exchange rates, the exchange rate is likely to fluctuate a lot and be difficult to control through monetary policy.

On balance, it would therefore appear that, from a macroeconomic viewpoint, flexible exchange rates dominate fixed exchange rates. This indeed appears to be the consensus that has emerged among economists and policy makers. The consensus goes like this: in general, flexible exchange rates are preferable. There are, however, two exceptions: first, when the central bank cannot be trusted to follow a responsible monetary policy under flexible exchange rates, a strong form of fixed exchange rates, such as a currency board or dollarisation, may provide a solution. Second, when a group of countries is already tightly integrated, a common currency may be the right solution.

Let's discuss in turn each of these two exceptions.

Hard pegs, currency boards and dollarisation

The second case for fixed exchange rates is very different from the first. It is based on the argument that there may be times when a country might want to limit its ability to use monetary policy. We shall look at this argument later (in Chapter 23), where we look at monetary policy in general. The essence of the argument is simple: look at a country that has had very high inflation in the recent past – perhaps because it was unable to finance its budget deficit by any means other than through money creation, resulting in high money growth and high inflation. Suppose the country decides to reduce money growth and inflation. One way of convincing financial markets that it is serious about doing this is to fix its exchange rate: the need to use the money supply to maintain the parity then ties the hands of the monetary authority.

To the extent that financial markets expect the parity to be maintained, they will stop worrying about money growth being used to finance the budget deficit.

Note the qualifier 'to the extent that financial markets expect the parity to be maintained'. Fixing the exchange rate is not a magic solution. The country also needs to convince financial investors that not only is the exchange rate fixed today, but it will also remain fixed in the future.

There are two ways it can do so:

- It can make the fixed exchange rate be part of a more general macroeconomic package. Fixing the exchange rate while continuing to run a large budget deficit will only convince financial markets that money growth will start again and that a devaluation is soon to come. When Israel was suffering from high inflation in the 1980s, an Israeli finance minister proposed such a measure as part of a stabilisation programme. His proposal was perceived as an attack on the sovereignty of Israel, and he was quickly fired.
- It can make it symbolically or technically harder to change the parity, an approach known as a **hard peg**.

An extreme form of a hard peg is simply to replace the domestic currency with a foreign currency. Because the foreign currency chosen is typically the dollar, this is known as **dollarisation**. Few countries are willing, however, to give up their currency and adopt

FOCUS
Currency boards in the Baltic countries

After regaining independence from the Soviet Union in the second half of 1991, the Baltic countries began economic reforms, of which currency reform was a major component. Estonia was the first country to abandon the Russian rouble and to introduce its own national currency in 1992. With the Argentinian experience with a currency board in the background – believed to have contributed importantly to monetary stability in a country that had in the past found it impossible to commit to fiscal discipline – Jeffrey Sachs, then Professor of Economics at Harvard University, proposed to Siim Kallas, then the Governor of the Bank of Estonia, that Estonia adopt a currency board arrangement (CBA).

The Estonian CBA ruled that the Bank of Estonia was committed to exchange local currency (including deposits of commercial banks) into foreign currency. The foreign currency that the kroon was pegged to was the Deutschmark (the ECU was initially considered as a peg, given the aspiration to ultimately join the EU, but such a peg would not have been as transparent as a well-known currency). The CBA allowed Estonia to immediately solve two problems:

- The problem of resisting demands for credit from the government and enterprises, as the CBA forbad central bank credit to both of them, and lending to banks could occur only under exceptional circumstances.
- The problem of managing an independent monetary policy, as the CBA left no scope for discretionary monetary policy.

The CBA also provided a framework for fiscal policy: any budget deficit had to be constrained to what could be financed in the domestic market outside the Bank of Estonia, which at that time was close to zero, implying that the budget needed to be roughly balanced. The kroon quickly became a symbol of the quest for independence and this enabled the government to introduce often painful adjustment measures (keeping the budget balanced, shutting down insolvent banks, pushing forwards an aggressive privatisation policy) which were of central importance in creating a stable macroeconomic environment.

Following Estonia, Lithuania also adopted a CBA in 1994. The CBA in Lithuania has also been associated with an improvement of macroeconomic stability: that is, a steady slowing of inflation. This in turn has had positive effects on output growth. Overall, currency boards have been useful in achieving macroeconomic stability in the Baltic countries' particular circumstances, but it can also be argued that the same results could have been achieved under a different exchange rate regime. In Lithuania, inflation had already been reduced after the introduction of the litas in mid-1993, so its importance should not be overplayed. Part of the reason for adopting a CBA – with inflation already on the fall – was precisely because of its effects on fiscal discipline: introducing a currency board, which prevents lending to the government, removed the temptation to use the central bank to finance the deficit.

The Estonian CBA worked for almost 20 years. On 1 January 2011 Estonia joined the European Monetary Union and adopted the euro.

Sources: Adalbert Knöbl, Andres Sutt and Basil Zavoico (1996), 'The Estonian Currency Board: its introduction and role in the early success of Estonia's transition to a market economy', *IMF Working Paper* 02/96. Iikka Korhonen (2000), 'Currency boards in the Baltic countries: what have we learned?', *Post-Communist Economies*, 12(1).

the currency of another country. A less extreme way is the use of a **currency board**. Under a currency board, a central bank stands ready to exchange foreign currency for domestic currency at the official exchange rate set by the government; furthermore, the bank cannot engage in open market operations – that is, buy or sell government bonds.

Perhaps the best-known example of a currency board is that adopted by Argentina in 1991, but abandoned in a crisis at the end of 2001. Economists differ on what conclusions one should draw from what happened in Argentina. Some conclude that currency boards are not hard enough: they do not prevent exchange rate crises. So, if a country decides to adopt a fixed exchange rate, it should go all the way and dollarise. Others conclude that adopting a fixed exchange rate is a bad idea. If currency boards are used at all, they should be used only for a short period of time, until the central bank has re-established its credibility and the country returns to a floating exchange rate regime. Some European countries – Estonia and Lithuania – offer counter-examples of success stories with currency boards. We describe it in detail in the Focus box 'Currency boards in the Baltic countries'. Although few would have expected that those currency board would work, it actually served well. Afterwards, other countries – Bulgaria and Bosnia-Herzegovina – adopted such an exchange rate arrangement and today currency boards are no longer regarded as historical peculiarities, nor as necessarily temporary arrangements.

◄ Hong Kong's currency board – another well-known example – has been in place for nearly three decades.

Common currency areas

Looking around the world, one sees many examples of groups of countries forming a currency union: that is, adopting a single currency run by a single central bank. This kind of arrangement applies to the euro area, where 17 countries have adopted a single currency. There are important arrangement also outside Europe. Six West African states created a new common currency for the region in 2003, and 11 members of the Southern African Development Community are debating whether to adopt the dollar or to create an independent monetary union possibly anchored to the South African rand. Six oil-producing countries (Saudi Arabia, United Arab Emirates, Bahrain, Oman, Qatar and Kuwait) have declared their intention to form a currency union by 2010.

◄ Section 19.3 in Chapter 19 will deal with this in depth.

The Eastern Caribbean Currency Area (ECCA) and the CFA zone in Africa are intermediate between the a currency union and a hard peg. In both cases, the countries have a joint currency and a joint central bank. However, the ECCA currency (Caribbean dollar) has been linked since 1976 to the US dollar (and, before that, to the British pound), and the CFA franc has been tied (except for one devaluation) to the French franc (and now to the euro).

Countries that operate under a fixed exchange rate regime are constrained to all have the same interest rate. But how costly is that constraint? If the countries face roughly the same macroeconomic problems and the same shocks, they will have chosen similar policies in the first place. Forcing them to have the same monetary policy may not be much of a constraint.

This argument was first explored by Robert Mundell, who looked at the conditions under which a set of countries might want to operate under fixed exchange rates or even adopt a common currency. For countries to constitute an **optimal currency area**, Mundell argued, they need to satisfy one of two conditions:

◄ This is the same Mundell who put together the *IS–LM* model we introduced earlier (in Chapter 9).

● The countries have to experience similar shocks. We just saw the rationale for this: if they experience similar shocks, then they would have chosen roughly the same monetary policy anyway.

● If the countries experience different shocks, they must have high factor mobility. For example, if workers are willing to move from countries that are doing poorly to countries that are doing well, factor mobility rather than macroeconomic policy can allow countries to adjust to shocks. When the unemployment rate is high in a country, workers leave that country to take jobs elsewhere, and the unemployment rate in that country decreases back to normal. If the unemployment rate is low, workers come to the country, and the unemployment rate in the country increases back to normal. The exchange rate is not needed.

Following Mundell's analysis, most economists believe, for example, that the common currency area composed of the 50 states of the USA is close to an optimal currency area. True, the first condition is not satisfied: individual states suffer from different shocks. California is more affected by shifts in demand from Asia than the rest of the USA, Texas is more affected by what happens to the price of oil and so on. But the second condition is largely satisfied. There is considerable labour mobility across states in the USA. When a state does poorly, workers leave that state. When it does well, workers come to that state. State unemployment rates quickly return to normal not because of state-level macro-economic policy but because of labour mobility.

Each US state could have its own currency that freely floated against other state currencies. But this is not the way things are: the USA is a common currency area, with one currency, the US dollar (whether it is optimal is an issue we will mention in Chapter 19).

Clearly, there are also many advantages of using a common currency. For firms and consumers within the USA, the benefits of having a common currency are obvious; imagine how complicated life would be if you had to change currency every time you crossed a state line. The benefits go beyond these lower transaction costs. When prices are quoted in the same currency, it becomes much easier for buyers to compare prices, and competition between firms increases, benefiting consumers. Given these benefits and the limited macroeconomic costs, it makes good sense for the USA to have a single currency.

In adopting the euro, Europe has made the same choice as the USA. When the process of conversion from national currencies to the euro ended in early 2002, the euro became the common currency for 11 European countries. The number of euro countries has now increased to 17. Is the economic argument for this new common currency area as compelling as it is for the USA? We will return to this later (in Chapter 19).

SUMMARY

- Even under a fixed exchange rate regime, countries can adjust their real exchange rate in the medium run. They can do this by relying on adjustments in the price level. Nevertheless, the adjustment can be long and painful. Exchange rate adjustments can allow the economy to adjust faster and thus reduce the pain that comes from a long adjustment.

- Exchange rate crises typically start when participants in financial markets believe a currency may soon be devalued. Defending the parity then requires very high interest rates, with potentially large adverse macroeconomic effects. These adverse effects may force the country to devalue, even if there were no initial plans for such a devaluation.

- The exchange rate today depends on both (1) the difference between current and expected future domestic interest rates and current and expected future foreign interest rates and (2) the expected future exchange rate. Any factor that increases current or expected future domestic interest rates leads to an increase in the exchange rate today. Any factor that increases current or expected future foreign interest rates leads to a decrease in the exchange rate today. Any factor that increases the expected future exchange rate leads to an increase in the exchange rate today.

- There is wide agreement among economists that exible exchange rate regimes generally dominate fixed exchange rate regimes, except in two cases:

  - When a group of countries is highly integrated and forms an optimal currency area (you can think of a common currency for a group of countries as an extreme form of fixed exchange rates among this group of countries). For countries to form an optimal currency area, they must face largely similar shocks, or there must be high labour mobility across these countries.

  - When a central bank cannot be trusted to follow a responsible monetary policy under exible exchange rates. In this case, a strong form of fixed exchange rates, such as dollarisation or a currency board, provides a way of tying the hands of the central bank.

KEY TERMS

gold standard 270

hard peg 278

dollarisation 278

currency board 279

optimal currency area 279

QUESTIONS AND PROBLEMS

QUICK CHECK

1. *Using the information in this chapter, label each of the following statements true, false or uncertain. Explain briefly.*

a. The UK's return to the gold standard caused years of high unemployment.

b. A sudden fear that a country is going to devalue may force an exchange rate crisis, even if the fear initially had no basis.

c. Because economies tend to return to their natural level of output in the medium run, there is a never a reason to devalue.

d. High labour mobility within Europe makes the euro area a good candidate for a common currency.

e. Changes in the expected level of the exchange rate far in the future have little effect on the current level of the exchange rate.

2. *Consider a country operating under fixed exchange rates, with aggregate demand and aggregate supply given by equations (12.1) and (12.2):*

$$AD: Y = Y\left(\frac{\bar{E}P}{P^*}, G, T\right)$$

$$AS: P = P^e(1 + \mu)F\left(1 - \frac{Y}{L}, z\right)$$

Assume that the economy is initially in medium-run equilibrium, with a constant price level and output equal to the natural level of output. Foreign output, the foreign price level and the foreign interest rate are fixed throughout the problem. Assume that expected (domestic) inflation remains constant throughout the problem.

a. Draw an *AD–AS* diagram for this economy.

b. Now suppose there is an increase in government spending. Show the effects on the *AD–AS* diagram in the short run and the medium run. How do output and the price level change in the medium run?

c. What happens to consumption in the medium run?

d. What happens to the real exchange rate in the medium run? (*Hint:* consider the effect on the price level you identified in part (b).) What happens to net exports in the medium run?

e. Given that the exchange rate is fixed, what is the domestic nominal interest rate? Does the increase in government spending affect the domestic nominal interest rate? What happens to the real interest rate in the medium run? (*Hint:* remember that expected inflation remains constant by assumption.) What happens to investment in the medium run?

f. In a closed economy, how does an increase in government spending affect investment in the medium run? (Refer to Chapter 9 if you need a refresher.)

g. Comment on the following statement: 'In a closed economy, government spending crowds out investment. In an open economy with fixed exchange rates, government spending crowds out net exports.'

3. Nominal and real interest parity

In equation (6.4), we wrote the nominal interest parity condition as

$$i_t \approx i_t^* - \frac{E_{t-1}^e - E_t}{E_t}$$

We can write the real interest parity condition in a manner analogous to equation (12.4):

$$r_t \approx r_t^* - \frac{(\varepsilon_{t-1}^e - \varepsilon_t)}{\varepsilon_t}$$

a. Interpret this equation. Under what circumstances will the domestic real interest rate exceed the foreign real interest rate?

Assume that the one-year nominal interest rate is 10% in the domestic economy and 6% in the foreign economy. Also assume that inflation over the coming year is expected to be 6% in the domestic economy and 3% in the foreign economy. Suppose that interest parity holds.

b. What is the expected nominal depreciation of the domestic currency over the coming year?

c. What is the expected real depreciation over the coming year?

d. If you expected a nominal appreciation of the currency over the coming year, should you hold domestic or foreign bonds?

4. Devaluation and interest rates

Consider an open economy with a fixed exchange rate, $\bar{E}$. Throughout the problem, assume that the foreign interest rate, i^*, remains constant.

a. Suppose that financial market participants believe that the government is committed to a fixed exchange rate. What is the expected exchange rate? According to the interest parity condition, what is the domestic interest rate?

b. Suppose that financial market participants do not believe that the government is committed to a fixed exchange rate. Instead, they suspect that the government will either devalue or abandon the fixed exchange rate altogether and adopt a flexible exchange rate. If the government adopts a flexible exchange rate, financial market participants expect the exchange rate to depreciate from its current fixed value, $\bar{E}$. Under these circumstances, how does the expected exchange rate compare to $\bar{E}$? How does the domestic interest rate compare to i^*?

c. Suppose that financial market participants feared a devaluation, as in part (b), and a devaluation actually occurs. The government announces that it will maintain a fixed exchange rate regime but changes the level of the fixed exchange rate to $\bar{E}'$, where $\bar{E}' < \bar{E}$. Suppose that financial market participants believe that the government will remain committed to the new exchange rate, $\bar{E}'$, and that there will be no further devaluations. What happens to the domestic interest rate after the devaluation?

d. Does a devaluation necessarily lead to higher domestic interest rates? Does fear of a devaluation necessarily lead to higher domestic interest rates?

DIG DEEPER

5. Exchange rate overshooting

a. Suppose there is a permanent 10% increase in M in a closed economy. What is the effect on the price level in the medium run? (*Hint: if you need a refresher, review the analysis in Chapter 9.*)

In a closed economy, we said that money was neutral because, in the medium run, a change in the money stock affected only the price level. A change in the money stock did not affect any real variables. A change in the money stock is also neutral in an open economy with flexible exchange rates. In the medium run, a change in the money stock will not affect the real exchange rate, although it will affect the price level and the nominal exchange rate.

b. Consider an open economy with a flexible exchange rate. Write the expression for the real exchange rate. Suppose there is a 10% increase in the money stock and assume that it has the same effect on the price level in the medium run that you found in part (a). If the real exchange rate and the foreign price level are unchanged in the medium run, what must happen to the nominal exchange rate in the medium run?

c. Suppose it takes n years to reach the medium run (and everyone knows this). Given your answer to part (b), what happens to E^e_{t+n} (the expected exchange rate for n periods from now) after a 10% increase in the money stock?

d. Consider equation (12.5). Assume that the foreign interest rate is unchanged for the next n periods. Also assume, for the moment, that the domestic interest rate is unchanged for the next n periods. Given your answer to part (c), what happens to the exchange rate today (at time t) when there is a 10% increase in the money stock?

e. Now assume that after the increase in the money stock, the domestic interest rate falls between time t and time $t + n$. Again, assume that the foreign interest rate is

unchanged. As compared to your answer to part (d), what happens to the exchange rate today (at time t)? Does the exchange rate move more in the short run than in the medium run?

The answer to part (e) is yes. In this case, the short-run depreciation is greater than the medium-run depreciation. This phenomenon is called overshooting, and may help to explain why the exchange rate is so variable.

6. Self-fulfilling exchange rate crises

Consider an open economy with a fixed exchange rate, $\bar{E}$. Suppose that, initially, financial market participants believe that the government is committed to the fixed exchange rate. Suddenly, however, financial market participants become fearful that the government will devalue or allow the exchange rate to float (a decision that everyone believes will cause the currency to depreciate).

a. What happens to the expected exchange rate, E^e_{t+1}? (See your answer to problem 4(b).)

Suppose that, despite the change in the expected exchange rate, the government keeps the exchange rate fixed today. Let UIP stand for the uncovered interest parity condition.

b. Draw an *IS–LM–UIP* diagram. How does the change in the expected exchange rate affect the *UIP* curve? As a result, how must the domestic interest rate change to maintain an exchange rate of $\bar{E}$?

c. Given your answer to part (b), what happens to the domestic money supply if the central bank defends the fixed exchange rate? How does the *LM* curve shift?

d. What happens to domestic output and the domestic interest rate? Is it possible that a government that was previously committed to a fixed exchange rate might abandon it when faced with a fear of depreciation (either through devaluation or abandonment of the fixed exchange rate regime)? Is it possible that unfounded fears about a depreciation can create a crisis? Explain your answers.

7. Devaluation and credibility

Consider an open economy with a fixed exchange rate, $\bar{E}$. Suppose that, initially, financial market participants believe that the government is committed to maintaining the fixed exchange rate. Let UIP stand for the uncovered interest parity condition.

Now suppose the central bank announces a devaluation. The exchange rate will remain fixed, but at a new level, $\bar{E}'$, such that $\bar{E}' < \bar{E}$. Suppose that financial market participants believe that there will be no further devaluations and that the government will remain committed to maintaining the exchange rate at $\bar{E}'$.

a. What is the domestic interest rate before the devaluation? If the devaluation is credible, what is the domestic interest rate after the devaluation? (See your answers to problem 4.)

b. Draw an *IS–LM–UIP* diagram for this economy. If the devaluation is credible, how does the expected exchange rate change? How does the change in the expected exchange rate affect the *UIP* curve?

c. How does the devaluation affect the *IS* curve? Given your answer to part (b) and the shift of the *IS* curve, what would happen to the domestic interest rate if there is no change in the domestic money supply?

d. Given your answer to part (c), what must happen to the domestic money supply so that the domestic interest rate achieves the value you identified in part (a)? How does the *LM* curve shift?

e. How is domestic output affected by the devaluation?

f. Suppose that devaluation is not credible in the sense that the devaluation leads financial market participants to expect another devaluation in the future. How does the fear of further devaluation affect the expected exchange rate? How will the expected exchange rate in this case, where devaluation is not credible, compare to your answer to part (b)? Explain in words. Given this effect on the expected exchange rate, what must happen to the domestic interest rate, as compared to your answer to part (a), to maintain the new fixed exchange rate?

EXPLORE FURTHER

8. Exchange rates and expectations

In this chapter, we emphasised that expectations have an important effect on the exchange rate. In this problem, we use data to get a sense of how large a role expectations play. You can show that the uncovered interest parity condition, equation (12.4), can be written as

$$\frac{(E_t - E_{t-1})}{E_{t-1}} \approx (i_t - i_t^*) - (i_{t-1} - i_{t-1}^*) + \frac{(E_t^e - E_{t-1}^e)}{E_{t-1}^e}$$

In words, the percentage change in the exchange rate (the appreciation of the domestic currency) is approximately equal to the change in the interest rate differential (between domestic and foreign interest rates) plus the percentage change in exchange rate expectations (the appreciation of the expected domestic currency value). We shall call the interest rate differential the spread.

a. Go to the website of the Bank of England (*www.bankofengland.co.uk*) and obtain data on the three-month Treasury bill rate for the past ten years. Download the data into a spreadsheet. Now go to the website of the European Central Bank (*www.ecb.int*) and download data on the three-month interbank rate (EURIBOR after 1999) for the same time period. For each month, subtract the UK interest rate from the euro interest rate to calculate the spread. Then, for each month, calculate the change in the spread from the preceding month. (Make sure to convert the interest rate data into the proper decimal form.)

b. At the website of the European Central Bank, obtain data on the monthly exchange rate between the euro and the UK pound for the same period as your data from part (a). Again, download the data into a spreadsheet. Calculate the percentage appreciation of the euro for each month. Using the standard deviation function in your software, calculate the standard deviation of the monthly appreciation of the euro. The standard deviation is a measure of the variability of a data series.

c. For each month, subtract the change in the spread (part (a)) from the percentage appreciation of the dollar (part (b)). Call this difference the *change in expectations*. Calculate the standard deviation of the change in expectations. How does it compare to the standard deviation of the monthly appreciation of the dollar?

There are some complications we do not take into account here. Our interest parity condition does not include a variable that measures relative asset demand. We explored the implications of changes in relative asset demands in problem 12 at the end of Chapter 7. In addition, changes in interest rates and expectations may be related. Still, the gist of this analysis survives in more sophisticated work. In the short run, observable economic fundamentals do not account for much of the change in the exchange rate. Much of the difference must be attributed to changing expectations.

Log on to **MyEconLab** and complete the studyplan exercises for this chapter to see how much you have learnt, and where you need to revise most.

MyEconLab

THE LONG RUN

The next three chapters focus on the long run. In the long run, what dominates is not fluctuations, but growth. So now we need to ask: what determines growth?

Chapter 13 The facts of growth

Chapter 13 looks at the facts of growth. It first documents the large increase in output that has taken place in rich countries over the past 50 years. Then, taking a wider look, it shows that, on the scale of human history, such growth is a recent phenomenon. And it is not a universal phenomenon: some countries are catching up, but many poor countries are suffering from no or low growth.

Chapter 14 Saving, capital accumulation and output

Chapter 14 focuses on the role of capital accumulation in growth. It shows that capital accumulation cannot by itself sustain growth, but that it does affect the level of output. A higher saving rate typically leads to lower consumption initially but to more consumption in the long run.

Chapter 15 Technological progress and growth

Chapter 15 turns to technological progress. It shows how, in the long run, the growth rate of an economy is determined by the rate of technological progress. It looks at the role of R&D in generating such progress. It returns to the facts of growth presented in Chapter 13 and shows how to interpret those facts in the light of the theory developed in Chapters 13–15.

Chapter 13

THE FACTS OF GROWTH

Our perceptions of how the economy is doing are often dominated by year-to-year fluctuations in economic activity. A recession leads to gloom, and an expansion to optimism. But if we step back to get a look at activity over longer periods – say, over many decades – the picture changes. Fluctuations fade. **Growth** – the steady increase in aggregate output over time – dominates the picture.

Figure 13.1 shows the evolution of GDP (in million 1990 PPP dollars) in some industrialised European economies (France, Germany and the UK) since 1890, compared to three poorer countries, Greece and Portugal in Europe, and Argentina. Notice how similar, although at different levels, were the evolutions of GDP before 1940, and how rapid was output growth in the first group of countries. In France, Germany and the UK, the years 1940–1945 correspond to the large decrease in output during the Second World War, and the years 2008–2009 correspond to the largest post-war recession. Note how small these two episodes appear compared to the steady increase in output over the past 100 years.

We now shift our focus from fluctuations to growth. Put another way, we turn from the study of the determination of output in the short and medium run – where fluctuations dominate – to the determination of output in the long run – where growth dominates. Our goal is to understand what determines growth, why some countries are growing while others are not, why some countries are rich while many others are still poor.

- Section 13.1 discusses a central measurement issue, namely how to measure the standard of living.

- Section 13.2 looks at growth in the USA and other rich countries over the past 50 years.

- Section 13.3 takes a broader look across both time and space.

- Section 13.4 then gives a primer on growth and introduces the framework that will be developed in the next chapters.

Figure 13.1

GDP in selected economies since 1890

Source: OECD.

13.1 MEASURING THE STANDARD OF LIVING

The reason we care about growth is that we care about the **standard of living**. Looking across time, we want to know by how much the standard of living has increased. Looking across countries, we want to know how much higher the standard of living is in one country relative to another. Thus, the variable we want to focus on, and compare either over time or across countries, is **output per person** rather than output itself.

A practical problem then arises: how do we compare output per person across countries? Countries use different currencies, thus output in each country is expressed in terms of its own currency. A natural solution is to use exchange rates: when comparing, say, the output per person of India to the output per person of the UK, we can compute Indian GDP per person in rupees, use the exchange rate to get Indian GDP per person in pounds, and compare it to UK GDP per person in pounds. This simple approach will not do, however, for two reasons:

◄ Output per person is also called *output per capita* (*capita* means 'head' in Latin). And given that output and income are always equal, it is also called *income per person*, or *income per capita*.

- Exchange rates can vary a lot (as we have learned in Chapter 8). For example, the pound decreased since the summer of 2008 by roughly 30% vis-à-vis the US dollar, the euro and other major currencies. But, surely, the standard of living in the UK did not decrease by 30% compared to the standard of living of the USA and of other European countries during the last year. Yet this is the conclusion we would reach if we were to compare GDP per person using exchange rates.
- The second reason goes beyond fluctuations in exchange rates. In 2006, income per person in India, using the current exchange rate, was $820, compared to $40,660 in the UK. Surely, no one could live on $820 per year in the UK. But people live on it – admittedly, not very well – in India, where the prices of basic goods – those goods needed for subsistence – are much lower than in the UK. The level of consumption of the average person in India, who consumes mostly basic goods, is not 50 (40,660 divided by 820) times smaller than that of the average person in the UK. This point applies to other countries besides the UK and India: in general, the lower a country's output per person, the lower the prices of food and basic services in that country.

So, when we focus on comparing standards of living, we get more meaningful comparisons by correcting for the two effects we just discussed – variations in exchange rates, and systematic differences in prices across countries. The details of construction are complicated, but the principle is simple: the numbers for GDP – and hence for GDP per person – are constructed using a common set of prices for all countries. Such adjusted real GDP numbers, which you can think of as measures of **purchasing power** across time or across countries, are called **purchasing power parity (PPP)** numbers. Further discussion is given in the Focus box 'The construction of PPP numbers'.

When comparing rich versus poor countries, the differences between PPP numbers and the numbers based on current exchange rates can be very large. Return to the comparison between India and the UK. We saw that, at current exchange rates, the ratio of GDP per person in the UK to GDP per person in India was 50. Using PPP numbers, the ratio is only 14. Although this is still a large difference, it is much smaller than the ratio we obtained using current exchange rates. Differences between PPP numbers and numbers based on current exchange rate are typically smaller when making comparisons among rich countries. Based on the numbers we saw earlier (in Chapter 1) – those numbers were constructed using current exchange rates – GDP per person in the USA in 2006 was equal to 125% of the GDP per person in Germany. Based on PPP numbers, GDP per person in the USA is in fact equal to 138% of GDP per person in Germany. More generally, PPP numbers suggest that the USA still has the highest GDP per person in the world.

The bottom line: when comparing standard of living across countries, make sure to use PPP numbers.

Let us end this section with three remarks before we move on and look at growth:

- What matters for people's welfare is their consumption rather than their income. One might therefore want to use consumption per person rather than output per person as a

FOCUS
The construction of PPP numbers

Consider two countries – let's call them the USA and Russia, although we are not attempting to fit the characteristics of those two countries very closely:

In the USA, annual consumption per person equals $20,000. People in the USA each buy two goods: every year, they buy a new car for $10,000, and spend the rest on food. The price of a yearly bundle of food in the USA is $10,000.

In Russia, annual consumption per person equals 60,000 roubles. People there keep their cars for 15 years. The price of a car is 300,000 roubles, so individuals spend on average 20,000 roubles – 300,000/15 – a year on cars. They buy the same yearly bundle of food as their US counterparts, at a price of 40,000 rubles.

Russian and US cars are of identical quality, and so are Russian and US food. (You may dispute the realism of these assumptions. Whether a car in country X is the same as a car in country Y is very much the type of problem confronting economists constructing PPP measures.) The exchange rate is such that one dollar is equal to 30 roubles. What is consumption per person in Russia relative to consumption per person in the USA?

One way to answer is by taking consumption per person in Russia and converting it into dollars using the exchange rate. Using that method, Russian consumption per person in dollars is $2,000 (60,000 roubles divided by the exchange rate, 30 roubles to the dollar). According to these numbers, consumption per person in Russia is only 10% of US consumption per person.

Does this answer make sense? True, Russians are poorer, but food is much cheaper in Russia. A US consumer spending all of his 20,000 dollars on food would buy 2 bundles of food ($20,000/$10,000). A Russian consumer spending all of his 60,000 roubles on food would buy 1.5 bundles of food (60,000 roubles/40,000 roubles). In terms of food bundles, the difference looks much smaller measure of the standard of living. (This is indeed what we do in the Focus box 'The construction of PPP numbers'.) Because the ratio of consumption to output is rather similar across countries, the ranking of countries is roughly the same, whether we use consumption per person or output per person.

- Thinking about the production side, one may be interested in differences in productivity rather than in differences in the standard of living across countries. In this case, the right measure is output per worker – or, even better, output per hour worked if the information about total hours worked is available – rather than output per person. Output per person and output per worker (or per hour) will differ to the extent that the ratio of the number of workers (or hours) to population differs across countries. Most of the difference between output per person in the USA and in Germany we noted earlier comes, for example, from differences in hours worked per person, rather than from differences in productivity. Put another way, German workers are about as productive as their US counterparts. However, they work fewer hours, so their standard of living is lower.

- The reason we ultimately care about the standard of living is presumably that we care about happiness. One may therefore ask the obvious question: does a higher standard of living lead to greater happiness? The answer is given in the Focus box 'Growth and happiness', that is: a qualified yes.

between US and Russian consumption per person. And given that one-half of consumption in the USA and two-thirds of consumption in Russia go to spending on food, this seems like a relevant computation.

Can we improve on our initial answer? Yes. One way is to use the same set of prices for both countries and then measure the quantities of each good consumed in each country using this common set of prices. Suppose we use US prices. In terms of US prices, annual consumption per person in the USA is obviously still $20,000. What is it in Russia? Every year, the average Russian buys approximately 0.07 car (one car every 15 years) and one bundle of food. Using US prices – specifically, $10,000 for a car and $10,000 for a bundle of food – gives Russian consumption per person as $((0.07 \times \$10,000) + (1 \times \$10,000)) = (\$700 + \$10,000) = \$10,700$. So, using US prices to compute consumption in both countries puts annual Russian consumption per person at $10,700/$20,000 = 53.5% of annual US consumption per person, a better estimate of relative standards of living than we obtained using our first method (which put the number at only 10%).

This type of computation, namely the construction of variables across countries using a common set of prices, underlies PPP estimates. Rather than using US dollar prices as in our example (why use US rather than Russian or, for that matter, French prices?), these estimates use average prices across countries. These average prices are called *international dollar prices*. Many of the estimates we use in this chapter are the result of an ambitious project known as the 'Penn World Tables'. (Penn stands for the University of Pennsylvania where the project is located.) Led by three economists – Irving Kravis, Robert Summers and Alan Heston – over the course of more than 40 years, researchers working on the project have constructed PPP series not only for consumption (as we just did in our example), but also more generally for GDP and its components, going back to 1950, for most countries in the world.

Note: For more on the construction of PPP numbers, go to the website *http://pwt.econ.upenn.edu*. (In the Penn tables, what is the ratio of Russian PPP GDP per person to US PPP GDP per person?) The IMF and the World Bank also construct their own set of PPP numbers. The IMF numbers are easily available on the IMF website, *www.imf.org*.

FOCUS
Growth and happiness

Does money lead to happiness? Or, put more accurately, does higher income per person lead to more happiness? The implicit assumption, when economists assess the performance of an economy by looking at its level of income per person or at its growth rate is that this is indeed the case. Early examinations of data on the relation between income and self-reported measures of happiness suggested that this assumption may not be right. They yielded what is now known as the **Easterlin paradox** (so named for Richard Easterlin, who was one of the first economists to look systematically at the evidence):

- Looking across countries, happiness in a country appeared to be higher the higher the level of income per person. The relation, however, appeared to hold only in relatively poor countries. Looking at rich countries, say, the set of OECD countries (look at Chapter 1 for the list), there appeared to be little relation between income per person and happiness.
- Looking over time, average happiness in rich countries did not seem to increase very much, if at all, with income. (There were no reliable data for poor countries.) In other words, in rich countries, growth did not appear to increase happiness.
- Looking across people within a given country, happiness appeared to be strongly correlated with income. Rich people were consistently happier than poor people. This was true in both poor and rich countries.

The first two facts suggested that, once basic needs were satisfied, higher income per person did not increase happiness. The third fact suggested that what was important was not the absolute level of income but the level of income relative to others.

If this interpretation is right, this has major implications for the way we think about the world and about economic policies. In rich countries, policies aimed at increasing income per person might be misdirected, as

what matters is the distribution of income rather than its average level. Globalisation and the diffusion of information, to the extent that it makes people in poor countries compare themselves not to rich people in the same country, but to people in richer countries may actually decrease rather than increase happiness. So, as you can guess, these findings have led to an intense debate and further research. As new data sets have become available, better evidence has accumulated. The state of knowledge and the remaining controversies are analysed in a recent paper by Betsey Stevenson and Justin Wolfers. Their conclusions are well summarised in Figure 13.2.

The figure contains a lot of information. Let's go through it step by step.

The horizontal axis measures PPP GDP per person for 131 countries. The scale is a **logarithmic scale**, so a given size interval represents a given percentage increase in GDP. The vertical axis measures average life satisfaction in each country. The source for this variable is a 2006 Gallup World Poll survey, which asked roughly a thousand individuals in each country the following question: 'Here is a ladder representing the "ladder of life"; let's suppose the top of the ladder represents the best possible life for you, and the bottom the worst possible life for you. On which step of the ladder do you feel you personally stand at the present time?' The ladder went from 0 to 10. The variable measured on the vertical axis is the average of the individual answers in each country.

Focus first on the dots representing each country, ignoring for the moment the lines that cross each dot. The visual impression is clear. There is a strong relation across countries between average income and average happiness. The index is around 4 in the poorest countries, around 8 in the richest. And, more importantly in view of the early Easterlin paradox, this relation appears to hold both for poor and rich countries.

13.2 GROWTH IN RICH COUNTRIES SINCE 1950

Let us start by looking, in this section, at growth in rich countries since 1950. In the next section, we shall look further back in time, and across a wider range of countries.

Table 13.1 shows the evolution of output per person (GDP divided by population, measured at PPP prices) for France, Japan, the UK and the USA since 1950. We have chosen these four countries not only because they are some of the world's major economic powers, but also because what has happened to them is broadly representative of what has happened in other advanced countries over the past half century or so.

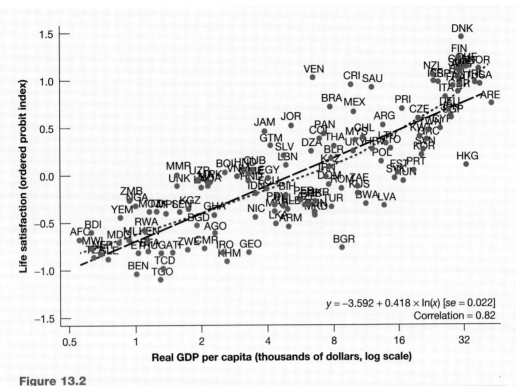

Figure 13.2

Life satisfaction and income per person

Source: Betsey Stevenson and Justin Wolfers, 'Economic growth and subjective well-being: reassessing the Easterlin Paradox', NBER Working Paper No. 14282. (**www.nber.org/papers/w14282**)

Focus now on the lines through each dot. The slope of each line reflects the estimated relation between life satisfaction and income across individuals within each country. Note first that all the lines slope upwards: this confirms the third leg of the Easterlin paradox: in each country, rich people are happier than poor people. Note also that the slopes of most of these lines are roughly similar to the slope of the relation across countries. This goes against the Easterlin paradox: individual happiness increases with income, whether this is because the country is getting richer, or because the individual becomes relatively richer within the country.

Stevenson and Wolfers draw a strong conclusion from their findings. While individual happiness surely depends on much more than income, it definitely increases with income. Thus, it is not a crime for economists to focus first on levels and growth rates of GDP per person. So, is the debate over? The answer is no. Even if one accepts this interpretation of the evidence, clearly, many other aspects of the economy matter for welfare, income distribution surely being one. And not everybody is convinced by the evidence. In particular, the evidence on the relation between happiness and income per person over time within a country is not as clear as the evidence across countries or across individuals presented in the figure. Given the importance of the question, the debate will continue for some time.

Sources: Betsey Stevenson and Justin Wolfers, 'Economic growth and subjective well-being: reassessing the Easterlin paradox', NBER Working Paper No. 14282, Spring 2008.

For a view closer to the Easterlin paradox, and a fascinating discussion of policy implications, read Richard Layard, *Happiness: Lessons from a New Science*, Penguin Books, 2005.

Table 13.1 The evolution of output per person in four rich countries since 1950

	Annual growth rate output per person (%)		Real output per person (2005 dollars)	
	1950–2009	1950	2009	2009/1950
France	2.5	7,112	30,821	4.3
Japan	3.9	3,118	31,958	10.2
UK	2.0	10,400	33,386	3.2
USA	1.9	13,183	41,102	3.1
Average	2.6	8,453	34,317	5.2

Source: Penn World Tables, **http://pwt.econ.upenn.edu**.

The data stop in 2009, the latest year (at this point) available in the Penn tables. The average in the last line is a simple unweighted average.

Table 13.1 yields two main conclusions:

- There has been a large increase in output per person.
- There has been convergence of output per person across countries.

Let's look at each of these points in turn.

The large increase in the standard of living since 1950

Look at the last column of the table. Output per person has increased by a factor of 3.1 since 1950 in the USA, by a factor of 4.3 in France and by a factor of 10.2 in Japan.

These numbers show what is sometimes called the *force of compounding*. In a different context, you probably have heard how saving even a little while you are young will build to a large amount by the time you retire. For example, if the interest rate is 3.9% a year, an investment of one dollar, with the proceeds reinvested every year, will grow to about 10 dollars ($[1 + 0.039]^{60}$) 60 years later. The same logic applies to growth rates. The average annual growth rate in Japan over the period 1950 to 2009 was equal to 3.9%. This high growth rate has led to a ten-fold increase in real output per person in Japan ➤ over the period.

> Most of the increase in Japan took place before 1990. As we saw earlier (in Chapter 9), since then, Japan has been in a prolonged economic slump, with very low growth.

> $1.01^{40} - 1 = 1.48 - 1 = 48\%$.

> Unfortunately, policy measures with ➤ such magic results have proven difficult to discover!

Clearly, a better understanding of growth, if it leads to the design of policies that stimulate growth, can have a very large effect on the standard of living. Suppose we could ➤ find a policy measure that permanently increased the growth rate by 1% per year. This would lead, after 40 years, to a standard of living 48% higher than it would have been ➤ without the policy – a substantial difference.

The convergence of output per person

The second and third columns of Table 13.1 show that the levels of output per person have converged (become closer) over time: the numbers for output per person are much more similar in 2009 than they were in 1950. Put another way, those countries that were behind have grown faster, reducing the gap between them and the USA.

In 1950, output per person in the USA was roughly twice the level of output per person in France and more than four times the level of output per person in Japan. From the perspective of Europe or Japan, the USA was seen as the land of plenty, where everything was bigger and better. Today these perceptions have faded, and the numbers explain why. Using PPP numbers, US output per person is still the highest, but, in 2009, it was only 20% above average output per person in the other three countries, a much smaller difference than in the 1950s.

> For the list of countries, see the ➤ appendix to Chapter 1.

> The figure includes only those OECD ➤ members where we have a reliable estimate of the level of output per person in 1950.

This **convergence** of levels of output per person across countries is not specific to the four countries we are looking at. It extends to the set of OECD countries. This is shown in Figure 13.3, which plots the average annual growth rate of output per person since 1950 against the initial level of output per person in 1950 for the set of countries that are members of the OECD today. There is a clear negative relation between the initial level of output per person and the growth rate since 1950: countries that were behind in 1950 have typically grown faster. The relation is not perfect: Turkey, which had roughly the same low level of output per person as Japan in 1950, has had a growth rate equal to only about half that of Japan. But the relation is clearly there.

Some economists have pointed to a problem in graphs like Figure 13.3. By looking at the subset of countries that are members of the OECD today, what we have done in effect is to look at a club of economic winners: OECD membership is not officially based on economic success, but economic success is surely an important determinant of membership. But when you look at a club whose membership is based on economic success, you will find that those who came from behind had the fastest growth: this is precisely why they made it to the club!

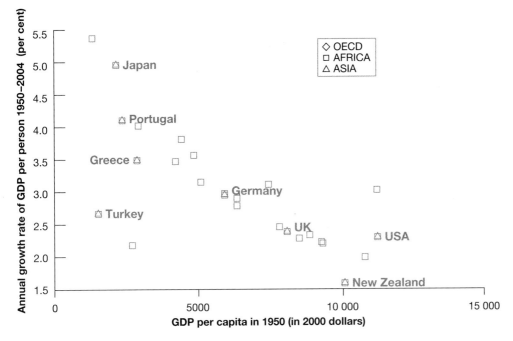

Figure 13.3

Growth rates of GDP per person since 1950 versus GDP per person in 1950 (OECD countries)

Countries with lower levels of output per person in 1950 have typically grown faster.

Source: Penn World Tables. The Czech Republic, Hungary and Poland are not included because of missing data.

The finding of convergence could come in part from the way we selected the countries in the first place.

So a better way of looking at convergence is to define the set of countries we look at not on the basis of where they are today – as we did in Figure 13.3 by taking today's OECD members – but on the basis of where they were in, say, 1950. For example, we can look at all countries that had an output per person of at least one-fourth of US output per person in 1950, then look for convergence within that group. It turns out that most of the countries in that group have indeed converged, and therefore convergence is not solely an OECD phenomenon. However, a few countries – Uruguay, Argentina, and Venezuela among them – have not converged. In 1950, those three countries had roughly the same output per person as France. In 2009, they had fallen far behind; their level of output per person stood only between one-fourth and one-half of the French level.

13.3 A BROADER LOOK ACROSS TIME AND SPACE

In the previous section, we focused on growth over the past 50 years in rich countries. Let's now put this in context, by looking at the evidence both over a much longer time span and a wider set of countries.

Looking across two millennia

Has output per person in the currently rich economies always grown at rates similar to the growth rates in Table 13.1? The answer is no. Estimates of growth are clearly harder to construct as we look further back in time. But there is agreement among economic historians about the main evolutions over the past 2,000 years.

From the end of the Roman Empire to roughly year 1500, there was essentially no growth of output per person in Europe: most workers were employed in agriculture, in which there was little technological progress. Because agriculture's share of output was so large, inventions with applications outside agriculture could only contribute little to overall production and output. Although there was some output growth, a roughly proportional increase in population led to roughly constant output per person.

This period of stagnation of output per person is often called the Malthusian era. Thomas Robert Malthus, an English economist, at the end of the eighteenth century, argued that this proportional increase in output and population was not a coincidence. Any increase in output, he argued, would lead to a decrease in mortality, leading to an increase in population until output per person was back to its initial level. Europe was in a **Malthusian trap**, unable to increase its output per person.

Eventually, Europe was able to escape that trap. From about 1500 to 1700, growth of output per person turned positive, but it was still small – only around 0.1% per year. It then increased to just 0.2% per year from 1700 to 1820. Starting with the Industrial Revolution, growth rates increased, but from 1820 to 1950 the growth rate of output per person in the USA was still only 1.5% per year. On the scale of human history, therefore, sustained growth of output per person – especially the high growth rates we have seen since 1950 – is definitely a recent phenomenon.

Figure 13.4 shows the evolution of the GDP per person in Western Europe since the year 960. The figure highlights the importance of technological innovation in raising GDP per capita. We shall study technological progress and growth more in depth later (in Chapter 15).

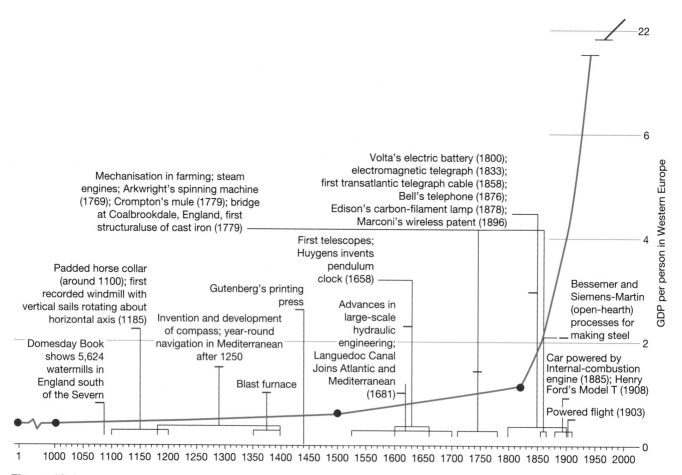

Figure 13.4

Take-off

It was only towards the end of the 1700s that mechanisation in England paved the way for the take-off in per capita income in Western Europe.

Looking across countries

We have seen how output per person has converged among OECD countries. But what about the other countries? Are the poorest countries also growing faster? Are they converging toward the USA, even if they are still far behind?

The answer is given in Figure 13.5, which plots the annual growth rate of output per person since 1960 against output per person for the year 1960, for 76 countries.

◀ The numbers for 1950 are missing for too many countries to use 1950 as the initial year, as we did in Figure 13.3.

The striking feature of Figure 13.5 is that there is no clear pattern: it is not the case that, in general, countries which were behind in 1960 have grown faster. Some have, but clearly many have not.

The cloud of points in Figure 13.5 hides, however, a number of interesting patterns which appear when we put countries into different groups. Note that we have used different symbols in the figure: the diamonds represent OECD countries; the squares represent African countries; the triangles represent Asian countries. Looking at patterns by groups yields three main conclusions:

- The picture for the OECD countries (for the rich countries) is much the same as in Figure 13.3, which looked at a slightly longer period of time (from 1950 onwards, rather than from 1960). Nearly all start at high levels of output per person (say, at least one-third of the US level in 1960), and there is clear evidence of convergence.

- Convergence is also visible for many Asian countries: most of the countries with the very high growth rates over the period are in Asia. Japan was the first one to take off. Starting a decade later, in the 1960s, four countries – Singapore, Taiwan, Hong Kong and South Korea, a group of countries sometimes called the **four tigers** – started catching up as well. In 1960, their average output per person was about 18% of the US level; by 2009, it had increased to 83% of US output. More recently, the major story has been China – both because of its very high growth rates, and because of its sheer size. Over the period, growth of output per person in China has been 4.4%. But, because it started very low, its output per person is still only about one-sixth of the US level.

- The picture is different, however, for African countries. Most African countries (represented by squares) were very poor in 1960, and most have not done well over the period. Many have suffered from either internal or external conflicts. Eight of them have had negative growth of output per person – an absolute decline in their standard of living between 1960 and 2009. Growth averaged –1% in the Central African Republic and –0.7% in Niger. As a result output per person in the Central African Republic in 2009 is 60% of its level in 1960. Some hope, however, comes from more recent numbers: growth of output per person in Sub-Saharan Africa, which averaged only 1.3% in the 1990s, was close to 5.0% in the 2000s.

◀ Paradoxically, the two fastest growing countries in Figure 13.3 are Botswana and Equatorial Guinea, both in Africa. In both cases, however, high growth reflects primarily favourable natural resources, diamonds in Botswana, oil in Guinea.

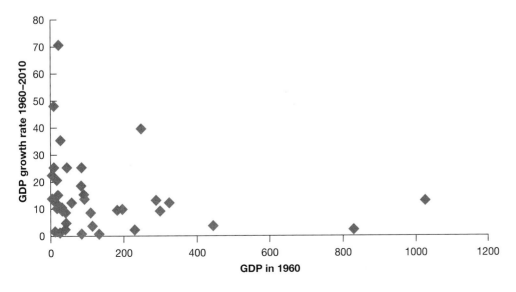

Figure 13.5

Growth rate of GDP per person since 1960, versus GDP per person in 1960 (2005 dollars) for 76 countries

There is no clear relation between the growth rate of output since 1960 and the level of output per person in 1960.

Source: Penn World Tables. The Czech Republic, Hungary and Poland are not included because of missing data.

Looking further back in time, the following picture emerges. For much of the first millennium, and until the fifteenth century, China probably had the world's highest level of output per person. For a couple of centuries, leadership moved to the cities of northern Italy. But, until the nineteenth century, differences across countries were typically much smaller than they are today. Starting in the nineteenth century, a number of countries, first in Western Europe, then in North and South America, started growing faster than others. Since then, a number of other countries, most notably in Asia, have started growing fast, and are converging. Many others, mainly in Africa, are not.

Our main focus, in this and the next chapter, will be primarily on growth in rich and emerging countries. We shall not take on some of the wider challenges raised by the facts we have just seen, such as why growth of output per person started in earnest in the nineteenth century, or why Africa has remained so poor. Doing so would take us too far into economic history and development economics. But these facts put into perspective the two basic facts we discussed earlier when looking at the OECD: neither growth nor convergence are a historical necessity.

> The distinction between growth theory and development economics is fuzzy. A rough distinction: growth theory takes many of the institutions of a country (for example, its legal system and its form of government) as given. Development economics asks what institutions are needed to sustain steady growth, and how they can be put in place.

13.4 THINKING ABOUT GROWTH: A PRIMER

To think about growth, economists use a framework developed originally by Robert Solow, from MIT, in the late 1950s. The framework has proven sturdy and useful, and we will use it here. This section provides an introduction. Later chapters (see Chapters 14 and 15) will provide a more detailed analysis, first of the role of capital accumulation and then of the role of technological progress in the process of growth.

> Solow's article, 'A contribution to the theory of economic growth', appeared in 1956. Solow was awarded the Nobel Prize in 1987 for his work on growth.

The aggregate production function

The starting point of any theory of growth must be an **aggregate production function**, a specification of the relation between aggregate output and the inputs in production.

The aggregate production function we introduced earlier (in Chapter 8) to study the determination of output in the short run and the medium run took a particularly simple form. Output was simply proportional to the amount of labour used by firms – more specifically, proportional to the number of workers employed by firms (equation (8.2)). So long as our focus was on fluctuations in output and employment, the assumption was acceptable. But now that our focus has shifted to growth, that assumption will no longer do: it implies that output per worker is constant, ruling out growth (or at least growth of output per worker) altogether. It is time to relax it. From now on, we will assume that there are two inputs – capital and labour – and that the relation between aggregate output and the two inputs is given by:

$$Y = F(K, N) \qquad [13.1]$$

As before, Y is aggregate output. K is capital – the sum of all the machines, plants and office buildings in the economy. N is labour – the number of workers in the economy. The function F, which tells us how much output is produced for given quantities of capital and labour, is the aggregate production function.

> The aggregate production function is
> $$Y = F(K, N)$$
> Aggregate output (Y) depends on the aggregate capital stock (K), and aggregate employment (N).

This way of thinking about aggregate production is an improvement on our treatment of it earlier (in Chapter 8). But it should be clear that it is still a dramatic simplification of reality. Surely, machines and office buildings play very different roles in production, and should be treated as separate inputs. Surely, workers with PhDs are different from school leavers; yet, by constructing the labour input as simply the number of workers in the economy, we treat all workers as identical. We will relax some of these simplifications later. For the time being, equation (13.1), which emphasises the role of both labour and capital in production will do.

The next step must be to think about where the aggregate production function, *F*, which relates output to the two inputs, comes from. In other words, what determines how much output can be produced for given quantities of capital and labour? The answer: the **state of technology**. A country with a more advanced technology will produce more output from the same quantities of capital and labour than will an economy with a primitive technology.

How should we define the state of technology? Should we think of it as the list of blueprints defining both the range of products that can be produced in the economy as well as the techniques available to produce them? Or should we think of it more broadly, including not only the list of blueprints, but also the way the economy is organised – from the internal organisation of firms, to the system of laws and the quality of their enforcement, to the political system, and so on? In the next two chapters, we will have in mind the narrower definition – the set of blueprints.

◀ The function *F* depends on the state of technology. The higher the state of technology, the higher *F*(*K*, *N*) for a given *K* and a given *N*.

Returns to scale and returns to factors

Now that we have introduced the aggregate production function, the next question is: what restrictions can we reasonably impose on this function?

Consider first a thought experiment in which we double both the number of workers and the amount of capital in the economy. What do you expect will happen to output? A reasonable answer is that output will double as well: in effect, we have cloned the original economy, and the clone economy can produce output in the same way as the original economy. This property is called **constant returns to scale**: if the scale of operation is doubled – that is, if the quantities of capital and labour are doubled – then output will also double:

$$2Y = F(2K, 2N)$$

Or more generally, for any number *x* (this will be useful below)

$$xY = F(xK, xN) \qquad [13.2]$$

We have just looked at what happens to production when both capital and labour are increased. Let's now ask a different question. What should we expect to happen if only one of the two inputs in the economy – say, capital – is increased?

◀ Constant returns to scale: $F(xK, xN) = xY$.

Surely output will increase. That part is clear. But it is also reasonable to assume that the same increase in capital will lead to smaller and smaller increases in output as the level of capital increases. In other words, if there is little capital to start with, a little more capital will help a lot. If there is a lot of capital to start with, a little more capital may make little difference. Why? Think, for example, of a secretarial pool, composed of a given number of secretaries. Think of capital as computers. The introduction of the first computer will substantially increase the pool's production, because some of the more time-consuming tasks can now be done automatically by the computer. As the number of computers increases and more secretaries in the pool get their own computers, production will further increase, although perhaps by less per additional computer than was the case when the first one was introduced. Once each and every secretary has a computer, increasing the number of computers further is unlikely to increase production very much, if at all. Additional computers might simply remain unused and left in their shipping boxes, and lead to no increase in output.

◀ Output here is secretarial services. The two inputs are secretaries and computers. The production function relates secretarial services to the number of secretaries and the number of computers.

We shall refer to the property that increases in capital lead to smaller and smaller increases in output as **decreasing returns to capital** (a property that will be familiar to those who have taken a course in microeconomics).

A similar argument applies to the other input, labour. Increases in labour, given capital, lead to smaller and smaller increases in output. (Return to our example, and think of what happens as you increase the number of secretaries for a given number of computers.) There are **decreasing returns to labour** as well.

Even under constant returns to scale, there are decreasing returns to each factor, keeping the other factor constant:

- There are decreasing returns to capital: given labour, increases in capital lead to smaller and smaller increases in output.
- There are decreasing returns to labour: given capital, increases in labour lead to smaller and smaller increases in output.

Figure 13.6

Output and capital per worker

Increases in capital per worker lead to smaller and smaller increases in output per worker.

Output per worker and capital per worker

The production function we have written down, together with the assumption of constant returns to scale, implies that there is a simple relation between output per worker and capital per worker.

To see this, set $x = 1/N$ in equation (13.2), so that

$$\frac{Y}{N} = F\left(\frac{K}{N}, \frac{N}{N}\right) = F\left(\frac{K}{N}, 1\right) \qquad [13.3]$$

Make sure you understand what is behind the algebra. Suppose capital and the number of workers both double. What happens to output per worker?

Note that Y/N is output per worker, K/N is capital per worker. So equation (13.3) says that the amount of output per worker depends on the amount of capital per worker. This relation between output per worker and capital per worker will play a central role in what follows, so let's look at it more closely.

The relation is drawn in Figure 13.6. Output per worker (Y/N) is measured on the vertical axis, and capital per worker (K/N) is measured on the horizontal axis. The relation between the two is given by the upward-sloping curve. As capital per worker increases, so does output per worker. Note that the curve is drawn so that increases in capital lead to smaller and smaller increases in output. This follows from the property that there are decreasing returns to capital: at point A, where capital per worker is low, an increase in capital per worker, represented by the horizontal distance AB leads to an increase in output per worker equal to the vertical distance A'B'. At point C, where capital per worker is larger, the same increase in capital per worker, represented by the horizontal distance CD (where the distance CD is equal to the distance AB) leads to a much smaller increase in output per worker, only C'D'. This is just like our secretarial pool example, where additional computers had less and less impact on total output.

Increases in capital per worker lead to smaller and smaller increases in output per worker as the level of capital per worker increases.

The sources of growth

We are now ready to return to our basic question: where does growth come from? Why does output per worker – or output per person, if we assume the ratio of workers to the population as a whole remains constant over time – go up over time? Equation (13.3) gives a first answer:

Increases in capital per worker: movements along the production function.

● Increases in output per worker (Y/N) can come from increases in capital per worker (K/N). This is the relation we just looked at in Figure 13.6. As (K/N) increases – that is, as we move to the right on the horizontal axis – (Y/N) increases.

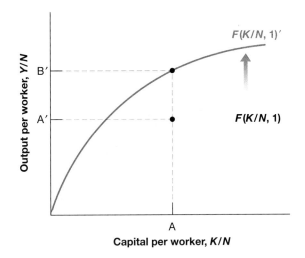

Figure 13.7

The effects of an improvement in the state of technology

An improvement in technology shifts the production function up, leading to an increase in output per worker for a given level of capital per worker.

- Or they can come from improvements in the state of technology that shift the production function, F, and lead to more output per worker given capital per worker. This is shown in Figure 13.7. An improvement in the state of technology shifts the production function up, from $F(K/N, 1)$ to $F(K/N, 1)$. For a given level of capital per worker, the improvement in technology leads to an increase in output per worker. For example, for the level of capital per worker corresponding to point A, output per worker increases from A′ to B′. (To go back to our secretarial pool example, a reallocation of tasks within the pool may lead to better division of labour and an increase in the output per secretary.)

◁ Improvements in the state of technology: shifts (up) of the production function.

Hence, we can think of growth as coming from **capital accumulation** and from **technological progress** – the improvement in the state of technology. We will see, however, that these two factors play very different roles in the growth process:

- Capital accumulation by itself cannot sustain growth. A formal argument will have to wait until later (see Chapter 14). But you can already see the intuition behind this from Figure 13.7. Because of decreasing returns to capital, sustaining a steady increase in output per worker will require larger and larger increases in the level of capital per worker. At some stage, the economy will be unwilling or unable to save and invest enough to further increase capital. At that stage, output per worker will stop growing.

    Does this mean that an economy's **saving rate** – the proportion of income that is saved – is irrelevant? No. It is true that a higher saving rate cannot permanently increase the growth rate of output.

    But a higher saving rate can sustain a higher level of output. Let us state this in a slightly different way. Take two economies that differ only in their saving rates. The two economies will grow at the same rate, but, at any point in time, the economy with the higher saving rate will have a higher level of output per person than the other. How this happens, how much the saving rate affects the level of output, and whether or not a country like the USA (which has a very low saving rate) should try to increase its saving rate, will be one of the topics we take up later (in Chapter 14).

- Sustained growth requires sustained technological progress. This really follows from the previous proposition: given that the two factors that can lead to an increase in output are capital accumulation and technological progress, if capital accumulation cannot sustain growth forever, then technological progress must be the key to growth. And it is. We will see later (in Chapter 15) that the economy's rate of growth of output per person is eventually determined by its rate of technological progress.

    This is very important. It means that in the long run, an economy that sustains a higher rate of technological progress will eventually overtake all other economies. This, of course, raises yet another question: what determines the rate of technological progress?

Recall the two definitions of the state of technology we discussed earlier: a narrow definition, namely the set of blueprints available to the economy; and a broader definition, which captures how the economy is organised, from the nature of institutions to the role of the government. What we know about the determinants of technological progress narrowly defined – the role of fundamental and applied research, the role of patent laws, the role of education and training – will be taken up later (in Chapter 15).

FOCUS
Why has per capita income in Europe decreased relative to the USA?

In the past two decades income per capita in European countries has decreased relative to the USA. To understand this, we must first understand what determines per capita income. A simple decomposition will help. If a country produces Y with a population of size L, we can decompose per capita income (Y/L) as follows:

$$\frac{Y}{L} = \frac{E}{L} \times \frac{\text{hours}}{E} \times \frac{Y}{\text{hours}}$$

The first term on the right is the ratio of employed workers (E) to the working-age population, thus labour force participation; the second term measures how many hours (per year) each worker works; and the third term measures productivity per hour: the amount of output produced per hour worked. This decomposition helps understand why per capita income in any country can increase or decrease over time. There may be three reasons (identified by the three terms on the right side):

● because fewer people work;
● because those who work work fewer hours;
● finally, because those who work, when they do, produce less.

Which of these factors explains the low per capita income in Europe relative to the USA? As shown in Table 13.2, the factors differ from country to country. The explanation for the low output per capita in Italy is, above all, the low labour force participation, while in Germany it is mainly a matter of too few hours worked by those who work. Instead, hourly productivity is sometimes higher in Europe than in the USA. For example, hourly productivity was 5% higher in Italy than in the USA in 2004.

Understanding this decomposition is clearly the first step to asking which policies are best suited to raising per capita income. For example, in Italy the priority is labour force participation: too few people work or are willing to work. And the problem is not only the participation rate of women – historically very low in Italy as in other Mediterranean countries; participation is low even among young people, especially in the age group between 24 and 29 years. In France and in Germany, the gap in per capita income with the USA is largely explained by fewer working hours per worker. Ireland was closer to the USA in 2004 than the three largest countries in continental Europe because participation and working hours per head were both higher.

Table 13.2 Decomposition of per capita income in some European countries compared to the USA, 2004

Country (USA = 100)	Output per capita	Participation	Hours worked per capita	Hourly productivity
Italy	75	−19	−11	5
France	77	−11	−15	3
Germany	75	−5	−21	1
Ireland	89	−6	−8	3

SUMMARY

- Over long periods, fluctuations in output are dwarfed by growth – the steady increase of aggregate output over time.

- Looking at growth in four rich countries (France, Japan, the UK and the USA) since 1950, two main facts emerge:

  - All four countries have experienced strong growth and a large increase in the standard of living. Growth from 1950 to 2009 increased real output per person by a factor of 3.1 in the USA, by a factor of 10.2 in Japan.

  - The levels of output per person across the four countries have converged over time. Put another way, those countries that were behind have grown faster, reducing the gap between them and the current leader, the USA.

- Looking at the evidence across a broader set of countries and a longer period, the following facts emerge:

  - On the scale of human history, sustained output growth is a recent phenomenon.

  - The convergence of levels of output per person is not a world-wide phenomenon. Many Asian countries are rapidly catching up, but most African countries have both low levels of output per person and low growth rates.

- To think about growth, economists start from an aggregate production function relating aggregate output to two factors of production: capital and labour. How much output is produced, given these inputs, depends on the state of technology.

- Under the assumption of constant returns, the aggregate production function implies that increases in output per worker can come either from increases in capital per worker or from improvements in the state of technology.

- Capital accumulation by itself cannot permanently sustain growth of output per person. Nevertheless, how much a country saves is very important because the saving rate determines the level of output per person, if not its growth rate.

- Sustained growth of output per person is ultimately due to technological progress. Perhaps the most important question in growth theory is what determines technological progress.

KEY TERMS

growth 286

standard of living 287

output per person 287

purchasing power, purchasing power parity (PPP) 288

Easterlin paradox 290

logarithmic scale 290

convergence 292

Malthusian trap 294

four tigers 295

aggregate production function 296

state of technology 297

constant returns to scale 297

decreasing returns to capital 297

decreasing returns to labour 297

capital accumulation 299

technological progress 299

saving rate 299

QUESTIONS AND PROBLEMS

QUICK CHECK

1. *Using the information in this chapter, label each of the following statements true, false or uncertain. Explain briefly.*

a. On a logarithmic scale, a variable that increases at 5% per year will move along an upward-sloping line with a slope of 0.05.

b. The price of food is higher in poor countries than it is in rich countries.

c. Evidence suggests that happiness in rich countries increases with output per person.

d. In virtually all the countries of the world, output per person is converging to the level of output per person in the USA.

e. For about 1,000 years after the fall of the Roman Empire, there was essentially no growth in output per person in Europe, because any increase in output led to a proportional increase in population.

f. Capital accumulation does not affect the level of output in the long run; only technological progress does.

g. The aggregate production function is a relation between output on one hand and labour and capital on the other.

2. *Assume that the average consumer in Mexico and the average consumer in the UK buy the quantities and pay the prices indicated in the following table:*

	Food		Transportation services	
	Price	Quantity	Price	Quantity
Mexico	5 pesos	400	20 pesos	200
UK	£1	1,000	£2	2,000

a. Compute UK consumption per capita in pounds.

b. Compute Mexican consumption per capita in pounds.

c. Suppose that £1 is worth 10 pesos. Compute Mexico's consumption per capita in pounds.

d. Using the purchasing power parity method and UK prices, compute Mexican consumption per capita in pounds.

e. Under each method, how much lower is the standard of living in Mexico than in the UK? Does the choice of method make a difference?

3. *Consider the production function* $Y = \sqrt{K} \sqrt{N}$.

a. Compute output when $K = 49$ and $N = 81$.

b. If both capital and labour double, what happens to output?

c. Is this production function characterised by constant returns to scale? Explain.

d. Write this production function as a relation between output per worker and capital per worker.

e. Let $K/N = 4$. What is Y/N? Now double K/N to 8. Does Y/N double as a result?

f. Does the relation between output per worker and capital per worker exhibit constant returns to scale?

g. Is your answer in (f) the same as your answer in (c)? Why or why not?

h. Plot the relation between output per worker and capital per worker. Does it have the same general shape as the relation in Figure 13.5? Explain.

DIG DEEPER

4. *The growth rates of capital and output*

Consider the production function given in problem 3. Assume that N is constant and equal to 1. Note that if $z = x^a$, *then* $g_z \approx a g_x$ *where* g_z *and* g_x *are the growth rates of z and x.*

a. Given the growth approximation here, derive the relation between the growth rate of output and the growth rate of capital.

b. Suppose we want to achieve output growth equal to 2% per year. What is the required rate of growth of capital?

c. In (b), what happens to the ratio of capital to output over time?

d. Is it possible to sustain output growth of 2% for ever in this economy? Why or why not?

5. *Between 1950 and 1973, France, Germany and Japan all experienced growth rates that were at least 2 percentage points higher than those in the USA. Yet the most important technological advances of that period were made in the USA. How can this be?*

EXPLORE FURTHER

6. *Convergence between Japan and the USA since 1950*

*Go to the website containing the Penn World Table (**http://pwt.econ.upenn.edu**) and collect data on the annual growth rate of GDP per person for the USA and Japan from 1951 to the most recent year available. In addition, collect the numbers for real GDP per person (chained series) for the USA and Japan in 1973.*

a. Compute the average annual growth rates of GDP per person for the USA and Japan for three time periods: 1951–1973, 1974 to the most recent year available and 1991 to the most recent year available. Did the level of real output per person in Japan tend to converge to the level of real output per person in the USA in each of these three periods? Explain.

b. Suppose that in every year since 1973, Japan and the USA had each achieved their average annual growth rates for the period 1951–1973. How would real GDP per person compare in Japan and the USA today (i.e. in the most recent year available in the Penn World Table)?

7. *Convergence in two sets of countries*

Go to the website containing the Penn World Table (http://pwt.econ.upenn.edu) and collect data on real GDP per person (chained series) from 1951 to the most recent year available for the USA, France, Belgium, Italy, Argentina, Venezuela, Chad and Madagascar.

a. Define for each country for each year the ratio of its real GDP to that of the USA for that year (so that this ratio will be equal to 1 for the USA for all years).

b. In one graph, plot the ratios for France, Belgium and Italy over the period for which you have data. Does your graph support the notion of convergence among France, Belgium, Italy and the USA?

c. Draw a graph with the ratios for Argentina, Venezuela, Chad and Madagascar. Does your new graph support the notion of convergence among Argentina, Venezuela, Chad, Madagascar and the USA?

8. *Growth successes and failures*

Go to the website containing the Penn World Table (http://pwt.econ.upenn.edu) and collect data on real GDP per capita (chained series) for 1970 for all available countries. Do the same for a recent year of data, say one year before the most recent year available in the Penn World Table. (If you choose the most recent year available, the Penn World Table may not have the data for some countries relevant to this question.)

a. Rank the countries according to GDP per person in 1970. List the countries with the ten highest levels of GDP per person in 1970. Are there any surprises?

b. Carry out the analysis in part (a) for the most recent year for which you collected data. Has the composition of the ten richest countries changed since 1970?

c. For each of the ten countries you listed in part (b), divide the recent level of GDP per capita by the level in 1970. Which of these countries has had the greatest proportional increase in GDP per capita since 1970?

d. Carry out the exercise in part (c) for all the countries for which you have data. Which country has had the highest proportional increase in GDP per capita since 1970? Which country had the smallest proportional increase? What fraction of countries have had negative growth since 1970?

e. Do a brief Internet search on either the country from part (c) with the greatest increase in GDP per capita or the country from part (d) with the smallest increase. Can you ascertain any reasons for the economic success, or lack of it, for this country?

---

*Log on to **MyEconLab** and complete the studyplan exercises for this chapter to see how much you have learnt, and where you need to revise most.*

MyEconLab

FURTHER READING

- Brad deLong has a number of fascinating articles on growth on his web page (*http://econ161.berkeley.edu/*). Read in particular 'Berkeley faculty lunch talk: main themes of twentieth century economic history', which covers many of the themes of this chapter.

- A broad presentation of facts about growth is given by Angus Maddison in *The World Economy: A Millenium Perspective* (Paris: OECD, 2001). The associated site

www.theworldeconomy.org has a large number of facts and data on growth over the last two millenia.

- Chapter 3 in *Productivity and American Leadership* by William Baumol, Sue Anne Batey Blackman and Edward Wolff (Cambridge, MA: MIT Press 1989) gives a vivid description of how life has been transformed by growth in the USA since the mid-1880s.

Chapter 14

SAVING, CAPITAL ACCUMULATION AND OUTPUT

Since 1950 OECD countries have had very different **saving rates** – the ratio of saving to GDP – from one another. Some countries have traditionally high saving rates, such as Japan (30%), Germany (24%) and Italy (30%). Can this explain why growth rates have been different across OECD countries? Can this also explain why growth rates in the USA have been lower than the rates in most other OECD countries in the past 50 years?

We have already given the basic answer to these questions earlier (at the end of Chapter 13). The answer is no. Over long periods – an important qualification to which we will return – an economy's growth rate does not depend on its saving rate. However, even if the saving rate does not permanently affect the growth rate, it does affect the level of output and the standard of living.

This chapter focuses on the effects of the saving rate on the level and the growth rate of output.

- Sections 14.1 and 14.2 look at the interactions between output and capital accumulation and the effects of the saving rate.

- Section 14.3 plugs in numbers to give a better sense of the magnitudes involved.

- Section 14.4 extends our discussion to take into account not only physical but also human capital.

14.1 INTERACTIONS BETWEEN OUTPUT AND CAPITAL

At the centre of the determination of output in the long run are two relations between output and capital:

- The amount of capital determines the amount of output being produced.
- The amount of output determines the amount of saving and, in turn, the amount of capital being accumulated over time.

Together, these two relations, which are represented in Figure 14.1 determine the evolution of output and capital over time. The green arrow captures the first relation, from capital to output. The blue and purple arrows capture the two parts of the second relation, from output to saving and investment, and from investment to the change in the capital stock. Let's look at each relation in turn.

The effects of capital on output

We started discussing the first of these two relations, the effect of capital on output, in section 13.3. There we introduced the aggregate production function and you saw that, under the assumption of constant returns to scale, we can write the following relation between output and capital per worker:

$$\frac{Y}{N} = F\left(\frac{K}{N}, 1\right)$$

Output per worker, Y/N, is an increasing function of capital per worker, K/N. Under the assumption of decreasing returns to capital, the effect of a given increase in capital per worker on output per worker decreases as the ratio of capital per worker gets larger. When capital per worker is already very high, further increases in capital per worker have only a small effect on output per worker.

To simplify notation, we will rewrite this relation between output and capital per worker simply as

$$\frac{Y}{N} = f\left(\frac{K}{N}\right)$$

where the function f represents the same relation between output and capital per worker as the function F:

$$f\left(\frac{K}{N}\right) \equiv F\left(\frac{K}{N}, 1\right)$$

In this chapter, we shall make two further assumptions:

- The first is that the size of the population, the participation rate and the unemployment rate are all constant. This implies that employment, N, is also constant. To see why, go back to the relations we saw earlier (in Chapter 2 and again in Chapter 8), between population, the labour force, unemployment and employment.

Suppose, for example, that the function F has the 'double square root' form:

$$F(K, N) = \sqrt{K}\sqrt{N}$$
$$\text{so } Y = \sqrt{K}\sqrt{N}.$$

Divide both sides by N, so

$$\frac{Y}{N} = \frac{\sqrt{K}\sqrt{N}}{\sqrt{N}} \longleftarrow N$$

Note that:

$$N \longrightarrow \frac{\sqrt{N}}{\sqrt{N}} = \frac{\sqrt{N}}{\sqrt{N}\sqrt{N}} = \frac{1}{\sqrt{N}}.$$

◄ Replacing in the preceding equation:

$$\frac{Y}{N} = \frac{\sqrt{K}}{\sqrt{N}} = \sqrt{\frac{K}{N}}$$

So, in this case, the function f giving the relation between output per worker and capital per worker is simply the square root function:

$$f\left(\frac{K}{N}\right) = \sqrt{\frac{K}{N}}$$

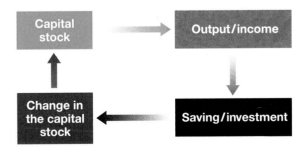

Figure 14.1

Capital, output and saving/investment

● The labour force is equal to population times the participation rate. So if population is constant, and the participation rate is constant, the labour force is also constant.

● Employment, in turn, is equal to the labour force times one minus the unemployment rate. If, for example, the size of the labour force is 100 million, and the unemployment rate is 5%, then employment is equal to 95 million (100 million times (1 − 0.05)). So, if the labour force is constant, and the unemployment rate is constant, employment is also constant.

Under these assumptions, output per worker, output per person, and output itself all move proportionately. Although we will usually refer to movements in output or capital *per worker*, to lighten the text we shall sometimes just talk about movements in output or capital, leaving out the 'per worker' or 'per person' qualification. The reason for assuming that N is constant is to make it easier to focus on how capital accumulation affects growth: if N is constant, the only factor of production that changes over time is capital. The assumption is not very realistic, however, so we will relax it in the next two chapters. Later (in Chapter 15), we will allow for steady population and employment growth. But this step is better left to later.

● The second assumption is that there is no technological progress, so the production function f (or, equivalently, F) does not change over time.

Again, the reason for making this assumption – which is obviously contrary to reality – is to focus just on the role of capital accumulation. Later (in Chapter 15), we shall introduce technological progress and see that the basic conclusions we derive here about the role of capital in growth also hold when there is technological progress. Again, this step is better left to later.

With these two assumptions, our first relation between output and capital per worker, from the production side, can be written as

$$\frac{Y_t}{N} = f\left(\frac{K_t}{N}\right) \tag{14.1}$$

where we have introduced time indexes for output and capital – but not for labour, N, which we assume to be constant, and so does not need a time index.

> From the production side: the level of capital per worker determines the level of output per worker.

In words: higher capital per worker leads to higher output per worker.

The effects of output on capital accumulation

To derive the second relation between output and capital accumulation, we proceed in two steps:

1. First, we derive the relation between output and investment.
2. Then we derive the relation between investment and capital accumulation.

Output and investment

To derive the relation between output and investment, we make three assumptions:

> Saving and investment need not be equal in an open economy (see Chapters 7 and 12). A country can save less than it invests, and borrow the difference from the rest of the world. This is indeed the case for the USA today.

● We continue to assume that the economy is closed. As we saw earlier (in Chapter 3, equation (3.10)), this means that investment, I, is equal to saving – the sum of private saving, S, and public saving, $T - G$:

$$I = S + (T - G)$$

> This assumption is again at odds with the situation in the USA today, where (as we saw in Chapter 1), the government is running a very large budget deficit. In other words, in the USA public saving is negative.

● To focus on the behavior of private saving, we assume public saving, $T - G$, is equal to zero. (We shall relax this assumption later when we focus on the effects of fiscal policy on growth.) With this assumption, the previous equation becomes

$$I = 8$$

Investment is equal to private saving.

● We assume that private saving is proportional to income, so

$$S = sY$$

The parameter s is the saving rate. It has a value between zero and 1. This assumption captures two basic facts about saving: first, the saving rate does not appear to systematically increase or decrease as a country becomes richer. Second, richer countries do not appear to have systematically higher or lower saving rates than poorer ones.

Combining these two relations, and introducing time indexes, gives a simple relation between investment and output:

$$I_t = sY_t$$

Investment is proportional to output: the higher the output, the higher the saving and thus the investment.

> ◄ You have now seen two specifications of saving behaviour (equivalently consumption behaviour): one for the short run earlier (in Chapter 3), and one for the long run in this chapter. You may wonder how the two specifications relate to each other, and whether they are consistent. The answer is yes. (A full discussion is given in Chapter 17.)

Investment and capital accumulation

The second step relates investment, which is a flow (the new machines produced and new plants built during a given period), to capital, which is a stock (the existing machines and plants in the economy at a point in time).

> ◄ Recall: flows are variables that have a time dimension (that is, they are defined per unit of time); stocks are variables that do not have a time dimension (they are defined at a point in time). Output, saving and investment are flows. Employment and capital are stocks.

Think of time as measured in years, so t denotes year t, $t + 1$ denotes year $t + 1$, and so on. Think of the capital stock as being measured at the beginning of each year, so K_t refers to the capital stock at the beginning of year t, K_{t+1} to the capital stock at the beginning of year $t + 1$, and so on.

Assume that capital depreciates at rate δ (the lower-case Greek letter delta) per year: that is, from one year to the next, a proportion δ of the capital stock breaks down and becomes useless. Equivalently, a proportion $(1 - \delta)$ of the capital stock remains intact from one year to the next.

The evolution of the capital stock is then given by

$$K_{t+1} = (1 - \delta) K_t + I_t$$

The capital stock at the beginning of year $t + 1$, K_{t+1}, is equal to the capital stock at the beginning of year t, which is still intact in year $t + 1$, $(1 - \delta) K_t$, plus the new capital stock put in place during year t, i.e. investment during year t, I_t.

We can now combine the relation between output and investment, and the relation between investment and capital accumulation to obtain the second relation we need in order to think about growth: the relation from output to capital accumulation.

Replacing investment by its expression from above, and dividing both sides by N (the number of workers in the economy) gives

$$\frac{K_{t+1}}{N} = (1 - \delta)\frac{K_t}{N} + s\frac{Y_t}{N}$$

In words: capital per worker at the beginning of year $t + 1$ is equal to capital per worker at the beginning of year t, adjusted for depreciation, plus investment per worker during year t, which is equal to the saving rate times output per worker during year t.

Expanding the term $(1 - \delta)K_t/N$ to $K_t/N - \delta K_t/N$, moving K_t/N to the left, and reorganising the right side, we have

$$\frac{K_{t+1}}{N} - \frac{K_t}{N} = s\frac{Y_t}{N} - \delta\frac{K_t}{N} \qquad [14.2]$$

In words: the change in the capital stock per worker – represented by the difference between the two terms on the left – is equal to saving per worker – represented by the first term on the right – minus depreciation – represented by the second term on the right. This equation gives us the second relation between output and capital per worker.

> ◄ From the saving side: the level of output per worker determines the change in the level of capital per worker over time.

14.2 THE IMPLICATIONS OF ALTERNATIVE SAVING RATES

We have derived two relations:

● From the production side, we have seen in equation (14.1) how capital determines output.
● From the saving side, we have seen in equation (14.2) how output in turn determines capital accumulation.

We can now put the two relations together and see how they determine the behaviour of output and capital over time.

Dynamics of capital and output

Replacing output per worker (Y_t/N) in equation (14.2) by its expression in terms of capital per worker from equation (14.1) gives

$$\frac{K_{t+1}}{N} - \frac{K_t}{N} = sf\left(\frac{K_t}{N}\right) - \delta\frac{K_t}{N} \qquad [14.3]$$

$$\underset{\text{from year } t \text{ to year } t+1}{\text{Change in capital}} = \underset{\text{during year } t}{\text{Investment}} - \underset{\text{during year } t}{\text{Depreciation}}$$

This relation describes what happens to capital per worker. The change in capital per worker from this year to next year depends on the difference between two terms:

$K_t/N \Rightarrow f(K_t/N) \Rightarrow sf(K_t/N)$

● Investment per worker, the first term on the right. The level of capital per worker this year determines output per worker this year. Given the saving rate, output per worker determines the amount of saving per worker and thus the investment per worker this year.

$K_t/N \Rightarrow \delta K_t/N$

● Depreciation per worker, the second term on the right. The capital stock per worker determines the amount of depreciation per worker this year.

If investment per worker exceeds depreciation per worker, the change in capital per worker is positive: capital per worker increases.

If investment per worker is less than depreciation per worker, the change in capital per worker is negative: capital per worker decreases.

Given capital per worker, output per worker is then given by equation (14.1)

$$\frac{Y_t}{N} = f\left(\frac{K_t}{N}\right)$$

Equations (14.3) and (14.1) contain all the information we need to understand the dynamics of capital and output over time. The easiest way to interpret them is to use a graph. We do this in Figure 14.2: output per worker is measured on the vertical axis, and capital per worker is measured on the horizontal axis.

In Figure 14.2, look first at the curve representing output per worker, $f(K_t/N)$, as a function of capital per worker. The relation is the same as in Figure 13.6: output per worker increases with capital per worker, but – because of decreasing returns to capital – the effect is smaller the higher the level of capital per worker.

Now look at the two curves representing the two components on the right of equation (14.3):

● The relation representing investment per worker, $sf(K_t/N)$, has the same shape as the production function except that it is lower by a factor s (the saving rate). Suppose the level of capital per worker is equal to K_0/N in Figure 14.2. Output per worker is then given by the distance AB, and investment per worker is given by the vertical distance AC, which is equal to s times the vertical distance AB. Thus, just like output per worker,

Figure 14.2

Capital and output dynamics

When capital and output are low, investment exceeds depreciation and capital increases. When capital and output are high, investment is less than depreciation and capital decreases.

investment per worker increases with capital per worker, but by less and less as capital per worker increases. When capital per worker is already very high, the effect of a further increase in capital per worker on output per worker, and by implication on investment per worker, is very small.

- The relation representing depreciation per worker, $\delta K_t/N$ is represented by a straight line. Depreciation per worker increases in proportion to capital per worker so the relation is represented by a straight line with slope equal to δ. At the level of capital per worker K_0/N, depreciation per worker is given by the vertical distance AD.

◀ To make the graph easier to read, we have assumed an unrealistically high saving rate. (Can you tell roughly what value we have assumed for *s*? What would be a plausible value for *s*?)

The change in capital per worker is given by the difference between investment per worker and depreciation per worker. At K_0/N, the difference is positive; investment per worker exceeds depreciation per worker by an amount represented by the vertical distance CD = AC − AD, so capital per worker increases. As we move to the right along the horizontal axis and look at higher and higher levels of capital per worker, investment increases by less and less, while depreciation keeps increasing in proportion to capital. For some level of capital per worker, K^*/N in Figure 14.2, investment is just enough to cover depreciation, and capital per worker remains constant. To the left of K^*/N, investment exceeds depreciation and capital per worker increases. This is indicated by the arrows pointing to the right along the curve representing the production function. To the right of K^*/N, depreciation exceeds investment, and capital per worker decreases. This is indicated by the arrows pointing to the left along the curve representing the production function.

Characterising the evolution of capital per worker and output per worker over time is now easy. Consider an economy that starts with a low level of capital per worker – say, K_0/N in Figure 14.2. Because investment exceeds depreciation at this point, capital per worker increases. And because output moves with capital, output per worker increases as well. Capital per worker eventually reaches K^*/N, the level at which investment is equal to depreciation. Once the economy has reached the level of capital per worker K^*/N, output per worker and capital per worker remain constant at Y^*/N and K^*/N, their long-run equilibrium levels.

◀ When capital per worker is low, capital per worker and output per worker increase over time. When capital per worker is high, capital per worker and output per worker decrease over time.

Think, for example, of a country that loses part of its capital stock, say, as a result of bombing during a war. The mechanism we have just seen suggests that, if the country has suffered larger capital losses than population losses, it will come out of the war with a low level of capital per worker: that is, at a point to the left of K^*/N. The country will then experience a large increase in both capital per worker and output per worker for some time. This describes well what happened after the Second World War to countries that

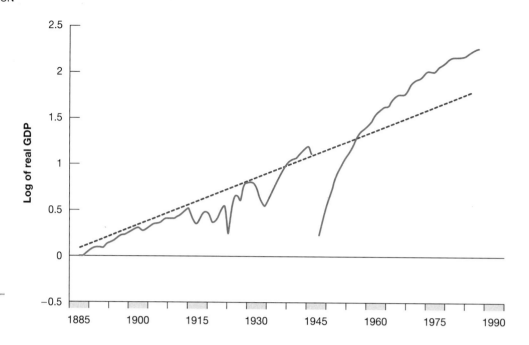

Figure 14.3

German log real GDP, 1885–1990

had proportionately larger destructions of capital than losses of human lives. Figure 14.3 shows that Germany experienced an extraordinary fast growth of output after 1945 (see the Focus box 'Capital accumulation and growth in France in the aftermath of the Second World War').

What does the model predict for ➤ post-war growth if a country suffers proportional losses in population and in capital? Do you find this answer convincing? What elements may be missing from the model?

If a country starts instead from a high level of capital per worker – that is, from a point to the right of K^*/N – then depreciation will exceed investment, and capital per worker and output per worker will decrease: the initial level of capital per worker is too high to be sustained, given the saving rate. This decrease in capital per worker will continue until the economy again reaches the point where investment is equal to depreciation and capital per worker is equal to K^*/N. From then on, capital per worker and output per worker will remain constant.

Steady-state capital and output

Let's look more closely at the levels of output per worker and capital per worker to which the economy converges in the long run. The state in which output per worker and capital per worker are no longer changing is called the **steady state** of the economy. Putting the left side of equation (14.3) equal to zero (in steady state, by definition, the change in capital per worker is zero), the steady-state value of capital per worker, K^*/N, is given by

$$sf\left(\frac{K^*}{N}\right) = \delta\frac{K^*}{N} \qquad [14.4]$$

The steady-state value of capital per worker is such that the amount of saving per worker (the left side) is just sufficient to cover depreciation of the capital stock per worker K^*/N is the long-run level of capital per ➤ (the right side).

worker.

Given steady-state capital per worker (K^*/N), the steady-state value of output per worker (Y^*/N), is given by the production function

$$\frac{Y^*}{N} = f\left(\frac{K^*}{N}\right) \qquad [14.5]$$

We now have all the elements we need to discuss the effects of the saving rate on output per worker, both over time and in steady state.

FOCUS

Capital accumulation and growth in France in the aftermath of the Second World War

When the Second World War ended in 1945, France had suffered some of the heaviest losses of all European countries. The losses in lives were large. More than 550,000 people had died, out of a population of 42 million. Relatively speaking, though, the losses in capital were much larger: it is estimated that the French capital stock in 1945 was about 30% below its pre-war value. A vivid picture of the destruction of capital is provided by the numbers in Table 14.1.

The model of growth we have just seen makes a clear prediction about what will happen to a country that loses a large part of its capital stock: the country will experience high capital accumulation and output growth for some time. In terms of Figure 14.2, a country with capital per

Table 14.1 Proportion of the French capital stock destroyed by the end of the Second World War

Railways	Tracks	6%
	Stations	38%
	Engines	21%
	Hardware	60%
Roads	Cars	31%
	Trucks	40%
Rivers	Waterways	86%
	Canal locks	11%
	Barges	80%
Buildings	(numbers)	
	Dwellings	1,229,000
	Industrial	246,000

Source: See source note for this box.

worker initially far below K^*/N will grow rapidly as it converges to K^*/N and output per worker converges to Y^*/N.

This prediction fares well in the case of post-war France. There is plenty of anecdotal evidence that small increases in capital led to large increases in output. Minor repairs to a major bridge would lead to the reopening of the bridge. Reopening the bridge would significantly shorten the travel time between two cities, leading to much lower transport costs. The lower transport costs would then enable a plant to get much needed inputs, increase its production, and so on.

More convincing evidence, however, comes directly from actual aggregate output numbers. From 1946 to 1950, the annual growth rate of French real GDP was a very high 9.6% per year. This led to an increase in real GDP of about 60% over the course of five years.

Was all of the increase in French GDP due to capital accumulation? The answer is no. There were other forces at work in addition to the mechanism in our model. Much of the remaining capital stock in 1945 was old. Investment had been low in the 1930s (a decade dominated by the Great Depression) and nearly nonexistent during the war. A good portion of the post-war capital accumulation was associated with the introduction of more modern capital and the use of more modern production techniques. This was another reason for the high growth rates of the post-war period.

Source: Gilles Saint-Paul, 'Economic reconstruction in France, 1945–1958', in Rudiger Dornbusch, Willem Nolling, and Richard Layard, eds, *Postwar Economic Reconstruction and Lessons for the East Today* (Cambridge, MA: MIT Press, 1993).

The saving rate and output

Let's return to the question asked at the beginning of the chapter: how does the saving rate affect the growth rate of output per worker? Our analysis leads to a three-part answer:

1. The saving rate has no effect on the long-run growth rate of output per worker, which is equal to zero.

    This conclusion is rather obvious: we have seen that, eventually, the economy converges to a constant level of output per worker. In other words, in the long run, the growth rate of output is equal to zero, no matter what the saving rate is.

    There is, however, a way of thinking about this conclusion that will be useful when we introduce technological progress later (in Chapter 15). Think of what would be needed to sustain a constant positive growth rate of output per worker in the long run. Capital per worker would have to increase. Not only that, but, because of decreasing returns to capital, it would also have to increase faster than output per worker. This

Figure 14.4

The effects of different saving rates

A country with a higher saving rate achieves a higher steady-state level of output per worker.

Some economists argue that the high output growth achieved by the Soviet Union from 1950 to 1990 was the result of such a steady increase in the saving rate over time, which could not be sustained forever. Paul Krugman has used ➤ the term 'Stalinist growth' to denote this type of growth – growth resulting from a higher and higher saving rate over time.

Note that the first proposition is a state- ➤ ment about the growth rate of output per worker. The second proposition is a statement about the level of output per worker.

implies that each year the economy would have to save a larger and larger fraction of its output and dedicate it to capital accumulation. At some point, the fraction of output it would need to save would be greater than one – something clearly impossible. This is why it is impossible, absent technological progress, to sustain a constant positive growth rate forever. In the long run, capital per worker must be constant, and so output per worker must be constant too.

2. Nonetheless, the saving rate determines the level of output per worker in the long run. Other things being equal, countries with a higher saving rate will achieve higher output per worker in the long run.

   Figure 14.4 illustrates this point. Consider two countries with the same production function, the same level of employment, and the same depreciation rate, but different saving rates, say s_0 and $s_1 > s_0$. Figure 14.4 draws their common production function, $f(K_t/N)$, and the functions showing saving/investment per worker as a function of capital per worker for each of the two countries, $s_0 f(K_t/N)$ and $s_1 f(K_t/N)$. In the long run, the country with saving rate s_0 will reach the level of capital per worker K_0/N and output per worker Y_0/N. The country with saving rate s_1 will reach the higher levels K_1/N and Y_1/N.

3. An increase in the saving rate will lead to higher growth of output per worker for some time, but not forever.

   This conclusion follows from the two propositions we just discussed. From the first, we know that an increase in the saving rate does not affect the long-run growth rate of output per worker, which remains equal to zero. From the second, we know that an increase in the saving rate leads to an increase in the long-run level of output per worker. It follows that, as output per worker increases to its new higher level in response to the increase in the saving rate, the economy will go through a period of positive growth. This period of growth will come to an end when the economy reaches its new steady state.

   We can use Figure 14.4 again to illustrate this point. Consider a country that has an initial saving rate of s_0. Assume that capital per worker is initially equal to K_0/N, with associated output per worker Y_0/N. Now consider the effects of an increase in the saving rate from s_0 to s_1. The function giving saving/investment per worker as a function of capital per worker shifts upwards from $s_0 f(K_t/N)$ to $s_1 f(K_t/N)$.

   At the initial level of capital per worker, K_0/N, investment exceeds depreciation, so capital per worker increases. As capital per worker increases, so does output per worker, and the economy goes through a period of positive growth. When capital per worker eventually reaches K_1/N, however, investment is again equal to depreciation, and

(Without technological progress)

Figure 14.5

The effects of an increase in the saving rate on output per worker

An increase in the saving rate leads to a period of higher growth until output reaches its new, higher steady-state level.

growth ends. From then on, the economy remains at K_1/N, with associated output per worker Y_1/N. The movement of output per worker is plotted against time in Figure 14.5. Output per worker is initially constant at level Y_0/N. After the increase in the saving rate, say, at time t, output per worker increases for some time until it reaches the higher level of output per worker Y_1/N, and the growth rate returns to zero.

We have derived these three results under the assumption that there was no technological progress, and, therefore, no growth of output per worker in the long run. But, as we will see (in Chapter 15), the three results extend to an economy in which there is technological progress. Let us briefly indicate how.

An economy in which there is technological progress has a positive growth rate of output per worker, even in the long run. This long-run growth rate is independent of the saving rate – the extension of the first result just discussed. The saving rate affects the level of output per worker, however – the extension of the second result. An increase in the saving rate leads to growth greater than steady-state growth rate for some time until the economy reaches its new higher path – the extension of our third result.

These three results are illustrated in Figure 14.6, which extends Figure 14.5 by plotting the effect an increase in the saving rate has on an economy with positive technological progress. The figure uses a logarithmic scale to measure output per worker: it follows that an economy in which output per worker grows at a constant rate is represented by a line with slope equal to that growth rate. At the initial saving rate, s_0, ◄ See the discussion of logarithmic the economy moves along AA. If, at time t, the saving rate increases to s_1, the economy scales in Appendix 2. experiences higher growth for some time until it reaches its new higher path, BB. On path BB, the growth rate is again the same as before the increase in the saving rate (that is, the slope of BB is the same as the slope of AA).

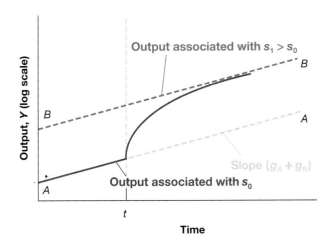

Figure 14.6

The effects of an increase in the saving rate on output per worker in an economy with technological progress

The increase in the saving rate leads to higher growth until the economy reaches its new, higher, balanced growth path.

The saving rate and consumption

Recall: saving is the sum of private plus ➤ public saving. Recall also: public saving ⇔ budget surplus; public dissaving ⇔ budget deficit.

Governments can affect the saving rate in various ways. First, they can vary public saving. Given private saving, positive public saving – a budget surplus, in other words – leads to higher overall saving. Conversely, negative public saving – a budget deficit – leads to lower overall saving. Second, governments can use taxes to affect private saving. For example, they can give tax breaks to people who save, making it more attractive to save, thus increasing private saving.

What saving rate should governments aim for? To think about the answer, we must shift our focus from the behaviour of output to the behaviour of consumption. The reason: what matters to people is not how much is produced, but how much they consume.

It is clear that an increase in saving must come initially at the expense of lower consumption (except when we think it helpful, we drop 'per worker' in this subsection and just refer to consumption rather than consumption per worker, capital rather than capital per worker, and so on): a change in the saving rate this year has no effect on capital this year and, consequently, no effect on output and income this year. So an increase in saving comes initially with an equal decrease in consumption.

Because we assume that employment ➤ is constant, we are ignoring the short-run effect of an increase in the saving rate on output we focused on earlier (in Chapter 3). In the short-run, not only does an increase in the saving rate reduce consumption given income, but it may also create a recession and decrease income further. We will return to a discussion of short-run and long-run effects of changes in saving at various points in the book. (See, for example, Chapter 18.)

Does an increase in saving lead to an increase in consumption in the long run? Not necessarily. Consumption may decrease, not only initially, but also in the long run. You may find this surprising. After all, we know from Figure 14.4 that an increase in the saving rate always leads to an increase in the level of output per worker. But output is not the same as consumption. To see why not, consider what happens for two extreme values of the saving rate:

● An economy in which the saving rate is (and has always been) zero is an economy in which capital is equal to zero. In this case, output is also equal to zero, and so is consumption. A saving rate equal to zero implies zero consumption in the long run.

● Now consider an economy in which the saving rate is equal to one: people save all their income. The level of capital, and thus output, in this economy will be very high. But because people save all of their income, consumption is equal to zero. What happens is that the economy is carrying an excessive amount of capital: simply maintaining that level of output requires that all output be devoted to replacing depreciation! A saving rate equal to one also implies zero consumption in the long run.

These two extreme cases mean that there must be some value of the saving rate between 0 and 1 that maximises the steady-state level of consumption. Increases in the saving rate below this value lead to a decrease in consumption initially, but to an increase in consumption in the long run. Increases in the saving rate beyond this value decrease consumption not only initially, but also in the long run. This happens because the increase in capital associated with the increase in the saving rate leads to only a small increase in output – an increase that is too small to cover the increased depreciation: in other words, the economy carries too much capital. The level of capital associated with the value of the saving rate that yields the highest level of consumption in steady state is known as the **golden-rule level of capital**. Increases in capital beyond the golden-rule level reduce steady-state consumption.

This argument is illustrated in Figure 14.7, which plots consumption per worker in steady state (on the vertical axis) against the saving rate (on the horizontal axis). A saving rate equal to zero implies a capital stock per worker equal to zero, a level of output per worker equal to zero, and by implication, a level of consumption per worker equal to zero. For s between 0 and s_G, (G for golden rule) a higher saving rate leads to higher capital per worker, higher output per worker and higher consumption per worker. For s larger than s_G, increases in the saving rate still lead to higher values of capital per worker and output per worker; but they now lead to lower values of consumption per worker: this is because the increase in output is more than offset by the increase in depreciation due to the larger capital stock. For $s = 1$, consumption per worker is equal to zero. Capital per worker and output per worker are high, but all of the output is used just to replace depreciation, leaving nothing for consumption.

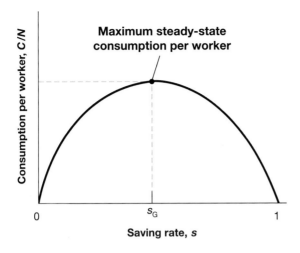

Figure 14.7

The effects of the saving rate on steady-state consumption per worker

An increase in the saving rate leads to an increase and then to a decrease in steady-state consumption per worker.

If an economy already has so much capital that it is operating beyond the golden rule, then increasing saving further will decrease consumption not only now, but also later. Is this a relevant worry? Do some countries actually have too much capital? The empirical evidence indicates that most OECD countries are actually far below their golden-rule level of capital. If they were to increase the saving rate, it would lead to higher consumption in the future – not lower consumption.

This means that, in practice, governments face a trade-off: an increase in the saving rate leads to lower consumption for some time, but higher consumption later. So what should governments do? How close to the golden rule should they try to get? That depends on how much weight they put on the welfare of current generations – who are more likely to lose from policies aimed at increasing the saving rate – versus the welfare of future generations – who are more likely to gain. Enter politics: future generations do not vote. This means that governments are unlikely to ask current generations to make large sacrifices, which in turn, means that capital is likely to stay far below its golden-rule level. These intergenerational issues are at the forefront of the current debate on social security reform in the USA. The Focus box 'Social security, saving and capital accumulation in Europe' explores this further.

FOCUS
Social security, saving and capital accumulation in Europe

Old-age pension programmes were introduced across Europe between the end of the nineteenth and the beginning of the twentieth century. The goal of these programmes was to make sure the elderly would have enough to live on. Over time, social security has become the largest government programme in almost every country, amounting to 44% of total expenditure on social protection in the EU (ranging from 25% in Ireland to 58% in Italy), with benefits paid to retirees exceeding 11% of GDP. For the majority of retirees, pension benefits account for most of their income. There is little question that, on their own terms, social security systems have been a great success, decreasing poverty among the elderly. There is also little question that they have led in many countries to a lower saving rate and therefore lower capital accumulation and lower output per person in the long run.

To understand why, we must take a theoretical detour. Think of an economy in which there is no social security system – one where workers have to save to provide for their own retirement. Now, introduce a pension system that collects taxes from workers and distributes benefits to the retirees. It can do so in one of two ways:

- One way is by taxing workers, investing their contributions in financial assets and paying back the principal plus the interest to the workers when they retire. Such a system is called a **fully funded system**: at any time, the system has funds equal to the accumulated contributions of workers, from which it will be able to pay out benefits to these workers when they retire.

● The other way is by taxing workers and redistributing the tax contributions as benefits to the current retirees. Such a system is called a **pay-as-you-go system**: the system pays benefits out as it goes, that is, as it collects them through contributions.

From the point of view of workers, the two systems are broadly similar. In both cases, the workers pay contributions when they work and receive benefits when they retire. What they receive, however, is slightly different in each case:

● What retirees receive in a fully funded system depends on the rate of return on the financial assets held by the fund.

● What retirees receive in a pay-as-you-go system depends on demographics – the ratio of retirees to workers – and on the evolution of the tax rate set by the system.

From the point of view of the economy, however, the two systems have very different implications:

● In the fully funded system, workers save less because they anticipate receiving benefits when they are old. The social security system saves on their behalf, by investing their contributions in financial assets. The presence of a social security system changes the composition of overall saving: private saving goes down and public saving goes up. But, to a first approximation, it has no effect on total saving and therefore no effect on capital accumulation.

● In the pay-as-you-go system, workers also save less because they again anticipate receiving benefits when they are old. But, now, the social security system does not save on their behalf. The decrease in private saving is not compensated by an increase in public saving. Total saving goes down and so does capital accumulation.

Most actual social security systems are somewhere between pay-as-you-go and fully funded systems. Most European countries have in place public pay-as-you-go pension schemes which are earnings-related: that is, the benefits are some fraction of the last salary, or of an average of salaries earned over the years. These are called 'defined benefit systems'. In the UK, instead, benefits are aimed at preventing poverty rather than providing income in retirement similar to that in working life. This basic pension is meant to be supplemented by funded private pension, and pension fund assets currently amount to more than 85% of UK GDP. Another exception is Denmark, which has a public pension system composed of two elements: a universal, pay-as-you-go scheme financed from general taxation, and a funded scheme financed from contributions from all employed individuals and organised in a separate fund.

In many countries, a shift to a fully funded system has been advocated by many parties, the main argument being that funding the social security systems would increase the saving rate. Such a shift could be achieved by investing, from now on, tax contributions in financial assets rather than distributing them as benefits to retirees. Under such a shift, the social security system would steadily accumulate funds and would eventually become fully funded. Martin Feldstein, an economist at Harvard University and an advocate of such a shift in the USA, has concluded that it could lead to a 34% increase of the capital stock in the long run.

How should we think about such a proposal? It would probably have been a good idea to fully fund the pension systems at the start: each country would have a higher saving rate. The capital stock would be higher, and output and consumption would also be higher. But we cannot rewrite history. The existing systems have promised benefits to retirees, and these promises have to be honoured. This means that, under the proposal we just described, current workers would, in effect, have to contribute twice – once to fund the system and finance their own retirement and then to finance the benefits owed to current retirees. This would impose a disproportionate cost on current workers. The practical implication is that, if it is to happen, the move to a fully funded system will have to be very slow, so that the burden of adjustment does not fall too much on one generation relative to the others. Indeed, some Eastern European countries such as Poland, Slovakia and the Baltic states, are currently implementing a partial shift to a funded system: a share of the contributions paid by workers is now being allocated to individual personal accounts and invested in the financial markets.

What are the potential drawbacks of such reforms? Consider the case in which workers are allowed, from now on, to make contributions to personal accounts instead of to the social security system, and to be able to draw from these accounts when they retire. By itself, this proposal would clearly increase private saving: workers will be saving more. But its ultimate effect on saving depends on how the benefits already promised to current workers and retirees by the social security system are financed. If these benefits are financed not through additional taxes but through debt finance, then the increase in private saving will be offset by an increase in deficits, that is a decrease in public saving: the shift to personal accounts would not increase the total saving rate of the economy. If, instead, these benefits are financed through higher taxes, then the saving rate will increase. But, in that case, current workers will have to both contribute to their personal accounts and pay the higher taxes. They will indeed pay twice.

14.3 GETTING A SENSE OF MAGNITUDES

How big an impact does a change in the saving rate have on output in the long run? For how long and by how much does an increase in the saving rate affect growth? How far is the USA from the golden-rule level of capital? To get a better sense of the answers to these questions, let's now make more specific assumptions, plug in some numbers, and see what we get.

Assume the production function is

$$Y = \sqrt{K}\sqrt{N} \qquad [14.6]$$

Output equals the product of the square root of capital and the square root of labour. (A more general specification of the production function known as the **Cobb–Douglas production function**, and its implications for growth, is given in the appendix to the chapter.)

◀ Check that this production function exhibits both constant returns to scale, and decreasing returns to either capital or labour.

Dividing both sides by N (because we are interested in output per worker), we get

$$\frac{Y}{N} = \frac{\sqrt{K}\sqrt{N}}{N} = \frac{\sqrt{K}}{\sqrt{N}} = \sqrt{\frac{K}{N}}$$

Output per worker equals the square root of capital per worker. Put another way, the production function, f, relating output per worker to capital per worker, is given by

◀ The second equality follows from:
$$\sqrt{N}/N = \sqrt{N}/(\sqrt{N}\sqrt{N})$$
$$= 1/\sqrt{N}$$

$$f\left(\frac{K_t}{N}\right) = \sqrt{\frac{K_t}{N}}$$

Replacing $f(K_t/N)$ with $\sqrt{K_t/N}$ in equation (14.3), we have

$$\frac{K_{t+1}}{N} - \frac{K_t}{N} = s\sqrt{\frac{K_t}{N}} - \delta\frac{K_t}{N} \qquad [14.7]$$

This equation describes the evolution of capital per worker over time. Let's look at what it implies.

The effects of the saving rate on steady-state output

How big an impact does an increase in the saving rate have on the steady-state level of output per worker?

Start with equation (14.7). In steady state the amount of capital per worker is constant, so the left side of the equation equals zero. This implies

$$s\sqrt{\frac{K^*}{N}} = \delta\frac{K^*}{N}$$

(We have dropped time indexes, which are no longer needed because in steady state K/N is constant. The asterisk is to remind you that we are looking at the steady-state value of capital.) Square both sides:

$$s^2\frac{K^*}{N} = \delta^2\left(\frac{K^*}{N}\right)^2$$

Divide both sides by (K/N) and reorganise:

$$\frac{K^*}{N} = \left(\frac{s}{\delta}\right)^2 \qquad [14.8]$$

Steady-state capital per worker is equal to the square of the ratio of the saving rate to the depreciation rate.

From equations (14.6) and (14.8), steady-state output per worker is given by

$$\frac{Y^*}{N} = \sqrt{\frac{K^*}{N}} = \sqrt{\left(\frac{s}{\delta}\right)^2} = \frac{s}{\delta} \qquad [14.9]$$

Steady-state output per worker is equal to the ratio of the saving rate to the depreciation rate.

A higher saving rate and a lower depreciation rate both lead to higher steady-state capital per worker (equation (14.8)) and higher steady-state output per worker (equation (14.9)). To see what this means, let's take a numerical example. Suppose the depreciation rate is 10% per year, and suppose the saving rate is also 10%. Then, from equations (14.8) and (14.9), steady-state capital per worker and output per worker are both equal to 1. Now suppose that the saving rate doubles, from 10% to 20%. It follows from equation (14.8) that in the new steady state, capital per worker increases from 1 to 4. And from equation (14.9), output per worker doubles, from 1 to 2. Thus, doubling the saving rate leads, in the long run, to doubling the output per worker: this is a large effect.

The dynamic effects of an increase in the saving rate

We have just seen that an increase in the saving rate leads to an increase in the steady-state level of output. But how long does it take for output to reach its new steady-state level? Put another way, by how much and for how long does an increase in the saving rate affect the growth rate?

To answer these questions, we must use equation (14.7) and solve it for capital per worker in year 0, in year 1, and so on.

Suppose that the saving rate, which had always been equal to 10%, increases in year 0 from 10% to 20% and remains at this higher value forever after. In year 0, nothing happens to the capital stock (recall that it takes one year for higher saving and higher investment to show up in higher capital). So, capital per worker remains equal to the steady-state value associated with a saving rate of 0.1. From equation (14.8):

$$\frac{K_0}{N} = (0.1/0.1)^2 = 1^2 = 1$$

In year 1, equation (14.7) gives

$$\frac{K_1}{N} - \frac{K_0}{N} = s\sqrt{\frac{K_0}{N}} - \delta\frac{K_0}{N}$$

With a depreciation rate equal to 0.1 and a saving rate now equal to 0.2, this equation implies

$$\frac{K_1}{N} - 1 = [(0.2)(\sqrt{1})] - [(0.1)1]$$

so

$$\frac{K_1}{N} = 1.1$$

In the same way, we can solve for K_2/N, and so on. Once we have determined the values of capital per worker in year 0, year 1, and so on, we can then use equation (14.6) to solve for output per worker in year 0, year 1, and so on. The results of this computation are presented in Figure 14.8. Panel (a) plots the level of output per worker against time. Y/N increases over time from its initial value of 1 in year 0 to its steady-state value of 2 in the long run. Panel (b) gives the same information in a different way, plotting instead the growth rate of output per worker against time. As panel (b) shows, growth of output per worker is highest at the beginning and then decreases over time. As the economy reaches its new steady state, growth of output per worker returns to zero.

The difference between investment and depreciation is greatest at the beginning. This is why capital accumulation and, in turn, output growth is highest at the beginning. ➤

What Figure 14.8 clearly shows is that the adjustment to the new, higher, long-run equilibrium takes a long time. It is only 40% complete after 10 years and it is 63% complete after 20 years. Put another way, the increase in the saving rate increases the growth rate

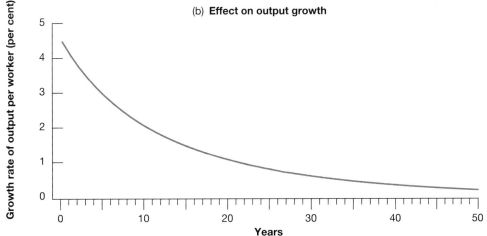

Figure 14.8

The dynamic effects of an increase in the saving rate from 10% to 20% on the level and the growth rate of output per worker

It takes a long time for output to adjust to its new, higher level after an increase in the saving rate. Put another way, an increase in the saving rate leads to a long period of higher growth.

of output per worker for a long time. The average annual growth rate is 3.1% for the first 10 years and it is 1.5% for the next ten. Although the changes in the saving rate have no effect on growth in the long run, they do lead to higher growth for a long time.

To go back to the question raised at the beginning of the chapter, can the low saving/investment rate in the USA explain why the US growth rate has been so low – relative to other OECD countries – since 1950? The answer would be yes if the USA had a higher saving rate in the past, and if this saving rate had fallen substantially in the past 50 years. If this were the case, it could explain the period of lower growth in the USA in the past 50 years along the lines of the mechanism in Figure 14.8 (with the sign reversed, as we would be looking at a decrease – not an increase – in the saving rate). But this is not the case: the US saving rate has been low for a long time. Low saving cannot explain the relative poor US growth performance over the past 50 years.

The saving rate and the golden rule

What is the saving rate that would maximise steady-state consumption per worker? Recall that, in steady state, consumption is equal to what is left after enough is put aside to maintain a constant level of capital. More formally, in steady state, consumption per worker is equal to output per worker minus depreciation per worker:

$$\frac{C}{N} = \frac{Y}{N} - \delta \frac{K}{N}$$

Table 14.2 The saving rate and the steady-state levels of capital, output and consumption per worker

Saving rate s	Capital per worker (K/N)	Output per worker (Y/N)	Consumption per worker (C/N)
0.0	0.0	0.0	0.0
0.1	1.0	1.0	0.9
0.2	4.0	2.0	1.6
0.3	9.0	3.0	2.1
0.4	16.0	4.0	2.4
0.5	25.0	5.0	2.5
0.6	36.0	6.0	2.4
–	–	–	–
1.0	100.0	10.0	0.0

Using equations (14.9) and (14.10) for the steady-state values of output per worker and capital per worker, consumption per worker is thus given by

$$\frac{C}{N} = \frac{s}{\delta} - \delta\left(\frac{s}{\delta}\right)^2 = \frac{s(1-s)}{\delta}$$

Using this equation, together with equations (14.9) and (14.10), Table 14.2 gives the steady-state values of capital per worker, output per worker, and consumption per worker for different values of the saving rate (and for a depreciation rate equal to 10%).

Steady-state consumption per worker is largest when s equals one-half. In other words, the golden-rule level of capital is associated with a saving rate of 50%. Below that level, increases in the saving rate lead to an increase in long-run consumption per worker. We saw earlier that the average saving rate has been very different across OECD countries since 1950. We can be quite confident that in countries with low saving rates, as in the USA, an increase in the saving rate would increase both output per worker and consumption per worker in the long run.

Check your understanding of the issues: using the equations in this section, argue the pros and cons of policy measures aimed at increasing the German saving rate.

14.4 PHYSICAL VERSUS HUMAN CAPITAL

We have concentrated so far on physical capital-machines, plants, office buildings, and so on. But economies have another type of capital: the set of skills of the workers in the economy, or what economists call **human capital**. An economy with many highly skilled workers is likely to be much more productive than an economy in which most workers cannot read or write.

The increase in human capital has been as large as the increase in physical capital over the past two centuries. At the beginning of the Industrial Revolution, only 30% of the population of the countries that constitute the OECD today knew how to read. Today, the literacy rate in OECD countries is above 95%. Schooling was not compulsory prior to the Industrial Revolution. Today it is compulsory, usually until the age of 16. Still, there are large differences across countries. Today, in OECD countries, nearly 100% of children get a primary education, 90% get a secondary education and 38% get a higher education. The corresponding numbers in poor countries, countries with GDP per person below $400, are 95%, 32% and 4%, respectively.

Even this comparison may be misleading because the quality of education can be quite different across countries.

How should we think about the effect of human capital on output? How does the introduction of human capital change our earlier conclusions? These are the questions we take up in this last section.

Extending the production function

The most natural way of extending our analysis to allow for human capital is to modify the production function relation (14.1) to read

$$\frac{Y}{N} = f\left(\frac{K}{N}, \frac{H}{N}\right) \qquad\qquad [14.10]$$
$$(+, +)$$

The level of output per worker depends on both the level of physical capital per worker, K/N, and the level of human capital per worker, H/N. As before, an increase in capital per worker, K/N, leads to an increase in output per worker. And an increase in the average level of skill, H/N, also leads to more output per worker. More skilled workers can do more complex tasks; they can deal more easily with unexpected complications. All of this leads to higher output per worker.

We assumed earlier that increases in physical capital per worker increased output per worker, but that the effect became smaller as the level of capital per worker increased. We can make the same assumption for human capital per worker: think of increases in H/N as coming from increases in the number of years of education. The evidence is that the returns to increasing the proportion of children acquiring a primary education are very large. At the very least, the ability to read and write allows people to use equipment that is more complicated but more productive. For rich countries, however, primary education – and, for that matter, secondary education – are no longer the relevant margin: most children now get both. The relevant margin is now higher education. We are sure it will come as good news to you that the evidence shows that higher education increases people's skills, at least as measured by the increase in the wages of those who acquire it. But, to take an extreme example, it is not clear that forcing everyone to acquire an advanced college degree would increase aggregate output very much. Many people would end up overqualified and probably more frustrated rather than more productive.

How should we construct the measure for human capital, H? The answer is: very much the same way we construct the measure for physical capital, K. To construct K, we just add the values of the different pieces of capital, so that a machine that costs \$2,000 gets twice the weight of a machine that costs \$1,000. Similarly, we construct the measure of H such that workers who are paid twice as much get twice the weight. Take, for example, an economy with 100 workers, half of them unskilled and half of them skilled. Suppose the relative wage of the skilled workers is twice that of the unskilled workers. We can then construct H as $((50 \times 1) + (50 \times 2)) = 150$. Human capital per worker, H/N, is then equal to $150/100 = 1.5$.

> ◄ Note that we are using the same symbol, *H*, to denote the monetary base (in Chapter 4), and human capital in this chapter. Both uses are traditional. Do not be confused.

> ◄ The rationale for using relative wages as weights is that they reflect relative marginal products. A worker who is paid three times as much as another is assumed to have a marginal product that is three times higher.
>
> An issue, however, is whether or not relative wages accurately reflect relative marginal products. To take a controversial example: in the same job, with the same seniority, women still often earn less than men. Is it because their marginal product is lower? Should they be given a lower weight than men in the construction of human capital?

Human capital, physical capital and output

How does the introduction of human capital change the analysis of the previous sections?

Our conclusions about physical capital accumulation remain valid: an increase in the saving rate increases steady-state physical capital per worker and therefore increases output per worker. But our conclusions now extend to human capital accumulation as well. An increase in how much society 'saves' in the form of human capital – through education and on-the-job training – increases steady-state human capital per worker, which leads to an increase in output per worker. Our extended model gives us a richer picture of how output per worker is determined. In the long run, it tells us that output per worker depends on both how much society saves and how much it spends on education.

What are the relative importance of human capital and physical capital in the determination of output per worker? A place to start is to compare how much is spent on formal education to how much is invested in physical capital. In the USA, spending on formal education is about 6.5% of GDP. This number includes both government expenditures on education and private expenditures by people on education. It is between one-third and one-half of the gross investment rate for physical capital (which is around 16%). But this comparison is only a first pass. Consider the following complications:

- Education, especially higher education, is partly consumption – done for its own sake – and partly investment. We should include only the investment part for our purposes. However, the 6.5% number in the preceding paragraph includes both.

How large is your opportunity cost ➤
relative to your tuition?

- At least for post-secondary education, the opportunity cost of a person's education are his or her foregone wages while acquiring the education. Spending on education should include not only the actual cost of education but also this opportunity cost. The 6.5% number does not include this opportunity cost.
- Formal education is only part of education. Much of what we learn comes from on-the-job training, formal or informal. Both the actual costs and the opportunity costs of on-the-job training should also be included. The 6.5% number does not include the costs associated with on-the-job training.
- We should compare investment rates net of depreciation. Depreciation of physical capital, especially of machines, is likely to be higher than depreciation of human capital. Skills deteriorate, but do so only slowly. And unlike physical capital, they deteriorate less quickly the more they are used.

For all these reasons, it is difficult to come up with reliable numbers for investment in human capital. Recent studies conclude that investment in physical capital and in education play roughly similar roles in the determination of output. This implies that output per worker depends roughly equally on the amount of physical capital and the amount of human capital in the economy. Countries that save more and/or spend more on education can achieve substantially higher steady-state levels of output per worker.

Endogenous growth

Note what the conclusion we just reached did say and did not say. It did say that a country that saves more or spends more on education will achieve a higher level of output per worker in steady state. It did not say that by saving or spending more on education a country can sustain permanently higher growth of output per worker.

We have mentioned Lucas once ➤
already in connection with the Lucas
critique (in Chapter 11).

This conclusion, however, has been challenged in the past two decades. Following the lead of Robert Lucas and Paul Romer, researchers have explored the possibility that the joint accumulation of physical capital and human capital might actually be enough to sustain growth. Given human capital, increases in physical capital will run into decreasing returns. And given physical capital, increases in human capital will also run into decreasing returns. But, these researchers have asked, what if both physical and human capital increase in tandem? Can't an economy grow forever just by having steadily more capital and more skilled workers?

Models that generate steady growth even without technological progress are called **models of endogenous growth** to reflect the fact that in those models – in contrast to the model we saw in earlier sections of this chapter – the growth rate depends, even in the long run, on variables such as the saving rate and the rate of spending on education. The jury on this class of models is still out, but the indications so far are that the conclusions we drew earlier need to be qualified, not abandoned. The current consensus is as follows:

- Output per worker depends on the level of both physical capital per worker and human capital per worker. Both forms of capital can be accumulated, one through physical investment, the other through education and training. Increasing either the saving rate and/or the fraction of output spent on education and training can lead to much higher levels of output per worker in the long run. However, given the rate of technological progress, such measures do not lead to a permanently higher growth rate.
- Note the qualifier in the last proposition: *given the rate of technological progress*. But is technological progress unrelated to the level of human capital in the economy? Can't a better educated labour force lead to a higher rate of technological progress? These questions take us to the topic of the next chapter, the sources and the effects of technological progress.

SUMMARY

- In the long run, the evolution of output is determined by two relations. (To make the reading of this summary easier, we shall omit 'per worker' in what follows.) First, the level of output depends on the amount of capital. Second, capital accumulation depends on the level of output, which determines saving and investment.

- These interactions between capital and output imply that, starting from any level of capital (and ignoring technological progress, the topic of Chapter 15), an economy converges in the long run to a steady-state (constant) level of capital. Associated with this level of capital is a steady-state level of output.

- The steady-state level of capital, and thus the steady-state level of output, depend positively on the saving rate. A higher saving rate leads to a higher steady-state level of output; during the transition to the new steady state, a higher saving rate leads to positive output growth. But (again ignoring technological progress) in the long run, the growth rate of output is equal to zero, and so does not depend on the saving rate.

- An increase in the saving rate requires an initial decrease in consumption. In the long run, the increase in the saving rate may lead to an increase or a decrease in consumption, depending on whether the economy is below or above the golden-rule level of capital, the level of capital at which steady-state consumption is highest.

- Most countries have a level of capital below the golden-rule level. Thus, an increase in the saving rate leads to an initial decrease in consumption followed by an increase in consumption in the long run. When considering whether or not to adopt policy measures aimed at changing a country's saving rate, policy makers must decide how much weight to put on the welfare of current generations versus the welfare of future generations.

- While most of the analysis of this chapter focuses on the effects of physical capital accumulation, output depends on the levels of both physical and human capital. Both forms of capital can be accumulated, one through investment, the other through education and training. Increasing the saving rate and/or the fraction of output spent on education and training can lead to large increases in output in the long run.

KEY TERMS

saving rate 304

steady state 310

golden-rule level of capital 314

fully funded system 315

pay-as-you-go system 316

Cobb–Douglas production function 317

human capital 320

models of endogenous growth 322

QUESTIONS AND PROBLEMS

QUICK CHECK

1. *Using the information in this chapter, label each of the following statements true, false or uncertain. Explain briefly.*

a. The saving rate is always equal to the investment rate.

b. A higher investment rate can sustain higher growth of output forever.

c. If capital never depreciated, growth could go on forever.

d. The higher the saving rate, the higher consumption in steady state.

e. We should transform social security from a pay-as-you-go system to a fully funded system. This would increase consumption both now and in the future.

f. When the capital stock is far below the golden-rule level, the government should give tax breaks for saving.

g. Education increases human capital and thus output. It follows that governments should subsidise education.

2. *Consider the following statement: 'The Solow model shows that the saving rate does not affect the growth rate in the long run, so we should stop worrying about the low saving rate. Increasing the saving rate wouldn't have any important effects on the economy.' Do you agree or disagree?*

3. *In Chapter 3 we saw that an increase in the saving rate can lead to a recession in the short run (i.e. the paradox of saving). We examined the issue in the medium run in a chapter problem at the end of Chapter 9. We can now examine the long-run effects of an increase in saving.*

Using the model presented in this chapter, what is the effect of an increase in the saving rate on output per worker likely to be after one decade? After five decades?

DIG DEEPER

4. *Discuss how the level of output per person in the long run would likely be affected by each of the following changes:*

a. The right to exclude saving from income when paying income taxes.

b. A higher rate of female participation in the labour market (but constant population).

5. *Suppose all European countries moved from the current pay-as-you-go social security system to a fully funded one, and financed the transition without additional government borrowing. How would the shift to a fully funded system affect the level and the rate of growth of output per worker in the long run?*

6. *Suppose that the production function is given by*

$$Y = 0.5\sqrt{K}\sqrt{N}$$

a. Derive the steady-state levels of output per worker and capital per worker in terms of the saving rate, s, and the depreciation rate, δ.

b. Derive the equation for steady-state output per worker and steady-state consumption per worker in terms of s and δ.

c. Suppose that $\delta = 0.05$. With your favourite spreadsheet software, compute steady-state output per worker and steady-state consumption per worker for $s = 0$, $s = 0.1$, $s = 0.2$, . . . , $s = 1$. Explain the intuition behind your results.

d. Use your favourite spreadsheet software to graph the steady-state level of output per worker and the steady-state level of consumption per worker as a function of the saving rate (i.e. measure the saving rate on the horizontal axis of your graph and the corresponding values of output per worker and consumption per worker on the vertical axis).

e. Does the graph show that there is a value of s that maximises output per worker? Does the graph show that there is a value of s that maximises consumption per worker? If so, what is this value?

7. *The Cobb–Douglas production function and the steady state. This problem is based on the material in the chapter appendix. Suppose that the economy's production function is given by*

$$Y = K^{a}N^{1-a}$$

and assume that $\alpha = 1/3$.

a. Is this production function characterised by constant returns to scale? Explain.

b. Are there decreasing returns to capital?

c. Are there decreasing returns to labour?

d. Transform the production function into a relation between output per worker and capital per worker.

e. For a given saving rate, s, and depreciation rate, δ, give an expression for capital per worker in the steady state.

f. Give an expression for output per worker in the steady state.

g. Solve for the steady-state level of output per worker when $s = 0.32$ and $\delta = 0.08$.

h. Suppose that the depreciation rate remains constant at $\delta = 0.08$, while the saving rate is reduced by half, to $s = 0.16$. What is the new steady-state output per worker?

8. *Continuing with the logic from problem 7, suppose that the economy's production function is given by $Y = K^{1/3}N^{2/3}$ and that both the saving rate, s, and the depreciation rate, δ, are equal to 0.10.*

a. What is the steady-state level of capital per worker?

b. What is the steady-state level of output per worker?

Suppose that the economy is in steady state and that, in period t, the depreciation rate increases permanently from 0.10 to 0.20.

c. What will be the new steady-state levels of capital per worker and output per worker?

d. Compute the path of capital per worker and output per worker over the first three periods after the change in the depreciation rate.

9. Deficits and the capital stock

For the production function, $Y = \sqrt{K}\sqrt{N}$, equation (14.8) gives the solution for the steady-state capital stock per worker.

a. Retrace the steps in the text that derive equation (14.8).

b. Suppose that the saving rate, s, is initially 15% per year, and the depreciation rate, δ, is 7.5%. What is the steady-state capital stock per worker? What is steady-state output per worker?

c. Suppose that there is a government deficit of 5% of GDP and that the government eliminates this deficit. Assume that private saving is unchanged so that national saving increases to 20%. What is the new steady-state capital stock per worker? What is the new steady-state output per worker? How does this compare to your answer to part (b)?

EXPLORE FURTHER

10. US saving

This question follows the logic of problem 9 to explore the implications of the US budget deficit for the long-run capital stock. The question assumes that the USA will have a budget deficit over the life of this edition of the text.

a. Go to the most recent *Economic Report of the President* (***www.gpoaccess.gov/eop/***). From Table B.32, get the numbers for gross national saving for the most recent year available. From Table B.1, get the number for US GDP for the same year. What is the national saving rate, as a percentage of GDP? Using the depreciation rate and the logic from problem 9, what would be the steady-state capital stock per worker? What would be steady-state output per worker?

b. In Table B.79 of the *Economic Report of the President*, get the number for the federal budget deficit as a percentage of GDP for the year corresponding to the data from part (a). Again, using the reasoning from problem 9, suppose that the federal budget deficit was eliminated and there was no change in private saving. What would be the effect on the long-run capital stock per worker? What would be the effect on long-run output per worker?

FURTHER READING

- The classic treatment of the relation between the saving rate and output is by Robert Solow, *Growth Theory: An Exposition* (New York: Oxford University Press, 1970).

- An easy-to-read discussion of whether and how to increase saving and improve education in the USA is given in Memoranda 23 to 27 in *Memos to the President: A Guide through Macroeconomics for the Busy Policymaker*, by Charles Schultze (the Chairman of the Council of Economic Advisers during the Carter administration), (Washington DC: Brookings Institution, 1992).

APPENDIX

The Cobb–Douglas production function and the steady state

In 1928, Charles Cobb (a mathematician) and Paul Douglas (an economist, who went on to become a US senator) concluded that the following production function gave a very good description of the relation between output, physical capital and labour in the USA from 1899 to 1922:

$$Y = K^\alpha N^{1-\alpha} \qquad [14A.1]$$

with α being a number between zero and 1. Their findings proved surprisingly robust. Even today, the production function (14A.1), now known as the **Cobb–Douglas production function**, still gives a good description of the relation between output, capital and labour in the USA, and it has become a standard tool in the economist's toolbox. (Verify for yourself that it satisfies the two properties we discussed in the text: constant returns to scale, and decreasing returns to capital and to labour.)

The purpose of this appendix is to characterise the steady state of an economy when the production function is given by (14A.1). (All you need to follow the steps is a knowledge of the properties of exponents.)

Recall that, in steady state, saving per worker must be equal to depreciation per worker. Let's see what this implies:

- To derive saving per worker, we must derive first the relation between output per worker and capital per worker implied by equation (14A.1). Divide both sides of equation (14A.1) by N:

$$Y/N = K^\alpha N^{1-\alpha}/N$$

Using the properties of exponents:

$$N^{1-\alpha}/N = N^{1-\alpha} N^{-1} = N^{-\alpha}$$

so, replacing in the preceding equation, we get

$$Y/N = K^\alpha N^{-\alpha} = (K/N)^\alpha$$

Output per worker, Y/N, is equal to the ratio of capital per worker, K/N, raised to the power α.

Saving per worker is equal to the saving rate times output per worker, so using the previous equation, it is equal to

$$s(K^*/N)^\alpha$$

- Depreciation per worker is equal to the depreciation rate times capital per worker:

$$\delta(K^*/N)$$

- The steady-state level of capital, K^*, is determined by the condition that saving per worker be equal to depreciation per worker, so

$$s(K^*/N)^\alpha = \delta(K^*/N)$$

To solve this expression for the steady-state level of capital per worker, K^*/N, divide both sides by $(K^*/N)^\alpha$:

$$s = \delta(K^*/N)^{1-\alpha}$$

Divide both sides by δ, and change the order of the equality:

$$(K^*/N)^{1-\alpha} = s/\delta$$

Finally, raise both sides to the power $1/(1 - \alpha)$:

$$(K^*/N) = (s/\delta)^{1/(1-\alpha)}$$

This gives us the steady-state level of capital per worker.

From the production function, the steady-state level of output per worker is then equal to

$$(y^*/N) = K/N^\alpha = (s/\delta)^{\alpha/(1-\alpha)}$$

Let's see what this last equation implies:

- In the text, we actually worked with a special case of an equation (14A.1), the case where $\alpha = 0.5$. (Taking a variable to the power 0.5 is the same as taking the square root of this variable.) If $\alpha = 0.5$, the preceding equation means

$$y^*/N = s/\delta$$

Output per worker is equal to the ratio of the saving rate to the depreciation rate. This is the equation we discussed in the text. A doubling of the saving rate leads to a doubling in steady-state output per worker.

- The empirical evidence suggests, however, that, if we think of K as physical capital, α is closer to one-third than to one-half. Assuming $\alpha = 1/3$, then $\alpha(1 - \alpha) = (1/3)/(1 - (1/3)) = (1/3)/(2/3) = 1/2$, and the equation for output per worker yields

$$y^*/N = (s/\delta)^{1/2} = \sqrt{s/\delta}$$

This implies smaller effects of the saving rate on output per worker than was suggested by the computations in the text. A doubling of the saving rate, for example, means that output per worker increases by a factor of $\sqrt{2}$, or only about 1.4 (put another way, a 40% increase in output per worker).

- There is, however, an interpretation of our model in which the appropriate value of α is close to 1/2, so the computations in the text are applicable. If, along the lines of section 14.4, we take human capital into account as well as physical capital, then a value of α around 1/2 for the contribution of this broader definition of capital to output is, indeed, roughly appropriate. Thus, one interpretation of the numerical results in section 14.3 is that they show the effects of a given saving rate, but that saving must be interpreted to include saving in both physical capital and in human capital (more machines, and more education).

Chapter 15

TECHNOLOGICAL PROGRESS AND GROWTH

Our conclusion (in Chapter 14) that capital accumulation cannot by itself sustain growth has a straightforward implication: sustained growth requires technological progress. This chapter looks at the role of technological progress in growth.

- Section 15.1 looks at the respective role of technological progress and capital accumulation in growth. It shows how, in steady state, the rate of growth of output per person is simply equal to the rate of technological progress. This does not mean, however, that the saving rate is irrelevant: the saving rate affects the level of output per person – but not its rate of growth.

- Section 15.2 turns to the determinants of technological progress, focusing in particular on the role of research and development (R&D).

- Section 15.3 returns to the facts of growth presented earlier (in Chapter 13), and interprets them in the light of what we have learned in this and the previous chapter.

15.1 TECHNOLOGICAL PROGRESS AND THE RATE OF GROWTH

In an economy in which there is both capital accumulation and technological progress, at what rate will output grow? To answer this question, we need to extend the model developed earlier (in Chapter 14) to allow for technological progress. To introduce technological progress into the picture, we must first revisit the aggregate production function.

Technological progress and the production function

Technological progress has many dimensions:

- It can lead to larger quantities of output for given quantities of capital and labour. Think of a new type of lubricant that allows a machine to run at a higher speed and so produce more.
- It can lead to better products. Think of the steady improvement in car safety and comfort over time.
- It can lead to new products. Think of the introduction of the CD or MP3 player, the fax machine, wireless communication technology in all its variants, flat-screen monitors and high-definition television.
- It can lead to a larger variety of products. Think of the steady increase in the number of breakfast cereals available at your local supermarket.

The average number of items carried by a supermarket increased from 2,200 in 1950 to 38,700 in 2010. To get a sense of what this means, see Robin ➤ Williams (who plays an immigrant from the Soviet Union) in the supermarket scene in the movie *Moscow on the Hudson*.

These dimensions are more similar than they appear. If we think of consumers as caring not about the goods themselves but about the services these goods provide, then they all have something in common: in each case, consumers receive more services. A better car provides more safety, a new product such as the fax machine or a new service such as wireless communication technology provides more communication services and so on. If we think of output as the set of underlying services provided by the goods produced in the economy, we can think of technological progress as leading to increases in output for given amounts of capital and labour. We can then think of the state of technology as a variable that tells us how much output can be produced from given amounts of capital and labour at any time. If we denote the state of technology by A, we can rewrite the production function as

As you saw in the Focus box 'Real GDP, ➤ technological progress and the price of computers' (in Chapter 2), thinking of products as providing a number of underlying services is the method used to construct the price index for computers.

$$Y = F(K, N, A)$$
$$(+, +, +)$$

This is our extended production function. Output depends on both capital and labour (K and N) and on the state of technology, A: given capital and labour, an improvement in the state of technology, A, leads to an increase in output.

For simplicity, we shall ignore human ➤ capital here. We return to it later in the chapter.

It will be convenient to use a more restrictive form of the preceding equation, however, namely

$$Y = F(K, AN) \qquad [15.1]$$

This equation states that production depends on capital and on labour multiplied by the state of technology. Introducing the state of technology in this way makes it easier to think about the effect of technological progress on the relation between output, capital and labour. Equation (15.1) implies that we can think of technological progress in two equivalent ways:

- Technological progress *reduces* the number of workers needed to produce a given amount of output. Doubling A produces the same quantity of output with only half the original number of workers, N.

AN is also sometimes called *labour in efficiency units*. The use of 'efficiency' for 'efficiency units' here and for 'efficiency wages' earlier (in Chapter 6) is a coincidence: the two notions are unrelated. ➤

- Technological progress *increases* the output that can be produced with a given number of workers. We can think of AN as the amount of **effective labour** in the economy. If the state of technology, A, doubles, it is as if the economy had twice as many workers. In other words, we can think of output being produced by two factors: capital, K, and effective labour, AN.

What restrictions should we impose on the extended production function (15.1)? We can build directly here on our earlier discussion (in Chapter 13).

Again, it is reasonable to assume constant returns to scale: for a given state of technology, A, doubling both the amount of capital, K, and the amount of labour, N, is likely to lead to a doubling of output:

$$2Y = F(2K, 2AN)$$

More generally, for any number x,

$$xY = F(xK, xAN)$$

It is also reasonable to assume decreasing returns to each of the two factors – capital and effective labour. Given effective labour, an increase in capital is likely to increase output, but at a decreasing rate. Symmetrically, given capital, an increase in effective labour is likely to increase output, but at a decreasing rate.

Earlier (see Chapter 13) it was convenient to think in terms of output per worker and capital per worker. That was because the steady state of the economy was a state where output per worker and capital per worker were constant. It is convenient here to look at output per effective worker and capital per effective worker. The reason is the same: as we shall soon see, in steady state, output per effective worker and capital per effective worker are constant.

To get a relation between output per effective worker and capital per effective worker, take $x = 1/AN$ in the preceding equation. This gives

$$\frac{Y}{AN} = F\left(\frac{K}{AN}, 1\right)$$

Or, if we define the function f so that $f(K/AN) \equiv F(K/AN, 1)$:

$$\frac{Y}{AN} = f\left(\frac{K}{AN}\right) \qquad [15.2]$$

In words: output per effective worker (the left side) is a function of capital per effective worker (the expression in the function on the right side).

The relation between output per effective worker and capital per effective worker is drawn in Figure 15.1. It looks very much the same as the relation we drew in Figure 13.2 between output per worker and capital per worker in the absence of technological progress. There, increases in K/N led to increases in Y/N, but at a decreasing rate. Here, increases in K/AN lead to increases in Y/AN, but at a decreasing rate.

◄ Per worker: divided by the number of workers, N. Per effective worker: divided by the number of effective workers, AN – the number of workers, N, times the state of technology, A.

◄ Suppose that F has the 'double square root' form:

$$Y = F(K, AN) = \sqrt{K}\sqrt{AN}$$

Then

$$\frac{Y}{AN} = \frac{\sqrt{K}\sqrt{AN}}{AN} = \frac{\sqrt{K}}{\sqrt{AN}}$$

So the function f is simply the square root function:

$$F(K/AN) = \sqrt{\frac{K}{AN}}$$

Interactions between output and capital

We now have the elements we need to think about the determinants of growth. Our analysis will parallel the analysis we did earlier (see Chapter 14). There we looked at the dynamics

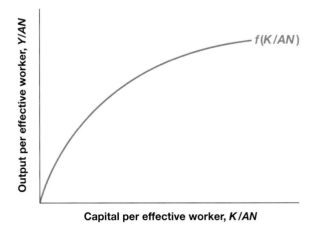

Figure 15.1

Output per effective worker versus capital per effective worker

Because of decreasing returns to capital, increases in capital per effective worker lead to smaller and smaller increases in output per effective worker.

Figure 15.2

The dynamics of capital per effective worker and output per effective worker

Capital per effective worker and output per effective worker converge to constant values in the long run.

of output per worker and capital per worker. Here we look at the dynamics of output per effective worker and capital per effective worker.

Earlier we characterised the dynamics of output and capital per worker using Figure 14.2. In that figure, we drew three relations:

The simple key to understanding the results in this section is that the results we derived for output per worker earlier (in Chapter 14) still hold in this chapter, but now for output per effective worker. For example, we saw that output per worker was constant in steady state. In this chapter, we shall see that output per effective worker is constant in steady state. And so on.

- The relation between output per worker and capital per worker.
- The relation between investment per worker and capital per worker.
- The relation between depreciation per worker – equivalently, the investment per worker needed to maintain a constant level of capital per worker – and capital per worker.

The dynamics of capital per worker, and by implication output per worker, were determined by the relation between investment per worker and depreciation per worker. Depending on whether investment per worker was greater or smaller than depreciation per worker, capital per worker increased or decreased over time, as did output per worker.

We shall follow the same approach in building Figure 15.2. The difference is that we focus on output, capital and investment per effective worker, rather than per worker.

- The relation between output per effective worker and capital per effective worker was derived in Figure 15.1. This relation is repeated in Figure 15.2: output per effective worker increases with capital per effective worker, but at a decreasing rate.
- Under the same assumptions as earlier (in Chapter 14) – that investment is equal to private saving, and the private saving rate is constant – investment is given by

$$I = S = sY$$

Divide both sides by the number of effective workers, AN, to get

$$\frac{I}{AN} = s\frac{Y}{AN}$$

Replacing output per effective worker, Y/AN, by its expression from equation (15.2) gives

$$\frac{I}{AN} = sf\left(\frac{K}{AN}\right)$$

The relation between investment per effective worker and capital per effective worker is drawn in Figure 15.2. It is equal to the upper curve – the relation between output per effective worker and capital per effective worker – multiplied by the saving rate, s. This gives us the lower curve.

- Finally, we need to ask what level of investment per effective worker is needed to maintain a given level of capital per effective worker. Earlier (in Chapter 14), for capital to be constant, investment had to be equal to the depreciation of the existing capital stock. Here, the answer is slightly more complicated. The reason is as follows: now that we allow for technological progress (so A increases over time), the number of effective workers, AN, increases over time. Thus, maintaining the same ratio of capital to effective workers (K/AN) requires an increase in the capital stock, K, proportional to the increase in the number of effective workers, AN. Let's look at this condition more closely.

Let δ be the depreciation rate of capital. Let the rate of technological progress be equal to g_A. Let the rate of population growth be equal to g_N. If we assume that the ratio of employment to the total population remains constant, the number of workers, N, also grows at annual rate g_N. Together, these assumptions imply that the growth rate of effective labour, AN, equals $g_A + g_N$. For example, if the number of workers is growing at 1% per year and the rate of technological progress is 2% per year, then the growth rate of effective labour is equal to 3% per year.

These assumptions imply that the level of investment needed to maintain a given level of capital per effective worker is therefore given by

$$I = \delta K + (g_A + g_N)K$$

Or equivalently,

$$I = (\delta + g_A + g_N)K \qquad [15.3]$$

An amount δK is needed just to keep the capital stock constant. If the depreciation rate is 10%, then investment must be equal to 10% of the capital stock just to maintain the same level of capital. And an additional amount, $(g_A + g_N)K$, is needed to ensure that the capital stock increases at the same rate as effective labour. If effective labour increases at 3% per year, for example, then capital must increase by 3% per year to maintain the same level of capital per effective worker. Putting δK and $(g_A + g_N)K$ together in this example: if the depreciation rate is 10% and the growth rate of effective labour is 3%, then investment must equal 13% of the capital stock to maintain a constant level of capital per effective worker. Dividing the previous expression by the number of effective workers to get the amount of investment per effective worker needed to maintain a constant level of capital per effective worker gives

$$\frac{I}{AN} = (\delta + g_A + g_N)\frac{K}{AN}$$

The level of investment per effective worker needed to maintain a given level of capital per effective worker is represented by the upward-sloping line, 'Required investment', in Figure 15.2. The slope of the line equals $(\delta + g_A + g_N)$.

Dynamics of capital and output

We can now give a graphical description of the dynamics of capital per effective worker and output per effective worker.

Consider a given level of capital per effective worker, say, $(K/AN)_0$ in Figure 15.2. At that level, output per effective worker equals the vertical distance AB. Investment per effective worker is equal to AC. The amount of investment required to maintain that level of capital per effective worker is equal to AD. Because actual investment exceeds the investment level required to maintain the existing level of capital per effective worker, K/AN increases.

Hence, starting from $(K/AN)_0$, the economy moves to the right, with the level of capital per effective worker increasing over time. This goes on until investment per effective worker is just sufficient to maintain the existing level of capital per effective worker, until capital per effective worker equals $(K/AN)^*$.

In the long run, capital per effective worker reaches a constant level, and so does output per effective worker. Put another way, the steady state of this economy is such that capital per effective worker and output per effective worker are constant and equal to $(K/AN)^*$ and $(Y/AN)^*$, respectively.

Earlier (in Chapter 14), we assumed $g_A = 0$ and $g_N = 0$. Our focus in this chapter is on the implications of technological progress, $g_A > 0$. But, once we allow for technological progress, introducing population growth $g_N > 0$ is straightforward. Thus, we allow for both $g_A > 0$ and $g_N > 0$.

The growth rate of the product of two variables is the sum of the growth rates of the two variables. (See Proposition 7 in Appendix 1 at the end of the book.)

If *Y/AN* is constant, *Y* must grow at the ➤ same rate as *AN*. So it must grow at rate $g_A + g_N$.

This implies that, in steady state, output, *Y*, is growing at the same rate as effective labour, *AN* (so that the ratio of the two is constant). Because effective labour grows at rate $g_A + g_N$, output growth in steady state must also equal $g_A + g_N$. The same reasoning applies to capital. Because capital per effective worker is constant in steady state, capital is also growing at rate $g_A + g_N$.

Stated in terms of capital or output per effective worker, these results seem rather abstract. But it is straightforward to state them in a more intuitive way, and this gives us our first important conclusion:

In steady state, the growth rate of output equals the rate of population growth, g_N, plus the rate of technological progress, g_A. By implication, the growth rate of output is independent of the saving rate.

To strengthen your intuition, let's go back to the argument we used earlier (in Chapter 14) to show that, in the absence of technological progress and population growth, the economy could not sustain positive growth forever.

● The argument went as follows: suppose the economy tried to sustain positive output growth. Because of decreasing returns to capital, capital would have to grow faster than output. The economy would have to devote a larger and larger proportion of output to capital accumulation. At some point there would be no more output to devote to capital accumulation. Growth would come to an end.

● Exactly the same logic is at work here. Effective labour grows at rate $g_A + g_N$. Suppose the economy tried to sustain output growth in excess of $g_A + g_N$. Because of decreasing returns to capital, capital would have to increase faster than output. The economy would have to devote a larger and larger proportion of output to capital accumulation. At some point this would prove impossible. Thus the economy cannot permanently grow faster than $g_A + g_N$.

The standard of living is given by output per worker (or, more accurately, output per person), not output per effective worker.

We have focused on the behaviour of aggregate output. To get a sense of what happens not to aggregate output, but rather to the standard of living over time, we must look instead at the behaviour of output per worker (not output per effective worker). Because output grows at rate $g_A + g_N$ and the number of workers grows at rate g_N, output per worker grows at rate g_A. In other words, when the economy is in steady state, output per worker grows at the rate of technological progress.

The growth rate of *Y/N* is equal to the ➤ growth rate of *Y* minus the growth rate of *N* (see Proposition 8 in Appendix 1 at the end of the book). So the growth rate of *Y/N* is given by $(g_Y - g_N) = (g_A + g_N) - g_N = g_A$.

Because output, capital, and effective labour all grow at the same rate, $g_A + g_N$, in steady state, the steady state of this economy is also called a state of **balanced growth**: in steady state, output and the two inputs, capital and effective labour, grow 'in balance', at the same rate. The characteristics of balanced growth will be helpful later in the chapter, and are summarised in Table 15.1.

On the balanced growth path (equivalently: in steady state, or in the long run):

● Capital per effective worker and output per effective worker are constant; this is the result we derived in Figure 15.2.

● Equivalently, capital per worker and output per worker are growing at the rate of technological progress, g_A.

Table 15.1 The characteristics of balanced growth

	Rate of growth of:
1 Capital per effective worker	0
2 Output per effective worker	0
3 Capital per worker	g_A
4 Output per worker	g_A
5 Labour	g_N
6 Capital	$g_A + g_N$
7 Output	$g_A + g_N$

- Or, in terms of labour, capital and output: labour is growing at the rate of population growth, g_N; capital and output are growing at a rate equal to the sum of population growth and the rate of technological progress, $g_A + g_N$.

The effects of the saving rate

In steady state, the growth rate of output depends only on the rate of population growth and the rate of technological progress. Changes in the saving rate do not affect the steady-state growth rate. But changes in the saving rate do increase the steady-state level of output per effective worker.

This result is best seen in Figure 15.3, which shows the effect of an increase in the saving rate from s_0 to s_1. The increase in the saving rate shifts the investment relation up, from $s_0 f(K/AN)$ to $s_1 f(K/AN)$. It follows that the steady-state level of capital per effective worker increases from $(K/AN)_0$ to $(K/AN)_1$, with a corresponding increase in the level of output per effective worker from $(Y/AN)_0$ to $(Y/AN)_1$.

Following the increase in the saving rate, capital per effective worker and output per effective worker increase for some time as they converge to their new higher level. Figure 15.4 plots output against time. Output is measured on a logarithmic scale. The economy is initially on the balanced growth path AA: output is growing at rate $g_A + g_N$ – so the slope of AA is equal to $g_A + g_N$. After the increase in the saving rate at time t, output grows faster for some period of time. Eventually, output ends up at a higher level than it would have been without the increase in saving. But its growth rate returns to $g_A + g_N$. In the new steady state, the economy grows at the same rate, but on a higher growth path BB. BB, which is parallel to AA, also has a slope equal to $g_A + g_N$.

Figure 15.4 is the same as Figure 14.5, which anticipated the derivation presented here.

(For a description of logarithmic scales, see Appendix 1 at the end of the book.)

When a logarithmic scale is used, a variable growing at a constant rate moves along a straight line. The slope of the line is equal to the rate of growth of the variable.

Figure 15.3

The effects of an increase in the saving rate (1)

An increase in the saving rate leads to an increase in the steady-state levels of output per effective worker and capital per effective worker.

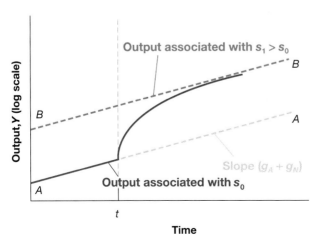

Figure 15.4

The effects of an increase in the saving rate (2)

The increase in the saving rate leads to higher growth until the economy reaches its new, higher, balanced growth path.

Let's summarise: in an economy with technological progress and population growth, output grows over time. In steady state, output per effective worker and capital per effective worker are constant. Put another way, output per worker and capital per worker grow at the rate of technological progress. Put yet another way, output and capital grow at the same rate as effective labour, and therefore at a rate equal to the growth rate of the number of workers plus the rate of technological progress. When the economy is in steady state, it is said to be on a balanced growth path.

The rate of output growth in steady state is independent of the saving rate. However, the saving rate affects the steady-state level of output per effective worker. And increases in the saving rate lead, for some time, to an increase in the growth rate above the steady-state growth rate.

15.2 THE DETERMINANTS OF TECHNOLOGICAL PROGRESS

We have just seen that the growth rate of output per worker is ultimately determined by the rate of technological progress. This leads naturally to the next question: what determines the rate of technological progress? This is the question we take up in this section.

'Technological progress' brings to mind images of major discoveries: the invention of the microchip, the discovery of the structure of DNA, and so on. These discoveries suggest a process driven largely by scientific research and chance rather than by economic forces. But the truth is that most technological progress in modern economies is the result of a humdrum process: the outcome of firms' **research and development (R&D)** activities. Industrial R&D expenditures account for between 2% and 3% of GDP in each of the four major rich countries we looked at earlier (in Chapter 13) (the USA, France, Japan and the UK). About 75% of the roughly one million US scientists and researchers working in R&D are employed by firms. US firms' R&D spending equals more than 20% of their spending on gross investment, and more than 60% of their spending on net investment – gross investment less depreciation.

Firms spend on R&D for the same reason they buy new machines or build new plants: to increase profits. By increasing spending on R&D, a firm increases the probability that it will discover and develop a new product. (We use 'product' as a generic term to denote new goods or new techniques of production.) If the new product is successful, the firm's profits will increase. There is, however, an important difference between purchasing a machine and spending more on R&D. The difference is that the outcome of R&D is fundamentally ideas. And, unlike a machine, an idea can potentially be used by many firms at the same time. A firm that has just acquired a new machine does not have to worry that another firm will use that particular machine. A firm that has discovered and developed a new product can make no such assumption.

This last point implies that the level of R&D spending depends not only on the **fertility** *of* the *research* process – how spending on R&D translates into new ideas and new products – but also on the **appropriability of research** results – the extent to which firms benefit from the results of their own R&D. Let's look at each aspect in turn.

The fertility of the research process

If research is very fertile – that is, if R&D spending leads to many new products – then, other things equal, firms will have strong incentives to spend on R&D; R&D spending and, by implication, technological progress will be high. The determinants of the fertility of research lie largely outside the realm of economics. Many factors interact here.

The fertility of research depends on the successful interaction between basic research (the search for general principles and results) and applied research and development (the application of these results to specific uses and the development of new products). Basic research does not lead, by itself, to technological progress. But the success of applied research and development depends ultimately on basic research. Much of the computer industry's development can be traced to a few breakthroughs, from the invention of the transistor to the invention of the microchip.

Some countries appear more successful at basic research; other countries are more successful at applied research and development. Studies point to differences in the education system as one of the reasons. For example, it is often argued that the French higher education system, with its strong emphasis on abstract thinking, produces researchers who are better at basic research than at applied research and development. Studies also point to the importance of a 'culture of entrepreneurship', in which a big part of technological progress comes from the ability of entrepreneurs to organise the successful development and marketing of new products – a dimension where the USA appears to be better than most other countries.

It takes many years, and often many decades, for the full potential of major discoveries to be realised. The usual sequence is one in which a major discovery leads to the exploration of potential applications, then to the development of new products and, finally, to the adoption of these new products. The Focus box 'The diffusion of new technology: hybrid corn' shows the results of one of the first studies of this process of the diffusion of ideas. Closer to us is the example of personal computers. Twenty-five years after the commercial introduction of personal computers, it often seems as if we have just begun discovering their uses.

◀ Earlier (in Chapter 14), we looked at the role of human capital as an input in production: more educated people can use more complex machines, or handle more complex tasks. Here, we see a second role of human capital: better researchers and scientists and, by implication, a higher rate of technological progress.

FOCUS
The diffusion of new technology: hybrid corn

New technologies are not developed or adopted overnight. One of the first studies of the diffusion of new technologies was carried out in 1957 by Zvi Griliches, a Harvard economist, who looked at the diffusion of hybrid corn in different states in the USA.

Hybrid corn is, in the words of Griliches, 'the invention of a method of inventing'. Producing hybrid corn entails crossing different strains of corn to develop a type of corn adapted to local conditions. The introduction of hybrid corn can increase the corn yield by up to 20%.

Although the idea of hybridisation was first developed at the beginning of the twentieth century, the first commercial application did not take place until the 1930s in the USA. Figure 15.5 shows the rate at which hybrid corn was adopted in a number of US states from 1932 to 1956.

The figure shows two dynamic processes at work. One is the process through which hybrid corns appropriate to

each state were discovered. Hybrid corn became available in southern states (Texas and Alabama) more than 10 years after it had become available in northern states (Iowa, Wisconsin and Kentucky). The other is the speed at which hybrid corn was adopted within each state. Within eight years of its introduction, practically all corn in Iowa was hybrid corn. The process was much slower in the south. More than 10 years after its introduction, hybrid corn accounted for only 60% of total acreage in Alabama.

Why was the speed of adoption higher in Iowa than in the South? Griliches' article showed that the reason was economic: the speed of adoption in each state was a function of the profitability of introducing hybrid corn. And profitability was higher in Iowa than in the southern states.

Source: Zvi Griliches, 'Hybrid corn: an exploration in the economics of technological change', *Econometrica*, October 1957, 25–4.

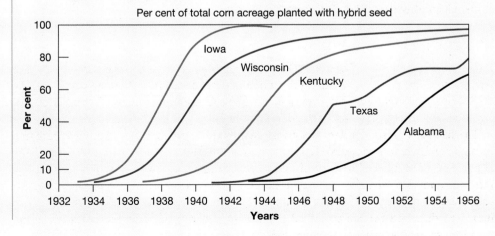

Per cent of total corn acreage planted with hybrid seed

Figure 15.5

Percentage of total corn acreage planted with hybrid seed, selected US states, 1932–1956

Source: Zvi Griliches, 'Hybrid corn: an exploration in the economics of technological change', *Econometrica*, October 1957, 25–4. *http://www.jstor.org/stable/pdfplus/ 1905380.pdf*

An age-old worry is that research will become less and less fertile, that most major discoveries have already taken place and that technological progress will now slow down. This fear may come from thinking about mining, where higher-grade mines were exploited first, and where we have had to exploit lower- and lower-grade mines. But this is only an analogy, and so far there is no evidence that it is correct.

The appropriability of research results

The second determinant of the level of R&D and of technological progress is the degree of appropriability of research results. If firms cannot appropriate the profits from the development of new products, they will not engage in R&D and technological progress will be slow. Many factors are also at work here.

The nature of the research process itself is important. For example, if it is widely believed that the discovery of a new product by one firm will quickly lead to the discovery of an even better product by another firm, there may be little payoff to being first. In other words, a highly fertile field of research may not generate high levels of R&D, because no company will find the investment worthwhile. This example is extreme, but revealing.

Even more important is the legal protection given to new products. Without such legal protection, profits from developing a new product are likely to be small. Except in rare cases where the product is based on a trade secret (such as Coca Cola), it will generally not take long for other firms to produce the same product, eliminating any advantage the innovating firm may have had initially. This is why countries have patent laws. **Patents** give a firm that has discovered a new product – usually a new technique or device – the right to exclude anyone else from the production or use of the new product for some time.

How should governments design patent laws? On the one hand, protection is needed to provide firms with the incentives to spend on R&D. On the other, once firms have discovered new products, it would be best for society if the knowledge embodied in those new products were made available to other firms and to people without restrictions. Take, for example, biogenetic research. Only the prospect of large profits is leading bioengineering firms to embark on expensive research projects. Once a firm has found a new product, and

Source: From Chappatte in L'Hebdo, www.globecartoon.com, copyright globecartoon.com

the product can save many lives, it would clearly be best to make it available at cost to all potential users. But if such a policy was systematically followed, it would eliminate incentives for firms to do research in the first place. So, patent law must strike a difficult balance. Too little protection will lead to little R&D. Too much protection will make it difficult for new R&D to build on the results of past R&D, and may also lead to little R&D. (The difficulty of designing good patent or copyright laws is illustrated in the cartoon about cloning.)

Countries that are less technologically advanced often have poorer patent protection. China, for example, is a country with poor enforcement of patent rights. Our discussion helps explain why. These countries are typically users rather than producers of new technologies. Much of their improvement in productivity comes not from inventions within the country, but from the adaptation of foreign technologies. In this case, the costs of weak patent protection are small, because there would be few domestic inventions anyway. But the benefits of low patent protection are clear: they allow domestic firms to use and adapt foreign technology without having to pay royalties to the foreign firms that developed the technology – which is good for the country.

◀ This type of dilemma is known as 'time inconsistency'. We shall see other examples and discuss it at length later (in Chapter 22).

The issues go beyond patent laws. To take two controversial examples: what is the role of open-source software? Should students download music, movies and even textbooks without making payments to the creators?

FOCUS
Another dimension of technological progress: management practices

For a given technology and a given human capital of its workers, the way a firm is managed also affects its performance. Some researchers actually believe that management practices might be stronger than many of the other factors that determine whether a business succeeds, including technological innovations. In a project* that examined management practices and performance of more than 4,000 medium-sized manufacturing operations in Europe, the USA and Asia, Nick Bloom of Stanford University and John Van Reenen of the London School of Economics found that firms across the globe that use the same technology but apply good management practices perform significantly better than those that do not. This suggests that improved management practice is one of the most effective ways for a firm to outperform its peers.

The most fascinating evidence of the importance of management practices comes from an experimental study conducted by Nick Bloom on a set of 20 Indian textile plants. To investigate the role of good management practices Bloom ran a field experiment providing free consulting on management practices to a randomly chosen subset of the 20 plants. Then he compared the performance of the firms that received management advice with that of the control plants – those that did not receive advice. He found that adopting good management practices raised productivity by 18% through improved quality and efficiency and reduced inventory.

A wonderful short video describes Bloom's Indian experiment. You can watch it at: ***www.gsb.stanford.edu/ multimedia/flv/100519-Bloom-5minute.html***.

* 'Why do management practices differ across firms and countries?' by Nick Bloom and John Van Reenen, *Journal of Economic Perspectives*, Spring 2010.

15.3 THE FACTS OF GROWTH REVISITED

We can now use the theory we have developed in this and the previous chapter to interpret some of the facts we saw earlier (in Chapter 13).

Capital accumulation versus technological progress in rich countries since 1985

Suppose we observe an economy with a high growth rate of output per worker over some period of time. Our theory implies this fast growth may come from two sources:

● It may reflect a high rate of technological progress under balanced growth.
● It may reflect instead the adjustment of capital per effective worker, K/AN, to a higher level. Such an adjustment leads to a period of higher growth, even if the rate of technological progress has not increased.

Can we tell how much of the growth comes from one source, and how much comes from the other? Yes. If high growth reflects high balanced growth, output per worker should be growing at a rate equal to the rate of technological progress (see Table 15.1, row 4). If high growth reflects instead the adjustment to a higher level of capital per effective worker, this adjustment should be reflected in a growth rate of output per worker that exceeds the rate of technological progress.

In the USA, for example, the ratio of ➤ employment to population decreased slightly from 60.1% in 1985 to 59.3% in 2009. Thus output per person and output per worker grew at virtually the same rate over this period.

Let's apply this approach to interpret the facts about growth in rich countries we saw in Table 15.1 earlier. This is done in Table 15.2, which gives, in column 1, the average rate of growth of output per worker, $g_Y - g_N$, and, in column 2, the average rate of technological progress, g_A, between 1985 and 2010 for a number of OECD countries. The rate of technological progress, g_A, is constructed using a method introduced by Robert Solow (the method and the details of construction are given in the appendix to this chapter).

The table leads to two conclusions. First, growth since 1985 has come from a higher growth rate of output per worker, exceeding the rate of technological progress. This is what we would expect when countries are adjusting to a higher level of capital per effective worker.

What would have happened to the growth rate of output per worker if these countries had had the same rate of technological progress, but no capital accumulation, during the period?

Note what this conclusion does not say. It does not say that capital accumulation was irrelevant. Capital accumulation was such as to allow these countries to maintain a roughly constant ratio of output to capital and achieve balanced growth. What it says is that, over the period, growth did not come from an unusual increase in capital accumulation – from an increase in the ratio of capital to output.

Second, convergence of output per worker between the USA and most of the other countries comes from higher technological progress, rather than from faster capital accumulation. France, Japan and the UK all started behind the USA in 1985. In all three countries the rate of technological progress has been higher than in the USA.

Table 15.2 Average annual rates of growth of output per worker and technological progress

	Rate of growth of output per worker (%) 1985–2010	Rate of technological progress (%) 1985–2010
Belgium	2.76	1.3
Canada	2.00	0.4
Denmark	2.79	0.7
Finland	3.16	1.7
France	2.49	0.9
Germany	2.77	0.8
Ireland	9.97	2.7
Italy	1.83	0.3
Japan	2.37	1.5
Netherlands	4.64	1.0
New Zealand	1.66	0.7
Spain	5.66	0.4
Sweden	2.47	0.9
UK	3.79	1.3
USA	2.52	1.1
Average	3.39	1.05

Note: data for Germany start from 1995.

Source: Based on data from OECD Statistics, Table: Country statistical profiles, Multi-factor productivity.
http://stats.oecd.org/#, © OECD

This is an important conclusion. One can think, in general, of two sources of convergence between countries. First, poorer countries are poorer because they have less capital to start with. Over time, they accumulate capital faster than the others, generating convergence. Second, poorer countries are poorer because they are less technologically advanced than the others. Thus, over time, they become more sophisticated, either by importing technology from advanced countries or developing their own. As technological levels converge, so does output per worker. The conclusion we can draw from Table 15.2 is that, in the case of rich countries, the more important source of convergence in this case is clearly the second one.

Capital accumulation versus technological progress in China

Going beyond growth in OECD countries, one of the striking facts was the high growth rates achieved by a number of Asian countries (see Chapter 13). This raises again the same questions as those we just discussed: do these high growth rates reflect fast technological progress, or do they reflect unusually high capital accumulation?

To answer the questions, we shall focus on China, because of its size, and because of the astonishingly high output growth rate, nearly 10%, it has achieved since the late 1970s. Table 15.3 gives the average rate of growth, g_Y, the average rate of growth of output per worker, $g_Y - g_N$, and the average rate of technological progress, g_A, for two periods, 1978 to 1995, and 1995 to 2007.

The table yields two conclusions. From the late 1970s to the mid-1990s, the rate of technological progress was close to the rate of growth of output per worker. China was roughly on a (very rapid) balanced growth path. Since 1995, however, while growth of output per worker has remained very high, the contribution of technological progress has decreased. Put another way, growth has come partly from unusually high capital accumulation – from an increase in the ratio of capital to output.

We can look at it another way. Recall, from Table 15.1 that under balanced growth, $g_K = g_Y = g_A + g_N$. To see what investment rate would be required if China had balanced growth, go back to equation (15.3), and divide both sides by output, y, to get

> ◀ **Warning:** Chinese data for output, employment and the capital stock (the latter is needed to construct g_A) are not as reliable as similar data for OECD countries. Thus, the numbers in the table should be seen as more tentative than the numbers in Table 15.2.

$$\frac{I}{Y} = (\delta + (g_A + g_N))\frac{K}{Y}$$

Let's plug in numbers for China for the period 1995–2007. The estimate of δ, the depreciation rate of capital in China, is 5% a year. As we just saw, the average value of g_A for the period was 6.0%. The average value of g_N, the rate of growth of employment, was 0.5%. The average value of the ratio of capital to output was 2.6. This implies a ratio of investment of output required to achieve balanced growth of (5.0% + 6.0% + 0.5%) × 2.6 = 30%. The actual average ratio of investment to output for 1995–2007 is, however, a much higher 39%. Thus, both rapid technological progress, and unusually high capital accumulation explain the high Chinese growth. If the rate of technological progress were to remain the same, this suggests that, as the ratio of capital to output stabilises, the Chinese growth rate will decrease somewhat, closer to 6% than to 9.4%.

Where does the technological progress in China come from? A closer look at the data suggests two main channels. First, China has transferred labour from the countryside, where

Table 15.3 Average annual rate of growth of output per worker and technological progress in China, 1978–2007

Period	Rate of growth of output (%)	Rate of growth of output per worker (%)	Rate of technological progress (%)
1978–1995	10.2	8.6	7.8
1995–2007	9.9	9.4	6.0

Source: Based on data from OECD Economic Surveys: China 2010, © OECD 2010 productivity is very low, to industry and services in the cities, where productivity is much higher. Second, China has imported the technology of more technologically advanced countries. It has, for example, encouraged the development of joint ventures between Chinese firms and foreign firms. Foreign firms have come with better technologies and, over time, Chinese firms have learned how to use them.

This leads to a more general point: the nature of technological progress is likely to be different in more and less advanced economies. The more advanced economies, being by definition at the **technological frontier**, need to develop new ideas and new processes, new products. They need to innovate. The countries that are behind can instead improve their level of technology by copying and adapting the new processes and products developed in the more advanced economies. They need to imitate. The further behind a country is, the larger the role of imitation relative to innovation. As imitation is likely to be easier than innovation, this can explain why convergence, both within the OECD, and in the case of China and other countries, typically takes the form of **technological catch-up**. It raises, however, yet another question: if imitation is so easy, why is it that so many other countries do not seem to be able to do the same and grow? This points to the broader aspects of technology we discussed earlier in the chapter. Technology is more than just a set of blueprints. How efficiently these blueprints can be used, and how productive an economy is, depend on its institutions, on the quality of its government and so on. We shall return to this issue in the next section.

Institutions and growth

How can institutions affect the ability of an economy to improve its technology? Economists have long recognised that economic growth is related not only to differences in the technology available to firms, but also to differences in how production is organised, and to differences in the quality of institutions that ultimaltely shape economic activity. But what are institutions? One of the first to offer a definition was Douglas North in 1990: 'Institutions are the rules of the game in a society or, more formally, are the humanly devised constraints that shape human interactions.' Therefore, institutions include a broad range of mechanisms that shape human interactions in different spheres – legal, social, political, cultural and economic.

Economic institutions matter for economic growth because they shape the way economic activity is organised and influence investments in physical and human capital, and technology and the organisation of production. Examples of economic institutions include the presence of markets – broadly defined as mechanisms that allow individuals to exchange goods and services, sometimes identified with the place where transactions happen, such as in street and flea markets – and property rights – the set of laws that regulate how property of resources is defined, and how individuals can control, benefit from and transfer property. Most countries in the world have adopted private property rights as a universal rule, but some of them have not – in China, for example, the land can only be owned by the state, whereas other resources and assets can be privately owned. Economists largely agree on the fact that the degree of government enforcement of property rights influences the economic incentives in an economy: if property rights are strongly enforced – that is, the owners of any kind of resources are protected against the possibility that others might succeed in overtaking their belongings or in preventing them from benefiting from their property – then individuals will have more incentives to invest in capital and technology. Economic institutions also influence the distribution of economic gains in a society by affecting the way income is distributed to different production factors (capital, land and labour).

How are economic institutions determined? They are determined by political institutions: that is, the government and all political decision-making bodies. Examples of political institutions include the form of government – for example, democracy versus dictatorship – and the constraints on politicians on how to make decisions (we will get back to these constraints in Chapter 23 when discussing fiscal and monetary policy decisions). Because economic institutions influence the distribution of resources, not all individuals and groups prefer the same set of economic instituons. This will lead to a conflict of interest among various groups over the choice of economic institutions, and those groups with most political power will ultimaltely decide for the whole society.

To illustrate the role of institutions in growth, history offers a lot of examples of countries that adopted or reformed their institutions in ways that postively or negatively affected their growth. In Europe, the seventeenth century witnessed major changes in the economic and political institutions that paved the way for the development of property rights and limits on monarchs' power, especially in England after the Civil War of 1642 and the Glorious Revolution of 1688, and in the Netherlands after the Dutch Revolt against the Hapsburgs. How did these major institutional changes take place? In England, for example, until the sixteenth century the king also possessed a substantial amount of de facto political power. Changes in the English land market and the expansion of Atlantic trade in the sixteenth and seventeenth centuries gradually increased the economic fortunes, and consequently the de facto power of landowners and merchants, who were able to field military forces capable of defeating the king. This de facto power overcame the Stuart monarchs in the Civil War and Glorious Revolution, and led to a change in political institutions that stripped the king of much of his previous power over policy. These changes in the distribution of political power led to major changes in economic institutions, strengthening the property rights of both land and capital owners and spurred a process of financial and commercial expansion. The consequence was rapid economic growth, culminating in the Industrial Revolution, and a very different distribution of economic resources from that in the Middle Ages.

Britain underwent a further important process of institutional change in the nineteenth century:

- First, it expanded democratic rights. The history of the rise of democracy in Britain is in many ways representative of the experiences of many other European countries. The 1832 reform established the right to vote based uniformly on the basis of property and income. It was passed in the context of rising popular discontent at the existing political status quo in Britain and there is little dissent amongst historians that it was passed to avoid social disturbances.

- Second, it began to invest more in education. The Education Act of 1870 committed the government to the systematic provision of universal education for the first time, and the school-leaving age was set at 11 in 1893, then in 1899 it increased to 12; as a result, the proportion of 10-year-olds enrolled in school that stood at 40 per cent in 1870 increased to 100 per cent in 1900).

Following changes in political institutions, economic institutions also began to change: the civil service was opened to public examination and made meritocratic; labour market legislation was introduced, fundamentally changing the nature of industrial relations in favour of workers; health and unemployment insurance, government-financed pensions, minimum wages, and a commitment to redistributive taxation were introduced. As a result of the fiscal changes, taxes as a proportion of National Product more than doubled in the 30 years following 1870, and then doubled again.

History also offers a few 'natural experiments' of institutional change that illustrate how economic performance diverged with the adoption of different institutions. One such experiment is Korea. Soon after the end of the Second World War and Japanese occupation, Soviet forces entered North Korea and took over the control from the Japanese. With the support of the USA, the influential nationalist leader Syngman Rhee, who was in favour of separation rather than a united communist Korea, won elections in the South in 1948, and the newly elected representatives in 1948 proceeded to draft a new constitution and established the Republic of Korea to the south of the 38th parallel. The North became the Democratic Peoples Republic of Korea, under the control of Kim Il-Sung. These two independent countries organised themselves in very different ways and adopted completely different sets of institutions. The North followed the model of Soviet socialism and the Chinese Revolution in abolishing private property of land and capital. The South instead maintained a system of private property and the government. Before this natural experiment in institutional change, North and South Korea shared the same history and cultural roots. In fact, Korea exhibited an unparalleled degree of ethnic, linguistic, cultural, geographic and economic homogeneity. There are few geographic distinctions between the North and South, and both share the same disease environment. Both countries share the same geographic possibilities in terms of access to markets and the cost of transportation. Other man-made initial economic conditions were also similar and, if anything, advantaged the North. For example, there was significant industrialisation during the colonial period with the expansion of both Japanese and indigenous firms. Yet this development was concentrated more in the North than the South. All in all, despite some potential advantages for the North, at the time of separation, North and South Korea had approximately the same income per capita. Since separation, the two Koreas have experienced dramatically diverging paths of economic development. By the late 1960s South Korea was transformed into one of the Asian miracle economies, experiencing one of the most rapid surges of economic prosperity in history while North Korea stagnated. By 2000 the level of income in South Korea was $16,100 while in North Korea it was only $1,000. By 2000 the South had become a member of the Organization of Economic Cooperation and Development, the rich nations club, while the North had a level of per-capita income about the same as a typical sub-Saharan African country. There is only one plausible explanation for the radically different economic experiences on the two Koreas after 1950: their very different institutions led to divergent economic outcomes.

More recently, a major example of a country that did reform its institutions and moved from stagnation to rapid growth is China. It can hardly be denied that the rapid growth in China since 1978 (which we wrote about in Chapter 1) was a result of policy and institutional reforms. Growth did not occur because of a change in culture, or in perceptions about which policies were needed to promote growth, but rather because of a shift in those who controlled the Communist Party. The new political élite since 1978 wanted to push through reforms, in contrast with the old élite who preferred not to change the way production decisions were implemented in the country.

The study of the economic impact of institutions has so far suggested that institutions are the very fundamental cause of economic growth in the long run, and of divergence in economic performance between rich and poor countries.

SUMMARY

- When we think about the implications of technological progress for growth, it is useful to think of technological progress as increasing the amount of effective labour available in the economy (that is, labour multiplied by the state of technology). We can then think of output as being produced with capital and effective labour.

- In steady state, output per effective worker and capital per effective worker are constant. Put another way, output per worker and capital per worker grow at the rate of technological progress. Put yet another way, output and capital grow at the same rate as effective labour, thus at a rate equal to the growth rate of the number of workers plus the rate of technological progress.

- When the economy is in steady state, it is said to be on a balanced growth path. Output, capital and effective labour are all growing 'in balance', that is, at the same rate.

- The rate of output growth in steady state is independent of the saving rate. However, the saving rate affects the steady-state level of output per effective worker. And increases in the saving rate will lead, for some time, to an increase in the growth rate above the steady-state growth rate.

- Technological progress depends on both (1) the fertility of research and development – how spending on R&D translates into new ideas and new products – and (2) the appropriability of the results of R&D – the extent to which firms benefit from the results of their R&D.

- When designing patent laws, governments must balance their desire to protect future discoveries and provide incentives for firms to do R&D, with their desire to make existing discoveries available to potential users without restrictions.

- France, Japan, the UK and the USA have experienced roughly balanced growth since 1950: growth of output per worker has been roughly equal to the rate of technological progress. Growth in China is a combination of a high rate of technological progress, and unusually high investment, leading to an increase in the ratio of capital to output.

KEY TERMS

effective labour, or labour in efficiency units 328

balanced growth 332

research and development (R&D) 334

fertility (of research) 334

appropriability of reseach 334

patents 336

technology frontier 340

technological catch-up 340

Solow residual 346

QUESTIONS AND PROBLEMS

QUICK CHECK

1. *Using the information in this chapter, label each of the following statements true, false or uncertain. Explain briefly.*

a. Writing the production function in terms of capital and effective labour implies that as the level of technology increases by 10%, the number of workers required to achieve the same level of output decreases by 10%.

b. If the rate of technological progress increases, the investment rate (the ratio of investment to output) must increase in order to keep capital per effective worker constant.

c. In steady state, output per effective worker grows at the rate of population growth.

d. In steady state, output per worker grows at the rate of technological progress.

e. A higher saving rate implies a higher level of capital per effective worker in the steady state and thus a higher rate of growth of output per effective worker.

f. Even if the potential returns from R&D spending are identical to the potential returns from investing in a new machine, R&D spending is much riskier for firms than investing in new machines.

g. The fact that one cannot patent a theorem implies that private firms will not engage in basic research.

h. Because eventually we will know everything, growth will have to come to an end.

2. R&D and growth

a. Why is the amount of R&D spending important for growth? How do the appropriability and fertility of research affect the amount of R&D spending?

How do each of the policy proposals listed in (b) through (e) affect the appropriability and fertility of research, R&D spending in the long run, and output in the long run?

b. An international treaty that ensures that each country's patents are legally protected all over the world.

c. Tax credits for each euro of R&D spending.

d. A decrease in funding of government-sponsored conferences between universities and corporations.

e. The elimination of patents on breakthrough drugs, so the drugs can be sold at low cost as soon as they are available.

3. Sources of technological progress: economic leaders versus developing countries

a. Where does technological progress come from for the economic leaders of the world?

b. Do developing countries have other alternatives to the sources of technological progress you mentioned in part (a)?

c. Do you see any reasons developing countries may choose to have poor patent protection? Are there any dangers in such a policy (for developing countries)?

DIG DEEPER

4. *For each of the economic changes listed in (a) and (b), assess the likely impact on the growth rate and the level of output over the next five years and over the next five decades.*

a. A permanent reduction in the rate of technological progress.

b. A permanent reduction in the saving rate.

5. Measurement error, inflation and productivity growth

Suppose that there are only two goods produced in an economy: haircuts and banking services. Prices, quantities and the number of workers occupied in the production of each good for year 1 and for year 2 are given below:

	Year 1			Year 2		
	P1	Q1	W1	P2	Q2	W2
Haircut	10	100	50	12	100	50
Banking	10	200	50	12	230	60

a. What is nominal GDP in each year?

b. Using year 1 prices, what is real GDP in year 2? What is the growth rate of real GDP?

c. What is the rate of inflation using the GDP deflator?

d. Using year 1 prices, what is real GDP per worker in year 1 and year 2? What is labour productivity growth between year 1 and year 2 for the whole economy?

Now suppose that banking services in year 2 are not the same as banking services in year 1. Year 2 banking services include telebanking that year 1 banking services did not include. The technology for telebanking was available in year 1, but the price of banking services with telebanking in year 1 was €13, and no one chose to purchase this package. However, in year 2, the price of banking services with telebanking was €12, and everyone chose to have this package (i.e. in year 2 no one chose to have the year 1 banking services package without telebanking). (Hint: assume that there are now two types of banking services: those with telebanking and those without. Rewrite the preceding table but now with three goods: haircuts and the two types of banking services.)

e. Using year 1 prices, what is real GDP for year 2? What is the growth rate of real GDP?

f. What is the rate of inflation using the GDP deflator?

g. What is labour productivity growth between year 1 and year 2 for the whole economy?

h. Consider this statement: 'If banking services are mismeasured – for example, by not taking into account the introduction of telebanking – we will overestimate inflation and underestimate productivity growth.' Discuss this statement in light of your answers to parts (a) through (g).

6. *Suppose that the economy's production function is*

$$Y = \sqrt{K} \sqrt{AN}$$

that the saving rate, s, is equal to 16%, and that the rate of depreciation, δ, is equal to 10%. Suppose further that the number of workers grows at 2% per year and that the rate of technological progress is 4% per year.

a. Find the steady-state values of the variables listed in (i) through (v).
   i. The capital stock per effective worker.
   ii. Output per effective worker.
   iii. The growth rate of output per effective worker.
   iv. The growth rate of output per worker.
   v. The growth rate of output.

b. Suppose that the rate of technological progress doubles to 8% per year. Re-compute the answers to part (a). Explain.

c. Now suppose that the rate of technological progress is still equal to 4% per year, but the number of workers now grows at 6% per year. Re-compute the answers to (a). Are people better off in (a) or in (c)? Explain.

7. *Discuss the potential role of each of the factors listed in (a) through (g) on the steady-state level of output per worker. In each case, indicate whether the effect is through A, through K, through H, or through some combination of A, K and H.*

a. geographic location

b. education

c. protection of property rights

d. openness to trade

e. low tax rates

f. good public infrastructure

g. low population growth

EXPLORE FURTHER

8. Growth accounting

The Appendix 'Constructing a measure of technological progress' shows how data on output, capital and labour can be used to construct estimates of the rate of growth of technological progress. We modify that approach in this problem to examine the growth of capital per worker. The function

$$Y = K^{1/3}(AN)^{2/3}$$

gives a good description of production in rich countries. Following the same steps as in the Appendix, you can show that

$$(2/3)g_A = g_Y - (2/3)g_N - (1/3)g_K$$
$$= (g_Y - g_N) - (1/3)(g_K - g_N)$$

where g_x denotes the growth rate of x.

a. What does the quantity $g_Y - g_N$ represent? What does the quantity $g_K - g_N$ represent?

b. Rearrange the preceding equation to solve for the growth rate of capital per worker.

c. Look at Table 15.2 in the chapter. Using your answer to part (b), substitute in the average annual growth rate of output per worker and the average annual rate of technological progress for the USA for the period 1950–2004 to obtain a crude measure of the average annual growth of capital per worker. (Strictly speaking, we should construct these measures individually for every year, but we limit ourselves to readily available data in this problem.) Do the same for the other countries listed in Table 15.2. How does the average growth of capital per worker compare across the countries in Table 15.2? Do the results make sense to you? Explain.

---

*Log on to **MyEconLab** and complete the studyplan exercises for this chapter to see how much you have learnt, and where you need to revise most.*

MyEconLab

FURTHER READING

- For more on growth, both theory and evidence, read *Leadership and Growth* edited by David Brady and Michael Spence (Washington DC: The World Bank, 2010); and D. Acemoglu and J. Robinson, 'Why Nations Fail', Random House, 2011.

- For more on patents, see *The Economist*, 'Survey on patents and technology', 20 October 2005.

- For more on growth in two large, fast-growing countries, read Barry Bosworth and Susan M. Collins, 'Accounting for growth: comparing China and India', *Journal of Economic Perspectives*, 22(1), 2008.

On two issues we have not explored in the text:

- Growth and global warming: read the 'Stern Review on the economics of climate change', 2006. You can find it at ***www.hm-treasury.gov.uk/independent_reviews/stern_review_economics_climate_change/stern_review_report.cfm***. (The report is very long. Read just the executive summary.)

- Growth and the environment: read *The Economist*, survey on 'The global environment; the great race', 4 July 2002.

APPENDIX

Constructing a measure of technological progress

In 1957, Robert Solow devised a way of constructing an estimate of technological progress. The method, which is still in use today, relies on one important assumption: that each factor of production is paid its marginal product.

Under this assumption, it is easy to compute the contribution of an increase in any factor of production to the increase in output. For example, if a worker is paid $30,000 a year, the assumption implies that her contribution to output is equal to $30,000. Now suppose that this worker increases the amount of hours she works by 10%. The increase in output coming from the increase in her hours will therefore be equal to $30,000 × 10%, or $3,000.

Let us write this more formally. Denote output by Y, labour by N, and the real wage by W/P. Then, we just established, the change in output is equal to the real wage multiplied by the change in labour:

$$\Delta Y = \frac{W}{P} \Delta N$$

Divide both sides of the equation by Y, divide and multiply the right side by N, and reorganise:

$$\frac{\Delta Y}{Y} = \frac{WN}{PY} \frac{\Delta N}{N}$$

Note that the first term on the right (WN/PY) is equal to the share of labour in output – the total wage bill in dollars divided by the value of output in dollars. Denote this share by α. Note that $\Delta Y/Y$ is the rate of growth of output, and denote it by g_Y. Note similarly that $\Delta N/N$ is the rate of change of the labour input, and denote it by g_N. Then the previous relation can be written as

$$g_Y = \alpha g_N$$

More generally, this reasoning implies that the part of output growth attributable to growth of the labour input is equal to $\alpha \times g_N$. If, for example, employment grows by 2%, and the share of labour is 0.7, then the output growth due to the growth in employment is equal to 1.4% (0.7 × 2%).

Similarly, we can compute the part of output growth attributable to growth of the capital stock. Because there are only two factors of production, labour and capital, and because the share of labour is equal to α, the share of capital in income must be equal to $(1 - \alpha)$. If the growth rate of capital is equal to g_K, then the part of output growth attributable to growth of capital is equal to $(1 - \alpha) \times g_K$. If for example, capital grows by 5%, and the share of capital is 0.3, then the output growth due to the growth of the capital stock is equal to 1.5% (0.3 × 5%).

Putting the contributions of labour and capital together, the growth in output attributable to growth in both labour and capital is equal to $(\alpha g_N + (1 - \alpha)g_K)$.

We can then measure the effects of technological progress by computing what Solow called the residual, the excess of actual growth of output, g_Y, over the growth attributable to growth of labour and the growth of capital $(\alpha g_N + (1 - \alpha)g_K)$:

$$\text{Residual} \equiv g_Y - [\alpha g_N + (1 - \alpha)g_K]$$

This measure is called the **Solow residual**. It is easy to compute: all we need to know to compute it are the growth rate of output, g_Y, the growth rate of labour, g_N, and the growth rate of capital, g_K, together with the shares of labour, α and capital, $(1 - \alpha)$.

To continue with our previous numerical examples, suppose employment grows by 4%, the capital stock grows by 5%, and the share of labour is 0.7 (and so the share of capital is 0.3). Then the part of output growth attributable to growth of labour and growth of capital is equal to 2.9% (0.7 × 2%) + (0.3 × 5%). If output growth is equal, for example, to 4%, then the Solow residual is equal to 1.1% (4% – 2.9%).

The Solow residual is sometimes called the rate of growth of total factor productivity (or the rate of TFP growth, for short). The use of 'total factor productivity' is to distinguish it from the rate of growth of labour productivity, which is defined as $g_Y - g_N$, the rate of output growth minus the rate of labour growth.

The Solow residual is related to the rate of technological progress in a simple way. The residual is equal to the share of labour multiplied by the rate of technological progress:

$$\text{Residual} = \alpha g_A$$

We shall not derive this result here. But the intuition for this relation comes from the fact that what matters in the production function $Y = F(K, AN)$ (equation (15.1)) is the product of the state of technology and labour, AN. We saw that to get the contribution of labour growth to output growth, we must multiply the growth rate of labour by its share. Because N and A enter the production function in the same way, it is clear that to get the contribution of technological progress to output growth, we must also multiply it by the share of labour.

If the Solow residual is equal to zero, so is technological progress. To construct an estimate of g_A, we must construct the Solow residual and then divide it by the share of labour. This is how the estimates of g_A presented in the text are constructed.

In the numerical example we saw earlier, the Solow residual is equal to 1.1%, and the share of labour is equal to 0.7. So, the rate of technological progress is equal to 1.6% (1.1%/0.7).

Keep straight the definitions of productivity growth you have seen in this chapter:

- Labour productivity growth (equivalently: the rate of growth of output per worker): $g_Y - g_N$
- The rate of technological progress: g_A

In steady state, labour productivity growth, $g_Y - g_N$, equals the rate of technological progress g_A. Outside of steady state, they need not be equal: an increase in the ratio of capital per effective worker, due for example to an increase in the saving rate, will cause $g_Y - g_N$ to be higher than g_A for some time.

Source: Robert Solow, 'Technical change and the aggregate production function', *Review of Economics and Statistics*, 1957, 312–20.

EXTENSIONS

Source: From www.CartoonStock.com, CartoonStock.com.

EXPECTATIONS

Expectations play an essential role in macroeconomics. Nearly all the economic decisions people and firms make – whether to buy a car, whether to buy bonds or to buy stocks, whether to build a new plant – depend on their expectations about future income, future profits, future interest rates and so on. All the previous chapters did not discuss expectations in depth. The next three chapters look more closely at the role of expectations in output fluctuations.

Chapter 16 Financial markets and expectations

Chapter 16 focuses on the role of expectations in financial markets. It first looks at the determination of bond prices and bond yields. It shows how we can learn about the course of expected future interest rates by looking at the yield curve. It then turns to stock prices, and shows how they depend on expected future dividends and interest rates. Finally, it discusses whether stock prices always reflect fundamentals, or may instead reflect bubbles or fads.

Chapter 17 Expectations, consumption and investment

Chapter 17 focuses on the role of expectations in consumption and investment decisions. The chapter shows how consumption depends partly on current income, partly on human wealth and partly on financial wealth. It shows how investment depends partly on current cash flow and partly on the expected present value of future profits.

Chapter 18 Expectations, output and policy

Chapter 18 looks at the role of expectations in output fluctuations. Starting from the *IS–LM* model, it modifies the description of the goods market equilibrium (the IS relation) to reflect the effect of expectations on spending. It revisits the effects of monetary and fiscal policy on output. It shows, for example, that, in contrast to the results derived in the core, a fiscal contraction can sometimes increase output, even in the short run.

Chapter 16

FINANCIAL MARKETS AND EXPECTATIONS

In our first pass at financial markets (in Chapter 4), we assumed that there were only two assets: money and one type of bond – a one-year bond. We now look at an economy with a richer and more realistic menu of non-money assets: short-term bonds, long-term bonds and stocks.

Our focus throughout this chapter will be on the role expectations play in the determination of asset prices, from bonds, to stocks, to houses. (The reason this belongs in a macroeconomics textbook is that, as you will see, not only are these prices affected by current and expected future activity, but they also in turn affect decisions which affect current activity. Understanding their determination is central to understanding fluctuations.)

● Section 16.1 introduces the concept of expected present discounted value.

● Section 16.2 looks at the determination of bond prices and bond yields. It shows how bond prices and yields depend on current and expected future short-term interest rates. It then shows how we can use the yield curve to learn about the expected course of future short-term interest rates.

● Section 16.3 looks at the determination of stock prices. It shows how stock prices depend on current and expected future profits, as well as on current and expected future interest rates. It then discusses how movements in economic activity affect stock prices.

● Section 16.4 looks more closely at two issues. First, the effect of perceptions of risk on asset prices. Second, the relevance of fads and bubbles – episodes where asset prices, stock or house prices in particular, appear to move for reasons unrelated to either current and expected future payments or interest rates.

16.1 EXPECTED PRESENT DISCOUNTED VALUES

Let's return to the example in section 5.1 of the manager considering whether or not to buy a new machine. On the one hand, buying and installing the machine involves a cost today. On the other, the machine allows for higher production, higher sales and higher profits in the future. The question facing the manager is whether the value of these expected profits is higher than the cost of buying and installing the machine. This is where the concept of expected present discounted value comes in handy: the **expected present discounted value** of a sequence of future payments is the value today of this expected sequence of payments. Once the manager has computed the expected present discounted value of the sequence of profits, her problem becomes simple. She compares two numbers, the expected present discounted value and the initial cost. If the value exceeds the cost, she should go ahead and buy the machine. If it does not, she should not.

As for the real interest rate, the practical problem is that expected present discounted values are not directly observable. They must be constructed from information on the sequence of expected payments and expected interest rates. Let's first look at the mechanics of construction.

Computing expected present discounted values

If the one-year nominal interest rate is i_t, lending one euro this year implies getting back $1 + i_t$ euros next year. Equivalently, borrowing one euro this year implies paying back $1 + i_t$ euros next year. In this sense, one euro this year is worth $1 + i_t$ euros next year. This relation is represented graphically in the first line of Figure 16.1.

Turn the argument around and ask: how much is one euro next year worth this year? The answer, shown in the second line of Figure 16.1, is $1/(1 + i_t)$ euros. Think of it this way: if you lend $1/(1 + i_t)$ euros this year, you will receive $1/(1 + i_t)$ times $(1 + i_t) = 1$ euro next year. Equivalently, if you borrow $1/(1 + i_t)$ euros this year, you will have to repay exactly one euro next year. So, one euro next year is worth $1/(1 + i_t)$ euros this year.

More formally, we say that $1/(1 + i_t)$ is the *present discounted value* of one euro next year. The word 'present' comes from the fact that we are looking at the value of a payment next year in terms of euros today. The word 'discounted' comes from the fact that the value next year is discounted, with $1/(1 + i_t)$ being the **discount factor**. (The one-year nominal interest rate, i_t, is sometimes called the **discount rate**.)

Because the nominal interest rate is always positive, the discount factor is always less than 1: a euro next year is worth less than a euro today. The higher the nominal interest rate, the lower the value today of a euro received next year. If $i = 5\%$, the value this year of a euro next year is $1/1.05 = 95$ cents. If $i = 10\%$, the value today of a euro next year is $1/1.10 = 91$ cents.

◄ i_t: discount rate.

$1/(1 + i_t)$: discount factor.

If the discount rate goes up, the discount factor goes down.

This year	Next year	2 years from now
€1	€$(1 + i_t)$	
€$\dfrac{1}{1 + i_t}$	€1	
€1		€$(1 + i_t)(1 + i_{t+1})$
€$\dfrac{1}{(1 + i_t)(1 + i_{t+1})}$		€1

Figure 16.1

Computing present discounted values

Now apply the same logic to the value today of a euro received two years from now. For the moment, assume that current and future one-year nominal interest rates are known with certainty. Let i_t be the nominal interest rate for this year, and i_{t+1} be the one-year nominal interest rate next year.

If, today, you lend one euro for two years, you will get $(1 + i_t)(1 + i_{t+1})$ euros two years from now. Put another way, one euro today is worth $(1 + i_t)(1 + i_{t+1})$ euros two years from now. This relation is represented in the third line of Figure 16.1.

What is one euro two years from now worth today? By the same logic as before, the answer is $1/(1 + i_t)(1 + i_{t+1})$ euros: if you lend $1/((1 + i_t)(1 + i_{t+1}))$ euros this year, you will get exactly one euro in two years. So, the present discounted value of a euro two years from now is equal to $1/(1 + i_t)(1 + i_{t+1})$ euros. This relation is shown in the last line of Figure 16.1. If, for example, the one-year nominal interest rate is the same this year and next, and equal to 5%, so $i_t = i_{t+1} = 5\%$, then the present discounted value of a euro in two years is equal to $1/(1.05)^2$, or about 91 cents today.

The general formula

Having gone through these steps, it is easy to derive the present discounted value for the case where both payments and interest rates can change over time.

Consider a sequence of payments in euros, starting today and continuing into the future. Assume for the moment that both future payments and future interest rates are known with certainty. Denote today's payment by €z_t, the payment next year by €z_{t+1}, the payment two years from today by €z_{t+2}, and so on.

The present discounted value of this sequence of payments – that is, the value in today's euros of the sequence of payments – which we shall call €V_t, is given by

$$€V_t = €z_t + \frac{1}{(1 + i_t)}€z_{t+1} + \frac{1}{(1 + i_t)(1 + i_{t+1})}€z_{t+2} + \cdots$$

Each payment in the future is multiplied by its respective discount factor. The more distant the payment, the smaller the discount factor, and thus the smaller today's value of that distant payment. In other words, future payments are discounted more heavily, so their present discounted value is lower.

We have assumed that future payments and future interest rates were known with certainty. Actual decisions, however, have to be based on expectations of future payments rather than on actual values for these payments. In our earlier example, the manager cannot be sure of how much profit the new machine will actually bring; nor does she know what interest rates will be in the future. The best she can do is get the most accurate forecasts she can, and then compute the expected present discounted value of profits, based on these forecasts.

How do we compute the expected present discounted value when future payments and interest rates are uncertain? Basically in the same way as before, but by replacing the known future payments and known interest rates with expected future payments and expected interest rates. Formally, denote expected payments next year by €z_{t+1}^e, expected payments two years from now by €z_{t+2}^e, and so on. Similarly, denote the expected one-year nominal interest rate next year by i_{t+1}^e, and so on (the one-year nominal interest rate this year, i_t, is known today, so it does not need a superscript 'e'). The expected present discounted value of this expected sequence of payments is given by

> This statement ignores an important issue – risk. If people dislike risk, the value of an uncertain (and therefore risky) payment, now or in the future, will be lower than the value of a riskless payment, even if both have the same expected value. We ignore this effect here. For a full treatment, you would have to take a course in finance.

$$€V_t = €z_t + \frac{1}{(1 + i_t)}€z_{t+1}^e + \frac{1}{(1 + i_t)(1 + i_{t+1}^e)}€z_{t+2}^e + \cdots \qquad [16.1]$$

'Expected present discounted value' is a heavy expression to carry: instead, for short, we will often just use **present discounted value**, or even just **present value**. Also, it will be convenient to have a shorthand way of writing expressions like equation (16.1). To denote the present value of an expected sequence for €z, we shall write $V(€z_t)$, or just $V(€z)$.

Using present values: examples

Equation (16.1) has two important implications:

- The present value depends positively on today's actual payment and expected future payments. An increase in either today's €z or any future €z^e leads to an increase in the present value.

  ◄ €z or future €z^e increase ⇒ €V increases.

- The present value depends negatively on current and expected future interest rates. An increase in either current i or any future i^e leads to a decrease in the present value.

  ◄ i or future i^e increase ⇒ €V decreases.

Equation (16.1) is not simple, however, and so it will help to go through some examples.

Constant interest rates

To focus on the effects of the sequence of payments on the present value, assume that interest rates are expected to be constant over time, so that $i_t = i^e_{t+1} = \cdots$, and denote their common value by i. The present value formula – equation (16.1) – becomes

$$€V_t = €z_t + \frac{1}{(1+i)}€z^e_{t+1} + \frac{1}{(1+i)^2}€z^e_{t+2} + \cdots \qquad [16.2]$$

In this case, the present value is a weighted sum of current and expected future payments, with weights that decline geometrically through time. The weight on a payment this year is 1, the weight on the payment n years from now is $(1/(1+i))^n$. With a positive interest rate, the weights get closer and closer to zero as we look further and further into the future. For example, with an interest rate equal to 10%, the weight on a payment 10 years from today is equal to $1/(1 + 0.10)^{10} = 0.386$, so that a payment of €1,000 in 10 years is worth €386 today. The weight on a payment in 30 years is $1/(1 + 0.10)^{30} = 0.057$, so that a payment of €1,000 30 years from today is worth only €57 today!

◄ The weights correspond to the terms of a geometric series. (See the discussion of geometric series in Appendix 1 at the end of the book.)

Constant interest rates and payments

In some cases, the sequence of payments for which we want to compute the present value is simple. For example, a typical fixed-rate 30-year mortgage requires constant euro payments over 30 years. Consider a sequence of equal payments – call them €z without a time index – over n years including this year. In this case, the present value formula in equation (16.2) simplifies to

$$€V_t = €z\left[1 + \frac{1}{(1+i)} + \cdots + \frac{1}{(1+i)^{n-1}}\right]$$

Because the terms in the expression in brackets represent a geometric series, we can compute the sum of the series, and get

$$€V_t = €z\frac{1 - [1/(1+i)^n]}{1 - [1/(1+i)]}$$

◄ By now, geometric series should not hold any secret, and you should have no problem deriving this relation. (But if you do, see Appendix 1 at the end of the book.)

Suppose you have just won one million euros from your state lottery and have been presented with a €1,000,000 cheque on TV. Afterwards, you are told that, to protect you from your worst spending instincts as well as from your many new 'friends', the state will pay you the million euros in equal yearly installments of €50,000 over the next 20 years. What is the present value of your prize today? Taking, for example, an interest rate of 6% per year, the preceding equation gives $V = €50,000(0.688)/(0.057) =$ or about €608,000. Not bad, but winning the prize did not make you a millionaire.

◄ What is the present value if i equals 4%? 8%? (Answers: €706,000, €530,000)

Constant interest rates and payments, forever

Let's go one step further and assume that payments are not only constant, but go on forever. Real-world examples are harder to come by for this case, but one example comes from nineteenth-century England, when the government issued *consols*, bonds paying a fixed yearly amount forever. Let €z be the constant payment. Assume that payments start next

Most *consols* were bought back by the British government at the end of the nineteenth century and early twentieth century. A few are still around. ►

year, rather than right away as in the previous example (this makes for simpler algebra). From equation (16.2), we have

$$€V_t = \frac{1}{(1+i)}€z + \frac{1}{(1+i)^2}€z + \cdots$$

$$= \frac{1}{(1+i)}\left(1 + \frac{1}{(1+i)} + \cdots\right)€z$$

where the second line follows by factoring out $1/(1+i)$. The reason for factoring out $1/(1+i)$ should be clear from looking at the term in brackets: it is an infinite geometric sum, so we can use the property of geometric sums to rewrite the present value as

$$€V_t = \frac{1}{(1+i)} \times \frac{1}{1-(1/(1+i))} \times €z$$

Or, simplifying (the steps are given in the application of Proposition 2 in Appendix 1 at the end of the book),

$$€V_t = \frac{€z}{i}$$

The present value of a constant sequence of payments $€z$ is simply equal to the ratio of $€z$ to the interest rate i. If, for example, the interest rate is expected to be 5% per year forever, the present value of a consol that promises €10 per year forever equals €10/0.05 = €200. If the interest rate increases and is now expected to be 10% per year forever, the present value of the consol decreases to €10/0.10 = €100.

Zero interest rates

Because of discounting, computing present discounted values typically requires the use of a calculator. There is, however, a case where computations simplify. This is the case where the interest rate is equal to zero: if $i = 0$, then $1/(1+i)$ equals one, and so does $(1/(1+i)^n)$ for any power n. For that reason, the present discounted value of a sequence of expected payments is just the sum of those expected payments. Because the interest rate is in fact typically positive, assuming the interest rate is zero is only an approximation. But it is a very useful one for back-of-the-envelope computations.

Nominal versus real interest rates and present values

So far, we have computed the present value of a sequence of euro payments by using interest rates in terms of euros – nominal interest rates. Specifically, we have written equation (16.1) as

$$€V_t = €z_t + \frac{1}{(1+i_t)}€z_{t+1}^e + \frac{1}{(1+i_t)(1+i_{t+1}^e)}€z_{t+2}^e + \cdots$$

where $i_t, i_{t+1}^e, \ldots$ is the sequence of current and expected future nominal interest rates, and $\$z_t, \$z_{t+1}^e, \$z_{t+2}^e, \ldots$ is the sequence of current and expected future euro payments.

Suppose we want to compute instead the present value of a sequence of real payments – that is, payments in terms of a basket of goods rather than in terms of euros. Following the same logic as before, we need to use the right interest rates for this case: namely interest rates in terms of the basket of goods – real interest rates. Specifically, we can write the present value of a sequence of real payments as

$$V_t = z_t + \frac{1}{(1+r_t)}z_{t+1}^e + \frac{1}{(1+r_t)(1+r_{t+1}^e)}z_{t+2}^e + \cdots \tag{16.3}$$

where $r_t, r_{t+1}^e, \ldots$ is the sequence of current and expected future real interest rates, $z_t, z_{t+1}^e, z_{t+2}^e, \ldots$ is the sequence of current and expected future real payments and V_t is the real present value of future payments.

These two ways of writing the present value turn out to be equivalent. That is, the real value obtained by constructing €V_t using equation (16.1) and dividing by P_t, the price level, is equal to the real value V_t obtained from equation (16.3), so

$$€V_t/P_t = V_t$$

In words: we can compute the present value of a sequence of payments in two ways. One way is to compute it as the present value of the sequence of payments expressed in euros, discounted using nominal interest rates, and then divided by the price level today. The other way is to compute it as the present value of the sequence of payments expressed in real terms, discounted using real interest rates. The two ways give the same answer.

FOCUS
How can inflation expectations be measured?

Inflation expectations can be measured in two ways:

1. *From surveys of consumers and firms.* In Europe, the forecasts of households and firms are calculated by *The Joint Harmonised EU Programme of Business and Consumer Surveys.* In particular, household expectations are constructed using the EU surveys question 6, which asks how, by comparison with the past 12 months, the respondents expect that consumer prices will develop in the next 12 months. Note from Figure 16.2 how inflation expectations measured through surveys tend to go down during recessions,

for example in the recent recession started in the summer of 2007.

In the UK, the Bank of England jointly with GfK NOP (a leading market research agency) runs the *Inflation Attitudes Survey*; questions are asked annually that cover perceptions of the relationship between interest rates and inflation and knowledge of who sets rates. In the USA, one such survey is conducted by the Survey Research Center at the University of Michigan.

2. *Comparing the yield on nominal government bonds with that on real government bonds of the same maturity.*

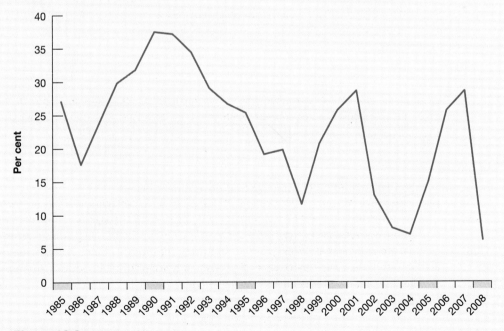

Figure 16.2

Expected inflation from consumers' surveys in the EU

Source: Eurostat.

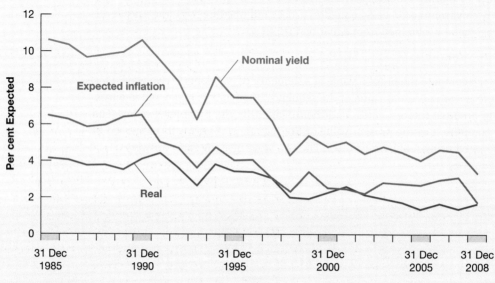

Figure 16.3

Expected inflation in the UK since 1985 computed as the difference between nominal and real yields

Source: Bank of England.

Figure 16.4

Expected inflation calculated on French indexed government bonds (OAT)

Source: Agence France Trésor.

Real bonds or indexed bonds are bonds that promise payments adjusted for inflation rather than fixed nominal payments. The UK was one of the first developed economies to issue index-linked bonds in 1981. As an example, Figure 16.3 shows expected inflation calculated as the difference between the nominal annual average yield on ten years' British Government Securities and the real annual average yield on ten years' British Government Securities.

In France the *Agence France Trésor* issues two types of real bonds: the OATi indexed to the French CPI and the OAT€ indexed to the euro area CPI. They also compute the implicit expected inflation rate (called 'point-mort d'inflation'), as shown in Figure 16.4 from January 2005 until June 2009. Note the impressive fall of expected inflation from July 2007 (beginning of the financial crisis) until November 2008 (when some major rescue packages were put in place in the UK and the USA).

Do we need both formulas? Yes. Which one is more helpful depends on the context. Take bonds, for example. Bonds typically are claims to a sequence of nominal payments over a period of years. For example, a 10-year bond might promise to pay €50 each year for 10 years, plus a final payment of €1,000 in the last year. So when we look at the pricing of bonds in the next section, we shall rely on equation (16.1) (which is expressed in terms of euro payments) rather than on equation (16.3) (which is expressed in real terms).

But sometimes, we have a better sense of future expected real values than of future expected euro values. You might not have a good idea of what your nominal income will be in 20 years: its value depends very much on what happens to inflation between now and then. But you might be confident that your nominal income will increase by at least as much as inflation – in other words, that your real income will not decrease. In this case, using equation (16.1), which requires you to form expectations of future nominal income, will be difficult. However, using equation (16.3), which requires you to form expectations of future real income, may be easier. For this reason, when we discuss consumption and investment decisions later (in Chapter 17), we shall rely on equation (16.3) rather than equation (16.1).

We now have the tools we need to look at the role of expectations in the economy. This is what we do in the next three sections.

16.2 BOND PRICES AND BOND YIELDS

Bonds differ in two basic dimensions:

- **Default risk** – the risk that the issuer of the bond (it could be a government or a company) will not pay back the full amount promised by the bond.
- **Maturity** – the length of time over which the bond promises to make payments to the holder of the bond. A bond that promises to make one payment of £1,000 in six months has a maturity of six months; a bond that promises £100 per year for the next 20 years and a final payment of £1,000 at the end of those 20 years has a maturity of 20 years.

In this section, we shall leave risk aside and focus on maturity. Bonds of different maturities each have a price and an associated interest rate called the *yield to maturity*, or simply the *yield*. Yields on bonds with a short maturity, typically a year or less, are called *short-term interest rates*. Yields on bonds with a longer maturity are called *long-term interest rates*.

On any given day, we observe the yields on bonds of different maturities, and so we can trace graphically how the yield depends on the maturity of a bond. This relation between maturity and yield is called the **yield curve**, or the **term structure of interest rates** (the word 'term' is synonymous with 'maturity'). Figure 16.5 gives, for example, two term

◄ Do not worry: we are just introducing the terms here. They will be defined and explained in this section.

◄ Term structure ≡ yield curve.

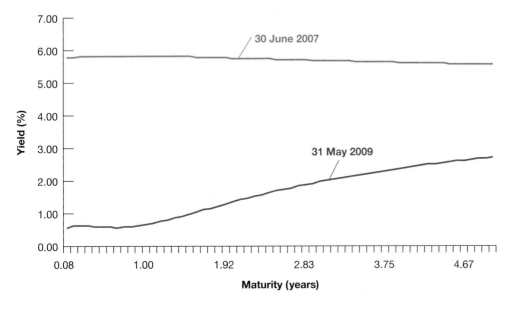

Figure 16.5

UK yield curves: June 2007 and May 2009

The yield curve, which was slightly downward sloping in June 2007, was sharply upward sloping in May 2009.

Source: Bank of England.

structures on British Government Securities on 30 June 2007, and on 31 May 2009. The choice of the two dates is not accidental; why we chose them will become clear shortly.

Note how, on 30 June 2007, the yield curve was slightly downward sloping, declining from a one-year interest rate of 5.83% to a five-year interest rate of 5.56%. In other words, long-term interest rates were slightly lower than short-term interest rates. Note how, almost

FOCUS
The vocabulary of bond markets

Understanding the basic vocabulary of financial markets will help make them less mysterious. Here is a basic vocabulary review.

- Bonds are issued by governments or by firms. If issued by the government or government agencies, the bonds are called **government bonds**. If issued by firms (corporations), they are called **corporate bonds**.
- Bonds are rated for their default risk (the risk that they will not be repaid) by rating agencies. The two major ones are the Standard and Poor's Corporation (S&P), and Moody's Investors Service. Moody's **bond ratings** range from AAA for bonds with nearly no risk of default, to C for bonds where the default risk is high. In August 2011, Standard and Poor's downgraded US government bonds from AAA to AA+, reflecting their worry about the large budget deficits, and creating a strong controversy. A lower rating typically implies that the bond has to pay a higher interest rate, or else investors will not buy it. The difference between the interest rate paid on a given bond and the interest rate paid on the bond with the highest (best) rating is called the **risk premium** associated with the given bond. Bonds with high default risk are sometimes called **junk bonds**.
- Bonds that promise a single payment at maturity are called **discount bonds**. The single payment is called the **face value** of the bond.
- Bonds that promise multiple payments before maturity and one payment at maturity are called **coupon bonds**. The payments before maturity are called **coupon payments**. The final payment is called the face value of the bond. The ratio of coupon payments to the face value is called the **coupon rate**. The **current yield** is the ratio of the coupon payment to the price of the bond.

   For example, a bond with coupon payments of £5 each year, a face value of £100, and a price of £80 has a coupon rate of 5% and a current yield of 5/80 = 0.0625 = 6.25%. From an economic viewpoint, neither the coupon rate nor the current yield are interesting measures. The correct measure of the interest rate on a bond is its yield to maturity, or simply yield; you can think of it as roughly the average interest rate paid by the bond over its life (the **life of a bond** is the amount of time left until the bond matures). We shall define the yield to maturity more precisely later in this chapter.

- In the UK, the government issues bonds called GILTS – a gilt is a UK government liability in sterling, issued by HM Treasury and listed on the London Stock Exchange. The government has concentrated issuance of conventional gilts around the 5-, 10- and 30-year maturity areas, but in May 2005 the Debt Management Dffice issued a new 50-year maturity conventional gilt. In Sweden, the government issues different types of nominal bonds. Nominal government bonds are interest-bearing securities with an annual coupon payment. Nominal bonds have maturities from 2 to 15 years. Approximately 45% of all borrowing consists of government bonds. T-bills are securities with short maturities (between three and six months). In all, around 20–25% of all borrowing takes place in T-bills.
- Bonds are typically nominal bonds: they promise a sequence of fixed nominal payments – payments in terms of domestic currency. There are, however, other types of bonds. Among them are **indexed bonds**, bonds that promise payments adjusted for inflation rather than fixed nominal payments. Instead of promising to pay, say, 100 pounds in a year, a one-year indexed bond promises to pay $100 \times (1 + \pi)$ pounds, whatever π, the rate of inflation that will take place over the coming year, turns out to be. Because they protect bondholders against the risk of inflation, indexed bonds are popular in many countries. In Europe, a certain number of countries issue indexed bonds, including the UK and France. They play a particularly important role in the UK, where, over the past 20 years, people have increasingly used them to save for retirement. By holding long-term indexed bonds, people can make sure that the payments they receive when they retire will be protected from inflation. Indexed bonds (called inflation-indexed bonds) were introduced in the USA in 1997. They account for less than 10% of US government bonds at this point, but their role will surely increase in the future.

two years later, on 31 May 2009, the yield curve was sharply upward sloping, increasing from a three-month interest rate of 0.64% to a five-year interest rate of 2.72%. In other words, long-term interest rates were now much higher than short-term interest rates.

Why was the yield curve downward sloping in June 2007 but upward sloping in May 2009? Put another way, why were long-term interest rates slightly lower than short-term interest rates in June 2007 but higher than short-term interest rates in May 2009? What were financial market participants thinking at each date? To answer these questions and, more generally, to think about the determination of the yield curve and the relation between short-term interest rates and long-term interest rates, we proceed in two steps:

1. First, we derive bond prices for bonds of different maturities.
2. Second, we go from bond prices to bond yields, and examine the determinants of the yield curve and the relation between short-term and long-term interest rates.

Bond prices as present values

In much of this section, we shall look at just two types of bonds, a bond that promises one payment of €100 in one year – a one-year bond, and a bond that promises one payment of €100 in two years – a two-year bond.

Once you understand how their prices and yields are determined, it will be easy to generalise our results to bonds of any maturity. We shall do so later.

Let's start by deriving the prices of the two bonds.

◄ Note that both bonds are discount bonds (see the Focus box).

- Given that the one-year bond promises to pay €100 next year, it follows from section 16.1 that its price, call it $€P_{1t}$, must be equal to the present value of a payment of €100 next year. Let the current one-year nominal interest rate be i_{1t}. Note that we now denote the one-year interest rate in year t by i_{1t} rather than simply by i_t as we did in earlier chapters. This is to make it easier for you to remember that it is the one-year interest rate. So,

$$€P_{1t} = \frac{€100}{1 + i_{1t}} \qquad [16.4]$$

The price of the one-year bond varies inversely with the current one-year nominal interest rate.

◄ We saw this relation earlier (in Chapter 4, section 4.2).

- Given that the two-year bond promises to pay €100 in two years, its price, call it $€P_{2t}$, must be equal to the present value of €100 two years from now:

$$€P_{2t} = \frac{€100}{(1 + i_{1t})(1 + i^e_{1t+1})} \qquad [16.5]$$

where i_{1t} denotes the one-year interest rate this year and i^e_{1t+1} denotes the one-year rate expected by financial markets for next year. The price of the two-year bond depends inversely on both the current one-year rate and the one-year rate expected for next year.

Arbitrage and bond prices

Before exploring further the implications of equations (16.4) and (16.5), let us look at an alternative derivation of equation (16.5). This alternative derivation will introduce you to the important concept of arbitrage.

Suppose you have the choice between holding one-year bonds or two-year bonds and what you care about is how much you will have one year from today. Which bonds should you hold?

- Suppose you hold one-year bonds. For every euro you put in one-year bonds, you will get $(1 + i_{1t})$ euros next year. This relation is represented in the first line of Figure 16.6.
- Suppose you hold two-year bonds. Because the price of a two-year bond is $€P_{2t}$, every euro you put in two-year bonds buys you $€1/€P_{2t}$ bonds today.

When next year comes, the bond will have only one more year before maturity. Thus, one year from today, the two-year bond will now be a one-year bond. Therefore the price

Figure 16.6

Returns from holding one-year and two-year bonds for one year

at which you can expect to sell it next year is $€P^e_{1t+1}$, which is the expected price of a one-year bond next year.

So for every euro you put in two-year bonds, you can expect to receive $€1/€P_{2t}$ times $€P^e_{1t+1}$, or, equivalently, $€P^e_{1t+1}/€P_{2t}$ euros next year. This is represented in the second line of Figure 16.6.

Which bonds should you hold? Suppose you, and other financial investors, care only about the expected return. (This assumption is known as the **expectations hypothesis**. It is a strong simplification: you, and other financial investors, are likely to care not only about the expected return, but also about the risk associated with holding each bond. If you hold a one-year bond, you know with certainty what you will get next year. If you hold a two-year bond, the price at which you will sell it next year is uncertain; holding the two-year bond for one year is risky. We will disregard this for now, but come back to it later.)

Under the assumption that you, and other financial investors, care only about expected return, it follows that the two bonds must offer the same expected one-year return. Suppose this condition was not satisfied. Suppose that, for example, the one-year return on one-year bonds was lower than the expected one-year return on two-year bonds. In this case, no one would want to hold the existing supply of one-year bonds, and the market for one-year bonds could not be in equilibrium. Only if the expected one-year return is the same on both bonds will financial investors be willing to hold both one-year bonds and two-year bonds.

If the two bonds offer the same expected one-year return, it follows from Figure 16.6 that

$$1 + i_{1t} = \frac{€P^e_{1t+1}}{€P_{2t}}$$ [16.6]

The left side gives the return per euro from holding a one-year bond for one year; the right side gives the expected return per euro from holding a two-year bond for one year. We shall call equations such as (16.6) – equations which state that the expected returns on two assets must be equal – **arbitrage** relations. Rewrite equation (16.6) as

> We use 'arbitrage' to denote the proposition that expected returns on two assets must be equal. Some economists reserve 'arbitrage' for the narrower proposition that riskless profit opportunities do not go unexploited.

$$€P_{2t} = \frac{€P^e_{1t+1}}{1 + i_{1t}}$$ [16.7]

Arbitrage implies that the price of a two-year bond today is the present value of the expected price of the bond next year. This raises the next question: what does the expected price of one-year bonds next year ($€P^e_{1t+1}$) depend on?

The answer is straightforward. Just as the price of a one-year bond this year depends on this year's one-year interest rate, the price of a one-year bond next year will depend on the one-year interest rate next year. Writing equation (16.4) for next year (year ($t + 1$)) and denoting expectations in the usual way, we get

$$€P^e_{1t+1} = \frac{€100}{(1 + i^e_{1t+1})}$$

> The relation between arbitrage and present values: arbitrage between bonds of different maturities implies that bond prices are equal to the expected present values of payments on these bonds.

The price of the bond next year is expected to equal the final payment, €100, discounted by the one-year interest rate expected for next year.

Replacing $€P^e_{1t+1}$ by $€100/(1 + i^e_{1t+1})$ in equation (16.7) gives

$$€P_{2t} = \frac{€100}{(1 + i_{1t})(1 + i^e_{1t+1})}$$ [16.8]

This expression is the same as equation (16.5). What we have shown is that arbitrage between one- and two-year bonds implies that the price of two-year bonds is the present value of the payment in two years, namely €100, discounted using current and next year's expected one-year interest rates.

From bond prices to bond yields

Having looked at bond prices, we now go on to bond yields. The basic point: bond yields contain the same information about future expected interest rates as bond prices. They just do so in a much clearer way.

To begin, we need a definition of the yield to maturity: the **yield to maturity** on an *n*-year bond, or, equivalently, the ***n*-year interest rate**, is defined as that constant annual interest rate that makes the bond price today equal to the present value of future payments on the bond.

This definition is simpler than it sounds. Take, for example, the two-year bond we introduced earlier. Denote its yield by i_{2t}, where the subscript 2 is there to remind us that this is the yield to maturity on a two-year bond or, equivalently, the two-year interest rate. Following the definition of the yield to maturity, this yield is the constant annual interest rate that would make the present value of €100 in two years equal to the price of the bond today. So, it satisfies the following relation:

$$€P_{2t} = \frac{€100}{(1 + i_{2t})^2} \qquad [16.9]$$

Suppose the bond sells for €90 today. Then, the two-year interest rate i_{2t} is given by $\sqrt{100/90} - 1$, or 5.4%. In other words, holding the bond for two years – until maturity – yields an interest rate of 5.4% per year.

◀ €90 = €100/(1 + i_{2t})² ⇒ (1 + i_{2t})² = €100/€90 ⇒ (1 + i_{2t}) = $\sqrt{€100/€90}$ ⇒ i_{2t} = 5.4%

What is the relation of the two-year interest rate to the current one-year interest rate and the expected one-year interest rate? To answer this question, look at equation (16.9) and equation (16.8). Eliminating $€P_{2t}$ between the two gives

$$\frac{€100}{(1 + i_{2t})^2} = \frac{€100}{(1 + i_{1t})(1 + i^e_{1t+1})}$$

Rearranging, we have

$$(1 + i_{2t})^2 = (1 + i_{1t})(1 + i^e_{1t+1})$$

This gives us the exact relation between the two-year interest rate, i_{2t}, the current one-year interest rate, i_{1t}, and next year's expected one-year interest rate, i^e_{t+1}. A useful approximation to this relation is given by

$$i_{2t} \approx \frac{1}{2}(i_{1t} + i^e_{1t+1}) \qquad [16.10]$$

◀ We used a similar approximation when we looked at the relation between the nominal interest rate and the real interest rate earlier (in Chapter 6). (See Proposition 3 in Appendix 1.)

Equation (16.10) simply says that the two-year interest rate is (approximately) the average of the current one-year interest rate and next year's expected one-year interest rate.

We have focused on the relation between the prices and yields of one-year and two-year bonds. But our results generalise to bonds of any maturity. For instance, we could have looked at bonds with maturities shorter than a year. To take an example: the yield on a bond with a maturity of six months is (approximately) equal to the average of the current three-month interest rate and next quarter's expected three-month interest rate. Or, we could have looked instead at bonds with maturities longer than two years. For example, the yield on a 10-year bond is (approximately) equal to the average of the current one-year interest rate and the one-year interest rates expected for the next nine years.

The general principle is clear: long-term interest rates reflect current and future expected short-term interest rates.

Interpreting the yield curve

The relations we just derived tell us what we need to interpret the slope of the yield curve. By looking at yields for bonds of different maturities, we can infer what financial markets expect short-term interest rates will be in the future.

Suppose we want to find out, for example, what financial markets expect the one-year interest rate to be one year from now. All we need to do is to look at the yield on a two-year bond, i_{2t}, and the yield on a one-year bond, i_{1t}. From equation (16.10), multiplying both sides by 2 and reorganising, we get

$$i^e_{1t+1} = 2i_{2t} - i_{1t} \qquad [16.11]$$

The one-year interest rate expected for next year is equal to twice the yield on a two-year bond minus the current one-year interest rate. Take, for example, the yield curve for 31 May 2009 shown in Figure 16.5.

On 31 May 2009, the one-year interest rate, i_{1t}, was 0.66%, and the two-year interest rate, i_{2t}, was 1.35%. From equation (16.11), it follows that, on 31 May 2009, financial markets expected the one-year interest rate one year later – that is, the one-year interest rate on 31 May 2010 – to equal $2 \times 1.35\% - 0.66\% = 2.04\%$ – that is, 1.4% higher than the one-year interest rate on 31 May 2009. In words: on 31 May 2009, financial markets expected the one-year interest rate to be substantially higher one year later.

More generally, when the yield curve is upward sloping – that is, when long-term interest rates are higher than short-term interest rates – this tells us that financial markets expect short-term rates to be higher in the future. When the yield curve is downward sloping – that is, when long-term interest rates are lower than short-term interest rates – this tells us that financial markets expect short-term interest rates to be lower in the future.

The yield curve and economic activity

We can now return to the question: why did the yield curve go from being downward sloping in June 2007 to being upward sloping in May 2009? Put another way, why did long-term interest rates go from being lower than short-term interest rates in June 2007 to much higher than short-term interest rates in May 2009?

First, the answer in short: because the financial crisis which started in the summer of 2007 turned into a full-fledged economic crisis in 2008, the Bank of England responded to the crisis by bringing short-term interest rates down. And because, even as the economy was still in recession, financial markets expected output to recover and expected short-term interest rates to return to higher levels in the future, leading long-term interest rates to fall by much less than short-term interest rates.

We shall extend the *IS–LM* model later (in Chapter 18) to explicitly take into account what we have learned about the role of expectations on decisions. For the moment, the basic *IS–LM* model will do.

It would be easy (and more realistic) to allow for constant, but positive (rather than zero) expected inflation. The conclusions would be the same.

To go through the answer step by step, let's use the *IS–LM* model we developed earlier (in Chapter 5). Think of the interest rate measured on the vertical axis as a short-term nominal interest rate. And to keep things simple, let's assume that expected inflation is equal to zero, so we do not have to worry about the distinction between the nominal and real interest rate we introduced earlier (in Chapter 11). This distinction is not central here.

In November 2000, economic indicators suggested that, after many years of high growth, the US economy had started to slow down. This slowdown was perceived as largely for the better: most economists believed output was above the natural level of output (equivalently, that the unemployment rate was below the natural rate), so a mild slowdown was desirable. And the forecasts were indeed for a mild slowdown, or what was called a **soft landing** of output back to the natural level of output.

The economic situation at the time is represented in Figure 16.7. The UK economy was at a point such as A, with interest rate i, and output Y. The level of output, Y, was believed to be above the natural level of output, Y_n. The forecasts were that the *IS* curve would gradually shift to the left, from *IS* to *IS'*, leading to a return of output to the natural level of

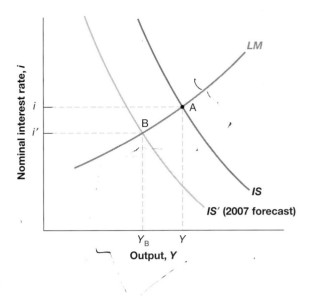

Figure 16.7

The UK economy as of June 2007

output Y_n, and a small decrease in the interest rate from i to i'. This small expected decrease in the interest rate was the reason why the yield curve was slightly downward sloping in June 2007.

Forecasts for a mild slowdown turned out, however, to be too optimistic. In 2008, the economic situation was worse than had been forecast. What happened is represented in Figure 16.8. There were two major developments:

- The reduction in spending was stronger than had been expected. In late 2008, spending in the UK slowed sharply. Instead of shifting from *IS* to *IS'* as forecast (see Figure 16.7), the *IS* curve shifted by much more, from *IS* to *IS''* in Figure 16.8. Had monetary policy remained unchanged, the economy would have moved along the *LM* curve, the equilibrium would have moved from A to B, leading to a decrease in output and a decrease in the short-term interest rate.
- There was more, however, at work. Realising that the slowdown was stronger than it had anticipated, the Bank of England shifted in early 2009 to a policy of monetary expansion, leading to a downward shift in the *LM* curve. As a result of this shift in the *LM* curve, the economy was, in May 2009, at a point like B' – rather than at point like B. Output was higher and the interest rate lower than they would have been in the absence of the monetary expansion.

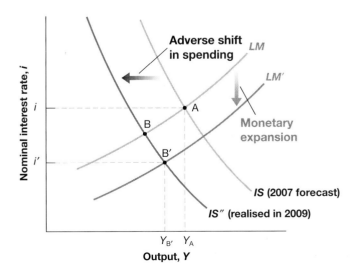

Figure 16.8

The UK economy from June 2007 to May 2009

From June 2007 to May 2009, a sharp reduction in spending, together with a monetary expansion, combined to lead to a decrease in the short-term interest rate.

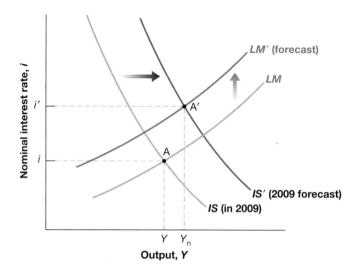

Figure 16.9

The expected path of the UK economy as of May 2009

In May 2009, financial markets expected that the economic stimulus stemming from monetary and fiscal policies would lead to a recovery in economic growth, hence to higher interest rates in the future.

In words: the decline in short-term interest rates – and therefore the decline at the short-term end of the yield curve from June 2007 to May 2009 – was the result of an unexpectedly large adverse shift in spending, combined with a strong response by the Bank of England aimed at limiting the size of the decrease in output. This still leaves one question: why was the yield curve upward sloping in June 2007? Equivalently, why were long-term interest rates higher than short-term interest rates?

To answer this question, we must look at what the markets expected to happen to the UK economy in the future, as of June 2007. This is represented in Figure 16.9. Financial markets expected two main developments:

- They expected a pickup in spending – a shift of the *IS* curve to the right, from *IS* to *IS'*. The reasons: some of the factors that had contributed to the adverse shift in the first half of 2007 were expected to turn more favourable. Investment spending was expected to pick up. Also, the tax cut passed in May 2009, to be implemented over the rest of the year, was expected to lead to higher consumption spending.
- They also expected that, once the *IS* curve started shifting to the right and output started to recover, the Bank of England would start shifting back to a tighter monetary policy. In terms of Figure 16.9, they expected the *LM* curve to shift up.

As a result of both shifts, financial markets expected the UK economy to move from point A to point A'; they expected both output to recover and short-term interest rates to increase. The anticipation of higher short-term interest rates was the reason why long-term interest rates remained high, and why the yield curve was upward sloping in June 2007.

Note that the yield curve in June 2007 was nearly flat for maturities up to one year. This tells us that financial markets did not expect interest rates to start rising until a year hence, that is before May 2010. Did they turn out to be right? Not quite. At the time of writing the Bank of England has not yet increased the short-term interest rate.

Let's summarise. We have seen in this section how bond prices and bond yields depend on current and future expected interest rates. By looking at the yield curve, we (and everybody else in the economy, from people to firms) learn what financial markets expect interest rates to be in the future. The Focus box, 'The yield curve and the liquidity trap', shows what can be learned by looking at the current yield curve.

FOCUS
The yield curve and the liquidity trap

Figure 16.10 shows the yield curve in the UK as of September 2011. At the short end, the interest rate is nearly equal to zero: this reflects the fact that the Bank of England has decreased the nominal interest rate as far as it could, namely zero, and the UK economy is now in the liquidity trap. What the yield curve tells us is that financial markets expect this to remain the case for many years: the one-year rate is equal to 0.10%, the two-year rate equal to 0.20%, the five-year rate is less than 1%. Only when we look at 10-year and 30-year horizons do the rates go up. In short, financial markets believe that the UK economy will remain weak, and thus the Bank of England will keep the nominal interest rate very low for a long time to come.

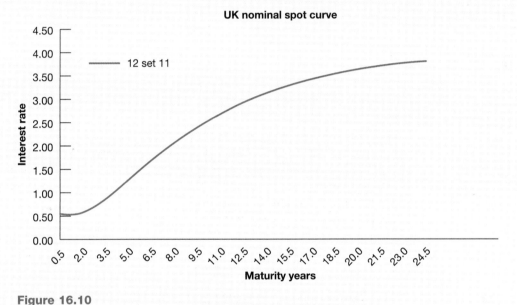

Figure 16.10

The yield curve in the UK as of September 2011

16.3 THE STOCK MARKET AND MOVEMENTS IN STOCK PRICES

So far, we have focused on bonds. But while governments finance themselves by issuing bonds, the same is not true of firms. Firms finance themselves in three ways. First, and this is the main channel for small firms, through bank loans. As we will see later (in Chapter 20), this channel has played a central role in the crisis; second, through **debt finance** – bonds and loans; and third, through **equity finance**, issuing **stocks** – or **shares**, as stocks are also called. Instead of paying predetermined amounts as bonds do, stocks pay **dividends** in an amount decided by the firm. Dividends are paid from the firm's profits. Typically dividends are less than profits, as firms retain some of their profits to finance their investment. But dividends move with profits: when profits increase, so do dividends.

Our focus in this section will be on the determination of stock prices. As a way of introducing the issues, let's look at the behaviour of an index of UK stock prices, the FT30. The FT30 index is based on the share prices of 30 British companies from a wide range of industry. The index, which began on 1 July 1935, is the oldest continuous index in the UK and one of the oldest in the world.

Similar indexes exist for other countries. In the US, the Standard & Poor's index reflects the average price of stocks, while the Dow Jones Industrial Index reflects movements of stocks of industrial firms only. The Nikkei Index reflects movements in stock prices in Tokyo and the CAC40 index reflects ◄ stock price movements in Paris.

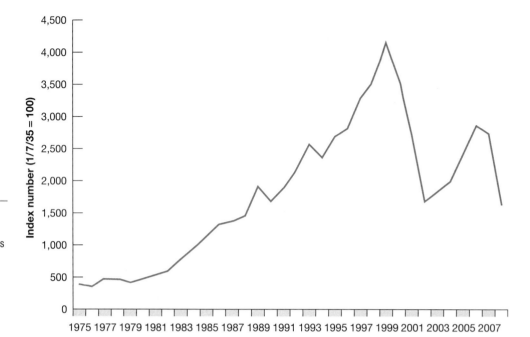

Figure 16.11

FT30 share index
July 1, 1935 = 100

Note the sharp increase in stock prices
in the 1990s, followed by the sharp
decrease in the early 2000s. Again
an increase until 2007, and then
a decrease since 2007.

Source: FTSE.

Figure 16.11 plots the FT30 since 1975 (the index is equal to 100 on 1 July 1935). The striking feature of the figure is obviously the sharp rise of the index during the 1990s, from 1,674 in 1990 to 4,157 in 1999, followed by a sharp fall in the early 2000s, from 3,574 in 2000 down to 1,670 in 2002. Then it increased again until 2006 but, in 2008, in the middle of the slowdown caused by the financial crisis of 2007, the index stood below its level in 2002. Why the long rise in the 1990s? Why the sharp fall in the early 2000s and more recently during the economic slowdown in 2007–2008? More generally, what determines the movement in stock prices, and how do stock prices respond to changes in the economic environment and macroeconomic policy? These are the questions we take up in this and the next section.

Stock prices as present values

What determines the price of a stock that promises a sequence of dividends in the future? (By now, we are sure the material in Chapter 11 has become second nature, and you already know the answer.) The stock price must equal the present value of future expected dividends.

Just as we did for bonds, let's derive this result from looking at the implications of arbitrage between one-year bonds and stocks. Suppose you face the choice of investing either in one-year bonds or in stocks for a year. What should you choose?

● Suppose you decide to hold one-year bonds. Then, for every euro you put in one-year bonds, you will get $(1 + i_{1t})$ euros next year. This payoff is represented in the upper line of Figure 16.12.
● Suppose you decide instead to hold stocks for a year. Let €Q_t be the price of the stock. Let €D_t denote the dividend this year, €D_{t+1}^e the expected dividend next year. Suppose we look at the price of the stock after the dividend has been paid this year – this price is

Figure 16.12

Returns from holding
one-year bonds or stocks
for one year

known as the *ex-dividend price* – so that the first dividend to be paid after the purchase of the stock is next year's dividend. (This is just a matter of convention; we could alternatively look at the price before this year's dividend has been paid. What term would we have to add?)

Holding the stock for a year implies buying a stock today, receiving a dividend next year and then selling the stock. As the price of a stock is $€Q_t$, every euro you put in stocks buys you $€1/€Q_t$ stocks. And for each stock you buy, you expect to receive $(€D_{t+1}^e + €Q_{t+1}^e)$, the sum of the expected dividend and the stock price next year. Therefore, for every euro you put in stocks, you expect to receive $(€D_{t+1}^e + €Q_{t+1}^e)/€Q_t$. This payoff is represented in the lower line of Figure 16.12.

Let's use the same arbitrage argument we used for bonds earlier. Assume financial investors care only about expected rates of return. Equilibrium then requires that the expected rate of return from holding stocks for one year be the same as the rate of return on one-year bonds:

$$\frac{(€D_{t+1}^e + €Q_{t+1}^e)}{€Q_t} = 1 + i_{1t}$$

◄ This ignores the fact that holding a stock is more risky than holding a bond. We take this up in the next section.

Rewrite this equation as

$$€Q_t = \frac{€D_{t+1}^e}{(1 + i_{1t})} + \frac{€Q_{t+1}^e}{(1 + i_{1t})} \qquad [16.12]$$

Arbitrage implies that the price of the stock today must be equal to the present value of the expected dividend plus the present value of the expected stock price next year.

The next step is to think about what determines $€Q_{t+1}^e$, the expected stock price next year. Next year, financial investors will again face the choice between stocks and one-year bonds. Thus, the same arbitrage relation will hold. Writing the previous equation, but now for time $t + 1$, and taking expectations into account gives

$$€Q_{t+1}^e = \frac{€D_{t+2}^e}{(1 + i_{1t+1}^e)} + \frac{€Q_{t+2}^e}{(1 + i_{1t+1}^e)}$$

The expected price next year is simply the present value next year of the sum of the expected dividend and price two years from now. Replacing the expected price $€Q_{t+1}^e$ in equation (16.12) gives

$$€Q_t = \frac{€D_{t+1}^e}{(1 + i_{1t})} + \frac{€D_{t+2}^e}{(1 + i_{1t})(1 + i_{1t+1}^e)} + \frac{€Q_{t+2}^e}{(1 + i_{1t})(1 + i_{1t+1}^e)}$$

The stock price is the present value of the expected dividend next year, plus the present value of the expected dividend two years from now, plus the expected price two years from now.

If we replace the expected price in two years as the present value of the expected price and dividends in three years and so on for n years, we get

$$€Q_t = \frac{€D_{t+1}^e}{(1 + i_{1t})} + \frac{€D_{t+2}^e}{(1 + i_{1t})(1 + i_{1t+1}^e)} + \cdots + \frac{€D_{t+n}^e}{(1 + i_{1t}) \cdots (1 + i_{1t+n-1}^e)}$$

$$+ \frac{€Q_{t+n}^e}{(1 + i_{1t}) \cdots (1 + i_{1t+n-1}^e)} \qquad [16.13]$$

Look at the last term in equation (16.13) – the present value of the expected price in n years. As long as people do not expect the stock price to explode in the future, then, as we keep replacing Q_{t+n}^e and n increases, this term will go to zero. To see why, suppose the interest rate is constant and equal to i. The last term becomes

$$\frac{€Q_{t+n}^e}{(1 + i_{1t}) \cdots (1 + i_{1t+n-1}^e)} = \frac{€Q_{t+n}^e}{(1 + i)^n}$$

A subtle point. The condition that people expect the price of the stock to converge to some value over time seems reasonable. Indeed, most of the time it is likely to be satisfied. When, however, prices are subject to rational bubbles (section 16.4), this is when people are expecting large increases in the stock price in the future, and this is when the condition that the expected stock price does not explode is not satisfied. This is why, when there are bubbles, the argument just given fails, and the stock price is no longer equal to the present value of expected dividends.

Suppose further that people expect the price of the stock to converge to some value, call it $€\bar{Q}$, in the far future. Then, the last term becomes

$$\frac{€Q^e_{t+n}}{(1+i)^n} = \frac{€\bar{Q}}{(1+i)^n}$$

If the interest rate is positive, this expression goes to zero as n becomes large. Equation (16.13) reduces to

$$€Q_t = \frac{€D^e_{t+1}}{(1+i_{1t})} + \frac{€D^e_{t+2}}{(1+i_{1t})(1+i^e_{1t+1})} + \cdots + \frac{€D^e_{t+n}}{(1+i_{1t})\cdots(1+i^e_{1t+n-1})} \qquad [16.14]$$

The price of the stock is equal to the present value of the dividend next year, discounted using the current one-year interest rate, plus the present value of the dividend two years from now, discounted using both this year's one-year interest rate and the next-year's expected one-year interest rate, and so on.

Equation (16.14) gives the stock price as the present value of nominal dividends, discounted by nominal interest rates. We know we can rewrite this equation to express the real stock price as the present value of real dividends, discounted by real interest rates. So we can rewrite the real stock price as:

$$Q_t = \frac{D^e_{t+1}}{(1+r_{1t})} + \frac{D^e_{t+2}}{(1+r_{1t})(1+r^e_{1t+1})} + \cdots \qquad [16.15]$$

Q_t and D_t, without a euro sign, denote the real price and real dividends at time t. The real stock price is the present value of future real dividends, discounted by the sequence of one-year real interest rates.

Two equivalent ways of writing the stock price:

This relation has two important implications:

- The *nominal* stock price equals the expected present discounted value of future nominal dividends, discounted by current and future nominal interest rates.
- The *real* stock price equals the expected present discounted value of future real dividends, discounted by current and future real interest rates.

- Higher expected future real dividends lead to a higher real stock price.
- Higher current and expected future one-year real interest rates lead to a lower real stock price.

Let's now see what light this relation sheds on movements in the stock market.

The stock market and economic activity

Figure 16.8 shows the large movements in UK stock prices over the past 30 years. It is not unusual for the price index to go up or down by 20% within a year. In 1997, the stock market went up by 17%; in 2002, it went down by 38%; in 2008 the stock market went down by 40%! Daily movements of 2% or more are not unusual. What causes these movements?

The first point to be made is that these movements should be, and they are for the most part, unpredictable. The reason is best understood by thinking in terms of the choice people have between stocks and bonds. If it were widely believed that, a year from now, the price of a stock was going to be 20% higher than today's price, holding the stock for a year would be unusually attractive, much more attractive than holding short-term bonds. There would be a very large demand for the stock. Its price would increase today to the point where the expected return from holding the stock was back in line with the expected return on other assets. In other words, the expectation of a high stock price next year would lead to a high stock price today.

You may have heard the proposition that stock prices follow a **random walk**. This is a technical term, but with a simple interpretation: something – it can be a molecule or the price of an asset – follows a random walk if each step it takes is as likely to be up as it is to be down. Its movements are therefore unpredictable.

There is indeed a saying in economics that it is a sign of a well-functioning stock market that movements in stock prices are unpredictable. The saying is too strong: at any moment, a few financial investors might have better information or simply be better at reading the future. If they are only a few, they may not buy enough of the stock to bid its price all the way up today. Thus, they may get large expected returns. But the basic idea is nevertheless right. The financial market gurus who regularly predict large imminent movements in the stock market are quacks. Major movements in stock prices cannot be predicted.

If movements in the stock market cannot be predicted, if they are the result of news, where does this leave us? We can still do two things:

- We can look back and identify the news to which the market reacted.
- We can ask 'what if' questions. For example: what would happen to the stock market if the central bank were to embark on a more expansionary policy, or if consumers were to become more optimistic and increase spending?

Let us look at two 'what if' questions, using the *IS–LM* model. To simplify, let's assume, as we did earlier, that expected inflation equals zero, so that the real interest rate and the nominal interest rate are equal.

A monetary expansion and the stock market

Suppose the economy is in a recession and the central bank decides to adopt a more expansionary monetary policy. The increase in money shifts the *LM* curve down in Figure 16.13, and equilibrium output moves from point A to point A′. How will the stock market react?

This assumes that the interest rate is positive to start with, so the economy is not in a liquidity trap.

The answer depends on what participants in the stock market expected monetary policy to be before the central bank's move. If they fully anticipated the expansionary policy, then the stock market will not react: neither its expectations of future dividends nor its expectations of future interest rates are affected by a move it had already anticipated. Thus, in equation (16.14), nothing changes, and stock prices will remain the same.

Suppose instead that the central bank's move is at least partly unexpected. In that case, stock prices will increase. They increase for two reasons: first, a more expansionary monetary policy implies lower interest rates for some time; second, it also implies higher output for some time (until the economy returns to the natural level of output), and therefore higher dividends. As equation (16.12) tells us, both lower interest rates and higher dividends – current and expected – will lead to an increase in stock prices.

On 30 September 1998 the US Fed lowered the target federal funds rate by 0.5%. This decrease was expected by financial markets, though, so the Dow Jones index remained roughly unchanged (actually, going down 28 points for the day).

Less than a month later, on 15 October 1998, the Fed lowered the target federal funds rate again, this time by 0.25%. In contrast to the September cut, that move by the Fed came as a complete surprise to financial markets. As a result, the Dow Jones index increased by 330 points on that day, an increase of more than 3%.

An increase in consumer spending and the stock market

Now consider an unexpected shift of the *IS* curve to the right, resulting, for example, from stronger-than-expected consumer spending. As a result of the shift, output in Figure 16.14(a) increases from A to A′.

Will stock prices go up? You might be tempted to say yes: a stronger economy means higher profits and higher dividends for some time. But this answer is incomplete, for at least two reasons.

First, the answer ignores the effect of higher activity on interest rates: the movement along the *LM* curve implies an increase in both output and interest rates. Higher output

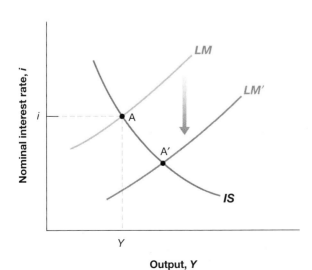

Figure 16.13

An expansionary monetary policy and the stock market

A monetary expansion decreases the interest rate and increases output. What it does to the stock market depends on whether financial markets anticipated the monetary expansion.

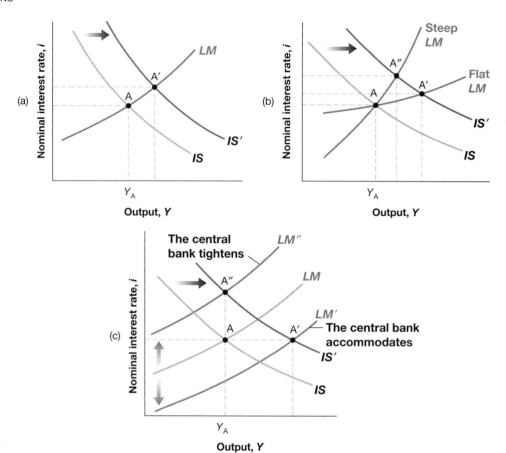

Figure 16.14

An increase in consumption spending and the stock market

(a) The increase in consumption spending leads to a higher interest rate and a higher level of output. What happens to the stock market depends on the slope of the *LM* curve and on the central bank's behaviour.

(b) If the *LM* curve is steep, the interest rate increases a lot, and output increases little. Stock prices go down. If the *LM* curve is flat, the interest rate increases little and output increases a lot. Stock prices go up.

(c) If the central bank increases the amount of money in the economy, the interest rate does not increase, but output does. Stock prices go up. If the central bank decides instead to keep output constant, the interest rate increases, but output does not. Stock prices go down.

leads to higher profits and, so, higher stock prices. Higher interest rates lead to lower stock prices. Which of the two effects, higher profits or higher interest rates, dominates? The answer depends on the slope of the *LM* curve. This is shown in Figure 16.14(b). A very flat *LM* curve leads to a movement from A to A″, with small increases in interest rates, large increases in output, and therefore an increase in stock prices. A very steep *LM* curve leads to a movement from A to A″, with large increases in interest rates, small increases in output, and therefore a decrease in stock prices.

Second, the answer ignores the effect of the shift in the *IS* curve on the central bank's behaviour. In practice, this is the effect that financial investors often care about the most. After receiving the news of unexpectedly strong economic activity, the main question among financial operators is: how will the central bank react?

- Will the central bank accommodate the shift in the *IS* curve, that is increase the money supply in line with money demand so as to avoid an increase in the interest rate?

  Central bank accommodation corresponds to a downward shift of the *LM* curve, from LM to LM′ in Figure 16.14(c). In this case, the economy will go from point A to point A′. Stock prices will increase, as output is expected to be higher and interest rates are not expected to increase.

- Will the central bank instead keep the same monetary policy, leaving the *LM* curve unchanged? In that case the economy will move along the *LM* curve. As we saw earlier, what happens to stock prices is ambiguous. Profits will be higher, but so will interest rates.

- Or will the central bank worry that an increase in output above Y_A may lead to an increase in inflation? This will be the case if the economy is already close to the natural level of output, if, in Figure 16.14(c), Y_A is close to Y_n. In this case, a further increase in output would lead to an increase in inflation, something that the central bank wants to avoid. A decision by the central bank to counteract the rightward shift of the *IS* curve with a

Another way of thinking about what happens is to think of the *LM* relation of an interest rate rule (as presented in the appendix to Chapter 5). Depending on how much the central bank increases the interest rate in response to the increase in output, the news will lead to an increase or a decrease in the stock market.

monetary contraction causes the *LM* curve to shift up, from *LM* to *LM″*, so the economy goes from A to A″ and output does not change. In that case, stock prices will surely go down: There is no change in expected profits, but the interest rate is now likely to be higher for some time.

FOCUS
Making (some) sense of (apparent) nonsense: why the stock market moved yesterday and other stories

Here are some quotes from the *Wall Street Journal* from April 1997 to August 2001. Try to make sense of them, using what you've just learned (and, if you have time, find your own quotes).

● April 1997. Good news on the economy, leading to an increase in stock prices:

> Bullish investors celebrated the release of market-friendly economic data by stampeding back into stock and bond markets, pushing the Dow Jones Industrial Average to its second-largest point gain ever and putting the blue-chip index within shooting distance of a record just weeks after it was reeling.

● December 1999. Good news on the economy, leading to a decrease in stock prices:

> Good economic news was bad news for stocks and worse news for bonds . . . The announcement of

stronger-than-expected November retail-sales numbers wasn't welcome. Economic strength creates inflation fears and sharpens the risk that the Federal Reserve will raise interest rates again.

● September 1998. Bad news on the economy, leading to an decrease in stock prices:

> Nasdaq stocks plummeted as worries about the strength of the US economy and the profitability of US corporations prompted widespread selling.

● August 2001. Bad news on the economy, leading to an increase in stock prices:

> Investors shrugged off more gloomy economic news, and focused instead on their hope that the worst is now over for both the economy and the stock market. The optimism translated into another 2% gain for the Nasdaq Composite Index.

Let's summarise: stock prices depend very much on current and future movements in activity. But this does not imply any simple relation between stock prices and output. How stock prices respond to a change in output depends on: (1) what the market expected in the first place, (2) the source of the shocks behind the change in output, and (3) how the market expects the central bank to react to the output change.

16.4 RISK, BUBBLES, FADS AND ASSET PRICES

Do all movements in stock and other asset prices come from news about future dividends or interest rates? The answer is no, for two different reasons. The first is variations in perceptions of risk. The second is deviations of prices from their fundamental value, namely bubbles or fads. Let's look at each one in turn.

Stock prices and risk

We have assumed so far that people cared only about expected return and did not take risk into account. Put another way, we have assumed that people were **risk neutral**. In fact, people, including financial investors, are **risk averse**. They care both about expected return – which they like – and risk – which they dislike.

Most of **finance theory** is indeed concerned with how people make decisions when they are risk averse, and what risk aversion implies for asset prices. Exploring these issues would take us too far from our purpose. But we can nevertheless explore a simple extension of our framework that captures the fact that people are risk averse and shows how to modify the arbitrage and the present value relations.

If people perceive stocks to be more risky than bonds, and people dislike risk, they are likely to require a risk premium to hold stocks rather than bonds. In the case of stocks, this risk premium is called the **equity premium**. Denote it by θ (the Greek lower-case letter theta). If θ is, for example, 5%, then people will hold stocks only if the expected rate of return on stocks exceeds the expected rate of return on short-term bonds by 5% a year.

In that case, the arbitrage equation between stocks and bonds becomes

$$\frac{\text{\euro}D^e_{t+1} + \text{\euro}Q^e_{t+1}}{\text{\euro}Q_t} = 1 + i_{1t} + \theta$$

The only change is the presence of θ on the right side of the equation. Going through the same steps as before (replacing Q^e_{t+1} by its expression at time $t + 1$, and so on), the stock price equals

$$\text{\euro}Q_t = \frac{\text{\euro}D^e_{t+1}}{(1+i_{1t}+\theta)} + \frac{\text{\euro}D^e_{t+2}}{(1+i_{1t}+\theta)(1+i^e_{1t+1}+\theta)} + \cdots + \frac{\text{\euro}D^e_{t+n}}{(1+i_{1t}+\theta)\cdots(1+i^e_{1t+n-1}+\theta)} \qquad [16.16]$$

The stock price is still equal to the present value of expected future dividends. But the discount rate here equals the interest rate plus the equity premium. Note that the higher the premium, the lower the stock price. Over the past 100 years in the USA, the average equity premium has been equal to roughly 5%. But (in contrast to the assumption we made earlier, where we took 0 to be constant) it is not constant. The equity premium appears, for example, to have decreased since the early 1950s, from around 7% to less than 3% today. And it may change quickly. Surely part of the stock market fall in 2008 was due not only to more pessimistic expectations of future dividends, but also to the large increase in uncertainty and the perception of higher risk by stock market participants.

Asset prices, fundamentals and bubbles

We have so far assumed that stock prices were always equal to their **fundamental value**, defined as the present value of expected dividends given in equation (15.11) (or

FOCUS
Famous bubbles: from tulipmania in seventeenth-century Holland to Russia in 1994 and the USA in 2008

Tulipmania in Holland

In the seventeenth century, tulips became increasingly popular in Western European gardens. A market developed in Holland for both rare and common forms of tulip bulbs.

The episode called the 'tulip bubble' took place from 1634 to 1637. In 1634, the price of rare bulbs started increasing. The market went into a frenzy, with speculators buying tulip bulbs in anticipation of even higher prices later. For example, the price of a bulb called 'Admiral Van de Eyck' increased from 1,500 guineas in 1634 to 7,500 guineas in 1637, equal to the price of a house at the time. There are stories about a sailor mistakenly eating bulbs, only to realise the cost of his 'meal' later. In early 1637, prices increased faster. Even the price of some common bulbs exploded, rising by a factor of up to 20 in January. But, in February 1637, prices collapsed. A few years later, bulbs were trading for roughly 10% of their value at the peak of the bubble.

Source: Taken from Peter Garber, 'Tulipmania', *Journal of Political Economy*, 1989, **97**, 535–60.)

The MMM pyramid in Russia

In 1994 a Russian 'financier', Sergei Mavrodi, created a company called MMM and proceeded to sell shares, promising shareholders a rate of return of at least 3,000% per year!

The company was an instant success. The price of MMM shares increased from 1,600 roubles (then worth £1) in February to 105,000 roubles (then worth £51) in July. And by July, according to the company claims, the number of shareholders had increased to 10 million.

The trouble was that the company was not involved in any type of production and held no assets, except for its 140 offices in Russia. The shares were intrinsically worthless. The company's initial success was based on a standard pyramid scheme, with MMM using the funds from the sale of new shares to pay the promised returns on the old shares. Despite repeated warnings by government officials, including Boris Yeltsin, that MMM was a scam and that the increase in the price of shares was a bubble, the promised returns were just too attractive to many Russian people, especially in the midst of a deep economic recession.

The scheme could work only as long as the number of new shareholders – and thus new funds to be distributed to existing shareholders – increased fast enough. By the end of July 1994, the company could no longer make good on its promises and the scheme collapsed. The company closed. Mavrodi tried to blackmail the government into paying the shareholders, claiming that not doing so would trigger a revolution or a civil war. The government refused, leading many shareholders to be angry at the government rather than at Mavrodi. Later on in the year, Mavrodi actually ran for Parliament, as a self-appointed defender of the shareholders who had lost their savings. He won!

Source: 'More murk in Moscow. MMM pyramid scheme investigation does not harm political ambitions of chairman Sergei Mavrodi', *Economist*, 5 November 1994.

The Madoff scandal of 2008

More recently, the scam perpetrated by Bernie Madoff, a Wall Street veteran, was the biggest financial fraud in history: a hole as big as $50 billion! The scheme was similar to the previous ones. For years, it seems, the returns paid to investors came, in part at least, not from real investment gains but from inflows from new clients. It might still have been going on, were it not for the global financial crisis.

The Madoff scandal of 2008 showed that investors presumed to be sophisticated, such as international bankers, can also be tricked into joining such a scheme by a promoter with a well-established reputation for financial skill. Why were they not suspicious of the unnaturally consistent returns? A former chairman of the NASDAQ stock market, Madoff has served on an advisory committee assembled by the Securities and Exchange Commission (SEC), America's main market watchdog.

Savvy marketing was another factor. Madoff, for example, only permitted one accounting firm, run by his brother-in-law, to perform audits on his hedge fund, claiming the need to keep his strategy secret. Moreover, investors had to be invited, lending his operation an air of exclusivity.

Source: 'Ponzi squared. Just when Wall Street needs it least, Bernie Madoff's pyramid scheme takes financial fraud to new lows', 15 December 2008, Economist.com.

equation (16.16) if we allow for a risk premium). Do stock prices always correspond to their fundamental value? Most economists doubt it. They point to Black October in 1929, when the US stock market fell by 23% in two days, and to 19 October 1987, when the Dow Jones index fell by 22.6% in a single day. They point to the amazing rise in the Nikkei index from around 13,000 in 1985 to around 35,000 in 1989, followed by a decline back to 16,000 in 1992. In each of these cases, they point to a lack of obvious news, or at least of news important enough to cause such enormous movements.

Instead, they argue that stock prices are not always equal to their fundamental value and that stocks are sometimes underpriced or overpriced. Overpricing eventually comes to an end, sometimes with a crash as in October 1929, or with a long slide as in the case of the Nikkei index.

> Recall that arbitrage is the condition that the expected rates of return on two financial assets be equal.

Under what conditions can such mispricing occur? The surprising answer is that it can occur even when investors are rational, and when arbitrage holds. To see why, consider the case of a truly worthless stock (that is, the stock of a company that all financial investors know will never make profits and will never pay dividends). Putting D^e_{t+1}, D^e_{t+2}, and so on, equal to zero in equation (16.15) yields a simple and unsurprising answer: the fundamental value of such a stock is equal to zero.

> The example is obviously extreme. But it makes the point most simply.

Might you nevertheless be willing to pay a positive price for this stock? Maybe. You might if you expect the price at which you can sell the stock next year to be higher than this year's price. And the same applies to a buyer next year: he may well be willing to buy at a high price if he expects to sell at an even higher price in the following year. This process suggests that stock prices may increase just because investors expect them to. Such movements in stock prices are called **rational speculative bubbles**: financial investors might well be behaving rationally as the bubble inflates. Even those investors who hold the stock at the time of the crash, and therefore sustain a large loss, may also have been rational. They may have realised there was a chance of a crash, but also a chance that the bubble would continue, and they could sell at an even higher price.

To make things simple, our example assumed the stock to be fundamentally worthless. But the argument is general and applies to stocks with a positive fundamental value as well. People might be willing to pay more than the fundamental value of a stock if they expect its price to further increase in the future. And the same argument applies to other assets, such as housing, gold and paintings. Three such bubbles are described in the Focus box, 'Famous bubbles: from tulipmania in seventeenth-century Holland to Russia in 1994 and the USA in 2008'.

> In a speculative bubble, the price of a stock is higher than its fundamental value. Investors are willing to pay a high price for the stock, in the anticipation of being able to resell the stock at an even higher price.

Are all deviations from fundamental values in financial markets rational bubbles? Probably not. The fact is that many financial investors are not rational. An increase in stock prices in the past, say, due to a succession of good news, often creates excessive optimism. If investors simply extrapolate from past returns to predict future returns, a stock may become 'hot' (high priced) for no reason other than its price has increased in the past. This is true not only of stocks, but also of houses (See the Focus box 'The increase in US housing prices in the USA in the 2000s: fundamentals or bubbles?') Such deviations of stock prices from their fundamental value are called fads. We are all aware of fads outside of the stock market; there are good reasons to believe they exist in the stock market as well.

We have focused in this chapter on how news about economic activity affects asset prices. But asset prices are more than just a sideshow. They affect economic activity by influencing consumption and investment spending. There is little question, for example, that the decline in the stock market was one of the factors behind the 2001 recession. Most economists also believe that the stock market crash of 1929 was one of the sources of the Great Depression, and that the large decline in the Nikkei is one of the causes of the long Japanese slump in the 1990s. These interactions between bond and stock markets, expectations and economic activity are the topics of the next two chapters.

FOCUS
The increase in US housing prices: fundamentals or bubbles?

Recall from earlier (in Chapter 1) that the trigger behind the current crisis was a decline in housing prices, starting in 2006 (see Figure 1.4 for the evolution of the housing price index). In retrospect, the large increase from 2000 on which preceded the decline is now widely interpreted as a bubble. But, in real time, as prices went up, there was little agreement as to what lay behind this increase.

Economists belonged to three camps. The pessimists argued that the price increases could not be justified by fundamentals. In 2005, Robert Shiller said: 'The home-price bubble feels like the stock-market mania in the fall of 1999, just before the stock bubble burst in early 2000, with all the hype, herd investing and absolute confidence in the inevitability of continuing price appreciation.'

To understand his position, let us go back to the derivation of stock prices in the text. We saw that, absent bubbles, we can think of stock prices as depending on current and expected future interest rates, and current and expected future dividends. The same applies to house prices: absent bubbles, we can think of house prices as depending on current expected future interest rates, and current and expected rents. In that context, pessimists pointed out that the increase in house prices was not matched by a parallel increase in rents. You can see this in Figure 16.15, which plots the price–rent ratio, i.e. the ratio of an index of house prices to an index of rents, from 1985 to today. After remaining roughly constant from 1985 to 1995, the ratio then increased by nearly 40%, reaching a peak in 2006, and declining since then. Furthermore, Shiller pointed out, surveys of house buyers suggested extremely high expectations of continuing large increases in housing prices, often in excess of 10% a year, and thus of large capital gains. As we saw earlier, if assets are valued at their fundamental value, investors should not be expecting very large capital gains in the future.

In European countries too, as well as in many advanced economies, real house prices have increased dramatically since the mid-1990s (Figure 16.16).

The optimists argued that there were good reasons for the price–rent ratio to go up. First, the real interest rate was decreasing, increasing the present value of rents. Second, the nominal interest rate was also decreasing, and this mattered because nominal, not real interest payments, are tax-deductible. Third, the mortgage market was changing: more people were able to borrow and buy a house; people who borrow, were able to borrow a larger proportion of the value of the house. Both of these factors led to an increase in demand, and thus an increase in

Figure 16.15

The US housing price–rent ratio since 1985

Source: Elod Takats 'Ageing and asset prices', Bank for International Settlements, Working Paper 318, 2010. *www.bis.org/publ/work318.pdf*

house prices. They also pointed out that, every year since 2000, the pessimists had kept predicting the end of the bubble, and prices continued to increase: the pessimists were losing credibility.

The third group was by far the largest, and remained agnostic (Harry Truman is reported to have said: 'Give me a one-handed economist! All my economists say, "On the one hand . . . on the other."'). They concluded that the increase in house prices reflected both improved fundamentals and bubbles, and that it was difficult to identify their relative importance.

What conclusions should you draw? That bubbles and fads are clearer in retrospect than while they are taking place. This makes the task of policy makers much harder: if they were sure it was a bubble, they should try to stop it before it gets too large, and then bursts. But they can rarely be sure until it is too late.

Source: 'Reasonable people did disagree: optimism and pessimism about the US housing market before the crash', Kristopher S. Gerardi, Christopher Foote and Paul Willen, Federal Reserve Bank of Boston, 10 September 2010, available at *www.bos.frb.org/economics/wp/index.htm*.

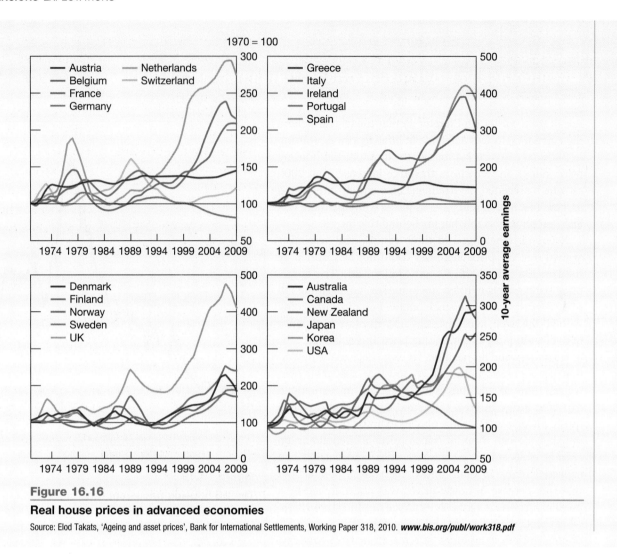

Figure 16.16

Real house prices in advanced economies

Source: Elod Takats, 'Ageing and asset prices', Bank for International Settlements, Working Paper 318, 2010. *www.bis.org/publ/work318.pdf*

SUMMARY

- Arbitrage between bonds of different maturities implies that the price of a bond is the present value of the payments on the bond, discounted using current and expected short-term interest rates over the life of the bond. Hence, higher current or expected short-term interest rates lead to lower bond prices.

- The yield to maturity on a bond is (approximately) equal to the average of current and expected short-term interest rates over the life of a bond.

- The slope of the yield curve – equivalently, the term structure – tells us what financial markets expect to happen to short-term interest rates in the future. A downward-sloping yield curve (when long-term interest rates are lower than short-term interest rates) implies that the market expects a decrease in short-term interest rates; an upward-sloping yield curve (when long-term interest rates are higher than short-term interest rates) implies that the market expects an increase in short-term rates.

- The fundamental value of a stock is the present value of expected future real dividends, discounted using current

and future expected one-year real interest rates. In the absence of bubbles or fads, the price of a stock is equal to its fundamental value.

- An increase in expected dividends leads to an increase in the fundamental value of stocks; an increase in current and expected one-year interest rates leads to a decrease in their fundamental value.

- Changes in output may or may not be associated with changes in stock prices in the same direction. Whether they are or not depends on (1) what the market expected in the first place, (2) the source of the shocks, and (3) how the market expects the central bank to react to the output change.

- Asset prices can be subject to bubbles and fads that cause the price to differ from its fundamental value. Bubbles are episodes in which financial investors buy an asset for a price higher than its fundamental value, anticipating to resell it at an even higher price. Fads are episodes in which, because of over-optimism, financial investors are willing to pay more for an asset than its fundamental value.

KEY TERMS

QUESTIONS AND PROBLEMS

QUICK CHECK

1. *Using the information in this chapter, label each of the following statements true, false or uncertain. Explain briefly.*

a. Junk bonds are bonds nobody wants to hold.

b. The price of a one-year bond decreases when the nominal one-year interest rate increases.

c. Given the Fisher hypothesis, an upward-sloping yield curve may indicate that financial markets are worried about inflation in the future.

d. Long-term interest rates typically move more than short-term interest rates.

e. An equal increase in expected inflation and nominal interest rates at all maturities should have no effect on the stock market.

f. A monetary expansion will lead to an upward-sloping yield curve.

g. A rational investor should never pay a positive price for a stock that will never pay dividends.

h. The value today of a nominal payment in the future cannot be greater than the nominal payment itself.

i. The real value today of a real payment in the future cannot be greater than the real payment itself.

2. *Determine the yield to maturity of each of the following bonds:*

a. A discount bond with a face value of €1,000, a maturity of three years, and a price of €800.

b. A discount bond with a face value of €1,000, a maturity of four years, and a price of €800.

c. A discount bond with a face value of €1,000, a maturity of four years, and a price of €850.

3. *Suppose that the annual interest rate this year is 5%, and financial market participants expect the annual interest rate to increase to 5.5% next year, to 6% two years from now and to 6.5% three years from now. Determine the yield to maturity on each of the following bonds.*

a. A one-year bond.

b. A two-year bond.

c. A three-year bond.

4. *Using the IS–LM model, determine the impact on stock prices of each of the policy changes described in (a) through (c). If the effect is ambiguous, explain what additional information would be needed to reach a conclusion.*

a. An unexpected expansionary monetary policy with no change in fiscal policy.

b. A fully expected expansionary monetary policy with no change in fiscal policy.

c. A fully expected expansionary monetary policy together with an unexpected expansionary fiscal policy.

5. *Choosing between different retirement plans*

You want to save €2,000 today for retirement in 40 years. You have to choose between two plans listed in (i) and (ii):

(i) *Pay no taxes today, put the money in an interest-yielding account and pay taxes equal to 25% of the total amount withdrawn at retirement.*

(ii) *Pay taxes equivalent to 20% of the investment amount today, put the remainder in an interest-yielding account and pay no taxes when you withdraw your funds at retirement.*

a. What is the expected present discounted value of each of these plans if the interest rate is 1%? 10%?

b. Which plan would you choose in each case?

6. Approximating the price of long-term bonds

The present value of an infinite stream of euro payments of €z (that starts next year) is €z/i when the nominal interest rate, i, is constant. This formula gives the price of a consol – a bond paying a fixed nominal payment each year, forever. It is also a good approximation for the present discounted value of a stream of constant payments over long but not infinite periods, as long as i is constant. Let's examine how close the approximation is.

a. Suppose that $i = 10\%$. Let $€z = 100$. What is the present value of the consol?

b. If $i = 10\%$, what is the expected present discounted value of a bond that pays €z over the next 10 years? 20 years? 30 years? 60 years? (*Hint:* use the formula from the chapter but remember to adjust for the first payment.)

c. Repeat the calculations in (a) and (b) for $i = 2\%$ and $i = 5\%$.

DIG DEEPER

7. Money growth and the yield curve

We have examined the effects of an increase in the growth rate of money on interest rates and inflation.

a. Draw the path of the nominal interest rate following an increase in the growth rate of money. Suppose that the lowest point in the path is reached after one year and that the long-run values are achieved after three years.

b. Show the yield curve just after the increase in the growth rate of money, one year later and three years later.

8. Interpreting the yield curve

a. What is the current price of the stock if the real interest rate is expected to remain constant at 5%? at 8%?

b. What does a steep yield curve imply about future inflation?

9. Stock prices and the risk premium

This problem is based on the appendix to this chapter.

Suppose a share is expected to pay a dividend of €1,000 next year, and the real value of dividend payments is expected to increase by 3% per year for ever after.

a. What is the current price of the stock if the real interest rate is expected to remain constant at 5%? at 8%?

Now suppose that people require a risk premium to hold stocks.

b. Redo the calculations in part (a) if the required risk premium is 8%.

c. Redo the calculations in part (a) if the required risk premium is 4%.

d. What do you expect would happen to stock prices if the risk premium decreased unexpectedly? Explain in words.

EXPLORE FURTHER

10. UK disinflation in the 1980s and the term structure

At the end of the 1970s, the UK inflation rate reached double digits. On 4 May 1979 Mrs Thatcher won the general election and was appointed Prime Minister. To reduce the inflation rate, the government instituted a Medium Term Financial Strategy (MTFS). In this problem, we will use yield curve data to judge whether the financial markets were indeed expecting the government to succeed in reducing the inflation rate.

Go to the data section of the website of the Bank of England (www.statistics.gov.uk/). Download the monthly data on the Consumer Price Index from 1970 to doday. Import it into your favourite spreadsheet program.

a. How can the government reduce inflation? How would this policy affect the nominal interest rate?

b. For each month, compute the annual rate of inflation as the percentage change in the Composite Price Index from last year to this year (i.e. over the preceding 12 months). In the same graph, plot the rate of inflation and the one-year interest rate from 1970 to today. When was the rate of inflation at its highest?

Now go to the website of the Bank of England (www.bankofengland.co.uk). Go to 'Statistics', then go to 'Interest rates and exchange rates', then to 'Yield curves' and finally to 'Government liabilities yield curve (monthly data)'. Download the Nominal 1970-latest data and open the spot curve spreadsheet (No. 4).

c. For each month, starting in 1970 and until the mid-1980s, draw the yield curve. To do this use the data in the Excel file which shows, for each month, the yield on government bonds with maturities ranging from 6 months, all the way to 20 years. (Doing this for each month is unnecessary and you would not see much with all those curves. Try drawing one yield curve per quarter.)

d. What does a declining yield curve imply about the expectations of financial market participants? As inflation was increasing in the late 1970s, what was happening to the yield curve? Were financial market participants expecting that trend to continue?

e. In 1979, the government announced that they would pursue a gradual reduction in the rate of growth of the money stock. Looking at the yield curves for 1979–1980, do you find any evidence of such an interpretation by financial market participants? Explain.

11. *Go to the Bank of England website cited in problem 10 and find the most recent observation on the term structure of interest rates ranging from three months to 30 years.*

Is the term structure upward sloping, downward sloping or flat? Why?

12. *Do a news search on the Internet about the most recent Governing Council of the ECB.*

a. What did the Governing Council decide about the interest rate?

b. What happened to stock prices on the day of the announcement?

c. To what degree do you think financial market participants were surprised by the Governing Council's announcement? Explain.

13. Inflation-indexed bonds

Some bonds issued by the British Treasury make payments indexed to inflation. These inflation-indexed bonds compensate investors for inflation. Therefore, the current interest rates on these bonds are real interest rates – interest rates in terms of goods. These interest rates can be used, together with nominal interest rates, to provide a measure of expected inflation. Let's see how.

*Go to the website of the Bank of England and get the most recent statistical release listing interest rates (**www.bankofengland.co.uk/publications/index.htm**). Find the current nominal interest rate on British Government Securities with a five-year maturity. Now find the current interest rate on 'inflation-indexed' securities with a five-year maturity. What do you think participants in financial markets think the average inflation rate will be over the next five years?*

---

*Log on to **MyEconLab** and complete the studyplan exercises for this chapter to see how much you have learnt, and where you need to revise most.*

MyEconLab

FURTHER READING

- There are many bad books written about the stock market. A good one, and one which is fun to read, is Burton Malkiel, *A Random Walk Down Wall Street*, 10th edn (New York: Norton, 2011).

- An account of some historical bubbles is given by Peter Garber in 'Famous first bubbles', *Journal of Economic Perspectives*, 1990, 4(2), 35–54.

Chapter 17

EXPECTATIONS, CONSUMPTION AND INVESTMENT

Having looked at the role of expectations in financial markets, we now turn to the role expectations play in determining the two main components of spending – consumption and investment. This description of consumption and investment will be the main building block of the expanded *IS–LM* model we shall develop later (in Chapter 18).

- Sections 17.1 and 17.2 look at consumption and show how consumption decisions depend not only on a person's current income but also on her expected future income and on financial wealth.

- Section 17.3 turns to investment and shows how investment decisions depend on current and expected profits, and on current and expected real interest rates.

- Section 17.4 looks at the movements in consumption and investment over time and shows how to interpret those movements in light of what you learned in this chapter.

17.1 CONSUMPTION THEORY AND THE ROLE OF EXPECTATIONS

How do people decide how much to consume and how much to save? Earlier (in Chapter 3), we assumed that consumption depended only on current income. But, even then, it was clear that consumption depended on much more, particularly on expectations about the future. We now explore how those expectations affect the consumption decision.

The modern theory of consumption, on which this section is based, was developed independently in the 1950s by Milton Friedman of the University of Chicago, who called it the **permanent income theory of consumption**, and by Franco Modigliani of MIT, who called it the **life cycle theory of consumption**. Each chose his label carefully. Friedman's 'permanent income' emphasised that consumers look beyond current income. Modigliani's 'life cycle' emphasised that consumers' natural planning horizon is their entire lifetime.

> ◀ Friedman received the Nobel Prize in economics in 1976; Modigliani received the Nobel Prize in economics in 1985.

The behaviour of aggregate consumption has remained a hot area of research ever since, for two reasons: one is simply the sheer size of consumption as a component of GDP and, therefore, the need to understand movements in consumption. The other is the increasing availability of large surveys of individual consumers, such as the British Household Panel Survey in the UK, the Survey of Household Income and Wealth SHIW in Italy, the German Socio Economic Panel Study, and the 'Enquête Budget de Famille' in France. These surveys, which were not available when Friedman and Modigliani developed their theories, have allowed economists to steadily improve their understanding of how consumers actually behave. This section summarises what we know today.

> ◀ Consumption spending accounts for 57% of total spending in the EU, 56% in the euro area, 64% in the UK, 49% in Denmark, 47% in Sweden and 46% in Ireland (from Chapter 3).

The very foresighted consumer

Let's start with an assumption that will surely – and rightly – strike you as extreme, but will serve as a convenient benchmark. We'll call it the theory of the very foresighted consumer. How would a very foresighted consumer decide how much to consume? He would proceed in two steps.

1. First, he would add up the value of the stocks and bonds he owns, the value of his current and savings accounts, the value of the house he owns minus the mortgage still due, and so on. This would give him an idea of his **financial wealth** and his **housing wealth**. He would also estimate what his after-tax labour income was likely to be over his working life, and compute the present value of expected after-tax labour income. This would give him an estimate of what economists call his **human wealth** to contrast it with his **non-human wealth**, defined as the sum of financial wealth and housing wealth.

> ◀ With a slight abuse of language, we shall use 'housing wealth' to refer not only to housing, but also to the other goods that the consumer may own, from cars to paintings and so on.

2. Adding his human wealth and non-human wealth, he would have an estimate of his **total wealth**. He would then decide how much to spend out of this total wealth. A reasonable assumption is that he would decide to spend a proportion of his total wealth such as to maintain roughly the same level of consumption each year throughout his life. If that level of consumption were higher than his current income, he would then borrow the difference. If it were lower than his current income, he would instead save the difference.

> ◀ Human wealth + non-human wealth = total wealth.

Let's write this formally. What we have described is a consumption decision of the form

$$C_t = C \text{ (total wealth}_t) \tag{17.1}$$

where C_t is consumption at time t, and (total wealth$_t$) is the sum of non-human wealth (financial plus housing wealth) and human wealth at time t (the expected present value, as of time t, of current and future after-tax labour income).

This description contains much truth: like the foresighted consumer, we surely do think about our wealth and our expected future labour income in deciding how much to consume today. But one cannot help thinking that it assumes too much computation and foresight on the part of the typical consumer.

To get a better sense of what that description implies and what is wrong with it, let's apply this decision process to the problem facing a typical student today.

An example

Let's assume you are 19 years old, with three more years of college before you start your first job. You may be in debt today, having taken out a loan to go to college. You may own a car and a few other worldly possessions. For simplicity, let's assume your debt and your possessions roughly offset each other, so that your non-human wealth is equal to zero. Your only wealth therefore is your human wealth, the present value of your expected after-tax labour income.

You expect your starting annual salary in three years to be around €40,000 (in 2011 euros) and to increase by an average of 3% per year in real terms, until your retirement at age 60. About 25% of your income will go to taxes.

> You are welcome to use your own numbers and see where the computation takes you.

Building on what you saw earlier (in Chapter 16), let's compute the present value of your labour income as the value of real expected after-tax labour income, discounted using real interest rates. Let Y_{Lt} denote real labour income in year t. Let T_t denote real taxes in year t. Let $V(Y_{Lt}^e - T_t^e)$ denote your human wealth – that is, the expected present value of your after-tax labour income – expected as of year t.

To make the computation simple, assume the real interest rate equals zero – so the expected present value is simply the sum of expected labour income over your working life and is therefore given by

$$V(Y_{Lt}^e - T_t^e) = (€40,000)(0.75)[1 + (1.03) + (1.03)^2 + \cdots + (1.03)^{38}]$$

The first term (€40,000) is your initial level of labour income, in year 2000 euros.

The second term (0.75) comes from the fact that, because of taxes, you keep only 75% of what you earn.

The third term $[1 + (1.03) + (1.03)^2 + \cdots + (1.03)^{38}]$ reflects the fact that you expect your real income to increase by 3% a year for 39 years (you will start earning income at age 22, and work until age 60).

Using the properties of geometric series to solve for the sum in brackets gives

$$V(Y_{Lt}^e - T_t^e) = (€40,000)(0.75)(72.2) = €2,166,000$$

Your wealth today, the expected value of your lifetime after-tax labour income, is around €2 million.

> The computation of the consumption level you can sustain is made easier by our assumption that the real interest rate equals zero. In this case, if you consume one less good today, you can consume exactly one more good next year, and the condition you must satisfy is simply that the sum of consumption over your lifetime is equal to your wealth. So, if you want to consume a constant amount each year, you just need to divide your wealth by the remaining number of years you expect to live.

How much should you consume? You can expect to live about 16 years after you retire, so that your expected remaining life today is 58 years. If you want to consume the same amount every year, the constant level of consumption that you can afford equals your total wealth divided by your expected remaining life, or €2,166,000/58 = €37,344 a year. Given that your income until you get your first job is equal to zero, this implies you will have to borrow €37,344 a year for the next three years, and begin to save when you get your first job.

The intertemporal budget constraint

By now you can see that an intertemporal perspective is crucial to understanding consumption decisions. To better understand the intertemporal choices of a consumer – i.e. what is 'behind' equation [17.1] – let us start from what you have probably already learned about consumer choices in your microeconomics course.

Let us assume for simplicity that all individuals are identical, namely that in our hypothetical world there is only one individual: the **representative consumer**. Assume that there are only two goods, 1 and 2, and denote by c_1 and c_2, y_1 and y_2, p_1 and p_2, respectively, the quantities of good 1 and good 2 consumed, the amounts of goods 1 and 2 owned by the consumer, called **endowments**, and the prices of goods 1 and 2. The consumer's budget constraint tells us that no one can spend more than he or she has. The value of consumption must be equal to the value of resources:

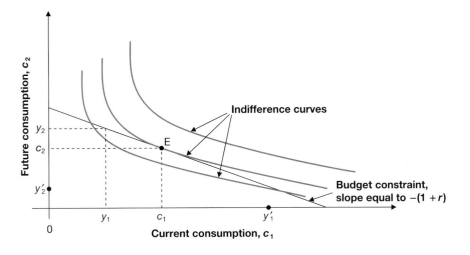

Figure 17.1

The intertemporal budget constraint

$$p_1c_1 + p_2c_2 = p_1y_1 + p_2y_2$$

or, if we express all in terms of good 1:

$$c_1 + \frac{p_2}{p_1}c_2 = y_1 + \frac{p_2}{p_1}y_2$$

Quantities c_1 and c_2 represent, respectively, consumption at time 1 – today – and at time 2 – tomorrow. The relative price p_1/p_2 is the price of current consumption in terms of future consumption: it corresponds to the real interest rate, r, which measures by how much future consumption can increase by lending one more unit of good today:

◀ Warning: the material in this section and in the next is a bit harder. However, persevere and you will find it useful.

$$1 + r = \frac{p_1}{p_2}$$

The budget constraint can therefore be rewritten as follows:

$$c_1 + \frac{1}{1+r}c_2 = y_1 + \frac{1}{1+r}y_2^e = V(y_t^e) \qquad t = 1, 2 \qquad [17.2]$$

where y_t^e is the expected endowment for tomorrow.

The interpretation is straightforward: the present discounted value of each individuals consumption – the sum of present and future consumption measured in terms of goods today – must be equal to the discounted present value of his or her endowments.

We can think of the endowment at time 1 as the sum of financial wealth and housing wealth with which the individual 'comes to the world', plus the net labour income. The expected endowment at time 2 can be thought of as the future labour income net of taxes. The present value of endowments is the total wealth of our consumer, which in turn is the sum of human wealth – the present discounted value of net labour income – plus the non-human wealth – his or her stock of financial wealth and housing wealth at a given time. However, until we consider endowments as exogenous, it is not necessary to distinguish the two components of wealth; let us then assume that y_1 is also labour income.

Let us go back to the budget constraint. It allows us to analyse consumption choices across two subsequent periods: for this reason we call it the **intertemporal budget constraint**. The intertemporal budget constraint is drawn in Figure 17.1. It represents all the combinations of current and future consumption (c_1, c_2) that the consumer can choose, given the present value of his or her endowments. Note that endowments (y_1, y_t^e) always satisfy the budget constraint: an individual can always choose to consume $c_1 = y_1$ and $c_2 = y_t^e$.

Intertemporal consumption decisions

Which of the possible intertemporal consumption paths is actually selected? Remember from your microeconomics course that consumer preferences may be represented by a utility function, which associates each basket (c_1, c_2) with a single value $U(c_1, c_2)$. Our representative consumer chooses the basket that maximises his or her utility, provided that it can be bought – that it does not violate the budget constraint.

In Figure 17.1, preferences are represented by a map of indifference curves. Each curve represents the combinations of current and future consumption that provide the same utility level – all the baskets among which the consumer is indifferent. The fact that each indifference curve is negatively-sloped and convex means that, compared to two 'unbalanced' consumption paths (i.e. one with high current consumption and low future consumption, another with low current consumption and high future consumption), the consumer prefers a more balanced path. The preference for a balanced consumption path over time is called **consumption smoothing**.

Graphically, the optimal choice is shown in Figure 17.1. The optimal combination of current and future consumption is the point along the budget constraint that lies on the outermost indifference curve. Except in the case of corner solutions, this corresponds to the point where the budget constraint is tangential to the higher indifference curve. The optimal choice is at point E. In the case represented in Figure 17.1, with endowments (y_1, y_2^e), the consumer borrows $c_1 - y_1$ in the current period and pays $y_2 - c_2$ in the future. Notice that the level of consumption E is also reachable by a consumer with endowments $(y_1', y_2^e)'$: he or she would save in the current period and borrow in the coming years.

To keep things quite simple, let us assume that the intertemporal utility function $U(c_1, c_2)$ is additive with respect to current and future consumption:

$$U(c_1, c_2) = u(c_1) + \frac{1}{1+\rho}u(c_2)$$

The function u is sometimes called instantaneous utility function, and can be interpreted as the flow of utility provided by consumption at a certain time, regardless of when the goods are consumed. Let us now assume that utility increases with the level of consumption, but increases in utility get smaller and smaller as consumption increases.

The parameter $\rho \geq 0$ is the **discount rate**. It measures the weight the consumer attaches to the future compared to the present:

- Case $\rho = 0$: the consumer attaches the same importance to increases in consumption, irrespective of the time in which they occur. In this case, starting from a perfectly balanced consumption path over time, $c_1 = c_2$, equal increases in c_1 and c_2 have the same impact on total utility.
- Case $\rho > 0$: the factor $1/(1 + \rho)$ is less than 1 – an increase of consumption increases total utility to a greater extent if it occurs in the current period rather than in the future. In other words, starting from a balanced consumption path, to maintain the same level of total utility, the consumer requires an increase of $1 + \rho$ units of c_2 to compensate for a reduction in consumption of one unit.

Note that $\rho > 0$ means that individuals are impatient: they prefer to consume today rather than tomorrow. At the point that identifies the optimal combination of present and future consumption, the slope of the indifference curve – the marginal substitution rate (MSR) between the two goods – is equal to slope of the budget constraint $1 + r$. If the utility function is additive, the optimal condition can be written as

$$\text{MRS} = \frac{\partial U(c_1, c_2)/\partial c_1}{\partial U(c_1, c_2)} = \frac{\partial u/\partial c_1}{\frac{1}{1+\rho}\partial u/\partial c_2} = 1 + r$$

and therefore:

$$\frac{\partial U/\partial c_1}{\partial U/\partial c_2} = \frac{1+r}{1+\rho} \qquad [17.3]$$

This condition tells us that if $r = \rho$ then, along the optimal consumption path, $c_1 = c_2$, the consumer chooses the same level of consumption in both periods because his or her impatience is exactly offset by the interest rate on his or her savings, r. When we explained the problem for a student, we said that probably he or she will choose a constant consumption path during his life. In that example, however, we described the student's preferences in words, without introducing a utility function. In the light of what we have just done – which, as we shall see, could easily be extended to two more periods – and if the preferences of our student is 'regular', then he will choose constant consumption over time only if $\rho = r$.

If instead $r > \rho$, the consumer will choose $c_1 < c_2$ (remember that we have assumed that marginal utility is decreasing). This result is quite intuitive: if the return on savings is sufficiently high, in particular higher than the discount rate, the consumer will find it more convenient to wait and postpone consumption in order to increase future consumption enough to compensate for his impatience. For example, if borrowing €23,340 in each of the three years of study before starting to work entailed paying very high interest, he would probably not borrow, and postpone higher levels of consumption to the future.

For the same reason, if $r < \rho$, the consumer will choose a decreasing consumption path, and hence $c_1 > c_2$. These conditions are very important because they allow us to answer the question: how do consumers behave, faced with a change in interest rates? The above optimal condition (equation (17.3)), together with the budget constraint (equation (17.2)), gives us a system of two equations in two unknowns, c_1 and c_2. This system can be solved to obtain the optimal values of c_1 and c_2 as functions of exogenous variables – the real interest rate and endowments.

In this section, expectations have not appeared explicitly in our equations. Note, however, that when our consumer, at time 1, chooses the level of his or her current and future consumption under the budget constraint, he or she must have a clue about his or her future labour income, y_2, and that is an expectation. The optimal consumption choices for the present and the future are thus functions of $V(y_t^e)$: that is, the present value of net current and expected future incomes, which we indicate with y_t^e.

17.2 TOWARD A MORE REALISTIC DESCRIPTION

In this section we give a more realistic description of consumption decisions by answering the question: if it is true that consumption decisions are made on a lifetime horizon, why is it that consumption reacts so much to changes in current income?

Why does consumption react so much to current income?

Let us go back to the computation made in the example in section 17.1. Your first reaction might be that it is a stark and slightly sinister way of summarising your life prospects. Your second reaction may be that while you agree with most of the elements that went into the computation, you surely do not intend to borrow €23,340 × 3 = €70,020 over the next three years. For example:

- You might not want to plan for constant consumption over your lifetime. Instead you may be quite happy to defer higher consumption until later. Student life usually does not leave much time for expensive activities. You may want to defer trips to the Galapagos Islands to later in life. You also have to think about the additional expenses that will come with having children, sending them to school and college, summer holidays and so on.
- You might find that the amount of maths and foresight involved in the computation we just went through far exceeds the amount you use in your own decisions. You may never have thought until now about exactly how much income you are going to make and for how many years. You might feel that most consumption decisions are made in a simpler, less forward-looking fashion.

- The computation of total wealth is based on forecasts of what is expected to happen. But things can turn out better or worse. What happens if you become unemployed or sick? How will you pay back what you borrowed? You might want to be prudent, making sure that you can adequately survive even the worst outcomes, and thus decide to borrow much less than €70,020.

- Even if you decide to borrow €70,020, you might have a hard time finding a bank willing to lend it to you. Why? The bank may worry that you are taking on a commitment you will not be able to afford if times turn bad and that you may not be able or willing to repay the loan.

These reasons, all good ones, suggest that to characterise consumers' actual behaviour, we must modify the description we gave earlier. The last three reasons in particular suggest that consumption depends not only on total wealth but also on current income.

Take the second reason: you may, because it is a simple rule, decide to let your consumption follow your income and not think about what your wealth might be. In that case, your consumption will depend on your current income, not on your wealth.

Now take the third reason: it implies that a safe rule may be to consume no more than your current income. This way, you do not run the risk of accumulating debt that you cannot repay if times turn bad.

Or take the fourth reason: it implies that you may have little choice anyway. Even if you wanted to consume more than your current income, you might be unable to do so because no bank will give you a loan.

If we want to allow for a direct effect of current income on consumption, what measure of current income should we use? A convenient measure is after-tax labour income, which we introduced when we defined human wealth. This leads to a consumption function of the form

$$C_t = C(\text{total wealth}_t, Y_{Lt} - T_t) \qquad [17.4]$$
$$(\quad + \quad , \quad + \quad)$$

where

$$W_t = W_t^F + W_t H + \sum_{i=0}^{T} \frac{Y_{t+i}^e - T_{t+i}^e}{(1+r)^i}$$

with the last element in the sum being the expected present discounted value of net income, EPDV$(Y - T)$, and where W is wealth.

In words: consumption is an increasing function of total wealth and of current after-tax labour income. Total wealth is the sum of non-human wealth (financial wealth plus housing wealth) and human wealth (the present value of expected after-tax labour income).

How much does consumption depend on total wealth (and therefore on expectations of future income), and how much does it depend on current income? The evidence is that most consumers look forward, in the spirit of the theory developed by Modigliani and Friedman. (See the Focus box 'Do people save enough for retirement?') But it is also true that we do observe that consumption reacts a lot to changes in current income. How can we explain this?

One possible explanation: liquidity constraints

Economic theory has given different explanations to justify the fact that consumption is very sensitive, or at least more sensitive than could be expected from the theory of consumptions based on expectations, to temporary changes in current income. As we said in the previous section, one possible explanation is that consumers cannot obtain credit as easily as the theory assumes. This means that consumers may be subject to liquidity constraints. To keep things simple, think of an extreme form of quantitative rationing, such that consumers have no means of getting credit – especially in period 1, when they are young and their

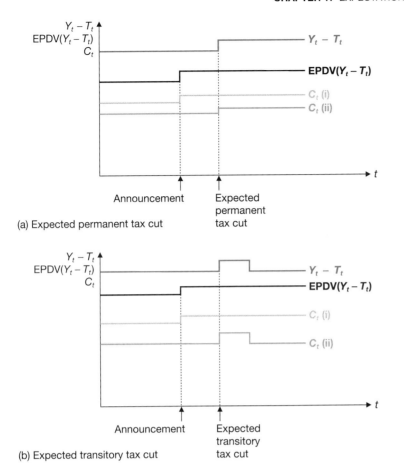

(a) Expected permanent tax cut

(b) Expected transitory tax cut

Figure 17.2

Two types of consumers (a, b)

(i) Consumers with no liquidity constraints can change consumption in line with changes in their EPDV($Y - T$).
(ii) Consumers with liquidity constraints can only consume out of their current disposable income.

endowments are likely to be low. In this case, current consumption cannot be greater than current income. Formally, this implies the presence, in addition to the inter-temporal budget constraint, of an additional constraint

$$c_1 \leq y_1$$

which allows us to better clarify the two results we have obtained in the previous section.

It may not be true that all consumers look forward when taking their consumption decisions. There are indeed two types of consumers. As Figure 17.2 shows, consumers who face no liquidity constraints because they are rich and have easy access to credit are more likely to give more weight to the expected future and to try to maintain roughly constant consumption over time. For example, prior to an announced tax cut in the near future, they can anticipate a future increase in their disposable income and increase the level of consumption accordingly. But some consumers, especially those who have temporarily low income and poor access to credit, are likely to consume their current income, regardless of what they expect will happen to them in the future. This is shown in Figure 17.2. A worker who becomes unemployed and has no financial wealth may have a hard time borrowing to maintain her level of consumption, even if she is fairly confident that she will soon find another job.

Putting things together: current income, expectations and consumption

Let's go back to what motivates this chapter – the importance of expectations in the determination of spending. Note first that, with consumption behaviour described by equation (17.4), expectations affect consumption in two ways:

How expectations of higher output in the future affect consumption today:

Expected future output increases
⇒ Expected future labour income increases
⇒ Human wealth increases
⇒ Consumption increases.

Expected future output increases
⇒ Expected future dividends increase
⇒ Stock prices increase
⇒ Non-human wealth increases
⇒ Consumption increases.

- Expectations affect consumption directly through human wealth: to compute their human wealth, consumers have to form their own expectations about future labour income, real interest rates and taxes.
- Expectations affect consumption indirectly, through non-human wealth – stocks, bonds and housing. Consumers do not need to do any computation here and can just take the value of these assets as given. As you saw in section 17.1, the computation is, in effect, done for them by participants in financial markets: the price of their stocks, for example, itself depends on expectations of future dividends and interest rates.

This dependence of consumption on expectations has, in turn, two main implications for the relation between consumption and income:

- Consumption is likely to respond less than one-for-one to fluctuations in current income. When deciding how much to consume, a consumer looks at more than his current income. If he concludes that the decrease in his income is permanent, he is likely to decrease consumption one-for-one with the decrease in income. But if he concludes that the decrease in his current income is transitory, he will adjust his consumption by less. In a recession, consumption adjusts less than one-for-one to decreases in income. This is because consumers know that recessions typically do not last for more than a few quarters and that the economy will eventually return to the natural level of output. The same is true in expansions: faced with an unusually rapid increase in income, consumers are unlikely to increase consumption by as much as income. They are likely to assume that the boom is transitory and that things will return to normal.
- Consumption may move even if current income does not change. The election of a charismatic president or prime minister who articulates the vision of an exciting future might

> Go back to the two consumption functions we used in the coresection.
>
> Looking at the short run (Chapter 3), we assumed $C = c_0 + c_1 Y$ (ignoring taxes here). This implied that, when income increased, consumption increased less than proportionately with income ($C_1 Y$ went down). This was appropriate because our focus was on fluctuations, on transitory movements in income.
>
> Looking at the long run (Chapter 14), we assumed that $S = sY$ or, equivalently, $C = (1 - s)Y$. This implied that when income increased, consumption increased proportionately with income ($C_1 Y$ remained the same).
>
> This was appropriate because our focus was on permanent – long-run – movements in income.

FOCUS
Do people save enough for retirement?

How carefully do people look forward when making consumption and saving decisions? One way to answer this question is to look at how much people save for retirement.

Table 17.1, taken from a study by Steven Venti, from Dartmouth, and David Wise, from Harvard, based on a **panel data set** called the Survey of Income and Program Participation gives the basic numbers. The table shows the mean level and the composition of (total) wealth for people between 65 and 69 years in 1991 – so, most of them are retired.

The first three components of wealth capture the various sources of retirement income. The first is the present value of social security benefits. The second is the value of the retirement plans provided by employers. And the third is the value of personal retirement plans. The last three components include the other assets held by consumers, such as bonds and stocks, and housing.

A mean wealth of $314,000 is substantial (for comparison, US per person personal consumption at the time of the study (1991) was $16,000). It gives an image

of forward-looking individuals making careful saving decisions and retiring with enough wealth to enjoy a comfortable retirement.

We must be careful, however: the high average may hide important differences across individuals. Some individuals may save a lot, others little. Another study, by Scholz, Seshadri and Khitatrakun, from the University

Table 17.1 Mean wealth of people, age 65–69, in 1991 (in thousands of 1991 dollars)

Social security pension	$100
Employer-provided pension	62
Personal retirement assets	11
Other financial assets	42
Home equity	65
Other equity	34
Total	$314

Source: From 'Choice, chance and wealth dispersion at retirement' in Ogura, S., Tachibanaki, T. and Wise, D. A. (eds) Aging Issues in United States and Japan, University of Chicago Press (Venti, S. and Wise, D. 2001) Table A.1 (c) 2001 by The National Bureau of Economic Research. All rights reserved.

lead people to become more optimistic about the future in general and about their own future income in particular, leading them to increase consumption even if their current income does not change.

One of the main worries macroeconomists had during the financial crisis of 2007 was that consumers would become pessimistic and consumption would drop, leading to a deeper recession. Unfortunately, this was in fact the case. Consumer confidence fell during 2008, and the financial crisis led to a fully fledged economic crisis.

17.3 INVESTMENT

How do firms make investment decisions? In our first pass at the answer earlier (see Chapter 5), we took investment to depend on the current interest rate and the current level of sales. We refined that answer earlier (in Chapter 16) by pointing out that what mattered was the real interest rate, not the nominal interest rate. It should now be clear that investment decisions, just as consumption decisions, depend on more than current sales and the current real interest rate. They also depend very much on expectations of the future. We now explore how those expectations affect investment decisions.

Just like the basic theory of consumption, the basic theory of investment is straightforward. A firm deciding whether to invest – say, whether to buy a new machine – must make a simple comparison. The firm must first compute the present value of profits it can expect from having this additional machine. It must then compare the present value of profits to the cost of buying the machine. If the present value exceeds the cost, the firm should buy the machine – invest; if the present value is less than the cost, then the firm should not buy the machine – not invest. This, in a nutshell, is the theory of investment. Let's look at it in more detail.

of Wisconsin, sheds light on this aspect. The study is based on another panel data set, called the Health and Retirement Study. The panel consists of 7,000 households whose heads of household were between 51 and 61 years at the time of the first interview in 1992, and which have been interviewed every two years since. The panel contains information about the level and the composition of wealth for each household, as well as on its labour income (if the individuals in the household have not yet retired). Based on this information, the authors construct a target level of wealth for each household, i.e. the wealth level that each household should have if it wants to maintain a roughly constant level of consumption after retirement. The authors then compare the actual wealth level to the target level for each household.

The first conclusion of their study is similar to the conclusion reached by Venti and Wise: on average, people save enough for retirement. More specifically, the authors find that more than 80% of households have wealth above the target level. Put the other way around, only 20% of households have wealth below the target. But these numbers hide important differences across income levels.

Among those in the top half of the income distribution, more than 90% have wealth that exceeds the target, often by a large amount. This suggests that these households plan to leave bequests, and so save more than what is needed for retirement.

Among those in the bottom 20% of the income distribution, however, fewer than 70% have wealth above the target. For the 30% of households below the target, the difference between actual and target wealth is typically small. But the relatively large proportion of individuals with wealth below the target suggests that there are a number of individuals who, through bad planning or bad luck, do not save enough for retirement. For most of these individuals, nearly all their wealth comes from the present value of social security benefits (the first component of wealth in Table 17.1), and it is reasonable to think that the proportion of people with wealth below target would be even larger if social security did not exist. This is indeed what the social security system was designed to do: to make sure that people have enough to live on when they retire. In that regard, it appears to be a success.

Sources: Steven Venti and David Wise, 'The wealth of cohorts: retirement and saving and the changing assets of older Americans', in Sylvester Schieber and John B. Shoven (eds) *Public Policy Toward Pensions*. MIT Press, 1997.
John Scholz, Ananth Seshadri and Surachai Khitatrakun, 'Are Americans saving "optimally" for retirement?', *Journal of Political Economy*, 2006, **114**(4), 607–643.

Investment and expected profit

Let's go through the steps a firm must take to determine whether to buy a new machine. (Although we refer to a machine, the same reasoning applies to the other components of investment – the building of a new factory, the renovation of an office complex, and so on.)

Depreciation

Look at cars in Cuba! ➤

To compute the present value of expected profits, the firm must first estimate how long the machine will last. Most machines are like cars. They can last nearly forever; but as time passes they become more and more expensive to maintain, and less and less reliable.

If the firm has a large number of machines, we can think of δ as the proportion of machines that die every year (Think of light bulbs – which work perfectly until they die). If the firm starts the year with K working machines and does not buy new ones, it will have only $K(1 - \delta)$ machines left one year later, and so on. ➤

Assume a machine loses its usefulness at rate δ (the Greek lowercase letter delta) per year. A machine that is new this year is worth only $(1 - \delta)$ machines next year, $(1 - \delta)^2$ machines in two years, and so on. The depreciation rate, δ, measures how much usefulness the machine loses from one year to the next. What are reasonable values for δ? This is a question that the statisticians in charge of computing how the US capital stock changes over time have had to answer. Based on their studies of depreciation of specific machines and buildings, they use numbers between 4% and 15% for machines, and between 2% and 4% for buildings and factories.

The present value of expected profits

The firm must then compute the present value of expected profits.

To capture the fact that it takes some time to put machines in place (and even more time to build a factory or an office building), let's assume that a machine bought in year t becomes operational – and starts depreciating – only one year later, in year $t + 1$. Denote profit per machine in real terms by Π.

This is an upper-case Greek pi as opposed to the lowercase Greek pi, which we use to denote inflation. ➤

If the firm buys a machine in year t, the machine will generate its first profit in year $t + 1$; denote this expected profit by $t + 1$. The present value, Π^e in year t, of this expected profit in year $t + 1$, is given by

$$\frac{1}{1 + r_t} \Pi^e_{t+1}$$

This term is represented by the arrow pointing left in the upper line of Figure 17.3. Because we are measuring profit in real terms, we are using real interest rates to discount future profits. This is one of the lessons we learned earlier (in Chapter 15).

Denote expected profit per machine in year $t + 2$ by Π^e_{t+2}. Because of depreciation, only $(1 - \delta)$ of the machine is left in year $t + 2$, so the expected profit from the machine is equal to $(1 - \delta)\Pi^e_{t+2}$. The present value of this expected profit as of year t is equal to

$$\frac{1}{(1 + r_t)(1 + r^e_{t+1})}(1 - \delta)\Pi^e_{t+2}$$

This computation is represented by the arrow pointing left in the lower line of Figure 17.3.

The same reasoning applies to expected profits in the following years. Putting the pieces together gives us the present value of expected profits from buying the machine in year t, which we shall call $V(\Pi^e_t)$:

$$V(\Pi^e_t) = \frac{1}{1 + r_t} \Pi^e_{t+1} + \frac{1}{(1 + r_t)(1 + r^e_{t+1})}(1 - \delta)\Pi^e_{t+2} + \cdots \qquad [17.5]$$

Figure 17.3

Computing the present value of expected profits

The expected present value is equal to the discounted value of expected profit next year, plus the discounted value of expected profit two years from now (taking into account the depreciation of the machine), and so on.

The investment decision

The firm must then decide whether or not to buy the machine. This decision depends on the relation between the present value of expected profits and the price of the machine. To simplify notation, let's assume the real price of a machine – that is, the machine's price in terms of the basket of goods produced in the economy – equals 1. What the firm must then do is to compare the present value of profits to 1.

If the present value is less than 1, the firm should not buy the machine: if it did, it would be paying more for the machine than it expects to get back in profits later. If the present value exceeds 1, the firm has an incentive to buy the new machine.

Let's now go from this one-firm one-machine example to investment in the economy as a whole.

Let I_t denote aggregate investment. Denote profit per machine, or more generally profit per unit of capital (where capital includes machines, factories, office buildings, and so on) for the economy as a whole by Π_t.

Denote the expected present value of profit per unit of capital by $V(\Pi_t^e)$, as defined in equation (17.3).

Our discussion suggests an investment function of the form

$$I_t = I[V(\Pi_t^e)] \qquad [17.6]$$
$$(+)$$

In words: investment depends positively on the expected present value of future profits (per unit of capital). The higher current or expected future profits, the higher the expected present value, and the higher the level of investment. The higher current or expected future real interest rates, the lower the expected present value, and thus the lower the level of investment.

If the present value computation the firm has to make strikes you as quite similar to the present value computation we saw earlier (in Chapter 16) for the fundamental value of a stock, you are right. This relation was first explored by James Tobin, from Yale University, who argued that, for this reason, there should indeed be a tight relation between investment and the value of the stock market. His argument and the evidence are presented in the Focus box 'Investment and the stock market'.

◄ Tobin received the Nobel Prize in economics in 1981.

A convenient special case

Before exploring further implications and extensions of equation (17.6), we will go through a special case where the relation between investment, profit and interest rates becomes very simple.

Suppose firms expect both future profits (per unit of capital) and future interest rates to remain at the same level as today, so that

$$\Pi_{t+1}^e = \Pi_{t+2}^e = \cdots = \Pi_t$$

and

$$r_{t+1}^e = r_{t+2}^e = \cdots = r_t$$

Economists call such expectations – expectations that the future will be like the present – **static expectations**. Under these two assumptions, equation (17.5) becomes

$$V(\Pi_t^e) = \frac{\Pi_t}{r_t + \delta} \qquad [17.7]$$

FOCUS
Investment and the stock market

Suppose a firm has 100 machines and 100 shares outstanding – one share per machine. Suppose the price per share is €2, and the purchase price of a machine is only €1. Obviously the firm should invest – buy a new machine – and finance it by issuing a share: each machine costs the firm €1 to purchase, but stock market participants are willing to pay €2 for a share corresponding to this machine when it is installed in the firm.

This is an example of a more general argument made by Tobin that there should be a tight relation between the stock market and investment. When deciding whether or not to invest, he argued, firms might not need to go through the type of complicated computation you saw in the text. In effect, the stock price tells firms how much the stock market values each unit of capital already in place. The firm then has a simple problem: compare the purchase price of an additional unit of capital to the price the stock market is willing to pay for it. If the stock market value exceeds the purchase price, the firm should buy the machine; otherwise, it should not.

Tobin then constructed a variable corresponding to the value of a unit of capital in place relative to its purchase price, and looked at how closely it moved with investment. He used the symbol q to denote the variable, and the variable has become known as **Tobin's q**. Its construction is as follows:

1. Take the total value of US corporations, as assessed by financial markets. That is, compute the sum of their stock market value (the price of a share times the number of shares). Compute also the total value of their bonds outstanding (firms finance themselves not only through stocks but also through bonds). Add together the value of stocks and bonds.
2. Divide this total value by the value of the capital stock of US corporations at replacement cost (the price firms would have to pay to replace their machines, their plants and so on).

The ratio gives us in effect the value of a unit of capital in place relative to its current purchase price. This ratio is Tobin's q. Intuitively, the higher the q, the higher the value of capital relative to its current purchase price, and the higher investment should be. (In the example at the start of the box, Tobin's q is equal to 2, so the firm should definitely invest.)

How tight is the relation between Tobin's q and investment? The answer is given in Figure 17.4, which plots two variables for each year from 1960 to 1999 for the USA.

Measured on the left vertical axis is the change in the ratio of investment to capital.

Measured on the right vertical axis is the change of Tobin's q. This variable has been lagged once. For 1987, for example, the figure shows the change in the ratio of investment to capital for 1987, and the change in Tobin's q for 1986 – that is, a year earlier. The reason for presenting the two variables this way is that the strongest relation in the data appears to be between investment this year

The present value of expected profits is simply the ratio of the profit rate – that is, profit per unit of capital – to the sum of the real interest rate and the depreciation rate. (The derivation is given in the appendix to this chapter.)

Replacing (17.7) in equation (17.6), investment is

$$I_t = I\left(\frac{\Pi_t}{r_t + \delta}\right) \qquad [17.8]$$

Investment is a function of the ratio of the profit rate to the sum of the interest rate and the depreciation rate.

The sum of the real interest rate and the depreciation rate is called the **user cost** or the **rental cost of capital**. To see why, suppose the firm, instead of buying the machine, rented it from a rental agency. How much would the rental agency have to charge per year? Even if the machine did not depreciate, the agency would have to ask for an interest charge equal to r_t times the price of the machine (we have assumed the price of a machine to be 1 in real terms, so r_t times 1 is just r_t): the agency has to get at least as much from buying and then renting the machine out as it would from, say, buying bonds. In addition, the rental agency would have to charge for depreciation, δ times the price of the machine, 1. Therefore:

> Such arrangements exist. For example, many firms lease cars and trucks from leasing companies.

Figure 17.4

Tobin's _q_ versus the ratio of investment to capital: annual rates of change, 1960–1999

and Tobin's _q_ last year. Put another way, movements in investment this year are more closely associated with movements in the stock market last year rather than with movements in the stock market this year; a plausible explanation is that it takes time for firms to make investment decisions, build new factories and so on.

The figure shows that there is a clear relation between Tobin's _q_ and investment. This is not because firms blindly follow the signals from the stock market, but because investment decisions and stock market prices depend very much on the same factors – expected future profits and expected future interest rates.

$$\text{rental cost} = (r_t + \delta)$$

Even though firms typically do not rent the machines they use, $(T_t + \delta)$ still captures the implicit cost – sometimes called the shadow cost – to the firm for using the machine for one year.

The investment function given by equation (17.8) then has a simple interpretation: investment depends on the ratio of profit to the user cost. The higher the profit, the higher is the level of investment. The higher the user cost, the lower is the level of investment.

This relation between profit, the real interest rate and investment hinges on a strong assumption: that the future is expected to be the same as the present. It is a useful relation to remember – and one that macroeconomists keep handy in their toolbox. It is time, however, to relax this assumption and return to the role of expectations in determining investment decisions.

Current versus expected profit

The theory we have developed implies that investment should be forward looking and should depend primarily on expected future profits. (Under our assumption that it takes

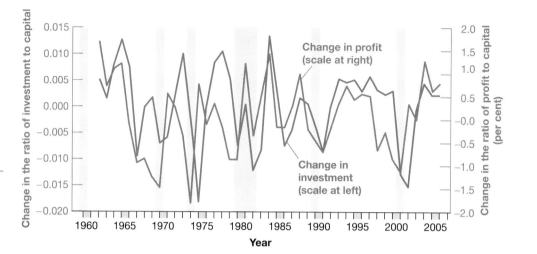

Figure 17.5

Figure 17.5

Changes in investment and changes in profit in the USA since 1960

Investment and profit move very much together.

a year for investment to generate profits, current profit does not even appear in equation (17.5).) One striking empirical fact about investment, however, is how strongly it moves with fluctuations in current profit.

This relation is shown in Figure 17.5, which plots yearly changes in investment and profit since 1960 for the US economy. Profit is constructed as the ratio of the sum of after-tax profits plus interest payments paid by US non-financial corporations, divided by their capital stock. Investment is constructed as the ratio of investment by US non-financial corporations to their capital stock. The shaded areas in the figure represent years in which there was a recession – a decline in output for at least two consecutive quarters of the year.

There is a clear positive relation between changes in investment and changes in current profit in Figure 17.5. Is this relation inconsistent with the theory we have just developed, which holds that investment should be related to the present value of expected future profits rather than to current profit? Not necessarily: if firms expect future profits to move very much like current profit, then the present value of those future profits will move very much like current profit, and so will investment.

Economists who have looked at the question more closely have concluded, however, that the effect of current profit on investment is stronger than would be predicted by the theory we have developed so far. How they have gathered some of the evidence is described in the Focus box 'Profitability versus cash flow'. On the one hand, some firms with highly profitable investment projects but low current profits appear to be investing too little. On the other hand, some firms that have high current profit appear sometimes to invest in projects of doubtful profitability. In short, current profit appears to affect investment, even after controlling for the expected present value of profits.

Why does current profit play a role in the investment decision? The answer lurks in section 17.1 where we discussed why consumption depends directly on current income; some of the reasons we used to explain the behavior of consumers also apply to firms:

● If its current profit is low, a firm that wants to buy new machines can get the funds it needs only by borrowing. It may be reluctant to borrow: although expected profits might look good, things may turn bad, leaving the firm unable to repay the debt. But if current profit is high, the firm might be able to finance its investment just by retaining some of its earnings and without having to borrow. The bottom line is that higher current profit may lead the firm to invest more.

● Even if the firm wants to invest, it might have difficulty borrowing. Potential lenders may not be convinced the project is as good as the firm says it is, and they may worry the firm will be unable to repay. If the firm has large current profits, it does not have to borrow and so does not need to convince potential lenders. It can proceed and invest as it pleases, and it is more likely to do so.

FOCUS
Profitability versus cash flow

How much does investment depend on the expected present value of future profits, and how much does it depend on current profit? In other words, which is more important for investment decisions: **profitability** (the expected present discounted value of future profits) or **cash flow** (current profit, the net flow of cash the firm is receiving now)?

The difficulty in answering this question is that, most of the time, cash flow and profitability move together. Firms that do well typically have both large cash flows and good future prospects. Firms that suffer losses often also have poor future prospects.

The best way to isolate the effects of cash flow and profitability on investment is to identify times or events when cash flow and profitability move in different directions and then to look at what happens to investment. This is the approach taken by Owen Lamont, an economist at Yale University. An example will help you understand Lamont's strategy.

Think of two firms, A and B. Both firms are involved in steel production. Firm B is also involved in oil exploration.

Suppose there is a sharp drop in the price of oil, leading to losses in oil exploration. This shock decreases firm B's cash flow. If the losses in oil exploration are large enough

to offset the profits from steel production, firm B might even show an overall loss.

The question we can now ask is: as a result of the fall in the price of oil, will firm B invest less in its steel operation than firm A does? If only the profitability of steel production matters, there is no reason for firm B to invest less in its steel operation than firm A. But if current cash flow also matters, the fact that firm B has a lower cash flow may prevent it from investing as much as firm A in its steel operation. Looking at investment in the steel operations of the two firms can tell us how much investment depends on cash flow versus profitability.

This is the empirical strategy followed by Lamont. He focused on what happened in 1986 when the price of oil in the USA dropped by 50%, leading to large losses in oil-related activities. He then looked at whether firms that had substantial oil activities cut investment in their non-oil activities relatively more than other firms in the same non-oil activities. He concludes that they did. He found that for every $1 decrease in cash flow due to the decrease in the price of oil, investment spending in non-oil activities was reduced by 10 to 20 cents. In short, current cash flow matters.

Source: Owen Lamont, 'Cash flow and investment: evidence from internal capital markets', *Journal of Finance*, 1997, **52**, 83–109.

In summary, to fit the investment behaviour we observe in practice, the investment equation is better specified as

$$I_t = I[V(\Pi_t^e), \Pi_t] \qquad [17.9]$$
$$(+, +)$$

In words: investment depends both on the expected present value of future profits and on the current level of profit.

Profit and sales

Let's take stock of where we are. We have argued that investment depends on both current and expected profit or, more specifically, current and expected profit per unit of capital. We need to take one last step: what determines profit per unit of capital? Answer: primarily two factors: (1) the level of sales and (2) the existing capital stock. If sales are low relative to the capital stock, profits per unit of capital are likely to be low as well.

Let's write this more formally. Ignore the distinction between sales and output, and let Y_t denote output – equivalently, sales. Let K_t denote the capital stock at time t. Our discussion suggests the following relation:

$$\Pi_t = \Pi\left(\frac{Y_t}{K_t}\right) \qquad [17.10]$$
$$(+)$$

Figure 17.6

Changes in profit per unit of capital versus changes in the ratio of output to capital in the USA since 1960

Profit per unit of capital and the ratio of output to capital move largely together.

Profit per unit of capital is an increasing function of the ratio of sales to the capital stock. For a given capital stock, the higher the sales, the higher the profit per unit of capital. For given sales, the higher the capital stock, the lower the profit per unit of capital.

How well does this relation hold in practice? Figure 17.6 plots yearly changes in profit per unit of capital (measured on the right vertical axis) and changes in the ratio of output to capital (measured on the left vertical axis) for the USA since 1960. As in Figure 17.5, profit per unit of capital is defined as the sum of after-tax profits plus interest payments by US non-financial corporations, divided by their capital stock, measured at replacement cost. The ratio of output to capital is constructed as the ratio of GDP to the aggregate capital stock.

The figure shows there is a tight relation between changes in profit per unit of capital and changes in the ratio of output to capital. Given that most of the year-to-year changes in the ratio of output to capital come from movements in output, and most of the year-to-year changes in profit per unit of capital come from movements in profit (capital moves slowly over time; the reason is that capital is large compared to yearly investment, so even large movements in investment lead to small changes in the capital stock), we can state the relation as follows: profit decreases in recessions, and increases in expansions.

Why is this relation between output and profit relevant here? Because it implies a link between current output and expected future output on the one hand and investment on the other: current output affects current profit, expected future output affects expected future profit, and current and expected future profits affect investment. For example, the anti-cipation of a long, sustained economic expansion leads firms to expect high profits, now

> High expected output ⇒
> High expected profit ⇒
> High investment today.

and for some time in the future. These expectations in turn lead to higher investment. The effect of current and expected output on investment, together with the effect of investment back on demand and output, will play a crucial role when we return to the determination of output (in Chapter 18).

17.4 THE VOLATILITY OF CONSUMPTION AND INVESTMENT

You will surely have noticed the similarities between our treatment of consumption and of investment behaviour in sections 17.1, 17.2 and 17.3:

● Whether consumers perceive current movements in income to be transitory or perma-nent affects their consumption decision. The more transitory they expect a current increase in income to be, the less they will increase their consumption.

● In the same way, whether firms perceive current movements in sales to be transitory or permanent affects their investment decisions. The more transitory they expect a current increase in sales to be, the less they revise their assessment of the present value of profits, and thus the less likely they are to buy new machines or build new factories. This is why, for example, the boom in sales that happens every year between Thanksgiving and Christmas does not lead to a boom in investment every year in December. Firms under- stand that this boom is transitory.

In the USA, retail sales are 24% higher on average in December than in other months. In France and Italy, sales are 60% higher in December.

But there are also important differences between consumption decisions and investment decisions:

● The theory of consumption we developed implies that, when faced with an increase in income consumers perceive as permanent, they respond with at most an equal increase in consumption. The permanent nature of the increase in income implies that they can afford to increase consumption now and in the future by the same amount as the increase in income. Increasing consumption more than one-for-one would require cuts in consumption later, and there is no reason for consumers to want to plan consumption this way.

● Now consider the behaviour of firms faced with an increase in sales they believe to be permanent. The present value of expected profits increases, leading to an increase in investment. In contrast to consumption, however, this does not imply that the increase in investment should be at most equal to the increase in sales. Rather, once a firm has decided that an increase in sales justifies the purchase of a new machine or the building of a new factory, it may want to proceed quickly, leading to a large but short-lived increase in investment spending. This increase in investment spending may exceed the increase in sales.

More concretely, take a firm that has a ratio of capital to its annual sales of, say, 3. An increase in sales of €10 million this year, if expected to be permanent, requires the firm to spend €30 million on additional capital if it wants to maintain the same ratio of capital to output. If the firm buys the additional capital right away, the increase in investment spending this year will equal three times the increase in sales. Once the capital stock has adjusted, the firm will return to its normal pattern of investment. This example is extreme because firms are unlikely to adjust their capital stock right away. But even if they do adjust their capital stock more slowly – say, over a few years – the increase in investment might still exceed the increase in sales for a while.

We can tell the same story in terms of equation (17.10). Because we make no distinction here between output and sales, the initial increase in sales leads to an equal increase in output, Y, so that Y/K – the ratio of the firm's output to its existing capital stock – also increases. The result is higher profit, which leads the firm to undertake more investment. Over time, the higher level of investment leads to a higher capital stock, K, so that Y/K decreases back to normal. Profit per unit of capital returns to normal, and so does investment. Thus, in response to a permanent increase in sales, investment may increase a lot initially, and then return to normal over time.

These differences suggest that investment should be more volatile than consumption. How much more? The answer is given in Figure 17.7, which plots yearly rates of change in consumption and investment in the UK since 1960. The shaded areas are years during which the UK economy was in recession. To make the figure easier to interpret, both rates of change are plotted as deviations from the average rate of change so that they are, on average, equal to zero.

The figure yields three conclusions:

● Consumption and investment usually move together. Recessions, for example, are typically associated with decreases in both investment and consumption. Given our discussion, which has emphasised that consumption and investment depend largely on the same determinants, this should not come as a surprise.

● Investment is much more volatile than consumption. Relative movements in investment range from −20% to 33%, while relative movements in consumption range only from −1% to 8%.

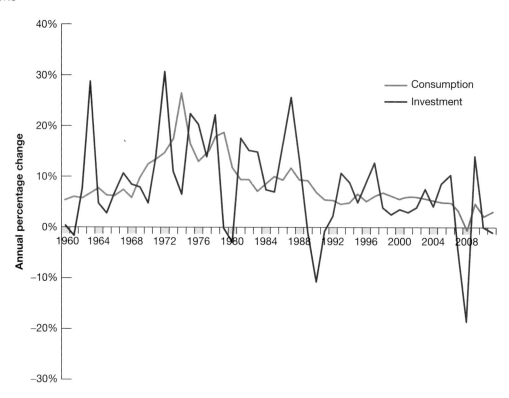

Figure 17.7

Rates of change of consumption and investment in the UK since 1960

Relative movements in investment are much larger than relative movements in consumption.

Source: Eurostat.

● Because the level of investment is much smaller than the level of consumption (recall that investment accounts for 16% of GDP versus 64% for consumption), changes in investment from one year to the next end up being of the same overall magnitude as changes in consumption. In other words, both components contribute roughly equally to fluctuations in output over time. Relative movements in *I* are larger than relative movements in *C*. But, because *I* accounts only for 16% of GDP in the UK (21% in EU-227) and *C* accounts for 64% in the UK (57% in EU-27), absolute movements in *I* and *C* are of roughly equal magnitude.

SUMMARY

● Consumption depends on both wealth and current income. Wealth is the sum of non-human wealth (financial wealth and housing wealth) and human wealth (the present value of expected after-tax labour income).

● The response of consumption to changes in income depends on whether consumers perceive these changes as transitory or permanent.

● Consumption is likely to respond less than one-for-one to movements in income. Consumption might move even if current income does not change.

● Investment depends on both current profit and the present value of expected future profits.

● Under the simplifying assumption that firms expect profits and interest rates to be the same in the future as

they are today, we can think of investment as depending on the ratio of profit to the user cost of capital, where the user cost is the sum of the real interest rate and the depreciation rate.

● Movements in profit are closely related to movements in output. Hence, we can think of investment as depending indirectly on current and expected future output movements. Firms that anticipate a long output expansion, and thus a long sequence of high profits, will invest. Movements in output that are not expected to last will have a small effect on investment.

● Investment is much more volatile than consumption. But, because investment accounts only for 16% of GDP and consumption accounts for 70%, movements in investment and consumption are of roughly equal magnitude.

KEY TERMS

permanent income theory of consumption 383

life cycle theory of consumption 383

financial wealth 383

housing wealth 383

human wealth 383

non-human wealth 383

total wealth 383

representative consumer 384

endowments 384

intertemporal budget constraint 385

consumption smoothing 386

discount rate 386

panel data sets 390

cash flow 394

static expectations 393

Tobin's q 394

user cost of capital, or rental cost of capital 394

profitability 397

QUESTIONS AND PROBLEMS

QUICK CHECK

1. *Using the information in this chapter, label each of the following statements true, false or uncertain. Explain briefly.*

a. For a typical university student, human wealth and non-human wealth are approximately equal.

b. Natural experiments, such as retirement, do not suggest that expectations of future income are a major factor affecting consumption.

c. Buildings and factories depreciate much faster than machines do.

d. A high value for Tobin's q indicates that the stock market believes that capital is overvalued, and thus investment should be lower.

e. Economists have found that the effect of current profit on investment can be fully explained by the effect of current profit on expectations of future profits.

f. Data from the past three decades in the USA suggest that corporate profits are closely tied to the business cycle.

g. Changes in consumption and investment typically occur in the same direction and at roughly the same magnitude.

2. *A consumer has non-human wealth equal to €100,000. She earns €40,000 this year and expects her salary to rise by 5% in real terms each year for the following two years. She will then retire. The real interest rate is equal to 0% and is expected to remain at 0% in the future. Labour income is taxed at a rate of 25%.*

a. What is this consumer's human wealth?

b. What is her total wealth?

c. If she expects to live for seven more years after retiring and wants her consumption to remain the same (in real terms) every year from now on, how much can she consume this year?

d. If she received a bonus of €20,000 in the current year only, with all future salary payments remaining as stated earlier, by how much could this consumer increase consumption now and in the future?

e. Suppose now that at retirement, social security will start paying benefits each year equal to 60% of this consumer's earnings during her last working year. Assume that benefits are not taxed. How much can she consume this year and still maintain constant consumption over her lifetime?

3. *A potato crisp manufacturer is considering buying another crisp-making machine that costs €100,000. The machine will depreciate by 8% per year. It will generate real profits equal to €18,000 next year, €18,000(1 – 8%) two years from now (that is, the same real profits but adjusted for depreciation), €18,000(1 – 8%)² three years from now and so on. Determine whether the manufacturer should buy the machine if the real interest rate is assumed to remain constant at each rate in (a) through (c).*

a. 5%

b. 10%

c. 15%

4. *Suppose that, at age 22, you have just finished university and have been offered a job with a starting salary of €40,000. Your salary will remain constant in real terms. However, you have also been accepted on to a postgraduate course. The course can be completed in two years. Upon graduation, you expect your starting salary to be 10% higher in real terms and to remain constant in real terms thereafter. The tax rate on labour income is 40%.*

a. If the real interest rate is zero and you expect to retire at age 60 (i.e. if you do not do the postgraduate course, you expect to work for 38 years total), what is the maximum you should be willing to pay in tuition to do the course?

b. What is your answer to part (a) if you expect to pay 30% in taxes?

DIG DEEPER

5. Individual saving and aggregate capital accumulation

Suppose that every consumer is born with zero financial wealth and lives for three periods: youth, middle age and old age.

Consumers work in the first two periods and retire in the last one. Their income is €5 in the first period, €25 in the second and €0 in the last one. Inflation and expected inflation are equal to zero, and so is the real interest rate.

a. What is the present discounted value of labour income at the beginning of life? What is the highest sustainable level of consumption such that consumption is equal in all three periods?

b. For each age group, what is the amount of saving that allows consumers to maintain the constant level of consumption you found in part (a)? (*Hint*: saving can be a negative number if the consumer needs to borrow in order to maintain a certain level of consumption.)

c. Suppose there are *n* people born each period. What is total saving in the economy? (*Hint*: add up the saving of each age group. Remember that some age groups may have negative saving.) Explain.

d. What is total financial wealth in the economy? (*Hint*: compute the financial wealth of people at the beginning of the first period of life, the beginning of the second period and the beginning of the third period. Add the three numbers. Remember that people can be in debt, so financial wealth can be negative.)

6. Borrowing constraints and aggregate capital accumulation

Continue with the set-up from problem 5, but suppose now that restrictions on borrowing do not allow young consumers to borrow. If we call the sum of income and total financial wealth 'cash on hand', then the borrowing restriction means that consumers cannot consume more than their cash on hand. In each age group, consumers compute their total wealth and then determine their desired level of consumption as the highest level that allows their consumption to be equal in all three periods. However, if at any time, desired consumption exceeds cash on hand, then consumers are constrained to consume exactly their cash on hand.

a. Calculate consumption in each period of life. Compare this answer to your answer to part (a) of problem 5, and explain any differences.

b. Calculate total saving for the economy. Compare this answer to your answer to part (c) of problem 5, and explain any differences.

c. Derive total financial wealth for the economy. Compare this answer to your answer to part (d) of problem 5, and explain any differences.

d. Consider the following statement: 'Financial liberalisation may be good for individual consumers, but it is bad for overall capital accumulation.' Discuss.

7. Saving with uncertain future income

Consider a consumer who lives for three periods: youth, middle age and old age. When young, the consumer earns €20,000 in labour income. Earnings during middle age are uncertain;

there is a 50% chance that the consumer will earn €40,000 and a 50% chance that the consumer will earn €100,000. When old, the consumer spends savings accumulated during the previous periods. Assume that inflation, expected inflation and the real interest rate equal zero. Ignore taxes for this problem.

a. What is the expected value of earnings in the middle period of life? Given this number, what is the present discounted value of expected lifetime labour earnings? If the consumer wishes to maintain constant expected consumption over her lifetime, how much will she consume in each period? How much will she save in each period?

b. Now suppose the consumer wishes, above all else, to maintain a minimum consumption level of €20,000 in each period of her life. To do so, she must consider the worst outcome. If earnings during middle age turn out to be €40,000, how much should the consumer spend when she is young to guarantee consumption of at least €20,000 in each period? How does this level of consumption compare to the level you obtained for the young period in part (a)?

c. Given your answer in part (b), suppose that the consumer's earnings during middle age turn out to be €100,000. How much will she spend in each period of life? Will consumption be constant over the consumer's lifetime? (*Hint*: when the consumer reaches middle age, she will try to maintain constant consumption for the last two periods of life, as long as she can consume at least €20,000 in each period.)

d. What effect does uncertainty about future labour income have on saving (or borrowing) by young consumers?

EXPLORE FURTHER

8. The movements of consumption and investment

*Go to the Eurostat website (**http://epp.eurostat.ec.europa.eu**) and download data for the years 1980 to the present date for personal consumption expenditures and gross private domestic investment for your country.*

a. On average, how much larger is consumption than investment?

b. Compute the change in the levels of consumption and investment from one year to the next, and graph them for the period 1980 to the present date. Are the year-to-year changes in consumption and investment of similar magnitude?

c. What do your answers in parts (a) and (b) imply about the average annual percentage changes of consumption and investment?

9. Consumer confidence and disposable income

*Go to the Eurostat website (**http://epp.eurostat.ec.europa.eu**) and download data on the Consumer Confidence Indicator for the latest available years. We will use this data series as our* *measure of consumer confidence. Now find the percentage change in real personal disposable income. Obtain these data for the latest available years.*

a. Before you look at the data, can you think of any reasons to expect consumer confidence to be related to disposable income? Can you think of reasons why consumer confidence would be unrelated to disposable income?

b. Calculate the average percentage change in personal disposable income over the entire period, and subtract this average from each observation of the percentage change in personal disposable income. Use this new data series as your measure of the change in personal disposable income. Now calculate the change in consumer con-

fidence as the change in the Consumer Confidence Indicator. Plot the change in consumer confidence against the change in personal disposable income (the measure you constructed in this part). Is there a clear relation (positive or negative) between the two variables? If you believe there is a relation, is it very tight? In other words, are there many observations that deviate greatly from the average relation?

c. Look at the data for 2008 and 2009. What happened to personal disposable income during these two years? What happened to consumer confidence? Why do you think consumer confidence behaved differently in these two time periods?

*Log on to **MyEconLab** and complete the studyplan exercises for this chapter to see how much you have learnt, and where you need to revise most.*

MyEconLab

APPENDIX

Derivation of the expected present value of profits under static expectations

You saw in the text (equation (17.5)) that the expected present value of profits is given by

$$V(\Pi_t^e) = \frac{1}{1+r_t}\Pi_{t+1}^e + \frac{1}{(1+r_t)(1+r_{t+1}^e)}(1-\delta)\Pi_{t+2}^e + \cdots$$

If firms expect both future profits (per unit of capital) and future interest rates to remain at the same level as today, so that $\Pi_{t+1}^e = \Pi_{t+2}^e = \cdots = \Pi_t$, and $r_{t+1}^e = r_{t+2}^e = \cdots = r_t$, the equation becomes

$$V(\Pi_t^e) = \frac{1}{1+r_t}\Pi_t + \frac{1}{(1+r_t)^2}(1-\delta)\Pi_t + \cdots$$

Factoring out $[1/(1+r_t)]\Pi_t$,

$$V(\Pi_t^e) = \frac{1}{1+r_t}\Pi_t\left(1 + \frac{1-\delta}{1+r_t} + \cdots\right) \qquad \text{[17A.1]}$$

The term in parentheses in this equation is a geometric series, a series of the form $1 + x + x^2 + \cdots$. So, from Proposition 2 (in Appendix 1 at the end of the book):

$$(1 + x + x^2 + \cdots) = \frac{1}{1-x}$$

Here x equals $(1-\delta)/(1+r_t)$, so

$$\left(1 + \frac{1-\delta}{1+r_t} + \left(\frac{1-\delta}{1+r_t}\right)^2 + \cdots\right) = \frac{1}{1-(1-\delta)/(1+r_t)}$$

$$= \frac{1+r_t}{r_t+\delta}$$

Replacing in equation (17A.1) gives

$$V(\Pi_t^e) = \frac{1}{1+r_t}\frac{1+r_t}{r_t+\delta}\Pi_t$$

Simplifying gives equation (17.5) in the text:

$$V(\Pi_t^e) = \frac{\Pi_t}{(r_t+\delta)}$$

Chapter 18

EXPECTATIONS, OUTPUT AND POLICY

Earlier (in Chapter 16), we saw how expectations affected asset prices, from bonds to stocks, to houses. We also saw (in Chapter 17) how expectations affected consumption decisions and investment decisions. In this chapter we put the pieces together and take another look at the effects of monetary and fiscal policy.

- Section 18.1 draws the major implication of what we have learned, namely that expectations of both future output and future interest rates affect current spending and therefore current output.

- Section 18.2 looks at monetary policy. It shows how the effects of monetary policy depend crucially on how expectations respond to policy: conventional monetary policy directly affects only the short-term interest rate. What happens to spending and output then depends on how changes in the short-term interest rate lead people and firms to change their expectations of future interest rates and future income and, by implication, lead them to change their decisions.

- Section 18.3 turns to fiscal policy. It shows how, in sharp contrast to the simple model you saw back in the core section, a fiscal contraction may, under some circumstances, lead to an increase in output, even in the short run. Again, how expectations respond to policy is at the centre of the story.

18.1 EXPECTATIONS AND DECISIONS: TAKING STOCK

Let's start by reviewing what we have learned, and then discuss how we should modify the characterisation of goods and financial markets – the *IS–LM* model – we developed in the core section.

Expectations, consumption and investment decisions

The theme earlier (see Chapter 17) was that both consumption and investment decisions depend very much on expectations of future income and interest rates. The channels through which expectations affect consumption and investment spending are summarised in Figure 18.1.

Note the many channels through which expected future variables affect current decisions, both directly and through asset prices:

- An increase in current and expected future after-tax real labour income, and/or a decrease in current and expected future real interest rates increase human wealth (the expected present discounted value of after-tax real labour income), which in turn leads to an increase in consumption.
- An increase in current and expected future real dividends, and/or a decrease in current and expected future real interest rates increase stock prices, which lead to an increase in non-human wealth and, in turn, to an increase in consumption.

Note that in the case of bonds, it is ➤ nominal rather than real interest rates which matter, because bonds are claims to dollars rather than goods in the future.

- A decrease in current and expected future nominal interest rates leads to an increase in bond prices, which leads to an increase in non-human wealth and, in turn, to an increase in consumption.
- An increase in current and expected future real after-tax profits, and/or a decrease in current and expected future real interest rates, increase the present value of real after-tax profits, which leads, in turn, to an increase in investment.

Expectations and the *IS* relation

A model that gave a detailed treatment of consumption and investment along the lines suggested in Figure 18.1 would be very complicated. It can be done – and, indeed, it is done in the large empirical models that macroeconomists build to understand the economy and analyse policy, but this is not the place for such complications. We want to capture the essence of what you have learned so far, how consumption and investment depend on expectations of the future – without getting lost in the details.

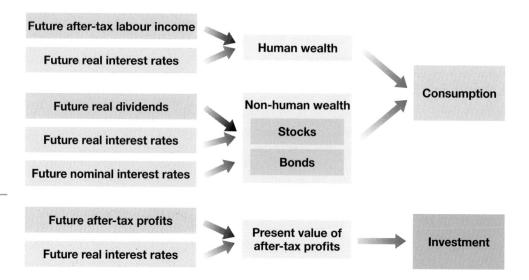

Figure 18.1

Expectations and spending: the channels

Expectations affect consumption and investment decisions, both directly and through asset prices.

To do so, let's make a major simplification. Let's reduce the present and the future to only two periods: (1) a current period, which you can think of as the current year, and (2) a future period, which you can think of as all future years lumped together. This way, we do not have to keep track of expectations about each future year.

This way of dividing time between 'today' and 'later' is the way many of us organise our own lives: think of 'things to do today' versus 'things that can wait'.

Having made this assumption, the question becomes: how should we write the *IS* relation for the current period? Earlier, we wrote the following equation for the *IS* relation:

$$Y = C(Y - T) + I(Y, r) + G$$

We assumed that consumption depended only on current income, and that investment depended only on current output and the current real interest rate. We now want to modify this to take into account how expectations affect both consumption and investment. We proceed in two steps.

First, we simply rewrite the equation in more compact form, but without changing its content. For that purpose, let's define aggregate private spending as the sum of consumption and investment spending:

$$A(Y, T, r) \equiv C(Y - T) + I(Y, r)$$

where *A* stands for **aggregate private spending** or, simply, **private spending**. With this notation we can rewrite the *IS* relation as

The reason for doing so is to group together the two components of demand, *C* and *I*, both of which depend on expectations. We continue to treat *G*, government spending, as exogenous – unexplained within our model.

$$Y = A(Y, T, r) + G \qquad [18.1]$$
$$(+, -, -)$$

The properties of aggregate private spending, *A*, follow from the properties of consumption and investment that we derived in earlier chapters:

- Aggregate private spending is an increasing function of income, *Y*: higher income (equivalently, output) increases consumption and investment.
- Aggregate private spending is a decreasing function of taxes, *T*: higher taxes decrease consumption.
- Aggregate private spending is a decreasing function of the real interest rate, *r*: a higher real interest rate decreases investment.

The first step only simplified notation. The second step is to extend equation (18.1) to take into account the role of expectations. The natural extension is to allow spending to depend not only on current variables but also on their expected values in the future period:

$$Y = A(Y, T, r, Y'^e, T'^e, r'^e) + G \qquad [18.2]$$
$$(+, -, -, +, -, -)$$

Primes denote future values and the superscript e denotes an expectation, so Y'^e, T'^e and r'^e denote future expected income, future expected taxes and the future expected real interest rate, respectively. The notation is a bit heavy, but what it captures is straightforward:

Notation: primes stand for values of the variables in the future period. The superscript e stands for 'expected'.

- Increases in either current or expected future income increase private spending.
- Increases in either current or expected future taxes decrease private spending.
- Increases in either the current or expected future real interest rate decrease private spending.

Y or Y'^e increase $\Rightarrow$ *A* increases.

T or T'^e increase $\Rightarrow$ *A* decreases.

r or r'^e increase $\Rightarrow$ *A* decreases.

With the goods market equilibrium now given by equation (18.2), Figure 18.2 shows the new *IS* curve for the current period. As usual, to draw the curve, we take all variables other than current output, *Y*, and the current real interest rate, *r*, as given. Thus, the *IS* curve is drawn for given values of current and future expected taxes, *T* and T'^e, for given values of expected future output, Y'^e, and for given values of the expected future real interest rate, r'^e.

The new *IS* curve, based on equation (18.2), is still downward sloping (for the same reason as in Chapter 5): a decrease in the current interest rate leads to an increase in spending. This increase in spending leads, through a multiplier effect, to an increase in output. We can say more, however: the new *IS* curve is much steeper than the *IS* curve we drew in earlier

Figure 18.2

The new *IS* curve

Given expectations, a decrease in the real interest rate leads to a small increase in output: the *IS* curve is steeply downward sloping. Increases in government spending or in expected future output shift the *IS* curve to the right. Increases in taxes, in expected future taxes or in the expected future real interest rate shift the *IS* curve to the left.

chapters. Put another way, everything else being the same, a large decrease in the current interest rate is likely to have only a small effect on equilibrium output.

To see why the effect is small, take point *A* on the *IS* curve in Figure 18.2, and consider the effects of a decrease in the real interest rate, from r_A to r_B. The effect of the decrease in the real interest rate on output depends on the strength of two effects: the effect of the real interest rate on spending given income, and the size of the multiplier. Let's examine each one:

● A decrease in the current real interest rate, given unchanged expectations of the future real interest rate, does not have much effect on spending. We saw why in the previous chapters: a change in only the current real interest rate does not lead to large changes in present values, and therefore does not lead to large changes in spending. For example, firms are not likely to change their investment plans very much in response to a decrease in the current real interest rate if they do not expect future real interest rates to be lower as well.

● The multiplier is likely to be small. Recall that the size of the multiplier depends on the size of the effect a change in current income (output) has on spending. But a change in current income, given unchanged expectations of future income, is unlikely to have a large effect on spending. The reason: changes in income that are not expected to last have only a limited effect on either consumption or investment. Consumers who expect their income to be higher only for a year will increase consumption, but by much less than the increase in their income. Firms which expect sales to be higher only for a year are unlikely to change their investment plans much, if at all.

> Suppose your firm decides to give all employees a one-time bonus of €10,000. You do not expect it to happen again. By how much will you increase your consumption this year? (If you need to, look at the discussion of consumption behaviour in Chapter 17.)

Putting things together, a large decrease in the current real interest rate – from r_A to r_B in Figure 18.2 – leads to only a small increase in output, from Y_A to Y_B. Put another way: the *IS* curve, which goes through points A and B, is steeply downward sloping.

A change in any variable in equation (18.2) other than Y and r shifts the *IS* curve:

● Changes in current taxes (T) or in current government spending (G) shift the *IS* curve.

An increase in current government spending increases spending at a given interest rate, shifting the *IS* curve to the right; an increase in taxes shifts the *IS* curve to the left. These shifts are represented in Figure 18.2.

● Changes in expected future variables also shift the *IS* curve.

An increase in expected future output, Y'^e, shifts the *IS* curve to the right: higher expected future income leads consumers to feel wealthier and spend more; higher expected future output implies higher expected profits, leading firms to invest more. Higher spending by consumers and firms leads, through the multiplier effect, to higher output. By a similar argument, an increase in expected future taxes leads consumers to decrease their current spending and shifts the *IS* curve to the left. And an increase in the expected future real interest rate decreases current spending, also leading to a decrease in output, shifting the *IS* curve to the left. These shifts are also represented in Figure 18.2.

The *LM* relation revisited

The *LM* relation we derived earlier (in Chapter 4) and have used until now was given by

$$\frac{M}{P} = YL(i) \qquad [18.3]$$

where *M/P* is the supply of money and *YL*(*i*) is the demand for money. Equilibrium in financial markets requires that the supply of money be equal to the demand for money. The demand for money depends on real income and on the short-term nominal interest rate – the opportunity cost of holding money. We derived this demand for money before thinking about expectations. Now that we have thought about them, the question is whether we should modify equation (18.3). The answer – we are sure this will be good news – is no.

Think of your own demand for money. How much money you want to hold today depends on your current level of transactions, not on the level of transactions you expect next year or the year after; there will be ample time for you to adjust your money balances to your transaction level if and when it changes in the future. And the opportunity cost of holding money today depends on the current nominal interest rate, not on the expected nominal interest rate next year or the year after. If short-term interest rates were to increase in the future, increasing the opportunity cost of holding money then, the time to reduce your money balances would be then, not now.

So, in contrast to the consumption decision, the decision about how much money to hold is myopic, depending primarily on current income and the current short-term nominal interest rate. We can still think of the demand for money as depending on the current level of output and the current nominal interest rate, and we can use equation (18.3) to describe the determination of the nominal interest rate in the current period.

Let's summarise. We have seen that expectations about the future play a major role in spending decisions. This implies that expectations enter the *IS* relation: private spending depends not only on current output and the current real interest rate, but also on expected future output and the expected future real interest rate. In contrast, the decision about how much money to hold is largely myopic: the two variables entering the *LM* relation are still current income and the current nominal interest rate.

18.2 MONETARY POLICY, EXPECTATIONS AND OUTPUT

In the basic *IS–LM* model we developed earlier (in Chapter 5), there was only one interest rate, *i*, which entered both the *IS* relation and the *LM* relation. When the central bank expanded the money supply, 'the' interest rate went down, and spending increased. From the previous three chapters, you have learned there are in fact many interest rates, and that we must keep at least two distinctions in mind:

- The distinction between the nominal interest rate and the real interest rate.
- The distinction between current and expected future interest rates.

The interest rate that enters the *LM* relation, which is the interest rate that the central bank affects directly, is the current nominal interest rate. In contrast, spending in the *IS*

Other distinctions may also be relevant. For example, during the initial part of the crisis, the interest rates charged by banks increased a lot relative to the rates on government bonds. We leave these aside here.

We leave aside 'unconventional' policies such as quantitative easing (see Chapter 19) here, but return to the issue below.

relation depends on both current and expected future real interest rates. Economists sometimes state this distinction even more starkly by saying that, while the central bank controls the short-term nominal interest rate, what matters for spending and output is the long-term real interest rate. Let's look at this distinction more closely.

From the short nominal rate to current and expected real rates

Recall from earlier (see Chapter 6) that the real interest rate is approximately equal to the nominal interest rate minus expected current inflation:

> Expected current inflation: inflation expected, as of today, for the current period (the current year).

$$r = i - \pi^e$$

Similarly, the expected future real interest rate is approximately equal to the expected future nominal interest rate minus expected future inflation:

> Expected future inflation: inflation expected, as of today, for the future period (all future years).

$$r'^e = i'^e - \pi'^e$$

When the central bank increases the money supply – decreasing the current nominal interest rate i – the effects on the current and the expected future real interest rates depend, therefore, on two factors:

- Whether the increase in the money supply leads financial markets to revise their expectations of the future nominal interest rate, I'^e.
- Whether the increase in the money supply leads financial markets to revise their expectations of both current and future inflation, π^e and π'^e. If, for example, the change in money leads financial markets to expect more inflation in the future – so π'^e increases – the expected future real interest rate, r'^e will decrease by more than the expected future nominal interest rate, i'^e.

> We explored the role of changing expectations of inflation on the relation between the nominal interest rate and the real interest rate earlier (in Chapter 6). Leaving changes in expected inflation aside will keep the analysis simpler here. You have, however, all the elements you need to think through what would happen if we also allowed expectations of current inflation and future inflation to adjust. How would these expectations adjust? Would this lead to a larger or a smaller effect on output in the current period?

To keep things simple, we shall ignore here the second factor – the role of changing expectations of inflation – and focus on the first, the role of changing expectations of the future nominal interest rate. Thus we shall assume that expected current inflation and expected future inflation are both equal to zero. In this case, we do not need to distinguish between the nominal interest rate and the real interest rate, as they are equal, and we can use the same letter to denote both. Let r denote the current real (and nominal) interest rate, and r'^e denote the expected future real (and nominal) interest rate.

> The *IS* relation is the same as equation (18.2). The *LM* relation is now in terms of the real interest rate – which, here, is equal to the nominal interest rate.

With this simplification, we can rewrite the *IS* and *LM* relations in equations (18.2) and (18.3) as

$$IS: \quad Y = A(Y, T, r, Y'^e, T'^e, r'^e) + G \qquad [18.4]$$

$$LM: \quad \frac{M}{P} = YL(r) \qquad [18.5]$$

The corresponding *IS* and *LM* curves are drawn in Figure 18.3. The vertical axis measures the current interest rate, r; the horizontal axis measures current output, Y. The *IS* curve is steeply downward sloping. We saw the reason earlier: for given expectations, a change in the current interest rate has a limited effect on spending and the multiplier is small. The *LM* is upward sloping: an increase in income leads to an increase in the demand for money; given the supply of money, the result is an increase in the interest rate. Equilibrium in goods and financial markets implies that the economy is at point A, on both the *IS* and the *LM* curves.

> There is no need to distinguish here between the real interest rate and the nominal interest rate: given zero expected inflation, they are the same.

Monetary policy revisited

Now suppose the economy is in recession, and the central bank decides to increase the money supply.

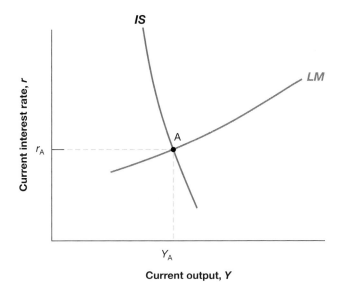

Figure 18.3

The new *IS–LM* curves

The *IS* curve is steeply downward sloping. Other things being equal, a change in the current interest rate has a small effect on output. The *LM* curve is upward sloping. The equilibrium is at the intersection of the *IS* and *LM* curves.

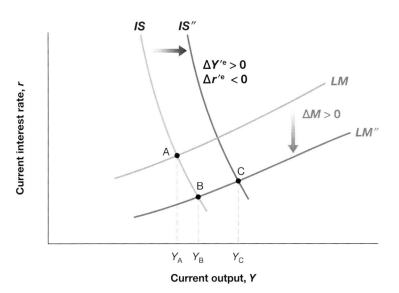

Figure 18.4

The effects of an expansionary monetary policy

The effects of monetary policy on output depend very much on whether and how monetary policy affects expectations.

Assume first that this expansionary monetary policy does not change expectations of either the future interest rate or future output. In Figure 18.4, the *LM* shifts down, from *LM* to *LM''*. (Because we have already used primes to denote future values of the variables, we shall use double primes, such as in *LM''*, to denote shifts in curves in this chapter.) The equilibrium moves from point A to point B, with higher output and a lower interest rate. The steep *IS* curve, however, implies that the increase in the money supply has only a small effect on output: changes in the current interest rate, unaccompanied by changes in expectations, have only a small effect on spending, and in turn a small effect on output.

◀ Given expectations, an increase in the money supply leads to a shift in the *LM*, and a movement down the steep *IS*. The result is a large decrease in *r*, a small increase in *Y*.

Is it reasonable, however, to assume that expectations are unaffected by an expansionary monetary policy? Isn't it likely that, as the central bank lowers the current interest rate, financial markets now anticipate lower interest rates in the future as well, along with higher future output stimulated by this lower future interest rate? What happens if they do? At a given current interest rate, prospects of a lower future interest rate and of higher future output both increase spending and output; they shift the *IS* curve to the right, from *IS* to *IS''*. The new equilibrium is given by point C. Thus, while the direct effect of the monetary expansion on output is limited, the full effect, once changes in expectations are taken into account, is much larger.

If the increase in money leads to an increase in *Y'^e* and a decrease in *r^e*, the *IS* curve shifts to the right, leading to a ◀ larger increase in *Y*.

FOCUS
The liquidity trap, quantitative easing and the role of expectations

At the time of writing, the scope for conventional monetary policy, namely a reduction in the nominal short-term interest rate, has simply disappeared. Since the end of 2008, the nominal short-interest rate is close to zero, and many OECD economies, including the USA, the UK and most other European economies have been in a liquidity trap. This has led many central banks to explore unconventional policies. These come by the name of 'quantitative easing', or 'credit easing'. (We will talk extensively about them in Chapter 19.) Here we look at the role of expectations in such unconventional policies.

First, the semantics: economists typically refer to **quantitative easing** to denote operations in which, while at the zero interest rate bound, the central bank continues to increase the money supply through open market operations, either by buying more T-bills or by buying longer maturity government bonds. The purpose of quantitative easing is to increase the money supply. Economists refer to 'credit easing' to operations where the central bank buys a specific type of asset: for example, mortgage-based securities, or even stocks. The focus is then not so much on the increase in the money supply but on the effects on the price or the interest rate on the specific asset being bought.

Why should such operations have any effect? After all, an increase in the money supply had no effect on the short-term nominal interest rate. As both bonds and money paid the same nominal interest rate, namely zero, people willingly held more money and fewer bonds in response to an open market operation, leaving the nominal interest rate unchanged and equal to zero. As we saw (late in Chapter 16), so long as expectations of future interest rates were unchanged, arbitrage between short- and long-term bonds implied that interest rates on longer-term bonds, also would not change. Nor would stock prices or other asset prices.

This simple argument is the reason many economists are sceptical that these unconventional policies can do much to increase spending and output. But, you can see that there is a number of qualifiers in the previous paragraph. If some of the assumptions we stated there are not correct, these policies may have an effect. Economists have identified three channels through which quantitative or credit easing may affect the economy:

- Arbitrage may not hold. Investors may, for example, think that an asset is so risky that they do not want to hold it at all. Or, and this happened during the crisis, investors may be short of funds and may have to sell

the asset, even if they wanted to keep it. This is known as a case of **fire sales**. In this case, by doing credit easing, i.e. by buying the asset, the central bank can replace these investors, increase the price of the asset and decrease the associated interest rate. Or, to take another example, if banks, for the reasons we will explain later (in Chapter 19), suddenly lose some of their funding and are forced to ration loans and turn down some borrowers, the central bank may be able to finance some of the borrowers. In short, when arbitrage fails, credit easing can work.

- Quantitative easing may affect expectations of future nominal interest rates. As this chapter makes clear, given inflation expectations, what matters is not so much the current nominal interest rate but future nominal interest rates. If the increase in the money supply is taken as a signal by markets that the central bank will continue to follow a very expansionary monetary policy in the future, and thus keep nominal interest rates low for a long time, this will increase spending today.

- Quantitative easing may affect expectations of inflation. In the strange world of the liquidity trap, higher expected inflation is good, as it leads to lower current and future expected real interest rates. Thus, if the large increase in the money supply leads people to expect more inflation in the future, this will also increase spending today.

None of these channels is a sure thing. The first is more likely to work during the acute phase of the crisis, when perceptions of risk are high, and some investors have to sell assets in a hurry. The other two work through expectations and are far from mechanical. If expectations of either future nominal interest rates or of inflation do not move, easing will have no effect on spending and, in turn, no effect on output.

What does the evidence suggest? To answer this, we can look at what has happened in the UK. Once the room for conventional monetary policy was exhausted, the Bank of England decided to use both credit and quantitative easing. In March 2009 it started to buy assets from the private sector. These assets were loans that banks had made to firms, or bonds that had been issued by firms and bought by banks or other investors. The Bank of England stated that the purpose of these purchases was to ease conditions in corporate credit markets and, ultimately, to raise nominal demand, precisely as we have seen in the previous section. By September 2009, these assets accounted for almost all assets held by the Bank of England (Figure 18.5). Because the value of a central bank's assets is equal to the value of its liabilities (namely money), assets bought by banks amounted to almost the entire UK money supply.

At the time of writing, we know that policy intervention did work to avoid a depression. Although one cannot attribute the turnaround observed in the summer of 2009 only to monetary and fiscal policy, the effects of the financial shock seem to have been serious but limited in time.

This is particularly striking if we compare the 2007–2010 crisis with what happened in the 1930s. Figure 18.6 compares the paths of industrial production in the 2007–2010 crisis with what happened after 1929. (We show industrial production, a very imperfect measure of output – industrial production accounts for 15–20% of total output in advanced economies – because this is the only measure of output available for the 1930s.) While output did fall, what happened is nothing like what happened after the financial crisis of 1929.

Figure 18.5

Quantitative easing in the UK

Loans to APF are the loans the Bank of England made to the legal entity (the Asset Purchase Facility) in charge of buying assets from the market on behalf of the Bank.

Source: Bank of England.

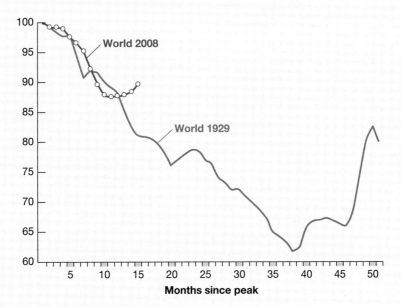

Figure 18.6

The 1930s and the 2007–2010 crisis: world industrial production

Source: Barry Eichengreen and K. H. O'Rourke, *A Tale of Two Depressions*, Voxeu.org, September 2009.

This is why macroeconomists working on monetary policy often argue that the ➤ task of a central bank is not only to adjust the short-term nominal interest rate, but also to 'manage expectations', so as to lead to predictable effects of changes in this interest rate on the economy. (More on this in Chapter 23.)

You have just learned an important lesson. The effects of monetary policy – the effects of any type of macroeconomic policy for that matter – depend crucially on its effect on expectations:

● If a monetary expansion leads financial investors, firms and consumers to revise their expectations of future interest rates and output, then the effects of the monetary expansion on output may be very large.
● But if expectations remain unchanged, the effects of the monetary expansion on output will be small.

The role of expectations is even more central in a case we have left aside, namely the case where the economy is in the liquidity trap, and the short-term rate is already equal to zero. The discussion of how monetary policy may still work in this case is taken up in the Focus box, 'The liquidity trap, quantitative easing and the role of expectations'.

We can link our discussion to our earlier discussion (in Chapter 16), about the effects of changes in monetary policy on the stock market. Many of the same issues were present there. If, when the change in monetary policy takes place, it comes as no surprise to investors, firms and consumers, then expectations will not change. The stock market will react only a little, if at all. And demand and output will change only a little, if at all. But, if the change comes as a surprise and is expected to last, expectations of future output will go up, expectations of future interest rates will come down, the stock market will boom and output will increase.

At this stage, you may have become very sceptical that macroeconomists can say much about the effects of policy or the effects of other shocks: if the effects depend so much on what happens to expectations, can macroeconomists have any hope of predicting what will happen? The answer is yes.

Saying that the effect of a particular policy depends on its effect on expectations is not the same as saying that anything can happen. Expectations are not arbitrary. The manager of a mutual fund who must decide whether to invest in stocks or bonds, the firm thinking

FOCUS
Rational expectations

Most macroeconomists today routinely solve their models under the assumption of rational expectations. This was not always the case. The past 40 years in macroeconomic research are often called the 'rational expectations' revolution.

The importance of expectations is an old theme in macroeconomics. But until the early 1970s, macroeconomists thought of expectations in one of two ways:

● One was as **animal spirits** (from an expression Keynes introduced in the *General Theory* to refer to movements in investment that could not be explained by movements in current variables). In other words, shifts in expectations were considered important but were left unexplained.
● The other was as the result of simple, backward-looking rules. For example, people were often assumed to have static expectations, that is, to expect the future to be like the present (we used this assumption when discussing the Phillips curve in Chapter 10, and when

exploring investment decisions in Chapter 17). Or people were assumed to have **adaptive expectations**: if, for example, their forecast of a given variable in a given period turned out to be too low, people were assumed to 'adapt' by raising their expectation for the value of the variable for the following period. For example, seeing an inflation rate higher than they had expected led people to revise upward their forecast of inflation in the future.

In the early 1970s, a group of macroeconomists led by Robert Lucas (at Chicago) and Thomas Sargent argued that these assumptions did not reflect the way people form expectations. (Robert Lucas and Thomas Sargent received the Nobel Prize in 1995 and 2011, respectively.) They argued that, in thinking about the effects of alternative policies, economists should assume that people have rational expectations, that people look into the future and do the best job they can in predicting it. This is not the same as assuming that people know the about whether or not to build a new plant, the consumer thinking about how much she should save for retirement, all give a lot of thought to what might happen in the future. We can think of each of them as forming expectations about the future by assessing the likely course of future expected policy and then working out the implications for future activity. If they do not do it themselves (surely most of us do not spend our time solving macroeconomic models before making decisions), they do so indirectly by watching TV and reading newsletters and newspapers, which in turn rely on the forecasts of public and private forecasters. Economists refer to expectations formed in this forward-looking manner as **rational expectations**. The introduction of the assumption of rational expectations is one of the important developments in macroeconomics in the past 35 years. It has largely shaped the way macroeconomists think about policy. It is discussed further in the Focus box 'Rational expectations'.

We could go back and think about the implications of rational expectations in the case of a monetary expansion we have just studied. It will be more fun to do this in the context of a change in fiscal policy, and this is what we now turn to.

18.3 DEFICIT REDUCTION, EXPECTATIONS AND OUTPUT

Recall the conclusions we reached in the core section about the effects of a budget deficit reduction:

- In the long run, a reduction in the budget deficit is good for the economy. In the medium run, a lower budget deficit implies higher saving and higher investment. In the long run, higher investment translates into higher capital and thus higher output.
- In the short run, however, a reduction in the budget deficit, unless it is offset by a monetary expansion, leads to lower spending and to a contraction in output.

> We discussed the short- and medium-run effects of changes in fiscal policy in section 9.5. We discussed the long-run effects of changes in fiscal policy in section 14.2.

future, but rather that they use the information they have in the best possible way.

Using the popular macroeconomic models of the time, Lucas and Sargent showed how replacing traditional assumptions about expectations formation by the assumption of rational expectations could fundamentally alter the results. We saw earlier (for example, in Chapter 11) how Lucas challenged the notion that disinflation necessarily required an increase in unemployment for some time. Under rational expectations, he argued, a credible disinflation policy might be able to decrease inflation without any increase in unemployment. More generally, Lucas and Sargent's research showed the need for a complete rethinking of macroeconomic models under the assumption of rational expectations, and this is what happened over the next two decades.

Most macroeconomists today use rational expectations as a working assumption in their models and analyses of policy. This is not because they believe that people always have rational expectations. Surely there are times when people, firms or financial market participants lose sight of reality and become too optimistic or too pessimistic. (Recall our discussion of bubbles and fads in Chapter 16.) But these are more the exception than the rule, and it is

not clear that economists can say much about those times anyway. When thinking about the likely effects of a particular economic policy, the best assumption to make seems to be that financial markets, people and firms will do the best they can to work out its implications. Designing a policy on the assumption that people will make systematic mistakes in responding to it is unwise.

Why did it take until the 1970s for rational expectations to become a standard assumption in macroeconomics? Largely because of technical problems. Under rational expectations, what happens today depends on expectations of what will happen in the future. But what happens in the future also depends on what happens today. Solving such models is hard. The success of Lucas and Sargent in convincing most macroeconomists to use rational expectations comes not only from the strength of their case, but also from showing how it could actually be done. Much progress has been made since in developing solution methods for larger and larger models. Today, a number of large macroeconometric models are solved under the assumption of rational expectations. (The simulation of the Taylor model presented in the Focus box on monetary policy in Chapter 9 was derived under rational expectations.)

It is this adverse short-run effect which – in addition to the unpopularity of increases in taxes or reductions in government programs in the first place – often deters governments from tackling their budget deficits: why take the risk of a recession now for benefits that will accrue only in the future?

In the recent past, however, a number of economists have argued that, under some conditions, a deficit reduction might actually increase output even in the short run. Their argument: if people take into account the future beneficial effects of deficit reduction, their expectations about the future might improve enough so as to lead to an increase – rather than a decrease – in current spending, thereby increasing current output. This section explores their argument. The Focus box 'Can a budget deficit reduction lead to an output expansion? Ireland in the 1980s' reviews some of the supporting evidence.

Assume the economy is described by equation (18.4) for the *IS* relation and equation (18.5) for the *LM* relation. Now suppose the government announces a programme to reduce the deficit, through decreases both in current spending, G, and in future spending, G'^e. What will happen to output this period?

The role of expectations about the future

Suppose first that expectations of future output (Y'^e) and of the future interest rate (r'^e) do not change. Then, we get the standard answer: the decrease in government spending in the current period leads to a shift of the *IS* curve to the left and so to a decrease in output.

The crucial question therefore is what happens to expectations. To answer this, let us go back to what we learned in the core section about the effects of a deficit reduction in the medium run and the long run:

- In the medium run, a deficit reduction has no effect on output. It leads, however, to a lower interest rate and to higher investment. (These were two of the main lessons of Chapter 9.) Let's review the logic behind each.

    Recall that, when we look at the medium run, we ignore the effects of capital accumulation on output. So, in the medium run, the natural level of output depends on the level of productivity (taken as given) and on the natural level of employment. The natural level of employment depends in turn on the natural rate of unemployment. If spending by the government on goods and services does not affect the natural rate of unemployment – and there is no obvious reason why it should – then changes in spending will not affect the natural level of output. Therefore, a deficit reduction has no effect on the level of output in the medium run.

    > In the medium run: output, *Y*, does not change, and investment, *I*, is higher. ➤

    Now recall that output must be equal to spending, and that spending is the sum of public spending and private spending. Given that output is unchanged and that public spending is lower, private spending must therefore be higher. Higher private spending requires a lower equilibrium interest rate: the lower interest rate leads to higher investment, and thus to higher private spending, which offsets the decrease in public spending and leaves output unchanged.

- In the long run – that is, taking into account the effects of capital accumulation on output – higher investment leads to a higher capital stock, and, therefore, a higher level of output.

    > In the long run: *I* increases
    > ⇒ *K* increases
    > ⇒ *Y* increases.

    (This was the main lesson of Chapter 14.) The higher the proportion of output saved (or invested; investment and saving must be equal for the goods market to be in equilibrium in a closed economy), the higher the capital stock, and thus the higher the level of output in the long run.

> The way this is likely to happen: forecasts by economists will show that these lower deficits are likely to lead to higher output and lower interest rates in the future. In response to these forecasts, long-term interest rates will decrease and the stock market will increase. People and firms, reading these forecasts and looking at bond and stock prices, will revise their spending plans and increase spending. ➤

We can think of our future period as including both the medium and the long run. If people, firms and financial market participants have rational expectations, then, in response to the announcement of a deficit reduction, they will expect these developments to take place in the future. Thus, they will revise their expectation of future output, Y'^e, up, and their expectation of the future interest rate, r'^e, down.

Back to the current period

We can now return to the question of what happens this period in response to the announcement and start of the deficit reduction programme. Figure 18.7 draws the *IS* and *LM* curves for the current period. In response to the announcement of the deficit reduction, there are now three factors shifting the *IS* curve:

- Current government spending, *G*, goes down, leading the *IS* curve to shift to the left. At a given interest rate, the decrease in government spending leads to a decrease in total spending and to a decrease in output. This is the standard effect of a reduction in government spending, and the only one taken into account in the basic *IS–LM* model.
- Expected future output, Y'^e, goes up, leading the *IS* curve to shift to the right. At a given interest rate, the increase in expected future output leads to an increase in private spending, increasing output.
- The expected future interest rate goes down, leading the *IS* curve to shift to the right. At a given current interest rate, a decrease in the future interest rate stimulates spending and increases output.

What is the net effect of these three shifts in the *IS* curve? Can the effect of expectations on consumption and investment spending offset the decrease in government spending? Without much more information about the exact form of the *IS* and *LM* relations and about the details of the deficit reduction programme, we cannot tell which shifts will dominate and whether output will go up or down. But our analysis tells us that both cases are possible – that output may go up in response to the deficit reduction. And it gives us a few hints as to when this might happen:

- Note that the smaller the decrease in current government spending, *G*, the smaller the adverse effect on spending today. Note also that the larger the decrease in expected future government spending, G'^e, the larger the effect on expected future output and interest rates, thus the larger the favourable effect on spending today. This suggests that **backloading** the deficit reduction programme towards the future, with small cuts today and larger cuts in the future is more likely to lead to an increase in output.
- On the other hand, backloading raises other issues. Announcing the need for painful cuts in spending, and then leaving them to the future, is likely to decrease the programme's **credibility** – the perceived probability that the government will do what it has promised when the time comes to do it.
- The government must play a delicate balancing act: enough cuts in the current period to show a commitment to deficit reduction; enough cuts left to the future to reduce the adverse effects on the economy in the short run.

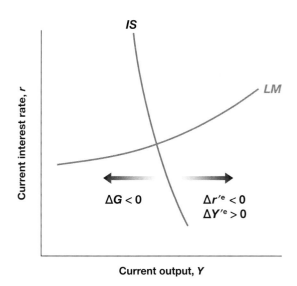

Figure 18.7

The effects of a deficit reduction on current output

When account is taken of its effect on expectations, the decrease in government spending need not lead to a decrease in output.

FOCUS
Can a budget deficit reduction lead to an output expansion?
Ireland in the 1980s

Ireland went through two major deficit reduction programs in the 1980s:

1. The first programme was started in 1982. In 1981, the budget deficit had reached a very high 13.0% of GDP. Government debt, the result of the accumulation of current and past deficits, was 77% of GDP, also a very high level. The Irish government clearly had to regain control of its finances. Over the next three years, it embarked on a programme of deficit reduction, based mostly on tax increases. This was an ambitious programme: had output continued to grow at its normal growth rate, the programme would have reduced the deficit by 5% of GDP.

   The results, however, were dismal. As shown in row 2 of Table 18.1, output growth was low in 1982 and negative in 1983. Low output growth was associated with a major increase in unemployment, from 9.5% in 1981 to 15% in 1984 (row 3). Because of low output growth, tax revenues – which depend on the level of economic activity – were lower than anticipated.

The actual deficit reduction, shown in row 1, was only of 3.5% of GDP. And the result of continuing high deficits and low GDP growth was a further increase in the ratio of debt to GDP to 97% in 1984.

2. A second attempt to reduce budget deficits was made starting in February 1987. At the time, things were still very bad. The 1986 deficit was 10.7% of GDP; debt stood at 116% of GDP, a record high in Europe at the time. This new programme of deficit reduction was different from the first. It was focused more on reducing the role of government and cutting government spending than on increasing taxes. The tax increases in the programme were achieved through a tax reform widening the tax base – increasing the number of households paying taxes – rather than through an increase in the marginal tax rate. The programme was again very ambitious: had output grown at its normal rate, the reduction in the deficit would have been 6.4% of GDP.

   The results of the second programme could not have been more different from the results of the first. The

Table 18.1 Fiscal and other macroeconomic indicators, Ireland, 1981–1984 and 1986–1989

	1981	1982	1983	1984	1986	1987	1988	1989
1 Budget deficit (% of GDP)	−13.0	−13.4	−11.4	−9.5	−10.7	−8.6	−4.5	−1.8
2 Output growth rate (%)	3.3	2.3	−0.2	4.4	−0.4	4.7	5.2	5.8
3 Unemployment rate (%)	9.5	11.0	13.5	15.0	17.1	16.9	16.3	15.1
4 Household saving rate (% of disposable income)	17.9	19.6	18.1	18.4	15.7	12.9	11.0	12.6

Source: OECD *Economic Outlook* database, June 1998.

More generally, our analysis suggests that anything in a deficit reduction programme that improves expectations of how the future will look is likely to make the short-run effects of deficit reduction less painful. Let us give two examples:

● Measures which are perceived by firms and financial markets as reducing some of the distortions in the economy may improve expectations and make it more likely that output increases in the short run. Take, for example, unemployment benefits. You saw earlier (in Chapter 8) that lower unemployment benefits lead to a decline in the natural rate of unemployment, resulting in a higher natural level of output. So, a reform of the social insurance system, which includes a reduction in the generosity of unemployment benefits, is likely to have two effects on spending and thus on output in the short run:
  ● One is an adverse effect on the consumption of the unemployed: lower unemployment benefits will reduce their income and their consumption.
  ● The other is a positive effect on spending through expectations: the anticipation of higher output in the future may lead to both higher consumption and higher investment.
  If the second effect dominates, the outcome might be an increase in overall spending, increasing output not only in the medium run but also in the short run. (An important

period 1987–1989 were years of strong growth, with average GDP growth exceeding 5%. The unemployment rate was reduced by 2%. Because of strong output growth, tax revenues were higher than anticipated, and the deficit was reduced by nearly 9% of GDP.

A number of economists have argued that the striking difference between the results of the two programs can be traced to the different reaction of expectations in each case. The first programme, they argue, focused on tax increases and did not change what many people saw as too large a role of government in the economy. The second programme, with its focus on cuts in spending and on tax reform, had a much more positive impact on expectations, and, therefore, a positive impact on spending and output.

Are these economists right? One variable, the household saving rate – defined as disposable income minus consumption, divided by disposable income – strongly suggests that expectations are an important part of the story. To interpret the behaviour of the saving rate, recall the lessons from earlier (see Chapter 17) about consumption behaviour. When disposable income grows unusually slowly or goes down – as it does in a recession – consumption typically slows down or declines by less than disposable income because people expect things to improve in the future. Put another way, when the growth of disposable income is unusually low, the saving rate typically comes down. Now look (in row 4) at what happened from 1981 to 1984: despite low growth throughout the period and a recession in 1983, the household saving rate actually increased slightly during that period. Put another way, people reduced their consumption by more than the reduction in their disposable income. The reason must be that they were very pessimistic about the future.

Now turn to the period 1986–1989. During that period, economic growth was unusually strong. By the same argument as in the previous paragraph, we would have expected consumption to increase less strongly, and thus the saving rate to increase. Instead, the saving rate dropped sharply, from 15.7% in 1986 to 12.6% in 1989. Consumers must have become much more optimistic about the future to increase their consumption by more than the increase in their disposable income.

The next question is whether this difference in the adjustment of expectations over the two episodes can be attributed fully to the differences in the two fiscal programs. The answer is surely no. Ireland was changing in many ways at the time of the second fiscal programme. Productivity was increasing much faster than real wages, reducing the cost of labour for firms. Attracted by tax breaks, low labour costs and an educated labour force, many foreign firms were relocating to Ireland and building new plants: these factors played a major role in the expansion of the late 1980s. Irish growth has been very strong ever since, with average output growth exceeding 6% since 1990. Surely, this long expansion is due to many factors. Nevertheless, the change in fiscal policy in 1987 probably played an important role in convincing people, firms – including foreign firms – and financial markets, that the government was regaining control of its finances. And the fact remains that the substantial deficit reduction of 1987–1989 was accompanied by a strong output expansion, not by the recession predicted by the basic *IS–LM* model.

Note: For a more detailed discussion, look at Francesco Giavazzi and Marco Pagano, 'Can severe fiscal contractions be expansionary? Tales of two small European countries', *NBER Macroeconomics Annual*, 1990, 75–110.

For a more systematic look at whether and when fiscal consolidations have been expansionary (and a mostly negative answer), see 'Will it hurt? Macroeconomic effects of fiscal consolidation', Chapter 3, *World Economic Outlook,* October 2010, 93–124.

caveat: even if a reduction in unemployment benefits increases output, this surely does not imply that unemployment benefits should be eliminated. Even if aggregate income goes up, we must worry about the effects on the distribution of income: the consumption of the unemployed goes down, and the pain associated with being unemployed goes up.)

- Or take an economy where the government has, in effect, lost control of its budget: government spending is high, tax revenues are low and the deficit is very large. In such an environment, a credible deficit reduction programme is also more likely to increase output in the short run. Before the announcement of the programme, people may have expected major political and economic trouble in the future. The announcement of a programme of deficit reduction may well reassure them that the government has regained control, and that the future is less bleak than they anticipated. This decrease in pessimism about the future may lead to an increase in spending and output, even if taxes are increased as part of the deficit reduction programme.

Let's summarise: a programme of deficit reduction may increase output even in the short run. Whether it does or does not depends on many factors, in particular:

- The credibility of the programme: will spending be cut or taxes increased in the future as announced?
- The timing of the programme: how large are spending cuts in the future relative to current spending cuts?
- The composition of the programme: does the programme remove some of the distortions in the economy?
- The state of government finances in the first place: how large is the initial deficit? Is this a 'last chance' programme? What will happen if it fails?

Note how far we have moved from the ➤ results earlier (see Chapter 3), where, by choosing spending and taxes wisely, the government could achieve any level of output it wanted. Here, even the direction of the effect of a deficit reduction on output is ambiguous.

More on current fiscal policy issues in ➤ Chapter 24.

This gives you a sense of both the importance of expectations in determining the outcome and of the complexities involved in the use of fiscal policy in such a context. And it is far more than an illustrative example. At the time of writing, it is at the centre of macroeconomic policy discussions As we have seen, the crisis has led to large increases in government debt and large budget deficits throughout advanced countries. Nearly all governments must now embark on a path of fiscal consolidation – of budget deficit reduction. The rate at which they should proceed, and whether they can hope that fiscal consolidation, if done right, will be expansionary rather than contractionary, are crucial issues. The analysis we have just gone through suggests the following conclusions.

- There should be a clear, politically credible plan for how fiscal consolidation will be carried out. The more credible the plan, the more people are convinced that fiscal consolidation will be effectively carried out in the medium and long term, the smaller the need for fiscal consolidation today, and thus the smaller the direct adverse effects of deficit reduction today.

At the time of writing, the interest rate on Italian and Spanish government debts are around 7%, nearly 6% higher than the interest rate on German government debt, which is considered safe.   ➤

- In most cases, governments should not expect miracles, and fiscal consolidation is likely to lead to lower growth in the short run. In a few cases, however, where financial markets are very worried about the fiscal situation – and where, as a result, the interest rate on government debt is already very high, such as in Italy and Spain – it may be that the decrease in the interest rate which would follow from a credible fiscal consolidation may offset the adverse direct effects.

SUMMARY

- Spending in the goods market depends on current and expected future output and on current and expected future real interest rates.

- Expectations affect demand and, in turn, affect output: changes in expected future output or in the expected future real interest rate lead to changes in spending and in output today.

- By implication, the effects of fiscal and monetary policy on spending and output depend on how the policy affects expectations of future output and real interest rates.

- Rational expectations is the assumption that people, firms, and participants in financial markets form expectations of the future by assessing the course of future expected policy and then working out the implications for future output, future interest rates and so on. Although it is clear that most people do not go through this exercise themselves, we can think of them as doing so indirectly by relying on the predictions of public and private forecasters.

- Although there are surely cases in which people, firms or financial investors do not have rational expectations, the assumption of rational expectations seems to be the best benchmark to evaluate the potential effects of alternative policies. Designing a policy on the assumption that people will make systematic mistakes in responding to it would be unwise.

- Changes in the money supply affect the short-term nominal interest rate. Spending, however, depends instead on current and expected future real interest rates. Thus, the effect of monetary policy on activity depends crucially on whether and how changes in the short-term nominal interest rate lead to changes in current and expected future real interest rates.

- A budget deficit reduction may lead to an increase rather than a decrease in output. This is because expectations of higher output and lower interest rates in the future may lead to an increase in spending which more than offsets the reduction in spending coming from the direct effect of the deficit reduction on total spending.

KEY TERMS

aggregate private spending, or private spending 407

quantitative easing 412

fire sales 412

adaptive expectations 414

animal spirits 414

rational expectations 415

backloading 417

credibility 417

QUESTIONS AND PROBLEMS

QUICK CHECK

1. *Using the information in this chapter, label each of the following statements true, false or uncertain. Explain briefly.*

a. Changes in the current one-year real interest rate are likely to have a much larger effect on spending than changes in expected future one-year real interest rates.

b. The introduction of expectations in the goods market model makes the *IS* curve flatter, although it is still downward sloping.

c. Current money demand depends on current and expected future nominal interest rates.

d. The rational expectations assumption implies that consumers take into account the effects of future fiscal policy on output.

e. Expected future fiscal policy affects expected future economic activity but not current economic activity.

f. Depending on its effect on expectations, a fiscal contraction may actually lead to an economic expansion.

g. Ireland's experience with deficit reduction programmes in 1982 and 1987 provides strong evidence against the hypothesis that deficit reduction can lead to an output expansion.

2. *During the late 1990s, many observers claimed that the USA had transformed into a New Economy, and this justified the very high values for stock prices observed at the time.*

a. Discuss how the belief in the New Economy, combined with the increase in stock prices, affected consumption spending.

b. Stock prices subsequently decreased. Discuss how this might have affected consumption.

3. *For each of the changes in expectations in (a)–(d), determine whether there is a shift in the IS curve, the LM curve, both curves or neither. In each case, assume that expected current and future inflation are equal to zero and that no other exogenous variable is changing.*

a. A decrease in the expected future real interest rate.

b. An increase in the current money supply.

c. An increase in expected future taxes.

d. A decrease in expected future income.

4. *Consider the following statement.*

'The rational expectations assumption is unrealistic because, essentially, it amounts to the assumption that every consumer has perfect knowledge of the economy.'

Discuss.

5. *A new head of state, who promised during the campaign that she would cut taxes, has just been elected. People trust that she will keep her promise, but expect that the tax cuts will be implemented only in the future. Determine the impact of the election on current output, the current interest rate, and current private spending under each of the assumptions in (a)–(c). In each case, indicate what you think will happen to Y'^e, r'^e and T'^e, and then how these changes in expectations affect output today.*

a. The central bank will not change its policy.

b. The central bank will act to prevent any change in future output.

c. The central bank will act to prevent any change in the future interest rate.

DIG DEEPER

6. The Clinton deficit reduction package

In 1992, the US deficit was $290 billion. During the presidential campaign, the large deficit emerged as a major issue. When President Clinton won the election, deficit reduction was the first item on the new administration's agenda.

a. What does deficit reduction imply for the medium run and the long run? What are the advantages of reducing the deficit?

In the final version passed by Congress in August 1993, the deficit reduction package included a reduction of $20 billion in its first year, increasing gradually to $131 billion four years later.

b. Why was the deficit reduction package back loaded? What are the advantages and disadvantages of this approach to deficit reduction?

In February 1993, President Clinton presented the budget in his State of the Union address. He asked Alan Greenspan, the Fed chairman, to sit next to First Lady Hillary Clinton during the delivery of the address.

c. What was the purpose of this symbolic gesture? How can the Fed's decision to use expansionary monetary policy in the future affect the short-run response of the economy?

7. A new central bank chairman

Suppose, in a hypothetical economy, that the chairman of the central bank unexpectedly announces that he will retire in one year. At the same time, the head of state announces her nominee to replace the retiring central bank chair. Financial market participants expect the nominee to be confirmed by the government. They also believe that the nominee will conduct a more contractionary monetary policy in the future. In other words, market participants expect the money supply to fall in the future.

a. Consider the present to be the last year of the current central bank chair's term and the future to be the time after that. Given that monetary policy will be more contractionary in the future, what will happen to future interest rates and future output (at least for a while, before output returns to potential GDP)? Given that these changes in future output and future interest rates are predicted, what will happen to output and the interest rate in the present? What will happen to the yield curve on the day of the announcement that the current central bank chair will retire in a year?

Now suppose that instead of making an unexpected announcement, the central bank chair is required by law to retire in one year (there are limits on the term of the central bank chair), and financial market participants have been aware of this for some time. Suppose, as in part (a), that the head of state nominates a replacement who is expected to conduct a more contractionary monetary policy than the current central bank chair.

b. Suppose financial market participants are not surprised by the choice of the head of state. In other words, market participants had correctly predicted who the president would choose as nominee. Under these circumstances, is the announcement of the nominee likely to have any effect on the yield curve?

c. Suppose instead that the identity of the nominee is a surprise and that financial market participants had expected the nominee to be someone who favoured an even more contractionary policy than the actual nominee. Under these circumstances, what is likely to happen to the yield curve on the day of the announcement? (*Hint*: be careful. Compared to what was expected, is the actual nominee expected to follow a more contractionary or more expansionary policy?)

d. On 24 October 2005, Ben Bernanke was nominated to succeed Alan Greenspan as chairman of the Federal Reserve. Do an Internet search and try to learn what happened in financial markets on the day the nomination was announced. Were financial market participants surprised by the choice? If so, was Bernanke believed to favour policies that would lead to higher or lower interest rates (as compared to the expected nominee) over the next three to five years? (You may also do a yield curve analysis of the kind described in problem 8 for the period around Bernanke's nomination. If you do this, use one-year and five-year interest rates.)

EXPLORE FURTHER

8. Deficits and interest rates

The dramatic increase in the German budget position after 1990 (from a surplus to a large and continuing deficit) has reinvigorated the debate about the effect of fiscal policy on interest rates. This problem asks you to review theory and evidence on this topic.

a. Review what theory predicts about fiscal policy and interest rates. Suppose there is an increase in government spending and a decrease in taxes. Use an *IS–LM* diagram to show what will happen to the nominal interest rate in the short run and the medium run. Assuming that there is no change in monetary policy, what does the *IS–LM* model predict will happen to the yield curve immediately after an increase in government spending and a decrease in taxes?

In the Winter of 1989–1990, following German Reunification, the need to assist residents in the former DDR – thus avoiding mass migration to the West – resulted in a sharp increase in actual and projected federal budget deficits. From a balanced budget in 1989, the deficit was project to increase to 2% of GDP in 1990 and 1991. In the Spring of 1990 these forecasts were revised and the projection for the deficit in 1991 went from 2% to 3% of GDP.

b. Go to the website of the Bundesbank (***www.bundesbank.de***) and find the section on 'Statistics'. Go to 'List all Series' and choose 'Interest Rates'. Download the yields on federal securities with annual residual maturity of one and ten years. Get the end-of-month data from 1989 to 1991.

c. For each month, subtract the one-year yield from the ten-year yield yield to obtain the interest rate spread. What happened to the interest rate spread as the budget picture worsened over the sample period? Is this result consistent with your answer to part (a)?

*Log on to **MyEconLab** and complete the studyplan exercises for this chapter to see how much you have learnt, and where you need to revise most.*

MyEconLab

EUROPE: PAST, PRESENT AND FUTURE

Since 1957, when six European countries (Belgium, the Federal Republic of Germany, France, Italy, Luxembourg and the Netherlands) decided to build a European Economic Community (EEC) based on a common market covering a whole range of goods and services, European economic integration has gone a long way further. It now includes 27 countries and the name has changed to European Union (EU); 17 among them have also formed a monetary union and share the same currency, the euro.

Chapter 19 The euro at fourteen: was it a good idea and why is it in trouble?

Chapter 19 describes the monetary history of Europe in the post-war period and explains how it was that it got to the euro. After 14 years of life, today the new currency has ended up in big trouble. We shall argue that the seeds of these troubles were planted long before the start of the recession which hit the world in 2008. We discuss the economic reasons for a monetary union and whether the euro area meets them, i.e. whether it is an optimal currency area. Then we describe the European Central Bank (ECB), and its performance up to the crisis. We close the chapter asking whether the EU countries that decided to stay out of the monetary union (Denmark, Sweden and the UK) did the right thing.

Chapter 20 The crisis

Chapter 20 is dedicated to the major macroeconomic event of the past 65 years – the years following the Second World War – the recession which started in 2008, and has been labelled The Great Recession, since it is by far the worst economic downturn since the Great Depression of the 1930s. We have briefly discussed the origin of the crisis in Chapter 1. This chapter takes off from there, analyses the triggers of the crisis and explains how a banking problem turned into a macroeconomic disaster. We also discuss the effects on Europe and on the countries which belong to the European monetary union in particular.

Chapter 21 High debt

When the crisis is over, its legacy will be high levels of government debt almost everywhere – something similar to what happens after a war. Chapter 21 looks at the problem of high government debt. Although, in principle, a high government deficit is neither good nor evil, government deficits can become a problem if they lead to the rapid accumulation of debt. This chapter gives you the tools to analyse whether government debt has become too high and to understand how a country can deal with its debt. It also discusses some notable episodes of debt reduction.

Chapter 19

THE EURO AT FOURTEEN: WAS IT A GOOD IDEA AND WHY IS IT IN TROUBLE?

On 1 January 1999, 12 countries of the European Union abandoned their national currencies to use a common currency, the euro. Up to 1 January 2002 the old national currencies continued to circulate, although linked by fixed exchange rates. Thereafter the euro replaced national currencies, which were quickly withdrawn from circulation. The birth of the euro is the most significant currency phenomenon that has happened in Europe in the post-war period, with important consequences for the future of European citizens.

The chapter consists of five sections:

● Section 19.1 reviews the monetary history of Europe, from the early experiments with the system of fixed exchange rates to the European Monetary System (EMS), until the signing of the Maastricht Treaty in 1991, when European countries formally decided to adopt a common currency.

● Section 19.2 discusses the economic reasons to form a monetary union and whether the euro area meets them, i.e. whether the countries that have adopted the euro form an optimal currency area.

● Section 19.3 describes the ECB – the common central bank of the countries that have adopted the euro – its institutional structure, goals and strategies.

● Section 19.4 reviews the first 13 years (1999–2011) of the euro, which has become the second most important world currency. Today the new currency is in big trouble. We shall argue that the seeds of these troubles were planted long before the start of the recession which hit the world in 2008.

● Section 19.5 asks why some European countries decided to opt out of the single currency, and whether the recent financial and economic turmoil has altered the incentives to adopt the euro.

19.1 THE MONETARY HISTORY OF EUROPE FROM POST-WAR TO THE PRESENT DAY

It is difficult to understand the process that led to the creation of the **European Economic and Monetary Union (EMU)** without understanding why Europeans have always tried to limit fluctuations between their currencies. In fact, the decision to adopt a common currency represents the ultimate attempt to fix exchange rates between European countries.

There are three reasons why Europeans have always been so concerned about the volatility of exchange rates between their currencies – more worried than, for example, the Americans or the Japanese:

- First, they live in very open economies, much more open compared to large non-European countries like Japan or the USA. Table 19.1 shows the '**degree of openness**' – measured as the sum of exports plus imports over total income – of European economies. It is around 50% in larger countries like France, Spain, Italy and the UK (slightly higher in Germany) and much higher, even higher than 100%, in small countries like Belgium, Luxembourg and the Netherlands.

  As we saw earlier (in Chapter 9), the higher the share of exports or imports in total income, the greater the effect, on the same income, of a change in the exchange rate. Therefore, exchange rate volatility among European currencies has a big impact on the national income of European countries. Considering that most European countries trade mainly with each other, and less with countries outside of Europe, when Europeans say they are concerned about fluctuations in exchange rates, their concern is primarily with exchange rate fluctuations within Europe.

  ◀ A degree of openness greater than 100% happens if, for instance, both exports and imports account for more than one-half of total income.

- Second, Europeans believe that the wide **exchange rate fluctuations** in Europe in the 1920s and 1930s contributed decisively to the crisis of national economies in the period between the wars. The attempts of some countries to increase their competitiveness to exit the Great Recession through currency devaluation prompted others to do the same and also to retaliate by defending their products with tariffs and duties. Eventually such **competitive devaluation** were ineffective and led to higher inflation everywhere and to the collapse of free trade, both of which are considered in no small measure responsible for the crisis of European democracies and the emergence of authoritarian regimes in the period between the two world wars. Politicians who worked in the 1950s for the creation

  ◀ The degree of openness of an economy can be measured as the ratio of exports to GDP or the ratio of imports to GDP: when the trade balance is zero, the two measures are clearly the same. In Table 21.1 we consider a measure that takes into account the fact that trade is usually not balanced: the sum of exports and imports.

Table 19.1 The degree of openness of European economies, (exports + imports)/GDP, 2008–2010

Euro area		non-euro area	
Austria	103.7	Norway	72.6
Belgium	154.3	UK	58.8
Cyprus	104.5	Sweden	93.3
Estonia	152.0	Denmark	96.9
Finland	79.8	Poland	82.4
France	53.0	Hungary	159.0
Germany	85.3		
Greece	48.8		
Ireland	167.7	USA	27.7
Italy	53.7	Japan	30.8
Luxembourg	261.6		
Malta	165.7		
Netherlands	138.2		
Portugal	69.9		
Slovakia	155.6		
Slovenia	126.2		
Spain	54.6		

Source: WTO Trade Statistics

of the first supranational European institutions (in particular, France's Robert Schuman, Germany's Konrad Adenauer and Italy's Alcide De Gasperi) believed that one of the main tasks of the new institutions was to avoid such an outcome through the creation of a monetary system that could avoid exchange rate fluctuations within Europe.

- A final factor is the common agricultural market. For many years – from the Treaty of Rome of 1958 until the Single Act of 1985 – the common agricultural market was the only tangible activity of the EU (at that time called the EEC, the European Economic Community), but it needed stable exchange rates. The price of agricultural products was the same in all European countries and was expressed in ECU. When a currency, say the French franc, devalued against the ECU – for example, because the franc was devalued relative to all other European currencies – the price of an ECU in terms of marks or lire fell. If ECU prices of agricultural products remained unchanged, prices in francs would increase and prices in marks would decrease. At this point, it was worth buying products in France where, after the devaluation, the price expressed in marks had fallen, and selling them in Germany, where the price in marks had remained unchanged. To avoid such a situation, any variation in exchange rates within the EU was accompanied by the introduction of import duties and tariffs: that is, instruments that removed the incentive to transfer all the French wheat to Germany. But import duties and tariffs were the very negation of the common market from which it all started.

These reasons explain why European countries have, since the end of the Second World War, tried to limit exchange rate fluctuations between their currencies. This was firstly achieved within the Bretton Woods system, an international monetary agreement signed in Bretton Woods (a town in the North East of the USA) in 1947, and successively within a regional monetary arrangement, the European Monetary System (EMS). This is what we turn to in the next two sections.

From Bretton Woods to the European Monetary System

From the late 1940s and until 1971, bilateral exchange rate volatility within Europe was limited by a common peg to the dollar. During those years, the international monetary system functioned as envisaged by the **Bretton Woods** agreements. The latter, in 1945, had created the International Monetary Fund, the institution responsible for overseeing the international monetary system. In the Bretton Woods system, each currency could not deviate from the dollar by more than 0.75% (below or above), so that the fluctuation band had a width of 1.50% around a central rate. Any changes in the central rate against the dollar had to be negotiated with and authorised by the IMF. Bilateral exchange rate fluctuations between pairs of European currencies were therefore limited within a band of 3%. With few exceptions – the revaluation of the central parity for the German mark in 1961, the devaluation of the parity for the French franc in 1969 – bilateral exchange rates in Europe remained stable for a long time.

In the early 1970s, however, the Bretton Woods system collapsed. In a first phase the band around the dollar was simply enlarged; then, as from March 1973, exchange rates began to fluctuate freely. Within Europe, the mark increased rapidly vis-à-vis the dollar; the Italian lira and the French franc were also revalued, but to a lesser extent, and therefore depreciated against the mark. The end of fixed exchange rates was therefore accompanied by wide fluctuations in the relative competitiveness of European countries.

Initially, the devaluations of the Italian lira and French franc, against the mark, benefited French and Italian products to the detriment of German goods. But the advantage was short-lived: the devaluations were soon accompanied by an increase in Italian and French inflation that eroded the initial competitive advantage. Once again, as it had been the case in the 1930s, the Europeans clashed with the ineffectiveness of the exchange rate as an instrument of economic policy: in the late 1970s inflation in Italy and the UK exceeded 20%, and in France it was close to 15%.

There is a book that describes in an ➤ illuminating way why, since the 1950s, Europeans have been so worried by exchange rate fluctuations: *International Currency Experience: Lessons from the Inter-War Period*, written in 1944 by Ragnar Nurske, an Estonian economist who, during the Second World War, worked at the Economic Department of the League of Nations, the institution that preceded the United Nations.

The ECU was not a real currency, but ➤ simply a unit of account, and was used as numeraire in transactions within the EU. 1 ECU = $\Sigma \alpha_i M_i$, where $\alpha_i M_i$ are the quantities of the various currencies included in the basket: 10 Deutschmarks, 1,000 Italian lire, etc. The value of an ECU in terms of, say, Italian lire or French francs, varied whenever bilateral exchange rates between European currencies changed.

The reason for the collapse of the Bretton Woods system was, essentially, the incompatibility between economic policy goals in Germany and in the USA. The USA had to fund the Vietnam war, and to do so needed low interest rates, which ended up in higher inflation. Germany was then ➤ forced, if it wanted to save the fixed parity between the Deutschmark and the US dollar, to accept the US inflation rate. But when Germany no longer accepted a higher inflation rate than the Bundesbank target, it increased interest rates and eventually the dollar devalued.

The European Monetary System

A return to stable exchange rates was the main reason that prompted European governments to create, in 1978, the **European Monetary System (EMS)**, an exchange rate agreement that essentially reproduced a small Bretton Woods system limited to European countries and in which the mark served as an anchor, the role played by the dollar during the years of Bretton Woods. In September 1992, the EMS also collapsed for reasons similar to those which, 20 years before, had led to the end of Bretton Woods: the incompatibility between German monetary policy goals, dictated by the needs of Germany's reunification (which had happened in 1989 after the fall of the Berlin Wall), and those of other European countries. The end of the EMS was accompanied once again by wide fluctuations in exchange rates: between September 1992 and March 1995 the Italian lira was devalued against the mark by almost 50%. This experience finally convinced the Europeans that only the adoption of a single currency would eliminate exchange rate fluctuations in Europe. Six years later, on 1 January 1999, the euro was born.

As we have seen, the EMS was the European response to the end of the Bretton Woods system and the high exchange rate volatility of the 1970s. The EMS allowed a period of relatively stable exchange rates but did not eliminate devaluations. Between 1979 and 1992 there were ten devaluations: in each case, the central parity of one or more European currencies were devalued against the mark. These devaluations were necessary because inflation in Germany remained consistently lower than in the rest of Europe. While exchange rates against the mark remained fixed, countries with relatively higher inflation would gradually lose their competitiveness and their trade balances would deteriorate. A devaluation was the way to restore equilibrium in the balance of payments. Within the EMS, however, devaluations were not unilateral, but collegial decisions. The decision to change the central parity against the mark – and the amount of the devaluation – required agreement by all the countries participating in the system as with the Bretton Woods system, when a devaluation required the approval of the IMF. This collective decision-making allowed countries with high inflation to be disciplined: if a country did not reduce its inflation rate, it could be punished by delaying the devaluation of its currency and by reducing the size of the devaluation when it happened. The result was that inflation gradually declined towards the German level. Italy, for example, entered the EMS with an inflation rate above 20%, which decreased gradually to 5%.

Let us now show how the EMS worked. When a currency reached the top margin of the fluctuation band – the maximum allowable devaluation against the Deutschmark (DM) – the central bank of that country had two options: raise interest rates in order to defend the exchange rate, or ask for a realignment, i.e. a devaluation of the central parity that implied the shift of the fluctuation band downwards. Figure 19.1 shows an example for the French franc (FF). The increases in interest rates in francs above interest rates in marks signal moments of weakness of the franc. In some cases, the interest rate differential vanishes because markets are convinced that there will not be a realignment; in other cases, the gap is closed after the realignment takes place as in March 1983, when the central parity of the franc was devalued by 8% relative to the DM.

As long as there were controls on capital flows – also known as foreign exchange controls – the defence of the exchange rate was relatively inexpensive for the peripheral countries. Consider, for example, the case of Italy: the rate on lira-denominated securities held in London could remain relatively high even for long periods, without any cost for Italy; the Italian public deficit continued to be financed at much lower rates. Capital controls worked then as a hidden tax because they actually forced savers to invest at lower rates than those that they would have obtained had they been allowed to purchase securities abroad.

Controls on capital flows allowed governments to defend the exchange rate even when the market believed that this should be devalued. They did not eliminate the need, sooner or later, to devalue – as they did not eliminate the inflation differentials – but allowed governments to delay devaluations. This autonomy disappeared on the day when foreign

◀ Foreign exchange controls are limitations imposed by governments on the purchase or sale of domestic currency by foreigners and/or of foreign currency by residents.

Figure 19.1

Differential between French and German three-month interest rates in the years of the EMS

When the interest rate differential widens, as at the beginning of 1983, this means that the market expects a devaluation of the French franc. The relation between expectations of a devaluation and the interest rate differential is explained in the Focus box 'Interest rate differentials and expected devaluations'.

FOCUS
Interest rate differentials and expected devaluations

To understand the relationship between expectations of a devaluation and the interest rate differential, consider the arbitrage condition between the returns on assets denominated in different currencies and write it as:

$$i^{FF} - i^{DM} = \frac{(DM/FF)^e_{t+1} - (DM/FF)_t}{(DM/FF)_t} = px + (1-p)0 = px$$

which corresponds to equation (7.4) if you replace:

$$i^{FF} = i_t, \; i^{DM} = i^*_t, \; (DM/FF)^e_{t+1} = E^e \text{ and } (DM/FF)_t = E_t.$$

Consider first the first two terms of this equation. Investors will continue to hold securities denominated in French francs, even when they expect a devaluation of the franc (when the right term in the first equality is positive) if their yield, i^{FF}, rises enough relative to the performance of similar securities denominated in marks (i.e. i^{DM}), thereby compensating for the losses they would suffer if the franc eventually devalues.

Now consider the second equality. The expected devaluation of the French franc relative to the DM can be expressed as the sum of two terms: the probability, p, that the devaluation occurs, multiplied by the amount of the devaluation, in the event it occurs – which we indicated with x – plus $(1p)$, the probability that no devaluation occurs, multiplied by zero. This expression shows how the ratio between the two interest rates fluctuates with changing market expectations about a devaluation (p).

The relationship between the French and the German rates shown in Figure 19.1 is a measure of market

expectations regarding the devaluation of the French franc. Figure 19.1 shows that when a spread emerges between French and German interest rates, this is because it is the French rate that moves, while the German rate is unchanged. This is a characteristic of exchange rate regimes built around a central currency, as the dollar in Bretton Woods and the Deutschmark in the EMS. If the system is under pressure – for example, because markets expect a devaluation – all of the adjustment is borne by peripheral countries, like France in our example. The core country never modifies its monetary policy to cope with the tensions of the system. For this reason, the country of the central currency (the Deutschmark in the EMS) is called the **anchor of the system**.

Figure 19.2 shows two series of interest rates in francs. The series called 'Euro-FF' shows the interest rates on securities denominated in French francs, but held outside of France, for example in London. The series called 'Dom-FF' indicates similar interest rates on securities held in France. The emergence of a differential (sometimes large, as in March 1983) between the two interest rates is due to **controls on capital flows**, also known as foreign exchange controls. These are laws that prevent citizens from holding financial assets abroad, even if denominated in the national currency. In 1983, for example, a French citizen could not hold securities in London even if denominated in French francs. In this way, the French authorities, like those of other European countries, ensured that the defence exchange controls – that had become incompatible with the integration of European financial market – were lifted. At that moment the EMS was doomed: without foreign exchange controls, the ability of domestic monetary authorities to maintain a fixed exchange rate depends on whether the market expects it to be sustainable or not. If the market is convinced that the exchange rate is sustainable, investors do not expect a devaluation, so interest rates remain the same as rates in Germany and defending the exchange rate involves no cost: the exchange rate remains fixed. Instead, if the market expects a devaluation, the domestic interest rates rise and domestic monetary authorities have no choice but to raise the white flag and devalue.

The first situation is unstable, however. If at time t a country's policy is perceived to be consistent with a fixed exchange rate, but investors expect that in future, at time $t+1$, it will no longer be the same – for example, after an election, a devaluation could happen even before the country experiences the change of government and even if this does not occur (as p becomes positive and the domestic interest rates rises. We will come back to this in the Focus box on 'Interest rate differentials and expected devaluations'). Fears of a devaluation can then become self-fulfilling, even if economic policy remains consistent with the fixed exchange rate.

of the exchange rate did not cause sharp increases in domestic rates.

Without foreign exchange controls, either one of the two following situations happens:

- The market is convinced that the exchange rate is sustainable, i.e. that the economic policy of the country is consistent with a fixed exchange rate. In this case, investors do not expect a devaluation ($p = 0$), so interest rates remain the same as rates in the central country

and defending the exchange rate involves no cost: the exchange rate remains fixed.

- The market expects a devaluation ($p > 0$). In this case, the domestic interest rates rise and domestic monetary authorities may have no choice but to raise the white flag and devalue.

Remember what the interest parity condition says: arbitrage by investors implies that the domestic interest rate must be equal to the foreign interest rate minus the expected appreciation rate of the domestic currency.

Figure 19.2

France: on-shore and off-shore three-month interest rates

Controls on capital flows allowed France to separate the internal financial market from the international market, especially in times preceding realignments.

When foreign exchange controls were removed (in the late 1980s) because they were incompatible with the single market, only two options were open to Europe:

● Abandon any attempt to stabilise exchange rates and move to a flexible exchange rate regime: that is, leaving it to the market to determine exchange rates between European currencies.
● Abandon exchange rates, adopting a common currency.

It is for this reason that European financial integration, combined with the old dislike by Europeans for flexible exchange rates, led as a natural consequence to monetary union.

The Maastrict Treaty

Although the crisis of the EMS probably accelerated the timetable for the creation of the euro, the decision to adopt a single currency came before, and was taken with the signing of the Treaty of the European Union in the Dutch city of Maastricht (which explains why it is commonly known as the **Maastricht Treaty**) in February 1992. The Treaty created a new supranational institution, the European Central Bank, the institution responsible for conducting monetary policy in the euro area.

The Maastricht Treaty also established some convergence criteria (which are described in the Focus box) that countries aspiring to enter the EMU had to meet. In the early 1990s, European countries, in fact, showed large macroeconomic differences: in particular, with regard to inflation and public deficits. Precisely because the single currency makes it obviously impossible to devalue, a condition for starting the EMU was therefore the convergence of macroeconomic variables, beginning with inflation.

The decision to name the new currency euro was adopted in December 1995 by the European Council. On the same occasion, the Council confirmed that EMU would definitely start on 1 January 1999: at that time, the exchange rate between the participating currencies would be irrevocably fixed while the new coins and notes were to be introduced on 1 January 2002.

The last step on the way towards EMU was taken on 3 May 1998, when the European Council agreed on which of the member states met the admission criteria and therefore

FOCUS
Criteria for admissions to the EMU set by the Maastrict Treaty

Inflation rate. The rate of inflation in the year preceding accession must not be more than 1.5 percentage points above that of the three best-performing member states in terms of price stability.

Public debt and deficits. The ratio of the government deficit to GDP must not exceed 3% unless:

● either the ratio has declined substantially and continuously and reached a level that comes close to the reference value; or, alternatively,
● the excess over the reference value is only exceptional and temporary and the ratio remains close to the reference value.

The ratio of government debt to GDP must not exceed 60% of GDP, unless the ratio is sufficiently diminishing and approaching the reference value at a satisfactory pace.

Exchange rate. Exchange rate movements must have been within the normal fluctuation margins provided for by the exchange-rate mechanism of the EMS, for at least two years, without devaluing against the currency of any other member state.

Long-term interest rate. Observed over a period of one year before the examination, a member state must show an average nominal long-term interest rate that does not exceed by more than 2 percentage points that of, at most, the three best-performing member states in terms of price stability. Interest rates shall be measured on the basis of long-term government bonds.

could enter EMU. There were 11 countries: Belgium, Germany, Spain, France, Ireland, Italy, Luxembourg, the Netherlands, Austria, Portugal and Finland. The months preceding the final decision on which countries would participate in EMU were particularly uncertain, especially as regards Italy, the country that started out more distant with regard to the convergence criteria imposed by the Maastricht Treaty. Greece was not allowed to join the first group (and did not join until 1 January 2001) because it did not comply with all the convergence criteria, and Sweden was not allowed because it has decided not to participate in the EMS (and being a member of the EMS for at least two years was a condition for admission to EMU). As regards the UK and Denmark, they were in special circumstances at that time. The UK, despite having ratified the Maastricht Treaty, had asked to postpone to a later date the choice of whether or not to join (the clause of 'opting-out'), while Denmark had linked the ratification of the Treaty to holding a new referendum, after one in July 1992 in which the Danes had rejected the euro. So far this referendum has not yet taken place. To member states that did not participate from the beginning (called states with a derogation), the Treaty guarantees the possibility of adopting the single currency at a later date. Seventeen countries now belong, the most recent members being Slovakia, Slovenia, Estonia, Cyprus and Malta.

19.2 IS EUROPE AN OPTIMAL CURRENCY AREA?

In section 19.1 we outlined the main stages of monetary integration among the EU countries. At this point, we pause to reflect on the purely economic reasons for forming a monetary union, highlighting the advantages and disadvantages that may result from the decision to adopt a common currency. In fact, we have so far not discussed the possible costs associated with that choice. Only with an analysis of costs and benefits is it possible to judge the welfare implications of the monetary union for European citizens. A group of countries is said to constitute an 'optimal currency area' only if the (macroeconomic and microeconomic) benefits from having just one currency outweigh the costs.

Robert Mundell, Nobel Prize laureate for economics in 1999, was the first economist to suggest, back in the late 1960s, that European countries might form an optimal currency area, pointing out the costs and benefits arising from the choice to abandon exchange rate flexibility forever. If we are to know whether the EU (or a group of countries in general) is an optimal currency area, the various benefits of forming a monetary union have to be compared to the costs which arise when countries give away exchange rate flexibility forever. (We summarise the costs and benefits of a monetary union in the Focus box 'Costs and benefits of a monetary union'.)

We are now ready to start answering our initial question: is the euro area an optimal currency area? To answer this question we need to understand to what extent European economies are likely to face asymmetric shocks. (Before answering, make sure you have read the Focus box.)

To answer the question whether or not the euro area is an optimal currency area, European macroeconomists have studied whether euro-area countries usually face similar shocks to one another (i.e. symmetric shocks), or whether instead different countries face different shocks (i.e. asymmetric shocks): for example, some countries register a decrease in aggregate demand while others experience increasing aggregate demand. Although a debate has been going on around this issue since before the beginning of EMU, conclusions are not clear-cut. Some studies find that in the run-up period to EMU and during all the 1990s, there has been an increasing synchronisation of GDP across the euro area and particularly of its two main components (consumption and investment). Evidence is more mixed regarding the following decade. Some countries seem to have experienced higher correlation of output movement with each other than before adopting the euro, but this is not the case for other countries. This leaves the chances open for asymmetric shocks to hit European countries, and thus for the need for different stabilisation policies.

FOCUS
Costs and benefits of a monetary union

The major benefits of joining a monetary union are both macroeconomic and microeconomic. As we mentioned earlier (in Chapter 12), the microeconomic benefits of a monetary union are:

- *Reduced uncertainty*. For example, the elimination of exchange rate fluctuations removes the uncertainty about interest rate differentials among member countries and hence the uncertainty about discounted present value of future profits (as you learned in Chapter 16).
- *Reduced transaction costs*. Before monetary union, in a trip through all European countries, the conversion costs from one currency to the next one would cost 47% of the initial sum. The European commission estimated such costs at 0.25–0.5% of EU GDP per year, not a negligible amount.
- *Price transparency*. Before monetary union, prices for identical goods (e.g. a given brand of car) differed substantially across European countries. A common currency, by easing price comparisons, has reduced price differentials (although price differences still exist due to local regulation, transport costs and tax differences).

The main macroeconomic benefits of a monetary union are:

- *Anti-inflationary reputation*. A country with a pro-inflationary reputation (e.g. Italy) may dramatically improve its reputation by forming a monetary union with a country with a very good reputation (e.g. Germany). Compared to a peg, a monetary union is more credible as it is irreversible (see Chapter 12). Notice, however, that a country could achieve the same outcome, while at the same time maintaining monetary independence, by simply making the central bank independent (e.g. the UK or Sweden).
- *Monetary policy coordination*. As we saw earlier (in Chapter 7), in the short run, a monetary expansion under flexible exchange rates leads to a depreciation, and it increases output at home at the expense of foreign output ('beggar-thy-neighbour policy'). Governments usually ignore these negative effects on other countries ('negative externalities'). Thus if all countries devalue without taking into account the effects on other countries, exchange rate will not move but everybody will lose. (The 1930s were an example of the dramatic costs of such policies.) A common currency eliminates such externalities.

- *European seignorage*. As we described in the Focus box 'Euro vs US dollar as a leading international reserve currency' (in Chapter 4), as the euro started playing the role of a reserve currency, its share in world reserves increased, and so did European seignorage. An increase of the share in world reserves from 20% to 30% is worth 0.5% of GDP.
- *Trade effects*. Last but not least, currency unions have positive effects on trade among member countries. According to recent studies on the trade effects of the euro, the common currency did boost intra-euro area trade by something between 5% and 10% on average (but divergent estimates exist, suggesting that the euro's trade effects might be even larger).

The main cost of sacrificing exchange rate flexibility between different countries, in the presence of rigidities in prices and wages, depends upon the magnitude of **asymmetric shocks** that might affect these countries. Economists define *asymmetric shocks* as those unexpected changes in demand and/or in aggregate supply that hit one country but not its main trading partners. A violent and sudden fall in demand for French wine, which has no effect on aggregate demand in Ireland, is an example of an asymmetric shock. Aggregate demand falls in France, but not in Ireland. To return to goods market equilibrium, the real exchange rate has to adjust, and this is easier under flexible than under fixed exchange rates.

To understand why this is the case, let us go back to our discussion of adjustment earlier (in Chapter 12). If the nominal exchange rate is fixed, a decrease of aggregate demand in France reduces output (if prices/wages are sticky in the short run, the real exchange rate is also sticky). If the nominal exchange rate between France and Ireland cannot be changed, the adjustment to such a shock will require lower prices, and thus lower wages, in France, relative to Ireland. Under flexible exchange rates, the nominal exchange rate would change to bring about the necessary change in the real exchange rate. This obviously cannot happen in a currency union where a change in the real exchange rate requires a change in domestic prices and wages. So a major cost of a monetary union is the loss of the exchange rate as an automatic stabiliser in the event of asymmetric shocks.

A second issue which has been debated among European macroeconomists is whether the euro itself can make business cycles more synchronised. Two factors have been emphasised:

- The most important one that has been discussed is **trade intensity** among euro area countries. The more countries trade with each other, the more likely it is that their economies become synchronised. As we have learned (in Chapter 9), an increase in income in one country will lead to an increased demand for both domestic and foreign goods, and therefore to an increase in imports from its trading partners. These other countries will also enjoy an increase in income due to increased foreign demand for their goods.

- Another, related, factor that will influence the degree of synchronisation of output and income among euro-area countries is industry specialisation. Asymmetric shocks are more likely between countries which produce different products, because different sectors are likely to face different demand and supply conditions. Therefore, European countries whose imports and exports are largely dominated by products belonging to the same sectors, i.e. where trade is largely intra-industry, should face less asymmetric shocks than countries whose trade flows mainly consist of different products (inter-industry trade).

◀ Intra-industry trade occurs when a country imports and exports the same type of goods or, more generally, goods belonging to the same sector: for example, one brand of cars versus another brand of cars.

Inter-industry trade occurs when a country imports and exports different goods, or goods belonging to different sectors: that is, cars versus umbrellas.

To the extent that asymmetric shocks have not totally disappeared, which factors might reduce the cost of adjusting to such shocks in a monetary union? One factor that could reduce the costs of a monetary union in the presence of asymmetric shocks among member countries is high labour mobility between regions. A favourite argument in the debate on how to deal with potential asymmetric shocks in Europe is to say that, if labour was mobile, the loss of exchange rate exibility would not be crucial. Labour mobility implies that if aggregate demand fell, in our example, in France, labour would migrate from France to other European countries, thus reducing the natural level of output in France and increasing the natural level of output in Ireland, and so re-establishing equilibrium without a change in the real exchange rate.

Labour mobility is a major absorber of asymmetric shocks in the USA. In the early 1990s, when the North East of the USA was hit by a local recession, a significant number of worker moved to the South West where the economy was booming. How mobile are workers among European countries? Table 19.2 shows the percentage of population which has moved residence from another EU-15 country since the year before relative to the total population of the country of residence, from 1995 until 2006. It shows no evidence of an expansion of intra-EU mobility both in the five years preceding the adoption of the euro and in the first five years of the new currency. However, there are measures of worker mobility within EU countries that show an increasing cross-border commuting rates in the majority of European countries both inside and outside the euro area. Still, when putting this numbers into international perspective, it appears that geographic mobility in Europe is very low compared to the USA where interstate mobility is around 2–2.5% (meaning that 2–2.5% of the population changed state every year) compared to only about 0.1% in Europe, and cross-border commuting is 3.7% in the USA compared to 1.4 in EU-12 and 0.5 in EU-15.

Table 19.2 Intra-EU mobility, 1995–2006

country	1995	2001	2006
Austria	0.1	0.3	0.2
Belgium	0.1		0.2
France	0.1	0.2	
Germany	0.1	0.1	0.1
Greece	0.1	0.1	0.03
Italy	0.1	0.1	
Portugal		0.1	0.1
Spain	0	0.1	0.2

Source: 'GEOGRAPHIC MOBILITY IN THE EUROPEAN UNION: OPTIMIZING ITS ECONOMIC AND SOCIAL BENEFITS', *IZA RESEARCH REPORT* No. 19, 2008, page 133.

In conclusion, considering simultaneously the possibility of asymmetric shocks and low labour mobility, it is difficult to argue that the euro area is an optimal monetary area. (In truth, if we consider Canada and the USA jointly, it is not necessarily true that the optimal currency area would match the political borders. Mundell, in a famous 1961 article, stated that, from an economic point of view, it would have been more efficient to divide North America in a longitudinal direction between east and west, rather than between north (Canada) and south (USA) as it has been historically divided.)

Based on the evidence described above, some economists argue that not only is Europe not an optimal currency area, but also not even individual European countries are. There is, however, a huge difference between the EU and a nation state. Nation states, unlike the EU, have a mechanism to deal with asymmetric shocks: a common fiscal policy which allows the use of transfers from one region to another (between the south and the north of the UK, for instance) to offset the effects of asymmetric shocks. The use of fiscal policy as a mechanism for redistribution between regions in order to protect against asymmetric shocks has been studied by several economists, and various studies have concluded that this role is extremely important. Between 20% and 30% of the effects of asymmetric shocks to the income of US states is compensated for by fiscal policy, i.e. by transfers from the Federal Government to individual states. Similar results apply to Canada and the UK. In the EU, fiscal policy cannot work because there are virtually no Europe-wide taxes, and therefore this means of adjusting to asymmetric shocks is precluded.

In the euro area, not only is there no common fiscal policy (and hence the possibility of fiscal transfers among countries) but also national governments are limited in their ability to use their fiscal policy as a means to respond to asymmetric shocks. As we shall see later (in Chapter 21), however, the crisis has reopened the debate about fiscal transfers across euro area states.

19.3 THE EUROPEAN SYSTEM OF CENTRAL BANKS: STRUCTURE AND OBJECTIVES

After examining the most significant stages of the process that led to the creation of the ECB, we now consider its organisational structure, its responsibilities and some elements of the monetary policy strategy that it pursues.

Monetary policy in the euro area is managed by the ECB, which, along with the 27 national central banks of all EU member states (regardless of whether they have adopted the euro), forms the **European System of Central Banks (ESCB)**. One key feature of the ECB is its independence with respect both to other European institutions and to the national governments of the countries that are part of the euro area. Article 7 of the Maastrict Treaty stresses independence unequivocally, arguing that 'neither a national central bank, nor any member of their decision-making bodies shall seek or take instructions from Community institutions or bodies, nor from the governments of the Member States'. The division of tasks between the ECB and national central banks is carried out as follows. Monetary policy decisions are centralised at the ECB, so that monetary policy at European level is unique, but its implementation decentralised to the national banks, which are responsible for carrying out open market operations in the individual countries.

- The decision-making bodies of the ECB are the Governing Council and the Executive Board. There is also a third body, called the General Council, which, however, has no decision-making powers.
- The Governing Council is composed of the six members of the Executive Board and the governors of the national central banks of the countries that are part of the euro area. This body is responsible for formulating monetary policy and establishing guidelines for its implementation. The Council normally meets twice a month (on Thursdays).
- The Executive Board comprises the President, the Vice-President and four other members selected from among persons of recognised reputation and experience in banking

and money matters by the European Council. The Executive Board implements monetary policy in accordance with the guidelines and decisions laid down by the Governing Council, giving instructions to national central banks. The Executive Board may be delegated certain powers when the Governing Council so decides.

- The General Council is composed of the President, the Vice-President and the governors of national central banks of all 27 countries that are part of the EU (the 17 countries which belong to the euro and the 10 which do not). This body has no decision-making capacity in the field of monetary policy but has some monitoring activities and may act in an advisory capacity. The groundwork for establishing the irrevocable conversion rates to be applied when the states that currently are not part of EMU are allowed to join is also among the responsibilities of the General Council.

An important aspect of the mode of operation of the governing bodies of the ECB concerns the process by which decisions are made. Both the Governing Council and the Executive Committee reach agreement by means of votes taken on the basis of two fundamental rules. The first rule is that each member holds one vote and the second is that decisions are taken by simple majority.

The first rule is particularly important: governors of central banks all have the same weight, regardless of the economic importance of the country of origin. Governors have not been assigned a weight proportional to the size of the economy of their country, such as in the IMF and in the World Bank, because such an arrangement would have suggested that the governors represent specific national interests.

Although the Treaty stipulates that the governors of national central banks (NCB) sit on the Governing Council in a personal capacity, the reality is that they end up reflecting the economic conditions of their respective countries. And, since NCB governors have 17 out of 23 seats on the Council, this makes decision making complicated particularly when economic conditions across EMU diverge. If we compare the structure of the ECB with that of another federal central bank, the Fed, we can see that the Fed's Federal Open Market Committee – the body that makes interest rate decisions in the USA – is slimmer, consisting of seven members appointed by the President of the USA and only five members belonging to the regional Federal Reserve Banks.

As regards the objectives of monetary policy in the euro area, Article 105.1 of the Treaty says the absolute priority of the ECB is to pursue price stability. Other goals, namely to support the economic policies of the EU, are formulated in a rather vague way and can be pursued only if they are compatible with price stability. The ECB has defined price stability as a rate of consumer price inflation close to but below 2%.

The ECB from its birth to the crisis: a tentative assessment

The relatively short life of the ECB (14 years since its creation) comes in two very different periods. Before the crisis the ECB's main task was to establish its reputation and to fine-tune its monetary policy operations. Both were not obvious tasks. Reputation could not simply be inherited from previous central banks, such as the Bundesbank, for example. Running monetary policy in an area where financial markets were still very much fragmented was also a big challenge. When the crisis hit the euro area, the ECB, like the Fed, had to drastically revise its approach to monetary policy. In this section we start evaluating the ECB's performance prior to the crisis. Later we shall discuss how the ECB responded to the crisis (in Chapter 20, which is fully devoted to it).

Nine years (1999–2007) is not a long enough period to be able to extrapolate from ECB decisions the rule that it followed.

One criticism often made is the claim that the ECB simply transposed to the whole of EMU the monetary policy rule formerly followed by the German central bank, the Bundesbank. To see whether this is a sound criticism, let us look at Figure 19.3. (To understand it, refer to the concept of the Taylor rule presented in Chapter 23.) This simple

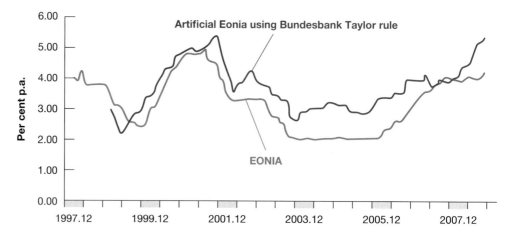

Figure 19.3

How different is the ECB from the Bundesbank?

Source: D.J.C. Smant, *ECB Interest Rate and Money Growth Rules*, Rotterdam, Erasmus University, mimeo.

rule for describing the behaviour of monetary authorities has proved a very usefull tool in interpreting and predicting the behaviour of central banks.

Using a simple formula, if we denote the interest rate set by the central bank at time t as i_t, the Taylor rule says that monetary authorities will set the interest rate based on the following formula:

$$i_t = a_0 + a_1(\pi^e_{t+1} - \pi^*) + a_2\frac{Y_t - Y^*}{Y^*}$$ [19.1]

where π^e_{t+1} indicates expected inflation for time $t + 1$, π^* is the inflation target, Y_t is GDP at time t, and Y^* is potential GDP, i.e. the level corresponding to full employment. Equation (19.1) includes expected inflation, since the central bank can do nothing to change current inflation: by changing interest rates, it can only hope to influence future inflation (where the term 'future' means one or two years from now) because of the time it takes for a change in interest rates to affect inflation. Using historical data on real GDP and expected inflation, econometrics allows us to estimate the values of the coefficients a_0, a_1 and a_2 in equation (19.1). In general, the higher the coefficient a_1 with respect to a_2, the greater is the concern of the central bank for inflation. When studying the behaviour of the Bundesbank until 1998, one finds values of a_1 in the order of 1.3 and a_2 in the order of 0.3.

Figure 19.3 shows the overnight interest rates set by the ECB since January 1999, the month the ECB came into existence (this overnight rate is called EONIA, ECB Overnight Interest Rate Average). To give some perspective, the chart reconstructs an artificial rate for EONIA before January 1999, using a weighted average of the overnight rates of the countries adopting the euro: this is the blue line. The pink line shows the interest rate that the ECB would have to set if it had behaved exactly like the Bundesbank – clearly a Bundesbank that had to face the same euro area variables, inflation and growth, which the ECB has faced. As you can see, after an initial period during which the ECB has actually shadowed the Bundesbank, the bank seems to have freed itself from the German legacy. Interest rates from 2001 onwards are significantly different (lower) than what the Bundesbank would have chosen if it were facing similar conditions for growth and inflation.

It is obviously still too early to write a history of the ECB. These exercises are used primarily to make the point that what matters for evaluating a central bank are the facts, not the words written in the treaties.

Eventually, the market is the best test of the effectiveness of a central bank's monetary policy when its ultimate objective by statute is to keep inflation under control. What does the market expect? Do financial operators expect that inflation will remain below the limit set by the ECB (2%) or do they think that it will exceed that limit? Figure 19.4 shows two measures of long-term inflation expectations. These are the measures the ECB itself uses to gain insights into the expectations of the private sector. As you will remember from earlier (see Chapter 16), there are two ways to measure expectations: one is based on surveys of private sector inflation expectations; another is based on comparisons between the yields

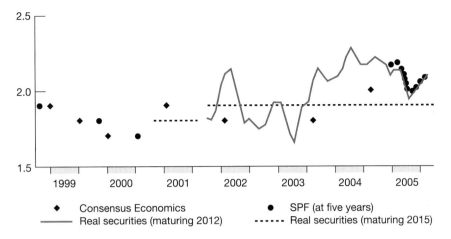

- ● Survey of Professional forecasters (SPF) (for 2014; left-hand scale)
- ▲ Consensus Economics (for 2014; left-hand scale)
- ■ Euro Zone Barometer (for 2013; left-hand scale)
- —— implied five-year forward break-even inflation rate
  five years ahead, seasonally adjusted (left-hand scale)
- - - - SPF probability of longer-term inflation being
  at or above 2% (right-hand scale)

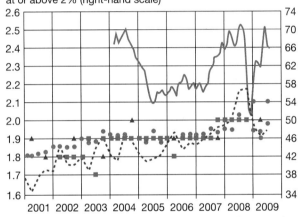

Sources: Consensus Economics, Euro Zone Barometer, Reuters and
ECB calculations.

Figure 19.4

**The ECB and expected
inflation**

Source: ECB, *Monthly Bulletin*, August 2009.

on inflation-indexed bond and the yields on nominal bonds. The Focus box 'Measures of euro area expectations of future inflation' summarises the available measures of euro area inflation expectations.

Figure 19.4 shows projections from two different groups of professional analysts (SPF and Consensus Economics) and from the Euro Zone Barometer, and the probability, calculated from the SPF projections, that future inflation will be at or above 2%. The blue line refers to breakeven inflation five years ahead. As you learned earlier (in Chapter 18), by comparing the yield spread between nominal and inflation-linked (or real) bonds, you can derive the implicit inflation expectations among financial market participants. These expectations are a little more volatile than the survey-based measures. In particular, notice the significant increase in market-based inflation expectations since mid-2007, i.e. since the beginning of the financial crisis. Until that time, financial markets were confident that the ECB would be able to keep inflation close to 2% for many years. Moreover, market-based measures were largely in line with survey-based measures. In 2008, financial markets expected that inflation would sharply decline in the near future due to the prospects of a widespread recession. However, since September of that year, market-based expectations have become more erratic and are no longer in line with survey-based measures. In fact, they seem to point to a significant increase in expected inflation in the near future. Such an increase does not suggest that financial markets expect a recovery in the near future, but

FOCUS
Measures of euro area expectations of future inflation

There are several available measures of inflation expectations in the euro area (see Table 19.3).

Survey-based measures

Survey-based measures provide direct measures of inflation expectations. There are several available surveys of private sector inflation expectations in the euro area:

- *The European Commission Consumer Survey on Inflation Expectations*. Every month since 1985, the European Commission has reported on consumers' expectations for consumer price trends over the following 12 months on the basis of a survey of nearly 20,000 consumers in the euro area. These consumer surveys are conducted at the national level and the results for the euro area are compiled by aggregating the country data.
- *The ECB Survey of Professional Forecasters (SPF)*. The SPF is a survey the ECB has carried out every quarter since the beginning of 1999. The SPF collects information on expectations for euro-area inflation, as well as for other relevant variables (mainly GDP growth and the unemployment rate) from a panel of more than 70 expert forecasters from financial or non-financial institutions that are based in the EU.
- *Euro Zone Barometer*. Since 2002, MJEconomics, a London-based consultancy, has been publishing its Euro Zone Barometer, which contains forecasts for euro area inflation one and two years ahead, also based on a panel of professional forecasters.

- *Consensus Economics' forecast*. Consensus Economics Inc., a private company, has published monthly average forecasts for major economic variables for several countries since 1989. It publishes the average forecast of professional forecasters for the euro area's inflation for the current year and the following one based on a panel of around 30 participants.

Financial-market based measures

- *Break-even inflation rates*. The difference between the yield on a nominal bond and that on an index-linked bond (i.e. on a bond that protects the principal against inflation) of the same maturity is often referred to as the 'break-even' inflation rate, as it would be the hypothetical rate of inflation at which the expected real – i.e. inflation-adjusted – return on the two bonds would be the same if both were held until maturity (as you learned in Chapter 16).
- *Inflation-linked swap rates*. Inflation-linked swap rates can be used as an additional source of information about market expectations of future inflation. In an inflation-linked swap agreement, an investor commits to a single payment on the basis of a fixed rate agreed at the beginning and, in return, receives payments based on realised inflation over the life of the contract.

Source: 'Measures of inflations expectations in the euro area', in *European Central Bank, Monthly Bulletin*, July 2006.

Table 19.3 Summary of available measures of euro area inflation more than 12 months ahead

Source	Agents	Frequency	Horizons
Survey-based measures			
EU Commission Consumer Survey	Consumers	Monthly	Twelve months ahead
ECB Survey of Professional Forecasters	Professional forecasters	Quarterly	Current and next calendar years (and rolling horizons one and two years ahead) Five years ahead
Consensus Economics	Professional forecasters	Monthly Biannual	Current and next calendar years Six to ten years ahead
Euro Zone Barometer	Professional forecasters	Monthly Quarterly	Current and next calendar years Four years ahead
Financial market-based measures			
Break-even inflation rates	Financial market participants	Intra-day	At present, between two and around 30 years ahead
Inflation-linked swap rates	Financial market participants	intra-day	Two to 30 years ahead

that it is largely due to an increase in real yields, i.e. yields of inflation-indexed bonds compared to nominal bonds yields. As you learned earlier (in Chapter 16), higher bond yields imply lower bond prices, as the price of a bond varies inversely with the nominal interest rate. Following the massive financial transactions carried out by several investors who wanted or needed to sell their bonds in the autumn of 2008, bond prices fell and real yields increased.

19.4 THE FIRST FOURTEEN YEARS OF THE EURO (1999–2013)

In the first 14 years of its existence, the euro has rapidly become the second most important world currency, challenging the US dollar. This is above all the effect of the economic size of the euro area which is a bit larger than the US both in terms of population (332 million people in the euro area, 312 in the US) and GDP, €12 trillion euros in the euro area, €11 trillion in the US. But it also reflects the rapidly acquired credibility of the new currency. This is suggested by three numbers:

- Before the euro, central banks worldwide held 70% of their reserves in US dollars, 14% in Deutschmarks and 3% in UK pounds (with other smaller currencies making up the difference). Today the share of the dollar has fallen to 65%, the share of the pound has slightly increased (to 4%) and the euro has jumped to 25%: a quarter of all reserves held by central banks is held in euros.
- The currency in which firms invoice the goods they export is another indicator of credibility. Japanese exporters, for instance, when they ship goods to the USA, will invoice 12% of exports in Japanese yen, 87% in dollars. When the new European currency was first introduced, the share of Japanese exports to Europe invoiced in euros was only 26%: today it is 42%.
- Another indicator of a currency's credibility is its use in denominating financial assets. Of all international bonds in circulation worldwide, 41% are denominated in euros, 37% in US dollars.

However, along with its successes, serious economic tensions have built up among the 17 countries that adopted the euro, to the point of questioning its very survival. The origin of these tensions is the emergence of two very different groups of countries in the euro area. A first group (Portugal, Greece, Spain, Ireland and, although to smaller degree, Italy) have run, year after year, current account deficits, meaning that they were spending more than they produced, borrowing from the rest of the world. The other EMU members, instead, have run current account surpluses, meaning that they were spending less than they produced, thus investing abroad, i.e. using their excess savings to buy foreign assets. At this stage it is useful to stop and remember what a country's current account represents. The current account (as we learned in Chapter 6) is the difference between how much a country produces and how much it spends. A current account deficit means that the sum of domestic spending (private consumption, plus government spending, plus investment) exceeds what the country produces and is paid for by borrowing from the rest of the world. Symmetrically, a current account surplus means that the country spends less than it produces and uses what is left to buy foreign assets, i.e. to invest abroad.

Table 19.4 shows the sum of the current account imbalances run by each country from 1999, the year EMU started, to 2008, the year the euro crisis began. In this period the euro area as a whole ran a current account surplus, but inside the area the periphery mostly borrowed from the centre. The fact that savings were flowing from the centre to the periphery is also clear from Table 19.5. This table shows which percentage of the total foreign assets owned by France and Germany is invested in the periphery. Consider Germany: in 1999 the share of total German foreign assets invested in the periphery was 10.8%. Ten years later this share had doubled to over 20%.

Table 19.4 Cumulated current accounts (per cent of GDP, 1999–2008)

Portugal	−91	Germany	+32
Greece	−85	Netherlands	+54
Spain	−60	Finland	+59
Ireland	−19	France	+3
Italy	−13	Euro area	+22

Source: Eurostat

Table 19.5 Share of the total foreign assets of France and Germany invested in Spain, Portugal, Greece and Ireland

	2001	2008
France	10.8	18.3
Germany	10.8	20.3

Source: IMF

Table 19.6 GDP per capita in 1998 (EU-15 = 100)

Portugal	50.40	Italy	92.10
Greece	54.30	Ireland	102.10
Spain	65.20	France	105.60
		UK	107.10
		Finland	108.40
		Netherlands	113.40
		Germany	114.70
		Sweden	122.90

Source: Eurostat

Tables 19.4 and 19.5 raise two questions: why did the periphery countries borrow so much, and why did the centre countries invest their excess savings in the periphery, instead, for instance, of investing in emerging markets? Understanding these issues is central to understanding what lies behind the euro crisis.

We shall proceed in two steps. First we explain why the fact that the periphery borrowed from the centre should not have come as a surprise. Then we explain what went wrong.

Table 19.6 shows the levels of GDP per capita in 1998, the year before the euro started. The income per capita in Portugal, Greece and Spain was half the average in the North. We learned earlier (in Chapters 18 and 19) that income per capita is determined, beyond other factors, by how much capital a country has: a low income per capita signals a relatively low stock of capital (as a per cent of GDP). The lower the capital stock, the higher the marginal benefit from adding some more capital, in other words the productivity of capital is higher in countries where the stock of capital is low. It is thus no surprise that capital flew to the periphery.

Let's go through an example: in 1998, in Germany, the ratio of the capital stock to GDP was 3.1; in Portugal, which had far less capital, it was 2.5. Now assume that output in both countries is produced using capital, K, and labour, L, and (to keep the reasoning simple) also assume that the two countries have the same technology, described by $Y = K^a L^{1-a}$. The productivity of capital (which can be computed asking by how much Y increases if K increases) is $a(Y/K)$. Now assume that $a = 0.3$, a number that is common to many countries. You are now ready to compute the productivity of capital in the two countries: it was 9.7% in Germany (0.3/3.1), 12% in Portugal (0.3/2.5). This example illustrates why it was no surprise that capital flew from Germany, where capital was abundant and its productivity relatively low, to Portugal, where capital was scarce and its productivity correspondingly higher. Investing in the periphery – and thus allowing the periphery to run current account deficits – was the rational thing to do for Germans and other Northern Europeans. So what

Table 19.7 Investment (per cent of GDP)

	1998	2008
Portugal	27	22
Greece	21	20
Ireland	22	26
Italy	19	19
Spain	23	29
Euro area	21	22

Source: Eurostat

Table 19.8 Housing construction (per cent of GDP)

	2000	2008
Ireland	8.2	14
Greece	7.0	8.5
Spain	6.0	9.0
Euro-15	5.9	6.2

Source: Eurostat

Table 19.9 Debt and deficits

	Government budget deficit % of GDP, average 2001–07	Government debt % of GDP, 2008
Euro area	2.3	70
Greece	6.1	100
Portugal	4.1	66
Spain	1.3	40
Ireland	1.0	44
Italy	3.1	106

Source: Eurostat

went wrong? Essentially that the centre invested its excess savings in the periphery, but the periphery used it largely to consume, not to invest.

Table 19.7 shows what happened to investment, as a share of GDP, in the first ten years of the euro. In all the countries of the periphery, except Ireland and Spain, investment either remained constant or fell back, while in the euro area as a whole it was slightly increasing. There is no evidence of an investment boom in the countries where capital should have flown. The important exceptions are Ireland and Spain, which did experience an investment boom, but limited to a particular type of investment: housing. Table 19.8 shows housing construction as a share of GDP: in both Ireland and Spain there was a housing boom, meaning that imported capital didn't go to finance productive investment, but a bubble in the housing market (that there was a bubble is suggested by what happened to the price of houses which in ten years increased by 300 per cent in Spain and 250 per cent in Ireland). Elsewhere, that is beyond Ireland and Spain, what did the capital flowing in from the centre finance? By and large it was used to increase consumption: mostly private consumption in Portugal, government spending in Greece (see Table 19.9). The experience of Italy was less clear-cut because the country, as shown in Table 19.4, imported only a small amount of capital from abroad. So what went wrong was not the fact that capital flowed from the rich euro area centre to the relatively poorer periphery, but the way that capital was used: not to invest and produce more goods, but simply to increase consumption, either directly or by acquiring houses whose prices were inflated by a real-estate bubble.

To understand why foreign borrowing turned into a crisis of the euro area, it is important to understand how households' savings were transferred from the centre to the periphery. This happened via banks, and this explains why banks are at the centre of the euro crisis. Let us start by going back to the balance sheet of banks that we studied earlier (in Chapter 4).

Table 19.10 The balance sheet of Spanish banks

Assets	Liabilities
Lending:	Deposits of Spanish residents
– mortages	Borrowing from French and German banks
– governement bonds	
Reserves	

Table 19.11 Total lending (per cent of GDP)

	Germany	France	Italy	Ireland	Greece	Spain	Portugal
2000	1.06	0.72	0.71	1.0	0.42	0.87	1.1
2008	0.95	0.95	0.97	2.02	0.85	1.7	1.5

Source: National Central Banks.

Tables 19.10 and 19.11 help us understand. The first, Table 19.10, shows the example of a bank in the periphery, say a Spanish bank. This bank finances itself with deposits from local residents and borrowing from banks located in the centre of the euro area, say France and Germany. It then uses these funds in part to lend to Spanish households in the form of housing mortgages, in part to buy government bonds. (As we learned, it also keeps some reserves at the central bank.) Total lending is the sum of mortgages plus bonds. Table 19.11 shows by how much total lending, as a share of GDP, grew in the euro area. The picture is very different across the various countries. In some countries (Germany and France) the ratio of total lending to GDP remained stable, or even fell as in Germany. In Spain, Ireland and Greece it doubled. What was happening is that Spanish, Irish, Greek and, to some extent, also Portuguese banks borrowed from French and German banks to finance loans to domestic households: these loans were mostly housing mortgages in Spain, consumer loans in Portugal. In Greece banks used the funds borrowed abroad mostly to lend to the government, buying its bonds.

In any case, at some point – as always happens following a consumption or a housing boom financed through foreign borrowing – banks in the centre got worried and stopped lending to banks in the periphery; when that happened, the borrowers started falling behind with their interest payments.

The mirror image of this cross-border lending among euro-area banks is that French and German banks ended up with very large exposures to the periphery. By March 2011, French banks, for instance (see Table 19.12), had lent a total of €612 billion to Italy, Greece, Spain, Portugal and Ireland: this was equivalent to 30% of French GDP. German banks too had a large exposure, equivalent 20% of the country's GDP. It is thus no surprise that the concern for the stability of banks soon turned into a concern for the country's public debt. If French banks were to lose, say, 50% of their loans to the periphery, and the government saved them to avoid a financial meltdown, French public debt would increase by 15% of GDP, a very sizable amount.

Table 19.12 Euro area banks: lending to other euro area countries (billion euros, March 2011)

Lending from: to:	Germany	France	Italy	Spain
Italy	167	364		39
Spain	164	135	35	
Greece	20	48	5	1
Portugal	38	25	6	81
Ireland	114	40	18	10
Σ lending	502	612	64	131
per cent of the country's GDP	20%	30%	4%	13%

Note: Lending is to public sector, banks and non-bank private sector. It includes exposures originating from derivative contracts, guarantees and credit commitments.
Source: BIS.

The bottom line is that concerns for the growth of public debt appeared both in the centre and in the periphery. In the centre for what we just discussed; in the periphery because, when local banks ran into trouble, governments had to bail them out. The most startling episode happened in Ireland. This was the country where the banks had issued the largest amount of real-estate mortgages. When the real-estate bubble burst, the government had to step in, providing €100 billion to the banks to avoid a meltdown of the financial system: this amount corresponds to 40% of Irish GDP and raised the debt–GDP ratio in Ireland from 47% of GDP in 2007 to 170% of GDP in 2011.

Who bears the responsibility for what happened? Certainly, financial regulators who did not prevent the lending boom to finance a housing bubble (in Ireland and Spain) or households' consumption (in Portugal) or the budget deficit (in Greece). Bankers in the centre were also ill-advised: they should have asked themselves whether all these loans to the periphery would ever have been paid back. This is very similar to what happened in the USA with lending to subprime borrowers (see Chapters 1 and 20).

This is where the euro area is at the time of writing (early 2013): between a rock and a hard place. During the first 13 years of the euro, banks in the periphery made loans that will be difficult to recover: their losses will be transferred to banks in France and Germany. Later (in Chapter 21) we discuss how it is that countries sometimes accumulate lots of public debt. In the case of the euro area, the origin of the increase in the public debt (as we will see in Chapter 21) is government intervention to bail out banks and the increase in the public deficit due to the increases in public spending to help economies out of the recession. This large increase in public debt then resulted in a loss of investors' confidence and in a debt crisis. The solution is to tighten fiscal rules (as are now being implemented in a new Treaty), rather than central banks' financing of the deficits.

Why did investors' confidence in the euro area government bonds collapse, while it did not in the UK and in the USA, where – and for the same reasons – debt ratios also increased sharply?

One reason is the different role central banks play. The ECB operated under a very strict mandate: it is not allowed to 'bail out' governments. Thus it cannot buy government bonds if this means (even indirectly) financing them. This prohibition does not apply to the Bank of England or to the Federal Reserve, both of which have bought large quantities of UK and US government bonds, respectively. For example, were an Italian public debt auction to fail, the ECB, differently from the Bank of England, could not intervene to buy Italian bonds. Some observers think this is the main weakness of the euro. Others think the euro was created precisely because national central banks lacked discipline and this had been the reason for high deficits and high inflation. Who is right will determine whether EMU will survive.

19.5 SHOULD THE OUTS JOIN?

Since its beginning, when the euro area consisted of 12 countries, five more have joined: Cyprus, Malta, Slovakia, Slovenia and Estonia. Yet major countries are still reluctant to do so, most notably Denmark, Sweden and the UK (but also Poland). In this section, we will briefly summarise the motivations and the political and economic events that accompanied the decision not to join EMU by two countries: Sweden, which did not opt out of EMU, but has not yet decided to join; and the UK which, like Denmark, explicitly postponed to a later date the decision whether to adopt the euro or not.

When the Swedish government negotiated its entry into the EU in 1993–1994, the negotiations did not include an exemption from adopting the euro. In contrast to Denmark and the UK, which did obtain such an exemption, Sweden is therefore required by EU law to join EMU and adopt the euro as soon as the convergence criteria specified in the Maastricht Treaty are fulfilled. Nevertheless, the Swedish Parliament (the Riksdag) decided in 1997 that Sweden would not join the Exchange Rate Mechanism (ERM) of the EMS, and the Swedish central bank (Sveriges Riksbank) has followed a policy of inflation targeting with a flexible exchange rate since 1993.

◄ Remember that the clause of 'opting out' refers to the choice to postpone the decision of whether or not to join at a later date.

As a consequence, in the assessments made by the European Commission prior to the launch of EMU in 1999 and every two years since 2000, Sweden has been judged not to fulfill the criterion regarding exchange rate stability, which requires the member state to participate in the ERM. Sweden therefore is a member state considered 'not yet ready' to participate in the EMU. A national referendum on Swedish participation in EMU was held in September 2003, and the result was a rejection of membership with 56% of the electorate voting against and 42% voting in favour. As a consequence, the Riksdag decision of 1997 remains in force, and Sweden remains out.

How should one consider the decision by a country not to join, from a purely economic point of view? In the case of Sweden, a recent study by Ulf Söderström (an economist at the Riksbank) looks at whether or not participation in the monetary union would be advantageous for the country. The business cycle since the mid-1990s has been closely correlated with the euro area economies: this would suggest that Sweden has overall been subject to similar shocks to those that hit the euro area. The study also showed that the exchange rate has acted to destabilise, rather than stabilise, the Swedish economy: this suggests that an independent monetary policy with a flexible exchange rate could be rather costly for Sweden. Finally, counterfactual simulations of a model of the Swedish economy suggest that Swedish inflation and GDP growth might have been slightly higher if Sweden had been a member of EMU since the launch in 1999, but also that GDP growth might have been more volatile.

In the UK, the euro has been a long-standing part of the debate about the implications of the country's integration into the EU. The UK affirmed its commitment to eventually adopting the euro in repeated official statements: in 1972, 1974, 1985 and 1989. But since 1974, UK policy makers have expressed reservations about economic and monetary union, which were finally made official with the securing of an 'opt-out' clause in the Maastrict Treaty that was executed in 1997.

A major element of the opposition to euro membership has taken the form of opposition to the perceived loss of political sovereignty, and some adherents to that argument regard it as a sufficient condition for rejecting the monetary union even if euro membership could be shown to be desirable on economic grounds. This seemed to be the stance taken by several members of the Conservative governments throughout the 1990s, but that position was decisively renounced as government policy when in 1997 the Blair Government stated that economic merits would be the only criteria for entry.

Shortly after its election in 1997, the Blair Government 'committed the UK to the principle of joining the single currency', but made any recommendation about actual entry conditional on five economic tests being passed. The five economic tests were:

1. Are business cycles and economic structures compatible so that we and others could live with euro interest rates on a permanent basis?
2. If problems emerge, is there sufficient exibility to deal with them?
3. Would joining EMU create better conditions for firms making long-term decisions to invest in Britain?
4. What impact would entry into EMU have on the financial services industry?
5. In summary, will joining EMU promote higher growth, stability and a lasting increase in jobs?

The UK Government determined in 1997 and 2003 that these tests had not yet been satisfied, and so did not proceed to a referendum on UK membership of the euro area. Until the recession that started in 2008, the prospects of the UK becoming a member of the euro area seemed remote. It's continuing good macroeconomic performance over 1997–2007, the success of the inflation targeting regime and the move to even greater seniority within the UK government of critics of membership (most notably when Gordon Brown moved from Chancellor of the Exchequer to Prime Minister) have all been factors reducing the likelihood of euro adoption.

Today, after the first 14 years of the euro experience, we can compare the monetary policy regimes followed by the European Central Bank and Bank of England since 1999, and thus we can try to assess the likely effect that monetary union would have had on UK economic performance. Economists studying the UK experience found that interest-rate variability would decline if the UK were to join EMU. Thus embracing the euro would appear to confer on the UK more stable interest rates.

Moreover, some economists suggest that the 'strong pound' period starting in 1996 and continuing for nearly a decade is a powerful argument in favour of euro adoption. Proponents of UK participation contend that the strong pound shifted UK employment from the exchange-rate-sensitive manufacturing sector to the financial services sector, and that the increase in employment in the latter has proved to be ephemeral.

Ex-post, set in the light of the today's troubles of the euro area, the decision not to join the euro area had one important benefit. Keeping a national currency meant that banks remained exposed to exchange rate risk when lending to euro area countries: this limited such lending. Swedish, Danish and British banks did not accumulate loans towards Spain, Greece or Portugal to the same extent that German or French banks did. When these countries ran into trouble, such troubles did not translate to the countries outside the euro area as they did to those that were members of the area. This was certainly an important benefit of non-membership.

Also, when the crisis hit Europe, the countries that had maintained a national currency were better able to use the exchange rate to offset the fall in demand produced by the crisis. Between 2007 and 2011 the UK pound devalued around 25% relative to the euro, the currency of Britain's main trading partners. Sweden and, to a minor extent, Denmark have had similar experiences since 2009, devaluing 13% and 0.2% respectively relative to the euro.

Still, using only economic arguments, it is difficult to come to an unambiguous answer about the pros and cons of euro membership. One must accept that an important factor in the decision to join is political. As a result of the current crisis, the euro area is transforming itself: it is not unlikely that ten years from now it will be a fiscal union as much as it is a monetary union, becoming much more similar to the USA. The countries that decide to remain outside the euro area will not take part in this process and will inevitably end up on the fringe of the EU: their influence on EU decisions will become increasingly weak. This will increase their distance from a euro area they had no part in shaping, making it increasingly difficult to join the future. It has already started to happen, with the decision by David Cameron, the UK Prime Minister, to threaten to pull the UK out of the EU.

SUMMARY

- The Europeans have always been concerned about the volatility of the exchange rate between their currencies. First, they live in very open economies, where international trade is an important component of national income. Second, the wide fluctuations in exchange rates in Europe in the 1920s and 1930s are seen as having contributed to the crisis of national economies in the period between the wars. A final factor is the Common Agricultural Market, which needs stable exchange rates to operate properly. After the collapse of the Bretton Woods system, the response of Europeans to the high volatility of exchange rates that had occurred in the 1970s was the EMS, an agreement of exchange limited to European countries where the mark acted as the anchor of the system. The EMS allowed a period of relatively stable exchange rates, but between 1979 and 1992 there were ten devaluations: in each case the central parity of

one or more European currencies were devalued against the mark.

- In the EMS devaluations were not unilateral decisions, but collegial; when a currency reached the top margin of fluctuation, the central bank of that country had two options: raise interest rates in order to defend the exchange or request a realignment: that is, a devaluation of the central parity.

- The Maastricht Treaty is a fundamental document for the history of European integration and for the birth of the euro. It established some convergence criteria that countries aspiring to enter the EMU were obliged to meet. The criteria adopted by the treaty concerned in particular: exchange rate stability, convergence of interest rates in the long run, inflation rates and two indicators of public finance: the deficit/GDP ratio and debt ratio.

KEY TERMS

European Economic and Monetary Union (EMU) 425

degree of openness 425

exchange rate fluctuations 425

competitive devaluation 425

Bretton Woods 426

European Monetary System (EMS) 427

anchor of the system 428

controls on capital flows 428

Maastricht Treaty 430

monetary policy 432

asymmetric shocks 432

trade intensity 433

European system of Central Bank (ESCB) 434

QUESTIONS AND PROBLEMS

QUICK CHECK

1. *Using the information in this chapter, label each of the following statements true, false or uncertain. Explain briefly.*

a. European countries have always been negatively affected by exchange rate volatility among their currencies (prior to euro adoption) because their economies are heavily integrated with one another.

b. A system of fixed exchange rates and a common currency are perfect substitutes.

c. Countries that form a monetary union have to set rules for their fiscal policies to maintain the stability of their exchange rate.

d. To be admitted to the European Monetary Union, countries must satisfy a set of minimum requirements based on a set of macroeconomic variables.

e. The European Central Bank pursues as its main objective the goal of price stability.

f. During its first ten years of life, the European Central Bank has *de facto* behaved as the Bundesbank would have done.

g. A group of countries is said to form an 'optimal currency area' only if the macroeconomic benefits from having just one currency outweigh the costs.

h. Since the introduction of the euro, price differentials have completely disappeared between euro member countries.

i. There exist divergent estimates about the positive trade effects of the euro on member countries, but all of them point to a significant increase in trade flows among member countries.

j. There is no cost of sacrificing exchange rate flexibility between different regions if wages and prices are perfectly flexible.

k. If wages and prices are not flexible, the main cost of sacrificing exchange rate flexibility between different regions depends on whether these regions face asymmetric shocks to aggregate demand.

l. Euro member countries have faced no asymmetric shocks in the first ten years of the euro: therefore the euro area can be considered an 'optimal currency area'.

2. *Describe why the European Monetary System was not an efficient mechanism to limit exchange rate volatility among European countries.*

3. *Describe which are the main benefits and costs of a monetary union.*

DIG DEEPER

4. The ECB open market operations

Describe the main open market operations carried out by the European Central Bank and their objectives. Visit the website of the European Central Bank and find the section on 'Open Market Operations'. Read the most recent 'Weekly Financial Statement' (the section about 'Items related to monetary policy operations') and collect the data about the Eurosystem's transactions during that week. Explain briefly what might be the reasons for the difference compared to the preceding week.

5. Import propensity and exchange rate changes

In Chapter 7 you learned that the higher the share of exports or imports in total income, the greater the effect, on the same income, of a change in the exchange rate. In this problem you will compare two economies with different propensities to import.

Suppose that exports and imports of country A and country B are described by the following relations:

$$X = X(Y^*, \varepsilon) = \alpha Y^* - b\varepsilon$$
$$IM = IM(Y^*, \varepsilon) = \alpha Y + \beta\varepsilon$$
$$NX = X - IM/\varepsilon$$

where the two countries differ only in terms of import propensity. Country A has a higher import propensity than country B ($\alpha_A > \alpha_B$).

a. Draw net exports as a function of output for each country in the same graph.

b. What is the slope of the net export function?

c. Is the relation between import propensity and Y_{TB} positive or negative? Explain briefly.

d. Does the import propensity impact on the sensitivity of net exports to changes in the exchange rate? (*Hint:* derive the net export function with respect to the exchange rate and see what happens to that derivative following a change in the exchange rate.)

e. How does this relates to the discussion about European countries being adverse to exchange rate volatility?

6. Monetary policy coordination

Among the benefits of a monetary union, the need for member countries to have monetary policy coordination prevents each member country from using monetary policy in an arbitrary manner. Illustrate in a graph the advantage, with respect to aggregate welfare, of member countries not being able to use expansionary monetary policies to increase domestic output at the expense of other members' output.

7. Monetary union vs exchange rate peg

Compare the pros and cons of a monetary union with those of an exchange rate peg.

EXPLORE FURTHER

8. The Taylor rule

In this chapter you learned that the way monetary authorities set interest rates can be described by the following formula, which is know as Taylor rule (from the name of an economist, John Taylor, who was observing the US economy in the 1980s):

$$R_t = a_0 + a_1(p^e_{t+1} - p^*) + a_2(y_t - y^*)$$

Go to the website of your country's central bank (the ECB if you are in the EMU), and download the data about potential GDP, real GDP, the rate of inflation and the short-term interest rate for the past ten years. Copy and paste them in your favourite spreadsheet.

a. Compute the average inflation for each year.

b. Assuming there is a target inflation of 2%, say what the real interest rate should have been if monetary authorities had followed the Taylor rule written above.

c. How would your answer change if the difference between potential output and actual output was bigger? Explain briefly.

9. Correlation between regional and aggregate GDP growth

In this problem you are asked to compute the correlation between regional and aggregate EA12 GDP growth for your country (or for another country of your choice).

a. Go to the Eurostat website (***http://epp.eurostat.ec. europa.eu/portal/page/portal/eurostat/home/***) and go to the section on 'Statistics' and then to the section on 'Regions and Cities'. In the 'Regional Economic Accounts', download the regional GDP growth for the regions of your country (NUTS 2 or 3 level) for the past ten years. Now download, from the main 'Statistics' section, the aggregate GDP growth for the Euro Area 12 (EA12) for the same years.

b. Compute the correlation between regional and national GDP growth for the two sub-periods. Are regions in your country more or less similar to each other in terms of growth?

c. Now compute the correlation between regional and aggregate EA12 GDP growth for the two sub-periods. Are the regions in your country more or less similar to the evolution of GDP in the EA12?

---

*Log on to **MyEconLab** and complete the studyplan exercises for this chapter to see how much you have learnt, and where you need to revise most.*

MyEconLab

FURTHER READING

- For an analysis of the role of the EMS in countries with high inflation you can read F. Giavazzi and M. Pagano, 'The advantage of tying one's hands: EMS discipline and central bank credibility', *European Economic Review*, **32**, 1055–75, 1988.

- If you want to know about European countries which tried to limit exchange rate flexibility before eventually deciding to adopt the euro, you should read F. Giavazzi and

A. Giovanninni, *Limiting Exchange Rate Flexibility: The European Monetary System* (MIT Press, 1989).

- On the intra-Euro area current account imbalance and its effect in triggering the Euro crisis see F. Giavazzi and L. Spaventa, 'Why the current account may matter in a monetary union', in Beblavý, M. et al. (eds) The Euro Area and the Financial Crisis, (Cambridge University Press, 2012).

Chapter 20

THE CRISIS

Since 2008, the world in general, and the USA and Europe in particular, have been going through an intense economic crisis. The trigger of the crisis was a problem in housing markets (predominantly in the USA but also in some European countries: the UK, Ireland and Spain) that quickly led to a financial crisis. Policy was used, but this quickly faced limits. And the recovery has been extremely slow.

The chapter has three sections:

● Section 20.1 looks at the trigger. The main question is how the initial trigger, namely a decline in housing prices, could lead to such a large recession. This forces us to have a closer look at the financial system and how it works.

● Section 20.2 looks at the limits of policy, the liquidity trap and the high public debt.

● Section 20.3 looks at why the recovery from the financial shocks is taking so long.

In the process, we shall build on the *IS–LM* and the *AS–AD* models. We shall need to extend both, but you will see how we build on them, and how they help organise both facts and thoughts.

20.1 FROM A HOUSING PROBLEM TO A FINANCIAL CRISIS

When, in 2006, housing prices started declining in the USA, most economists forecast that this would lead to a decrease in demand, and a slowdown in growth. Few, however, anticipated that it would lead to a major financial crisis and, in turn, to a major macro-economic crisis. This section looks at how a housing problem turned into a major financial crisis.

Housing prices and sub-prime mortgages in the USA and in Europe

Figure 20.1 shows the evolution of an index of US house prices from 2000 onwards. The index is known as the Case–Shiller index, named for the two economists who constructed it. The index is normalised to equal 100 in January 2000. You can see the large increase in prices in the early 2000s, followed by a large decrease since then. From a value of 100 in 2000, the index increased to 226 in mid-2006. Starting in 2006, however, the index first stabilised, and then started declining. By the end of 2008, at the start of the financial crisis, the index was down to 162. At the time of writing (early 2013) it stood at 156.

> ◀ Just as for the price of oil, we should look at a real price index rather than a nominal price index. But inflation was low during that period, so it would not make a large difference.

Was the sharp price increase from 2000 to 2006 justified? In retrospect, and given the collapse later on, surely not. But, in real time, when prices were increasing, economists were not so sure. Some increase in prices was clearly justified:

- The 2000s were a period of unusually low interest rates. As a result, mortgage rates were also low, increasing the demand for housing and thus pushing up the price.
- Other factors were also at work. **Mortgage lenders** became increasingly willing to make loans to more risky borrowers. These mortgages, known as **sub-prime mortgages**, or sub-primes for short, had existed since the mid-1990s but became more prevalent in the 2000s. By 2006, about 20% of all US mortgages were sub-primes. Was it necessarily bad? Again, at the time, this was seen by most economists as a positive development: it allowed more people to buy homes and – under the assumption that housing prices would continue to increase, so the value of the mortgage would decrease over time relative to the price of the house – looked safe both for lenders and for borrowers. Judging from the past, the assumption that housing prices would not decrease also seemed reasonable: as you can see from the figure, they had not decreased: for example, during the 2000–2001 recession.

> ◀ Even if people did not finance the purchase of a house by taking a mortgage, low interest rates would lead to an increase in the price of houses. Remember (from Chapter 17) that lower interest rates increase the present discounted value of an asset, so that houses sell for higher current prices due to their future expected value being discounted at a lower interest rate.

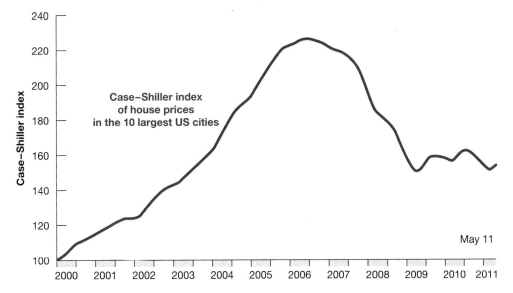

Figure 20.1

US housing prices since 2000

Housing prices increased sharply from 2000 to 2006, only to decline since then.

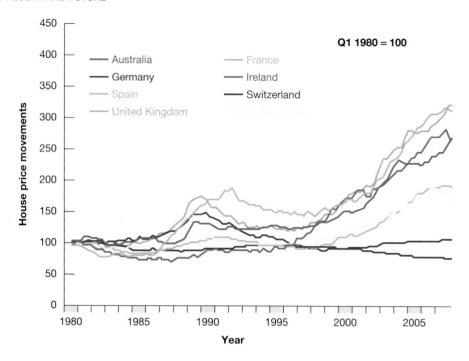

Figure 20.2

'Real' house prices in eight countries

Source: Bank for International Settlement.

Some economists were worried even as prices were going up. Robert Shiller, one of the two economists behind the Case–Shiller index, was among them, warning that the price increase was a bubble which would most likely crash later.

Some of these loans became known as NINJA loans (for no income, no job, no assets).

Some mortgages offered very low interest rates at the beginning. The low rates were known as 'teaser rates'. The rates then increased sharply after a few months or a few years.

The increase in house prices since the late 1990s was not a phenomenon limited to the USA. As shown in Figure 20.2, in some European countries house prices increased even more. In the UK and Ireland by 2007, house prices were three times their level in 1980, compared with just around two times in the USA. In Spain they had increased two-and-a-half times.

In retrospect, again, these developments were much less benign than most economists thought. First, housing prices could go down, as became evident from 2006 on. When this happened, many borrowers found themselves in a situation where the mortgage they owed now exceeded the value of their house. Second, it became clear that, in many cases, the mortgages were in fact much riskier than either the lender pretended, or the borrower understood. In many cases, borrowers had taken mortgages with low initial interest rates and thus low initial interest payments, probably not fully realising that payments would increase sharply later. Even if house prices had not declined, many of these borrowers would have been unable to make mortgage payments.

Thus, as house prices turned around and many borrowers defaulted, many banks found themselves faced with large losses. In mid-2008, losses on mortgages were estimated to be around $300 billion. This is obviously a large number, but, relative to the size of the US economy, it is not a very large one: $300 billion is about 2% of US GDP. One might have thought that the US financial system could absorb the shock, and that the adverse effect on output would be limited.

This was not to be. And while the trigger of the crisis was indeed the decline in housing prices, its effects were enormously amplified. Even those economists who had anticipated the housing price decline did not realize how strong amplification mechanisms would be. To understand them, we must return to the role of banks.

The role of banks

See section 4.3.

Earlier (in Chapter 4), we looked at the role of banks in the determination of the money supply. Their important characteristic in that context was that they issued money or, more precisely, that they had deposit accounts as liabilities. Here, we shall focus on their more general role as financial intermediaries, institutions which intermediate funds between lenders and borrowers.

	Assets	Liabilities	Capital	Leverage
Bank A	€100	€80	€20	5
Bank B	€100	€95	€ 5	20

Figure 20.3

Bank assets, capital and liabilities

Figure 20.3 shows a (much simplifed) bank balance sheet. Consider first Bank A. The bank has assets of €100, liabilities of €80 and capital of €20. You can think of the owners of the bank as having put €20 of their own funds, borrowed €80, and bought assets for €100. As we saw earlier (in Chapter 4), the liabilities may be deposit accounts or borrowing from investors and other banks. The assets may be reserves (central bank money), loans to consumers and to frms, mortgages, government bonds or other forms of securities.

Earlier (in Chapter 4), we focused on the choice between holding reserves and holding bonds, and ignored capital. But, for our purposes, introducing capital is important. Suppose that a bank did not hold any capital. Then, if, for any reason, the assets it held went down in value, and the liabilities remained the same, liabilities would exceed assets, and the bank would be bankrupt. It is thus essential for the bank to hold enough capital to limit the risk that it goes bankrupt.

How can things go wrong, even if the bank holds some capital, as in our example? First, the assets may decline in value by so much that the capital the bank holds is not enough to cover losses. In our example, this will happen if the value of the assets decreases below €80. The bank will become insolvent. This is not, however, the only way the bank can get in trouble. Suppose that some of the investors that have lent to the bank want their funds back right away. If the bank can sell some of its assets, it can get the funds and pay the investors. But it may be difficult for the bank to sell the assets quickly: calling back loans is difficult; some securities may be hard to sell. The problem of the bank in this case is not solvency, but illiquidity. The bank is still solvent, but it is illiquid. The more liquid its liabilities, or the less liquid its assets, the more likely the bank is to find itself in trouble.

What happened in this crisis is a combination of all these factors: banks had too little capital. Liabilities were very liquid. Assets were often very illiquid. The outcome was a combination of both solvency and liquidity problems, which quickly paralysed the financial system. We now look at it in more detail.

Leverage

Consider two banks. As in Figure 20.3, bank A has assets of €100, liabilities of €80 and capital of €20. Its **capital ratio** is defined as the ratio of capital to assets and is thus equal to 20%. Its **leverage ratio** is defined as the ratio of assets to capital (the inverse of the capital ratio) and is thus equal to 5. Bank B has assets of €100, liabilities of €95 and capital of €5. Thus, its capital ratio is equal to 5% and its leverage ratio equal to 20.

Now suppose that some of the assets in each of the two banks go bad. For example, some borrowers cannot repay their loans. Suppose, as a result, that for both banks the value of the assets decreases from €100 to €90. Bank A now has assets of €90, liabilities of €80 and capital of €90 − €80 = €10. Bank B has assets of €90, liabilities of €95 and, thus, negative capital of €5 (€90 − €95). Its liabilities exceed its assets: in other words, it is bankrupt. This is indeed what happened during the crisis: many banks were highly leveraged, so that even limited losses very much increased the risk of bankruptcy.

Why was leverage so high? The example suggests a simple answer: higher leverage means higher expected profit. Suppose, for example, that assets pay an expected rate of return of 5%, and liabilities pay an expected rate of return of 4%. Then the owners of bank A have an expected rate of return on their capital of (€100 × 5% − €80 × 4%)/€20 = 9%, the owners of Bank B have an expected rate of return of (€100 × 5% − €95 × 4%)/€5 = 24%, so more than twice as high. But, as the example we just saw also makes clear, leverage also increases risk: the higher the leverage, the more likely the bank is to go bankrupt. What happened throughout the 2000s is that banks decided to get a higher return and thus to take on more risk as well.

One wishes that the balance sheets of banks were that simple and transparent. Had it been the case, the crisis would have been much more limited.

See the Focus box, 'Bank runs, deposit insurance and wholesale funding' (in Chapter 4).

Some liabilities may actually pay a zero rate of return. Recall (from Chapter 4) that a large part of these liabilities is deposit accounts, which typically pay at most a low interest rate.

Why did they do so? This is the subject of much discussion. There appears to be a number of reasons. First, banks probably underestimated the risk they were taking: times were good, and, in good times, banks, just like people, tend to underestimate the risk of bad times. Second, the compensation system and bonus payments also gave incentives to managers to go for high expected returns without fully taking risk into account. Third, while financial **regulation** required banks to keep their capital ratio above some minimum, banks found new ways of avoiding the regulation, by creating new financial structures such as SIVs. What these are and how banks used them is explained in the Focus box 'Increasing leverage and alphabet soup'.

FOCUS
Increasing leverage and alphabet soup. SIVs, AIG and CDSs

SIV stands for **structured investment vehicle**. Think of it as a virtual bank, created by an actual bank. On the liability side, it borrows from investors, typically in the form of short-term debt. On the asset side, it holds various forms of securities. To reassure the investors that they will get repaid, the SIV typically has a guarantee from the actual bank that, if needed, the bank will provide funds to the SIV.

While the first SIV was set up by Citigroup in 1988, SIVs rapidly grew in size in the 2000s. You may ask why banks did not simply do all these things on their own balance sheet, rather than create a separate vehicle. The main reason was to be able to increase leverage. If the banks had done these operations themselves, it would have shown up on their balance sheet and they would have been subject to regulatory capital requirements, forcing them to hold enough capital to limit the risk of bankruptcy. But, it turns out, doing these operations through an SIV did not require banks to put capital down. For that reason, through setting up SIVs, banks could increase leverage and increase expected profits, and they did.

When housing prices started declining, and many mortgages turned bad, the securities held by the SIVs decreased in value. Investors became reluctant to lend to the SIVs, out of fear that they may be insolvent. The banks that had created the SIVs had to honour their obligations by paying investors, but had limited capital to do so. It became clear that banks had in effect created a **shadow banking system**, and that leverage of the banking system as a whole (i.e including the shadow banking part) was much higher than had been perceived. Small losses could lead to bankruptcies. As of October 2008, no SIVs were left; they had either closed, or all their assets and liabilities had been transferred to the banks that had created them.

AIG stands for **American International Group**. It is an insurance company which, in the 2000s, had what looked like a good idea at the time. It would sell not only regular insurance but also insurance against default risk through the sale of **credit default swaps**, or **CDS** for short. If a bank was worried about default on a security it held in its portfolio, it could buy a CDS from AIG which promised to pay the bank in case of default on the security. For this, AIG charged the bank a price that was supposed to reflect the probability of such a default. For banks, it was an attractive deal as, by buying insurance, the securities they held became riskless and thus decreased the capital that banks had to hold (the less risky the asset, the smaller the amount of capital required by regulation). AIG, being an insurance company rather than a bank, did not have to hold capital against the promises it was making.

When housing prices started declining, however, AIG had to make good on many of its promises, but it just did not have the funds to do so, and so could not provide the insurance. Thus, suddenly, banks realised that, without the insurance, their assets were much riskier than they had assumed, and that they did not have the capital needed to sustain losses. Again, leverage of the financial system (including now the banks, the SIVs, and CDS issuers such as AIG) was much higher than had been perceived. As we shall see below, the US government decided it had to provide funds to AIG to make payments. The alternative would have led not only to default of AIG, but also to the potential default of many banks holding CDSs. As of the end of 2009, the government had advanced more than $180 billion to AIG, which AIG used to pay the banks as promised. Since then, AIG has been steadily reimbursing the US government, and is expected to fully repay the loan. By 23 August 2013 the US government was fully reimbursed and earned in the overall operations a net profit of 17.7 billion dollars.

Complexity

Another important development of the 1990s and the 2000s was the growth of **securitisation**. Traditionally, the financial intermediaries that made loans or issued mortgages kept them on their balance sheet. This had obvious drawbacks. A local bank, with local loans and mortgages on its books, was very much exposed to the local economic situation. When, for example, oil prices had come down sharply in the mid-1980s and Texas was in recession, many local banks went bankrupt. Had they had a more diversified portfolio of mortgages, say, mortgages from many parts of the country, these banks might have avoided bankruptcy.

This is the idea behind securitisation. Securitisation is the creation of securities based on a bundle of assets: for example, a bundle of loans or a bundle of mortgages. For instance, a **mortgage-based security**, or **MBS** for short, is a title to the returns from a bundle of mortgages, with the number of underlying mortgages often in the tens of thousands. The advantage is that many investors, who would not want to hold individual mortgages, will be willing to buy and hold these securities. This increase in the supply of funds from investors is, in turn, likely to decrease the cost of borrowing.

One can think of further forms of securitisation. For example, instead of issuing identical claims to the returns on the underlying bundle of assets, one can issue different types of securities. For example, one can issue two types of securities: **senior** securities which have first claims on the returns from the bundle, and **junior** securities which come after, and pay only if something is left after the senior securities have been paid. Senior securities will appeal to investors who want little risk, junior securities will appeal to investors who are willing to take more risk. Such securities, known as **collateralised debt obligations**, or **CDOs**, were first issued in the late 1980s but, again, grew in importance in the 1990s and 2000s. Securitisation went even further, with the creation of CDOs on CDOs, or CDO^2, i.e. CDO securities based on an underlying bundle of CDOs, and so on.

Securitisation would seem like a good idea, a way of diversifying risk and getting a larger group of investors involved in lending to households or firms. And, indeed, it is. But it also came with a large cost, which became clear only during the crisis. It was a risk that **rating agencies**, those firms that assess the risk of various securities, had largely missed: when underlying mortgages went bad, assessing the value of the underlying bundles in the MBSs or, even more so, of the underlying MBSs in the CDOs, was extremely hard to do. These assets came to be known as **toxic assets**. It led investors to assume the worst and be very reluctant either to hold them or to continue lending to those institutions that did hold them.

Liquidity

Yet another development of the 1990s and 2000s was the development of other sources of finance than deposit accounts by banks (the 80 euros they borrowed in our example above). Increasingly, they relied on borrowing from other banks or other investors, in the form of short-term debt, to finance the purchase of their assets, a process known as **wholesale funding**. SIVs, the financial entities set up by banks, which we saw earlier, were entirely funded through such wholesale funding.

Wholesale funding again would seem like a good idea, giving banks more flexibility in the amount of funds they can use to make loans or buy assets. But it has a cost, which again became clear during the crisis. If investors or other banks, worried about the value of the assets held by the bank, decide to stop lending to the bank, the bank may find itself short of funds and be forced to sell some of its assets. If these assets are complex and hard to sell, it may have to sell them at very low prices.

We now have all the elements we need to explain what happened when housing prices declined, and why this led first to a major financial crisis.

Amplification mechanisms

As the crisis got worse, solvency and liquidity concerns increased sharply, each reinforcing the other:

> ◄ This is the modern equivalent of bank runs, when people ran to the bank to take their money out. Deposit insurance has largely eliminated that risk. But, now, it is investors, not depositors, who can decide to take their money out. (See the Focus box 'Bank runs, deposit insurance and wholesale funding' in Chapter 4.)

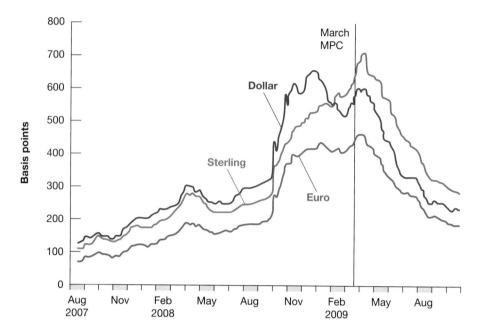

Figure 20.4

The Ted Spread since 2007

The rate spread, which reflects the risk banks perceived in lending to each other, went sharply up in September 2008.

- When housing prices declined, and some mortgages went bad, high leverage implied a sharp decline in the capital of banks. This in turn forced them to sell some of their assets. Because these assets were often hard to value, they had to sell them at very low prices – often referred to as **fire sale prices**. This, in turn, decreased the value of similar assets remaining on their balance sheet or on the balance sheet of other banks, leading to a further decline in capital, forcing further sales of assets and further declines in prices.
- The complexity of the securities (MBSs, CDOs) and of the true balance sheets of banks (banks and their SIVs) made it very difficult to assess the solvency of banks and their risk of bankruptcy. Thus, investors became very reluctant to continue to lend to them, and wholesale funding came to a stop, forcing further asset sales and price declines. Even banks became very reluctant to lend to each other. This is shown in Figure 20.4, which shows the difference between the riskless rate (measured by the rate of three-month government bonds) and the rate at which banks are willing to lend to each other (known as the **Libor rate**). This difference is known as the Ted spread.

  If banks perceived no risk in lending to each other, the Ted spread would be equal to zero. And, indeed, until mid-2007, it was very close to zero. Note, however, how it became larger in the second half of 2007 and then increased sharply in September 2008. Why then? Because, on 15 September 2008, Lehman Brothers, a major bank with more than $600 billion in assets, declared bankruptcy, leading financial participants to conclude that many, if not most, other banks and financial institutions were indeed at risk.

By mid-September, both mechanisms were in full force. The financial system had become paralysed: banks had basically stopped lending to each other or to anybody else. Quickly, what had been largely a financial crisis turned into a macroeconomic crisis.

20.2 THE USE AND LIMITS OF POLICY

The immediate effects of the financial crisis on the macroeconomy were twofold: first, a large increase in the interest rates at which people and firms could borrow; second, a dramatic decrease in confidence.

- Figure 20.5 shows the effect of the financial crisis on different interest rates. The first interest rate is the rate on ten-year government bonds. The second and third are the rates charged by the bond markets to two different types of firms, corresponding to different risk ratings. Firms with a **AAA** rating are considered the safest, firms with a **BBB**

Figure 20.5

Yields on US government bonds, AAA and BBB corporate bonds, since 2007

In 2008, the financial crisis led to a sharp decrease in the rates at which firms could borrow.

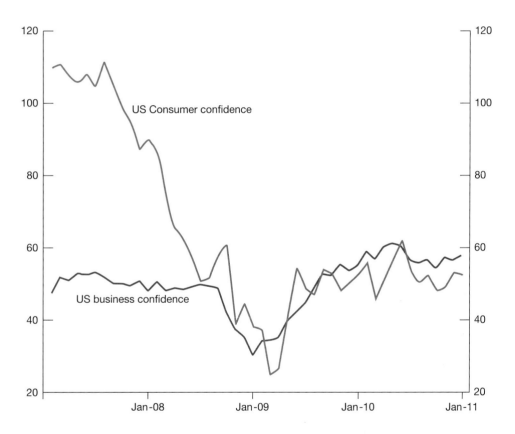

Figure 20.6

US consumer and business confidence, 2007–2010

The financial crisis led to a sharp drop in confidence, which bottomed in early 2009.

Source: *www.tradingeconomics.com/ united-states/business-confidence*

are considered less safe. In normal times, AAA firms can borrow at a rate close to the rate on government bonds; BBB firms borrow at a higher rate, but the difference is typically small, of the order of 1%. You can see that this was indeed the case at the start of 2007. But, as you can also see, the difference increased from mid-2007 on, and, while the rate on government bonds remained very low, the rates on both AAA and BBB bonds jumped in September to very high levels. Suddenly, borrowing became extremely expensive for most firms. And for the firms too small to issue bonds and thus depending on bank credit, it became nearly impossible to borrow at all.

● Figure 20.6 shows the effects of the financial crisis on expectations. The events of September 2008 triggered wide anxiety among consumers and firms. Thoughts of another Great Depression and, more generally, confusion and fear about what was happening in the financial system led to a large drop in confidence. The evolution of consumer

See the Focus box, 'The Lehman bankruptcy, fears of another Great Depression, and shifts in the consumption function' (in Chapter 3).

confidence and business confidence indexes for the USA are shown in Figure 20.6. Both indexes are normalised to equal 100 in January 2007. Note how consumer confidence, which had started declining in mid-2007, took a sharp drop in the fall of 2008 and reached a low of 22 in early 2009, a level far below previous historical lows. Associated with this collapse in confidence was a large decrease in the stock market (see chapter 1). The result of lower confidence and lower stock prices was a sharp decrease in consumption.

International spillover

The sharp contraction of the US economy rapidly translated to the rest of the world, and to Europe in particular, through three channels:

- Some European banks were directly exposed to the US housing market having bought securities whose underlying assets were US housing mortgages (MBS and CDOs).
- Trade flows contracted, both because demand was contracting due to the fall in consumers' confidence (Figure 20.7) and because trade credit dried up.
- The increase in the US interest rates translated to European interest rates, making it difficult also for firms outside the US to borrow (Figure 20.8).

Moreover, as we have seen in section 20.1, the increase and the following turnaround in house prices – which was at the origin of the crisis – was not limited to the USA. House prices had increased in Europe as well, in some countries (the UK, Ireland and Spain) by an even greater amount than in the USA. And when in Europe also house prices started to decrease, the effect of their fall was amplified by the same factors that amplified it in the USA. Figure 20.9 shows to what extent these factors resulted in a worldwide synchoronised fall in output.

Initial policy responses

The USA

Higher interest rates, the inability to borrow, lower stock prices and lower confidence all combined to decrease the demand for goods. In terms of the *IS-LM* model, there was a sharp

Figure 20.7

The fall in consumers' confidence spread to Europe and Japan

Source: IMF, *World Economic Outlook*, April 2009, p. 4.

Figure 20.8

The increase in interest rates in the USA translated to European rates

The 'spreads' shown in the figure are the difference between the interest rate on a corporate bond and that on a government bond of the same maturity.

Source: IMF, *World Economic Outlook*, April 2009, p. 7.

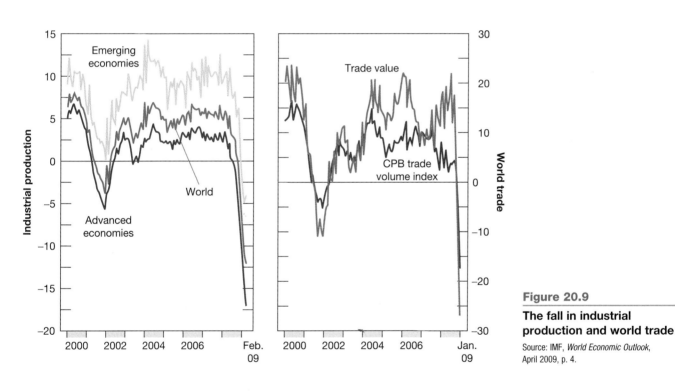

Figure 20.9

The fall in industrial production and world trade

Source: IMF, *World Economic Outlook*, April 2009, p. 4.

adverse shift of the *IS* curve. In the face of this large decrease in demand, policy makers did not remain passive.

The most urgent measures were aimed at strengthening the financial system:

● In order to prevent a run by depositors, Federal deposit insurance was increased from $100,000 to $250,000 per account. Recall, however, that much of the funding of banks came not from deposits but from the issuance of short-term debt to investors. In order to allow the banks to continue to fund themselves through wholesale funding, the US government offered a program guaranteeing new debt issues.

- The Fed provided widespread liquidity to the financial system. We have seen that, if investors wanted to take their funds back, the banks had no alternative but to sell some of these assets, often at fire sale prices. In many cases, this would have meant bankruptcy. To avoid this, the Fed put in place a number of **liquidity facilities** to make it easier to borrow from the Fed. It allowed not only banks but also other financial institutions to borrow from the Fed. Finally, it increased the set of assets that financial institutions could use as **collateral** when borrowing from the Fed (collateral refers to the asset a borrower pledges when borrowing from a lender. If the borrower defaults, the asset then goes to the lender). Together, these facilities allowed banks and financial institutions to pay back investors without having to sell the assets. It also decreased the incentives of investors to ask for their funds, as these facilities decreased the risk that banks would go bankrupt.

- The US government introduced a program, called the **Troubled Asset Relief Program**, or **TARP**, aimed at cleaning up banks. The initial goal of the $700 billion program, introduced in October 2008, was to remove the complex assets from the balance sheet of banks, thus decreasing uncertainty, reassuring investors and making it easier to assess the health of each bank. The Treasury, however, faced the same problems as private investors. If these complex assets were going to be exchanged for, say, Treasury bills, at what price should the exchange be done? Within a few weeks, it became clear that the task of assessing the value of each of these assets was extremely hard and would take a long time, and the initial goal was abandoned. The new goal became to increase the capital of banks. This was done by the government acquiring shares and thus providing funds to most of the largest US banks. By increasing their capital ratio, and thus decreasing leverage, the goal of the program was to allow them to avoid bankruptcy and, over time, return to normal. As of the end of September 2009, total spending under the TARP was $360 billion, of which $200 billion was spent through the purchase of shares in banks. At the time of writing, most banks have bought back their shares and have reimbursed the government. The final cost of TARP is expected to be small, perhaps even zero.

- All these measures were aimed at providing liquidity to financial institutions, avoiding unnecessary bankruptcies and allowing the financial system to function again. Worried, however, that some markets were slow to recover, the Fed directly intervened by purchasing private securities in these markets. In particular, given the importance of the housing sector in the crisis, it bought mortgage-backed securities. Today, the Fed is still the main buyer of these securities.

Europe

The ECB too responded to the crisis through a mix of conventional and non-conventional monetary policies. As a standard monetary intervention to stimulate economic activity, official interest rates were cut in a sequence of steps, bringing the main refinancing rate down from 4.25% to 1% in the space of six months. Moreover, it modified its operational framework and used an exceptional set of non-standard policy tools to address the crisis:

- European banks were granted access to essentially unlimited liquidity at a fixed interest rate at maturities of up to a year. This was a big change, since previously the ECB used to auction a given amount of liquidity and let competition between the banks determine the interest rate.

- When the ECB provides liquidity to a bank it does so by exchanging liquidity for some of the assets the bank owns. For example, the bank transfers some of the government bonds it owns to the ECB in exchange for cash, for a period of, say, six months. At the end of the six months, the bank buys back the bonds from the ECB. Thus the liquidity provided by the ECB is only temporary and does not permanently affect the stock of money in circulation. An important innovation introduced during the crisis is a list of assets the ECB would accept in such operations: not only government bonds, as it did in the past, but also private assets – for example, bank loans to private clients. This also made liquidity more easily available to banks.

● The ECB also provided liquidity to banks buying from them a particular type of bonds, called 'covered bonds'. These are bonds issued by banks and guaranteed by a flow of interest payments the bank will receive – for instance, from its housing mortgages. Thus the only difference between the purchase by the ECB of covered bonds and the Fed TARP program is that the Fed would buy mortgage-based securities directly, while the ECB would buy them indirectly through the banks. Thus the Fed was directly exposed to the risk that the mortgages might not be repaid, while the ECB was somewhat protected by the banks – in the sense that if the mortgages went sour and the banks had enough capital, the ECB would still be repaid.

Fiscal and monetary policies were used aggressively as well.

Fiscal policy

When the size of the adverse shock became clear, the governments of the 20 largest world economies (the G-20) came together and turned to fiscal policy using a combination of tax cuts and increases in spending. Figure 20.10 shows the effect of these fiscal actions on government budget deficits. In the advanced economies, those more seriously hit by the adverse shock, budget deficits increased, on average, from 1% of GDP before the crisis, to 9% in 2009.

The fiscal program adopted in the USA in 2009 by the newly elected Obama administration (the **American Recovery and Reinvestment Act**) was one of the largest. It called for $780 billion in new measures, in the form of both tax reductions and spending increases, over 2009 and 2010. The US budget deficit increased from 2.7% of GDP in 2007 to a very high 12.7% in 2009. As in other countries, the increase was largely the mechanical effect of ◄ the crisis, as a decrease in output leads automatically to a decrease in tax revenues and to an increase in transfer programs, such as unemployment benefits. But it was also the result of the specific measures in the fiscal program aimed at increasing either private or public spending.

Figure 1.4 (in Chapter 1) showed the path of the US budget deficits since 1990. You can see how unusual these large deficits are.

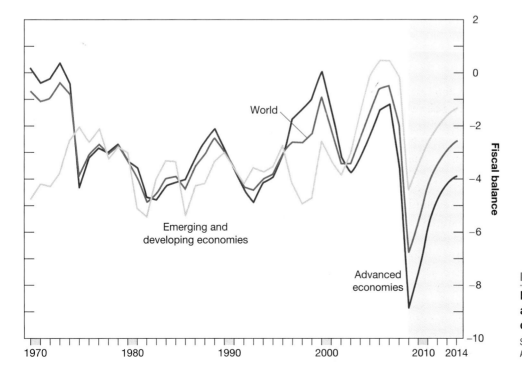

Figure 20.10

Fiscal balances in advanced, emerging and developing economies

Source: IMF, *World Economic Outlook*, April 2009, p. 30.

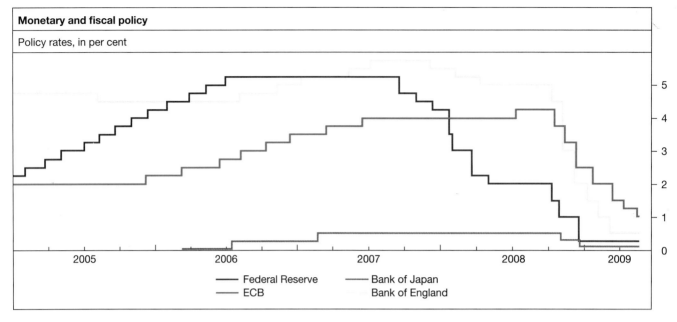

Figure 20.11

Policy rates

Central banks responded to the crises lowering interest rates throughout the world

Source: Economic Outlook, March 2009.

Monetary policy

Figure 20.11 shows the evolution of the interest rate, quarterly since January 2005 in the USA, the UK, the euro area and Japan. The interest rates in the figure are the rates directly controlled by monetary policy. You can see how, starting in the fall of 2007, the Fed started decreasing the federal funds rate, slowly at first, and then faster as it became clear that the crisis was leading to a sharp decrease in demand. By January 2009, the federal funds was, for all practical purposes, down to zero – they could not go lower. The Bank of England also followed the Fed, bringing interest rates down to zero, while the ECB stopped only slightly above, at 1.

Still, this combination of financial, fiscal and monetary measures was not enough to avoid a large decrease in output, both in the USA and in other advanced economies, especially in Europe, and recovery was slow thereafter. One would hope that fiscal and monetary policies could help strengthen the recovery, but, as we shall see now, both face sharp limits.

The limits of policies, monetary and fiscal

Since the end of 2008, the central banks of major advanced economies had decreased the interest rate to zero. Therefore (as you learned in Chapter 6), they could not do more: the economy had fallen in a **liquidity trap**. Conventional monetary policy, i.e. monetary policy using open market operations aimed at decreasing the interest rate, could do nothing more to increase output. The question is whether some unconventional measures may still be used. This is what central banks around the world have explored since 2008.

FOCUS
The Irish crisis

Ireland has been among the countries worst affected by the recession that started in 2008, with a cumulative nominal GDP decline of 21% from the end of 2007 until mid-2010. Since in those years the price level was falling, on average, at the rate of 2% per year, the fall in real GDP was even larger. Moreover, after a long period of budget surpluses, the fiscal balance dropped to a deficit of 10–12% of GDP during 2009–2011.

The main factor behind these developments has been a boom–bust cycle in the Irish property market. A real-estate boom, both family homes and commercial property, had been the main driver of Irish economic growth between 2003 and 2007. In turn, rising property prices had led to strong growth in private consumption (since, as we learned in Chapter 16, houses are the largest component of households' wealth), which also contributed to strong growth of GDP. Moreover, increasing tax revenues (driven by the increase in property taxes which follow the rise in house prices) enabled the government to increase public spending, while maintaining a budget surplus. The expansion in property investment was fuelled by rapid credit expansion, largely provided by local banks. In turn, these banks relied on funding from international financial markets, which resulted in a major increase in the country's net external liabilities. The mirror image of this foreign borrowing (as we learned in Chapter 7) was a current account deficit. The current account balance shifted from near zero in 2003 to a deficit close to 6% of GDP in 2007.

Already by the autumn of 2006, there were clear signs that the property sector had passed its peak. However, the hope was that the decline in property prices and construction-related activity would be gradual and could be offset by economic expansion in other areas. Indeed, economic activity continued to be strong during 2007. However, at the onset of the financial crisis, in early 2008, Irish banks started to find it more and more difficult to maintain funding in international wholesale markets.

Since then, Ireland has grappled with a triple crisis:

- *Massive losses in the banking system.* All banks have suffered considerable losses due to the fall in house prices which constitute the guarantee for the mortgages issued to Irish households. The most extreme losses were incurred by one bank that turned out to have had very a weak corporate governance – Anglo-Irish Bank (which had grown very rapidly through aggressive

property-related lending) – and whose losses have been by far the largest contributor to the overall losses in the Irish banking system. Anglo-Irish was nationalised in early 2009. In addition, a smaller mutual bank – Irish Nationwide Building Society (INBS) – has also incurred catastrophic property-related losses.
- *Severe decline in economic activity.* As banks cut credit lines and stopped new lending, this amplified the downturn in the property sector and in the economy at large. The increase in bad loans further curtailed the supply of credit by Irish banks. The credit squeeze amplified the recessionary effect of the fall in private consumption. Unemployment climbed from 4.6% in 2007 to 14% in 2011. In contrast to many other advanced economies, the export sector was a stabilising factor, with the decline in output concentrated in the domestically oriented sectors of the economy.
- *Rapid deterioration in the fiscal position.* Increased market concerns about the sustainability of the Irish fiscal position and, more generally, the uncertainty surrounding estimates of total loan losses in the Irish banking system pushed up the spread on Irish sovereign debt (Figure 20.12). This in turn added to the budget deficit by raising the interest cost of the debt. In just five years the ratio of public debt to GDP jumped from 25% to above 110%.

Overall, the main source of the Irish crisis was the failure to regulate the banking sector in avoiding the massive exposure to the real-estate bubble. This was especially problematic under EMU, since access to the area-wide financial markets meant that the scope for Irish banks to take on too much risk was amplified.

When it became impossible for the Irish government to raise funds on the market, it had to turn to the IMF and the European Union for financial support. This came in the form of a three-year deal agreed with the IMF and the EU. The total financial package under deal is valued at €85 billion, which is about 54% of 2010 Irish GDP. €17.5 billion of the total is domestically sourced, because the funds were to be supplied by the Irish National Pension Reserve Fund, and, in part, by the cash balances held by the agency responsible for managing the national debt (the National Treasury Management Agency). The remaining €67.5 billion are evenly split, with €22.5 billion from the Europeans; €22.5 billion from the IMF; and €22.5 billion from the European Financial Stability Fund

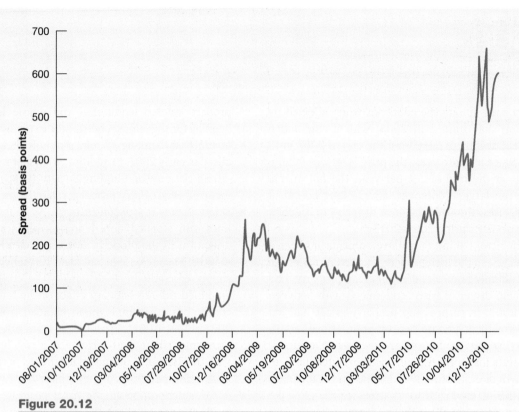

Figure 20.12

Spread between ten-year bonds: Ireland over Germany (1 August 2007 to 13 December 2010)

Source: Philip R. Lane (2011), 'The Irish crisis', *CEPR Discussion Papers* No. 8287.
www.cepr.org/pubs/dps/DP8287.asp

(EFSF) and from bilateral loans (from the UK, Sweden and Denmark).

The deal requires Ireland to reduce the risk in the banking system by downsizing the banking sector, through asset sales and deleveraging, with the aim that the loan–deposit ratio falls from 160% in 2010 to 120% by end of 2013. The goal is that these banking sector reforms will result in a smaller, less risky and better capitalised banking system. By summer 2011, there has been considerable progress towards these goals and it is projected that the official funding required for the banks will be far below that projected in the EU/IMF deal.

Equally important is the macroeconomic adjustment Ireland has been able to accomplish in just a couple of years. In 2008 Ireland was running a current account deficit as large as 6% of GDP, meaning that Ireland was spending 6% more than it was producing, borrowing the balance from the rest of the world (mostly from other euro area countries); by 2011 this had turned into a 1% surplus. Ireland is the only crisis-hit country in the euro area which has been able to eliminate its macroeconomic imbalance so rapidly.

Source: Philip R. Lane (2011), 'The Irish crisis', *CEPR Discussion Papers* No. 8287.

We have seen that the interest rate was equal to zero, and so further purchases of bonds could not decrease the interest rate. In our *IS–LM* model, there is only one type of bonds, one interest rate and, thus, nothing more monetary policy can do. But, in reality, there are many types of bonds, many interest rates. Some of these interest rates are higher than the interest rate on bonds. This suggests the following unconventional monetary policy: rather than buying Treasury bills through open market operations, the central bank could buy other bonds, for example, mortgages – loans made by banks to households – or gilts – government bonds which promise payment over, say, 10 or 20 years. By doing so, it may be able to decrease the interest rate on those bonds or mortgages. These lower interest rates can help increase demand.

Lehman   APF Phase II

Figure 20.13

Quantitative easing in the UK

Loans to APF are the loans the Bank of England made to the legal entity (the Asset Purchase Facility) in charge of buying assets from the market on behalf of the Bank.

Source: Bank of England.

Such a policy goes under the name of **credit easing** or **quantitative easing** and this is indeed what some central banks, in particular the Fed and the Bank of England, have done at various times during this crisis. Figure 20.13 shows the cumulative purchases of gilts (which constituted most of the assets purchased by the APF) of various maturities (from 3–5 years to more than 25 years) by the Bank of England during the crisis. Overall, the Bank of England bought 200 billion pounds worth of gilts, a bit more that 10% of UK GDP and 15% of the total outstanding stock of UK government bonds. Did these purchases reduce long-term interest rates? The Bank of England has estimated that its quantitative easing operation has reduced the interest rate on gilts by approximately 1%, a significant effect given that interest rates on gilts averaged, at that time, between 1.5% and 2.5%. The effect of this reduction in interest rates is estimated (by the Bank of England) to have increased the level of GDP by 1.5% to 2%, also not a negligible amount.

How helpful is quantitative easing? The evidence is mixed. It takes very large purchases by the central bank to decrease, for example, the interest rate on gilts, and, even then, the decrease in that interest rate is small.

Some economists have argued, however, that quantitative easing may actually work through another channel. Like open market operations, quantitative easing is achieved by buying assets, in this case bonds or mortgages, and paying for them by issuing money. It thus increases the money supply. Recall that (in the strange world of the liquidity trap we learned above in Chapter 5), higher expected inflation is good, as it reduces the real interest rate and thus stimulates spending. So, to the extent that the increase in the money supply leads people and firms to expect more inflation, this decreases the real interest rate and thus increases output. How convincing is that argument? The evidence from Japan where the central bank has used quantitative easing is not very supportive. It does not appear that large increases in the money supply lead people to expect higher inflation in the future.

To summarise: when conventional monetary policy can no longer be used, central banks still have a few tools in their hand. These tools, however, may have rather limited effects.

A recurrent theme of this book is that both monetary policy and fiscal policy can be used to affect demand and, in turn, output. So, even if monetary policy has reached sharp limits, isn't fiscal policy the solution? The answer is that fiscal policy also can reach limits. The problem is that, if the demand for goods does not recover over time by itself, if people or firms do not eventually become more optimistic and increase spending, the government must continue to run deficits to sustain higher demand and output. Continuing large deficits lead, however, to steadily higher public debt.

We shall look at the precise relation between debt and deficits later (in Chapter 21). But the notion that deficits lead to higher debt is straightforward.

In advanced countries, the ratio of government debt to GDP has increased from 46% in 2006 to 70% in 2011; in the USA, the ratio has increased from 42% in 2006 to 72% in 2011. High debt implies that, sooner or later, either taxes will have to increase or spending will have to decrease, or the government will be unable to repay the debt back. And when investors become worried about repayment of the debt, they start asking for higher interest rates on government bonds, making it even harder for the government to repay the debt. These worries are already leading to higher interest rates in a number of European countries. They have not yet led to higher interest rates on government bonds in the USA. But the risk that they might in the future is forcing the US government to reduce its budget deficit, and thus limit the contribution of fiscal policy to demand and to the recovery.

More on this in Chapter 21.

20.3 THE SLOW RECOVERY

While output growth is now positive in the USA and in some European countries, the recovery is very slow. Under current forecasts, unemployment is predicted to remain high for many years. Looking at what has happened in Japan since the 1990s, these worries are justified: for nearly two decades, Japan has been in an economic slump. As the Focus box 'Japan, the liquidity trap, and fiscal policy' shows, zero interest rates and large budget deficits have not succeeded in getting the Japanese economy back to normal.

FOCUS
Japan, the liquidity trap and fiscal policy

In the early 1990s, the Japanese stock market, which had boomed earlier, suddenly crashed. The **Nikkei index**, a broad index of Japanese stock prices, had gone up from 7,000 in 1980 to 35,000 at the beginning of 1990. Then, within two years, it went down to 16,000, and continued to decline after that, reaching a trough of 7,000 in 2003 (As we write, the Nikkei index is around 8,500). This decline in stock prices was followed by a decline in spending, and,

in response to the decline in spending, the Japanese central bank cut the interest rate. As you can see from Figure 20.14, by the mid-1990s, the interest rate was down to less than 1%, and it has remained below 1% since then.

With little room left for using monetary policy, fiscal policy was used to sustain demand. Figure 20.15 shows the evolution of government spending and revenues as a percentage of GDP since 1990. You can see the dramatic

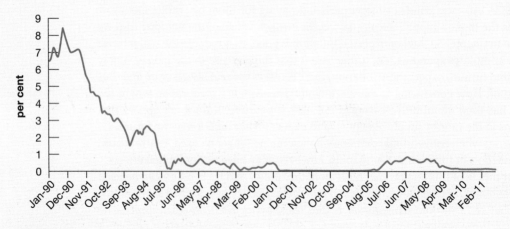

Figure 20.14

The interest rate in Japan since 1990

Why is the recovery so slow?

Some economists point to the aggregate supply side. They argue that the banking crisis has decreased the natural level of output, so that it would be wrong to think that we can go back to the pre-crisis level of output. More accurately, taking into account that output typically grows over time, it would be wrong to think that output can return to its old pre-crisis trend line. The weak recovery that we observe may be the best the economy can deliver. Indeed, the evidence from a large number of past banking crises, summarised in the Focus box 'Do banking crises affect output in the medium run?', suggests that, indeed, output remains below its old pre-crisis trend line for many years, if not forever. One can think of a number of reasons why this may be. The banking crisis may affect the efficiency of the banking system for a long time, leading to lower productivity (again relative to trend). Some of the new regulations introduced to decrease the risk of another financial crisis, such as increases in the capital ratio that banks must maintain, may indeed decrease risk; but they may also make intermediation between borrowers and lenders more costly, thus decreasing the natural level of output.

It may indeed be that the economy cannot return to its pre-crisis trend line. But in the context of the USA today, however, this does not appear sufficient to explain the slow recovery. It is hard to think that the unemployment rate, which is now around 9%, is not much higher than the natural unemployment rate, which most economists put at less than

> We saw earlier (in Chapter 10) how some shocks, such as a permanent increase in the price of oil, can lead to a lower natural level of output. The financial crisis provides another potential example.

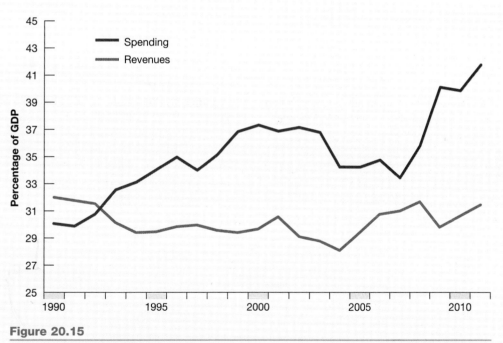

Figure 20.15

Government spending and revenues (as a percentage of GDP), Japan, since 1990

Source: International Monetary Fund, *World Economic Outlook Database*, September 2001.

increase in spending from the early 1990s on. Much of the increased spending has taken the form of public work projects, and a joke circulating in Japan is that, by the time the Japanese economy has recovered, the entire shoreline of the Japanese archipelago will be covered in concrete. The result of this strong fiscal expansion, however, has been a sharp increase in debt. The ratio of government debt to GDP, which stood at 13% of GDP in 1991, is now above 120%. Meanwhile, the Japanese economy is still in a slump: GDP growth, which averaged 4.4% in the 1980s, was down to 1.4% in the 1990s, and 0.9% in the 2000s. What has happened in Japan since 1990 is a tough warning to other advanced countries that it may take a long time to recover.

6% before the crisis. In other words, what we are observing seems to be a rate of unemployment far above the underlying natural rate and, by implication, a level of output far below its natural level. So, most economists point to the aggregate demand side. For the time being, insufficient aggregate demand, they argue, is the issue.

They point first to the limits of policy we have examined earlier. In a typical recovery, monetary and fiscal policy can be used to hasten the return of output to its natural level. In the current crisis, they can play at best a limited role. There is no room left for conventional monetary policy, and the effects of unconventional monetary policy are limited and uncertain. Worries about debt are putting strong pressure on the government to reduce the deficit, to pursue fiscal consolidation rather than fiscal expansion.

They also point out that, in the presence of the liquidity trap, not only does conventional monetary policy not work, but the process of adjustment which typically takes output back to its natural level in the medium run also fails. (Recall from Chapter 10 how the mechanism typically works.)

A decrease in output below its natural level leads to a decrease in the price level (at least relative to its trend). This leads to an increase in the real money stock, which in turn leads to a decrease in the interest rate. The decrease in the interest rate leads then to an increase in spending, which in turn leads to an increase in output. The process goes on until output has returned to its natural level. The process can be made faster by using either monetary policy, that is by increasing the money stock, which leads to a larger decrease in the interest rate, or fiscal policy, which increases demand directly. At the core of the adjustment is the aggregate demand relation (equation (9.3) in Chapter 9):

$$Y = Y\left(\frac{M}{P}, G, T\right)$$

Now think about what happens when the economy is in the liquidity trap, with the interest rate equal to zero. In this case, an increase in the real money stock, M/P, whether it comes from an increase in M or from a decrease in P, has no effect on the interest rate, which remains equal to zero. So not only does monetary policy not affect spending, but the adjustment mechanism which returns output to its natural level in the AS–AD model also does not work: the decrease in the price level leads to a higher real money stock, but does not lead to a lower interest rate and does not lead to higher spending.

Let's formally introduce this in our AS–AD model. If the economy is in the liquidity trap, the aggregate demand relation takes the following form:

$$Y = Y(G, T)$$

As before, increases in government spending or decreases in taxes increase demand. But in the liquidity trap, aggregate demand no longer depends on the real money stock.

What may then happen to the economy is represented in Figure 20.16, using the AS–AD model. Aggregate supply is still represented by an upward sloping curve in the figure: the higher the level of output, the higher the price level, given the expected price level. Conversely, and more relevant for our case, the lower the output, the lower is the price level. The aggregate demand relation is now vertical. For given values of G, T, aggregate demand does not depend on the real money stock and thus does not depend on the price level.

Suppose that the initial aggregate supply and demand curves are given by AS and AD respectively, so the initial equilibrium is at point A, with output, Y, below the natural level, Y_n. In other words, output is low, and the economy is in the liquidity trap. As output is below its natural level, the aggregate supply curve shifts down over time. (Recall the mechanism: low output implies high unemployment, which puts downward pressure on wages and, in turn, on prices.) The equilibrium moves over time from A to B to C: the price level keeps decreasing, but this does not lead to an increase in output.

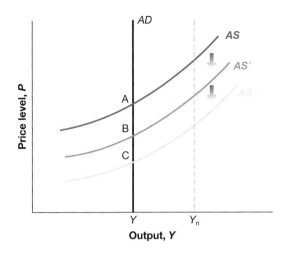

Figure 20.16

The liquidity trap and adjustment failure

So is there any hope that the economy will eventually return to normal? Yes. There are a number of reasons to think that aggregate demand will eventually recover. Eventually, the damage done to the banking system should slowly be repaired. Very low housing investment and thus a stable housing stock, together with a growing population, should eventually lead to an increase in prices and higher housing investment in the future. Also, some types of consumption and investment cannot be deferred forever. Low purchases of consumer durables and of equipment now imply higher purchases later: eventually, cars and machines break down and must be replaced. Economists sometimes refer to this mechanism as **pent-up demand**: demand which does not take place today is pent up, and increases demand in the future. Still, this may all take time, and, at the time of writing, a strong recovery appears to be far in the future.

FOCUS
Do banking crises affect output in the medium run?

Leaving aside the current crisis, there is a lot of evidence that banking crises lead to large decreases in output in the short run. But do they have an effect on output in the medium run? Or put in terms of our model, do they affect the natural level of output?

To answer this question, researchers at the IMF looked at a number of banking crises across many countries from 1970 to 2002. They defined banking crises as episodes where there were either bank runs or a large number of bank failures. They identified 88 such crises. In each case, they looked at the behaviour of GDP in the years following the crisis.

Using econometrics, they reached two conclusions. First, financial crises typically lead to a decrease in output relative to trend, even in the medium run. Second, while this conclusion holds on average, there is a lot of variation across countries. Some countries go back to trend, while others suffer large decreases.

The flavour of their results is given in Figure 20.17, which shows what happened in four countries following a banking crisis: Mexico after 1994, Korea after 1997, Sweden after 1991 and Thailand after 1997. In all four cases, there were major bank failures. For each country, the figure shows the evolution of GDP (the blue line), relative to the pre-crisis trend (the red line). You can see that, in three of the cases, Korea, Sweden and Thailand, there was a large decrease in output relative to the pre-crisis trend, and this decrease was still largely present five years after the crisis. In other words, five years after the crisis, the rate of growth of GDP was roughly the same as before the crisis, but the level of GDP was lower than it would have been without the crisis.

Can we tell why banking crises affect output, even in the medium run? The same researchers also looked at what happened to employment, and what happened to productivity as a result of the crisis. They concluded that,

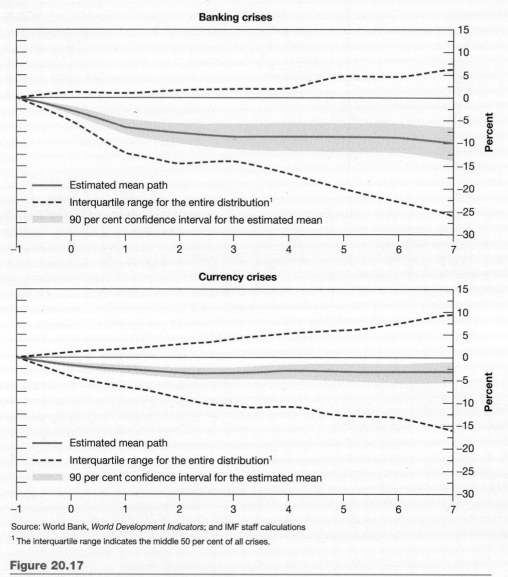

Source: World Bank, *World Development Indicators*; and IMF staff calculations

[1] The interquartile range indicates the middle 50 per cent of all crises.

Figure 20.17

The evolution of output after four banking crises

Per cent of pre-crisis trend; mean difference from year $t = -1$; first year of crisis at $t = 0$; years on x-axis.

Source: *World Economic Outlook*, October 2009 Chapter 4.

www.imf.org/external/pubs/ft/weo/2009/02/index.htm#ch4fig

on average, the decline in output was one-third due to a decrease in employment and two-thirds due to a decrease in productivity (all relative to trend). This suggests that the banking system plays an important role in the economy. Banking crises weaken the ability of the banking system to allocate funds to the right borrowers. This, in turn, makes the economy less productive.

Reference: 'What's the damage? Medium-term output dynamics after financial crises', *World Economic Outlook*, October 2009, Chapter 4.

SUMMARY

- The trigger of the crisis was a decrease in housing prices, starting in 2006. The increase in house prices since the late 1990s was not a phenomenon limited to the United States. In some European countries (UK, Ireland and Spain), prices increased even more.

- The effect of lower housing prices was considerably amplified by the effects on the banking system. Because they had very low capital ratios, some banks became insolvent. Because the assets they held were highly complex, their value in the face of a decrease in housing prices and defaults on mortgages was highly uncertain, investors became reluctant to lend to banks, and many banks became illiquid. Banks became unwilling to lend to each other, or to anybody else.

- Much higher interest rates, and in some cases, the inability to borrow at all, led to a large decrease in spending. Worries about another Great Depression led to sharp declines in confidence, and a further decrease in spending. The financial crisis led to a macroeconomic crisis and a large deficit in output. The sharp contraction of the US economy rapidly translated to the rest of the world, to Europe in particular, due to the exposure of banks to the US housing market bubble, the contraction of international trade flows and the increase of US interest rates.

- Fiscal, monetary and financial policies were used. They probably prevented an even larger decline in output but did not prevent the recession both in the USA and in other advanced economies. Both fiscal and monetary

policies now face sharp limits. Conventional monetary policy no longer works. The interest rate in the USA, UK and Europe has declined to zero. Unconventional monetary policy measures, such as credit easing and quantitative easing, were used by the Fed and the Bank of England. Also, the ECB responded to the crisis through a mix of conventional and non-conventional monetary policies.

- While output growth is now positive in the USA and in some European countries, the recovery is slow. There is strong pressure on the US government to start reducing deficits now.

- The recovery is slow, and unemployment in the USA is expected to remain high for some time. It may be that the financial crisis has done lasting damage to the banking system, and the natural level of output has decreased, relative to trend. However, there are a number of reasons to think that aggregate damand will recover, due to the pent-up demand mechanism, although currently a strong demand-led recovery appears far in the future.

KEY TERMS

mortgage lenders 449

sub-prime mortgages (sub-primes) 449

capital ratio 451

leverage ratio 451

structured investment vehicle (SIV) 452

shadow banking system 452

American International Group (AIG) 452

credit default swap (CDS) 452

securitisation 453

mortgage-based security (MBS) 453

senior securities 453

junior securities 453

collateralised debt obligation (CDO) 453

rating agencies 453

toxic assets 453

wholesale funding 453

fire sale prices 454

Libor rate 454

AAA, BBB 454

liquidity facilities 458

collateral 458

Troubled Asset Relief Program (TARP) 458

American Recovery and Reinvestment Act 459

liquidity trap 460

credit easing 463

quantitative easing 463

Nikkei index 464

pent-up demand 467

QUESTIONS AND PROBLEMS

QUICK CHECK

1. *Using the information in this chapter, label each of the following statements true, false or uncertain. Explain briefly.*

a. The origins of the recession which began in 2008 can be found in a financial crisis caused by poor functioning of the entire banking system.

b. The boom in house prices since 2000 in the USA did not contribute to the financial crisis because there were sound reasons for the rise in prices.

c. Financial liberalisation was at the origin of the financial crisis; hence a way to prevent another such crisis is strong regulation of the banking system.

d. Banks like to have high leverage because it leads to higher profit, and this is the reason why they expanded lending to sub-prime borrowers.

e. The main channel of transmission of the financial crisis around the world was the participation of other countries' banks in US financial institutions.

f. The major policy response to the crisis was a severe credit tightening to prevent the banking system from lending to sub-prime borrowers.

2. Active monetary policy

a. Consider an economy with output below the natural level of output. How could the central bank use monetary policy to return the economy to its natural lever of output? Illustrate your answer in an *IS–LM* diagram.

b. Again, suppose that output is below the natural level. This time, however, assume that the central bank does not change monetary policy. Under normal circumstances, how does the economy return to its natural level of output? Illustrate your answer in an *IS–LM* diagram.

c. Considering your answer to part (b), if the central bank does nothing, what is likely to happen to expected inflation? How does this change in expected inflation affect the *IS–LM* diagram? Does output move closer to the natural level?

d. Consider the following policy advice: 'Because the economy always returns to the natural level of output on its own, the central bank does not need to concern itself with recessions.' Do your answers to parts (a)–(c) support this advice?

DIG DEEPER

3. Leverage

Suppose that Bank A has €500 of assets and €80 of capital. Bank B has €400 of assets and €100 of capital.

a. Define and compute the leverage for Bank A and Bank B.

b. Now suppose that the value of the assets falls by 10 for each bank. How does the leverage change for each of the two banks?

c. Suppose neither bank succeeds in restoring capital at the original level. By how much will loans have to decrease if both banks want to maintain the original leverage?

4. Monetary policy in the presence of a liquidity trap

Consider the following IS–LM model:

$$C = 100 + 0.25YD$$
$$T = 200$$
$$G = 350$$
$$I = 150 + 0.25Y - 500i$$
$$(M/P)^d = 2Y - 2000i$$
$$M/P = 2000$$

a. Derive the *IS* relation.

b. Derive the *LM* relation.

c. Solve for the equilibrium real output.

d. Solve for the equilibrium interest rate.

e. Now suppose that autonomous consumption decreases from 100 to 50. Solve for the equilibrium real output and interest rate. Compare the change in the equilibrium level of output with the change in autonomous consumption. Explain briefly.

f. Suppose that the central bank tries to increase the equilibrium real output by increasing the money supply by 10%. Solve for the equilibrium real output and interest rate. Do you think the central bank intervention is effective in increasing the equilibrium real output? Explain briefly.

g. Which alternative measures can the central bank adopt to increase the equilibrium real output?

EXPLORE FURTHER

5. The external finance premium and the cost of bank loans

Consider the following IS–LM model:

$$C = 150 + \tfrac{1}{3}YD$$
$$T = 300$$
$$G = 300$$
$$I = 150 + \tfrac{1}{3}Y - 10,000\rho$$
$$\rho = i + x$$
$$(M/P)^d = 2Y - 20,000i$$
$$M/P = 2,600$$

a. Imagine the external finance premium (x) is zero. Derive the *IS* relation.

b. Derive the *LM* relation.

c. Solve for the equilibrium real output and interest rate.

d. What is the cost of bank loans and the equilibrium level of investment?

e. Now suppose that firms' capital drops following a severe slump in stock prices and banks charge an external finance premium (x) on loans to firms equal to 0.5%. How does the cost of bank loans change? What is the new equilibrium level of investment? How does this affect the equilibrium real output? Explain briefly.

---

*Log on to **MyEconLab** and complete the studyplan exercises for this chapter to see how much you have learnt, and where you need to revise most.*

MyEconLab

FURTHER READING

- There are already many good books on the crisis. Among them, Michael Lewis's *The Big Short* (W.W. Norton, 2010), and Gillian Tett's *Fool's Gold* (Free Press, 2009) both show how the financial system became increasingly risky until it finally collapsed. Both read like detective novels, with a lot of action and fascinating characters.

  On the different responses of the ECB and the FED to the current crisis, you can read 'Central Banks in Times of Crisis', European Parliament, June 2012

- *In Fed We Trust* (Crown Buiness, 2009), written in 2009 by David Wessel, the economics editor of the *Wall Street Journal*, describes how the Fed reacted to the crisis. It also makes for fascinating reading.

  On the Bank of England's response to the financial crisis, you can read the documents available at: *www.bankofengland.co.uk/about/pages/response/index/aspx*

Chapter 21

HIGH DEBT

Why do economists worry so much when governments run large budget deficits and accumulate debt quickly? In answering this question, they argue that debt slows capital accumulation, puts at risk the stability of the economic system and makes it extremely difficult to conduct monetary policy.

In principle, a high government deficit is neither good nor evil. Deficits (and surpluses) can help to redistribute the burden of taxation over time. Deficits become a problem when they result in rapid accumulation of debt, and also because, as we shall discuss, reducing a high debt, once it has been created, can take a long time, often many decades. This is why high debt will turn out to be the most long-lasting consequence of the financial crisis that started in 2008.

This chapter is in three parts:

- Section 21.1 studies the budget constraint of government – namely the relationship between debt, deficit, government spending and taxes – and examines its consequences.

- Section 21.2 examines which factors determine the evolution over time – the dynamics – of the debt-to-GDP ratio, and what determines debt accumulation.

- Section 21.3 introduces a political theory of debt that will help us understand some historical episodes of large build-ups and subsequent reductions in public debt.

21.1 THE GOVERNMENT'S BUDGET CONSTRAINT

Suppose that the government, starting from a situation of **balanced budget**, decides to cut taxes while keeping public expenditure unchanged, thereby creating a **budget deficit**. What will happen to debt over time? Will the government eventually be forced to increase taxes? If so, by how much: by more than its original cut? To answer these questions, let us start from a definition of the budget deficit. We can write the budget deficit in year t as:

$$deficit_t = rB_{t-1} + G_t - T_t \qquad [21.1]$$

All variables are in real terms, that is measured in units of real output, not in euros or pounds. B_{t-1} is public debt at the end of year $t-1$, i.e. at the beginning of year t. We define B as all the bonds and bills issued by the government and held by the private sector (at home or abroad) but excluding those held by the central bank. r is the real interest rate, which for the time being we assume to be constant. rB_{t-1} represents the real interest paid on government bonds in circulation. G_t is government spending on goods and services in year t. T_t are taxes less transfers in year t. We do this because what matters, at least for this discussion, are the net sums paid by households to the state, that is the taxes households pay minus what they receive from the state, such as unemployment benefits and pensions.

The budget deficit is equal to spending on goods and services, plus interest payments, minus taxes less transfers.

Equation (21.1) has two characteristics:

- First, we measure interest in real terms – that is, not considering the actual interest payments (which are calculated as the nominal interest rate times the stock of debt), but real interest payments, i.e. the real interest rate on existing debt. This is in fact the proper way to measure interest payments. In Brazil, for instance, in the early 1990s, when inflation was running at 50% per year, nominal interest payments were very large because the nominal interest rate was as high as 50%: but the real interest rate (the nominal minus expected inflation) was close to zero: debt was not really a burden for the state. However, the official measures of the deficit are based on actual expenditure and thus on nominal interest payments: as a result, they give a distorted picture of state finances. In Brazil, for instance, the official deficit was extremely high, but the deficit corrected for inflation was not as large. (To see how you can compute the deficit adjusted for inflation starting from the official measure of the deficit, look at the Focus box 'How to compute the budget deficit corrected for inflation').

> Remember there is a (sometimes big) difference between the official deficit and the deficit adjusted for inflation.

- To remain consistent with our definition of G as public spending on goods and services, we continue to assume that G includes neither interest payments nor transfers. Transfers are subtracted from T. The official measures of public spending include transfers, and they define revenues as taxes rather than as net taxes. This is simply an accounting convention: adding transfers to expenses or subtracting them from taxes obviously makes a difference when you compute G and T, but it is irrelevant when you compute the deficit.

> Recall that in our definition of public debt, this includes only the securities held by private investors, not those purchased by the central bank.

When a government faces a budget deficit, it may ask the central bank to finance it. In this case, what the government technically does is to sell bonds to the central bank. Alternatively, it may sell the bonds directly to private investors.

Earlier (in Chapter 14) we learned the link between s, money creation (what happens when the central bank buys government bonds) and inflation. In this chapter, however, to keep things simple we assume that the only means of **deficit financing** is selling securities to private investors.

In this case, the budget constraint of the government simply says that the increase in government debt in year t must be equal to the deficit in year t:

$$B_t - B_{t-1} = deficit_t$$

FOCUS

How to compute the budget deficit corrected for inflation

Official measures of the <u>budget deficit</u> are constructed (omitting the time index) as the sum of nominal interest, iB, more government spending on goods and services, G, minus taxes net of transfers, T:

$$\text{official deficit} = iB + G - T$$

This is a measure of the change in nominal debt. If it is positive, the government is spending more than it collects and must therefore issue new debt. If it is negative, the government reimburses part of the existing debt.

But this measure is not suitable to calculate the change in real debt, i.e. the variation in what the government will have to pay in terms of goods rather than money.

To understand why, suppose that the official measure of the deficit is equal to zero: the government does not issue or repay any securities. Suppose that inflation is positive and equal to 10%. In this case, at the end of the year, the real value of debt will be reduced by 10%. So, if we define, as we should, the deficit as the change in the real value of debt, the government recorded a budget surplus equal to 10% of the initial value of the debt.

In general: if B is the debt and inflation is π, the official measure of the deficit overstates the correct measure by an amount equal to πB. The correct, inflation-adjusted measure of the deficit is in fact equal to:

$$iB + G - T - \pi B = rB + G - T$$

where $r = i - \pi$ is the real interest rate.* The correct measure of the deficit is thus equal to the real interest plus government spending minus taxes net of transfers, i.e. the measure that we use in the text.

The difference between the official and the proper measure is equal to πB. This means that the higher the rate of inflation (π) or the level of debt (B), the more imprecise is the official measure of the deficit. In countries where inflation and debt are both very high, the official measure could indicate a very large deficit, even in the presence of a decreasing real debt. For this reason, we should always take inflation into account whenever we derive conclusions on fiscal policy.

Figure 21.1 shows the official measure and the inflation-adjusted deficit for the UK since 1949. Both measures show a strong decline occurring after 1976, an improvement at the end of the 1980s, followed by a sharp deterioration in the mid-1990s, a significant improvement around 2000 and a further deterioration since 2006.

*Note that here r is the nominal interest rate minus actual inflation: it should be called the real effective interest rate to distinguish it from the real interest rate (which we defined in Chapter 11 as the nominal interest rate less expected inflation).

Figure 21.1

Official and inflation-adjusted budget deficits for the UK, 1949–2006

So if the government runs a deficit, government debt increases. If the government has a surplus, debt decreases. Using our definition of the deficit, we can write the government budget constraint as:

$$B_t - B_{t-1} = rB_{t-1} + (G_t - T_t) \qquad [21.2]$$

Finally, if we move to the right of the equation and we reorganise the terms, we get:

$$B_t = (1 + r)B_{t-1} + G_t - T_t \qquad [21.3]$$

Debt at the end of year t is equal to $(1 + r)$ times debt at the end of year $t - 1$, plus the **primary deficit**, which is equal to the total deficit minus interest payments, that is $G_t - T_t$. This relation will be very useful in the next sections.

Current and future taxes

We now use equation (21.3) to run an experiment. We want to study the effect on the evolution of debt and future taxes of a tax cut in year 0. We start from a situation in which, up to year 0, the budget had always been in balance, so that debt is zero. In year 0, the government cuts taxes by 1 for one year (the amount is irrelevant, since we are computing everything in real terms; think of the tax cut as a reduction equivalent to 1 unit of output). Then, debt at the end of year 0, B_0, will be equal to 1. What happens next? Let us consider several cases:

- Repayment in year 1 – suppose the government decides to repay the whole debt in year 1. From equation (21.3), the budget constraint in year 1 is given by:

$$B_1 = (1 + r)B_0 + (G_1 - T_1)$$

  If all debt is repaid in year 1 then, at the end of year 1, debt will be equal to zero: replacing B_0 with 1 and B_1 with 0, the previous equation becomes:

$$T_1 - G_1 = (1 + r)1 = 1 + r$$

  To repay the debt in year 1, the government must therefore create, in year 1, a **primary surplus** equal to $(1 + r)$ units of goods. This can happen in two ways: by reducing spending or by increasing taxes. Here we assume that the adjustment is done through taxes, while spending remains unchanged. It follows that a tax cut of 1 in year 0 must be compensated by an increase in taxes by $(1 + r)$ in year 1. The path of taxes and debt corresponding to this case is shown in Figure 21.2(a) (assuming $r = 10\%$). The blue areas represent the deviations of taxes from their initial level, and pink areas represent the debt level.

- Repayment after t years – suppose now that the government decides to wait for t years before raising taxes to repay the debt. In this case, from year 1 to year t, the primary deficit will be equal to zero. Let's see what the effects are on the debt level at the beginning of year t (or at the end of year $t - 1$). In year 1, the primary deficit is equal to zero. Then, in equation (23.3), debt at the end of year 1 is equal to:

Repayment means that the government buys back securities held by private investors.

$$B_1 = (1 + r)B_0 + 0 = 1 + r$$

where the last equality comes from our initial hypothesis according to which $B_0 = 1$. In year 2, with a primary deficit still equal to zero, debt at the end of the year is:

$$B_2 = (1 + r)B_1 + 0 = (1 + r)(1 + r) = (1 + r)^2$$

Solving for the debt level in year 3 and subsequent years, it is clear that, as long as the government maintains a primary deficit equal to zero, the debt grows at a rate equal to the interest rate, and therefore debt at the end of year t_1 is given by:

$$B_{t-1} = (1 + r)^{t-1} \qquad [21.4]$$

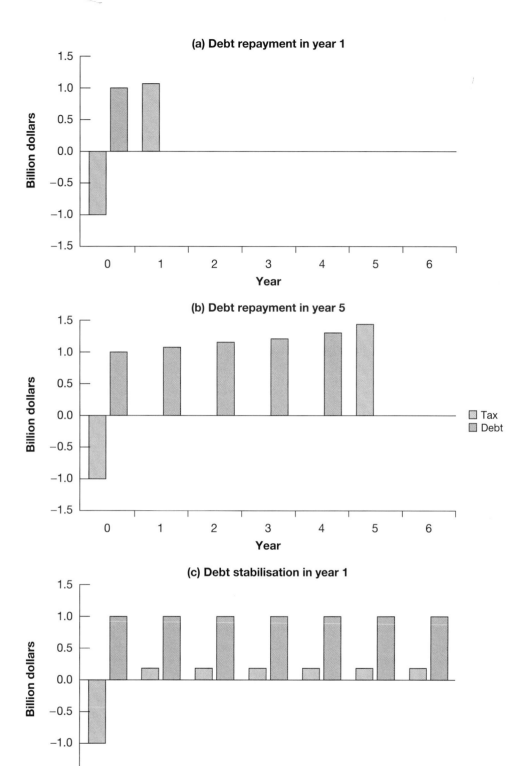

Figure 21.2

Tax reduction, debt repayment and debt stabilisation

(a) If debt is entirely repaid in year 1, a tax reduction equal to 1 in year 0 must be compensated by an increase in taxes by $(1 + r)$ in year 1.

(b) If debt is entirely repaid in year t, a tax reduction equal to 1 in year 0 must be compensated by an increase in taxes by $(1 + r)^t$ in year 1.

(c) If debt is stabilised from year 1 onwards, then taxes must be permanently higher by $(1 + r)$ from year 1 onwards.

Although taxes have been reduced only in year 0, the debt increases continuously from year 0 onwards, at a rate equal to the interest rate. The reason is simple: while the primary deficit is zero, the debt is now positive, as is the interest accruing on the debt itself. Each year, the government must issue more debt to pay interest on existing debt. In year t, the year in which the government decides to repay the debt, the budget constraint is given by:

$$B_t = (1 + r)B_{t-1} + (G_t - T_t)$$

If the debt is fully repaid in year t, B_t (the debt at the end of year t) will be equal to zero. Substituting B_t with zero and B_{t-1} with its expression from equation (21.4), we obtain:

$$0 = (1 + r)(1 + r)^{t-1} + (G_t - T_t)$$

By rearranging terms and moving $(G_t - T_t)$ to the left side, we get:

$$T_t = G_t = (1 + r)^t$$

To repay the debt, the government should produce a primary surplus equal to units of goods. If the adjustment is done only through taxation, the initial tax cut of 1 in year 0 implies, after t years and during a single year, a tax increase equal to $(1 + r)^t$. The path of taxes and debt related to this case is shown in Figure 21.2(b).

This example allows you to draw a first important conclusion. If government spending remains unchanged, a reduction of taxes today must be offset by an increase in future taxes. The longer the government waits before raising taxes, or the higher the real interest rate, the greater the increase in taxes will have to be.

Debt and primary surpluses

So far we have assumed that the government fully repays its debt. Let us see what happens if the government decides instead to stabilise the debt, i.e. to keep B constant at the level achieved in year 1.

From equation (21.3), the budget constraint in year 1 is given by:

$$B_1 = (1 + r)B_0 + (G_1 - T_1)$$

Debt stabilisation means keeping debt equal to a given level, in our case the level of year 0, so that debt at the end of year 1 will be equal to the debt at the end of year 0, $B_1 = B_0 = 1$. Substituting into the above, we obtain:

$$1 = (1 + r) + (G_1 - T_1)$$

Rearranging terms and moving $G_1 - T_1$ to the left, we get:

$$T_1 - G_1 = (1 + r) - 1 = r$$

To avoid a further increase of debt in year 1, the government must achieve a primary surplus equal to the real interest on existing debt (remember that the level of the debt stabilises at 1). The government must do the same in subsequent years: every year, the primary surplus must be sufficient to cover interest payments, so as to leave the existing level of debt unchanged. The path of taxes and debt is shown in Figure 21.2(c): the debt is equal to 1 from year 1 onwards. Taxes are higher from year 1 onwards, by an amount equal to r.

The logic of this argument extends directly to cases where the government decides to wait for t years before stabilising the debt. Since the moment when the government decides to stabilise the debt, it will have to generate primary surpluses sufficient to pay interest payments accrued until then. Of course the longer the government waits to stabilise, the higher the level of debt, the higher the interest payments and the higher the required level of taxes.

This example suggests a second conclusion. The legacy of past deficits is a higher current debt. To stabilise the debt, the government must run a primary surplus equal to the interest on existing debt. The longer the government waits before stabilising the debt, the more painful the stabilisation will be.

> Stabilisation means that the government wants to keep the amount of existing debt constant.

21.2 THE EVOLUTION OF THE DEBT-TO-GDP RATIO

So far we have studied the evolution of the level of public debt in real terms (that is, measured in units of goods). But in an economy where output grows over time, the relevant variable is the ratio of government debt to GDP. By using this, we can tell if the debt is too high, where 'too' must be defined in relation to the ability of the government to repay the debt.

The government budget constraint in terms of GDP

To see how our previous conclusions change, let us move from equation (21.3) to an equation that expresses the evolution of **debt-to-GDP ratio** or **debt ratio**. To do this we need to carry out some further steps. Let's divide both sides of equation (23.3) by real output, Y_t, to get:

$$\frac{B_t}{Y_t} = (1+r)\frac{B_{t-1}}{Y_t} + \frac{G_t - T_t}{Y_t}$$

Rewriting, on the right side, B_{t-1}/Y_t as $(B_t/Y_{t-1})(Y_{t-1}/Y_T)$ (in other words, multiplying the numerator and denominator by Y_{t-1}), the relationship becomes:

$$\frac{B_t}{Y_t} = (1+r)\left(\frac{Y_{t-1}}{Y_t}\right)\frac{B_{t-1}}{Y_{t-1}} + \frac{G_t - T_t}{Y_t}$$

Now that each term is expressed in terms of GDP at time t, we can simplify this expression. By defining g, the growth rate of output, we have $Y_{t-1}/Y_t = 1/(1+g)$. Moreover, by approximating $(1+r)/(1+g)$ with $r - g$ (which is a good enough approximation if the real interest rate and the growth rate of output are relatively small numbers), we can rewrite the previous equation as:

$$\frac{B_t}{Y_t} = (1+r-g)\frac{B_{t-1}}{Y_{t-1}} + \frac{G_t - T_t}{Y_t} \qquad [21.5]$$

Finally, moving B_{t-1}/Y_{t-1} to the left, we get:

$$\frac{B_t}{Y_t} - \frac{B_{t-1}}{Y_{t-1}} = (r-g)\frac{B_{t-1}}{Y_{t-1}} + \frac{G_t - T_t}{Y_t} \qquad [21.6]$$

This equation tells us that the change in the debt ratio is equal to the sum of two terms:

- The first is the difference between the real interest rate and the rate of growth of GDP, multiplied by the debt ratio at the end of the previous period (and thus at the beginning of the current period). This term refers to interest payments, in real terms, corrected for the growth rate of real GDP. Depending on whether the real interest rate is higher or lower than the growth rate of real GDP, this term is a factor that increases or reduces the debt ratio. Therefore, r and g have opposite effects on the dynamics of the debt ratio.
- The second term is the ratio of the primary deficit to GDP. The primary balance relative to GDP has a positive or negative effect on the growth of debt, respectively, in the case of a deficit ($G_t - T_t > 0$) or a surplus ($G_t - T_t < 0$).

> ◁ The growth rate of the economy is as important as the real interest rate in determining the growth rate of the debt/GDP ratio.

Lets now compare equation (21.6), which describes the evolution of the debt ratio, with equation (21.2), which describes the evolution of the debt level. The difference is the presence of $(r - g)$ in equation (21.6) rather than r in equation (21.2). The reason for this difference is simple. Suppose that the primary deficit is zero. In this case, the debt level will increase at a rate equal to the real interest rate, r. But, if GDP grows, the debt/GDP ratio will grow more slowly; it will grow at a rate equal to real interest rate minus the rate of growth of output, $r - g$. If the rate of growth of the economy is greater than the real interest rate, that is, if $r - g$ is negative, the debt ratio will not only grow more slowly, but it will also decline from year to year.

The debt ratio in the long run

Equation (21.6) – or, equivalently, equation (21.5) – allows us to analyse the change in the debt ratio from one year to the next. But we can look further ahead and ask whether the

FOCUS
A qualitative solution of difference equations

The simplest mathematical tool to study the dynamics of a variable is a difference equation: an expression that relates a variable with its past values. In its simplest form, a difference equation can be written as:

$$y_t = A + \beta y_t - 1 \qquad [21.7]$$

where y_t is the value that variable y takes at time t. In equation (21.7) y_t depends on its past values and on an exogenous variable, A. β is, instead, a simple constant, which from now on we will call a parameter.

Since y_t depends on a single lagged value, equation (21.7) is called a first-order difference equation.

We can study the qualitative properties of a difference equation by means of a chart. Equation (21.7), for example, can be represented graphically on a Cartesian plane, as shown in Figure 21.3.

The vertical axis shows variable y_t and the horizontal axis shows variable y_{t-1}. The 45° line identifies the points where $y_t = y_{t-1}$, whereas curve C represents equation (21.7) with a slope lower than 1 and a vertical intercept $A > 0$. Point y, the intersection between curve C and the 45° line, is, as we shall see, the equilibrium steady state.

From this graph, we can apply an iterative method. Indeed, if we choose a value of y_0 at time zero, shown on the horizontal axis, we can derive the value of y_1, the

Figure 21.3

A stable equilibrium ($\beta < 1$)

vertical axis through the curve C. The value of y_1 can then be shown on the horizontal line through the 45° line (having a slope equal to 1, this line identifies all the points for which the abscissa is equal to the order). The transfer of y_1 from the vertical to the horizontal axis can be done with the 45° line. Once the value of y_1 on the horizontal axis is

debt ratio, given all the other variables, will tend to stabilise or will instead tend to diverge, that is to shoot off to plus infinity or to zero.

At this point you could make a small (but very useful) investment by learning the basics of differential equations: read the Focus box 'A qualitative solution of difference equations'. Otherwise you can skip directly to the next section.

The Focus box teaches you how to solve this simple difference equation:

$$y_t = \beta y_{t-1} + A$$

where y_t is a generic dynamic variable, β a parameter and A a constant, can be applied to the equation which describes how the debt/GDP ratio evolves through time:

$$\frac{B_t}{Y_t} = (1 + r - g)\frac{B_{t-1}}{Y_{t-1}} + \frac{G_t - T_t}{Y_t}$$

where Y_t is the debt ratio, the parameter β is $1 - r - g$ and the exogenous variable A is $(G_t - T_t)/Y_t$. As we want to study the evolution of the debt ratio, given all other variables, we assume that the government runs primary deficits (or surpluses) in relation to GDP that are constant over time, namely that $(G_t - T_t)/Y_t$ is constant. To keep things simple, we also assume that r and g are constant. To analyse the dynamics of the debt ratio a few graphs can help us. First, in Figure 21.5, we rewrite equation (21.5) representing the debt ratio at time t in terms of its value in the previous period. This equation is a line of slope $1 - r - g$ and

Solving a simple differential equation is not difficult, but to keep things simple here we will solve it only graphically.

identified, we can repeat the same reasoning, finding the value of y_2 on the vertical axis through the curve C. The iteration stops when there is no difference between two successive values of y_t. At this point, there is no more dynamics and the value of y_t coincides with that of steady state, y.

We would reach the same result if we started from an initial value of y greater than y_t, such as y_0'. Again, as shown by the arrows in Figure 21.3, the value of y is reached over time. The only difference is that starting from an initial value $y_0 < y$ the dynamic equation (21.7) generates successively larger values of y_t until you reach stationary equilibrium. Instead, where $y_0' > y$, the dynamic equation generates, moving from one period to another, smaller and smaller values, always leading to the value of y.

So, if the curve C has slope less than 1, the equilibrium point y is reached regardless of the starting value of y_t. A balance that has these characteristics is called a stable equilibrium.

Things are different if the slope is greater than 1, as shown in Figure 21.4. In this case, if we start from a starting value lower than y, the dynamic equation generates smaller and smaller values over time, gradually moving away from the point of equilibrium.

The same divergent trend occurs if you choose as the initial value $y_0' > y$. In other words, if the slope of the equation (21.7) is greater than 1, the steady-state equilibrium is unstable because, starting from different values of y, it gradually moves away from equilibrium. Equilibrium can be achieved only by choosing a value of y_0 equal to y.

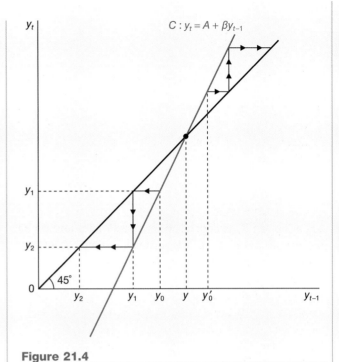

Figure 21.4

The unstable equilibrium ($\beta > 1$)

The main rule to be drawn from this analysis is that the dynamic adjustment of a first-order difference equation toward equilibrium steady state is different depending on the value of β and of the initial value of y_t. In particular, the nature of the equilibrium steady state changes according to β: it is stable if $\beta < 1$, unstable if $\beta > 1$.

intercept $(G_t - T_t)/Y_t$ (remember that we are assuming that the primary budget balance is a constant fraction of GDP). On the same figure, we also show the 45° straight line which allows us to project values from the vertical to the horizontal axis, as time goes by.

We have seen that the change in the debt-to-GDP ratio depends on whether the government runs primary surpluses or deficits, and on whether the real interest rate is higher or lower than the growth rate of GDP. Before we solve the equation graphically, you can already guess that two main cases can arise:

● *The normal case* – On most occasions, the growth rate of GDP is smaller than the real interest rate. Equation (21.5) is a straight line with slope greater than 1. What happens to the debt ratio in the long run? If the initial debt is positive (as it usually is), then the government needs primary surpluses to stabilise the debt ratio. The economic intuition is as follows. The interest rate is the rate at which the government accumulates debt because of interest due on the debt inherited from the past. If the government pays such interest by issuing new debt, rather than by means of primary surpluses, the debt ratio will continue to grow at a rate equal to the interest rate. Real GDP, however, grows at rate g – less than r – therefore the debt-to-GDP ratio increases over time. This is true even if the government maintains a primary budget balance and, even more so, if it runs primary deficits. In summary, if the growth rate is lower than the real interest rate, in the case of a positive debt inherited from the past and of primary deficits, the debt ratio increases, gradually diverging away from its equilibrium value. We can now ask what

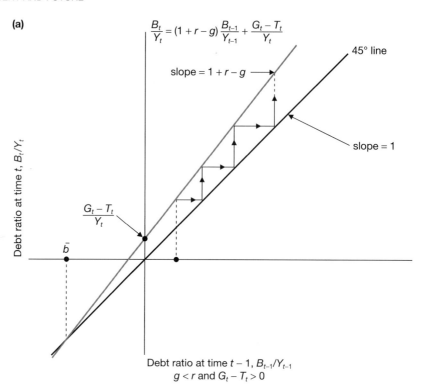

(a)

$$\frac{B_t}{Y_t} = (1 + r - g)\frac{B_{t-1}}{Y_{t-1}} + \frac{G_t - T_t}{Y_t}$$

Debt ratio at time $t-1$, B_{t-1}/Y_{t-1}
$g < r$ and $G_t - T_t > 0$

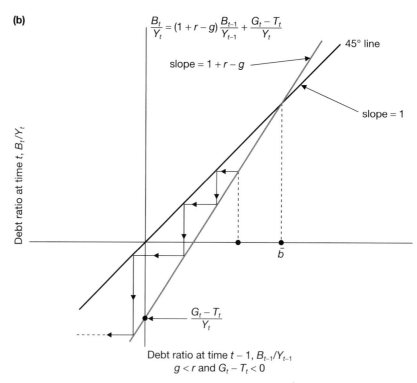

(b)

$$\frac{B_t}{Y_t} = (1 + r - g)\frac{B_{t-1}}{Y_{t-1}} + \frac{G_t - T_t}{Y_t}$$

Debt ratio at time $t-1$, B_{t-1}/Y_{t-1}
$g < r$ and $G_t - T_t < 0$

Figure 21.5

The dynamics of the debt-to-GDP ratio in the long run

(a) If $g < r$, and if the country has past debt and runs primary deficits ($G_t - T_t > 0$), then the debt ratio increases going farther away from equilibrium.

(b) Even if $g < r$, and if initial debt is positive, the debt ratio decreases over time if the government runs 'adequate' primary surpluses ($G_t - T_t < 0$).

(c) If $g > r$, the debt ratio converges to the equilibrium level despite the presence of primary deficits ($G_t - T_t > 0$).

(d) If $g > r$ and the government runs primary surpluses ($G_t - T_t < 0$), then the debt ratio always converges to its equilibrium level.

options a government has if it wishes to stop this exponential growth in the debt ratio. The answer is simple: it must finance the servicing of the debt with adequate primary surpluses.

- *The more exotic case* – Although less frequent, it can happen that the GDP growth rate exceeds the real interest rate. Equation (21.5) is then described by a straight line with slope lower than one ($1 + r - g < 1$). The straight line representing equation (21.5) therefore has a lower slope than the 45° line, which has a slope equal to 1. What happens to the debt ratio in the long run? The debt-to-GDP ratio over time will converge to its steady

(c)

(d)

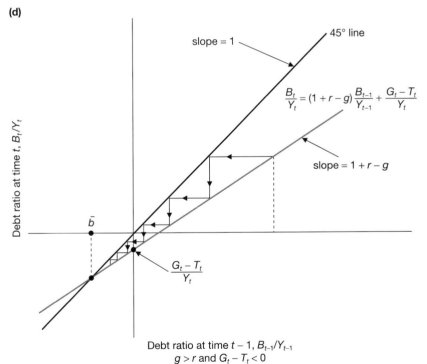

Figure 21.5

(Cont'd)

state value, which we indicate with $\bar{b}$. The economic intuition is as follows: the interest rate determines the speed at which the debt grows if interest payments are financed by issuing new debt. The rate of output growth instead determines the speed at which GDP grows. So, if the primary budget is balanced, and the growth rate exceeds the interest rate, the debt ratio converges to zero. If the government continues running constant primary deficits, the debt ratio continues to converge, but at a value of the debt such that the reduction in the debt ratio due to the fact that the growth rate is greater than the interest rate exactly offsets the increase in the ratio due to primary deficits. In summary, if the growth rate of output is greater than the interest rate, whatever the value of the debt inherited from the past and even in the presence of primary deficits, the debt ratio always converges to its steady-state value. In the case, therefore, where g exceeds r, the government should not necessarily service the debt using primary surpluses, as constant deficits are compatible with a constant debt-to-GDP ratio.

Since all variables are constant in the steady-state equilibrium, to find B/Y just ask, in equation (21.5), what if $B_t/Y_t = (B_{t-1}/Y_{t-1}) = \bar{b}$, to obtain:

$$\bar{b} = \frac{(G_t - T_t)/\bar{Y}}{g - r}$$

where $\bar{G}$, $\bar{T}$, $\bar{Y}$ and $\bar{b}$ are steady-state values, which is positive for $g > r$ and $G_t > T_t$, but also for g, r and $\bar{G}$, $\bar{Y}$: in equilibrium the government is a debtor.

In Figure 21.5 we describe all the possible cases arising, those with $g < r$ (cases a and b) and those with $g > r$ (cases c and d).

The evolution of the debt ratio in some European countries

The analysis conducted so far provides the framework for studying the trend in the debt ratio of some European countries. The 1960s were a decade of strong growth throughout Europe, so strong that the average growth rate exceeded the real interest rate almost everywhere: $r - g$ was negative, and most countries succeeded in reducing the debt ratio (which had increased during the Second World War) without the need to generate large primary surpluses.

The 1970s, in contrast, were a period of much lower growth, but also of very low real interest rates (sometimes negative): $r - g$ on average was still negative, and this further reduced debt ratios. In the early 1980s (after the appointment of Paul Volker as Chairman of the Fed and the resulting shift in US monetary policy) the situation changed dramatically. Real interest rates increased and growth rates slowed down. To avoid an increase in the debt-to-GDP ratio, many countries should have created large budget surpluses. But this did not happen and the result was a sharp increase in debt ratios. Just before the crisis, the public debts in the euro area accounted on average for less than 70% of GDP, more or less the same ratio as when the euro was introduced, and 10 percentage points higher than in the early 1990s. During the crisis, the primary balance turned from positive to negative in many European countries (in the UK, it had already been negative since 2002). Therefore, from 2007 to 2011, the debt ratio increased by several percentage points, 20% on average in the euro area (from 66% to almost 86%).

Table 21.1 shows the increase in the debt-to-GDP ratio during the crisis across Europe. In some countries the increase was very large: in Ireland it increased by 83 percentage points (from 25% to 108%); in Spain the debt ratio more than doubled in just five years; in Portugal it increased from 68 to 101%.

In EU-27 outside of the euro area, the experiences of individual countries were very varied. The debt ratio increased by 40 percentage points in the UK, up to 84% of GDP, but much less in countries which were less affected by the financial and economic crisis, such as Denmark (up 16 percentage points from 28% to 44%) and Sweden (where the debt ratio actually declined from 40% to 36%).

The origin of debt increases is also different country by country. Recall from section 21.1 that the debt ratio (B/Y) can increase for several reasons: for slow growth (which reduces Y), for $(r - g) > 0$ (which increases interest payments more than the income generated in the country), for primary deficits (which add to the stock of outstanding debt) and for public interventions in the financial system (such as the bailout of banks). When decomposing the increase in public debt into these factors, it turns out that European countries also differ as regards the origin of the increase in their debt ratios.

Table 21.1 Breakdown of the increase in the debt-to-GDP ratio between 2007 and 2011

Country	B/Y in 2011	Increase in B/Y from 2007 to 2011	Primary balance of which:	Cyclical components	Discretionary increase in the primary deficit	Interest rate and growth	Public interventions in the financial system
					due to:		
Ireland	87	62	36	30	6	15	12
Greece	134	38	20	25	−5	15	3
Spain	73	36	26	20	6	7	3
Portugal	91	28	16	15	1	9	2
France	89	25	16	16	6	6	3
Netherlands	70	24	7	7	6	4	11
Slovenia	45	22	12	12	4	4	6
Finland	55	20	0	−4	4	3	17
Belgium	100	17	2	0	2	9	6
Italy	119	16	−1	−2	1	15	2
Germany	82	16	2	2	1	8	6
Slovakia	44	15	15	2	13	1	−1
Austria	73	13	2	4	1	6	5
UK	87	42	28			5	9

Source: European Commission (2010), 'Public finances in EMU – 2010', *European Economy*, 4, and Barry Eichengreen, Robert Feldman, Jeffrey Liebman, Jurgen von Hagen and Charles Wyplosz (2011), *Public Debts: Nuts, Bolts and Worries*. London: Centre for Economic Policy Research.

In the four countries with the largest increases – Spain, Portugal, Ireland and Greece – the recession explains most of the increase in the debt ratio, which was already high before the crisis. In other countries – Belgium, Italy and Germany – the main source of the debt increase were unfavourable interest rates compared to the growth rate of their economies. In some countries, such as the Netherlands and Finland, most of the increase was due to the bailout (or purchase) of banks (ABN Amro was the largest case).

The dangers of a very high public debt

We have seen that the higher the level of public debt, the higher the primary surplus (in the normal case $r > g$) needed to keep that debt level stable, i.e. to prevent it from growing. But large primary surpluses require high taxes (remember that so far we are assuming that G remains constant), which introduce distortions in the economy. The recent experience of some European countries with a debt ratio above 100% shows an additional cost: the risk of a vicious circle that can make it difficult or impossible to conduct monetary policy with the only objective being to keep inflation under control.

To understand why, let us return to equation (21.5), which describes the evolution of the debt-to-GDP ratio:

$$\frac{B_t}{Y_t} - \frac{B_{t-1}}{Y_{t-1}} = (r - g)\frac{B_{t-1}}{Y_{t-1}} + \frac{G_t - T_t}{Y_t}$$

Consider a country with a high debt ratio, say 100%. Suppose that the real interest rate is equal to 3%, and that the growth rate is 2%. The first term on the right side of the equation is equal to $(3\% - 2\%) \times 100\% = 1\%$ of GDP. Suppose further that the government generates a primary surplus of 1%, a level just sufficient to maintain a constant debt ratio – in this case, the right side of the equation is equal to $1\% + (-1\%) = 0\%$.

Suppose now that for some reason – for example, because of a political scandal which increases the perception of risk in the country – investors begin to demand higher returns for holding government bonds denominated in the currency of that country. Suppose further that the central bank wishes to defend the exchange rate (as we have discussed in Chapter 12), and in order to do so increases the interest rate from 3% to 6%. Finally, suppose that the higher interest rate triggers a recession, so that the growth rate falls to 0%. Let us now turn to taxes: $r - g$ is equal to $6\% - 0\% = 6\%$.

With an increase of $r - g$ to 6%, to maintain a constant debt ratio, the government should increase its primary surplus by five points, from 1% to 6%. It is at this point that the country may enter a vicious circle.

To increase the primary surplus, the government raises taxes, but tax hikes are unpopular; they generate even more political uncertainty and further increase the risk premium and, therefore, interest rates. The fiscal tightening induced by the first increase in interest rates then generates an even deeper recession, further reducing the rate of growth. The increase in the interest rate and the lower growth rate result in higher $r - g$, making it even more difficult to stabilise the debt ratio.

Alternatively, suppose that the government is unable or unwilling to increase the budget surplus by 5% of GDP. Debt increases, and with it the concern of financial markets: if the government was not able to change the primary surplus, the debt-to-GDP ratio would grow indefinitely. The result is that investors will ask for a further interest rate increase. The easiest way in which to exit the vicious circle is by resorting to monetary financing of the deficit. But once investors realise it, the prospects of higher inflation push up nominal interest rates futher, and so forth. These are not just intellectual speculations. In Italy, in the early 1990s, the Bribesville scandals and frequent political crises triggered a series of speculative attacks on the Italian lira, making it necessary to increase interest rates, which resulted in large deficits and a growing debt ratio. The lesson is that countries with high debt should reduce it rapidly.

See the Focus box on 'Debt and sovereign spreads'.

FOCUS
Debt and foreign spreads

The increase in the debt-to-GDP ratio of many European countries during the crisis has raised concerns among investors about the possibility that governments could eventually find themselves unable to repay their debts. The fear that governments could renege on their debt – a possibility that is referred to as sovereign default – started to make it increasingly difficult for some countries to find investors willing to buy newly issued bonds, unless the return on those bonds were to rise enough to compensate them for the risk they were taking upon by buying them. This is how it was that returns on bonds issued by some countries – those countries whose debt-to-GDP ratios had increased the most during the crisis, namely Ireland, Greece and Portugal – started to increase to very high levels (Figure 21.6).

In normal times, returns on sovereign debt are below 6%. A return of 6% or more indicates that investors have serious doubts about the ability of a country to repay its debt, and therefore on the merit of credit of that country – also known as creditworthiness. Usually the return of bonds issued by a country are benchmarked against that of the most creditworthy country – Germany among European countries. The difference between the return on a German bond (called Bund) and the return on bonds issued by another country is called 'spread', or 'sovereign spread'.

Figure 21.6

Long-term sovereign bond spread in Ireland, Portugal and Greece, 2010–2011

Source: 'Mispricing of sovereign risk and multiple equilibria in the Eurozone', Paul De Grauwe, Yuemei Ji, Voxeu.org, 23 January 2012

How and at what speed should they reduce it? The answer is: through many years, perhaps decades, of primary surpluses. A good example is the UK in the nineteenth century. At the end of the wars against Napoleon, in the early 1800s, Britain had accumulated a debt ratio in excess of 200%. Reducing that ratio took almost a century: it was only by 1900 that the ratio dropped to 30%. The prospect of many decades of fiscal austerity is not encouraging. The result is that, when the level of debt is large, the idea of repudiating it may become attractive. The reasoning is very simple. To repudiate the debt – i.e. to cancel it, in whole or in part – is an attractive solution for the economy. This allows an immediate decrease in taxes and, hence, in the distortions associated with them. It also reduces the risk of potential vicious circles. But repudiation carries with it a bigger problem, i.e. the problem of time inconsistency (which we will discuss in Chapter 23). If the government fails to honour its promise to repay the debt, it will find it very difcult to borrow again in the future: following a default, financial markets will be very reluctant to buy new government securities. In other words, what seems the best today may not be so in the long term. The repudiation of the debt must be considered a last resort, and probably not a good solution even in situations of extremely high debt, exceeding even those of many countries today. In addition, **debt repudiation** could produce a fall in consumption, as households see the value of their wealth, at least the portion invested in government bonds, reduced. (This is why governments, if they have the choice, prefer to default on securities issued abroad and held by non-resident investors, which of course has other consequences for the international reputation of the country.)

We can go a step further and ask whether sovereign spreads can inform us of what investors think about the possibility that a government might not repay its debt. Let us go through an example by considering Greek sovereign spreads. At the time of writing, an investor who buys a ten-year Greek government bond (in euros) receives a 25% return, 23 percentage points more than the return on a ten-year bond issued by the German government (and also denominated in euros). We can compute investors' expectations of a default in a simple way.

Assume that in case of default Greece repays nothing, then – calling p the probability of default and assuming that investors are indifferent between Greek and German bonds, provided that they have the same expected return – we can write:

$$2\% = (1-p) \times 25\% + p \times 0$$

which implies $p = 92\%$. The term on the left-hand side is the (sure) return on German bonds and on the right-hand side is the expected return on a Greek bond.

Figure 21.7 uses the above expression to show how investors' expectations of a Greek default have evolved since the start of the Greek crisis in early 2010. The expectations of a Greek default was around 66% in January 2010. An 'orderly' (i.e. agreed with investors) Greek default eventually happened in 2012.

Figure 21.7

Model-implied sovereign default probabilities for Greece

Solid lines denote the median and 90% confidence interval probabilities for in-sample debt-to-GDP ratios. Dashed lines denote the median and 90% confidence interval probabilities for out-of-sample debt-to-GDP ratios.

21.3 THE RETURN FROM A HIGH DEBT

At the end of the previous section, we saw that if the stock of public debt, as a ratio to GDP, reaches a very high level, the situation can escalate and lead to a debt crisis: for instance, the government finds it impossible to issue new debt except at extraordinary high interest rates. We can then ask why, in such a case, policy makers wait rather than immediately introduce adequate measures to adjust the budget. One of the reasons why corrective measures are often late and inadequate is that debt crises are largely unpredictable events, and governments tend to be short-sighted: until the crisis hits, they are reluctant to admit that a crisis can burst. Therefore governments often do not perceive the urgency for an adjustment.

A second reason is that fiscal stabilisation is often the result of a political struggle between different groups and between their political representatives. Various economic groups (the young and the old, rentiers and entrepreneurs, etc.) are likely to be affected differently by some of the measures that may be introduced to reduce a high debt. The various groups that make up a society will try to use their political pressure to defend their economic interests. To avoid losing political consensus, and thereby opening social conflicts, governments tend to delay the fiscal correction, allowing debt to grow to the point where it triggers a financial crisis.

How to reduce a high debt?

What are the options open to a government that wants to stabilise or reduce a high and growing debt ratio? There are only three ways (in the normal case $r > g$) to achieve this goal:

- Generate sufficient primary surpluses; to do so the government can cut spending and transfers or increase taxes.
- Resort to monetary financing by the central bank.
- Repudiate the debt, in whole or in part; this means that the government erases, at least in part, the existing debt, or introduces taxes on government securities that were not foreseen when investors had purchased those securities.

Generating primary surpluses is the most virtuous way to reduce a high debt. However, it is also the most difficult way. To cut spending is politically costly, and sometimes it is not socially viable: imposing new and higher taxes is an unpopular choice, and there is a limit to the tax burden beyond which the cost (especially the political cost) of collecting more taxes becomes too high. In this case, a tax plan consistent with the budget constraint becomes unfeasible.

The government can then convince the central bank to print money by purchasing government bonds. Given the initial level of debt and given the path of public spending, monetary financing reduces the tax levy required for debt relief. However, recourse to the issuing of money is not free of charge because inflation is also a form, albeit a peculiar one, of taxation. An increase in the money supply increases inflation and reduces the real value of existing nominal debt and of the cash held by citizens. Inflation therefore acts like a tax – the inflation tax. Inflation reduces the disposable income of households because it forces them to spend part of their income just to maintain the real value of the money stock or of the government bonds they wish to hold constant.

Inflating the debt away can be done in different ways: directly (by issuing money) or indirectly (through a decrease in the real value of debt, if the maturity is long enough).

Finally, the government may decide to cancel all or part of the debt. Even if, as we have seen, repudiation is in some ways a good solution – it reduces the distortions caused by high tax rates – the result is the breaking up of the relationship of trust between the government and investors, who may no longer be willing to buy public debt. If this happens, the government loses the ability to run deficits in order to distribute over time the burden of an unexpected high expenditure.

Towards a political theory of debt

At first glance, the three ways to finance the budget deficit and reduce debt accumulation – discussed above – may seem very different. In reality, these are different forms of taxation that differ only because they fall on different economic groups. Repudiation, for example, can be treated as a tax on wealth that affects those who hold securities. The inflation tax affects those who hold nominal assets not protected by inflation (money and bonds).

It becomes important, therefore, to take into account the fact that government debt and the economic policy choices needed to reduce it have significant effects on income distribution. This idea has been developed in a recent branch of the economic literature which lies on the border between economics and political science. This literature has proposed a **political theory of government debt**. In particular, some economists argue that the choice of who should pay for the reduction of a high debt is essentially a problem of redistribution of income and wealth between economic groups. When the different economic groups are represented politically, it is also possible to establish a relationship between the degree of a country's political stability, distributional conflict and evolution of deficits and debt. Before showing how these ideas can help to understand the different solutions adopted in certain historical episodes of high public debt, we need to take a few more steps.

First, let us distinguish between a stable and an unstable political scenario. A political situation is stable if a political party has a solid majority and controls economic policy decisions. A political situation is unstable if each group has enough power to block a measure that is damaging some groups, but not enough to turn it around. In this case, fiscal adjustment may not be politically feasible. There is no way to resolve the dispute over which items of expenditure should be cut, or which taxes increased, and this prevents the government from reaching a decision, thus undermining its ability to reduce the deficit. In the end, the government must either monetise the debt or repudiate it. As we shall see, this assumption seems a good description of what happened in Germany and France in the first half of the 1920s.

If, instead, the political situation is stable, a political party has enough power to start a fiscal adjustment because it is strong enough to impose the burden of adjustment on others. This was the case in France in the mid-1920s and in the UK in the post-war period. The case of the USA after the Second World War is an example of a reduction in public debt that has not given rise to fights among different social and political groups. But this was only possible because of the high growth rates of income recorded in those years, which contributed to the reduction of the debt ratio.

Suppose that society can be divided into three groups:

- Rentiers (from the French '*rente*' which means 'annuity') hold wealth in the form of government bonds, i.e. securities which pay an annuity every year.
- Entrepreneurs hold wealth in the form of physical capital that produces profits.
- Workers own human wealth, which produces their salaries.

Each of these interest groups will seek to avoid the burden of adjustment and shift it onto someone else. Rentiers are opposed both to explicit debt repudiation and to an inflation tax, which reduces the real value of debt and, as such, is an implicit form of repudiation. If average debt maturity is short, and hence holders of securities are protected from inflation by the changes in interest rates, then rentiers prefer the inflation tax to debt repudiation. Rentiers also look favourably on various forms of tax increases, whether direct or indirect. Entrepreneurs are opposed to taxes on capital, but not to debt repudiation nor to monetary financing or to taxes on consumer goods and income. Workers prefer taxes on wealth and capital, and the repudiation of debt, while being opposed to indirect taxes, particularly on consumer goods. They are affected by inflation if wages are not indexed, but they can be made better off by an increase in employment induced by a monetary expansion.

Four episodes of reduction of a high public debt

Historical experiences provide us with illuminating examples of how some countries have emerged from situations of high debt by taking very different solutions. We shall describe the experience of Germany, France and the UK at the end of the First World War and the case of the USA at the end of the Second World War.

Germany in the inter-war period

Germany financed military spending during the First World War mainly through borrowing. During the war period, in fact, fiscal revenue accounted for a negligible fraction of overall spending, and the resulting budget deficit was financed by issuing debt, especially short-term debt. But how did Germany plan to repay this debt? Like all the countries that took part in the conflict, it hoped to win the war and shift the debt burden onto the defeated countries. But Germany lost the war and at the end of the conflict found itself with a very high debt stock.

After the war, the German political situation was particularly unstable. Following on from the military defeat, the old nationalistic regime, ruled by aristocrats and the military, collapsed. The Communist Party began to gain broad support but, rather than a communist revolution, what happened was the birth of a new democratic regime, the Weimar Republic. The political situation remained, however, quite unstable. The democratic regime was very weak, threatened both by the workers' unrest linked to the communist movement and, at the other extreme, by the forces of the old regime and new movements of far-right nationalists.

In the first half of the 1920s, the debt problem was aggravated by the high budget deficits accumulated by the Weimar government. In part, these deficits were related to the reparations Germany had to pay to the winners of the war, to France in particular. In reality, reparations accounted for no more than one-third of the deficits in those years. The main reason for the deficits of the years 1920–1923 was a political impasse in fiscal policy. The proposal of drastic tax reforms had further weakened an already weak political situation, making it extremely difficult for the government to collect taxes. For example, the Socialists' proposal to levy an extraordinary tax on firms' capital and profits encountered violent opposition from nationalists and, obviously, from the entrepreneurs. Similarly, the proposal by entrepreneurs to raise income tax was rejected by the Socialists. The result was that no significant measure was introduced until 1922. The need to strike a compromise between the new and the old regimes had undermined the ability and willingness of the government to increase taxes. The political and fiscal policy impasse of these years left, as the only solution, monetisation which led to hyperinflation. One of effects of the German hyperinflation was the total cancellation of the debt that had existed at the end of the war. By the autumn of 1922, the debt did not exceed 5% of its real value in 1919. This dramatic reduction of wealth struck especially the middle class, which held the largest share of government debt. The reduction of wealth owned by the middle class worsened the income distribution, which is one of the reasons for the subsequent collapse of democratic institutions.

France in the inter-war period

In the decade that followed the end of the First World War, the question of who should pay the cost of the debt issued to finance the conflict monopolised the political debate in France. The debt was a particularly difficult problem due both to its size – the public debt represented about 150% of GDP – and its composition – the short-term debt constituted 32% of the total. In the years 1919–1926, the political situation in France was very unstable: in a few years, Socialist and Conservative governments alternated one after another. But in the second half of the decade political instability decreased: in 1926 the right won the final fight and was able to form a stable conservative government headed by Raymond Poincaré.

At the beginning of the decade, there seemed to be an easy solution to the French public debt problem: have the Germans pay for it through reparations. It was only at the end of 1922, and after the occupation of the Ruhr, that the French began to understand that

German taxpayers would not be able to pay. Then an endless debate began between the opposition, on the one hand, and the conservatives on the other. The left denounced the unfairness of the tax structure, maintaining that, although income taxes were very progressive, only 20% of tax revenue was collected through income taxes. The high incidence of indirect taxes meant that the tax burden fell mostly on the less wealthy. The left, therefore, proposed a unique and progressive tax. At the other extreme, the conservatives opposed progressive income taxes, proposing much more reliance on indirect taxes. The distributional conflict made the political situation increasingly volatile; the French franc was hit by speculation and inflation went up. In fact, the fear of a capital levy made the public unwilling to buy government bonds. As a result, the government had to repay the bonds coming to maturity with monetary financing. In 1926 France was probably on the verge of hyperinflation.

At this point, Raymond Poincaré assumed the leadership of a new Conservative government and announced a drastic stabilisation programme. The element that made this programme different from previous attempts at fiscal adjustment was simply the greater political stability. The programme was credible because the political opponents had been defeated. Inflation ended abruptly, even before the government had started the fiscal adjustment.

> Only when Poincaré introduced a bill to shift the tax burden off bondholders did the demand for government bonds recover and inflation stop.

The UK in the inter-war period

Even in the UK, the debt was very high at the end of the First World War: the debt-to-GDP ratio had reached 130% in 1919. The policies adopted in the UK, however, were very different from those in Germany and France. What distinguished the UK from Germany and France? The answer is simple: the degree of political stability. As we have seen, both in Germany and in France, the political situation at the end of the conflict was very unstable. In the UK, instead, except for two brief Labour governments, in 1924 and in 1930, the Conservative Party ruled continuously throughout the 1920s and 1930s. Democratic institutions were very solid and, despite very high unemployment, were never really threatened by the risk of a social revolt. This made it possible to introduce fiscal and monetary contractions, whose main objective was the stability of sterling and its return to its pre-war value, thus allowing a return to the gold standard. At the same time, the government produced budget surpluses in order to reduce the high public debt. The UK was one of the very few European countries where no expansionary fiscal policies were implemented to promote economic recovery.

Throughout the 1920s, and until the second half of the 1930s, fiscal surpluses, however, were not sufficient to reduce public debt. In this period, interest rates greatly exceeded the rate of growth of GDP. In 1923, the debt reached 170% of GDP and remained above 150% up to 1936. The debt-to-GDP ratio only started to decline in the second half of the 1930s, 15 years after the war.

Who bore the burden of debt reduction in the UK? Certainly not those who had bought government securities, since there was no form of repudiation, either explicitly or implicitly through inflation. The burden of adjustment was borne primarily by taxpayers. Among them, those in the less wealthy classes were especially affected, because of an increasingly regressive tax system. For example, the introduction of taxes on specific products (tea, sugar, tobacco, milk, etc.) had a signicant regressive effect.

The United States after the Second World War

The debt accumulated by the USA at the end of the Second World War was very close, in relation to GDP, to the debt ratio in the UK after the First World War. In both cases, moreover, the political situation was relatively stable. That is why both the UK and the US governments were able to start a fiscal adjustment without being forced to resort to repudiation. The USA, however, had greater success than the UK: 15 years after the end of the Second World War, the debt-to-GDP ratio was halved; in the UK, in contrast, 15 years passed before the debt ratio began to fall. So what distinguished the USA in the 1950s from the UK in the 1920s? During the period 1948–1968, the average growth rate of GDP in the

USA was 4%, while real interest rates did not exceed 0.5%. Unlike the case of the UK, in the USA budget surpluses were accompanied by rapid output growth that exceeded the level of real interest rates. There is a simple but important lesson: it is easier to reduce a high debt when the economy is growing.

SUMMARY

- Governments, like households and individuals, can spend less or more than the amount of their revenues. When public spending exceeds taxes, a government runs a budget deficit. When public spending is lower than taxes, a government runs a budget surplus.

- In principle, a high government deficit is neither good nor evil. Deficits (and surpluses) can actually help to redistribute the burder of taxation over time. But deficits become a problem when they result in rapid accumulation of debt.

- To tell whether government debt is too high, the relevant variable to look at is the ratio of government debt-to-GDP. Whether debt is too high must be defined in relation to the ability of government to repay the debt.

- To stabilise the debt, the government must run a primay surplus equal to the interest on existing debt. The longer the government waits before stabilising the debt, the more painful the stabilisation wiil be.

- When $r > g$, the reduction of the debt ratio requires primary surpluses. When $r < g$, a country can reduce the debt ratio without the need to generate primary surpluses.

- The massive use of fiscal policy to help the economies of many European countries to face the recession that started in 2008 resulted in a signicant deterioration of primary balances that turned from positive to negative in most cases. These large budget deficits caused a dramatic increase in the debt ratio, which doubled in several countries.

KEY TERMS

balanced budget 472

budget deficit 472

deficit financing 472

primary deficit 474

primary surplus 474

debt stabilisation 476

debt-to-GDP ratio, or debt ratio 477

debt repudiation 485

political theory of government debt 487

QUESTIONS AND PROBLEMS

QUICK CHECK

1. *Using the information in this chapter, label each of the following statements true, false or uncertain. Explain briefly.*

a. Official measures of the budget deficit are constructed as the difference between government spending and taxes net of transfers.

b. The central bank can finance the government budget deficit.

c. In a debt stabilisation the government decreases the amount of existing debt.

d. If real GDP growth is lower than the real interest rate, the debt/GDP ratio will increase even if the government runs a primary deficit.

e. The 1960s and 1970s in Europe were decades of high growth and negative debt/GDP ratio.

f. Debt repudiation is the more efficient solution to the problem of high debt in a country.

g. The ways of reducing high debt differ because they fall on different population groups.

h. The war reparations were the main reason for the deficits of the years 1919–1923 in Germany.

i. Both the USA and the UK started successful fiscal adjustments after the Second World War.

j. The official measure of the budget deficit are biases because of the inflation rate.

2. *Consider an economy in which the official budget deficit is 4% of GDP, the debt-to-GDP ratio is 100%, the nominal interest rate is 10% and the inflation rate is 7%.*

a. What is the relationship between the primary balance and GDP?

b. What is the balance adjusted for inflation as a percentage of GDP?

c. Suppose that production is down 2% compared to natural levels. What is the cyclically adjusted balance ratio to GDP adjusted for inflation and balance/GDP?

d. Suppose instead that production is initially at its natural level, and that output growth remains constant at the normal rate of 2%. Does the debt ratio increase or decrease?

3. *Suppose that in a country's public debt, inflation and the rate of GDP growth are all equal to zero, and that the interest rate is 5%. In year t, the country recorded a deficit of 10% of GDP, and in year t + 1 onwards eliminates the primary deficit.*

Calculate the deficit (as percentage of GDP) in years $t + 1$ and $t + 2$.

DIG DEEPER

4. *Consider the economy described in problem 2 and assume that there is a fixed exchange rate. Suppose, further, that financial investors fear that the debt level is too high, and that the government may have to devalue to stimulate production (and thus tax revenues) and reduce debt. Financial investors expect a devaluation of 10%. In other words, the expected exchange rate, E^e_{t+1}, decreases by 10% from its previous value.*

a. We recall the uncovered interest parity condition: if the foreign interest rate is and remains equal to 10%, what happens when the domestic interest rate decreases by 10%?

b. Suppose that domestic inflation remains unchanged. What happens to the real interest rate nationally? What will happen to the rate of growth?

c. What happens to the official budget deficit and to the deficit adjusted for inflation?

d. Suppose that the growth rate declines from 2% to 0%. What happens to the change in the debt/GDP? (We assume that the primary balance ratio to GDP remains unchanged, although the decrease in growth rate may reduce tax revenues.)

e. Were investors' fears justified?

5. *Consider the data of the previous year but assume that the country has primary surpluses of less than 2% of GDP instead of 1% of GDP.*

a. Calculate the debt ratio in 2009, 2010 and 2011.

b. In light of the results, do you think that primary surpluses of 1% should be considered 'good' with a view to reducing the debt ratio.

EXPLORE FURTHER

6. *Consider an economy where the ratio of debt to GDP is 40%, the primary deficit is 4% of GDP, the rate of growth is 3% and the real interest rate is 3%.*

a. Using a spreadsheet, calculate the debt ratio after ten years, assuming that the primary deficit remains at 4% of GDP each year as the economy grows at the normal rate of growth each year and that the real interest rate remains constant at 2%.

b. Suppose that the real interest rate increases to 5%, but that everything else remains as in part (a). Calculate the debt ratio after ten years.

c. Suppose that the rate of growth falls to 1% and that the economy will grow at the normal rate each year. Everything else remains as in part (a). Calculate the debt ratio after ten years. Compare your answer with that in (b).

d. Returning to the assumptions of part (a), suppose that the policy makers decide that a debt ratio above 50% is dangerous. Check that the immediate reduction of the primary deficit of 1% retained for ten years will lead to a debt ratio of 50% after ten years. What level of primary deficit will be necessary to maintain a debt ratio of 50%?

e. Following on from (d), suppose that policy makers wait five years before changing the tax policy. For five years, the primary deficit remains at 4% of GDP. What is the debt ratio after five years? Suppose that after five years economic policy makers decide to reduce the debt ratio to 50%. From year 6 to year 10, what is the constant primary deficit level which will lead to a debt ratio of 50% at the end of 10?

f. Suppose that the policy makers decide to enact the policy in part (d) or part (e). If these policies lead to a reduction in the rate of output growth for a time, how will they affect the level of primary deficit needed to achieve a debt ratio of 50% after ten years?

g. What policy – the one in part (d) or the one in part (e) – do you think is more dangerous for the stability of the economy?

---

*Log on to **MyEconLab** and complete the studyplan exercises for this chapter to see how much you have learnt, and where you need to revise most.*

MyEconLab

FURTHER READING

- Chapter 13 of the volume by R. Farmer, *Macroeconomics* (Cincinnati, OH, South-Western College Publishing, 1998), analyses the dynamics of debt and deficits in line with the discussion of this chapter.

- For an illuminating analysis of how various countries have emerged from situations of high debt, you can read A. Alesina, *The End of Large Public Debts, in High Public Debt: The Italian Experience*, edited by F. Giavazzi and L. Spaventa (Cambridge, Cambridge University Press, 1988).

SHOULD POLICY MAKERS BE RESTRAINED?

Nearly every chapter of this book has looked at the role of policy. The next two chapters put it all together.

Chapter 22 Policy and policy makers: what do we know?

Chapter 22 asks two questions: given the uncertainty about the effects of macroeconomic policy, wouldn't it be better not to use policy at all? And, even if policy can in principle be useful, can we trust policy makers to carry out the right policy? The bottom line: uncertainty limits the role of policy. Policy makers do not always do the right thing. But, with the right institutions, policy can help and should be used.

Chapter 23 Monetary and fiscal policy rules and constraints

Chapter 23 looks at monetary and fiscal policies. It reviews what we have learned and then focuses on two issues. The first is the optimal rate of inflation: high inflation is bad, but how low a rate of inflation should the central bank aim for? The second is the design of policy: should the central bank target money growth or should it target inflation? What rule should the central bank use to adjust the interest rate? Then it looks at fiscal policy, reviewing what we have learned and looking more closely at the implications of the government budget constraint for the relation between debt, spending and taxes. Next, it considers several issues, from how wars should be financed, to the dangers of accumulation of too high a level of debt. It ends with a description of the current budget situation in advanced countries, especially in the USA and Europe, and a discussion of the problems on the horizon.

Chapter 22

POLICY AND POLICY MAKERS: WHAT DO WE KNOW?

At many points in this book, we saw how the right mix of fiscal policy and monetary policy could help a country out of a recession, improve its trade position without increasing activity and igniting inflation, slow down an overheating economy, stimulate investment and capital accumulation, and so on.

This conclusion, however, appears to be at odds with frequent demands that policy makers be tightly restrained: in Europe, the countries that adopted the euro signed a 'Stability and Growth Pact', which required them to keep their budget deficit under 3% of GDP or else face large fines. Monetary policy is also under fire. For example, the charter of the central bank of New Zealand, written in 1989, defines monetary policy's role as the maintenance of price stability, to the exclusion of any other macroeconomic goal.

This chapter looks at the case for such restraints on macroeconomic policy.

● Sections 22.1 and 22.2 look at one line of argument, namely that policy makers may have good intentions, but they end up doing more harm than good.

● Section 22.3 looks at another – more cynical – line, that policy makers do what is best for them, which is not necessarily what is best for the country.

On 15 January 2004, the German cartoonist, Horst Haitzinger, took an ironic look ('It was self-defence, honest!') at the uncomfortable position of Hans Eichel, German Finance Minister, who was attempting to justify the position of the Federal Republic of Germany (FRG) before the Court of Justice of the European Communities regarding its failure to comply with the Stability and Growth Pact.

Source: Haitzinger, Horst. Haitzinger Karikaturen 2004. München: Bruckmann, 2004, p. 9. *http://www.ena.lu?lang=2&doc=23469*.

22.1 UNCERTAINTY AND POLICY

A blunt way of stating the first argument in favour of policy restraints is that those who know little should do little (and the crisis that started in 2008 that so few economists had anticipated is a humbling reminder of how little most of us know). The argument has two parts: macroeconomists, and by implication the policy makers who rely on their advice, know little; they should therefore do little. Let's look at each part separately.

How much do macroeconomists actually know?

Macroeconomists are like doctors treating cancer. They know a lot, but there is a lot they don't know.

Take an economy with high unemployment, where the central bank is considering the use of monetary policy to increase economic activity. Think of the sequence of links between an increase in money and an increase in output – all the questions the central bank faces when deciding whether and by how much to increase the money supply:

- Is the current high rate of unemployment above the natural rate of unemployment, or has the natural rate of unemployment itself increased (Chapters 10 and 11)?
- If the unemployment rate is close to the natural rate of unemployment, isn't there a risk that monetary expansion will lead to a decrease in unemployment below the natural rate of unemployment and cause an increase in inflation (Chapters 10 and 11)?
- By how much will the change in the money supply decrease the short-term interest rate (Chapter 4)? What will be the effect of the decrease in the short-term interest rate on the long-term interest rate (Chapter 16)? By how much will stock prices increase (Chapter 16)? By how much will the currency depreciate (Chapter 7)?
- How long will it take for lower long-term interest rates and higher stock prices to affect investment and consumption spending (Chapter 17)? How long will it take for the J-curve effects to work themselves out and for the trade balance to improve (Chapter 7)? What is the danger that the effects come too late, when the economy has already recovered?

When assessing these questions, central banks – or macroeconomic policy makers in general – do not operate in a vacuum. They rely in particular on macroeconometric models. The equations in these models show how these individual links have looked in the past. But different models yield different answers. This is because they have different structures, different lists of equations and different lists of variables.

We will consider two cases: a fiscal policy and a monetary policy shock. Let us first start with a monetary policy shock.

Consider a case where the euro area economy is growing at its normal growth rate; call this the *baseline* case. Suppose now, that over a period of a year, the ECB increases the nominal short-term interest rate by a 1% point. What will happen to the output in the euro area?

Table 22.1 shows the deviation of output from the baseline predicted by each of four models available for the euro area (the characteritics of these models are described in the

Table 22.1 The response of output to a monetary shock: predictions from four models

Year	Model 1	Model 2	Model 3	Model 4
1	−0.19	−0.20	−0.16	−0.57
2	−0.30	−0.14	−0.22	−0.10
3	−0.28	−0.02	−0.11	−0.03
5	−0.17	−0.02	−0.04	−0.02
10	−0.01	0.02	0.0	−0.01

Note: the first-year monetary policy multipliers are greater in Model 4 than in the other three models.

Source: Kenneth F. Wallis, 'Comparing economic models of the euro economy'. *Economic Modeling*, 2004, **21**, 735–758.

Focus box 'Macroeconometric models for the euro area'. All four models predict that output decreases for some time after the increase in the short-term nominal interest rate. What is reported in the table is the value of the monetary policy multipliers you have learned earlier (in Chapter 5). The four models predict different impacts of the increase in the short-term interest rate on output. After one year, the average deviation of output from the baseline is negative. The range of answers goes from nearly no change (−0.16% in

FOCUS
Macroeconometric models for the euro area

There are many major macro models for the euro area:

- The Area-Wide Model (AWM) of the European Central Bank (Fagan et al., 2001) treats the euro area as a single economy. It corresponds to a conventional national economy macro model, with the rest of the world treated as exogenous. Although this includes the three EU members that have not adopted the single currency, and Greece, which did not join the third stage of EMU until 1 January 2001, in the current model the rest of the world is proxied by a four-country aggregate, comprising the USA, Japan, the UK and Switzerland.

And three well-established multicountry models, namely:

- MULTIMOD Mark III, developed in the Research Department of the International Monetary Fund in Washington, DC (Laxton et al., 1998). This model contains separate models for each of the Group of Seven (G7) countries – the USA, Canada, Japan, France, Germany, Italy, UK – and for an aggregate grouping of 14 smaller industrial countries. The remaining economies of the world are then aggregated into two separate blocks of developing and transition economies. Each of the industrial country models has the structure of a complete national-economy model, whereas the two remaining blocks are modelled in much less detail.

The following two models NIGEM and QUEST are more disaggregated, each having complete country models for each EU member (taking the Belgium–Luxembourg Economic Union as a single entity) and a finer division of the rest of the world.

- NIGEM, developed at the National Institute of Economic and Social Research, London (Barrell et al., 2001). After separate country models for the remaining three G7 members, NIGEM has six intermediate-size models consisting of a very basic description of the domestic economy (output and prices) together with

trade volume and price equations and the balance of payments; these relate to Australasia, Mexico, Norway, S. Korea, Switzerland and the Visegrad economies (Czech Republic, Hungary, Poland). Finally, there are seven simpler trade-and-payments models for China, OPEC, Developing Europe, Africa, Latin America, other LDCs and the rest of East Asia.

- The QUEST model of the European Commission (Roeger and in't Veld, 1997) separately models the USA and Japan, then describes the rest of the world by 11 trade-and-payments models. Four of these relate to the larger remaining OECD countries (Australia, Canada, Norway, Switzerland) and seven to various groups of countries, very much as above (Central and Eastern Europe, the rest of the OECD, OPEC, the former Soviet Union, dynamic Asian economies, the rest of Asia and the rest of Africa and Latin America).

All the models describe the economy as you have learned in the previous chapters: the economy tends to its medium-run equilibrium with output equal to the natural level of output and employment equal to the natural rate of unemployment. All the models incorporate what you have learned about the behaviour of economic agents: that is, they suppose that financial markets, firms and households take their economic decisions based on their rational expectations about the future.

References:
Fagan, G., Henry, J. and Mestre, R., 'An area-wide model (AWM) for the euro area, *Working Paper No. 42*, European Central Bank, Frankfurt, 2001.

Laxton, D., Isard, P., Faruqee, H., Prasad, E. and Turtelboom, B., 'Multimod MARK III: the core dynamic and steady-state models', *Occasional Paper No. 164*, International Monetary Fund, Washington DC, 1998.

Barrell, R., Dury, K., Hurst, I. and Pain, N., 'Modeling the world economy: the National Institute Global Economic Model'. Presented at an ENEPRI workshop on Simulation Properties of Macroeconometric Models, CEPII, Paris, 2001.

Roeger, W. and in't Veld, J., 'QUEST II. A multi country business cycle and growth model', *European Economy. Economic Papers*, 1997, **123**, Brussels.

Source: This box is taken from Kenneth F. Wallis 'Comparing economic models of the euro economy', *Economic Modeling*, 2004, **21**, 735–758.

Table 22.2 The response of output to a fiscal shock (a reduction in GDP equivalent to 1% of euro area GDP): predictions from two models

Year	Model 1	Model 2
1	−1.35	−1.48
2	−0.52	0.23
3	0.09	0.24
5	0.22	0.11
10	0.03	0.00

Note: The first-year fiscal policy multipliers are well above 1 in both models.

Source: Kenneth F. Wallis 'Comparing economic models of the euro economy', *Economic Modeling*, 2004, **21**, 735–758.

Model 3) to −0.75%, a range of 0.41%. Two years out, the average deviation is −0.19%; the range is down to 0.20%. But two models (Model 1 and Model 3) predict a higher second-year monetary policy multiplier compared to the first-year multiplier: that is, they predict that the largest negative impact on output of an increase in the short-term interest rate happen after two years. On the other hand, Model 4 and Model 2 predict that the largest impact on output happen in the first year. Five years out, the average deviation is −0.06%, but the answers range from −0.02% to −0.17%. Ten years out, the average deviation is 0%, but the answers range from −0.01% to 0.02%. Admittedly, the range of answers is not as large as it was in macroeconometric models used in the 1980s, where the range of answers was much larger than it is now. But still, if we measure uncertainty by the range of answers from this set of models, there is a certain amount of uncertainty about the effects of policy.

Now consider a case where the euro area economy is growing at its normal growth rate; call this the baseline case. Suppose now, that over the period of a year, government spending is reduced by 1% of GDP, area-wide. What will happen to the output in the euro area? Table 22.2 shows the effect on GDP to the fiscal contraction. Only two models are included in the table, Model 1 and Model 2, which can provide area-wide results. The responses of GDP to the fiscal contraction show wide variation, with impact multipliers well in excess of 1 on Model 1 and Model 2, 1.35 and 1.48 respectively. In both cases the change in investment accounts for most of the reduction in GDP.

Should uncertainty lead policy makers to do less?

Should uncertainty about the effects of policy lead policy makers to do less? In general, the answer is yes. Consider the following example, which builds on the simulations we just looked at.

Suppose the euro area economy is in recession. The ECB is considering using monetary policy to expand output. To concentrate on uncertainty about the effects of policy, let's assume that the ECB knows everything else for sure. By how much should the ECB decrease the short-term nominal interest rate?

Taking the average of the responses from the different models in Table 22.1 (but with the opposite sign), a decrease in short-term nominal interest rate of 1% leads to a 0.28% increase in output in the first year. Suppose the ECB takes this average relation as holding with certainty. What it should then do is straightforward. To achieve 1% more output growth requires the ECB to decrease the short-term interest rate by 1%/0.28 = 3.6%. The ECB should therefore decrease the interest rate by 3.6%.

Suppose the ECB actually decreases rates by 3.6%. But let's now take into account uncertainty, as measured by the range of responses of the different models in Table 22.2. Recall that the range of responses of output to a 1% decrease in interest rates after one year varies from −0.16% to −0.57%; equivalently, a 1% decrease in interest rates leads to a range of increases in output from 0.16% to 0.57%. These ranges imply that a decrease in interest rates of 3.6% leads, across models, to an output response anywhere between 0.58% and 2%.

This example relies on the notion of multiplicative uncertainty that, because the effects of policy are uncertain, more active policies lead to more uncertainty. See William Brainard, 'Uncertainty and the effectiveness of policy', *American Economic Review*, 1967, **57**, 411–425.

The conclusion is clear: given the range of uncertainty about the effects of monetary policy on output, decreasing interest rates by 3.6% would be irresponsible. If the effects of interest rates on output are as weak as suggested by one of the 4 models, output growth at the end of the year would increase by just around half percentage point. Given this uncertainty, the ECB should consider carefully whether and by how much to decrease the short-term interest rate. (In fact, as the short-term interest rate is much lower than 3.6% in the euro area, the ECB, to help the economy out of the crisis that started in 2008, had no such option as to reduce rates by as much as 3.6%, and had to resort to other forms of monetary policy, i.e. quantitative easing, as you learned in Chapter 22).

Uncertainty and restraints on policy makers

Let's summarise: there is substantial uncertainty about the effects of macroeconomic policies. This uncertainty should lead policy makers to be more cautious and to use less active policies. Policies should be broadly aimed at avoiding prolonged recessions, slowing down booms and avoiding inflationary pressure. The higher the unemployment or the higher the inflation, the more active the policies should be. But they should stop well short of **fine-tuning**, of trying to achieve constant unemployment or constant output growth.

Friedman and Modigliani are the same two economists who independently developed the modern theory of consumption (see Chapter 17).

These conclusions would have been controversial 20 years ago. Back then, there was a heated debate between two groups of economists. One group, headed by Milton Friedman from Chicago, argued that because of long and variable lags, activist policy is likely to do more harm than good. The other group, headed by Franco Modigliani from MIT, had just built the first generation of large macroeconometric models and believed that economists' knowledge was becoming good enough to allow for increasingly fine-tuning of the economy. Today, most economists recognise there is substantial uncertainty about the effects of policy. They also accept the implication that this uncertainty should lead to less active policies.

Differences of opinion are more pronounced on the effects of fiscal rather than monetary policy. During the crisis that started in 2008 there was widespread agreement on the need to use monetary policy both to offset the shock to aggregate demand and to compensate the shift in the demand for money (the crisis induced people to hold more money and fewer bonds for any given level of the interest rate). Whether to use government spending to offset the shock to aggregate demand was more controversial. In the USA, the UK and Ireland, governments relied extensively on fiscal policy: in the USA the budget deficit increased from 2.2% of GDP in 2006 to 13.6% in 2009; in the UK from 2.7% to 15.5%, in Ireland the budget shifted from a 3% surplus in 2006 to a 12% deficit in 2009. Continental Europe did much less: Germany for instance increased the deficit from 1.5% of GDP in 2006 to 4% in 2009. Underlying these differences in policies lie differences in views about the effects of a fiscal stimulus, with the Europeans less convinced than the Anglo-Saxons that an increase in public spending translates into higher GDP growth.

Note, however, that what we have developed so far is an argument for *self-restraint by* policy makers, not for *restraints on* policy makers. If policy makers understand the implications of uncertainty – and there is no particular reason to think they don't – they will, on their own, follow less active policies. There is no reason to impose further restraints, such as the requirement that money growth be constant or that the budget be balanced. Let's now turn to arguments for restraints *on* policy makers.

22.2 EXPECTATIONS AND POLICY

One of the reasons why the effects of macroeconomic policy are uncertain is the interaction of policy and expectations. How a policy works, and sometimes whether it works at all, depends not only on how it affects current variables but also on how it affects expectations about the future (this was the main theme of Chapter 18). The importance of expectations for policy goes, however, beyond uncertainty about the effects of policy. This brings us to a discussion of *games*.

Until 30 years ago, macroeconomic policy was seen in the same way as the control of a complicated machine. Methods of **optimal control**, developed initially to control and guide rockets, were being increasingly used to design macroeconomic policy. Economists no longer think this way. It has become clear that the economy is fundamentally different from a machine, even from a very complicated one. Unlike a machine, the economy is composed of people and firms who try to anticipate what policy makers will do, and who react not only to current policy but also to expectations of future policy. Hence, macroeconomic policy must be thought of as a **game** between the policy makers and 'the economy' – more concretely, the people and the firms in the economy. So, when thinking about policy, what we need is not **optimal control theory** but rather **game theory**.

> Even machines are becoming smarter: HAL, the computer in the 1968 movie *2001 A Space Odyssey*, starts anticipating what humans in the spaceship will do. The result is not a happy one. (See the movie.)

Warning: when economists say 'game', they do not mean 'entertainment': they mean **strategic interactions** between **players**. In the context of macroeconomic policy, the players are the policy makers on one side and people and firms on the other. The strategic interactions are clear: what people and firms do depends on what they expect policy makers to do. In turn, what policy makers do depends on what is happening in the economy.

Game theory has given economists many insights, often explaining how some apparently strange behaviour makes sense when one understands the nature of the game being played. One of these insights is particularly important for our discussion of restraints here: sometimes you can do better in a game by giving up some of your options. To see why, let's start with an example from outside economics – governments' policies toward hostage takers.

> Game theory has become an important tool in all branches of economics. Both the 1994 and the 2005 Nobel Prizes in Economics were awarded to game theorists: in 1994 to John Nash from Princeton, John Harsanyi from Berkeley and Reinhard Selten from Germany. (John Nash's life is portrayed in the movie *A Beautiful Mind*); in 2005 to Robert Aumann from Israel and Tom Schelling from Harvard.

Hostage takings and negotiations

Most governments have a stated policy that they will not negotiate with hostage takers. The reason for this stated policy is clear: to deter hostage taking by making it unattractive to take hostages.

Suppose, despite the stated policy, somebody is taken hostage. Now that the hostage taking has taken place anyway, why not negotiate? Whatever compensation the hostage takers demand is likely to be less costly than the alternative – the likelihood that the hostage will be killed. So the best policy would appear to be: announce that you will not negotiate, but if somebody is taken hostage, negotiate.

Upon reflection, it is clear this would in fact be a very bad policy. Hostage takers' decisions do not depend on the stated policy, but on what they expect will actually happen if they take a hostage. If they know that negotiations will actually take place, they will rightly consider the stated policy as irrelevant. And hostage takings will take place.

So what is the best policy? Despite the fact that once hostage takings have taken place, negotiations typically lead to a better outcome, the best policy is for governments to commit *not* to negotiate. By giving up the option to negotiate, they are likely to prevent hostage takings in the first place.

Let's now turn to a macroeconomic example, based on the relation between inflation and unemployment.

As you will see, exactly the same logic is involved.

> This example was developed by Finn Kydland, from Carnegie Mellon, and Edward Prescott, then from Minnesota and now at Arizona State University, in 'Rules rather than discretion: the inconsistency of optimal plans', *Journal of Political Economy*, 1977, 3, 85. Kydland and Prescott were awarded the Nobel Prize in Economics in 2004.

Inflation and unemployment revisited

Recall the relation between inflation and unemployment we derived earlier (equation (10.9) in Chapter 10, with the time indexes omitted for simplicity):

$$\pi = \pi^e - \alpha(u - u_n) \qquad [22.1]$$

Inflation, π, depends on expected inflation, π^e, and on the difference between the actual unemployment rate, u, and the natural unemployment rate, u_n.

The coefficient α captures the effect of unemployment on inflation, given expected inflation: when unemployment is above the natural rate, inflation is lower than expected; when unemployment is below the natural rate, inflation is higher than expected.

Suppose the central bank announces it will follow a monetary policy consistent with zero inflation. On the assumption that people believe the announcement, expected inflation, π^e, as embodied in wage contracts is equal to zero, and the central bank faces the following relation between unemployment and inflation:

$$\pi = -\alpha(u - u_n) \qquad [22.2]$$

If the central bank follows through with its announced policy, it will choose an unemployment rate equal to the natural rate; from equation (22.2), inflation will be equal to zero, just as the central bank announced and people expected. Achieving zero inflation and an unemployment rate equal to the natural rate is not a bad outcome. But it would seem the central bank can actually do even better.

- Recall (from Chapter 10) that in the USA α is roughly equal to 1. So equation (22.2) implies that, by accepting just 1% inflation, the central bank can achieve an unemployment rate of 1% below the natural rate of unemployment. Suppose the central bank – and everybody else in the economy – finds the trade-off attractive, and decides to decrease unemployment by 1% in exchange for an inflation rate of 1%. This incentive to deviate from the announced policy once the other player has made his move – in this case, once wage setters have set the wage – is known in game theory as the **time inconsistency** of optimal policy. In our example, the central bank can improve the outcome this period by deviating from its announced policy of zero inflation: by accepting some inflation, it can achieve a substantial reduction in unemployment.

- Unfortunately, this is not the end of the story. Seeing that the central bank has increased money by more than it announced it would, wage setters are likely to wise up and begin to expect positive inflation of 1%. If the central bank still wants to achieve an unemployment rate 1% below the natural rate, it will have to achieve 2% inflation. However, if it does achieve 2%, wage setters are likely to increase their expectations of inflation further, and so on.

- The eventual outcome is likely to be high inflation. Because wage setters understand the central bank's motives, expected inflation catches up with actual inflation, and the central bank will eventually be unsuccessful in its attempt to achieve an unemployment rate below the natural rate. In short, attempts by the central bank to make things better lead in the end to things being worse. The economy ends up with the *same unemployment rate* that would have prevailed if the central bank had followed its announced policy, but with *much higher inflation*.

How relevant is this example? Very relevant. We can read the history of the Phillips curve (see Chapter 10) and the increase in inflation in the 1970s as coming precisely from the Fed's attempts to keep unemployment below the natural rate of unemployment, leading to higher and higher expected inflation, and higher and higher actual inflation. In that light, the shift of the original Phillips curve can be seen as the adjustment of wage setters' expectations to the central bank's behaviour.

So what is the best policy for the central bank to follow in this case? It is to make a credible commitment that it will not try to decrease unemployment below the natural rate. By giving up the option of deviating from its announced policy, the central bank can achieve unemployment equal to the natural rate of unemployment and zero inflation. The analogy with the hostage taking example is clear: by credibly committing not to do something that would appear desirable at the time, policy makers can achieve a better outcome: no hostage takings in our earlier example, no inflation here.

A refresher:
Given labour market conditions, and given their expectations of what prices will be, firms and workers set nominal wages. Given the nominal wages firms have to pay, firms then set prices. So, prices depend on expected prices and labour market conditions. Equivalently, price inflation depends on expected price inflation and labour market conditions. This is what is captured in equation (22.1).

For simplicity, we assume the central bank can choose the unemployment rate – and by implication, the inflation rate – exactly. In doing so, I ignore the uncertainty about the effects of policy. This was the topic of section 22.1, but it is not central here.

If $\alpha = 1$, equation (22.2) implies $\pi = -(u - u_n)$. If $\pi = 1\%$, then $(u - u_n) = -1\%$.

Remember that the natural rate of unemployment is neither natural nor best in any sense (see Chapters 8 and 10). It may be reasonable for the central bank and everyone else in the economy to prefer an unemployment rate lower than the natural rate of unemployment.

Establishing credibility

How can a central bank credibly commit not to deviate from its announced policy?

One way to establish its credibility is for the central bank to give up – or to be stripped by law of – its policy-making power. For example, the mandate of the central bank can be defined by law in terms of a simple rule, such as setting money growth at 0% forever. (An alternative, which we discussed in Chapter 12, is to adopt a hard peg, such as a currency board or even dollarisation: in this case, instead of giving up its ability to use money growth, the central bank gives up its ability to use the exchange rate and the interest rate.)

Such a law surely takes care of the problem of time inconsistency. But the tight restraint it creates comes close, however, to throwing the baby out with the bathwater. We want to prevent the central bank from pursuing too high a rate of money growth in an attempt to lower unemployment below the natural unemployment rate. But – subject to the restrictions discussed in section 22.1 – we still want the central bank to be able to expand the money supply when unemployment is far above the natural rate, and contract the money supply when unemployment is far below the natural rate. Such actions become impossible under a constant-money-growth rule. There are indeed better ways to deal with time inconsistency. In the case of monetary policy, our discussion suggests various ways of dealing with the problem.

A first step is to make the central bank independent. Politicians, who face frequent re-elections, are likely to want lower unemployment now, even if it leads to inflation later. Making the central bank independent, and making it difficult for politicians to fire the central banker, makes it easier for the central bank to resist the political pressure to decrease unemployment below the natural rate of unemployment.

This may not be enough, however. Even it is not subject to political pressure, the central bank will still be tempted to decrease unemployment below the natural rate: doing so leads to a better outcome in the short run. So, a second step is to give incentives to the central bankers to take the long view – that is, to take into account the long-run costs from higher inflation. One way of doing so is to give them long terms in office, so they have a long horizon and have the incentives to build credibility.

A third step may be to appoint a 'conservative' central banker, somebody who dislikes inflation very much and is therefore less willing to accept more inflation in exchange for less unemployment when unemployment is at the natural rate. When the economy is at the natural rate, such a central banker will be less tempted to embark on a monetary expansion. Thus, the problem of time inconsistency will be reduced.

These are the steps many countries have taken over the past two decades. Central banks have been given more independence. Central bankers have been given long terms in office. And governments typically have appointed central bankers who are more 'conservative' than the governments themselves – central bankers who appear to care more about inflation and less about unemployment than the government. (See the Focus box 'Was Alan Blinder wrong in speaking the truth?')

Figure 22.1 suggests that this approach has been successful. The vertical axis gives the average annual inflation rate in 18 OECD countries for the period 1960–1990. The horizontal axis gives the value of an index of 'central bank independence', constructed by looking at a number of legal provisions in the bank's charter – for example, whether and how the government can remove the head of the bank. There is a striking inverse relation between the two variables, as summarised by the regression line: more central bank independence appears to be systematically associated with lower inflation.

Time consistency and restraints on policy makers

Let's summarise what we have learned in this section:

We have examined arguments for putting restraints on policy makers, based on the issue of time inconsistency.

A warning:

Figure 22.1 shows correlation, not necessarily causality. It may be that countries that dislike inflation tend both to give more independence to their central bankers and have lower inflation. (This is another example of the difference between correlation and causality – discussed in Appendix 2 at the end of the book.)

Figure 22.1

Inflation and central bank independence

Across OECD countries, the higher the degree of central bank independence, the lower the rate of inflation.

Source: Vittorio Grilli, Donato Masciandaro and Guido Tabellini, 'Political and monetary institutions and public financial policies in the industrial countries', *Economic Policy*, October 1991, 341–392.

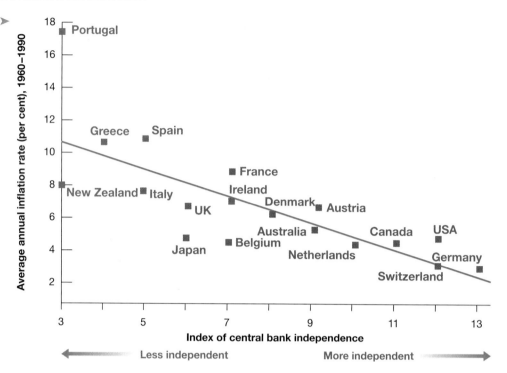

FOCUS
Was Alan Blinder wrong in speaking the truth?

In the summer of 1994, President Clinton appointed Alan Blinder, an economist from Princeton, Vice-Chairman (in effect, second in command) of the Federal Reserve Board. A few weeks later, Blinder, speaking at an economic conference, indicated his belief that the Fed has both the responsibility and the ability, when unemployment is high, to use monetary policy to help the economy recover. This statement was badly received. Bond prices fell, and most newspapers ran editorials critical of Blinder.

Why was the reaction of markets and newspapers so negative? It was surely not that Blinder was wrong. There is no doubt that monetary policy can and should help the economy out of a recession. Indeed, the Federal Reserve Bank Act of 1978 requires the Fed to pursue full employment as well as low inflation.

The reaction was negative because, in terms of the argument we developed in the text, Blinder revealed by

his words that he was not a conservative central banker, that he cared about unemployment as well as inflation. With the unemployment rate at the time equal to 6.1%, close to what was thought to be the natural rate of unemployment at the time, markets interpreted Blinder's statements as suggesting that he might want to decrease unemployment below the natural rate. Interest rates increased because of higher expected inflation – bond prices decreased.

The moral of the story: whatever views central bankers may hold, they should try to look and sound conservative. This is why many heads of central banks are reluctant to admit, at least in public, the existence of any trade-off between unemployment and inflation, even in the short run.

We have looked at the case of monetary policy. But similar issues arise in the context of fiscal policy. For instance, we have discussed (in Chapter 21) the issue of debt repudiation – the option for the government to cancel its debt obligations – and can see that the conclusions are very similar to the case of monetary policy.

When issues of time inconsistency are relevant, tight restraints on policy makers – like a fixed-money-growth rule in the case of monetary policy, or a balanced budget rule in the case of fiscal policy – can provide a rough solution. But the solution has large costs because it prevents the use of macroeconomic policy altogether. Better solutions typically involve designing better institutions (like an independent central bank or a better budget process) that can reduce the problem of time inconsistency while, at the same time, allowing the use of policy for the stabilisation of output.

22.3 POLITICS AND POLICY

We have assumed so far that policy makers were *benevolent* – that they tried to do what was best for the economy. However, much public discussion challenges that assumption: politicians or policy makers, the argument goes, do what is best for themselves, and this is not always what is best for the country.

You have heard the arguments: politicians avoid the hard decisions, they pander to the electorate, partisan politics leads to gridlock and nothing ever gets done. Discussing the flaws of democracy goes far beyond the scope of this book. What we can do here is to briefly review how these arguments apply to macroeconomic policy, then look at the empirical evidence and see what light it sheds on the issue of policy restraints.

Games between policy makers and voters

Many macroeconomic policy decisions involve trading off short-run losses against long-run gains – or, conversely, short-run gains against long-run losses.

Take, for example, tax cuts. By definition, tax cuts lead to lower taxes today. They are also likely to lead to an increase in activity and, therefore, to an increase in pre-tax income, for some time. But unless they are matched by equal decreases in government spending, they lead to a larger budget deficit and to the need for an increase in taxes in the future. If voters are short-sighted, the temptation for politicians to cut taxes may prove irresistible. Politics may lead to systematic deficits, at least until the level of government debt has become so high that politicians are scared into action.

Now move on from taxes to macroeconomic policy in general. Again suppose that voters are short-sighted. If the politicians' main goal is to please voters and get re-elected, what better policy than to expand aggregate demand before an election, leading to higher growth and lower unemployment? True, growth in excess of the normal growth rate cannot be sustained, and eventually the economy must return to the natural level of output: higher growth now must be followed by lower growth later. But with the right timing and short-sighted voters, higher growth can win elections. Thus, we might expect a clear **political business cycle**, with higher growth on average before elections than after elections.

The arguments we have just laid out are familiar; you have heard them before, in one form or another. And their logic is convincing. The question is: how well do they fit the facts?

Take, first, deficits and debt. The argument above would lead you to expect that budget deficits and high government debt have always been and always will be there. Figure 22.2, which gives the evolution of the ratio of government debt to GDP in the UK since 1900, shows that the reality is more complex.

Look first at the evolution of the ratio of debt to GDP from 1900 to 1980. Note that each of the three build-ups in debt was associated with special circumstances: the First World War for the first build-up, the Great Depression for the second and the Second World War for the third. These were times of unusually high military spending or unusual declines in output. Adverse circumstances not pandering to voters were clearly behind the large deficit and the resulting increase in debt during each of these three episodes. Note also how, in each case, the build-up was followed by a steady decrease in debt. In particular, note how the ratio of debt to GDP, which was as high as 250% around 1950, was steadily reduced to a post-war low below 50% in the early 1990s.

Figure 22.2

The evolution of the ratio of UK debt-to-GDP since 1900

The three major build-ups of debt since 1900 have been associated with the First World War, the Great Depression and the Second World War.

Source: *Bank of England Statistical Abstract*, Part 1, 2000 edition, Table 15.2 (cited in HM Treasury, *Public Finances Databank*, October 2001).

Table 22.3 **The evolution of the ratio of UK debt-to-GDP since 1900**

	Year of the administration				
	First	Second	Third	Fourth	Average
Conservative Party	1.48	1.26	1.29	1.39	1.35
Labour Party	1.34	1.65	1.89	0.82	1.50
Average	1.40	1.47	1.59	1.16	1.43

Source: Bank of England Statistical Abstract, Part 1, 2000 edition, Table 15.2 (cited in HM Treasury, Public Finances Databank, Octorber 2001).

Let us now return to the political-business-cycle argument, that policy makers try to get high output growth before the elections so they will be re-elected. If the political business cycle were important, we would expect to see faster growth before elections than after. Table 22.3 gives average output growth rates for each of the first four years of each UK government from the second Wilson administration in 1974, until the third Blair administration ended in 2007, distinguishing between Conservative and Labour governments. Look at the last line: growth has not been highest on average in the last year of a ministry; actually, average growth in the fourth years of a ministry was the lowest compared to average growth in previous years. Moreover, the average difference across years is small: 1.16% in the fourth year of an administration versus 1.40% in the first year. (We shall return later in this chapter to the other interesting feature in the table the difference between Conservative and Labour governments.) However, if you look at Conservative and Labour governments separately, you will notice that the former achieved on average higher growth in the fourth year of a ministry with respect to the second and third years, which is not the case with Labour governments. It would seem that the Conservatives, unlike their opponents, tried to stimulate the economy towards the end of their ministries to win elections. Overall, there is still little evidence of manipulation – or at least of successful manipulation – of the economy to win elections.

Games between policy makers

Another line of argument shifts the focus from games between politicians and voters to games between policy makers.

Suppose, for example, that the party in power wants to reduce spending but faces opposition to spending cuts in Parliament. One way of putting pressure both on Parliament and on the future parties in power is to cut taxes and create deficits. As debt increases over time, the increasing pressure to reduce deficits may in turn force Parliament and the future parties in power to reduce spending – something they would not have been willing to do otherwise.

Or suppose that, either for the reason we just saw or for any other reason, the country is facing large budget deficits. Both parties want to reduce the deficit, but they disagree about the way to do it: one party wants to reduce deficits primarily through an increase in taxes; the other wants to reduce deficits primarily through a decrease in spending. Both parties may hold out on the hope that the other side will give in first. Only when debt has increased sufficiently, and it becomes urgent to reduce deficits, will one party give up. Game theorists refer to these situations as **wars of attrition**. The hope that the other side will give in leads to long and often costly delays. Such wars of attrition happen often in the context of fiscal policy, and deficit reduction occurs long after it should.

Wars of attrition arise in other macroeconomic contexts, such as during episodes of hyperinflation. Hyperinflations come from the use of money creation to finance large budget deficits. Although the need to reduce those deficits is usually recognised early on, support for stabilisation programmes – which include the elimination of those deficits – typically comes only after inflation has reached such high levels that economic activity is severely affected.

Another example of games between political parties is the movements in economic activity brought about by the alternation of parties in power. Conservatives typically worry more than Labour about inflation. They worry less than Labour about unemployment. So we would expect Labour governments to show stronger growth – and thus less unemployment and more inflation – than Conservative governments. This prediction appears to fit the facts quite well. Look at Table 22.3 again. Average growth has been 1.50% during Labour governments, compared to 1.35% during Conservative governments. The most striking contrast is in the third year, 1.89% during Labour governments, compared to 1.29% during Conservative governments.

This raises an intriguing question: why is the effect so much stronger in the administrations' third year? The theory of unemployment and inflation we developed earlier (in Chapter 11) suggests a possible hypothesis: there are lags in the effects of policy, so it takes more than two years for a new government to affect the economy. And sustaining higher growth than normal for too long would lead to increasing inflation, so even a Labour government would not want to sustain higher growth throughout its term. Thus, differences in growth rates tend to decline in the fourth year of Labour and Conservative governments and to be much closer to each other towards the end of a ministry – more so than in the third year. In fact, during Labour governments, growth actually declined in the fourth year compared to the first three years.

SUMMARY

- The effects of macroeconomic policies are always uncertain. This uncertainty should lead policy makers to be more cautious and to use less active policies. Policies must be broadly aimed at avoiding prolonged recessions, slowing down booms and avoiding inflationary pressure. The higher the level of unemployment or inflation, the more active the policies should be. But they should stop short of fine-tuning, of trying to maintain constant unemployment or constant output growth.

- Using macroeconomic policy to control the economy is fundamentally different from controlling a machine. Unlike a machine, the economy is composed of people and firms who try to anticipate what policy makers will do, and who react not only to current policy but also to expectations of future policy. In this sense, macroeconomic policy can be thought of as a game between policy makers and people in the economy.

- When playing a game, it is sometimes better for a player to give up some of his or her options. For example: when a hostage taking occurs, it is better to negotiate with the hostage takers. But a government that credibly commits to not negotiating with hostage takers – a government that gives up the option of negotiation – is actually more likely to deter hostage takings from occurring.

- The same argument applies to various aspects of macroeconomic policy. By credibly committing not to use monetary policy to decrease unemployment below the natural rate of unemployment, a central bank can alleviate fears that money growth will be high, and in the process decrease both expected and actual inflation. When issues of time inconsistency are relevant, tight restraints on policy makers – such as a fixed-money-growth rule in the case of monetary policy – can provide a rough solution. But the solution can have large costs if it prevents the use of macroeconomic policy altogether. Better methods typically involve designing better institutions (such as an independent central bank) that can reduce the problem of time inconsistency without eliminating monetary policy as a macroeconomic policy tool.

- Another argument for putting restraints on policy makers is that policy makers may play games either with the public or among themselves, and these games may lead to undesirable outcomes. Politicians may try to fool a short-sighted electorate by choosing policies with short-run benefits but large long-term costs – for example, large budget deficits. Political parties may delay painful decisions, hoping that the other party will make the adjustment and take the blame. In cases like this, tight restraints on policy, such as a constitutional amendment to balance the budget, again provide a rough solution. Better ways typically involve better institutions and better ways of designing the process through which policy and decisions are made.

KEY TERMS

QUESTIONS AND PROBLEMS

QUICK CHECK

1. *Using the information in this chapter, label each of the following statements true, false or uncertain. Explain briefly.*

a. There is so much uncertainty about the effects of monetary policy that we would be better off not using it.

b. Elect a Labour government if you want low unemployment.

c. There is clear evidence of political business cycles in the UK: low unemployment during election campaigns and higher unemployment the rest of the time.

d. Rules are ineffective in reducing budget deficits.

e. Governments would be wise to announce a no-negotiation policy with hostage takers.

f. If hostages are taken, it is clearly wise for governments to negotiate with hostage takers, even if the government has announced a no-negotiation policy.

g. When a central bank announces a target inflation rate, it has no incentive to deviate from the target.

2. Implementing a political business cycle

You are the economic adviser to a newly elected prime minister. In four years she will face another election. Voters want a low unemployment rate and a low inflation rate. However, you believe that voting decisions are influenced heavily by the values of unemployment and inflation in the last year before the election, and that the economy's performance in the first three years of a prime minister's administration has little effect on voting behaviour.

Assume that inflation last year was 10%, and that the unemployment rate was equal to the natural rate. The Phillips curve is given by

$$\pi_t = \pi_{t-1} - \alpha(\mu_t - \mu_n)$$

Assume that you can use fiscal and monetary policy to achieve any unemployment rate you want for each of the next four years. Your task is to help the prime minister achieve low unemployment and low inflation in the last year of her administration.

a. Suppose you want to achieve a low unemployment rate (i.e. an unemployment rate below the natural rate) in the year before the next election (four years from today). What will happen to inflation in the fourth year?

b. Given the effect on inflation you identified in part (a), what would you advise the prime minister to do in the early years of her administration to achieve low inflation in the fourth year?

c. Now suppose the Phillips curve is given by

$$\pi_t = \pi_t^e - \alpha(\mu_t - \mu_n)$$

In addition, assume that people form inflation expectations, π_t^e, based on consideration of the future (as opposed to looking only at inflation last year) and are aware that the prime minister has an incentive to carry out the policies you identified in parts (a) and (b). Are the policies you described in parts (a) and (b) likely to be successful? Why or why not?

3. *Suppose the government amends the constitution to prevent government officials from negotiating with terrorists.*

What are the advantages of such a policy? What are the disadvantages?

4. *New Zealand rewrote the charter of its central bank in the early 1990s to make low inflation its only goal.*

Why would New Zealand want to do this?

DIG DEEPER

5. Political expectations, inflation and unemployment

Consider a country with two political parties, Labour and Conservative. Labour care more about unemployment than Conservative, and Conservative care more about inflation than Labour. When Labour are in power, they choose an inflation rate of π_L, and when the Conservatives are in power, they choose an inflation rate of π_C. We assume that $\pi_L > \pi_C$.

The Phillips curve is given by

$$\pi_t = \pi_t^e - \alpha(\mu_t - \mu_n)$$

An election is about to be held. Assume that expectations about inflation for the coming year (represented by π_t^e) are formed before the election. (Essentially, this assumption means that wages for the coming year are set before the election.) Moreover, Labour and Conservative have an equal chance of winning the election.

a. Solve for expected inflation, in terms of π_L and π_C.

b. Suppose Labour win the election and implement their target inflation rate, π_L. Given your solution for expected inflation in part (a), how will the unemployment rate compare to the natural rate of unemployment?

c. Suppose the Conservatives win the election and implement their target inflation rate, π_C. Given your solution for expected inflation in part (a), how will the unemployment rate compare to the natural rate of unemployment?

d. Do these results fit the evidence in Table 22.3? Why or why not?

e. Now suppose that everybody expects Labour to win the election, and Labour indeed win. If Labour implement their target inflation rate, how will the unemployment rate compare to the natural rate?

6. Deficit reduction as a prisoner's dilemma game

Suppose there is a budget deficit. It can be reduced by cutting military spending, by cutting social security, or by cutting both. Labour have to decide whether to support cuts in social security. The Conservatives have to decide whether to support cuts in military spending.

The possible outcomes are represented in the following table:

		Social security cuts	
		Yes	**No**
Defence cuts	Yes	$(C = 1, L = -2)$	$(C = -2, L = 3)$
	No	$(C = 3, L = -2)$	$(C = -1, L = -1)$

The table presents payoffs to each party under the various outcomes. Think of a pay-off as a measure of happiness for a given party under a given outcome. If Labour vote for social security cuts and the Conservatives vote against cuts in military spending, the Conservatives receive a pay-off of 3 and Labour receive a pay-off of –2.

a. If the Conservatives decide to cut military spending, what is the best response of Labour? Given this response, what is the pay-off for the Conservatives?

b. If the Conservatives decide not to cut military spending, what is the best response of Labour? Given this response, what is the pay-off for the Conservatives?

c. What will the Conservatives do? What will Labour do? Will the budget deficit be reduced? Why or why not? (A game with a pay-off structure like the one in this problem, and which produces the outcome you have just described, is known as a *prisoner's dilemma*.) Is there a way to improve the outcome?

EXPLORE FURTHER

7. Games, pre-commitment and time inconsistency in the news

Current events offer abundant examples of disputes in which the parties are involved in a game, try to commit themselves to lines of action in advance and face issues of time inconsistency. Examples arise in the domestic political process, international affairs and labour–management relations.

a. Choose a current dispute (or one resolved recently) to investigate. Do an Internet search to learn the issues involved in the dispute, the actions taken by the parties to date and the current state of play.

b. In what ways have the parties tried to pre-commit to certain actions in the future? Do they face issues of time inconsistency? Have the parties failed to carry out any of their threatened actions?

c. Does the dispute resemble a prisoner's dilemma game (a game with a pay-off structure like the one described in problem 6)? In other words, does it seem likely (or did it actually happen) that the individual incentives of the parties will lead them to an unfavourable outcome – one that could be improved for both parties through cooperation? Is there a deal to be made? What attempts have the parties made to negotiate?

d. How do you think the dispute will be resolved (or how has it been resolved)?

FURTHER READING

- If you want to learn more on these issues, some very useful references are *Political Economy in Macroeconomics*, by Alan Drazen (Princeton, NJ: Princeton University Press, 2000) and *Political Economics: Explaining Economic Policy*, by Torsten Persson and Guido Tabellini (The MIT Press, 2002).

- A leading proponent of the view that governments misbehave and should be tightly restrained is James Buchanan, from George Mason University. Buchanan received the Nobel Prize in 1986 for his work on public choice. Read, for example, his book with Richard Wagner, *Democracy in Deficit: The Political Legacy of Lord Keynes* (New York: Academic Press, 1977).

- For an interpretation of the increase in inflation in the 1970s as the result of time inconsistency, see 'Did time consistency contribute to the great inflation?', by Henry Chappell and Rob McGregor, *Economics & Politics*, 2004, **16**, 233–251.

Chapter 23

MONETARY AND FISCAL POLICY RULES AND CONSTRAINTS

Nearly every chapter has said something about monetary policy. This chapter puts all these things together and ties up the remaining loose ends.

Let's first briefly review what you have learned about monetary policy:

- In the short run, monetary policy affects the level of output as well as its composition:
  - An increase in money leads to a decrease in interest rates and a depreciation of the currency.
  - Both of these lead to an increase in the demand for goods and an increase in output.

- In the medium run and the long run, monetary policy is neutral:
  - Changes in either the level or the rate of growth of money have no effect on output or unemployment.
  - Changes in the level of money lead to proportional increases in prices.
  - Changes in the rate of nominal money growth lead to corresponding changes in the inflation rate.

Let's also review what you have learned about fiscal policy:

- In the short run, a budget deficit (triggered, say, by an increase in government spending) increases demand and output. What happens to investment spending is ambiguous.

- In the medium run, output returns to the natural level of output. The interest rate and the composition of spending are different, however. The interest rate is higher, and investment spending is lower.

- In the long run, lower investment leads to a lower capital stock and, therefore, a lower level of output.

With these effects in mind, this chapter looks at the goals and methods of monetary and fiscal policy today. The chapter is divided in three sections.

The first two sections deal with monetary policy rules:

- Section 23.1 discusses what inflation rate central banks should try to achieve in the medium and long run, in other words what is the optimal inflation rate.

- Section 23.2 discusses how monetary policy should be designed both to achieve this inflation rate in the medium and long run, and to reduce output fluctuations in the short run.

The last section deals with fiscal policy rules and constraints:

● Section 23.3 examines a number of fiscal policy issues where the government budget constraint plays a central role, from the proposition that deficits do not really matter, to tax distortions. It then describes some notable cases of fiscal policy rules around the world: the rules imposed by the Stability and Growth Pact on the members of the European Monetary Union, the Golden Rule recently introduced in the UK and the balanced budget rule in the USA.

23.1 THE OPTIMAL INFLATION RATE

Table 23.1 shows how inflation has steadily gone down in rich countries since the early 1980s. In 1981, average inflation in the OECD was 11.9%; in 2011, it was down to 1.2%. In 1981, 2 countries (out of 30) had an inflation rate below 5%; by 2008, the number had increased to 25.

> The five countries with inflation above 5%: Iceland, with 5.8%; Luxembourg, with 7.1%; Mexico, with 6.6%; Norway, with 7.7%; and Turkey, with 13.0%.

Does this mean that most central banks have now achieved their goal? Dr should they aim for an even lower inflation rate, perhaps 0%? The answer depends on the costs and benefits of inflation.

The costs of inflation

Earlier we saw (in Chapter 11) how very high inflation, say a rate of 30% a month or more, can disrupt economic activity. The debate in OECD countries today, however, is not about the costs of inflation rates of 30% a month or more. Rather, it centres on the advantages of, say, 0% versus 3% inflation a year. Within that range, economists identify four main costs of inflation: (1) shoe-leather costs, (2) tax distortions, (3) money illusion and (4) inflation variability.

Shoe-leather costs

> (From Chapter 11): In the medium run, the real interest rate is not affected by inflation. The increase in inflation is reflected one-for-one in an increase in the nominal interest rate. This is called the Fisher effect.

In the medium run, a higher inflation rate leads to a higher nominal interest rate, and so to a higher opportunity cost of holding money. As a result, people decrease their money balances by making more trips to the bank – thus the expression **shoe-leather costs**. These trips would be avoided if inflation were lower, and people could be doing other things instead, working more or enjoying leisure.

During hyperinflations, shoe-leather costs can become quite large. But their importance in times of moderate inflation is limited. If an inflation rate of 3% leads people to go the bank, say, one more time every month, or to do one more transaction between their money market fund and their current account every month, this hardly qualifies as a major cost of inflation.

Table 23.1 Inflation rates in OECD countries since 1981

Year	1981	1985	1990	1995	2000	2005	2010	2011
OECD average	11.9%	7.3%	7.0%	6.1%	4.1%	2.6%	3.6%	1.2%
Number of countries with inflation below 5%	2	11	11	22	23	29	25	27

Source: OECD *Economic Outlook* database.

Tax distortions

The second cost of inflation comes from the interaction between the tax system and inflation.

Consider, for example, the taxation of capital gains. Taxes on capital gains are typically based on the change in the price of the asset between the time it was purchased and the time it is sold. This implies that the higher the rate of inflation, the higher is the tax. An example will make this clear:

- Suppose inflation has been running at $\pi\%$ a year for the past ten years.
- Suppose you bought your house for €50,000 ten years ago, and you are selling it today for €50,000 times $(1 + \pi\%)^{10}$ – so its real value is unchanged.
- If the capital gains tax is 30%, the effective tax rate on the sale of your house – defined as the ratio of the tax you pay to the price for which you sell your house – is

$$(30\%)\frac{50,000(1 + \pi\%)^{10} - 50,000}{50,000(1 + \pi\%)^{10}}$$

◀ The numerator of the fraction equals the sale price minus the purchase price. The denominator is the sale price.

- Because you are selling your house for the same real price at which you bought it, your real capital gain is zero, so you should not be paying any tax. Indeed, if $\pi = 0$ – if there has been no inflation – then the effective tax rate is 0. But if $\pi = 3\%$, then the effective tax rate is 7.6%: despite the fact that your real capital gain is zero, you end up paying a high tax.

The problems created by the interactions between taxation and inflation extend beyond capital gains taxes. Although we know that the real rate of return on an asset is the real interest rate, not the nominal interest rate, income for the purpose of income taxation includes nominal interest payments, not real interest payments. Or, to take yet another example, until the early 1980s in the USA, the income levels corresponding to different income tax rates were not increased automatically with inflation. As a result, people were pushed into higher tax brackets as their nominal income – but not necessarily their real income – increased over time, an effect known as *bracket creep*.

You might argue this cost is not a cost of inflation per se, but rather the result of a badly designed tax system. In the house example we just discussed, the government could eliminate the problem if it indexed the purchase price to the price level – that is, it adjusted the purchase price for inflation since the time of purchase – and computed the tax on the difference between the sale price and the adjusted purchase price. Under that computation, there would be no capital gains and therefore no capital gains tax to pay. But because tax codes rarely allow for such systematic adjustment, the inflation rate matters and leads to distortions.

◀ Some economists argue the costs of bracket creep were much larger. As tax revenues steadily increased, there was little pressure on the government to control spending. The result, they argue, was an increase in the size of the government spending in the 1960s and 1970s far beyond what would have been desirable.

Money illusion

The third cost comes from **money illusion** – the notion that people appear to make systematic mistakes in assessing nominal versus real changes. A number of computations that would be simple when prices are stable become more complicated when there is inflation. When they compare their income this year to their income in previous years, people have to keep track of the history of inflation. When they choose between different assets or deciding how much to consume or save, they have to keep track of the difference between the real interest rate and the nominal interest rate. Casual evidence suggests that many people find these computations difficult and often fail to make the relevant distinctions. Economists and psychologists have gathered more formal evidence, and it suggests that inflation often leads people and firms to make incorrect decisions (see the Focus box 'Money illusion'.) If this is the case, then a simple solution is to have zero inflation.

Inflation variability

This cost comes from the fact that higher inflation is typically associated with more variable inflation. And more variable inflation means financial assets such as bonds, which promise fixed nominal payments in the future, become riskier.

A good and sad movie about surviving ➤
on a fixed pension in post–war Italy is
Umberto D, made by Vittorio de Sica
in 1952.

Take a bond that pays €1,000 in ten years. With constant inflation over the next ten years, not only the nominal value, but also the real value of the bond in ten years is known with certainty – we can compute exactly how much a euro will be worth in ten years. But with variable inflation, the real value of €1,000 in ten years becomes uncertain. The more variability there is, the more uncertainty it creates. Saving for retirement becomes more difficult. For those who have invested in bonds, lower inflation than they expected means a better retirement; but higher inflation may mean poverty. This is one of the reasons retirees, for whom part of income is fixed in money terms, typically worry more about inflation than other groups in the population.

You might argue, as in the case of taxes, that these costs are not due to inflation per se, but rather to the financial markets' inability to provide assets that protect their holders against inflation. Rather than issuing only nominal bonds (bonds that promise a fixed nominal amount in the future), governments or firms could also issue indexed bonds – bonds that promise a nominal amount adjusted for inflation, so people do not have to worry about the real value of the bond when they retire. Indeed (as we saw in Chapter 16), a number of countries, including the UK, France and Sweden, have now introduced such bonds, so people can better protect themselves against movements in inflation.

FOCUS
Money illusion

There is a lot of anecdotal evidence that many people fail to adjust properly for inflation in their financial computations. Recently, economists and psychologists have started looking at money illusion more closely. In a recent study, two psychologists, Eldar Shafir from Princeton and Amos Tversky from Stanford, and one economist, Peter Diamond from MIT, designed a survey aimed at finding how prevalent money illusion is and what causes it. Among the many questions they asked of people in various groups (people at Newark International Airport, people at two New Jersey shopping malls, and a group of Princeton undergraduates) is the following:

Suppose Adam, Ben and Carl each received an inheritance of $200,000 and each used it immediately to purchase a house. Suppose each sold his house one year after buying it. Economic conditions were, however, different in each case:

● During the time Adam owned the house, there was a 25% deflation – the prices of all goods and services decreased by approximately 25%. A year after Adam bought the house, he sold it for $154,000 (23% less than what he had paid).

● During the time Ben owned the house, there was no inflation or deflation – the prices of all goods and services did not change significantly during the year. A year after Ben bought the house, he sold it for $198,000 (1% less than what he had paid).

● During the time Carl owned the house, there was a 25% inflation – the prices of all goods and services increased by approximately 25%. A year after Carl bought the house, he sold it for $246,000 (23% more than what he had paid).

Please rank Adam, Ben and Carl in terms of the success of their house transactions. Assign '1' to the person who made the best deal and '3' to the person who made the worst deal.

In nominal terms, Carl clearly made the best deal, followed by Ben, followed by Adam. But what is relevant is how they did in real terms – adjusting for inflation. In real terms, the ranking is reversed: Adam (with a 2% real gain), made the best deal, followed by Ben (with a 1% loss), followed by Carl (with a 2% loss).

The survey's answers were the following:

Rank	Adam	Ben	Carl
1st	37%	15%	48%
2nd	10%	74%	16%
3rd	53%	11%	36%

Carl was ranked first by 48% of the respondents, and Adam was ranked third by 53% of the respondents. These answers suggest that money illusion is very prevalent. In other words, people (even Princeton undergraduates) have a hard time adjusting for inflation.

The benefits of inflation

Inflation is actually not all bad. One can identify three benefits of inflation: (1) seignorage, (2) the option of negative real interest rates for macroeconomic policy and (3) (somewhat paradoxically) the use of the interaction between money illusion and inflation in facilitating real wage adjustments.

Seignorage

Money creation – the ultimate source of inflation – is one of the ways in which the government can finance its spending. Put another way, money creation is an alternative to borrowing from the public or raising taxes.

The government typically does not 'create' money to pay for its spending. Rather, the government issues and sells bonds, and spends the proceeds. But if the bonds are bought by the central bank, which then creates money to pay for them, the result is the same: other things equal, the revenues from money creation – that is, seignorage – allow the government to borrow less from the public or to lower taxes.

How large is seignorage in practice? Seignorage is often an important source of government finance in countries with very high inflation rates. But its importance in OECD economies today, and for the range of inflation rates we are considering, is much more limited. Take the case of the USA. The ratio of the monetary base – the money issued by the Fed (see Chapter 4) – to GDP is about 6%. An increase in nominal money growth of 3% per year (which eventually leads to a 3% increase in inflation) would lead therefore to an increase in seignorage of $3\% \times 6\%$, or 0.18% of GDP.

This is a small amount of revenues to get in exchange for 3% more inflation.

Therefore, while the seignorage argument is sometimes relevant (for example, in economies that do not yet have a good fiscal system in place), it hardly seems relevant in the discussion of whether OECD countries today should have, say, 0% versus 3% inflation.

◁ Let H denote the monetary base – the money issued by the central bank. Then

$$\frac{\text{Seignorage}}{Y} = \frac{\Delta H}{PY} = \frac{\Delta H}{H}\frac{H}{PY}$$

where $\Delta H/H$ is the rate of growth of the monetary base, and H/PY is the ratio of the monetary base to nominal GDP.

The option of negative real interest rates

This argument follows from our discussion of the liquidity trap and its macroeconomic implications (in Chapter 5). A numerical example will help here.

- Consider two economies, both with a natural real interest rate equal to 2%.
- In the first economy, the central bank maintains an average inflation rate of 3%, so the nominal interest rate is on average equal to $2\% + 3\% = 5\%$.
- In the second economy, the central bank maintains an average inflation rate of 0%, so the nominal interest rate is on average equal to $2\% + 0\% = 2\%$.
- Suppose both economies are hit by a similar adverse shock, which leads, at a given interest rate, to a decrease in spending and a decrease in output in the short run.
- In the first economy, the central bank can decrease the nominal interest rate from 5% to 0%, a decrease of 5%. Under the assumption that expected inflation does not change immediately, and remains equal to 3%, the real interest rate decreases from 2% to −3%. This is likely to have a strong positive effect on spending, and help the economy recover.
- In the second economy, the central bank can only decrease the nominal interest rate from 2% to 0%, a decrease of 2%. Under the assumption that expected inflation does not change right away, and remains equal to 0%, the real interest rate decreases only by 2%, from 2% to 0%. This small decrease in the real interest rate may not increase spending by very much.

◁ (From Chapter 11): The natural real interest rate is the real interest rate implied by equilibrium in the goods market when output is equal to its natural level.

In short, an economy with a higher average inflation rate has more scope to use monetary policy to fight a recession. An economy with a low average inflation rate may find itself unable to use monetary policy to return output to the natural level of output. This possibility is far from being just theoretical. Japan faced precisely such a limit on monetary policy, and its recession turned into a slump. In the early 2000s, many economists worried that other countries may also be at risk. Many countries, including the USA, had low inflation and low nominal interest rates. If, for any reason, some of these countries had been faced with further adverse shocks to spending, the room for monetary policy to help avoid a decline in output would clearly have been limited. Fortunately, there were no adverse shocks, and the issue has disappeared from the front pages. It is likely, however, to come back in the future.

Money illusion revisited

Paradoxically, the presence of money illusion provides at least one argument for having a positive inflation rate.

To see why, consider two situations. In the first, inflation is 3%, and your wage goes up by 1% in nominal terms – in euros. In the second, inflation is 0% and your wage goes down by 2% in nominal terms. Both lead to the same 2% decrease in your real wage, so you should be indifferent. The evidence, however, shows that many people will accept the real wage cut more easily in the first case than in the second case.

Why is this example relevant to our discussion? Because, as you saw earlier (in Chapter 14), the constant process of change that characterises modern economies means some workers must sometimes take a real pay cut. Thus, the argument goes, the presence of inflation allows for these downward real-wage adjustments more easily than when there is no inflation. This argument is plausible. Economists have not established its importance; but, because so many economies now have very low inflation, we may soon be in a position to test it.

> See, for example, the results of a survey of managers by Alan Blinder and Don Choi, in 'A shred of evidence on theories of wage rigidity', *Quarterly Journal of Economics*, 1990, **105**(4), 1003–1015.

> A conflict of metaphors: because inflation makes these real wage adjustments easier to achieve, some economists say inflation 'greases the wheels' of the economy. Others, emphasising the adverse effects of inflation on relative prices, say that inflation 'puts sand' in the economy.

The optimal inflation rate: the current debate

At this stage, the debate in OECD countries is largely between those who think some inflation – say, 3% – is fine and those who want to achieve price stability – that is, 0% inflation.

Those who want an inflation rate around 3% emphasise that the costs of 3% versus 0% inflation are small and that the benefits of inflation are worth keeping. They argue that some of the costs of inflation could be avoided by indexing the tax system and issuing more indexed bonds. They also argue that getting inflation down from its current rate to zero would require some increase in unemployment for some time, and that this transition cost may well exceed the eventual benefits.

Those who want to aim for 0% make the point that 0% is a very different target rate from all others: it corresponds to price stability. This is desirable in itself. Knowing that the price level will be roughly the same in 10 or 20 years as it is today simplifies a number of complicated decisions and eliminates the scope for money illusion. Also, given the time consistency problem facing central banks (discussed in Chapter 22), credibility and simplicity of the target inflation rate are important. They believe price stability can achieve these goals better than a target inflation rate of 3%.

The debate is not settled. For the time being, most central banks appear to be aiming for low but positive inflation – that is, inflation rates between 2% and 3%.

23.2 MONETARY POLICY RULES

Until the 1990s the design of monetary policy typically centred around nominal money growth. Central banks chose a nominal money growth target for the medium run. And they thought about short-run monetary policy in terms of deviations of nominal money growth from that target. In the past decade, however, this design has evolved. Most central banks have adopted an inflation rate target rather than a nominal money growth rate target. And they think about short-run monetary policy in terms of movements in the nominal interest rate rather than in terms of movements in the rate of nominal money growth. Let's first look at what they did earlier, before turning to what they do now.

Money growth targets and target ranges

Until the 1990s, monetary policy in many OECD countries was typically conducted as follows:

- The central bank chose a target rate for nominal money growth corresponding to the inflation rate it wanted to achieve in the medium run. If, for example, it wanted to achieve an inflation rate of 4% and the normal rate of growth of output (the rate of growth implied by the rate of technological progress and the rate of population growth) was 3%, the central bank chose a target rate of nominal money growth of 7%.
- In the short run, the central bank allowed for deviations of nominal money growth from the target. If, for example, the economy was in a recession, the central bank increased nominal money growth above the target value, so as to allow for a decrease in the interest rate and a faster recovery of output. In an expansion, it might do the reverse to slow down output growth.
- To communicate to the public both what it wanted to achieve in the medium run and what it intended to do in the short run, the central bank announced a range for the rate of nominal money growth it intended to achieve. Sometimes, this range was presented as a commitment from the central bank; sometimes, it was presented simply as a forecast rather than as a commitment.

Over time, central banks became disenchanted with this way of conducting monetary policy. Let's now see why.

Money growth and inflation revisited

The design of monetary policy around nominal money growth is based on the assumption that there is a close relation between inflation and nominal money growth in the medium run. The problem is that, in practice, this relation is not very tight. If nominal money growth is high, inflation will also be high; and if nominal money growth is low, inflation will be low. But the relation is not tight enough that, by choosing a rate of nominal money growth, the central bank can achieve precisely its desired rate of inflation, not even in the medium run.

The relation between inflation and nominal money growth is shown in Figure 23.1, which plots ten-year averages of the inflation rate against ten-year averages of the growth

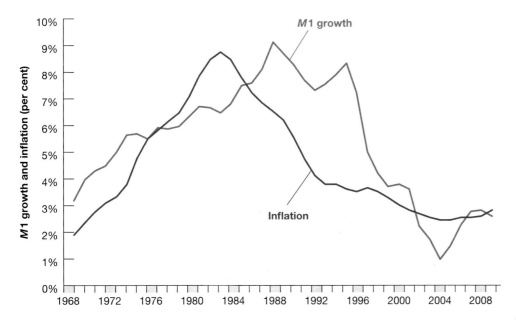

Figure 23.1

_M_1 growth and inflation in the UK: ten-year averages since 1968

There is no tight relation between _M_1 growth and inflation – not even in the medium run.

rate of the money stock since 1968 (so the numbers for inflation and for money growth for 2000, for example, are the average inflation rate and the average growth rate of money from 1991 to 2000) in the UK. The inflation rate is constructed using the CPI as the price index. The growth rate of nominal money is constructed using $M1$ as the measure for the money stock. The reason for using ten-year averages should be clear: in the short run, changes in nominal money growth affect mostly output, not inflation. It is only in the medium run that a relation between nominal money growth and inflation should emerge. Taking ten-year averages of both nominal money growth and inflation is a way of detecting such a medium-run relation.

Figure 23.1 shows that, for the UK since 1968, the relation between $M1$ growth and inflation has not been very tight. True, both went up at the beginning of the period, and both have come down since. But note how inflation started declining in the early 1980s, while nominal money growth remained high for another decade and came down only in the 1990s. Average inflation from 1982 to 1992 was down to 3.8%, while average money growth over the same period was still running at 7.5%. Since 2006, average inflation and average money growth have remained closer, around 0.2%.

Why is the relation between $M1$ growth and inflation not tighter? Because of shifts in the demand for money. An example will help. Suppose, as the result of the introduction of credit cards, people decide to hold only half the amount of money they held before: in other words, the real demand for money decreases by half. In the medium run, the real money stock must also decrease by half. For a given nominal money stock, the price level must double.

Even if the nominal money stock were to remain constant, there would still be a period of inflation as the price level doubles. During this period, there will be no tight relation between nominal money growth (which is zero) and inflation (which is positive).

From equation (5.3) (the *LM* equation): the real money supply (the left side) must be equal to the real demand for money (the right side):

$$\frac{M}{P} = YL(i)$$

If, as a result of the introduction of credit cards, the real demand for money halves, then

$$\frac{M}{P} = \frac{1}{2}YL(i)$$

For a given level of output and a given interest rate, M/P must also halve. Given M, this implies P must double.

FOCUS
The unsuccessful search for the right monetary aggregate

The reason why the demand for money shifts over time goes beyond the introduction of credit cards. To understand why, we must challenge an assumption we have maintained until now, namely that there is a sharp distinction between money and other assets. In fact, there are many financial assets that are close to money. They cannot be used for transactions – at least not without restrictions – but they can be exchanged for money at little cost. In other words, these assets are very **liquid**; this makes them attractive substitutes for money. Shifts between money and these assets are the main factor behind shifts in the demand for money.

Take, for example, money market fund shares. Money market funds are financial intermediaries that hold as assets short-maturity securities (typically, Treasury bills in the USA or BTS in the UK) and have deposits (or shares, as they are called) as liabilities. The funds pay depositors an interest rate close to the T-bill rate minus the administrative costs of running the fund. Deposits can be exchanged for money on notice and at little cost. Most money market funds allow depositors to write cheques but only above a certain amount, typically $500. Because of this restriction, money market funds are not included in **$M1$**. When these funds were introduced in the mid-1970s, people were able for the first time to hold a very liquid asset while receiving an interest rate close to that on T-bills. Money market funds quickly became very attractive, increasing from nothing in 1973 to $321 billion in 1989. (In comparison, chequeable deposits were $280 billion in 1989.) Many people reduced their bank account balances and moved to money market funds. In other words, there was a large negative shift in the demand for money.

The presence of such shifts between money and other liquid assets led central banks to construct and report measures that include not only money, but also other liquid assets. These measures are called **monetary aggregates**, and come under the names of $M2$, **$M3$** and so on. The narrowest definition of money supply in common use is $M0$. The definition of $M0$ used in the UK is bank notes and coins in circulation, plus banks' deposits with the

Frequent and large shifts in money demand created serious problems for central banks. They found themselves torn between trying to keep a stable target for money growth and staying within announced bands (in order to maintain credibility), or adjusting to shifts in money demand (in order to stabilise output in the short run, and inflation in the medium run). Starting in the early 1990s, a dramatic rethinking of monetary policy took place, based instead on inflation targeting rather than money growth targeting, and the use of interest rate rules. Let's look at the way monetary policy is conducted today.

Inflation targeting

In many countries, central banks have defined as their primary goal the achievement of a low inflation rate, both in the short run and in the medium run. This is known as **inflation targeting**.

- Trying to achieve a given inflation target in the medium run would seem, and indeed is, a clear improvement over trying to achieve a nominal money growth target. After all, in the medium run, the primary goal of monetary policy is to achieve a given rate of inflation. Better to have an inflation rate as the target than a nominal money growth target, which, as you have seen, may not lead to the desired rate of inflation.
- Trying to achieve a given inflation target in the short run would appear to be much more controversial. Focusing exclusively on inflation would seem to eliminate any role monetary policy could play in reducing output fluctuations. But, in fact, this is not the case. To see why, return to the Phillips curve relation between inflation, π_t, lagged inflation, π_{t-1}, and the deviation of the unemployment rate, u_t, from the natural rate of unemployment, u_n (equation (10.10)):

Bank of England. $M0$ is also known as the wide monetary base. This term refers to the fact that the money measured by $M0$ supplies the base on which other forms of money (such as bank deposits) are based.

In the UK, $M2$ includes notes and coins in circulation with the public; plus UK private sector's non-interest-bearing sterling sight deposits with banks in the UK; plus UK private sector's interest-bearing retail sterling deposits with banks in the UK. In the USA, $M2$ – which is also sometimes called **broad money** – includes $M1$ (currency and chequeable deposits) plus money market mutual fund shares, money market deposit accounts (the same as money market shares, but issued by banks rather than money market funds) and time deposits (deposits with an explicit maturity of a few months to a few years and with a penalty for early withdrawal). In 2006, $M2$ was $7.0 trillion, compared to $1.3 trillion for $M1$.

The construction of $M2$ and other monetary aggregates would appear to offer a solution to our earlier problem: if most of the shifts in the demand for money are between $M1$ and other assets within $M2$, the demand for $M2$ should be more stable than the demand for $M1$, and so there should be a tighter relation between $M2$ growth and inflation than between $M1$ growth and inflation. If so, the central bank could choose targets for $M2$ growth rather than for $M1$ growth. This is indeed the solution that many central banks adopted. But it did not work well, for two reasons:

- The relation between $M2$ growth and inflation is no tighter than the relation between $M1$ growth and inflation.
- More importantly, while the central bank controls $M1$, it does not control $M2$. If people shift from T-bills to money market funds, this will increase $M2$ – which includes money market funds, but does not include T-bills. There is little the central bank can do about this increase in $M2$. Thus, $M2$ is a strange target: it is neither under the direct control of the central bank, nor what the central bank ultimately cares about.

In short, the relation between inflation and the growth of monetary aggregates such as $M2$ and $M3$ is no tighter than the relation between inflation and the growth rate of $M1$. And the central bank has little control over the growth of these monetary aggregates anyway. This is why, in most countries, monetary policy has shifted its focus from monetary aggregates – be it $M1$, $M2$ or $M3$ – to inflation.

$$\pi_t = \pi_{t-1} - \alpha(u_t - u_n)$$

Let the inflation rate target be π^*. Suppose the central bank could achieve its inflation target exactly in every period. Then, the relation would become:

$$\pi^* = \pi^* - \alpha(u_t - u_n)$$

$0 = -\alpha(u_t - u_n) \Rightarrow u_t = u_n$

➤ The unemployment rate, u_t, would always equal u_n, the natural rate of unemployment; by implication, output would always be equal to the natural level of output. In effect, inflation targeting would lead the central bank to act in such a way as to eliminate all deviations of output from its natural level.

The intuition: if the central bank saw that an adverse demand shock were going to lead to a recession, it would know that, with out a monetary expansion, the economy would experience a decline in inflation below the target rate of inflation. To maintain stable inflation, the central bank would then rely on a monetary expansion to avoid the recession. The converse would apply to a favourable demand shock: fearing an increase in inflation above the target rate, the central bank would rely on a monetary contraction to slow down the economy and keep output at the natural level of output. As a result of this active monetary policy, output would remain at the natural level of output all the time.

The result we have just derived – that inflation targeting eliminates deviations of output from its natural level – is too strong, however, for two reasons:

- The central bank cannot always achieve the rate of inflation it wants in the short run. So suppose that, for example, the central bank was not able to achieve its desired rate of inflation last year, so π_{t-1} is higher than π^*. Then it is not clear that the central bank should try to hit its target this year, and achieve $\pi_t = \pi^*$: the Phillips curve relation implies that such a decrease in inflation would require a potentially large increase in unemployment. We return to this issue below.
- Like all other macroeconomic relations, the Phillips curve relation above does not hold exactly. It will happen that, for example, inflation increases even when the unemployment is at the natural rate of unemployment. In this case, the central bank will face a more difficult choice: whether to keep unemployment at the natural rate and allow inflation to increase, or to increase unemployment above the natural rate to keep inflation in check.

These qualifications are important, but the basic point remains: Inflation targeting makes good sense in the medium run and allows monetary policy to stabilise output around its natural level in the short run.

Table 23.1 shows how inflation has steadily gone down in rich countries since the early 1980s. In 1981, average inflation in OECD countries was 11.9%; in 2008, it was down to 3.6%. In 1981, two countries (out of 30) had inflation rates below 5%; in 2008, the number had increased to 25.

Does this mean that most central banks have now achieved their goal? Or should they aim for an even lower inflation rate, perhaps 0%? The answer depends on the costs and benefits of inflation.

FOCUS
Inflation targeting in Sweden

Sweden started the transition to a new monetary regime in January 1993. Two months before (on 19 November 1992), the fixed exchange rate regime had been abandoned and the krona – following a very costly but failed attempt to defend the parity – had been allowed to float. Soon thereafter (on 14 January 1993), the Riksbank announced that monetary policy would be run based on an inflation targeting regime, and the first prototype *Inflation Report* was published in June of that year. The inflation target was set at 2%.

The Riksbank Act of 1999 greatly increased the independence of the central bank along several dimensions, in particular by creating an independent Executive Board with long-term appointments that are protected from severance from employment and that can neither seek nor take instructions when fulfilling their monetary policy duties.

How was Swedish monetary policy run? In evaluating Swedish monetary policy over the past decade, we examine several questions: (1) whether it produced good economic performance in the long run; (2) were policy rates set appropriately; and (3) what has been the relationship between monetary policy and the exchange rate?

IT and Sweden's overall economic performance
Monetary policy is unable to affect a country's level of potential output. What it can and should do is try to minimise fluctuations of actual output around potential output but, as we argued in this chapter, the best way to do this is not by focusing on output or employment targets, but rather on the path of inflation. One way to evaluate whether the Swedish monetary policy regime during the past ten years has been successful thus consists in looking at the volatility of output along with the behaviour of inflation and inflation expectations.

Figure 23.2 computes the volatility of the output gap over four sub-periods: 1980–1989, the years preceding the banking crisis; 1990–1994, the period characterised by the banking and subsequently the exchange rate crises; 1995–1998, the early years of the new monetary policy regime, before the Riksbank had gained full independence; and finally 1999–2005. The volatility of the output gap is lower since 1999, compared with its level in the 1980s: the standard deviation is 1.1 in the more recent period, compared with 1.6 in the 1980s. This means a 30% reduction in output volatility.

Figure 23.3 shows inflation expectations at various horizons. For each year the grey lines show inflation

Figure 23.2

Output gap (GDP) (level of standard deviation)

Source: Francesco Giavazzi and Frederic S. Mishkin, *An Evaluation of Swedish Monetary Policy Between 1995 and 2005*, Finance Committee, Swedish Parliament.

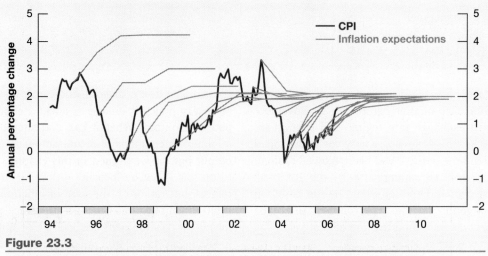

Figure 23.3

CPI and money market inflation expectations (annual percentage change)

Source: Francesco Giavazzi and Frederic S. Mishkin, *An Evaluation of Swedish Monetary Policy Between 1995 and 2005*, Finance Committee, Swedish Parliament.

expectations at 1, 2, 3, 4 and 5-years horizons. The message from Figures 23.2 and 23.3 is very clear: the new monetary policy regime has allowed Sweden to stabilise inflation expectations with no loss in terms of higher output volatility: on the contrary, output volatility has also been reduced.

The shift in inflation expectations is consistent with the observation that the transition to inflation targeting has produced a dramatic change in the process driving Swedish inflation. This is clear from Figure 23.4 which shows the path of Swedish inflation. Inflation has come down sharply but, in addition, its process has changed. Statistical tests of the inflation time-series show that up to 1993 (more precisely, for the decade 1984–1993) it is not possible to reject the hypothesis that inflation drifted without a firm anchor, i.e. that the inflation time-series was non-stationary. The statistical test indicates that there is a 43% chance that over the decade there was no anchor. On the contrary, for the inflation targeting period over the years 1994–2003, the corresponding probability is just 0.27%, which means that inflation was stationary. Inflation targeting has succeeded in establishing a solid nominal anchor.

What have been the effects on unemployment? Unemployment in Sweden has been higher in the past 15 years

than it had been before the crisis of the early 1990s (Figure 23.5): it was fluctuating between 1.5% and 3.5%, and has now shifted to a range about 3 points higher. As we have argued (in Chapter 10), however, because there is no long-run trade-off between inflation and employment, there was little that monetary policy could do to shift unemployment back to the old range. There are a large number of studies of the reasons for the rise in Swedish unemployment, a phenomenon shared by other European countries. This is not the place to get into this discussion. Our point is simply that such a rise cannot be attributed to the shift in monetary policy.

Still, monetary policy can affect fluctuations of employment within the new range. We have just seen that over the past decade fluctuations in output and employment have not been wider than they had been in the past, but it would not be fair to stop here. For instance, unemployment has moved towards the top of the new range at a time, 2002–2005, when inflation has constantly undershot the 2% target.

Source: Francesco Giavazzi and Frederic S. Mishkin, *An Evaluation of Swedish Monetary Policy Between 1995 and 2005*, Finance Committee, Swedish Parliament.

Figure 23.4

Swedish inflation assessed using different measures (annual percentage change)

Source: Francesco Giavazzi and Frederic S. Mishkin, *An Evaluation of Swedish Monetary Policy Between 1995 and 2005*, Finance Committee, Swedish Parliament.

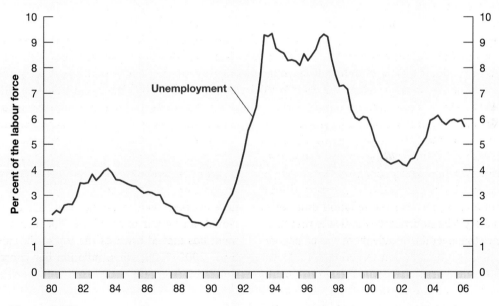

Figure 23.5

Open unemployment in Sweden (per cent of the labour force), seasonally adjusted

Source: Francesco Giavazzi and Frederic S. Mishkin, *An Evaluation of Swedish Monetary Policy Between 1995 and 2005*, Finance Committee, Swedish Parliament.

Interest rate rules

The question is then how to achieve the inflation target. Inflation is clearly not under the direct control of the central bank. In answer to this question, John Taylor, from Stanford University, argued that, since the central bank affects spending through the interest rate, the central bank should think directly in terms of the choice of an interest rate rather than a rate of nominal money growth. He then suggested a rule that the central bank should follow to set the interest rate. This rule, which is now known as the **Taylor rule** goes as follows:

- Let π_t be the rate of inflation, and π^* be the target rate of inflation.
- Let i_t be the nominal interest rate, and i^* be the target nominal interest rate – the nominal interest rate associated with the target rate of inflation π^* in the medium run.
- Let u_t be the unemployment rate, and u_n be the natural unemployment rate.

> In the medium run, the real interest rate is equal to the natural real interest rate, r_n, so the nominal interest rate moves one-for-one with the inflation rate: if r_n = 2% and the target inflation rate π^* = 3%, then the target nominal interest rate i^* = 2% + 3% = 5%. If the target inflation rate π^* is 0%, then i^* = 2% + 0% = 2% (see Chapter 11).

Think of the central bank as choosing the nominal interest rate, i. (Recall, from Chapter 4, that, through open market operations, the central bank can achieve any short-term nominal interest rate that it wants.) Then, Taylor argued, the central bank should follow the following rule:

$$i_t = i^* + a(\pi_t - \pi^*) - b(u_t - u_n)$$

where a and b are positive coefficients.

Let's look at what the rule says:

- If inflation is equal to target inflation ($\pi_t = \pi^*$), and the unemployment rate is equal to the natural rate of unemployment ($u_t = u_n$), then the central bank should set the nominal interest rate, i_t, equal to its target value, i^*. This way, the economy can stay on the same path, with inflation equal to the target inflation rate, and unemployment equal to the natural rate of unemployment.

- If inflation is higher than the target ($\pi_t > \pi^*$), the central bank should increase the nominal interest rate, i_t, above i^*. This higher interest rate will increase unemployment, and this increase in unemployment will lead to a decrease in inflation.

  The coefficient a should therefore reflect how much the central bank cares about unemployment versus inflation. The higher a is, the more the central bank will increase the interest rate in response to inflation, the more the economy will slow down, the more unemployment will increase, and the faster inflation will return to the target inflation rate.

  In any case, Taylor pointed out, a should be larger than 1. Why? Because what matters for spending is the real interest rate, not the nominal interest rate. When inflation increases, the central bank, if it wants to decrease spending and output, must increase the real interest rate. In other words, it must increase the nominal interest rate more than one-for-one with inflation.

- If unemployment is higher than the natural rate of unemployment ($\pi > \pi_n$), the central bank should decrease the nominal interest rate. The lower nominal interest rate will increase output, leading to a decrease in unemployment. Like the coefficient a, the coefficient b should reflect how much the central bank cares about unemployment relative to inflation. The higher b is, the more the central bank will be willing to deviate from target inflation to keep unemployment close to the natural rate of unemployment.

In stating this rule, Taylor did not argue that it should be followed blindly: many other events, such as an exchange rate crisis, or the need to change the composition of spending on goods, and thus the mix between monetary policy and fiscal policy, justify changing the nominal interest rate for other reasons than those included in the rule. But, he argued, the rule provided a useful way of thinking about monetary policy: once the central bank has chosen a target rate of inflation, it should try to achieve it by adjusting the nominal interest rate. The rule it should follow should take into account not only current inflation but also current unemployment.

Since it was first introduced, the Taylor rule has generated a lot of interest, both from researchers and from central banks:

- Interestingly, researchers looking at the behaviour of both the Fed in the USA and the Bundesbank in Germany have found that, although neither of these two central banks thought of itself as following a Taylor rule, this rule actually describes their behaviour over the past 15–20 years quite well.
- Other researchers have explored whether it is possible to improve on this simple rule: for example, whether the nominal interest rate should be allowed to respond not only to current inflation but also to expected future inflation.
- Yet other researchers have discussed whether central banks should adopt an explicit interest rate rule and follow it closely, or whether they should use the rule more informally and feel free to deviate from the rule when appropriate. We shall return to this issue in discussing the behaviour of the Fed in the next section.
- In general, most central banks have now shifted from thinking in terms of nominal money growth to thinking in terms of an interest rate rule. Whatever happens to nominal money growth as a result of following such a nominal interest rate rule is increasingly seen as unimportant, both by the central banks and by financial markets.

23.3 FISCAL POLICY RULES AND CONSTRAINTS

In this section we describe some issues where the government budget constraint plays a central role. Then we tackle a much debated topic in fiscal policy: the reasons why countries participating in a monetary union should follow some fiscal policy rules.

Three issues in fiscal policy

Having looked at the mechanics of the government budget constraint, we can now take up three issues in which this constraint plays a central role.

Ricardian equivalence

How does taking into account the government budget constraint (in Chapter 21) affect the way we should think of the effects of deficits on output?

One extreme view is that when the government budget constraint is taken into account, neither deficits nor debt have an effect on economic activity! This argument is known as the **Ricardian equivalence** proposition. David Ricardo, a nineteenth-century English economist, was the first to articulate its logic. His argument was further developed and given prominence in the 1970s by Robert Barro, then at the University of Chicago, now at Harvard University. For this reason, the argument is also known as the **Ricardo–Barro proposition**.

The best way to understand the logic of the proposition is to use the example of tax changes.

◄ While Ricardo stated the logic of the argument, he also argued that there were many reasons it would not hold in practice. In contrast, Barro argues that not only is the argument logically correct, but it is also a good description of reality.

● Suppose that the government decreases taxes by 1 (again think 1 billion euros) this year. As it does so, it announces that, to repay the debt, it will increase taxes by $1 + r$ next year. What will be the effect of the initial tax cut on consumption?

● One possible answer is: no effect at all. Why? Because consumers realise that the tax cut is not much of a gift: lower taxes this year are exactly offset, in present value, by higher taxes next year. Put another way, their human wealth – the present value of after-tax labour income – is unaffected. Current taxes go down by 1, but the present value of next year's taxes goes up by $(1 + r)/(1 + r)$, and the net effect of the two changes is exactly equal to zero.

● Another way of coming to the same answer – this time looking at saving rather than looking at consumption – is as follows. To say that consumers do not change their consumption in response to the tax cut is the same as saying that private saving increases one-for-one with the deficit. So the Ricardian equivalence proposition says that, if a government finances a given path of spending through deficits, private saving will increase one-for-one with the decrease in public saving, leaving total saving unchanged. The total amount left for investment will not be affected. Over time, the mechanics of the government budget constraint imply that government debt will increase. But this increase will not come at the expense of capital accumulation.

Under the Ricardian equivalence proposition, the long sequence of deficits and the increase in government debt that characterised the OECD until the late 1990s are no cause for worry. As governments were dissaving, the argument goes, people were saving more in anticipation of the higher taxes to come. The decrease in public saving was offset by an equal increase in private saving. Total saving was therefore unaffected, and so was investment. OECD economies have the same capital stock today that they would have had if there had been no increase in debt. High debt is no cause for concern.

The increase in taxes in t years is ▷ $(1 + r)^{t-1}$. The discount factor for a euro t years from now is $1/(1 + r)^{t-1}$. So the value of the increase in taxes t years from now as of today is $(1 + r)^{t-1}/(1 + r)^{t-1} = 1$.

How seriously should you take the Ricardian equivalence proposition? Most economists would answer: seriously, but not seriously enough to think that deficits and debt are irrelevant. A major theme of this book has been that expectations matter, that consumption decisions depend not only on current income but also on expected future income. If it were widely believed that a tax cut this year was going to be followed by an offsetting increase in taxes next year, the effect on consumption would indeed probably be small. Many consumers would save most or all of the tax cut in anticipation of higher taxes next year. (Replace year with month or week, and the argument becomes even more convincing.)

Of course, tax cuts rarely come with the announcement of corresponding tax increases a year later. Consumers have to guess when and how taxes will eventually be increased. This fact does not by itself invalidate the Ricardian equivalence argument: no matter when taxes will be increased, the government budget constraint still implies that the present value of future tax increases must always be equal to the decrease in taxes today. Take the second example we looked at earlier (in Chapter 22) in which the government waits t years to increase taxes, and so increases taxes by $(1 + r)^{t-1}$. The present value in year 0 of this expected tax increase is $(1 + r)^{t-1}/(1 + r)^{t-1} = 1$; exactly equal to the original tax cut. The change in human wealth from the tax cut is still zero.

But insofar as future tax increases appear more distant and their timing more uncertain, consumers are in fact more likely to ignore them. This may be the case because they expect to die before taxes go up or, more likely, because they just do not think that far into the future. In either case, Ricardian equivalence is likely to fail.

So, it is safe to conclude that budget deficits have an important effect on activity – although perhaps a smaller effect than we thought before going through the Ricardian

Figure 23.6

Ricardian equivalence illustrated

Source: Mark McHugh, Across the Street Blog, M. C. Escher, *Economist*, 21 February 2009.

equivalence argument. In the short run, larger deficits are likely to lead to higher demand and to higher output. In the long run, higher government debt lowers capital accumulation and, as a result, lowers output.

Deficits, output stabilisation and the cyclically adjusted deficit

The fact that budget deficits do, indeed, have long-run adverse effects on capital accumulation and, in turn, on output, does not imply that fiscal policy should not be used to reduce output fluctuations. Rather, it implies that deficits during recessions should be offset by surpluses during booms, so as not to lead to a steady increase in debt.

◀ Note the analogy with monetary policy: the fact that higher money growth leads in the long run to more inflation does not imply that monetary policy should not be used for output stabilisation.

To help assess whether fiscal policy is on track, economists have constructed deficit measures that tell what the deficit would be, under existing tax and spending rules, if output were at the natural level of output. Such measures come under many names, ranging from the **full-employment deficit**, to the **mid-cycle deficit**, to the **standardised employment deficit**, to the **structural deficit** (the term used by the OECD). We shall use **cyclically adjusted deficit**, the term we find the most intuitive.

◀ Ignore output growth in this section, and so ignore the distinction between stabilising the debt and stabilising the debt-to-GDP ratio. (Verify that the argument extends to the case where output is growing.)

The cyclically adjusted deficit gives a simple benchmark against which to judge the direction of fiscal policy: if the actual deficit is large but the cyclically adjusted deficit is zero, then current fiscal policy is consistent with no systematic increase in debt over time. The debt will increase as long as output is below the natural level of output; but as output returns to its natural level, the deficit will disappear and the debt will stabilise.

It does not follow that the goal of fiscal policy should be to maintain a cyclically adjusted deficit equal to zero at all times. In a recession, the government may want to run a deficit large enough that even the cyclically adjusted deficit is positive. In that case, the fact that the cyclically adjusted deficit is positive provides a useful warning. The warning is that the return of output to its natural level will not be enough to stabilise the debt: the government will have to take specic measures, from tax increases to cuts in spending, to decrease the deficit at some point in the future.

The theory underlying the concept of cyclically adjusted deficit is simple; the practice of it has proven tricky. To see why, we need to look at how measures of the cyclically adjusted deficit are constructed. Construction requires two steps. First, establish how much lower the deficit would be if output were, say, 1% higher. Second, assess how far output is from its natural level.

- The first step is straightforward. A reliable rule of thumb is that a 1% decrease in output leads automatically to an increase in the deficit of 0.5% of GDP. This increase occurs because most taxes are proportional to output, whereas most government spending does not depend on the level of output. This means that a decrease in output, which leads to a decrease in revenues and not much change in spending, naturally leads to a larger deficit.

    If output is, say, 5% below its natural level, the deficit as a ratio to GDP will therefore be about 2.5% larger than it would be if output were at the natural level of output. (This effect of activity on the deficit has been called an **automatic stabiliser**: a recession naturally generates a deficit, and therefore a fiscal expansion, which partly counteracts the recession.)

- The second step is more difficult. Recall (from Chapter 8) that the natural level of output is the output level that would be produced if the economy were operating at the natural rate of unemployment. Too low an estimate of the natural rate of unemployment will lead to too high an estimate of the natural level of output and, therefore, to too optimistic a measure of the cyclically adjusted decit.

    This difficulty explains in part what happened in Europe in the 1980s. Based on the assumption of an unchanged natural unemployment rate, the cyclically adjusted deficits of the 1980s did not look that bad: if European unemployment had returned to its level of the 1970s, the associated increase in output would have been sufficient to re-establish budget balance in most countries. But, it turned out, much of the increase in unemployment reflected an increase in the natural unemployment rate, and unemployment remained very high during the 1980s. As a result, the decade was characterised by high deficits and large increases in debt ratios in most countries.

Wars and deficits

Wars typically bring about large budget deficits. As you saw earlier (in Chapter 22), the two largest increases in US government debt in the twentieth century took place during the First and Second World Wars.

Is it right for governments to rely so much on deficits to finance wars? After all, war economies are usually operating at low unemployment, so the output stabilisation reasons for running deficits we examined earlier are irrelevant. The answer, nevertheless, is yes. In fact, there are two good reasons to run deficits during wars:

- The first is distributional – Deficit finance is a way to pass some of the burden of the war to those alive after the war, and it seems only fair for future generations to share in the sacrifices the war requires.
- The second is more narrowly economic – Deficit spending helps reduce tax distortions.

Lets look at each reason in turn.

1. *Passing on the burden of the war*

Wars lead to large increases in government spending. Consider the implications of financing this increased spending either through increased taxes or through debt. To distinguish this case from our earlier discussion of output stabilisation, let's also assume that output is fixed at the natural level of output:

- Suppose the government relies on deficit finance. With government spending sharply up, there will be a very large increase in the demand for goods. Given our assumption that output stays the same, the interest rate will have to increase enough to maintain equilibrium. Investment, which depends on the interest rate, will decrease sharply.
- Suppose instead that the government finances the spending increase through an increase in taxes – say, income taxes. Consumption will decline sharply. Exactly how much depends on consumers' expectations: the longer they expect the war to last, the longer they will expect higher taxes to last, and the more they will decrease their consumption. In any case, the increase in government spending will be partly offset by a decrease in consumption. Interest rates will increase by less than they would have increased under deficit spending, and investment will therefore decrease by less.

In short, for a given output, the increase in government spending requires either a decrease in consumption and/or a decrease in investment. Whether the government relies on tax increases or deficits determines whether consumption or investment does more of the adjustment when government spending goes up.

How does this affect who bears the burden of the war? The more the government relies on deficits, the smaller the decrease in consumption during the war and the larger the decrease in investment. Lower investment means a lower capital stock after the war and, therefore, lower output after the war. By reducing capital accumulation, deficits become a way of passing some of the burden of the war on to future generations.

> ◁ Assume that the economy is closed, so that $Y = C + I + G$. Suppose that G goes up and Y remains the same. Then, $C + I$ must go down. If taxes are not increased, most of the decrease will come from a decrease in I. If taxes are increased, most of the decrease will come from a decrease in C.

2. *Reducing tax distortions*

There is another argument for running deficits, not only during wars but, more generally, in times when government spending is exceptionally high. Think, for example, of reconstruction after an earthquake, or the costs involved in the reunification of Germany in the early 1990s. (See the Focus box 'German unication, interest rates and the EMS' in Chapter 7).

The argument is as follows: if the government were to increase taxes in order to finance the increase in spending, tax rates would have to be very high. Very high tax rates can lead to very high economic distortions: faced with very high income tax rates, people work less or engage in illegal, untaxed activities. Rather than moving the tax rate up and down to always balance the budget, it is better (from the point of view of reducing distortions) to maintain a relatively constant tax rate to smooth taxes. **Tax smoothing** implies running large deficits when government spending is exceptionally high, and small surpluses the rest of the time.

Politics and fiscal restraints

Earlier we saw that politics can sometimes lead to long and lasting budget deficits (games between policy makers in Chapter 22). Can rules be put in place to limit these adverse effects?

One approach tried in the USA is to use a constitutional amendment to balance the budget; such an the amendment proposed by the Republicans in 1994 would surely eliminate the problem of deficits. But, just like a constant-money-growth rule in the case of monetary policy, it would eliminate the use of fiscal policy as a macroeconomic instrument altogether. This is just too high a price to pay.

A better approach is to put in place rules that put limits on either deficits or debt. This is harder than it sounds. Rules such as limits on the ratio of the deficit to GDP or the ratio of debt to GDP are more flexible than a balanced budget requirement; but they may still not be flexible enough if the economy is affected by particularly bad shocks. In the euro area, this has been made clear by the problems faced by the Stability and Growth Pact (on which you can learn more by reading the Focus box 'Why did the SGP fail?'). More flexible or more complex rules, such as rules that allow for special circumstances, or rules that take into account the state of the economy, are harder to design and, especially, harder to enforce. For example, allowing the deficit to be higher if the unemployment rate is higher than the natural rate requires having a simple and unambiguous way of computing the natural rate – a nearly impossible task.

A complementary approach is to put in place mechanisms to reduce deficits, were such deficits to arise. Consider, for example, a mechanism that triggers automatic spending cuts when the deficit gets too large. Suppose the budget deficit is too large, and it is desirable to cut spending across the board by 5%. Members of Parliament will find it difficult to explain to their constituency why their favourite spending programme was cut by 5%. Now suppose the deficit triggers automatic across-the-board spending cuts of 5% without any government action. Knowing that other programmes will be cut, Members of Parliament will accept cuts in their favourite programmes more easily. They will also be better able to deflect the blame for the cuts: members of Parliament who succeed in limiting the cuts to their favourite programme to, say, 4% (by convincing Parliament to make deeper cuts in some other programmes in order to maintain the lower overall level of spending) can then return to their constituents and claim that they successfully prevented even larger cuts.

This was indeed the approach used in the UK. The UK government specified two key fiscal rules that provided benchmarks against which the performance of fiscal policy could be judged:

- *The golden rule* – Over the economic cycle, until 2009, the government will borrow only to invest and not to fund current spending; this rule was officially adopted by former Chancellor of the Exchequer, Prime Minister Gordon Brown. The government will meet the golden rule if, on average over a complete economic cycle, the current budget is in balance or surplus.
- *The sustainable investment rule* – Public sector net debt as a proportion of GDP will be held over the economic cycle at a stable and prudent level. The Chancellor has stated that, other things being equal, net debt will be maintained below 40% of GDP over the current economic cycle, in accordance with the sustainable investment rule.

This was also the approach which was used to reduce deficits in the USA in the 1990s. The Budget Enforcement Act, passed in 1990 and extended by new legislation in 1993 and 1997, introduced two main rules:

- It imposed constraints on spending. Spending was divided into two categories: discretionary spending (roughly: spending on goods and services, including defence) and mandatory spending (roughly: transfer payments to individuals). Constraints, called spending caps, were set on discretionary spending for the following five years. These caps were set in such a way as to require a small but steady decrease in discretionary spending (in real terms). Explicit provisions were made for emergencies. For example, spending on Operation Desert Storm during the Gulf War in 1991 was not subject to the caps.

- It required that a new transfer programme could be adopted only if it could be shown that it would not increase deficits in the future (either by raising new revenues or by decreasing spending on an existing programme). This rule is known as the pay-as-you-go rule, or the PAYGO rule.

The focus on spending rather than on the deficit itself had one important implication. If there was a recession, hence a decrease in revenues, the deficit could increase without triggering a decrease in spending. This happened in 1991 and 1992 when, because of the recession, the deficit increased despite the fact that spending satisfied the constraints imposed by the caps. This focus on spending had two desirable effects: it allowed for a larger fiscal deficit during a recession – a good thing from the point of view of macroeconomic policy; and it decreased the pressure to break the rules during a recession – a good thing from a political point of view.

By 1998, deficits were gone and, for the first time in 20 years, the federal budget was in surplus. Not all of the deficit reduction was due to the Budget Enforcement Act rules: a decrease in defence spending due to the end of the Cold War and a large increase in tax revenues due to the strong expansion of the second half of the 1990s were important factors. But there is wide agreement that the rules played an important role in making sure that decreases in defence spending and increases in tax revenues were used for deficit reduction rather than for increases in other spending programmes.

Once budget surpluses appeared, however, Congress became increasingly willing to break its own rules. Spending caps were systematically broken, and the PAYGO rule was allowed to expire in 2002. At the time of this writing, deficits are large and predicted to remain so for many years to come. It is clear that, although spending caps and PAYGO rules were essential in reducing deficits in the 1990s, they did not prevent large deficits from reappearing in the 2000s. This is leading some economists and policy makers to conclude that, in the end, nothing short of a constitutional amendment can do the job of avoiding deficits. The issue is likely to rise again to the forefront of discussions of fiscal policy in the future.

Following years of deficits, the Netherlands started to build – in the early 1980s – original arrangements combining rules and institutions. The key rule is a path for the budget ceiling, set for the duration of each parliament. The institutional set-up relies on an explicit agreement among coalition parties before they take office and valid until the next election. The Netherlands has performed better than the other European countries. Its public debt has been reduced from 1993 onward, until the onset of the financial and economic crisis. Even though part of the measured (gross) debt reduction is related to asset sales and to natural gas revenues, it seems the Netherlands has become fiscally disciplined following the adoption of its new fiscal policy regime.

Germany adopted a constitutional rule in 2009, due to be fully implemented in 2016, following a scheme firstly introduced in Switzerland and known as 'debt brake'. The debt brake is a rule specifying that the federal budget must be balanced over time, not year by year; therefore, deficits must be compensated by surpluses within a certain span of time. This rule has reversed the past trend of debt accumulation, and the reversal has continued throughout the crisis.

We now return to the euro area and ask why the members of the monetary union have thought it necessary to accompany it with the fiscal rules.

FOCUS
Why the EMU needs fiscal rules

Why impose fiscal rules on countries participating in a monetary union?

The crisis that hit the euro area since early 2010 (discussed in Chapter 20) is a reminder of how important it is for members of a monetary union to constrain their fiscal policies, i.e. to adopt fiscal rules. As we illustrated in the Focus box, 'Debt and sovereign spreads' (in Chapter 21), the euro area sovereign debt crisis has at its roots the large increases in the debt-to-GDP ratios of many countries in the euro area. These increases in government debt were largely the consequence of the government deficits accumulated during the crisis in an effort to help economies out of the recession by adopting expansionary fiscal policies (in a situation where conventional monetary policy, as we saw in Chapter 21, was largely ineffective).

Yet, even before the crisis, European countries had already accumulated a large stock of public debt. Even euro area countries, who faced common constraints on their debt-to-GDP ratios and primary deficits (as envisaged by the Maastrict criteria we described in the Focus box 'Criteria for admissions to the EMU set by the Maastrict Treaty' in Chapter 19), had not been disciplined in managing their budgets for a long time before the crisis forced them to resort to fiscal intervention that further deteriorated their budget balances. Indeed, almost all euro area countries (with the only exceptions of Luxembourg and Finland) have failed to meet the 3% criterion on their budget deficit for quite a number of years – some countries only a few times (Belgium for 3 years; Austria, Ireland, Netherlands and Spain for 4 years, Germany for 5 years), but some other countries for most of the time since the introduction of the euro (France for 7 years, Italy for 8 years, Portugal for 10 years, Greece for 13 years).

Why did countries run those deficits and accumulate large amounts of public debt? There are a number of reasons why European countries – and, in general, advanced countries – tend to systematically run budget deficits:

- As we explained earlier (in Chapter 22), governments are often inclined to increase public spending and/or cut taxes before elections, to maximise the probability of being re-elected.

- Even in non-election times, governments tend to spend above their means and pass part of the burden of current public spending to future generations.

- Finally, the advanced countries' population is ageing, which means high spending on public pensions relative to the contributions paid by the population in working age.

For countries adopting a common currency, it is even more important to maintain fiscal discipline, because (as we saw in Chapter 19) a common currency means that monetary policy can no longer be used to increase output, and fiscal policy is the only policy tool in case of recessions. Hence it is appropriate that the member countries of a monetary union are subject to constraints on their fiscal policies. There are two main reasons for that:

- *To correct the incentive to pass on the costs of fiscal expansion.*

  In a closed economy, when the government increases the budget deficit, by cutting taxes or by increasing government spending, income growth is compensated by the increase in interest rates – the *IS* curve moves to the right, but the *LM* curve does not move, the new equilibrium income is higher, but interest rates are also higher, slightly reducing private demand. In an open economy with a fixed exchange rate – the case of a monetary union – the smaller the size of the country which increases the deficit relative to the area to which the exchange rate is anchored, the smaller will be the increase in the interest rate. If the country is very small, the interest rate of the rest of the world does not move, whatever the small country does.

  EMU is an intermediate case. Consider, for example, the effect of fiscal expansion in France. First, income will grow, not only in France, but also in the rest of the EMU, through the indirect effect of the increase in French imports (see the Focus box 'Fiscal multipliers in an open economy' in Chapter 7). So the demand for money grows in EMU. If the ECB keeps the supply of money unchanged, euro interest rates increase. This, similarly to what happens in a closed economy, crowds out private demand and reduces the positive impact of fiscal expansion. How much interest rates increase depends, of course, on the size of the French economy compared to the rest of EMU. If it were not France but, for example, Slovenia to increase the budget deficit, the effect on total demand in the euro area would be negligible and euro interest rates would not move, just as in the case of a small open economy with fixed exchange rates. But if France increases its deficit, euro interest rates will rise.

Let us now consider the position of the various countries in EMU. What happens in France is exactly what would have happened in a system of fixed exchange rates: an increase in demand, partly mitigated by an increase in international interest rates. The other countries suffer from higher interest rates without the benefit of an expansionary fiscal policy, or at least without a direct benefit: they have a small benefit indirectly through the increase in French imports. So while in France, despite rising interest rates, income certainly grows, the effect in the rest of the EMU is ambiguous: income might also fall. And there is also another effect. Since the EMU as a whole has a flexible exchange rate with the rest of the world, the euro exchange rate will appreciate, for example against the dollar. The larger the country that has increased its budget deficit (France in our example), the larger this appreciation will be. An appreciation of the exchange rate reduces exports of all euro area countries, not only French exports.

What can other countries do? As they are members of a monetary union, they cannot control the supply of money; they can choose between putting up with the effect of the French fiscal expansion, which for them could be negative, or also implementing a fiscal expansion. This example suggests why the member countries of a monetary union wish to agree on the type of fiscal policy that each of them will implement, that is, adopt common fiscal rules.

● *To prevent financial crisis in one country spreading to all other members.*

Suppose that in a certain month financial markets were unwilling to buy all the bonds that the Greek government wished to issue to finance the deficit in that month and, above all, to pay for the bonds that reach maturity in that month. Before the monetary union was formed, what would have happened is probably an intervention by the Bank of Greece: to prevent the government from going bankrupt, the Bank of Greece would have purchased the unsold securities or, rather, those unsold at the interest rate above which the government was unwilling to go. The supply of money would be increased, but this was basically a lesser evil than bankruptcy.

What other countries fear is that the ECB would have to do the same, with the effect of increasing the supply of money across the euro area. This explains why both the Maastricht Treaty and the criteria for admission to EMU, as well as the rules of the Stability and Growth Pact, state that high-debt countries must quickly reduce their stocks of public debt. But there is another concern. EMU speeds up financial integration among member countries: this means that financial assets move more easily between member countries because they are now all denominated in the same currency, and there is no longer a foreign exchange risk. Consequently, Greek government securities are held, to a greater extent than before the euro, by banks and insurance companies in France and Germany and also by households in those countries. A bankruptcy of the Greek government would hit the other countries to a greater extent, compared to the years before the euro. This explains why EMU increases concern over countries with high public debt and also why, to avoid bankruptcy in a member state, the ECB would be forced to increase the supply of money to protect savers throughout the whole EMU. (What has happened in Greece – a euro country – since 2010 is a vivid reminder of their problems.)

There are different ways countries can impose constraints on their fiscal policies: they can adopt fiscal numerical rules and/or establish fiscal institutions responsible for ensuring fiscal discipline. The best way to understand what they are and how they work is to give you a flavour of the experiences of some European countries over the recent past.

SUMMARY

On the optimal rate of inflation:

- Inflation is down to very low levels in most OECD countries. One question facing central banks is whether they should try to achieve price stability – that is, zero inflation.

- The main arguments for zero inflation are:

  - Inflation, together with an imperfectly indexed tax system, leads to tax distortions.

  - Because of money illusion, inflation leads people and firms to make incorrect decisions.

  - Higher inflation typically comes with higher inflation variability, creating more uncertainty and making it more difficult for people and firms to make decisions.

  - As a target, price stability has a simplicity and a credibility that a positive inflation target does not have.

- There are also arguments for maintaining low but positive inflation:

  - Positive revenues from nominal money growth seignorage allow for decreases in taxes elsewhere in the budget. However, this argument is quantitatively unimportant when comparing inflation rates of 0.

  - Positive actual and expected inflation allow the central bank to achieve negative real interest rates, an option that can be useful when fighting a recession.

  - Positive inflation allows firms to achieve real wage cuts when needed without requiring nominal wage cuts.

  - Further decreasing inflation from its current rate to zero would require an increase in unemployment for some time, and this transition cost might exceed whatever benefits come from zero inflation.

On the design of monetary policy:

- Traditionally, the design of monetary policy was focused on nominal money growth. But because of the poor relation between inflation and nominal money growth, this approach has been abandoned by most central banks.

- Central banks now typically focus on an inflation rate target rather than a nominal money growth rate target. And they think about monetary policy in terms of determining the nominal interest rate rather than in terms of determining the rate of nominal money growth.

- The Taylor rule gives a useful way of thinking about the choice of the nominal interest rate. The rule states that the central bank should move its interest rate in response to two main factors: the deviation of the inflation rate from the target rate of inflation, and the deviation of the unemployment rate from the natural rate of unemployment. A central bank that follows this rule will stabilise activity and achieve its target inflation rate in the medium run.

- The government budget constraint gives the evolution of government debt as a function of spending and taxes. One way of expressing the constraint is that the change in debt (the deficit) is equal to the primary deficit plus interest payments on the debt. The primary deficit is the difference between government spending on goods and services, G, and taxes net of transfers, T.

- If government spending is unchanged, a decrease in taxes must eventually be offset by an increase in taxes in the future. The longer the government waits to increase taxes or the higher the real interest rate, the higher the eventual increase in taxes.

- The legacy of past deficits is higher debt. To stabilise the debt, the government must eliminate the deficit. To eliminate the deficit, it must run a primary surplus equal to the interest payments on the existing debt.

- Under the Ricardian equivalence proposition, a larger deficit is offset by an equal increase in private saving. Deficits have no effect on demand and on output. The accumulation of debt does not affect capital accumulation. When Ricardian equivalence fails, larger deficits lead to higher demand and higher output in the short run. The accumulation of debt leads to lower capital accumulation and thus to lower output in the long run.

- Member countries of a monetary union should impose constraints on their fiscal policy for two reasons: to correct the incentive of small countries to pass on the cost of a fiscal expansion to other member countries and to prevent a financial crisis in a country spreading to all other members.

KEY TERMS

shoe-leather costs 510

money illusion 511

liquid asset 516

*M*I 516

*M*3 516

monetary aggregate 516

broad money (*M*2) 517

inflation targeting 517

Taylor rule 522

Ricardian equivalence 524

Ricardo–Barro
proposition 524

full-employment deficit 526

mid-cycle deficit 526

standardised employment
deficit 526

structural deficit 526

cyclically adjusted
deficit 526

automatic stabiliser 526

tax smoothing 528

QUESTIONS AND PROBLEMS

QUICK CHECK

1. *Using the information in this chapter, label each of the following statements true, false or uncertain. Explain briefly.*

a. The most important argument in favour of a positive rate of inflation in OECD countries is seignorage.

b. The ECB should target *M*2 growth because it moves quite closely with inflation.

c. Fighting inflation should be the ECB's only purpose.

d. Because most people have little trouble distinguishing between nominal and real values, inflation does not distort decision making.

e. The ECB uses **reserve requirements** as its primary instrument of monetary policy.

f. The higher the inflation rate, the higher the effective tax rate on capital gains.

g. If Ricardian equivalence holds, then an increase in income taxes will affect neither consumption nor saving.

h. Tax smoothing and deficit finance help spread the burden of war across generations.

2. *Explain how each of the developments listed in (a)–(d) would affect the demand for M1 and M2.*

a. Banks reduce penalties on early withdrawal from time deposits.

b. The government forbids the use of money market funds for cheque-writing purposes.

c. The government legislates a tax on all ATM transactions.

d. The government decides to impose a tax on all transactions involving government securities with maturities more than one year.

3. Taxes, inflation and home ownership

In this chapter, we discussed the effect of inflation on the effective capital-gains tax rate on the sale of a home. In this question, we explore the effect of inflation on another feature of the tax code – the deductibility of mortgage interest.

Suppose you have a mortgage of €50,000. Expected inflation is p^e, and the nominal interest rate on your mortgage is i. Consider two cases:

   i. $\pi^e = 0\%$; $i = 4\%$

   ii. $\pi^e = 10\%$; $i = 14\%$

a. What is the real interest rate you are paying on your mortgage in each case?

b. Suppose you can deduct nominal mortgage interest payments from your income before paying income tax. Assume that the tax rate is 25%. So, for each euro you pay in mortgage interest, you pay 25 cents less in taxes, in effect getting a subsidy from the government for your mortgage costs. Compute, in each case, the real interest rate you are paying on your mortgage, taking into account this subsidy.

c. Considering only the deductibility of mortgage interest (and not capital-gains taxation), is inflation good for homeowners?

4. Inflation targets

Consider a central bank that has an inflation target, p^*. The Phillips curve is given by

$$\pi_t - \pi_{t-1} = \alpha(u_t - u_n)$$

a. If the central bank is able to keep the inflation rate equal to the target inflation rate every period, will there be dramatic fluctuations in unemployment?

b. Is the central bank likely to be able to hit its inflation target every period?

c. Suppose the natural rate of unemployment, u_n, changes frequently. How will these changes affect the central bank's ability to hit its inflation target? Explain.

DIG DEEPER

5. *Suppose you have been elected to Parliament. One day, one of your colleagues makes the following statement:*

> The central bank chair is the most powerful economic policy maker in our country. We should not turn over the keys to the economy to someone who was not elected and therefore has no accountability. Parliament should impose an explicit Taylor rule on the central bank. Parliament should choose not only the target inflation rate but also the relative weight on the inflation and unemployment targets. Why should the preferences of an individual substitute for the will of the people, as expressed through the democratic and legislative processes?

Do you agree with your colleague? Discuss the advantages and disadvantages of imposing an explicit Taylor rule on the central bank.

6. Inflation targeting and the Taylor rule in the *IS–LM* model

*This problem is based on David Romer's 'Short-Run Fluctuations', which is available on his website (**http://emlab.berkeley.edu/ users/dromer/index.shtml**). Consider a closed economy in which the central bank follows an interest rate rule. The IS relation is given by*

$$Y = C(Y - T) + I(Y, r) + G$$

where r is the real interest rate.

The central bank sets the nominal interest rate according to the rule

$$i = i^* + \alpha(\pi^e - \pi^*) + b(Y - Y_n)$$

where π^e is expected inflation, π^* is the target rate of inflation and Y_n is the natural level of output. Assume that a > 1 and b > 0. The symbol i^* is the interest rate the central bank chooses when expected inflation equals the target rate and output equals the natural level. The central bank will increase the nominal interest rate when expected inflation rises above the target or when output rises above the natural level.

(Note that the Taylor rule described in this chapter uses actual inflation instead of expected inflation, and it uses unemployment instead of output. The interest rate rule we use in this problem simplifies the analysis and does not change the basic results.)

Real and nominal interest rates are related by

$$r = i - \pi^e$$

a. Define the variable r^* as $r^* = i^* - \pi^*$. Use the definition of the real interest rate to express the interest rate rule as

$$r = r^* + (a - 1)(\pi^e - \pi^*) + b(Y - Y_n)$$

(*Hint*: subtract p^* from each side of the nominal interest rate rule and rearrange the right-hand side of the equation.)

b. Graph the *IS* relation in a diagram, with r on the vertical axis and Y on the horizontal axis. In the same diagram, graph the interest rate rule (in terms of the real interest rate) you derived in part (a) for given values of p^e, p^* and Y_n. Call the interest rate rule the monetary policy (*MP*) relation.

c. Using the diagram you drew in part (b), show that an increase in government spending leads to an increase in output and the real interest rate in the short run.

d. Now consider a change in the monetary policy rule. Suppose the central bank reduces its target inflation rate, p^*. How does the fall in p^* affect the *MP* relation? (Remember that $a > 1$.) What happens to output and the real interest rate in the short run?

7. *Consider the economy described in problem 6.*

a. Suppose the economy starts with $Y - Y_n$ and $\pi^e = \pi^*$.

b. Now suppose there is an increase in π^e. Assume that Y_n does not change. Using the diagram you drew in problem 6(b), show how the increase in p^e affects the *MP* relation. (Again, remember that $a > 1$.) What happens to output and the real interest rate in the short run?

c. Without attempting to model the dynamics of inflation explicitly, assume that inflation and expected inflation will increase over time if $Y > Y_n$, and that they will decrease over time if $Y < Y_n$. Given the effect on output you found in part (a), will π^e tend to return to the target rate of inflation, π^*, over time?

d. Redo part (a), but assuming this time that $a < 1$. How does the increase in π^e affect the *MP* relation when $a < 1$? What happens to output and the real interest rate in the short run?

e. Again assume that inflation and expected inflation will increase over time if $Y < Y_n$ and that they will decrease over time if $Y > Y_n$. Given the effect on output you found in part (c), will π^e tend to return to the target rate of inflation, π^*, over time? Is it sensible for the parameter a (in the interest rate rule) to take values less than one?

8. *Consider an economy characterised by the following facts:*

   i.   *The official budget deficit is 3% of GDP.*

   ii. *The debt-to-GDP ratio is 100%.*

   iii. *The nominal interest rate is 8%.*

   iv. *The inflation rate is 6%.*

a. What is the primary deficit/surplus ratio to GDP?

b. What is the inflation-adjusted deficit/surplus ratio to GDP?

c. Suppose that output is 2% below its natural level. What is the cyclically adjusted, inflation-adjusted deficit/surplus ratio to GDP?

d. Suppose, instead, that output begins at its natural level and that output growth remains constant at the normal rate of 2%. How will the debt-to-GDP ratio change over time?

EXPLORE FURTHER

9. Ricardian equivalence and fiscal policy

First consider an economy in which Ricardian equivalence does not hold (i.e. an economy like the one we have described in this text).

a. Suppose the government starts with a balanced budget. Then, there is an increase in government spending, but there is no change in taxes. Show in an *IS–LM* diagram the effect of this policy on output in the short run. How will the government finance the increase in government spending?

b. Suppose, as in part (a), that the government starts with a balanced budget and then increases government spending. This time, however, assume that taxes increase by the same amount as government spending. Show in an *IS–LM* diagram the effect of this policy on output in the short run. (It may help to recall the discussion of the multiplier in Chapter 3. Does government spending or tax policy have a bigger multiplier?) How does the output effect compare with the effect in part (a)?

Now suppose Ricardian equivalence holds in this economy. (Parts (c) and (d) do not require use of diagrams.)

c. Consider again an increase in government spending with no change in taxes. How does the output effect compare to the output effects in parts (a) and (b)?

d. Consider, again, an increase in government spending combined with an increase in taxes of the same amount. How does this output effect compare to the output effects in parts (a) and (b)?

e. Comment on each of the following statements:

   i. 'Under Ricardian equivalence, government spending has no effect on output.'

   ii. 'Under Ricardian equivalence, changes in taxes have no effect on output.'

10. Current monetary policy

Problem 10 in Chapter 4 asked you to consider the current stance of monetary policy. Here, you are asked to do so again, but with the additional understanding of monetary policy you have gained in this and previous chapters.

Go to the website of the ECB and download either the press release you considered in Chapter 4 (if you did problem 10) or the most recent press release of the Governing Council.

a. What is the stance of monetary policy, as described in the press release?

b. Is there evidence that the GC considers both inflation and unemployment in setting interest rate policy, as would be implied by the Taylor rule?

c. Does any of the language of the press release seem to be aimed at increasing the credibility of the ECB (as committed to low inflation) or at affecting inflation expectations?

FURTHER READING

- 'Modern central banking', written by Stanley Fischer for the 300th anniversary of the Bank of England (published in Forrest Capie, Stanley Fischer, Charles Goodhart and Norbert Schnadt (eds), *The Future of Central Banking*, Cambridge University Press, Cambridge, UK, 1995), provides a nice discussion of the current issues in central banking. (Stanley Fischer is now governor of the Central Bank of Israel.) Read also 'What central bankers could learn from academics – and vice versa', by Alan Blinder, *Journal of Economic Perspectives*, 1997, **11**(2), 319.

- On inflation targeting, read Ben Bernanke and Frederic Mishkin, 'Inflation targeting: a new framework for monetary policy?' *Journal of Economic Perspectives*, 1997, **11**(2), 97–116. (This article was written by Ben Bernanke before he became chairman of the ECB. Frederic Mishkin, on leave from Columbia University, is currently a member of the Board of Governors of the Federal Reserve.)

- For more detail on how the ECB operates, read Glenn Hubbard, *Money, the Financial System, and the Economy*, (Reading, MA: Addison-Wesley, 5th edn, 2004).

- For more on monetary policy under Alan Greenspan, read N. Gregory Mankiw, 'U.S. monetary policy during the 1990s', in *American Economic Policy in the 1990s* (Cambridge, MA: MIT Press, 2001).

- For a more relaxing read, see Bob Woodward, *Maestro: Greenspan's Fed and the American Boom* (New York: Simon & Schuster, 2001).

- The modern statement of the Ricardian equivalence proposition is Robert Barro's 'Are government bonds net wealth?', *Journal of Political Economy*, December 1974, 1095–117.

APPENDIX

The time inconsistency problem: Barro and Gordon model

The Robert Barro and David Gordon model is a clear example of an economic policy model with strategic interaction between different players, in this case, between the monetary policy authority and the private sector.

The model consists of two equations. The first one is the Phillips curve, expressed in terms of production levels instead of employment rate:

$$\pi = \pi^e - \alpha(u - u_N)$$

If $Y = N$, $u = 1 - Y/L$. We can rewrite the Phillips curve as:

$$y = y_N + b(\pi - \pi^e) \qquad [23A.1]$$

with $b = L/\alpha > 0$. If $\pi = \pi^e$, $y = y_N$. When $\pi > \pi^e$, $y > y_N$.

The central bank wants to minimise the fluctuations of inflation around the optimal inflation rate, $\pi^* = 0$, and the fluctuation of production around the optimal production level, $y^* = ky_N$.

The central bank's preferences are described by the *loss function*:

$$L = a(\pi - \pi^*)^2 + (y - ky_N)^2 \qquad [23A.2]$$

with $a > 0$, $k > 1$ and $\pi^* = 0$. a is the relative weight that the central bank gives to inflation fluctuations, with respect to production fluctuations, around desired values. The higher is a, the higher is the central bank's concern about inflation stabilisation with respect to production stabilisation.

To consider both the central bank loss function and the Phillips curve, we substitute y in the loss function:

$$L = a\pi^2 + [b(\pi - \pi^e) + (1 - k)y_N]^2 \qquad [23A.3]$$

To introduce time, let's consider a one-year period. At the beginning of the period workers and firms sign a contract that establish the nominal wage level of the period. After the nominal wages have been fixed, the central bank decides the monetary policy, determining the inflation rate. When workers and firms sign the contract, they fix the nominal wages on the basis of their expected inflation rate.

Let's assume that the central bank announces before the wages are fixed that $\pi^* = 0$. If the central bank is trusted by agents, $\pi^e = 0$. If the central bank respects the commitment, it will fix $\pi^* = 0$, so that $\pi = \pi^e$ and $y = y_N$.

However, once the contract is signed, the incentives of the central bank change and maintaining the commitment is no longer optimal for the bank. In fact, once salaries are fixed, it becomes optimal for the central bank to produce some unexpected inflation to increase the production in equilibrium.

The central bank has to minimise the loss function, given the expectations of the private sector about the inflation rate incorporated in the nominal wages.

From equation (23A.3) we derive:

$$\frac{\partial L}{\partial \pi} = 2a\pi + 2b[(1 - k)y_N + b(\pi - \pi^e)] = 0$$

From which we obtain the optimal inflation rate:

$$\pi = \frac{b}{a + b^2}[(k - 1)y_N + b\pi^e] \qquad [23A.4]$$

If $\pi^e = 0$, we will see that the optimal inflation rate for the central bank is not equal to zero:

$$\pi^f = \frac{b}{a + b^2}[(k - 1)y_N]$$

The production level that is possible to obtain if the central bank deviates from its commitment and fixes the inflation level that minimises its loss is:

$$y^f = y_N + b\left[\frac{b(k - 1)y_N}{a + b^2} - 0\right] = \frac{a + kb^2}{a + b^2}y_N > y_N$$

However, in the real world, the central bank cannot achieve this equilibrium (i.e. *first-best* equilibrium). The private sector understands the incentive to deviate and it does not believe in the commitment announced by the central bank at the beginning of the period: $\pi^e > 0$. In particular, if $\pi^e = \pi$, effective inflation will be:

$$\pi^d = \frac{b(k - 1)}{a}y_N$$

and the production level will be equal to the natural level:

$$y^d = y_N$$

The result is that production does not increase and at same time there is an increase in inflation, a worse situation than the *pre-commitment* case, also called *second-best* equilibrium. The case where the private sector does not trust the central bank when it announces its commitment is called *discretionary* or *third-best* equilibrium.

Substituting the values of effective and expected inflation in the loss function, we can compute the central bank's loss in the three cases:

First best (inflationary surprise):

$\pi^e = 0$ and $\pi = \pi^f$ $\qquad L^f = \dfrac{a}{a + b^2}(k - 1)^2 y_N^2$

Second best (pre-commitment):

$\pi^e = \pi = 0$ $\qquad L^p = (k - 1)^2 y_N^2$

Third best (discretionary):

$\pi^e = 0$ and $\pi = \pi^f$ $\qquad L^d = \dfrac{a + b^2}{a}(k - 1)^2 y_N^2$

Because $L^f = \dfrac{a}{a+b^2}L^p < L^p$ and $L^d = \dfrac{a+b^2}{a}L^p > L^p$, we can verify that $L^f < L^p < L^d$.

The *pre-commitment* case is better than the one with discretionality. Given the production level, inflation is lower if the central bank respects the commitment and it is trusted by the private sector. The best policy is to achieve the *second-best* equilibrium maintaining the commitment, because in an attempt to obtain the *first-best*, the central bank would fall in the *third-best* equilibrium.

EPILOGUE

Chapter 24

THE STORY OF MACROECONOMICS

We have spent 23 chapters presenting the framework that most economists use to think about macroeconomic issues, the major conclusions they draw, and the issues on which they disagree. How this framework has been built over time is a fascinating story. It is the story we want to tell in this chapter.

- Section 24.1 starts at the beginning of modern macroeconomics – with Keynes and the Great Depression.

- Section 24.2 turns to the *neoclassical synthesis*, a synthesis of Keynes's ideas with those of earlier economists – a synthesis that dominated macroeconomics until the early 1970s.

- Section 24.3 describes the *rational expectations critique*, the strong attack on the neoclassical synthesis that led to a complete overhaul of macroeconomics, starting in the 1970s.

- Section 24.4 gives you a sense of the main lines of research up to the crisis.

- Section 24.5 takes a first pass at assessing the effects of the crisis on macroeconomics.

24.1 KEYNES AND THE GREAT DEPRESSION

The history of modern macroeconomics starts in 1936, with the publication of Keynes's *General Theory of Employment, Interest, and Money*. As he was writing the *General Theory*, Keynes confided to a friend: 'I believe myself to be writing a book on economic theory which will largely revolutionize – not, I suppose at once but in the course of the next ten years, the way the world thinks about economic problems.'

Keynes was right. The book's timing was one of the reasons for its immediate success. The Great Depression was not only an economic catastrophe, but also an intellectual failure for the economists working on **business cycle theory** – as macroeconomics was then called. Few economists had a coherent explanation for the Depression, either for its depth or for its length. The economic measures taken by the Roosevelt administration as part of the New Deal had been based on instinct rather than on economic theory. The *General Theory* offered an interpretation of events, an intellectual framework and a clear argument for government intervention.

The *General Theory* emphasised **effective demand** – what we now call *aggregate demand*. In the short run, Keynes argued, effective demand determines output. Even if output eventually returns to its natural level, the process is slow at best. One of Keynes's most famous quotes is: 'In the long run, we are all dead.'

In the process of deriving effective demand, Keynes introduced many of the building blocks of modern macroeconomics:

- The relation of consumption to income, and the multiplier, which explains how shocks to demand can be amplified and lead to larger shifts in output.
- **Liquidity preference** (the term Keynes gave to the demand for money), which explains how monetary policy can affect interest rates and aggregate demand.
- The importance of expectations in affecting consumption and investment; and the idea that *animal spirits* (shifts in expectations) are a major factor behind shifts in demand and output.

The *General Theory* was more than a treatise for economists. It offered clear policy implications, and they were in tune with the times: waiting for the economy to recover by itself was irresponsible. In the midst of a depression, trying to balance the budget was not only stupid, it was dangerous. Active use of fiscal policy was essential to return the country to high employment.

24.2 THE NEOCLASSICAL SYNTHESIS

Within a few years, the *General Theory* had transformed macroeconomics. Not everybody was converted, and few agreed with it all. But most discussions became organised around it.

By the early 1950s a large consensus had emerged, based on an integration of many of Keynes's ideas and the ideas of earlier economists. This consensus was called the **neoclassical synthesis**. To quote from Paul Samuelson, in the 1955 edition of his textbook, *Economics* – the first modern economics textbook:

> In recent years, 90 per cent of American economists have stopped being 'Keynesian economists' or 'Anti-Keynesian economists.' Instead, they have worked toward a synthesis of whatever is valuable in older economics and in modern theories of income determination. The result might be called neo-classical economics and is accepted, in its broad outlines, by all but about five per cent of extreme left-wing and right-wing writers.

The neoclassical synthesis was to remain the dominant view for another 20 years. Progress was astonishing, leading many to call the period from the early 1940s to the early 1970s the golden age of macroeconomics.

Progress on all fronts

The first order of business after the publication of the *General Theory* was to formalise mathematically what Keynes meant. Although Keynes knew mathematics, he had avoided using it in the *General Theory*. One result was endless controversies about what Keynes meant and whether there were logical flaws in some of his arguments.

The *IS–LM* model

A number of formalisations of Keynes's ideas were offered. The most influential one was the *IS–LM* model, developed by John Hicks and Alvin Hansen in the 1930s and early 1940s. The initial version of the *IS–LM* model (which was actually very close to the version presented in Chapter 5 of this text) was criticised for emasculating many of Keynes's insights: expectations played no role, and the adjustment of prices and wages was altogether absent. Yet the *IS–LM* model provided a basis from which to start building and, as such, it was immensely successful. Discussions became organised around the slopes of the *IS* and *LM* curves, what variables were missing from the two relations, what equations for prices and wages should be added to the model, and so on.

Theories of consumption, investment and money demand

Keynes had emphasised the importance of consumption and investment behaviour and of the choice between money and other financial assets. Major progress was soon made along all three fronts.

In the 1950s, Franco Modigliani (then at Carnegie Mellon, later at MIT) and Milton Friedman (at the University of Chicago) independently developed the theory of consumption (see Chapter 16). Both insisted on the importance of expectations in determining current consumption decisions.

James Tobin, from Yale, developed the theory of investment, based on the relation between the present value of profits and investment. The theory was further developed and tested by Dale Jorgenson from Harvard. (You saw this theory in Chapter 16.)

Tobin also developed the theory of the demand for money and, more generally, the theory of the choice between different assets based on liquidity, return and risk. His work has become the basis not only for an improved treatment of financial markets in macroeconomics but also for finance theory in general.

Growth theory

In parallel with the work on fluctuations, there was a renewed focus on growth. In contrast to the stagnation in the period before the Second World War, most countries were growing fast in the 1950s and 1960s. Even if they experienced fluctuations, their standard of living was increasing rapidly. The growth model developed by MIT's Robert Solow in 1956 (which you saw in Chapters 13 and 14) provided a framework to think about the determinants of growth. It was followed by an explosion of work on the roles that saving and technological progress play in determining growth.

Macroeconometric models

All these contributions were integrated in larger and larger macroeconometric models. The first US macroeconometric model, developed by Lawrence Klein from the University of Pennsylvania in the early 1950s, was an extended *IS* relation with 16 equations. With the development of the National Income and Product Accounts (making available better data) and the development of econometrics and of computers, the models quickly grew in size. The most impressive effort was the construction of the MPS model (MPS stands for MIT–Penn–SSRC, for the two universities and the research institution – the Social Science Research Council – involved in its construction), developed during the 1960s by a group led by Modigliani. Its structure was an expanded version of the *IS–LM* model, plus a Phillips curve mechanism. But its components – consumption, investment and money demand – all reflected the tremendous theoretical and empirical progress made since Keynes.

Keynesians versus monetarists

With such rapid progress, many macroeconomists – those who defined themselves as **Keynesians** – came to believe that the future was bright. The nature of fluctuations was becoming increasingly well understood; the development of models allowed policy decisions to be made more effectively. The time when the economy could be fine-tuned, and recessions all but eliminated, seemed not far in the future.

This optimism was met with scepticism by a small but influential minority, the **monetarists**. The intellectual leader of the monetarists was Milton Friedman. Although Friedman saw much progress being made – and was himself the father of one of the major contributions to macroeconomics, the theory of consumption – he did not share in the general enthusiasm.

He believed that the understanding of the economy remained very limited. He questioned the motives of governments as well as the notion that they actually knew enough to improve macroeconomic outcomes.

In the 1960s, debates between 'Keynesians' and 'monetarists' dominated the economic headlines. The debates centred around three issues: (1) the effectiveness of monetary policy versus fiscal policy, (2) the Phillips curve and (3) the role of policy.

Monetary policy versus fiscal policy

Keynes had emphasised *fiscal* rather than *monetary* policy as the key to fighting recessions. And this had remained the prevailing wisdom. The *IS* curve, many argued, was quite steep: changes in the interest rate had little effect on demand and output. Thus, monetary policy did not work very well. Fiscal policy, which affects demand directly, could affect output faster and more reliably.

Friedman strongly challenged this conclusion. In their 1963 book *A Monetary History of the United States, 1867–1960*, Friedman and Anna Schwartz painstakingly reviewed the evidence on monetary policy and the relation between money and output in the USA over a century. Their conclusion was not only that monetary policy was very powerful but that movements in money did explain most of the fluctuations in output. They interpreted the Great Depression as the result of a major mistake in monetary policy, a decrease in the money supply due to bank failures – a decrease that the Fed could have avoided by increasing the monetary base but had not.

Friedman and Schwartz's challenge was followed by a vigorous debate and by intense research on the respective effects of fiscal policy and monetary policy. In the end, a consensus was reached. Both fiscal policy and monetary policy clearly affected the economy. And if policy makers cared about not only the level but also the composition of output, the best policy was typically a mix of the two.

The Phillips curve

The second debate focused on the Phillips curve. The Phillips curve was not part of the initial Keynesian model. But because it provided such a convenient (and apparently reliable) way of explaining the movement of wages and prices over time, it had become part of the neoclassical synthesis. In the 1960s, based on the empirical evidence up until then, many Keynesian economists believed that there was a reliable trade-off between unemployment and inflation, even in the long run.

Milton Friedman and Edmund Phelps (from Columbia University) strongly disagreed. They argued that the existence of such a long-run trade-off flew in the face of basic economic theory. They argued that the apparent trade-off would quickly vanish if policy makers actually tried to exploit it – that is, if they tried to achieve low unemployment by accepting higher inflation. As you saw earlier (in Chapter 10) when we studied the evolution of the Phillips curve, Friedman and Phelps were definitely right. By the mid-1970s, the consensus was indeed that there was no long-run trade-off between inflation and unemployment.

The role of policy

The third debate centred on the role of policy. Sceptical that economists knew enough to stabilise output and that policy makers could be trusted to do the right thing, Friedman argued for the use of simple rules, such as steady money growth (a rule we discussed in Chapter 23). Here is what he said in 1958:

> A steady rate of growth in the money supply will not mean perfect stability even though it would prevent the kind of wide fluctuations that we have experienced from time to time in the past. It is tempting to try to go farther and to use monetary changes to offset other factors making for expansion and contraction [. . .] The available evidence casts grave doubts on the possibility of producing any fine adjustments in economic activity by fine adjustments in monetary policy – at least in the present state of knowledge. There are thus serious limitations to the possibility of a discretionary monetary policy and much danger that such a policy may make matters worse rather than better.
>
> Political pressures to 'do something' in the face of either relatively mild price rises or relatively mild price and employment declines are clearly very strong indeed in the existing state of public attitudes. The main moral to be drawn from the two preceding points is that yielding to these pressures may frequently do more harm than good.
>
> (Source: 'The supply of money and changes in prices and output',
> Testimony to Congress, 1958.)

This debate on the role of macroeconomic policy has not been settled (see Chapter 22). The nature of the arguments has changed a bit, but they are still with us today.

24.3 THE RATIONAL EXPECTATIONS CRITIQUE

Despite the battles between Keynesians and monetarists, macroeconomics around 1970 looked like a successful and mature field. It appeared to successfully explain events and guide policy choices. Most debates were framed within a common intellectual framework. But within a few years, the field was in crisis. The crisis had two sources.

One was events. By the mid-1970s, most countries were experiencing *stagflation*, a word created at the time to denote the simultaneous existence of high unemployment and high inflation. Macroeconomists had not predicted stagflation. After the fact and after a few years of research, a convincing explanation was provided, based on the effects of adverse supply shocks on both prices and output. (We discussed the effects of such shocks in Chapter 7.) But it was too late to undo the damage to the discipline's image.

The other was ideas. In the early 1970s, a small group of economists – Robert Lucas from Chicago; Thomas Sargent, then from Minnesota and now at New York University; and Robert Barro, then from Chicago and now at Harvard – led a strong attack against mainstream macroeconomics. They did not mince words. In a 1978 paper, Lucas and Sargent stated:

> That the predictions [of Keynesian economics] were wildly incorrect, and that the doctrine on which they were based was fundamentally flawed, are now simple matters of fact, involving no subtleties in economic theory. The task which faces contemporary students of the business cycle is that of sorting through the wreckage, determining what features of that remarkable intellectual event called the Keynesian Revolution can be salvaged and put to good use, and which others must be discarded.

The three implications of rational expectations

Lucas and Sargent's main argument was that Keynesian economics had ignored the full implications of the effect of expectations on behaviour. The way to proceed, they argued, was to assume that people formed expectations as rationally as they could, based on the information they had.

Thinking of people as having *rational expectations* had three major implications, all highly damaging to Keynesian macroeconomics.

The Lucas critique

The first implication was that existing macroeconomic models could not be used to help design policy. Although these models recognised that expectations affect behaviour, they did not incorporate expectations explicitly. All variables were assumed to depend on current and past values of other variables, including policy variables. Thus, what the models captured was the set of relations between economic variables as they had held in the past under past policies. Were these policies to change, Lucas argued, the way people formed expectations would change as well, making estimated relations – and, by implication, simulations generated using existing macroeconometric models – poor guides to what would happen under these new policies. This critique of macroeconometric models became known as the **Lucas critique**. To take again the history of the Phillips curve as an example, the data up to the early 1970s had suggested a trade-off between unemployment and inflation. As policy makers tried to exploit that trade-off, it disappeared.

Rational expectations and the Phillips curve

The second implication was that when rational expectations were introduced in Keynesian models, these models actually delivered very un-Keynesian conclusions. For example, the models implied that deviations of output from its natural level were short-lived, much more so than Keynesian economists claimed.

This argument was based on a re-examination of the aggregate supply relation. In Keynesian models, the slow return of output to the natural level of output came from the slow adjustment of prices and wages through the Phillips curve mechanism. An increase in money, for example, led first to higher output and to lower unemployment. Lower unemployment then led to higher nominal wages and to higher prices. The adjustment continued until wages and prices had increased in the same proportion as nominal money, until unemployment and output were both back at their natural levels.

But this adjustment, Lucas pointed out, was highly dependent on wage setters' backward-looking expectations of inflation. In the MPS model, for example, wages responded only to current and past inflation and to current unemployment. But once the assumption was made that wage setters had rational expectations, the adjustment was likely to be much faster. Changes in money, to the extent that they were anticipated, might have no effect on output: for example, anticipating an increase in money of 5% over the coming year, wage setters would increase the nominal wages set in contracts for the coming year by 5%. Firms would in turn increase prices by 5%. The result would be no change in the real money stock, and no change in demand or output.

Within the logic of the Keynesian models, Lucas therefore argued, only *unanticipated changes in money* should affect output. Predictable movements in money should have no effect on activity. More generally, if wage setters had rational expectations, shifts in demand were likely to have effects on output for only as long as nominal wages were set – a year or so. Even on its own terms, the Keynesian model did not deliver a convincing theory of the long-lasting effects of demand on output.

Optimal control versus game theory

The third implication was that if people and firms had rational expectations, it was wrong to think of policy as the control of a complicated but passive system. Rather, the right way was to think of policy as a game between policy makers and the economy. The right tool was not *optimal control*, but *game theory*. And game theory led to a different vision of policy. A striking example was the issue of *time inconsistency* discussed by Finn Kydland (then at Carnegie Mellon, now at UC Santa Barbara) and Edward Prescott (then at Carnegie Mellon, now at Arizona State University), an issue that we discussed earlier (in Chapter 22): good intentions on the part of policy makers could actually lead to disaster.

To summarise: when rational expectations were introduced, Keynesian models could not be used to determine policy; Keynesian models could not explain long-lasting deviations of output from the natural level of output; the theory of policy had to be redesigned using the tools of game theory.

The integration of rational expectations

As you might have guessed from the tone of Lucas and Sargent's quote, the intellectual atmosphere in macroeconomics was tense in the early 1970s. But, within a few years, a process of integration (of ideas, not people, because tempers remained high) had begun, and it was to dominate the 1970s and the 1980s.

Fairly quickly, the idea that rational expectations was the right working assumption gained wide acceptance. This was not because macroeconomists believed that people, firms and participants in financial markets always form expectations rationally. But rational expectations appeared to be a natural benchmark, at least until economists have made more progress in understanding whether, when and how actual expectations systematically differ from rational expectations.

Work then started on the challenges raised by Lucas and Sargent.

The implications of rational expectations

First, there was a systematic exploration of the role and implications of rational expectations in goods markets, in financial markets and in labour markets. Much of what was discovered has been presented in this book. For example:

- Robert Hall, then from MIT and now at Stanford, showed that if consumers are very foresighted (in the sense defined in Chapter 17), then changes in consumption should be unpredictable: the best forecast of consumption next year would be consumption this year! Put another way, changes in consumption should be very hard to predict. This result came as a surprise to most macroeconomists at the time, but it is in fact based on a simple intuition: if consumers are very foresighted, they will change their consumption only when they learn something new about the future. But, by definition, such news cannot be predicted. This consumption behaviour, known as the **random walk of consumption**, became the benchmark in consumption research thereafter.
- Rudiger Dornbusch from MIT showed that the large swings in exchange rates under flexible exchange rates, which had previously been thought of as the result of speculation by irrational investors, were fully consistent with rationality. His argument (which we saw in Chapter 12) was that changes in monetary policy can lead to long-lasting changes in nominal interest rates; changes in current and expected nominal interest rates lead in turn to large changes in the exchange rate. Dornbusch's model, known as the *overshooting* model of exchange rates, became the benchmark in discussions of exchange-rate movements.

Wage and price setting

Second, there was a systematic exploration of the determination of wages and prices, going far beyond the Phillips curve relation. Two important contributions were made by Stanley Fischer, then at MIT, now governor of the Central Bank of Israel, and John Taylor, then from Columbia University and now at Stanford. Both showed that the adjustment of prices and wages in response to changes in unemployment can be slow *even under rational expectations*.

Fischer and Taylor pointed out an important characteristic of both wage and price setting, the **staggering** of wage and price decisions. In contrast to the simple story we told earlier, where all wages and prices increased simultaneously in anticipation of an increase in money, actual wage and price decisions are staggered over time. So there is not one sudden synchronised adjustment of all wages and prices to an increase in money. Rather, the adjustment is likely to be slow, with wages and prices adjusting to the new level of money through a process of leapfrogging over time. Fischer and Taylor thus showed that the second issue raised by the rational-expectations critique could be resolved, that a slow return of output to the natural level of output can be consistent with rational expectations in the labour market.

The theory of policy

Third, thinking about policy in terms of game theory led to an explosion of research on the nature of the games being played, not only between policy makers and the economy but also between policy makers – between political parties, or between the central bank and the government, or between governments of different countries. One of the major achievements of this research was the development of a more rigorous way of thinking about fuzzy notions such as 'credibility', 'reputation' and 'commitment'. At the same time, there was a distinct shift in focus from 'what governments should do' to 'what governments actually do', an increasing awareness of the political constraints that economists should take into account when advising policy makers.

In short: by the end of the 1980s, the challenges raised by the rational-expectations critique had led to a complete overhaul of macroeconomics. The basic structure had been extended to take into account the implications of rational expectations or, more generally, of forward-looking behaviour by people and firms. As you have seen, these themes have played a central role in this text.

24.4 RECENT DEVELOPMENTS UP TO THE CRISIS

From the late 1980s to the crisis, three groups dominated the research headlines: the new classicals, the new Keynesians and the new growth theorists. (Note the generous use of the word 'new'. Unlike producers of laundry detergents, economists stop short of using 'new and improved'. But the subliminal message is the same.)

New classical economics and real business cycle theory

The rational-expectations critique was more than just a critique of Keynesian economics. It also offered its own interpretation of fluctuations. Instead of relying on imperfections in labour markets, on the slow adjustment of wages and prices, and so on, to explain fluctuations, Lucas argued, macroeconomists should see how far they could go in explaining fluctuations as the effects of shocks in competitive markets with fully flexible prices and wages.

This research agenda was taken up by the **new classicals**. The intellectual leader is Edward Prescott, and the models he and his followers developed are known as **real business cycle (RBC) models**. Their approach was based on two premises.

The first was methodological. Lucas had argued that, in order to avoid earlier pitfalls, macroeconomic models should be constructed from explicit micro-foundations, i.e. utility maximisation by workers, profit maximisation by firms and rational expectations. Before the development of computers, this was hard, if not impossible, to achieve: models constructed in this way would have been too complex to solve analytically. Indeed, much of the art of macroeconomics was in finding simple shortcuts to capture the essence of a model while keeping the model simple enough to solve (it still remains the art of writing a good textbook . . .) The development of computing power made it possible to solve such models numerically, and an important contribution of RBC theory was the development of more and more powerful numerical methods of solution, allowing for the development of richer and richer models.

The second was conceptual. Until the 1970s, most fluctuations had been seen as the result of imperfections, of deviations of actual output from a slowly moving natural level of output. Following up on Lucas's suggestion, Prescott argued in a series of influential contributions that fluctuations could indeed be interpreted as coming from the effects of technological shocks in competitive markets with fully flexible prices and wages. In other words, he argued that movements in actual output could be seen as movements in – rather than as deviations from – the natural level of output. As new discoveries are made, he argued, productivity increases, leading to an increase in output. The increase in productivity leads to an increase in the wage, which makes it more attractive to work, leading workers to work more. Productivity increases therefore lead to increases in both output and employment, just as we observe in the real world. Fluctuations were desirable features of the economy, not something policy makers should try to reduce.

Not surprisingly, this radical view of fluctuations was criticised on many fronts. Technological progress is the result of very many innovations, each taking a long time to diffuse throughout the economy (see Chapter 15). It is hard to see how this process could generate anything like the large short-run fluctuations in output that we observe in practice. It is also hard to think of recessions as times of technological *regress*, times in which productivity and output both go down. Finally, as we have seen, there is strong evidence that changes in money, which have no effect on output in RBC models, in fact have strong effects on output in the real world. Still, the conceptual RBC approach proved influential and useful. It reinforced an important point, that not all fluctuations in output are deviations of output from its natural level, but movements in the natural level itself.

New Keynesian economics

The term 'new Keynesians' denotes a loosely connected group of researchers who shared a common belief that the synthesis that emerged in response to the rational-expectations critique was basically correct. But they also shared the belief that much remained to be learned about the nature of imperfections in different markets and about the implications of those imperfections for macroeconomic fluctuations.

There was further work on the nature of **nominal rigidities**. As we saw earlier in this chapter, Fischer and Taylor had shown that with staggering of wage or price decisions, output can deviate from its natural level for a long time. This conclusion raised a number of questions. If staggering of decisions is responsible, at least in part, for fluctuations, why don't wage setters/price setters synchronise decisions? Why aren't prices and wages adjusted more often? Why aren't all prices and all wages changed, say, on the first day of each week? In tackling these issues, George Akerlof (from Berkeley) and N. Gregory Mankiw (from Harvard University) derived a surprising and important result, often referred to as the **menu cost** explanation of output fluctuations.

Each wage setter or price setter is largely indifferent as to when and how often he or she changes his or her own wage or price (for a retailer, changing the prices on the shelf every day versus every week does not make much of a difference to the store's overall profits). Therefore, even small costs of changing prices – like the costs involved in printing a new menu, for example – can lead to infrequent and staggered price adjustment. This staggering leads to slow adjustment of the price level and to large aggregate output fluctuations in response to movements in aggregate demand. In short, decisions that do not matter much at the individual level (how often to change prices or wages) lead to large aggregate effects (slow adjustment of the price level, and shifts in aggregate demand that have a large effect on output).

Another line of research focused on the imperfections in the labour market. We have discussed (see Chapter 8) the notion of *efficiency wages* – the idea that wages, if perceived by workers as being too low, may lead to shirking by workers on the job, to problems of morale within the firm, to difficulties in recruiting or keeping good workers, and so on. One influential researcher in this area was Akerlof, who explored the role of 'norms', the rules that develop in any organisation – in this case, the firm – to assess what is fair or unfair. This research led him and others to explore issues previously left to research in sociology and psychology, and to examine their macroeconomic implications. In another direction, Peter Diamond (from MIT), Dale Mortensen (from Cornell) and Christopher Pissarides (from the London School of Economics) looked at the labour market as the market characterised by constant reallocation, large flows, and bargaining between workers and firms, a characterisation which has proven extremely useful (and which we relied upon in Chapter 8).

Yet another line of research, which turned out to be precious when the crisis took place, explored the role of imperfections in credit markets. Most macro models assumed that monetary policy worked through interest rates, and that firms could borrow as much as they wanted at the market interest rate. In practice, many firms can borrow only from banks. And banks often turn down potential borrowers, despite the willingness of these borrowers to pay the interest rate charged by the bank. Why this happens, and how it affects our view of how monetary policy works, was the focus of research by, in particular, Ben Bernanke (then from Princeton, and now the Chairman of the Fed) and Mark Gertler (from New York University).

New growth theory

After being one of the most active topics of research in the 1960s, growth theory had gone into an intellectual slump. From the late 1980s on, however, growth theory made a strong comeback. The set of new contributions went under the name of **new growth theory**.

Two economists, Robert Lucas (the same Lucas who spearheaded the rational-expectations critique) and Paul Romer, then from Berkeley, now at Stanford, played an important role in defining the issues. When growth theory faded in the late 1960s, two major issues were left largely unresolved.

One issue was the role of increasing returns to scale – whether, say, doubling capital and labour can actually cause output to more than double. The other was the determinants of technological progress. These are the two major issues on which new growth theory concentrated.

Our previous discussion of the effects of R&D on technological progress (in Chapter 11) and of the interaction between technological progress and unemployment (in Chapter 15), reflect some of the advances made on this front. An important contribution here was the work of Philippe Aghion (from Harvard University) and Peter Howitt (from Brown University) who developed a theme first explored by Joseph Schumpeter in the 1930s, the notion that growth is a process of *creative destruction*, in which new products are constantly introduced, making old ones obsolete. Institutions which slow this process of reallocation, for example by making it harder to create new firms or by making it more expensive for firms to layoff workers, may slow down the rate of technological progress, and thus decrease growth.

Research also tried to identify the precise role of specific institutions in determining growth. Andrei Shleifer (from Harvard University) explored the role of different legal systems in affecting the organisation of the economy, from financial markets to labour markets, and, through these channels, the effects of legal systems on growth. Daron Acemoglu (from MIT) explored how to go from correlations between institutions and growth – democratic countries are on average richer – to causality from institutions to growth: does the correlation tell us that democracy leads to higher output per person, or does it tell us that higher output per person leads to democracy, or that some other factor lead to both more democracy and higher output per person? Examining the history of former colonies, he argued that their growth performance has been very much shaped by the type of institutions put in place by their colonisers, thus showing a strong causal role of institutions on economic performance.

Towards an integration

In the 1980s and 1990s, discussions between these three groups, and in particular between 'new classicals' and 'new Keynesians', were often heated. New Keynesians would accuse new classicals from relying on an implausible explanation of fluctuations and ignoring obvious imperfections; new classicals would in turn point to the ad hoc nature of some of the new Keynesian models. From the outside – and indeed sometimes from the inside – macroeconomics looked like a battlefield rather than a research field.

By the 2000s, a synthesis appeared, however, to be emerging. Methodologically, it built on the RBC approach and its careful description of the optimisation problems of people and firms. Conceptually, it recognised the potential importance, emphasised by the RBC and the new growth theory, of changes in the pace of technological progress. But it also allowed for many of the imperfections emphasised by the new Keynesians, from the role of bargaining in the determination of wages, to the role of imperfect information in credit and financial markets, to the role of nominal rigidities in creating a role for aggregate demand to affect output. There was no convergence on a single model or on a single list of important imperfections, but there was broad agreement on the framework and on the way to proceed.

A good example of this convergence was the work of Michael Woodford (from Columbia), and of Jordi Galí (from Pompeu Fabra in Catalonia). Woodford, Gali and a number of co-authors developed a model, known as the *New-Keynesian model*, that embodies utility and profit maximisation, rational expectations and nominal rigidities. You can think of it as a high-tech version of the model that was presented earlier (in Chapter 10). This model proved extremely useful and influential in the redesign of monetary policy – from the focus on inflation targeting to the reliance on interest rate rules (which we described in Chapter 23). It led to the development of a class of larger models which build on its simple structure, but allow for a longer menu of imperfections, and thus must be solved numerically. These models, which are now standard workhorses in most central banks, are known as 'dynamic stochastic general equilibrium', or DSGE, models.

24.5 FIRST LESSONS FROM THE CRISIS

Just at the time at which a new synthesis appeared to be in sight, and macroeconomists felt that they had the tools do understand the economy and design policy, the crisis started and, at the time of this writing, is still continuing. We saw in section 24.1 how the Great Depression had led to a dramatic reassessment of macroeconomics and started the Keynesian revolution. One may ask: will this crisis have the same effect on macroeconomics, leading yet to another revolution? It is too early to say, but out guess is: probably not.

There is no question that the crisis reflects a major intellectual failure on the part of macroeconomics. The failure is in not realising that such a large crisis *could happen*, that the characteristics of the economy were such that a relatively small shock, in this case the decrease in housing prices, could lead to a major financial and macroeconomic world crisis. The source of the failure, in turn, was a lack of focus on the role of the financial institutions in the economy. (To be fair, a few macroeconomists, who were looking more closely at the financial system, sounded the alarm, best-known among them being Nouriel Roubini, from New York University, and the economists at the Bank for International Settlements in Basel, whose job it is to follow financial developments closely.)

By and large, the financial system and the complex role of banks and other financial institutions in the intermediation of funds between lenders and borrowers was ignored in most

macroeconomic models. There were exceptions. Work by Doug Diamond (from Chicago) and Philip Dybvig (from Washington University in Saint Louis) in the 1980s had clarified the nature of bank runs (which we examined in Chapter 4): illiquid assets and liquid liabilities created a risk of runs even for solvent banks. The problem could only be avoided by the provision of liquidity by the central bank if and when needed. Work by Bengt Holmstrom and Jean Tirole (both from MIT, Tirole is now at the University of Toulouse, France) showed that liquidity issues were endemic to a modern economy. Not only banks, but also firms could well find themselves in a position where they were solvent, but illiquid, unable to raise the additional cash to finish a project or unable to repay investors when they wanted repayment. An important paper by Andrei Shleifer, called 'The limits of arbitrage' showed ◄ Holmstrom, Tirole
that, after a decline in an asset price below its fundamental value, investors might not be able to take advantage of the arbitrage opportunity; indeed, they themselves may be ◄ 'The limits of arbitrage', by Andrei
forced to sell the asset, leading to a further decline in the price and a further deviation Shleifer and Robert W. Vishny, *Journal*
from fundamentals. Behavioural economists, for example, Richard Thaler (from Chicago), *of Finance*, 1997, 52(1), 35–55.
pointed to the way in which individuals differ from the rational individual model typically used in economics, and drew implications for financial markets.

Thus, most of the elements needed to understand the crisis were available. Much of the work, however, was carried out outside macroeconomics, in the fields of finance or corporate finance. The elements were not integrated in a consistent macroeconomic model, and their interactions were poorly understood. Leverage, complexity, liquidity, the factors which (as we saw in Chapter 9) combined to create the crisis, were nearly fully absent from the macroeconomic models used by central banks.

Three years into the crisis, things have changed dramatically. Not surprisingly, researchers have turned their attention to the financial system, and the nature of macro financial linkages. Further work is taking place on the various pieces, and these pieces are starting to be integrated in the large macroeconomic models. The lessons for policy are also being drawn, be it on the use of macro prudential tools or the dangers of very high public debt. There is still a long way to go, but, in the end, our macroeconomic models will be richer, with a better understanding of the financial system. Yet, if history is any guide, the economy will be hit by yet another type of shock we have not thought about.

The lessons of the crisis probably go beyond that, however. The Great Depression had, rightly, led most economists to question the macroeconomic properties of a market economy and to suggest a larger role for government intervention. The crisis is raising similar questions. Both the new classical and new Keynesian models had in common the belief that, in the medium run at least, the economy naturally returned to its natural level. The new classicals took the extreme position that output was always at its natural level. The new Keynesians took the view that, in the short run, output would likely deviate from its natural level. But they maintained that, eventually, in the medium run, natural forces would return the economy to the natural level. The Great Depression, the long slump in Japan, were obviously well known, but were seen as aberrations, reflecting largely policy mistakes, and there was a wide belief that these mistakes could be avoided. Many economists today believe that this optimism was excessive. After nearly four years at the liquidity trap, it is clear that the usual adjustment mechanism, namely, a decrease in interest rates in response to low output, is not operational. It is also clear that the room for policy, be it monetary policy or fiscal policy, is also limited.

If there is a consensus, it might be that with respect to small shocks, and normal fluctuations, the adjustment process works; but that, in response to large, exceptional shocks, the normal adjustment process may fail, the room for policy may be limited, and it may take a long time for the economy to repair itself. For the moment, the priority is for researchers to better understand what has happened, and for policy makers to use their remaining room to steer the world economy back to health.

SUMMARY

- The history of modern macroeconomics starts in 1936, with the publication of Keynes's *General Theory of Employment, Interest and Money*. Keynes's contribution was formalised in the *IS–LM* model by John Hicks and Alvin Hansen in the 1930s and early 1940s.

- The period from the early 1940s to the early 1970s can be called the golden age of macroeconomics. Among the major developments were the development of the theories of consumption, investment, money demand and portfolio choice; the development of growth theory and the development of large macroeconometric models.

- The main debate during the 1960s was between Keynesians and monetarists. Keynesians believed developments in macroeconomic theory allowed for better control of the economy. Monetarists, led by Milton Friedman, were more sceptical of the ability of governments to help stabilise the economy.

- In the 1970s, macroeconomics experienced a crisis. There were two reasons. One was the appearance of stagflation, which came as a surprise to most economists. The other was a theoretical attack led by Robert Lucas. Lucas and his followers showed that when rational expectations were introduced, (1) Keynesian models could not be used to determine policy, (2) Keynesian models could not explain long-lasting deviations of output from its natural level and (3) the theory of policy needed to be redesigned, using the tools of game theory.

- Much of the 1970s and 1980s was spent integrating rational expectations into macroeconomics. As is reflected in this text, macroeconomists are now much more aware of the role of expectations in determining the effects of shocks and policy and of the complexity of policy than they were two decades ago.

- Recent research in macroeconomic theory, up to the crisis, proceeded along three lines. New classical economists explored the extent to which fluctuations can be explained as movements in the natural level of output, as opposed to movements away from the natural level of output. New Keynesian economists explored more formally the role of market imperfections in fluctuations. New growth theorists explored the determinants of technological progress. These lines were increasingly overlapping, and, on the eve of the crisis, a new synthesis appeared to be emerging.

- The crisis reflects a major intellectual failure on the part of macroeconomics – the failure to understand the macroeconomic importance of the financial system. While many of the elements needed to understand the crisis had been developed before the crisis, they were not central to macroeconomic thinking and were not integrated in large macroeconomic models. Much research is now focused on macro financial linkages.

- The crisis has also raised a larger issue about the adjustment process through which output returns to their natural level. If there is a consensus, it might be that with respect to small shocks, and normal fluctuations, the adjustment process works, and policy can accelerate the return; but that, in response to large, exceptional shocks, the normal adjustment process may fail, the room for policy may be limited, and it may take a long time for the economy to repair itself.

KEY TERMS

business cycle theory 541

effective demand 541

liquidity preference 541

neoclassical synthesis 541

Keynesians 543

monetarists 543

Lucas critique 545

random walk of consumption 546

staggering (of wage and price decisions) 547

new classicals 547

real business cycle (RBC) models 547

new Keynesians 548

nominal rigidities 548

menu cost 548

new growth theory 549

FURTHER READING

- Two classics are J.M. Keynes, *The General Theory of Employment, Money and Interest* (London: Macmillan Press, 1936), and Milton Friedman and Anna Schwartz, *A Monetary History of the United States, 1867–1960* (Princeton, NJ: Princeton University Press, 1963). Warning: the first makes for hard reading, and the second is a heavy volume.

- For an account of macroeconomics in textbooks since the 1940s, read Paul Samuelson's, 'Credo of a lucky textbook author', *Journal of Economic Perspectives*, Spring 1997, 153–60.

- In the introduction to *Studies in Business Cycle Theory* (Cambridge, MA: MIT Press, 1981), Robert Lucas develops his approach to macroeconomics and gives a guide to his contributions.

- The paper that launched real business cycle theory is Edward Prescott, 'Theory ahead of business cycle measurement', *Federal Reserve Bank of Minneapolis Review*, Fall 1986, 9–22. It is not easy reading.

- For more on new Keynesian economics, read David Romer, 'The new Keynesian synthesis', *Journal of Economic Perspectives*, Winter 1993, 5–22.

- For more on new growth theory, read Paul Romer, 'The origins of endogenous growth', *Journal of Economic Perspectives*, Winter 1994, 3–22.

- For a detailed look at the history of macroeconomic ideas, with in-depth interviews of most of the major researchers, read Brian Snowdon and Howard Vane, *Modern Macroeconomics: Its Origins, Development and Current State*, (Cheltenham: Edward Elgar, 2005).

- For two points of view on the state of macroeconomics pre-crisis, read V.V. Chari and Patrick Kehoe, 'Macroeconomics in practice: how theory is shaping policy', and N. Greg Mankiw, 'The macroeconomist as scientist and engineer', *Journal of Economic Perspectives*, Fall 2006.

- For a sceptical view of financial markets, and the contributions of Thaler and Shleifer among others, read *The Myth of the Rational Market: A History of Risk, Reward, and Delusion on Wall Street* by Justin Fox (New York, Harper Collins, 2009).

- For an assessment of macroeconomic policy post-crisis, read *In the Wake of the Crisis: Leading Economists Reassess Economic Policy*, edited by Olivier Blanchard et al. (Cambridge: MIT Press, 2012).

- If you want to learn more about macroeconomic issues and theory, most economics journals are heavy on mathematics and are hard to read. But a few make an effort to be more friendly. The *Journal of Economic Perspectives* in particular has non-technical articles on current economic research and issues. The *Brookings Papers on Economic Activity*, published twice a year, analyse current macroeconomic problems. So does *Economic Policy*, published in Europe, which focuses more on European issues.

- Most regional Federal Reserve Banks also publish reviews with easy-to-read articles; these reviews are available free of charge. Among these are the *Economic Review* published by the Cleveland Fed, the *Economic Review* published by the Kansas City Fed, the *New England Economic Review* published by the Boston Fed, and the *Review* published by the Minneapolis Fed.

- More advanced treatments of current macroeconomic theory – roughly at the level of a first graduate course in macroeconomics – are given by David Romer, *Advanced Macroeconomics* (New York: McGraw-Hill, 4th edn, 2011) and by Olivier Blanchard and Stanley Fischer, *Lectures on Macroeconomics* (Cambridge, MA: MIT Press, 1989).

APPENDIX 1 A maths refresher

This appendix presents the mathematical tools and the mathematical results that are used in this book.

Geometric series

Definition:

A geometric series is a sum of numbers of the form

$$1 + x + x^2 + \cdots + x^n$$

where x is a number that may be greater or smaller than 1 and x^n denotes x to the power n, that is x times itself n times.
Examples of such series are:

- The sum of spending in each round of the multiplier (Chapter 3). If c is the marginal propensity to consume, then the sum of increases in spending after $n + 1$ rounds is given by

$$1 + c + c^2 + \cdots + c^n$$

- The present discounted value of a sequence of payments of €1 each year for n years (Chapter 15), when the interest rate is equal to i:

$$1 + \frac{1}{1+i} + \frac{1}{(1+i)^2} + \cdots + \frac{1}{(1+i)^{n-1}}$$

We usually have two questions we want to answer when encountering such a series:

1. What is the sum?
2. Does the sum explode as we let n increase, decrease or does it reach a finite limit? If so, what is that limit?

The following propositions tell you what you need to know to answer these questions.

Proposition 1 tells you how to compute the sum.

Proposition 1:

$$1 + x + x^2 + \cdots + x^n = \frac{1 - x^{n+1}}{1 - x} \qquad \text{[A1.1]}$$

Here is the proof: multiply the sum by $(1 - x)$, and use the fact that $x^a x^b = x^{a+b}$ (that is, add exponents when multiplying):

$$(1 + x + x^2 + \cdots + x^n)(1 - x) = 1 + x + x^2 + \cdots + x^n$$
$$- x - x^2 \cdots - x^n - x^{n+1}$$
$$= 1 \qquad\qquad - x^{n+1}$$

All the terms on the right except for the first and the last cancel. Dividing both sides by $(1 - x)$ gives equation (A1.1).

This formula can be used for any x and any n. If, for example, x is 0.9 and n is 10, then the sum is equal to 6.86. If x is 1.2 and n is 10, then the sum is 32.15.

Proposition 2 tells you what happens as n gets large.

Proposition 2:

If x is less than 1, the sum goes to $1/(1 - x)$ as n gets large. If x is equal to or greater than 1, the sum explodes as n gets large.

Here is the proof: if x is less than 1, then x^n goes to 0 as n gets large. Thus, from equation (A1.1), the sum goes to $1/(1 - x)$. If x is greater than 1, then x^n becomes larger and larger as n increases, $1 - x^n$ becomes a larger and larger negative number, and the ratio $(1 - x^n)/(1 - x)$ becomes a larger and larger positive number. Thus, the sum explodes as n gets large.

Application from Chapter 17:

Consider the present value of a payment of €1 forever, starting next year, when the interest rate is i. The present value is given by

$$\frac{1}{(1+i)} + \frac{1}{(1+i)^2} + \cdots \qquad \text{[A1.2]}$$

Factoring out $1/(1 + i)$, rewrite this present value as

$$\frac{1}{(1+i)}\left[1 + \frac{1}{(1+i)} + \cdots\right]$$

The term in brackets is a geometric series, with $x = 1/(1 + i)$. As the interest rate, i, is positive, x is less than 1. Applying Proposition 2, when n gets large, the term in brackets equals

$$\frac{1}{1 - \dfrac{1}{(1+i)}} = \frac{(1+i)}{(1+i-1)} = \frac{(1+i)}{i}$$

Replacing the term in brackets in the previous equation with $(1 + i)/i$ gives:

$$\frac{1}{(1+i)}\left[\frac{(1+i)}{i}\right] = \frac{1}{i}$$

The present value of a sequence of payments of €1 per year forever, starting next year, is equal to €1 divided by the interest rate. If i is equal to 5% per year, the present value equals €1/0.05 = €20.

Useful approximations

Throughout this book, we use a number of approximations that make computations easier. These approximations are most reliable when the variables x, y, z are small, say between 0% and 10%. The numerical examples in Propositions 3–10 are based on the values $x = 0.05$ and $y = 0.03$.

Proposition 3:

$$(1 + x)(1 + y) \approx (1 + x + y) \qquad [\text{A1.3}]$$

Here is the proof: Expanding $(1 + x)(1 + y)$ gives $(1 + x)(1 + y) = 1 + x + y + xy$. If x and y are small, then the product xy is very small and can be ignored as an approximation (for example, if $x = 0.05$ and $y = 0.03$, then $xy = 0.0015$). So $(1 + x)(1 + y)$ is approximately equal to $(1 + x + y)$.

For the values x and y above, for example, the approximation gives 1.08 compared to an exact value of 1.0815.

Proposition 4:

$$(1 + x)^2 \approx 1 + 2x \qquad [\text{A1.4}]$$

The proof follows directly from Proposition 3, with $y = x$. For the value of $x = 0.05$, the approximation gives 1.10, compared to an exact value of 1.1025.

Application from Chapter 16:
From arbitrage, the relation between the two-year interest rate and the current and the expected one-year interest rates is given by

$$(1 + i_{2t})^2 = (1 + i_{1t})(1 + i_{1t+1}^e)$$

Using Proposition 4 for the left side of the equation gives

$$(1 + i_{2t})^2 \approx 1 + 2i_{2t}$$

Using Proposition 3 for the right side of the equation gives

$$(1 + i_{1t})(1 + i_{1t+1}^e) \approx 1 + i_{1t} + i_{1t+1}^e$$

Using this expression to replace $(1 + i_{1t})(1 + i_{1t+1}^e)$ in the original arbitrage relation gives

$$1 + 2i_{2t} = 1 + i_{1t} + i_{1t+1}^e$$

Or, reorganising,

$$i_{2t} = \frac{(i_{1t} + i_{1t+1}^e)}{2}$$

The two-year interest rate is approximately equal to the average of the current and the expected one-year interest rates.

Proposition 5:

$$(1 + x)^n \approx 1 + nx \qquad [\text{A1.5}]$$

The proof follows by repeated application of Propositions 3 and 4. For example, $(1 + x)^3 = (1 + x)^2(1 + x) \approx (1 + 2x)(1 + x)$ by Proposition 4, $\approx (1 + 2x + x) = 1 + 3x$ by Proposition 3.

The approximation becomes worse as n increases, however. For example, for $x = 0.05$ and $n = 5$, the approximation gives 1.25, compared to an exact value of 1.2763. For $n = 10$, the approximation gives 1.50, compared to an exact value of 1.63.

Proposition 6:

$$\frac{(1 + x)}{(1 + y)} \approx (1 + x - y) \qquad [\text{A1.6}]$$

Here is the proof. Consider the product $(1 + x - y)(1 + y)$. Expanding this product gives $(1 + x - y)(1 + y) = 1 + x + xy - y^2$. If both x and y are small, then xy and y^2 are very small, so $(1 + x - y)(1 + y) \approx (1 + x)$. Dividing both sides of this approximation by $(1 + y)$ gives the proposition above.

For the values of $x = 0.05$ and $y = 0.03$, the approximation gives 1.02, while the correct value is 1.019.

Application from Chapter 14:
The real interest rate is defined by

$$(1 + r_t) = \frac{(1 + i_t)}{(1 + \pi_t^e)}$$

Using Proposition 6 gives

$$(1 + r_t) \approx (1 + i_t - \pi_t^e)$$

Simplifying,

$$r_t \approx i_t - \pi_t^e$$

This gives us the approximation we use at many points in this book: the real interest rate is approximately equal to the nominal interest rate minus expected inflation.

These approximations are also very convenient when dealing with growth rates. Define the rate of growth of x by $g_x = \Delta x / x$, and similarly for z, g_z, y and g_y. The following numerical examples are based on the values $g_x = 0.05$ and $g_y = 0.03$.

Proposition 7:

If $z = xy$, then

$$g_z \approx g_x + g_y \qquad [\text{A1.7}]$$

Here is the proof. Let Δz be the increase in z when x increases by Δx and y increases by Δy. Then, by definition:

$$z + \Delta z = (x + \Delta x)(y + \Delta y)$$

Divide both sides by z. The left side becomes

$$\frac{z + \Delta z}{z} = \left(1 + \frac{\Delta z}{z}\right)$$

The right side becomes

$$\frac{(x + \Delta x)(y + \Delta y)}{z} = \frac{(x + \Delta x)(y + \Delta y)}{x \qquad y}$$

$$= \left(1 + \frac{\Delta x}{x}\right)\left(1 + \frac{\Delta y}{y}\right)$$

where the first equality follows from the fact that $z = xy$, the second equality from simplifying each of the two fractions.

Using the expressions for the left and right sides gives

$$\left(1 + \frac{\Delta z}{z}\right) = \left(1 + \frac{\Delta x}{x}\right)\left(1 + \frac{\Delta y}{y}\right)$$

Or, equivalently,

$$(1 + g_z) = (1 + g_x)(1 + g_y)$$

From Proposition 3, $(1 + g_z) \approx (1 + g_x + g_y)$, or, equivalently,

$$g_z \approx g_x + g_y$$

For $g_x = 0.05$ and $g_y = 0.03$, the approximation gives $g_z = 8\%$, while the correct value is 8.15%.

Application from Chapter 15:

Let the production function be of the form $Y = NA$, where Y is production, N is employment and A is productivity. Denoting the growth rates of Y, N and A by g_Y, g_N and g_A, respectively, Proposition 7 implies

$$g_Y \approx g_N + g_A$$

The rate of output growth is approximately equal to the rate of employment growth plus the rate of productivity growth.

Proposition 8:

If $z = x/y$, then

$$g_z \approx g_x - g_y \qquad \text{[A1.8]}$$

Here is the proof. Let Δz be the increase in z, when x increases by Δx and y increases by Δy. Then, by definition:

$$x + \Delta z = \frac{x + \Delta x}{y + \Delta y}$$

Divide both sides by z. The left side becomes

$$\frac{(z + \Delta z)}{z} = \left(1 + \frac{\Delta z}{z}\right)$$

The right side becomes

$$\frac{(x + \Delta x)}{(y + \Delta y)}\frac{1}{z} = \frac{(x + \Delta x)y}{(y + \Delta y)x} = \frac{(x + \Delta x)/x}{(y + \Delta y)/y} = \frac{1 + (\Delta x/x)}{1 + (\Delta y/y)}$$

where the first equality comes from the fact that $z = x/y$, the second equality comes from rearranging terms and the third equality comes from simplifying.

Using the expressions for the left and right sides gives:

$$1 + \Delta z/z = \frac{1 + (\Delta x/x)}{1 + (\Delta y/y)}$$

Or, substituting,

$$1 + g_z = \frac{1 + g_x}{1 + g_y}$$

From Proposition 6, $(1 + g_z) \approx (1 + g_x - g_y)$, or, equivalently,

$$g_z \approx g_x - g_y$$

For $g_x = 0.05$ and $g_y = 0.03$, the approximation gives $g_z = 2\%$, while the correct value is 1.9%.

Application from Chapter 11:

Let aggregate demand be given by $Y = \gamma M/P$, where Y is output, M is nominal money, P is the price level and γ is a constant. It follows from Propositions 7 and 8 that:

$$g_Y \approx g_\gamma + g_M - \pi$$

where π is the rate of growth of prices, equivalently the rate of inflation. As γ is constant, g_γ is equal to zero. Thus,

$$g_Y \approx g_M - \pi$$

The rate of output growth is approximately equal to the rate of growth of nominal money minus the rate of inflation.

Functions

We use functions informally in this book, as a way of denoting how a variable depends on one or more other variables.

In some cases, we look at how a variable Y moves with a variable X. We write this relation as

$$Y = f(X)$$
$$(+)$$

A plus sign below X indicates a positive relation: an increase in X leads to an increase in Y. A minus sign below X indicates a negative relation: an increase in X leads to a decrease in Y.

In some cases, we allow the variable Y to depend on more than one variable. For example, we allow Y to depend on X and Z:

$$Y = f(X, Z)$$
$$(+, -)$$

The signs indicate that an increase in X leads to an increase in Y, and that an increase in Z leads to a decrease in Y.

An example of such a function is the investment function (5.1) in Chapter 5:

$$I = I(Y, i)$$
$$(+, -)$$

This equation says that investment, I, increases with production, Y, and decreases with the interest rate, i.

In some cases, it is reasonable to assume that the relation between two or more variables is a **linear relation**. A given increase in X always leads to the same increase in Y. In that case, the function is given by:

$$Y = a + bX$$

This relation can be represented by a line giving Y for any value of X.

The parameter a gives the value of Y when X is equal to zero. It is called the **intercept** because it gives the value of Y when the line representing the relation 'intercepts' (crosses) the vertical axis.

The parameter b tells us by how much Y increases when X increases by 1. It is called the **slope** because it is equal to the slope of the line representing the relation.

A simple linear relation is the relation $Y = X$, which is represented by the 45° line and has a slope of 1. Another example of a linear relation is the consumption function (3.2) in Chapter 3:

$$C = c_0 + c_1 Y_D$$

where C is consumption and Y_D is disposable income. c_0 tells us what consumption would be if disposable income were equal to zero. c_1 tells us by how much consumption increases when income increases by 1 unit; c_1 is called the marginal propensity to consume.

Logarithmic scales

A variable that grows at a constant growth rate increases by larger and larger increments over time. Take a variable X that grows over time at a constant growth rate, say at 3% per year:

- Start in year 0 and assume that $X = 2$. So a 3% increase in X represents an increase of 0.06 (0.03 × 2).
- Go to year 20. X is now equal to $2(1.03)^{20} = 3.61$. A 3% increase now represents an increase of 0.11 (0.03 × 3.61).
- Go to year 100. X is equal to $2(1.03)^{100} = 38.4$. A 3% increase represents an increase of 1.15 (0.03 × 38.4), so an increase about 20 times larger than in year 0.

If we plot X against time using a standard (linear) vertical scale, the plot looks like Figure A1.1(a). The increases in X become larger and larger over time (0.06 in year 0, 0.11 in year 20 and 1.15 in year 100). The curve representing X against time becomes steeper and steeper.

Another way of representing the evolution of X is to use a *logarithmic scale* to measure X on the vertical axis. The property of a logarithmic scale is that the same *proportional* increase in this variable is represented by the same vertical distance on the scale. So the behaviour of a variable such as X, which increases by the same proportional increase (3%) each year, is now represented by a line. Figure A1.1(b) represents the behaviour of X, this time using a logarithmic scale on the vertical axis. The fact that the relation is represented by a line indicates that X is growing at a constant rate over time. The higher the rate of growth, the steeper the line.

In contrast to X, economic variables such as GDP do not grow at a constant growth rate every year. Their growth rate may be higher in some decades and lower in others. A recession may lead to a few years of negative growth. Yet, when looking at their evolution over time, it is often more informative to use a logarithmic scale than a linear scale. Let's see why.

Figure A1.2(a) plots real US GDP from 1890–2006 using a standard (linear) scale. Because real US GDP is about 46 times bigger in 2006 than in 1890, the same proportional increase in GDP is 46 times bigger in 2006 than in 1890. So the curve representing the evolution of GDP over time becomes steeper and steeper over time. It is very difficult to see from the figure whether the US economy is growing faster or slower than it was 50 years ago or 100 years ago.

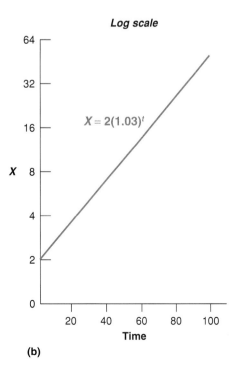

Figure A1.1

(a) The evolution of X using a linear scale.

(b) The evolution of X using a logarithmic scale.

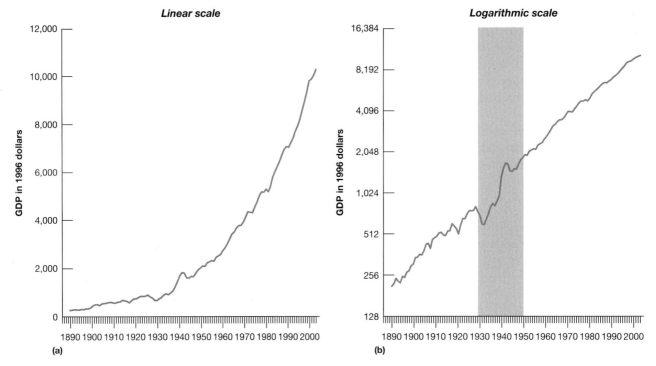

Figure A1.2

(a) US GDP since 1890 using a linear scale.

(b) US GDP since 1890 using a logarithmic scale.

Figure A1.2(b) plots US GDP from 1890–2006, now using a logarithmic scale. If the growth rate of GDP was the same every year – so the proportional increase in GDP was the same every year – the evolution of GDP would be represented by a line – the same way as the evolution of X was represented by a line in Figure A1.1(b). Because the growth rate of GDP is not constant from year to year – so the proportional increase in GDP is not the same every year – the evolution of GDP is no longer represented by a line. Unlike in Figure A1.2(a), GDP does not explode over time, and the graph is more informative. Here are two examples:

- If, in Figure A1.2(b), we were to draw a line to fit the curve from 1890–1929 and another line to fit the curve from 1950–2003 (the two periods are separated by the shaded area in Figure A1.2(b)), the two lines would have roughly the same slope. What this tells us is that the

average growth rate was roughly the same during the two periods.
- The decline in output from 1929–1933 is very visible in Figure A1.2(b). So is the strong recovery of output that follows. By the 1950s, output appears to be back to its old trend line. This suggests that the Great Depression was not associated with a permanently lower level of output.

Note, in both cases, that you could not have derived these conclusions by looking at Figure A1.2(a), but you can derive them by looking at Figure A1.2(b). This shows the usefulness of using a logarithmic scale.

KEY TERMS

linear relation 556   intercept 557   slope 557

How do we know that consumption depends on disposable income? How do we know the value of the propensity to consume?

To answer these questions, and more generally, to estimate behavioural relations and find out the values of the relevant parameters, economists use *econometrics* – the set of statistical techniques designed for use in economics. Econometrics can get very technical, but the basic principles behind it are simple.

Our purpose in this appendix is to show you these basic principles. We shall do so using as an example the consumption function introduced in Chapter 3, and we shall concentrate on estimating c_1, the propensity to consume out of disposable income.

Changes in consumption and changes in disposable income

The propensity to consume tells us by how much consumption changes for a given change in disposable income. A natural first step is simply to plot changes in consumption versus changes in disposable income and see how the relation between the two looks. You can see this in Figure A2.1.

The vertical axis in Figure A2.1 measures the annual change in consumption minus the average annual change in consumption, for each year from 1970–2006. More precisely, let C_t denote consumption in year t. Let ΔC_t denote $C_t - C_{t-1}$, the change in consumption from year $t - 1$ to year t. Let ΔC denote the average annual change in consumption since 1970. The variable measured on the vertical axis is constructed as $\Delta C_t - \overline{\Delta C}$. A positive value of the variable represents an increase in consumption larger than average, while a negative value represents an increase in consumption smaller than average.

Similarly, the horizontal axis measures the annual change in disposable income, minus the average annual change in disposable income since 1970, $\Delta Y_{Dt} - \overline{\Delta Y_D}$.

A particular square in the figure gives the deviations of the change in consumption and disposable income from their respective means for a particular year between 1970 and 2006. In 2006 for example, the change in consumption was higher than average by $50 billion; the change in disposable income was higher than average by $67 billion. (For our purposes, it is not important to know which year each square refers to, just what the set of points in the diagram looks like. So, except for 2006, the years are not indicated on Figure A2.1.)

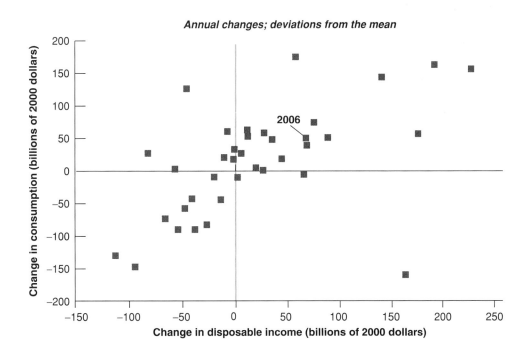

Annual changes; deviations from the mean

Figure A2.1

Changes in consumption vs changes in disposable income, since 1970

There is a clear positive relation between changes in consumption and changes in disposable income.

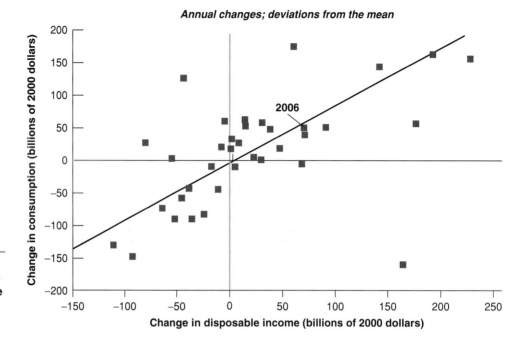

Annual changes; deviations from the mean

Figure A2.2

Changes in consumption and changes in disposable income: the regression line

The regression line is the line that fits the scatter of points best.

Figure A2.1 suggests two main conclusions:

- There is a clear positive relation between changes in consumption and changes in disposable income. Most of the points lie in the upper-right and lower-left quadrants of the figure: when disposable income increases by less than average, so typically does consumption.
- The relation between the two variables is good but not perfect. In particular, some points lie in the upper-left quadrant: these points correspond to years when smaller-than-average changes in disposable income were associated with higher-than-average changes in consumption.

Econometrics allows us to state these two conclusions more precisely and to get an estimate of the propensity to consume. Using an econometrics software package, we can find the line that fits the cloud of points in Figure A2.1 best. This line-fitting process is called **ordinary least squares (OLS)**. The estimated equation corresponding to the line is called a **regression** and the line itself is called the **regression line**. The term *least squares* comes from the fact that the line has the property that it minimises the sum of the squared distances of the points to the line – thus gives the 'least' 'squares'. The word *ordinary* comes from the fact that this is the simplest method used in econometrics.

In our case, the estimated equation is given by

$$(\Delta C_t - \overline{\Delta C}) = 0.77(\Delta Y_{Dt} - \overline{\Delta Y_D}) = \text{residual} \qquad [A2.1]$$
$$\bar{R} = 0.58$$

The regression line corresponding to this estimated equation is drawn in Figure A2.2. Equation (A2.1) reports two important numbers (econometrics packages give more

information than those reported here; a typical printout, together with further explanations, is given in the Focus box 'A guide to understanding econometric results'):

- The first important number is the estimated propensity to consume. The equation tells us that an increase in disposable income of $1 billion above normal is typically associated with an increase in consumption of $0.77 billion above normal. In other words, the estimated propensity to consume is 0.77. It is positive but smaller than 1.
- The second important number is $\bar{R}^2$, which is a measure of how well the regression line fits:

Having estimated the effect of disposable income on consumption, we can decompose the change in consumption for each year into that part that is due to the change in disposable income – the first term on the right in equation (A2.1) – and the rest, which is called the **residual**. For example, the residual for 2006 is indicated in Figure A2.2 by the vertical distance from the point representing 2006 to the regression line. (The point representing 2006 happens to be nearly on the regression line, so the vertical distance is very small.)

If all the points in Figure A2.2 were exactly on the estimated line, all residuals would be 0; all changes in consumption would be explained by changes in disposable income. As you can see, however, this is not the case. $\bar{R}^2$ is a statistic that tells us how well the line fits. $\bar{R}^2$ is always between 0 and 1. A value of 1 would imply that the relation between the two variables is perfect, that all points are exactly on the regression line. A value of 0 would imply that the computer can see no relation between the two variables. The value of $\bar{R}^2$ of 0.58 in

FOCUS
A guide to understanding econometric results

In your readings, you may run across results of estimation using econometrics. Here is a guide, which uses the slightly simplified, but otherwise untouched computer output for equation (A2.1):

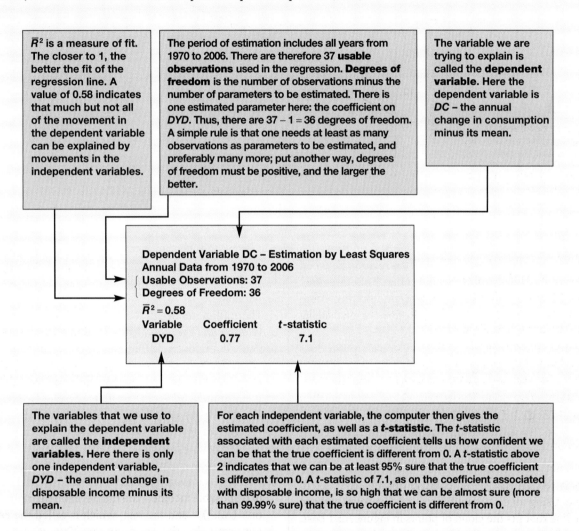

$\bar{R}^2$ is a measure of fit. The closer to 1, the better the fit of the regression line. A value of 0.58 indicates that much but not all of the movement in the dependent variable can be explained by movements in the independent variables.

The period of estimation includes all years from 1970 to 2006. There are therefore 37 **usable observations** used in the regression. **Degrees of freedom** is the number of observations minus the number of parameters to be estimated. There is one estimated parameter here: the coefficient on *DYD*. Thus, there are $37 - 1 = 36$ degrees of freedom. A simple rule is that one needs at least as many observations as parameters to be estimated, and preferably many more; put another way, degrees of freedom must be positive, and the larger the better.

The variable we are trying to explain is called the **dependent variable**. Here the dependent variable is *DC* – the annual change in consumption minus its mean.

Dependent Variable DC – Estimation by Least Squares
Annual Data from 1970 to 2006
Usable Observations: 37
Degrees of Freedom: 36

$\bar{R}^2 = 0.58$

Variable	Coefficient	*t*-statistic
DYD	0.77	7.1

The variables that we use to explain the dependent variable are called the **independent variables**. Here there is only one independent variable, *DYD* – the annual change in disposable income minus its mean.

For each independent variable, the computer then gives the estimated coefficient, as well as a *t*-statistic. The *t*-statistic associated with each estimated coefficient tells us how confident we can be that the true coefficient is different from 0. A *t*-statistic above 2 indicates that we can be at least 95% sure that the true coefficient is different from 0. A *t*-statistic of 7.1, as on the coefficient associated with disposable income, is so high that we can be almost sure (more than 99.99% sure) that the true coefficient is different from 0.

equation (A2.1) is high, but not very high. It confirms the message from Figure A2.2: movements in disposable income clearly affect consumption, but there is still quite a bit of movement in consumption that cannot be explained by movements in disposable income.

Correlation versus causality

We have established so far that consumption and disposable income typically move together. More formally, we have seen that there is a positive **correlation** – the technical term for 'co-relation' – between annual changes in consumption and annual changes in disposable income. And we have interpreted this relation as showing **causality** – that an increase in disposable income causes an increase in consumption.

We need to think again about this interpretation. A positive relation between consumption and disposable income may reflect the effect of disposable income on consumption. But it may also reflect the effect of consumption on disposable income. Indeed, the model we developed in Chapter 3 tells us that if, for any reason, consumers decide to spend

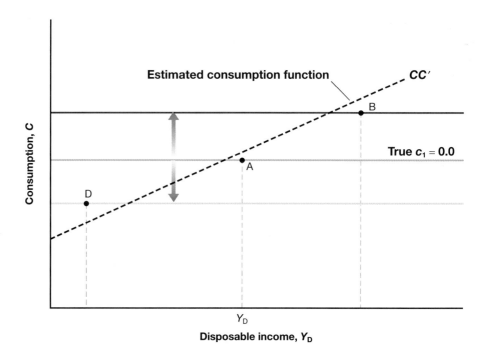

Figure A2.3

A misleading regression

The relation between disposable income and consumption comes from the effect of consumption on income rather than from the effect of income on consumption.

more, then output, and therefore income and, in turn, disposable income will increase. If part of the relation between consumption and disposable income comes from the effect of consumption on disposable income, interpreting equation (A2.1) as telling us about the effect of disposable income on consumption is not right.

An example will help here: suppose consumption does not depend on disposable income, so that the true value of c_1 is 0. (This is not very realistic, but it will make the point most clearly.) So draw the consumption function as a horizontal line (a line with a 0 slope) in Figure A2.3. Next, suppose that disposable income equals Y_D, so that the initial combination of consumption and disposable income is given by point A.

Now suppose that, because of improved confidence, consumers increase their consumption, so the consumption line shifts up. If demand affects output, then income and, in turn, disposable income, increase, so that the new combination of consumption and disposable income will be given by, say, point B. If, instead, consumers become more pessimistic, the consumption line shifts down, and so does output, leading to a combination of consumption and disposable income given by point D.

If we look at that economy, we observe points A, B and D. If, as we did earlier, we draw the best-fitting line through these points, we estimate an upward-sloping line, such as CC', and so estimate a positive value for propensity to consume, c_1. Remember, however, that the true value of c_1 is 0. Why do we get the wrong answer – a positive value for c_1 when the true value is 0? Because we interpret the positive relation between disposable income and consumption as showing the effect of disposable income on

consumption when, in fact, the relation reflects the effect of consumption on disposable income: higher consumption leads to higher demand, higher output and higher disposable income.

There is an important lesson here: *the difference between correlation and causality*. The fact that two variables move together does not imply that movements in the first variable cause movements in the second variable. Perhaps the causality runs the other way: movements in the second variable cause movements in the first variable. Or perhaps, as is likely to be the case here, the causality runs both ways: disposable income affects consumption, *and* consumption affects disposable income.

Is there a way out of the correlation-versus-causality problem? If we are interested – and we are – in the effect of disposable income on consumption, can we still learn that from the data? The answer yes, but only by using more information.

Suppose we *knew* that a specific change in disposable income was not caused by a change in consumption. Then, by looking at the reaction of consumption to *this* change in disposable income, we could learn how consumption responds to disposable income; we could estimate the propensity to consume.

This answer would seem to simply assume away the problem: how can we tell that a change in disposable income is not due to a change in consumption? In fact, sometimes we can tell. Suppose, for example, that the government embarks on a major increase in defence spending, leading to an increase in demand and, in turn, an increase in output. In that case, if we see both disposable income and consumption increase, we can safely assume that the movement in consumption reflects the effect of disposable income on consumption, and thus estimate the propensity to consume.

This example suggests a general strategy:

- Find exogenous variables – that is, variables that affect disposable income but are not in turn affected by it.
- Look at the change in consumption in response not to all changes in disposable income – as we did in our earlier regression – but in response to those changes in disposable income that can be explained by changes in these exogenous variables.

By following this strategy, we can be confident that what we are estimating is the effect of disposable income on consumption, and not the other way around.

The problem of finding such exogenous variables is known as the **identification problem** in econometrics. These exogenous variables, when they can be found, are called **instruments**. Methods of estimation that rely on the use of such instruments are called **instrumental variable methods**.

When equation (A2.1) is estimated using an instrumental variable method – using current and past changes in government defence spending as the instruments – rather than ordinary least squares, as we did earlier, the estimated equation becomes

$$(\Delta C_t - \overline{\Delta C}) = 0.62(\Delta Y_{Dt} - \overline{\Delta Y_D})$$

Note that the coefficient on disposable income, 0.62, is smaller than 0.77 in equation (A2.1). This decrease in the estimated propensity to consume is exactly what we would expect: our earlier estimate in equation (A2.1) reflected not only the effect of disposable income on consumption, but also the effect of consumption on disposable income. The use of instruments eliminates this second effect, which is why we find a smaller estimated effect of disposable income on consumption.

This short introduction to econometrics is no substitute for a course in econometrics. But it gives you a sense of how economists use data to estimate relations and parameters, and to identify causal relations between economic variables.

KEY TERMS

ordinary least squares (OLS) 560

regression, regression line 560

residual, $\bar{R}^2$ 560

dependent variable, independent variables 561

usable observations, degrees of freedom 561

t-statistic 561

correlation, causality 561

identification problem 563

instruments, instrumental variable methods 563

GLOSSARY

AAA, BBB In the jargon of credit rating agencies, letter codes are assigned to each bond to indicate its quality. AAA refers to a prime grade while BBB refers to lower grade.

above the line, below the line In the balance of payments, the items in the *current account* are above the line drawn to divide them from the items in the *capital account*, which appear below the line.

accelerationist Phillips curve See *modified Phillips curve.*

adaptive expectations A backward-looking method of forming expectations by adjusting for past mistakes.

adjusted nominal money growth Nominal money growth minus normal output growth.

aggregate demand relation The demand for output at a given price level. It is derived from equilibrium in goods and financial markets.

aggregate output The total amount of output produced in the economy.

aggregate private spending The sum of all nongovernment spending. Also called *private spending.*

aggregate production function The relation between the quantity of aggregate output produced and the quantities of inputs used in production.

aggregate supply relation The price level at which firms are willing to supply a given level of output. It is derived from equilibrium in the labour market.

AIG (American International Group) An American multinational insurance corporation.

American Recovery and Reinvestment Act Commonly referred to as the Stimulus or The Recovery Act, an economic stimulus package enacted by the 111th United States Congress in February 2009 and signed into law on 17 February 2009, by President Barack Obama. The primary objective for ARRA was to save and create jobs almost immediately. Secondary

objectives were to provide temporary relief programs for those most impacted by the recession and invest in infrastructure, education, health and 'green' energy.

anchor of the system A currency which is the basis for movements of other currencies.

animal spirits A term introduced by Keynes to refer to movements in investment that could not be explained by movements in current variables.

appreciation (nominal) An increase in the price of domestic currency in terms of foreign currency. Corresponds to an increase in the exchange rate.

appropriability of research The extent to which firms benefit from the results of their research and development efforts.

arbitrage The proposition that the expected rates of return on two financial assets must be equal. Also called *risky arbitrage* to distinguish it from *riskless arbitrage*, the proposition that the actual rates of return on two financial assets must be the same.

asymmetric shocks Shifts in demand which hit two different countries in opposiste ways.

automatic stabiliser The fact that a decrease in output leads, under given tax and spending rules, to an increase in the budget deficit. This increase in the budget deficit in turn increases demand and thus stabilises output.

autonomous spending The component of the demand for goods that does not depend on the level of output.

backloading Deferring the payment until specified conditions have been implemented.

balance of payments A set of accounts that summarise a country's transactions with the rest of the world.

balanced budget A budget in which taxes are equal to government spending.

balanced growth The situation in which output, capital and effective labour all grow at the same rate.

band (for exchange rates) The limits within which the exchange rate is allowed to move under a fixed exchange rate system.

bank reserves Holdings of central bank money by banks. The difference between what banks receive from depositors and what they lend to firms or hold as bonds.

bank run Simultaneous attempts by depositors to withdraw their funds from a bank.

bargaining power The relative strength of each side in a negotiation or a dispute.

barter The exchange of goods for other goods rather than for money.

base year When constructing real GDP by evaluating quantities in different years using a given set of prices, the year to which this given set of prices corresponds.

behavioural equation An equation that captures some aspect of behaviour.

bilateral exchange rate The real exchange rate between two countries.

bond A financial asset that promises a stream of known payments over some period of time.

bond rating The assessment of a bond based on its default risk.

broad money See *M2.*

Bretton Woods System of monetary management that established the rules for commercial and financial relations among the world's major industrial states in the mid-twentieth century. It included an obligation for each country to adopt a monetary policy that maintained the exchange rate of its currency within a fixed value – plus or minus one percent – in terms of gold.

BRICs (or 'the BRIC countries') Acronym – first coined by Goldman Sachs in 2001 – that refers to the fast-growing developing economies of Brazil, Russia, India and China.

budget deficit The excess of government expenditures over government revenues.

budget surplus The excess of government revenues over government expenditures.

business cycle convergence Close relationship between economy-wide fluctuations in production or economic activity in different countries.

business cycle theory A class of macroeconomic models in which business cycle fluctuations to a large extent can be accounted for by either real or nominal shocks (see also real business cycle models).

business cycles See *output fluctuations*.

capital account In the balance of payments, a summary of a country's asset transactions with the rest of the world.

capital account balance The net result of public and private international investment flowing in and out of a country. This includes foreign direct investment, portfolio investment (such as changes in holdings of stocks and bonds) and other investments (such as changes in holdings in loans, bank accounts, and currencies).

capital account deficit An imbalance in a nation's balance of payments capital account in which payments made by the country for purchasing foreign assets exceed payments received by the country for selling domestic assets. In other words, investment by the domestic economy in foreign assets is less than foreign investment in domestic assets.

capital account surplus An imbalance in a nation's balance of payments capital account in which payments received by the country for selling domestic assets exceed payments made by the country for purchasing foreign assets. In other words, investment by the domestic economy in foreign assets is greater than foreign investment in domestic assets.

capital accumulation Increase in the capital stock.

capital controls Restrictions on the foreign assets domestic residents can hold, and on the domestic assets foreigners can hold.

capital ratio A ratio of a bank capital to its assets.

cash flow The net flow of cash a firm is receiving.

causality A relation between cause and effect.

central bank accommodation Increase in the money supply by the central bank (usually in the presence of contractionary fiscal policies).

central bank money Money issued by the central bank. Also known as the *monetary base* and *high-powered money*.

central parity The reference value of the exchange rate around which the exchange rate is allowed to move under a fixed exchange rate system. The centre of the *band*.

Cobb–Douglas production function A standard production function which is applied to describe how much output two inputs into a production process make, with the hypothesis of constant returns to scale.

collateral In lending agreements, collateral is a borrower's pledge of specific property to a lender, to secure repayment of a loan.

collateralised debt obligation (CDO) A type of asset-backed security. To create a CDO, a corporate entity is constructed to hold assets as collateral and to sell packages of cash flows to investors. CDOs are a promise to pay cash flows to investors in a prescribed sequence, based on how much cash flow the CDO collects from the pool of bonds or other assets it owns.

collective bargaining Wage bargaining between unions and firms.

competitive devaluation In a fixed exchange rate system, an official lowering of the value of a country's currency, by which the monetary authority formally sets a new fixed rate with respect to a foreign reference currency, done with the aim to improve domestic growth by shifting demand away from imports onto domestically produced goods.

constant returns to scale The proposition that a proportional increase (or decrease) of all inputs leads to the same proportional increase (or decrease) in output.

consumption (C) Goods and services purchased by consumers.

consumption function A function that relates consumption to its determinants.

consumption smoothing Preference for a consumption path that is constant over time.

contractionary open market operation An open-market operation in which the central bank sells bonds to decrease the money supply.

controls on capital flows Regulations preventing residents of a country from holding foreign denominated assets or currency and non-residents from holding domestic denominated assets or currency.

convergence The tendency for countries with lower output per capita to grow faster, leading to convergence of output per capita across countries.

corporate bond A bond issued by a corporation.

correlation A measure of the way two variables move together. A positive correlation indicates that the two variables tend to move in the same direction. A negative correlation indicates that the two variables tend to move in opposite directions. A correlation of zero indicates that there is no apparent relation between the two variables.

cost of living The cost of maintaining a certain standard of living in a certain region or country.

coupon bond A bond that promises multiple payments before maturity and one payment at maturity.

coupon payments The payments before maturity on a coupon bond.

coupon rate The ratio of the coupon payment to the face value of a coupon bond.

crawling peg An exchange rate mechanism in which the exchange rate is allowed to move over time according to a pre-specified formula.

credibility The degree to which people and markets believe that a policy announcement will actually be implemented and followed through.

credit default swaps (CDS) A financial agreement that the seller of the CDS will compensate the buyer in case of loan default.

credit easing Policy tools used by central banks to make credit more readily available in the event of a financial crisis, such as the one experienced in 2007–2008.

currency Coins and notes.

currency board An exchange rate system in which: (i) the central bank stands ready to buy or sell foreign currency at the official exchange rate; (ii) the central bank cannot engage in open-market operations, that is buy or sell government bonds.

current account In the balance of payments, the summary of a country's payments to and from the rest of the world.

current account balance The net revenues that arise from a country's international sales and purchases of goods and services plus net international transfers.

current account deficit An excess of expenditure over receipts on current account in a country's balance of payments. See also *current account balance*.

current account surplus Excess of receipts over expenditure on current account in a country's balance of payments. See also *current account balance*.

current yield The ratio of the coupon payment to the price of a coupon bond.

cyclically adjusted deficit A measure of what the government deficit would be under existing tax and spending rules, if output were at its natural level. Also called a *full-employment deficit, midcycle deficit, standardised employment deficit*, or *structural deficit*.

debt finance Financing based on loans or the issuance of bonds.

debt ratio See *debt-to-GDP ratio*.

debt repudiation A unilateral decision by a debtor not to repay its debt.

debt stabilisation Convergence of the debt ratio to a steady-state level.

debt-to-GDP ratio The ratio of debt to gross domestic product. Also called simply the *debt ratio*.

decreasing returns to capital The property that increases in capital lead to smaller and smaller increases in output as the level of capital increases.

decreasing returns to labour The property that increases in labour lead to smaller and smaller increases in output as the level of labour increases.

default risk (or credit risk) The risk of loss due to a debtor's non-payment of a loan or other line of credit (either the principal or interest (coupon) or both).

deficit financing (or **deficit spending**) Deficit spending is the amount by which a government spending exceeds income over a particular period of time, also called simply 'deficit', or 'budget deficit', the opposite of budget surplus.

deflation Negative inflation.

degree of openness Ratio of exports (and/or imports) to GDP.

degrees of freedom The number of usable observations in a *regression* minus the number of parameters to be estimated.

demand for domestic goods The demand for domestic goods by people, firms and governments, both domestic and foreign. Equal to the domestic demand for goods plus net exports.

dependent variable A variable whose value is determined by one or more other variables.

deposit account A current account, savings account or other type of bank account that allows money to be deposited and withdrawn by the account holder.

deposit insurance Measure implemented in many countries to protect bank depositors, in full or in part, from losses caused by a bank's inability to pay its debts when due.

depreciation (nominal) A decrease in the price of domestic currency in terms of a foreign currency. Corresponds to a decrease in the exchange rate.

devaluation A decrease in the exchange rate in a fixed exchange rate system.

discount bond A bond that promises a single payment at maturity.

discount factor The value today of a (euro other national currency unit) at some time in the future.

discount rate (i) The interest rate used to discount a sequence of future payments. Equal to the nominal interest rate when discounting future nominal payments and to the real interest rate when discounting future real payments. (ii) The interest rate at which the central bank lends to banks. (iii) In the context of intertemporal consumption decisions, it is the rate at which an individual discounts future consumption.

discouraged worker A person who has given up looking for employment.

disinflation A decrease in inflation.

disposable income (Y_D) The income that remains once consumers have received transfers from the government and paid their taxes.

dividends The portion of a corporation's profits that the firm pays out each period to its shareholders.

dollarisation The use of dollars in domestic transactions in a country other than the USA.

domestic demand for goods The sum of consumption, investment and government spending.

duration of unemployment The period of time during which a worker is unemployed.

dynamics Movements of one or more economic variables over time.

easterlin paradox A paradox according to which within a given country people with higher incomes are more likely to report being happy. However, in international comparisons, the average reported level of happiness does not vary much with national income per person, at least for countries with income sufficient to meet basic needs.

econometrics The application of mathematical and statistical techniques to test and develop hypothesis provided by economic theory.

effective demand Quantity of goods and services that consumers are actually buying at the current market price.

effective labour The number of workers in an economy times the state of technology.

effective real exchange rate See *multilateral exchange rate*.

efficiency wage The wage at which a worker is performing a job most efficiently or productively.

efficiency wage theories Economists call the theories that link the *productivity* or the *efficiency* of workers to the wage they are paid efficiency wage theories.

emerging economies Countries with low output per person, and high growth.

employment Total number of individuals who are employed.

employment protection Employment protection refers both to regulations concerning hiring (e.g. rules favouring disadvantaged groups, conditions for using temporary or fixed-term contracts, training requirements) and firing (e.g. redundancy procedures, mandated prenotification periods and severance payments, special requirements for collective dismissals and short-time work schemes).

endogenous variable A variable that depends on other variables in a model and is thus explained within the model.

endowment Amount of goods owned by an individual.

EONIA Acronym for Euro Overnight Index Average – a rate used as a benchmark for the markets in the European system of central banks. It is calucalte by taking the weighted average of all the overnight offer rates in the market.

equilibrium The equality between demand and supply.

equilibrium condition The condition that supply be equal to demand.

equilibrium in the goods market The condition that the supply of goods be equal to the demand for goods.

equity finance Financing based on the issuance of shares.

equity premium Risk premium required by investors to hold stocks rather than short-term bonds.

EU-15 The original group of 15 countries that formed the European Union including the three new member countries that joined in 1995 (Austria, Finland and Sweden).

EU-27 The group of 27 countries that joined the European Union until 2007. It includes the 15 members of EU-15 plus Cyprus, Czech Republic, Estonia, Hungary, Latvia, Lithuania, Malta, Poland, Slovakia and Slovenia that joined in 2004, and Bulgaria and Romania that joined in 2007.

European Central Bank (ECB) One of the world's most important central banks, responsible for monetary policy covering the 16 member States of the Eurozone. It was established by the European Union in 1998 with its headquarters in Frankfurt, Germany.

European Economic and Monetary Union (EMU) Consists of three stages coordinating economic policy, achieving economic convergence and culminating with the adoption of the euro, the EU's single currency. All member states of the European Union are expected to participate in the EMU. All member states, except Denmark and the UK, have committed themselves by treaty to join EMU. Sixteen member states of the European Union have entered the third stage and have adopted the euro as their currency. Denmark, Estonia, Latvia, and Lithuania are the current participants in the exchange rate mechanism. Of the pre-2004 members, the UK and Sweden have not joined ERM II and Denmark remains in ERM without proceeding to the third stage.

European Monetary System (EMS) Arrangement established in 1979 under the Jenkins European Commission where most nations of the European Economic Community (EEC) linked their currencies to prevent large fluctuations relative to one another.

European System of Central Banks (ESCB) The European Central Bank (ECB) and the national central banks (NCBs) of all the 27 European Union (EU) Member States.

exchange rate fluctuation In a flexible exchange rate system, the free movement of the exchange rate.

exogenous variable A variable that is not explained within a model but, rather, is taken as given.

expansion A period of positive GDP growth.

expansionary open market operation An open-market operation in which the central bank buys bonds to increase the money supply.

expectations hypothesis The hypothesis that financial investors are risk neutral, which implies that expected returns on all financial assets have to be equal.

expectations-augmented Phillips curve See *modified Phillips curve*.

expected present discounted value The value today of an expected sequence of future payments. Also called *present discounted value* or *present value*.

exports (X) The purchases of domestic goods and services by foreigners.

face value (on a bond) The single payment at maturity promised by a discount bond.

fertility (of research) The degree to which spending on research and development translates into new ideas and new products.

final good Goods that are ultimately consumed rather than used in the production of another good.

finance theory Field that deals with investment making decisions.

financial intermediary A financial institution that receives funds from people, firms or other financial institutions, and uses these funds to make loans or buy financial assets.

financial investment The purchase of financial assets.

financial markets The markets in which financial assets are bought and sold.

financial wealth The value of all of one's financial assets minus all financial liabilities. Sometimes called *wealth*, for short.

fine-tuning A macroeconomic policy aimed at precisely hitting a given target, such as constant unemployment or constant output growth.

fine-tuning operations – A non-regular open market operation executed by the Eurosystem, mainly to deal with unexpected liquidity fluctuations in the market.

fire sale prices Extremely discounted prices, typically when the seller faces bankruptcy or other impending distress.

fire sales A sale of goods (or assets) at extremely discounted prices.

fiscal consolidation See *fiscal contraction*.

fiscal contraction A policy aimed at reducing the budget deficit through a decrease in government spending or an increase in taxation. Also called *fiscal consolidation*.

fiscal expansion An increase in government spending or a decrease in taxation, which leads to an increase in the budget deficit.

fiscal policy A government's choice of taxes and spending.

fiscal policy multiplier The increase in aggregate demand following a €1 increase in government spending (or following increases in other components of autonomous demand of the same amount).

Fisher effect or Fisher hypothesis The proposition that, in the long run, an increase in nominal money growth is reflected in an identical increase in both the nominal interest rate and the inflation rate, leaving the real interest rate unchanged.

fixed exchange rate An exchange rate between the currencies of two or more countries that is fixed at some level and adjusted only infrequently.

fixed investment See *investment (I)*.

flexible exchange rate Exchange rate between two currencies, free to fluctuate.

flow A variable that can be expressed as a quantity per unit of time (such as income).

foreign exchange Foreign currency; all currencies other than the domestic currency of a given country.

four tigers The four Asian economies of Singapore, Taiwan, Hong Kong and South Korea.

full-employment deficit See *cyclically adjusted deficit.*

fully funded system A retirement system in which the contributions of current workers are invested in financial assets, with the proceeds (principal and interest) given back to the workers when they retire.

fundamental value (of a stock) The present value of expected dividends.

game *Strategic interactions* between *players.*

game theory The prediction of outcomes from *games.*

GDP adjusted for inflation See *real GDP.*

GDP at constant prices See *real GDP.*

GDP at current prices See *nominal GDP.*

GDP deflator The ratio of nominal GDP to real GDP; a measure of the overall price level. Gives the average price of the final goods produced in the economy.

GDP growth The growth rate of real GDP in year *t*; equal to $(Y_t - Y_{t-1})/Y_{t-1}$.

GDP in terms of goods See *real GDP.*

geometric series A mathematical sequence in which the ratio of one term to the preceding term remains the same. A sequence of the form $1 + c + c^2 + \cdots + c^n$.

gold standard A system in which a country fixed the price of its currency in terms of gold and stood ready to exchange gold for currency at the stated parity.

golden-rule level of capital The level of capital at which steady-state consumption is maximised.

government bond A bond issued by a government or a government agency.

government spending (G) The goods and services purchased by regional, and local governments.

government transfers Payments made by the government to individuals that are not in exchange for goods or services. Example: social security payments.

gross domestic product (GDP) A measure of aggregate output in the national income accounts.

gross national product (GNP) A measure of aggregate output in the national income accounts.

growth The steady increase in aggregate output over time.

hard peg The exchange rate to which a country commits under a fixed exchange rate system.

Harmonised Index of Consumer Prices (HICP) An indicator of inflation and price stability for the European Central Bank (ECB). It is a consumer price index which is compiled according to a methodology that has been harmonised across EU countries. The euro area HICP is a weighted average of price indices of member states who have adopted the euro.

hedonic pricing An approach to calculating real GDP that treats goods as providing a collection of characteristics, each with an implicit price.

heterodox stabilisation programme A stabilization programme that includes incomes policies.

high-powered money See *central bank money.*

hires Workers newly employed by firms.

housing wealth The value of the housing stock.

human capital The set of skills possessed by the workers in an economy.

human wealth The labour-income component of wealth.

hyperinflation Very high inflation.

identification problem In econometrics, the problem of finding whether correlation between variables *X* and *Y* indicates a causal relation from *X* to *Y*, or from *Y* to *X*, or both. This problem is solved by finding exogenous variables, called *instruments*, that affect *X* and do not affect *Y* directly, or affect *Y* and do not affect *X* directly.

identity An equation that holds by definition, denoted by the sign ≡.

imports (IM) The purchases of foreign goods and services by domestic consumers, firms and the government.

income The flow of revenue from work, rental income, interest and dividends.

incomes policies Government policies that set up wage and/or price guidelines or controls.

independent variable A variable that is taken as given in a relation or in a model.

index number A number, such as the GDP deflator, that has no natural level and is thus set to equal some value (typically 1 or 100) in a given period.

indexed bond A bond that promises payments adjusted for inflation.

inflation A sustained rise in the general level of prices.

inflation rate The rate at which the price level increases over time.

inflation targeting The conduct of monetary policy to achieve a given inflation rate over time.

inflation tax The product of the rate of inflation and real money balances.

instrumental variable methods In econometrics, methods of estimation that use *instruments* to estimate causal relations between different variables.

instruments In econometrics, the exogenous variables that allow the identification problem to be solved.

interbank market Foreign exchange market where banks exchange different currencies. The interbank market is an important segment of the foreign exchange market.

intercept In a linear relation between two variables, the value of the first variable when the second variable is equal to zero.

interest parity condition See *uncovered interest parity.*

interest rate rule Rule followed by the central bank to determine the desired level of the interest rate.

intermediate good A good used in the production of a final good.

International Monetary Fund (IMF) The principal international economic organisation. Publishes the *World Economic Outlook* annually and the *International Financial Statistics (IFS)* monthly.

intertemporal budget constraint Budget constraint that applies to consumption choices over subsequent periods of time.

inventory investment The difference between production and sales.

investment (I) Purchases of new houses and apartments by people, and purchases of new capital goods (machines and plants) by firms.

investment income In the current account, income received by domestic residents from their holdings of foreign assets.

IS **curve** A downward-sloping curve relating output to the interest rate. The curve corresponding to the *IS relation*, the equilibrium condition for the goods market.

IS **relation** An equilibrium condition stating that the demand for goods must be equal to the supply of goods, or equivalently that investment must be equal to saving. The equilibrium condition for the goods market.

J-curve A curve depicting the initial deterioration in the trade balance caused by a real depreciation, followed by an improvement in the trade balance.

junior securities Securities that rank lower than senior securities in regards to the owner's claims on assets and income in the event of the issuer becoming insolvent.

junk bond A bond with a high risk of default.

Keynesians A group of macroeconomic schools of thought based on the ideas of twentieth-century economist John Maynard Keynes. Keynesian economists believe that, in the short run, productive activity is influenced by effective demand (total spending in the economy), and that effective demand does not necessarily equal aggregate supply (the total productive capacity of the economy).

labour force The sum of those employed and those unemployed.

Labour Force Survey (LFS) Statistical survey conducted in EU member countries annually designed to capture data about the labour market.

labour hoarding The practice of retaining workers during a period of low product demand rather than laying them off.

labour in efficiency units See *effective labour*.

labour productivity The ratio of output to the number of workers.

layoffs Workers who lose their jobs either temporarily or permanently.

leavers Workers who leave their jobs for better alternatives.

leverage ratio In general, capital to assets ratio.

Libor rate The interest rate(s) banks pay when borrowing from each other.

life (of a bond) See *maturity*.

life cycle theory of consumption The theory of consumption, developed initially by Franco Modigliani, which emphasises that the planning horizon of consumers is their lifetime.

linear relation A relation between two variables such that a one-unit increase in one variable always leads to an increase of n units in the other variable.

liquid asset An asset that can be sold easily and at little cost.

liquidity As a financial term, it indicates money and assets at prompt disposal.

liquidity facilities These were emergency measures taken by the US Federal Reserve in 2009 to mitigate the disruption in financial markets by introducing or expanding liquidity facilities, providing support to specific institutions, and engaging in direct purchases of assets.

liquidity preference Refers to the demand for money, considered as liquidity. The concept was first developed by John Maynard Keynes in his book *The General Theory of Employment, Interest and Money* (1936) to explain determination of the interest rate by the supply and demand for money.

liquidity trap The case where nominal interest rates are equal to zero, and monetary policy cannot, therefore, decrease them further.

LM **curve** An upward-sloping curve relating the interest rate to output. The curve corresponding to the *LM relation*, the equilibrium condition for financial markets.

LM **relation** An equilibrium condition stating that the demand for money must be equal to the supply of money. The equilibrium condition for financial markets.

logarithmic scale A scale in which the same proportional increase is represented by the same distance on the scale, so that a variable that grows at a constant rate is represented by a straight line.

long run A period of time extending over decades.

Lucas critique The proposition, put forth by Robert Lucas, that existing relations between economic variables may change when policy changes. An example is the apparent trade-off between inflation and unemployment, which may disappear if policy makers try to exploit it.

*M*1 A 'narrow' money aggregate that comprises currency in circulation and overnight deposits.

*M*2 An 'intermediate' monetary aggregate that comprises *M*1 plus deposits with an agreed maturity of up to two years and deposits redeemable at notice of up to three months.

*M*3 A 'broad' monetary aggregate that comprises *M*2 plus repurchase agreements, money market fund shares and units as well as debt securities with a maturity of up to two years.

Maastricht Treaty (formally, the **Treaty on European Union**, **TEU**) Treaty signed in 1992 in Maastricht, the Netherlands between the members of the European Community and entered into force in 1993. It created the European Union and led to the creation of the euro. The treaty led to the creation of the euro currency, and created what is commonly referred to as the pillar structure of the European Union. This conception of the Union divides it into the European Community (EC) pillar, the Common Foreign and Security Policy (CFSP) pillar, and the Justice and Home Affairs (JHA) pillar.

Malthusian trap Following Malthus' theory that population increase would outpace increases in the means of subsistence, indicates a steady decrease in the amount of resources available to each individual over time.

mark-up The ratio of price to marginal cost. It is a measure of market power across firms or industries.

Marshall–Lerner condition The condition under which a real depreciation leads to an increase in net exports.

maturity The length of time over which a financial asset (typically a bond) promises to make payments to the holder.

medium run A period of time between the *short run* and the *long run*.

menu cost A menu cost is the cost to a firm resulting from changing its prices. The name stems from the cost of restaurants literally printing new menus, but economists use it to refer to the costs of changing prices in general.

mid-cycle deficit See *cyclically adjusted deficit*.

minimum wage Lowest hourly rate an employer can pay an employee. In some countries (such as the US) the minimum wage is set by a statute while in others (such as the UK) it is set by the wage council of each industry.

models of endogenous growth Models in which accumulation of physical and human capital can sustain growth even in the absence of technological progress.

modified Phillips curve The curve that plots the change in the inflation rate against the unemployment rate. Also called an *expectations-augmented Phillips curve* or an *accelerationist Phillips curve*.

monetarists A group of macroeconomic schools of thought based on the strong belief that the economy's performance is determined almost entirely by changes in the money supply.

monetary aggregate The market value of a sum of liquid assets. *M1* is a monetary aggregate that includes only the most liquid assets.

monetary base See *central bank money.*

monetary contraction A change in monetary policy, which leads to an increase in the interest rate. Also called *monetary tightening.*

monetary expansion A change in monetary policy, which leads to a decrease in the interest rate.

monetary policy The use of the money stock by the central bank to affect interest rates and, by implication, economic activity and inflation.

monetary–fiscal policy mix The combination of monetary and fiscal policies in effect at a given time.

monetary tightening See *monetary contraction.*

money Those financial assets that can be used directly to buy goods.

money illusion The proposition that people make systematic mistakes in assessing nominal versus real changes.

money market funds Financial institutions that receive funds from people and use them to buy short-term bonds.

money multiplier The increase in the money supply resulting from a one-euro increase in central bank money.

mortgage lender A person or company that makes a mortage loan, that is, a loan secured by real property.

mortgage-based securities (MBS) A security backed by a mortgage loan; it represents a claim on the cash flows from mortgage loans.

multilateral exchange rate (multilateral real exchange rate) The real exchange rate between a country and its trading partners, computed as a weighted average of bilateral real exchange rates. Also called the *trade-weighted real exchange rate* or *effective real exchange rate.*

multiplier The ratio of the change in an *endogenous variable* to the change in an *exogenous variable* (for example, the ratio of the change in output to a change in autonomous spending).

narrow banking Restrictions on banks that would require them to hold only short-term government bonds.

natural level of employment The level of employment that prevails when unemployment is equal to its natural rate.

natural level of output The level of production that prevails when employment is equal to its natural level.

natural rate of unemployment The unemployment rate at which price and wage decisions are consistent.

neoclassical synthesis Neoclassical synthesis is a post-war academic movement in economics that attempts to absorb the macroeconomic thought of John Maynard Keynes into the thought of neoclassical economics.

net capital flows Capital flows from the rest of the world to the domestic economy, minus capital flows to the rest of the world from the domestic economy.

net exports (X – IM) The difference between exports and imports. Also called the *trade balance.*

net transfers received In the current account, the net value of foreign aid received minus foreign aid given.

neutrality of money The proposition that an increase in nominal money has no effect on output or the interest rate, but is reflected entirely in a proportional increase in the price level.

new classicals A school of thought in macroeconomics that builds its analysis entirely on a neoclassical framework. Specifically, it emphasises the importance of rigorous foundations based on microeconomics, especially rational expectations.

new growth theory A group of recent growth models that argues that economic growth comes endogenously from investment in human capital, innovation and knowledge.

new Keynesians New Keynesian economics is a school of contemporary macroeconomics that strives to provide microeconomic foundations for Keynesian economics. It developed partly as a response to criticisms of Keynesian macroeconomics by adherents of *new classical* macroeconomics.

Nikkei index The most widely quoted average of Japanese equities, similar to the Dow Jones Industrial Average.

nominal exchange rate The price of domestic currency in terms of foreign currency. The number of units of foreign currency you can get for one unit of domestic currency.

nominal GDP The sum of the quantities of final goods produced in an economy times their current price.

nominal interest rate The interest rate in terms of the national currency. It tells us how many euros (for example) one has to repay in the future in exchange for borrowing €1 today.

nominal rigidities The slow adjustment of nominal wages and prices to changes in economic activity.

non-accelerating inflation rate of unemployment (NAIRU) The unemployment rate at which inflation neither decreases nor increases. See *natural rate of unemployment.*

non-employment rate The ratio of population minus employment, to population.

non-human wealth The financial and housing component of wealth.

non-residential investment The purchase of new capital goods by firms: *structures* and *producer durable equipment.*

normal growth rate The rate of output growth needed to maintain a constant unemployment rate.

not in the labour force The number of people who are neither employed nor looking for employment.

n-year interest rate See *yield to maturity.*

Okun's law The relation between GDP growth and the change in the unemployment rate.

OPEC Organisation of Petroleum Exporting Countries.

open market operation The purchase or sale of government bonds by the central bank for the purpose of increasing or decreasing the money supply.

openness in factor markets The opportunity for firms to choose where to locate production, and for workers to choose where to work and whether or not to migrate.

openness in financial markets The opportunity for financial investors to choose between domestic and foreign financial assets.

openness in goods markets The opportunity for consumers and firms to choose between domestic and foreign goods.

optimal control The control of a system (a machine, a rocket, an economy) by means of mathematical methods.

optimal control theory The set of mathematical methods used for *optimal control.*

optimal currency area Also known as optimum currency area, it is a geographical region in which it would maximise economic efficiency to have the entire region share a single currency.

ordinary least squares A statistical method to find the best-fitting relation between two or more variables.

Organisation for Economic Cooperation and Development (OECD) An international organisation that collects and studies economic data for many countries. Most of the world's rich countries belong to the OECD.

orthodox stabilisation programme A stabilisation programme that does not include incomes policies.

out of the labour force Individuals who do not have a job but are not looking for one.

output fluctuations Movements in output around its trend. Also called *business cycles.*

output per person A country's gross domestic product divided by its population.

panel data set A data set that gives the values of one or more variables for many individuals or many firms over some period of time.

paradox of saving The result that an attempt by people to save more may lead both to a decline in output and to unchanged saving.

parameter A coefficient in a behavioural equation.

participation rate The ratio of the labour force to the non-institutional civilian population.

patent The legal right granted to a person or firm to exclude anyone else from the production or use of a new product or technique for a certain period of time.

pay-as-you-go system A retirement system in which the contributions of current workers are used to pay benefits to current retirees.

pent-up demand When the demand for a service or product is unusually strong. Pent-up demand is used by economists to describe a strong return to spending following a period of decreased spending.

permanent income theory of consumption The theory of consumption, developed by Milton Friedman, that emphasises that people make consumption decisions based not on current income, but on their notion of permanent income.

Phillips curve The curve that plots the relation between movements in inflation and unemployment. The original Phillips curve captured the relation between the inflation rate and the unemployment rate. The *modified Phillips curve* captures the relation between (i) the change in the inflation rate and (ii) the unemployment rate.

players The participants in a *game.* Depending on the context, players may be people, firms, governments and so on.

point-year of excess employment A difference between the actual unemployment rate and the natural unemployment rate of one percentage point for one year.

policy mix See *monetary–fiscal policy mix.*

political business cycle Fluctuations in economic activity caused by the manipulation of the economy for electoral gain.

political theory of government debt A theory about the political process through which the level of government debt is decided.

population in working age Population aged between 15 and 64 years.

present discounted value See *expected present discounted value.*

present value See *expected present discounted value.*

price level The general level of prices in an economy.

price-setting relation The relation between the price chosen by firms, the nominal wage and the mark-up.

primary deficit Government spending, excluding interest payments on the debt, minus government revenues. (The negative of the *primary surplus.*)

primary surplus Government revenues minus government spending, excluding interest payments on the debt.

private saving (*S*) Saving by the private sector. The value of consumers' disposable income minus their consumption.

private spending See *aggregate private spending.*

production function A mathematical function that elates physical output of a production process to physical inputs or factors of production.

profitability The expected present discounted value of profits.

propagation mechanism The dynamic effects of a *shock* on output and its components.

propensity to consume (*c*₁) The effect on consumption of an additional euro disposable income.

propensity to save (1 − *c*₁) The effect on saving of an additional dollar of disposable income. (Equal to one minus the marginal propensity to consume.)

public saving (*T* − *G*) Saving by the government; equal to government revenues minus government spending. Also called the *budget surplus.* (A *budget deficit* represents public dissaving.)

purchasing power Income in terms of goods.

purchasing power parity (PPP) A method of adjustment used to allow for international comparisons of GDP.

quantitative easing An extreme form of monetary policy used to stimulate an economy where interest rates are either at, or close to, zero. Normally, a central bank stimulates the economy indirectly by lowering interest rates but when it cannot lower them any further it can purchases financial assets (mostly short-term), including government paper and corporate bonds, from financial institutions (such as banks) using money it has created out of nothing.

quotas Restrictions on the quantities of goods that can be imported.

$\bar{R}^2$ A measure of fit, between zero and one, from a *regression*. An $\bar{R}^2$ of zero implies that there is no apparent relation between the variables under consideration. An $\bar{R}^2$ of 1 implies a perfect fit: all the *residuals* are equal to zero.

random walk The path of a variable whose changes over time are unpredictable.

rate of growth of multifactor productivity See *Solow residual*.

rating agencies Companies that assign credit ratings for issuers of certain types of debt obligations as well as the debt instruments themselves.

rational expectations The formation of expectations based on rational forecasts, rather than on simple extrapolations of the past.

rational speculative bubble An increase in stock prices based on the rational expectation of further increases in prices in the future.

real appreciation An increase in the relative price of domestic goods in terms of foreign goods. An increase in the real exchange rate.

real business cycle (RBC) models A class of macroeconomic models in which business cycle fluctuations to a large extent can be accounted for by real (in contrast to nominal) shocks.

real depreciation A decrease in the relative price of domestic goods in terms of foreign goods. An increase in the real exchange rate.

real exchange rate The relative price of domestic goods in terms of foreign goods.

real GDP A measure of aggregate output. The sum of quantities produced in an economy times their price in a base year. Also known as *GDP in terms of goods*, *GDP in constant dollars* or *GDP adjusted for inflation*.

real GDP per capita Real GDP divided by population.

real interest rate The interest rate in terms of goods. It tells us how many goods one has to repay in the future in exchange for borrowing the equivalent one good today.

recession A period of negative GDP growth. Usually refers to at least two consecutive quarters of negative GDP growth.

regression The output of *ordinary least squares*. Gives the equation corresponding to the estimated relation between variables, together with information about the degree of fit and the relative importance of the different variables.

regression line The best-fitting line corresponding to the equation obtained by using *ordinary least squares*.

regulation In the context of the banking sector, regulations are a form of government regulation which subjects banks to certain requirements, restrictions and guidelines.

rental cost of capital See *user cost*.

representative consumer The representative consumer hypothesis assumes that all individuals are identical, or that there is only one (representative) individual.

research and development (R&D) Spending aimed at discovering and developing new ideas and products.

reservation wage The wage that would make a worker indifferent between working and being unemployed.

reserve ratio The ratio of bank reserves to chequeable deposits.

reserve requirements The minimum amount of reserves that banks must hold in proportion to chequeable deposits.

residential investment The purchase of new homes and apartments by people.

residual The difference between the actual value of a variable and the value implied by the *regression line*. Small residuals indicate a good fit.

revaluation An increase in the exchange rate in a fixed exchange rate system.

Ricardian equivalence The proposition that neither government deficits nor government debt have an effect on economic activity. Also called the *Ricardo–Barro proposition*.

Ricardo–Barro proposition See *Ricardian equivalence*.

risk averse A person is risk averse if he/she prefers to receive a given amount for sure to an uncertain amount with the same expected value.

risk neutral A person is risk neutral if he/she is indifferent between receiving a given amount for sure or an uncertain amount with the same expected value.

risk premium The difference between the interest rate paid on a given bond and the interest rate paid on a bond with the highest rating.

sacrifice ratio The number of point-years of excess unemployment needed to achieve a decrease in inflation of 1%.

saving The sum of private and public saving, denoted by S.

saving rate The proportion of income that is saved.

savings The accumulated value of past saving. Also called *wealth*.

securitisation Financial practice of pooling various types of contractual debt such as residential mortgages, commercial mortgages, auto loans or credit card debt obligations and selling said consolidated debt as bonds.

seignorage The revenues from the creation of money.

senior securities Securities (usually debt) that, in the event the issuer goes bankrupt, must be repaid before other creditors receive any payment.

separations Workers who are leaving or losing their jobs.

shadow banking system The collection of non-bank financial intermediaries that provide services similar to traditional commercial banks. It includes entities such as hedge funds, money market funds and *structured investment vehicles (SIV)*.

share A financial asset issued by a firm that promises to pay a sequence of payments, called dividends, in the future. Also called *stock*.

shocks Movements in the factors that affect aggregate demand and/or aggregate supply.

shoe-leather costs The costs of going to the bank to take money out of a chequeing account.

short run A period of time extending over a few years at most.

slope In a linear relation between two variables, the amount by which the first variable increases when the second increases by one unit.

soft landing A smooth reduction in economic growth, which does not entail a recession.

Solow residual The excess of actual output growth over what can be accounted for by the growth in capital and labour.

stabilisation programme A government program aimed at stabilising the economy (typically stopping high inflation).

stagflation The combination of stagnation and inflation.

staggering of wage decisions The fact that different wages are adjusted at different times, making it impossible to achieve a synchronised decrease in nominal wage inflation.

standard of living Level of material comfort as measured by the goods and services available to an individual, group or country.

standardised employment deficit See *cyclically adjusted deficit.*

state of technology The degree of technological development in a country or industry.

static expectations See *adaptive expectations.*

statistical discrepancy A difference between two numbers that should be equal, coming from differences in sources or methods of construction for the two numbers.

steady state In an economy without technological progress, the state of the economy where output and capital per worker are no longer changing. In an economy with technological progress, the state of the economy where output and capital per effective worker are no longer changing.

stock A variable that can be expressed as a quantity at a point in time (such as wealth). Also a synonym for *share.*

stocks An alternative term for inventories.

strategic interactions An environment in which the actions of one player depend on and affect the actions of another player.

structural deficit See *cyclically adjusted deficit.*

structural rate of unemployment See *natural rate of unemployment.*

structured investment vehicle (SIV) An operating finance company established to earn a spread between its assets and liabilities like a traditional bank. The strategy of SIVs was to borrow money by issuing short-term securities, such as commercial paper and medium-term notes and public bonds, at low interest rates and then lend that money by buying longer-term securities at higher interest rates, with the difference in rates going to investors as profit.

sub-prime mortgages Mortgages accorded to borrowers with weakened credit histories including payment delinquencies, and possibly more severe problems such as charge-offs, judgments, and bankruptcies. These borrowers have reduced repayment capacity as measured by credit scores or debt-to-income ratios.

System of National Accounts (SNA) The System of National Accounts (SNA) consists of a coherent, consistent and integrated set of macroeconomic accounts, balance sheets and tables based on a set of internationally agreed concepts, definitions, classifications and accounting rules. (SNA 1.1) The System of National Accounts 1993 (SNA) has been prepared under the joint responsibility of the United Nations, the International Monetary Fund, the Commission of the European Communities, the OECD and the World Bank.

tariffs Taxes on imported goods.

tax smoothing The principle of keeping tax rates roughly constant, so that the government runs large deficits when government spending is exceptionally high and small surpluses the rest of the time.

Taylor rule A rule, suggested by John Taylor, telling a central bank how to adjust the nominal interest rate in response to deviations of inflation from its target, and of the unemployment rate from the natural rate.

technological catch-up The process through which countries or firms come near to the technology frontier over time.

technology frontier The highest level reached upon a technological path.

technological progress An improvement in the state of technology.

term structure of interest rates See *yield curve.*

time inconsistency In game theory, the incentive for one player to deviate from his or her previously announced course of action once the other player has moved.

Tobin's *q* The ratio of the value of the capital stock, computed by adding the stock market value of firms and the debt of firms, to the replacement cost of capital.

total wealth The sum of human wealth and non-human wealth.

toxic assets A popular term for certain financial assets whose value has fallen significantly and for which there is no longer a functioning market, so that such assets cannot be sold at a price satisfactory to the holder. The term became common during the crisis that started in 2008.

tradable goods Goods that compete with foreign goods in domestic or foreign markets.

trade balance The difference between exports and imports. Also called *net exports.*

trade deficit A negative trade balance, that is, imports exceed exports.

trade intensity The volume of trade between any two pairs of countries.

trade surplus A positive trade balance, that is, exports exceed imports.

Troubled Asset Relief Program (TARP) A program of the US government to purchase assets and equity from financial institutions to strengthen its financial sector that was signed into law by US President George W. Bush on 3 October 2008. It was a component of the government's measures in 2008 to address the subprime mortgage crisis.

_t_-statistic A statistic associated with an estimated coefficient in a regression that indicates how confident one can be that the true coefficient differs from zero.

uncovered interest parity An arbitrage relation stating that domestic and foreign bonds must have the same expected rate of return, expressed in terms of a common currency.

unemployment Total number of individuals who are not employed and are looking for a job.

unemployment rate The ratio of the number of unemployed to the labour force.

unemployment insurance Payment made by the state or other agencies to unemployed persons, conditional on some eligibilities conditions that vary country by country.

usable observation An observation for which the values of all the variables under consideration are available for *regression* purposes.

user cost of capital The cost of using capital over a year, or a given period of time. The sum of the real interest rate and the depreciation rate. Also called the *rental cost of capital*.

value added The value a firm adds in the production process, equal to the value of its production minus the value of the intermediate inputs it uses in production.

wage indexation A rule that automatically increases wages in response to an increase in prices.

wage–price spiral The mechanism by which increases in wages lead to increases in prices, which lead in turn to further increases in wages, and so on.

wage-setting relation The relation between the wage chosen by wage setters, the price level, and the unemployment rate.

war of attrition When both parties to an argument hold their grounds, hoping that the other party will give in.

wealth See *financial wealth*.

wholesale funding A method that banks use in addition to core demand deposits to finance operations.

yield curve The relation between yield and maturity for bonds of different maturities. Also called the *term structure of interest rates*.

yield to maturity The constant interest rate that makes the price of an n-year bond today equal to the present value of future payments. Also called the *n-year interest rate*.

SYMBOLS USED IN THIS BOOK

Symbol	Term	Introduced in Chapter
$(\ )^d$	Superscript^d means demanded	
$(\ )^e$	Superscript^e means expected	
A	Aggregate private spending	18
	Also: Autonomous spending/labour productivity/states of technology	5, 9, 15
α	Effect on the inflation rate of the unemployment rate, given expected inflation	10
B	Goverment debt	21
B/Y	Debt ratio	21
$\bar{b}$	Steady-state value of debt ratio	21
β	Effect of an increase in output growth on the unemployment rate	11
C	Consumption	3
CU	Currency	4
c	Proportion of money held as currency	4
c_0	Consumption when disposable income equals zero	3
c_1	Propensity to consume	3
D	Deposit accounts	4
	Also: Real dividend on a stock	16
$\text{\euro}D$	Nominal dividend on a stock	16
δ	Depreciation rate	14
E	Nominal exchange rate (price of domestic currency in terms of foreign currency)	6
$\bar{E}$	Fixed nominal exchange rate	12
E^e	Expected future exchange rate	6
ε	Real exchange rate	6
G	Government spending	3
g_A	Growth rate of technological progress	15
g_K	Growth rate of capital	15
g_m	Growth rate of nominal money	11
g_N	Growth rate of population	15
g, g_y	Growth rate of output	11
$\bar{g}_y$	Normal rate of growth of output	11
H	High powered money/monetary base/central bank money	4
	Also: Human capital	14
I	Fixed investment	3
IM	Imports	3
i	Nominal interest rate	4
i_1	One-year nominal interest rate	16
i_2	Two-year nominal interest rate	16
i^*	Foreign nominal interest rate	6
K	Capital stock	11
L	Labour force	2
M	Money stock (nominal)	4
M^d	Money demand (nominal)	4
M^s	Money supply (nominal)	4

m	Propensity to import	18
μ	Markup of prices over wages	8
N	Employment	2
N_n	Natural level of employment	8
NX	Net exports	6
P	GDP deflator/CPI/price level	2
P^*	Foreign price level	6
π	Inflation	2
Π	Profit per unit of capital	17
Q	Real stock price	16
$\unicode{x20AC}Q$	Nominal stock price	16
R	Bank reserves	4
r	Real interest rate	11
S	Private saving	3
s	Private saving rate	14
T	Net taxes (taxes paid by consumers minus transfers)	3
θ	Reserve ratio of banks	4
U	Unemployment	2
u	Unemployment rate	2
u_n	Natural rate of unemployment	8
V	Present value of a sequence of real payments z	15
$\unicode{x20AC}V$	Present value of a sequence of nominal payments $\pounds z$	15
W	Nominal wage/wealth	8, 17
Y	Real GDP/output/production	2
$\unicode{x20AC}Y$	Nominal GDP	2
Y_D	Disposable income	3
Y_L	Labour income	17
Y_n	Natural level of output	8
Y^*	Foreign output	6
X	Exports	3
Z	Demand for goods	3
z	Factors that affect the wage, given unemployment	8

INDEX